CMP

Acknowledgement for the front cover illustration is made to G. Tanyeli and U. Tanyeli for the use of Figure 5, on page 20, from their paper in Section 1.

Structural Repair and Maintenance of Historical Buildings

Editor:
C.A. Brebbia

Computational Mechanics Publications
Southampton Boston

Birkhäuser Verlag Basel Boston Berlin

C.A. BREBBIA

Computational Mechanics Institute
Ashurst Lodge
Ashurst, Southampton
SO4 2AA
U.K.

British Library Cataloguing in Publication Data
Brebbia, C.A. (Carlos Alberto), 1938-
    Structural repair and maintenance of
    historical buildings
    1. Great Britain. Buildings of historical
    importance. Conservation and restoration.
    I. Title.
    363.6'9'0941

Library of Congress Catalog Card Number 89-60103

ISBN 1-85312-021-9 Computational Mechanics Publications Southampton
ISBN 0-945824-06-8 Computational Mechanics Publications Boston
ISBN 3-7643-2302-7 Birkhäuser Verlag Basel Boston Berlin
ISBN 0-8176-2302-7 Birkhäuser Verlag Boston Basel Berlin

Printed in Great Britain by Unwin Brothers Limited, Old Woking, Surrey.

CONTENTS

SECTION 1 - HISTORICAL AND CULTURAL ASPECTS

SECTION 2 - MASONRY AND OTHER MATERIAL PROBLEMS

SECTION 6 - REPAIRS AND STRENGTHENING

SECTION 7 - RESTORATION

SECTION 8 - COMPUTER AIDED SIMULATION

PREFACE

A substantial amount of work has recently been carried out by Scientists and Engineers and Architects interested in Structural Studies, Repairs and Maintenance of Historical Buildings and Ancient Monuments. This work has been supported by many organizations in different parts of the world and has involved the commitment of considerable financial resources. This book brings together the experiences of different researchers and scientists who have been involved in the solution of these problems. Its contents describe the technical expertise gained by the specialists when solving problems related to the behaviour of historical buildings. Sections of the book describe the nature and the assessment of the problems and others, the solution adopted for the repairs and strengthening of the structures.

The book contains the edited version of some of the papers presented at the 1st International Conference on Structural Repairs and Maintenance of Historical Buildings, held in Florence, Italy in April of 1989. The meeting was the first of its type and was convened to discuss case studies in addition to the more scientific aspects of the problems, trying to learn from past experience and mistakes. The result of the conference, i.e. this volume, is of importance to all scientists, architects and engineers in government, industry and academia who are actively involved in the preservation of our historical heritage. It is hoped that this work will stimulate research into this important topic and point the way ahead for years to come.

Southampton
April 1989

SECTION 1 - HISTORICAL AND CULTURAL ASPECTS

The Care of Masonry Buildings
The Engineer's Contribution

J. Heyman

*Department of Engineering, University of Cambridge,
Cambridge CB2 1PZ*

Why should an engineer be involved at all in the care of
historical buildings? This is a question which it is not
really easy to answer. Visually, one is always aware when an
engineer intervenes - it can be seen that foundations are being
underpinned, or that steel reinforcement is being introduced
into a masonry structure in the neighbourhood of cracks, and
these are clearly engineering activities. But the mere
observation of a particular engineering activitiy does not
necessarily answer the question of why that activity is being
carried out. Are the cracks dangerous in some way? Is
settlement compromising the stability of the whole structure?

Indeed, although large masonry structures require more or
less continuous inspection and maintenance, this is not to
check their stability (for they seem to be extraordinarily
stable), but to make sure that the stone is not weathering too
severely, that water is not penetrating, that cracks are not
extending, and so on. Such inspection will draw attention to
the existence of settlements, to the general distortion of the
structure, to the presence of cracks. Small "cosmetic" defects
will be remedied immediately, but it seems that every so often
more extensive structural work is undertaken. In the second
half of the eighteenth century, for example, and again a
hundred years later, and again now at the end of the twentieth
century, many major works of restoration are recorded.

It is perhaps fashion that impels a society to a renewed
interest in its cultural heritage at intervals of about a
hundred years. Keen interest will loosen purse strings; with
money expert advice may be sought and experts usually advise
the spending of more money. The very fact that an engineer is
engaged will normally lead to engineering work being carried
out.

The typical, indeed the archetypal, question asked of the

engineer is: Is this crack dangerous? It is the question that
was asked of Poleni about the dome of St Peter's, Rome in the
middle of the eighteenth century, and to which in 1748 he gave
the courageous answer: No.   For once, then, a proposal was
made for non-intervention; Poleni was, naturally, not believed
(everyone could see that the dome was cracked), and engineering
work was carried out.

The modern, careful, engineer does not encourage brutal
intervention.   Confronted with a crack, he will make
calculations based upon the latest developments of his
structural art, in an attempt to decide precisely what action
to take.   These numerical calculations will be based upon a
survey of the building in question, and will try to determine
the force system within the building.   That is, how does the
structure carry its loads (whether these be due to self-weight,
to wind or to earthquake)? Having determined the force system,
the engineer will probably move into a slightly remoter realm
of stresses, those abstract quantities which result from
calculation, can never be measured, but can nevertheless be
related to known limiting stresses for the material of the
building.

In making these calculations the engineer is trying to
convince himself that the structure can satisfy each of the
three major structural criteria, those of strength, stiffness
and stability.   The structure must be strong enough to carry
whatever loads are imposed, it must not deflect unduly, and it
must not develop large unstable displacements, either locally
or overall.

Now an ancient structure - the Roman Pantheon, for
example, a Greek temple, or a Gothic cathedral - seems
intuitively to be strong enough; loading has not, over the
centuries, caused failure to occur by fracture of the material.
It is true that local spalling and crushing of masonry may
sometimes be seen, but this does not appear to affect the
structural integrity of the whole.   In fact, mean stresses are
very low in masonry structures when compared with the strength
of the material (low stresses are a feature of any structure,
whether timber or stone, designed to last through the
centuries).

Similarly, the engineer is unlikely to worry about unduly
large working deflexions of say the vault of a Gothic
cathedral.   The passage of the years may have lead to more or
less gross deformations of the vault, but it is still stable;
the engineer will walk on its upper surface without engendering
any visible further deflexion.   Strength and stiffness do not
lie in the foreground of masonry design.

It is the third structural criterion, that of stability,
that is important, although it is satisfied in rather a curious

way. It turns out that all that is necessary to ensure the stability of a masonry structure is for the internal forces to lie within the boundaries of the masonry. Thus for the simple voussoir arch of Fig. 1, it may be imagined that each stone is

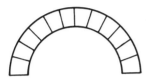

in equilibrium under its own weight and reactive forces with its neighbours. The positions of these reactive forces define a "line of thrust" for the arch, and stability will be assured if the line of thrust lies wholly within the masonry.

Figure 1

The engineer, then, will calculate structural forces in order (in terms of the simple example of Fig. 1) to determine a line of thrust; he will then check that the line of thrust lies within the masonry. This was precisely Poleni's intention, and Poleni understood that the calculation of the thrust line was not a simple matter. He knew, however, of Hooke's statement: "As hangs the flexible line, so, but inverted, will stand the rigid arch". Figure 2 reproduces one of Poleni's illustrations; the shape of the tensile loaded string (a catenary) is exactly the same as that of an arch carrying the same loads in compression.

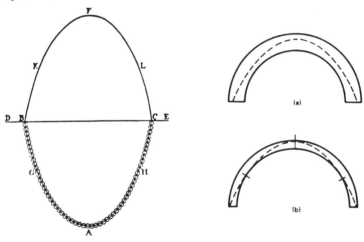

Figure 2   Figure 3

Thus the weights of the voussoirs of the arch of Fig. 1 would lead to a hanging chain of a certain shape; that shape is shown inverted as the line of thrust in Fig. 3(a). The line of thrust lies within the masonry; this is the demonstration that the arch is safe. Poleni used precisely this technique in his analysis of the dome of St Peter's. For a two-dimensional arch which he devised as a (legitimate) analogue of the dome, he determined experimentally the shape of the hanging chain. The fact that this chain lay (as a thrust line) within the surfaces of the dome was his proof, and stated as such by him, that the dome was stable, despite the cracks.

It will be appreciated that the shape of the thrust line for the arch of Fig. 3(b) is exactly the same as that for the arch of Fig. 3(a). The arch of Fig. 3(b) has, however, much slenderer dimensions, and has been drawn in fact so that it only just contains the structural forces. An arch of this thickness would, theoretically, be just stable; any accidental disturbance of the geometry, however, or a slight asymmetry of loading, would lead to the possibility of the thrusts being no longer containable within the masonry.

A notion has been derived, therefore, of an assessment of safety based upon a satisfactory geometry; the arch must have a sufficient thickness to contain the thrust line, and indeed the arch of Fig. 3(a) might be said to have a "geometrical factor of safety" of about 2, when its thickness is compared with that of the "minimum" arch of Fig. 3(b). Ideas of safety based upon stress have, for the moment, receded from view; mean stresses in the two arches of Fig. 3 are small. It is the shape of the arch compared with the shape dictated by the structural forces (the thrust line) that is of importance.

The arch is a simple structure whose behaviour can be visualised, and which can be set up as a model for experiment in the laboratory. The problem facing the engineer is to find equivalent internal structural forces for a complex real structure, say a complete Gothic cathedral. What he seeks (and it will be seen that his goal is, on the one hand, mistaken, and, on the other, in any case not achievable) is a representation of the actual state of the structure. He may proceed, as did Poleni, experimentally, but he has also the whole apparatus of modern structural theory at his disposal.

If then, he proceeds by calculation, the first equation he will write is that of statical equilibrium. If he can solve this equation straight away then the main problem has been solved (and, technically, the structure is statically determinate). Generally, however, the equilibrium equations standing alone are insoluble; the structure is statically indeterminate (hyperstatic). There are many possible equilibrium states, and to determine the actual state requires the use of other equations of structural analysis.

For example, the thrust line of Fig. 3(a) is only one of an infinite number of such lines, each representing a possible state of equilibrium of the arch. If the chain in Fig. 2 is made slightly shorter, or the span slightly increased, the resulting inverted shape will still remain within the thickness of the masonry sketched in Fig. 3(a). To determine the "actual" position the other two equations of structural analysis must be used. First, a statement may be made of the material properties, so that internal deformation of the arch can be related to the internal forces. Secondly, an overall geometrical statement will relate the deformed arch to any imposed external or internal restraints; in Fig. 3(a), for example, the arch rests firmly on rigid foundations, and, however the arch deforms, the displacements at the abutments must be zero.

The elastic design method postulates a (linear) elastic law of deformation, and certain boundary conditions must be assumed. In this way enough equations become available for the solution of the hyperstatic problem; a unique position may be found for the thrust line in Fig. 3(a). Now the solution of the structural equations for a hyperstatic structure is extremely sensitive to very small variations in the boundary conditions. If one of the fixed abutments in the arch of Fig. 3(a) should suffer a small displacement this would be accompanied by a large shift in the position of the thrust line. (Small in this connexion implies a displacement within the thickness of the lines in Fig. 3(a) – the eye would detect no difference between the original and the displaced states.)

It is certain that one of the abutments of the arch will suffer an (unpredictable) small displacement, and this then puts in question the whole rationale of elastic analysis. There is no sensible answer to the question: What is the actual state of the structure? If the abutments were known to behave in a certain predictable way, then the boundary conditions could perhaps be specified; if the elasticity of the stone were assumed uniform, or indeed if the different elasticities of stone and mortar could be allowed for (as Castigliano attempted), then elastic constants could perhaps be assigned. In this case the "actual" state of the structure could be calculated, but in truth the quantities assumed in the analysis are not knowable with the degree of accuracy that would make the resulting calculations trustworthy.

Further, the values of the assumed quantities are ephemeral; a severe gale, a slight earth tremor, a change in water table will produce an entirely different state for the structure. Elastic analysis, in fact, calculates only one of an infinite number of possible equilibrium states for a hyperstatic structure; the calculated state cannot be observed in practice, as repeated tests on real structures have shown. Thus any method of analysis based upon elastic concepts must be viewed with great suspicion if it claims to lead to results which somehow represent the "real" state of the structure.

Any method which involves the assignment of a numerical value for Young's modulus will be, by definition, an elastic method. It will entrain assumptions about the relative elastic properties of neighbouring parts of the structure; it will probably ignore internal constraints on deformation, such as the fact that neighbouring blocks of masonry make imperfect contact, leading to voids in the structure; and it will probably ignore the real small movements of foundations.   Thus elastic finite elements, for example, are a very imperfect tool for the analysis of masonry, and experiments on elastic models suffer from the same defects.   Further, masonry is essentially a unilateral material, capable of satisfactory behaviour in compression but virtually incapable of carrying tension; a photoelastic model, then, displaying compressive and tensile stresses, is a poor representation of reality.

If, then, elastic methods are suspect, how should the engineer proceed?   Even if the elastic equations are not relevant, common sense would seem to indicate that a severe gale, easily survived but leading to a completely different state of the structure, cannot really have weakened the structure.   Common sense is supported by both theory and experiment.   If two seemingly identical structures, but actually with different small imperfections so that they are in very different states of working stress, are loaded slowly to collapse, the collapse loads (that is, the strength of the structure) will be found to be the same.

It was this observation which led to the development of the so-called plastic theory of structures, applicable to any case where the ultimate collapse state is a ductile quasi-stable process (and therefore to steel and to reinforced-concrete frames and, as it turns out, to masonry, but not to structures made, for example, from glass or cast iron, which are brittle).   The plastic designer does not, however, envisage that his structure will actually collapse.   He performs a hypo-thetical limiting calculation within the conceptual framework of the plastic theorems, and has the knowledge that these calculations are safe.

In detail, the designer constructs one possible state of equilibrium for the structure under the action of the given loads, and then checks that the actual proportions of the structure are such that the internal forces associated with the equilibrium state can be carried safely.   In this sense he has reached common ground with the elastic designer.   The elastic designer believes that he has established the actual equilibrium state, whereas the "plastic" designer does not attempt to find the "actual" solution, but is content to have established one of the infinitely many possible solutions. Both designers then proceed in the same way in their detailed assessment of the structure.

The "equilibrium" approach to structural analysis is not such a blunt tool as might at first be supposed.   Even if the search for the actual state of equilibrium is abandoned, nevertheless limits may be found for the values of important structural quantities.   If the chain of Fig. 2 is made too

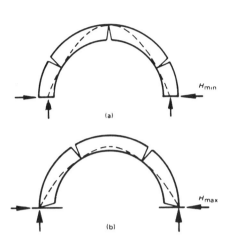

Figure 4

short, for example, then there will be no way in which the corresponding inverted chain may be made to fit within the arch of Fig. 3(a), and the same applies if the chain is made too long. Indeed, the limiting positions of the line of thrust are sketched in Fig. 4; each corresponds to a separate equilibrium state, with different structural forces being called into play in order to maintain the equilibrium of the arch. The forces are calculable, and the abutment thrust, for example, may be found to lie within upper and lower limits.

The "equilibrium" analyst can, in fact, derive a set of forces for his structure and can begin to make basic engineering judgments. From the values of abutment thrust for the arch the foundation pressures may be calculated as lying within a certain bracketed range, and the science of modern soil mechanics may be used to determine whether or not reinforcement is needed in this area (say by underpinning or piling).

Similarly, a good estimate may be made of the values of the stresses within the structure; these are normally extremely low in an ancient structure, as has been mentioned, but indications may again be given for the need for local attention. However, in general the engineer will be satisfied that there is no danger of overall failure caused by high stresses in the structure.

Above all, an equilibrium analysis leads to the notion of "geometrical safety" of the structure. Do the internal forces lie comfortably within the masonry? If so, then the structure is safe against small but hostile movements of the environment, against unforeseen loading, and indeed against irregularities in the construction. And the more comfortably the forces lie within the masonry, then the safer is the structure – these are qualitative statements, but precise numerical quantities can be assigned to geometrical factors of safety.

On such a general basis of equilibrium theory applied to constructions made of unilateral material – masonry – the engineer can begin to interpret what he finds in practice. For example, in passing under a masonry bridge he will be likely to see a crack running under the soffit of the arch at or near the crown, and he will deduce that the abutments of the bridge have given way slightly, the span of the bridge has increased while the abutment thrust has dropped to its lowest value, and a "hinge" has developed at the crown as sketched in Fig. 4(a). To the question "Is this crack dangerous?" the answer is: No, not in itself.   The hinging crack at the crown indicates that the abutments have spread, possibly a long time ago.   If there is no indication of recent movement then Poleni's judgement is correct; the structure is in a stable state, and no engineering intervention is indicated (cracks may have to be pointed to keep out water, but not to strengthen the construction).

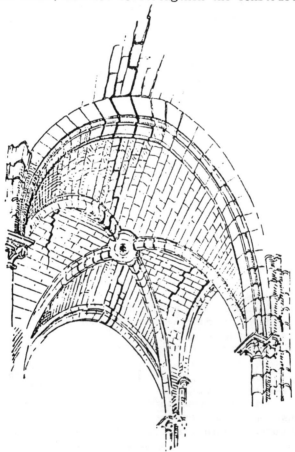

Figure 5

The conclusion from this simple example of a crack in an arch may be applied to much more complex structures.   The typical fissures sketched in Fig. 5, for example, result from an almost standard spread of the abutment system of a Romanesque or Gothic cathedral; the cracks near the crown are "hinging" cracks similar to those sketched in Fig. 4, but "Sabouret's cracks", parallel to these and between 1 and 2 metres from the sides of the vault, represent complete separation of the masonry (if one stands on the upper surface of the vault, the floor of the cathedral may be seen through the fissure). Similarly, the meridional cracks observed by Poleni in the dome of St Peter's, starting from the drum and dying away towards the crown, result from a spread of the lower circumference of the dome. In all these instances the structures are safe if the movements that engendered the defects have now ceased.

A prime precept thus emerges to guide the engineer in his intervention into the structure of an ancient building. It is to leave well alone, unless there are other indications that intervention is necessary. More precisely:

1   If there is evidence of continuing distortion of the structure, or if it is known that permanent forces might act to distort the structure in future, or that abutments are continuing to give way, then steps should be taken to stabilize the geometry of the structure as a whole, and in its present state (there is no need to restore the geometry to a supposed initial perfection).

2   If, on the contrary, there is no evidence of continuing distortion, and if, for example, it seems that soil has consolidated under foundations, then the structure may be left safely in its permanently deformed but stable state.

To these two principles may be added a third to counter a possible hidden defect, of which an example can occur in the construction of a thick load-bearing medieval wall. Typically, the wall will have two well-constructed skins, but the rubble fill may well have decayed; calculated mean stresses are low, but the loads are in fact carried on the two skins, and perhaps dangerously high stresses can arise.

3   Loose masonry and rubble infill must be consolidated to a sufficient strength (which need not necessarily be as high as that of the best close-coursed masonry).

If these three principles are followed, then some unnecessary restoration work may be avoided. The principles imply an effective faith in the structure itself, if this does not transgress into the field of anthropomorphic fancy. And indeed the essence of the "equilibrium" approach is at once comforting and humbling. If the clever engineer can find one possible way in which the structure can comfortably support its loads, then he can be assured that the structure itself is at least as clever as the engineer; the structure will itself find at least as comfortable a way.

BIBLIOGRAPHY

1   Poleni, G.   Memorie istoriche della gran cupola del Tempio Vaticano, Padova, 1748.
2   Heyman, J.   Chronic defects in masonry vaults: Sabouret's cracks, Monumentum, Vol. 26, p. 131, 1983.
3   Heyman, J.   Poleni's problem.   Proceedings of the Institution of Civil Engineers, Part 1, Vol. 84, p. 737, 1988.

Structural Use of Iron in Ottoman Architecture (from the 15th to the Early 19th Century)

G. Tanyeli and U. Tanyeli

Faculty of Architecture, Istanbul Technical University, Istanbul, Turkey

Abstract

This paper has to be an introductory summary because of the amazing abundance of its subject material, which has not been evaluated and published properly until now. Therefore, in spite of its all-embracing title, which aims to cover a period of four hundred years, we are not able to draw a detailed picture of the structural use of wrought-iron in Ottoman architecture beyond showing a general view of it. Also we cannot claim to have covered all aspects of the research with the same depth, because historical information, both in architecture and writing, is not easily available for the whole period.

Categories of the Iron Elements

What has been previously published on the structural use of iron in Ottoman Turkey was restricted mainly to elements such as clamps, pins and ties. In the Ottoman archives there are numerous documents in which big quantities of iron for important buildings are ordered, but, naturally, they never stated where and how the iron was employed. The most detailed information in the use of iron in architecture is in an 18th century treatise. The author of the treatise, one Ahmed Efendi [1], narrated the process of construction of the Mosque of Nuruosmaniye (1748-1755); and as a part of his narrative he wrote of the reinforcement of the structure with iron rings at several levels of the building. However, precise observations on buildings give valuable clues which show that Ottoman architecture developed an iron-using tradition as much as two centuries before the treatise of Nuruosmaniye. Structural use of iron in Ottoman architecture can be divided into five groups.

Clamps and Pins

Before 1450 Ottoman architecture used iron only as clamps and pins and these uses were rather limited. Even after 1450 for at least a forty year period, clamps were employed only where they were unavoidable. For instance, in the kitchen block of the Palace of Edirne (third quarter of the 15th century) masonry fastened with clamps was used only in the piers, and the walls were built in an alternate brick and stone construction, because this was relatively cheap. The mosque of the Bayezid Complex which was built after 15 or 20 years in the same city (1484-88) proves that the clamped ashlar masonry reached its standard technique here. The mosque's riverside position and the rise of the river bed in the course of five centuries damaged the facade of the building with numerous little cracks, because extreme and constant dampness is over-corrosive for the clamps below the surface. Thanks to the damage on the facade, many clamps are now easy to see, and it seems that all the stone blocks are fastened with them. Besides clamps, there is sufficient information on the use of vertical pins which were installed in the minarets and seen in the restoration works; e.g. Kulaç [2]. From the late 15th and early 16th century onwards masonry fastened with pins and clamps was a standard technique for minaret construction. This made us think that in the mid-16th century, minaret-building techniques reached their constructive climax, which continues up to the end of the 19th century. In a country like Turkey which is situated on an earthquake belt, it is natural to understand quickly that it is not possible to build a slender tower structure like an Ottoman minaret with only the cohesive quality of the mortar. Some iron elements, clamps and pins, are needed to resist the lateral thrusts. Lateral thrusts which oblige architects to employ pins, may also affect the voussoirs of arches and the balustrade and parapet slabs; this necessity was understood in Ottoman architecture at least as early as the mid-15th century.

Around the 1550's, clamps and pins became widely applied iron elements in Ottoman masonry construction, and new sorts of clamps also appeared. For example, contrary to the normal Ottoman clamp which seldom exceeds 50 cm, a new long clamp, called "Frengî" (European), appeared in the mid-16th century. We do not know why this clamp was named "European". Ahmed Efendi [1] states that it was at least 75 cm long. "Frengî" clamps were generally used to tie stone brackets to the main building behind them like those on the Golden Horn facade of the Harem of Topkapi Palace in Istanbul (c.1660s). The clamps of these brackets are approximately 2m long.

There is no experimental research on the structural behaviour of the clamps in the masonry of Ottoman buildings. We have to be content with some *a priori* suppositions. The first supposition is that the behaviour of the clamped masonry is more satisfactory than ordinary masonry against tensile stresses; the second one is that the clamps function especially while the building is under construction. Ottoman masonry construction consists of two wythes, which are made with stone blocks fastened with clamps, and an infill which is a sort of concrete (horasan) plus rubble stone. The main problem with this technique is to prevent the deformation of the wythes during the settlement of the infill. The Romans who first used this masonry technique solved the problem by setting the infill gradually in layers, but this was a time-wasting practice. The Ottoman clamped masonry technique makes the wythes rise rapidly before the infill becomes solidified. This speedy construction process also made the infill more coherent than that which was set in layers like the Roman *opus caementitium*.

Iron beams

Towards the 1550s iron bars began to be used as beams in Ottoman buildings. The main reason for the emergence of iron beams was, perhaps, the need for building floor systems which can not be constructed with ordinary vaulting. As a measure of fire protection, timber floors were eliminated from the field of monumental building design. For example, according to Silahdar [3], the Sultan ordered that iron elements, instead of timber ones, had to be used in the restoration of the palace after the disastrous fire of 1665, for fear of fire. Mainstone [4] stated that the first European attempts to use iron as floor beams were also related to the demand for building fireproof floor systems. These fireproof floor systems which were built according to the will of the Sultan are still visible in some areas of the palace (Fig. 1). In the basement of Vâlide Dairesi there is an interesting example of it, which is formed with 300cm long triplets of iron beams (each has a section of 10 x 8.5 cm) that carry 250 cm long secondary beams, (8.5 x 7 cm) which are placed at 35 cm intervals and the spaces between the secondary beams are spanned with shallow brick vaults or "jack arches". This is a very simple solution, but the system which was applied in the gallery floors of some mosques is even simpler than that. The wrought-iron beams in them are placed simply in parallel rows to span a minimum of 4 m. Examples of this method are now perceptible - if not visible - because of the cracks, present on the plastered surface of the gallery ceilings of many important mosques. For example: Rüstem Paşa (Istanbul 1561-62) and Selimiye Mosques (Edirne, 1569-75).

In some cases iron beams are not the primary components of the structural system, but they function as extra safety precautions which can support the system. For example, in the ceiling of the vestibule of Hadim Hasan Paşa Medrese (1595-96) in Istanbul, thin iron bars (10 cm x 2 cm) were used under the stone floor slabs to support them against accidental loads. The aim of the designer here was to eliminate a structural weakness by using an iron auxiliary element. This sort of element can be observed in many similar forms and in numerous places, especially in architecturally unimportant parts of the building. For instance, some stone door and window lintels were supported by thin iron bars. In the 18th century these auxiliary iron elements became more functional and aesthetically more gratifying, as in the ceiling system of the side porticos of the Laleli Mosque (1759-1763) which was constructed with marble slabs. Though these marble slabs are self-supported structural units, the architect preferred to strengthen them by using square-section iron bars which were rotated 45° along their horizontal axes and concealed in the pointings between the slabs whose touching surfaces were cut to make V-formed canals.

In all the examples which were discussed above, iron was generally used to substitute for timber without taking due advantage of its specific qualities. Iron was employed as a slender stone lintel or as a fireproof timber joist. Because of this, all the known iron beams of the period have rectangular sections. There is not a single example of any experiment with another cross- section form. This means that Ottoman builders never understood the importance of the section form of the iron beam for employing its load-carrying capacity. There are numerous examples in which cross-sections have not been used effectively; i.e. the major principal axis of the beam is placed horizontally in many cases.

In Ottoman architecture, the iron beams were simply-supported structural elements. Generally, the ends of the iron bar were bent so as to form "L"s, then they were inserted into the holes which were prepared on the block of stone and the holes were filled with molten lead. It is obvious that this system of anchorage is no different from that of the clamps. Sometimes iron rods were not anchored; their ends were only placed on the masonry construction (for example, in the structure in Fig. 1) without being bent. However, the solution to the supports of the iron tensile rods is not so simple. It seems that Ottoman engineering was more successful in tensile iron rods and created its best solutions in this sort of structural problem.

Singular structural ties

The simplest example of iron in a tensile bar is the stuctural tie. This sort of tie functions as a stiffener in vaults and arches. The first iron arch ties appeared in Ottoman architecture after 1450. Early ties are timber struts. Iron ties which were employed in the vaulting were a late innovation; the first examples of them were used in the mid-16th century. For example, the ties which stiffen the barrel vaults of the side galleries in Kara Ahmet Paşa Mosque (after 1558) are among the early examples of iron vault ties. Tie rods can effectively be used only in barrel vaults, and the barrel vault was the most disliked structural shell in Ottoman architecture. These architectural limitations made vault ties rather rare. They were generally employed in secondary parts of the buildings. Arch ties were also rare used independently. The tie rods of the hexahedral semidomes of Süleymaniye Mosque which function as independent arch ties are a good example.

The best known and most widely applied type of singular structural tie is the composite system which consists of several tie rods that cross on the vertical axis of a column or a pier. The role of these rods, which bind the column of the pier to another column, pier or wall, is to stiffen the structural system. For example, four main piers of the Süleymaniye Mosque were tied in three directions with iron rods. The system in the Kara Ahmet Paşa Mosque is even more interesting (Fig.2). The main dome was supported in this building by six columns, two of which are placed on the axis parallel to the *kibla* wall, and these columns are stabilised in three directions with iron rods. The use of structural tie rods in the courtyard colonnades was also a widespread practice in Ottoman architecture. There are numerous examples of it from the mid-15th century up to the 19th.

In Ottoman technology the supports for iron rods which were employed in tension were prepared with the help of an artifact called "simid" (ring) in Turkish. A "simid" was a rectangular wrought-iron ring which was placed in the masonry construction and, after the anchorage, buried in it. The end of a rod was bent to form an L, then placed in the "simid" and was tightly packed with scrap iron pieces, or in early buildings, with gravel; and finally molten lead was cast into the "simid" to fix the end (or ends) of the rod (or rods). After this operation the iron rod became partly buried in the masonry. It was usual to coat the buried part of it with lead 0.5 or 1.0 cm thick. The intention of the coating was, without doubt, to protect the iron from corrosion. The "simid" support is an expensive and time-wasting method of anchorage. Because of this, perhaps, a new method of anchorage, "kiliç" (literally "sword" in Turkish), was invented in the mid-17th century. As far as we know, the oldest examples of it can be seen in Köprülü Library and in Misir Çarşisi (covered market), c. 1640 and 1663 respectively. In this method of anchorage the rods were never joined to each other as in the "simid", but they function as independent ties. The application process of the tie which is anchored with "kiliçs" at first is not very different from that of the ties with "simids". First, a groove was prepared at a certain level of the wall on which the tie would be placed, and after the tie was wet molten lead was poured into the groove. The tie was at least 15 or 20 cm longer than the wall , and both ends of the tie which were left outside the surface of the wall were pierced vertically to place little vertical iron bars ("kiliçs") in the holes. Although it is not easy to determine precisely the development of the "kiliç", it can be supposed that two new types of "kiliçs", concealed and half-concealed types, appeared at the beginning of the 18th century. A half-concealed "kiliç" is hidden in a socket on the surface of the outer wall of the building. A concealed "kiliç" is totally hidden in the masonry construction (Fig.3).

The appearance of the "kiliç' proves that structural iron, which was employed prior to the 1650s only in the most important buildings, became widespread from the mid-

17th century onwards in all sorts of buildings; even for ordinary commercial structures in Istanbul. Especially in the multi-storey buildings, storeys above the ground floor level are always reinforced with iron tie rods stiffened with "kiliçs" - sometimes more than one in each wall. In a city like Istanbul which is shaken frequently by earthquakes iron reinforcements are extremely important. However, it cannot be assumed that the iron support and joint elements, called "simid", were dismissed after the invention of the "kiliç". When the designer did not want to show the iron rods on the surface of the wall and wanted to join tie rods to each other, within the masonry construction, he preferred to use "simids" such as those in the Nuruosmaniye Mosque and the Çirağan Palace, even as late as the 1860s. But it is important to point out that the "simids" for the latter were not made by the native technology but were industrially produced in Britain.

Iron Ring Systems

In Ottoman architecture the first buildings which were reinforced with iron ring systems appeared in the second half of the 16th century. Nevertheless, we have to be careful regarding this problem because iron ring systems are seldom visible. In at least two 16th century tomb structures iron ring reinforcements are partly visible. Both buildings, the tombs of Süleyman the Magnificent and Selim II, were designed by Sinan and built respectively in 1566-70 and 1577 in Istanbul. Some of their iron reinforcements are concealed and some of them are visible. In the tomb of Süleyman the Magnificent the building was reinforced at three levels: the first at the top of the capitals of the deambulatorium (visible); the second at the top of the capitals of the columns of the domed inner core (also visible) and the third, at the base of the outer dome (concealed). The first one is not structurally very important as a component of the main system, but the other two, especially the latter, are extremely necessary elements (Fig. 4).

In the tomb of Selim II (Fig. 5) there is a concealed tensile ring and some other iron reinforcements which are partly visible - they cross a stairwell transversely at different levels - besides a ring system at the top of the capitals of the octagonal inner core. It seems that the concealed ring encircles the building at the level of the base of the outer dome. We supposed that what can be partly seen in the window openings in the lower part of the outer dome is another continuous iron reinforcement necessary to tighten the shell to carry horizontal tensile stresses. Perhaps because of this "probable" tensile ring, the outer dome is almost without cracks in spite of its thinness and 21 m diameter. Moreover, the outer dome of Süleyman's tomb, which lacks, above the level of the base, a tensile ring, is full of cracks.

The techniques for detecting iron in these buildings are still insufficient. This makes a complete understanding of the structural use of iron in Ottoman architecture impossible. We are almost ignorant of the iron reinforcements in the largest 16th and 17th century buildings except for the visible tie rods. For example, it is not possible to draw a complete plan of the iron elements in the Süleymaniye Mosque, but a comparative cross-analysis can reveal some problems. We re-evaluated the information in Barkan [5], and according to our estimation the total weight of the iron rods which were employed in the Sultan Ahmet Complex, which is 55% as large as the Süleymaniye Complex, was thrice the weight of those which were used on the Süleymaniye. This means that the iron rods which are unconcealed in the Süleymaniye have to be the total of the iron mentioned in the documents, except perhaps for a tensile ring hidden in the main dome. On the contrary, Sultan Ahmet Mosque has to consist of many more concealed iron reinforcements. It can be concluded that, from the 1550s to the early 17th century, iron ring systems became more widely used. The increase in the use of iron reinforcements continued in

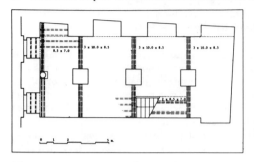

Fig. 1   Floor system in the basement
         of Vâlide Dairesi. Plan

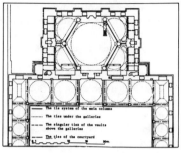

Fig. 2   Iron reinforcements in
         Kara Ahmet Paşa Mosque.
         Plan

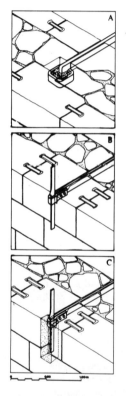

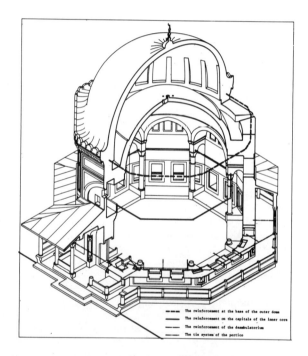

Fig. 3   Types of anchorage: Fig. 4   Iron reinforcements in the tomb of
         A. Simid, B. Ordi-   Süleyman the Magnificent. Isometric
         nary Kılıç, C. Half-   perspective
         hidden Kılıç.

the 17th and the 18th centuries. For instance, the Hekimoğlu Ali Paşa Mosque (1734) was reinforced at least at two levels. Possibly there is a third tensile ring on the lower part of the dome (Fig. 6). Three sides of the building were also reinforced at the gallery level with iron rods. In the Hekimoğlu Ali Paşa Mosque, one can observe an interesting novelty; here, the section form of the iron tensile rods is not rectangular but circular (Ø9.5 cm) but they were made partially rectangular where they were embedded in the wall for anchorage.

The climax of the Ottoman architectural iron technology is the Nuruosmaniye Mosque (1748-55). According to the documentary evidence, which was given by Ahmed Efendi [1] and insufficiently evaluated by Kuban [6], it was reinforced with iron rods at nine levels, four of them are almost easily visible. What is also astonishing in the Nuruosmaniye is that the iron reinforcements at the level of the columns of the gallery were horizontally triangulated. This triangulation can be observed neither in the buildings of the past nor in the successors of the Nuruosmaniye. (Fig. 7).

The most probable explanation of the "invention " of the iron ring systems is the unsatisfactory response of the ordinary masonry construction to tensile stresses. To make this defect disappear, clamped masonry is the first among the solutions. But, along with the increase in the span of the vaulting, it can be concluded that the capacity of the clamped masonry became too low to carry the horizontal tensile stresses. This makes the installation of iron reinforcements into the masonry structural system an unavoidable necessity. Nevertheless, one can suppose that, in many cases, iron tensile rings were placed in other sections of the buildings which are not affected by tensile stresses under normal conditions. It seems that this sort of reinforcement functions only under accidental loadings such as those generated by earthquakes.

Iron reinforcement as an afterthought

All the types of iron elements discussed above were also employed for making repairs and alterations in existing buildings. For example, important cracks were fastened with gigantic clamps, like those at the main arches of the Mihrimah Mosque (1562-65), which was damaged by the earthquake of 1766, and photographed by Gurlitt [7] in the 1890s; or new structural elements which were added to existing structures were stiffened by binding them to the old building with rows of clamps.

In many places iron beams substitute for arches which were removed to alter the buildings. There are even iron arches which replace removed masonry arches such as those in the Yemiş Odasi in the Topkapi Palace. In this tiny structure there is a wrought-iron arch in the place of the two demolished arches on the front facade of the original building (Fig. 8). The best examples of the category of the "iron as an afterthought" are tensile rings. Many buildings were encircled at the level of the drum of the dome or at the lower levels of the building mass with iron elements. For instance, the cracked dome of the Ayas Paşa Mosque (1528) in Saray, was reinforced with an iron ring on the drum. An octagonal 15th century building, Tütünsüz Baba Türbesi in Edirne, was also reinforced with a tensile ring. Both examples employ "belts" which were made with hinged iron rods (9 x 0.6 cm), each one approximately 3m long. Both reinforcements might be applied in the early 18th century if they were contemporaneous with the other alterations in these buildings. In the Kalenderhane Mosque, originally a 12th century Byzantine church, the tensile ring on the drum of the main dome is rather different from those observed on the former buildings. The drum of the Kalenderhane which has a diameter of 8.20 m is reinforced with two iron rings that have cross-sections of 8 x 7 cm. The first

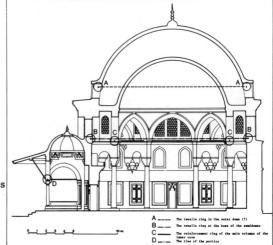

Fig. 5 Iron reinforcements
in the tomb of
Selim II. Longi-
tudinal section.

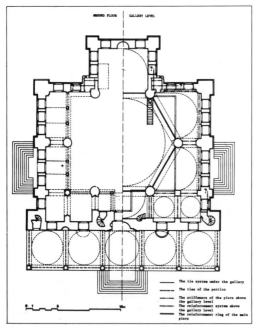

Fig. 6 Iron reinforcements in
Hekimoğlu Ali Paşa Mosque. Plan

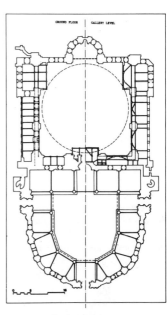

Fig. 7 Iron reinforcements
in Nuruosmaniye
Mosque. Plan

ring encircles the cracked structure on the outside, contrary to the second one which was placed, curiously enough, inside it, and these two were tied to each other with iron bars which can be seen within the windows of the drum. These rings, perhaps, were applied in 1747 when the building was completely restored. It probably substitutes for the original timber reinforcing ring whose empty grooves are still visible.

Conclusion

In the second half of the 19th century Ottoman architectural iron technology became gradually old fashioned. The change began with the import of European iron. Nevertheless, architects at first preferred to use European iron in the traditional Ottoman way. The real destructive force upon the Ottoman iron technology was the large scale application of cast-iron in architecture. When this European architectural invention reached Ottoman Turkey, traditional wrought-iron lost all its importance. From this time onwards, what was imported to Turkey was not the technology or the material, but industrially produced cast-iron elements, even in the form of prefabricated "packages" of buildings. Ottoman architecture, perhaps the most abundantly iron-using pre-industrial tradition in the world, could not resist this industrial invasion.

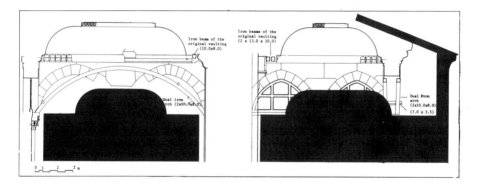

Fig. 8   The dual iron arch in the Yemiş Odası in Topkapı Palace. Sections.

References

1. Efendi, Ahmed. Târih-i Câm-i Şerîf-i Nûri Osmanî, supplement to Târih-i Osmanî Encümeni Mecmuasi, İstanbul, 1335-1337, 1917-1919.

2. Kulaç, Ü. Türk Taş Minarelerinde Döner Merdiven ve Metal Bahlanti Ememanlarinin Yatay Yükleri Karşilamadaki İşleveri, pp. 235-240, I. Uluslararasi Türk-İslam Bilim ve Teknoloji Tarihi Kongresi 14-18 Eylül 1981-Bildiriler, Vol. 1, İTÜ Mimarlik Fakültesi, Istanbul, 1981.

3. Silahdar Findiklili Mehmed Ağa. Silagdar Tarigi, Vol. 1. Devlet Matbaasi, Istanbul, 1928.

4. Mainstone, R. Developments in Structural Form, the M.I.T. Press, Cambridge, Mass., 1975.

5. Barkan, Ö.L., Süleymaiye Cami ve İmareti İnşaati (1550-1557). Cedvel No. 18, Vol. 2, pp. 296-302, TTK Publications, Andara, 1979.

6. Kuban, Notes on Building Technology of the 18th Century, the Building of the Mosque of Nuruosmaniye at Istanbul, According to Târih-i Camii Şerif-i Nur-u Osmanî, pp. 271-293, I. Uluslararasi Türk-İslam Bilim ve Teknoloji Tarihi Kongresi 14-18 Eylül 1981-Bildiriler, Vol. 5, İTÜ Mimarlik Fakültesi, Istanbul, 1981.

7. Gurlitt, C. Die Baukunst Konstantinopels, Vol. 4, E. Wasmuth, Berlin, 1912.

A Structural Study of the Michelangelo and Della Porta Designs for the St. Peter's Dome

Elwin C. Robison
School of Architecture and Environmental Design, Kent State University, Kent, Ohio, USA

Abstract

An axisymmetric finite element analysis of the dome designs for St. Peter's by Giacomo Della Porta and Michelangelo Buonarroti shows a similar structural behavior for both projects. Della Porta's taller, pointed dome has smaller tensile hoop forces, but Michelangelo's hemispherical design is still a viable project, requiring only about 60% more tensile reinforcement at the haunches.

Text

The dome of St. Peter's, Vatican is one of the great domes of the Renaissance, both in terms of architectural significance and physical size. As the central basilica of the western church, it was the focus of attention of Italian architects and builders during the years of its demolition and rebuilding from 1506 through 1689. Much of this attention was centered on the design and construction of the dome, as it is the crowning element visible to the city and the largest dome constructed in Italy since Brunelleschi's Santa Maria del Fiore in Florence, completed over a century before.

The project for the new St. Peter's began with plans for a tomb for Pope Julius II. A new chapel appended to the old Constantinian basilica of St. Peter's was proposed, but the dilapidated condition of the old cathedral together with the ambition of both Pope Julius II and his architect Donato Bramante encouraged the decision to tear the old church down and replace it with a building fitting as the focus of the western church. Bramante's design for St. Peter's was based on antique precedent and centrally-planned church designs which Leonardo had developed while he and Bramante worked together in Milan. The Greek cross plan magnificently combined the dual roles of the primary church of the Roman Catholic faith and martyrium--symbolically significant because of the western church's claim of authority through St. Peter. The altar, located on the traditional site of St. Peter's burial, was to be positioned at the center of the Greek cross, directly underneath the Pantheon-inspired dome.

Construction proceeded rapidly on the new edifice but at Bramante's death in 1516 only the four central piers and adjacent nave barrel vaults were completed. A succession of architects were appointed to direct the St. Peter's fabbrica in the ensuing years, resulting in significant alterations to Bramante's original scheme. Most of these architects wished to abandon Bramante's Greek cross plan in favor of a Latin cross plan with a longer nave to accommodate large throngs of pilgrims. However, little was accomplished with these changed plans because the usual financial and political impediments were augmented by both a premature death of the architect (in the case of Raphael Sansio), and inordinate amounts of time being consumed in design and model-building (in the case of Antonio da Sangallo). This period of indecision and sporadic work ended in 1546 with the appointment of Michelangelo as chief architect. Because of his fame as an artist he was able to overrule competing political factions (most significantly the 'setta sangallesca') and make significant progress on construction. More importantly, he recognized the merits of Bramante's centralized design, and clarified it by creating a single subsidiary space circulating around the emboldened piers of the crossing.

Michelangelo was in his 60's when he was appointed architect of St. Peter's. It became apparent that Michelangelo, an old man, would not live to see the dome completed. He therefore had a definitive wooden model built from 1558-61 to act as a guide to workmen so that no confusion would . suspend construction upon his death. Despite careful planning, however, changes in the papacy suspended work on the dome for 24 years following Michelangelo's death in 1564.

Ten years later, under the papacy of Gregory XIII, Giacomo Della Porta was appointed as architect and remained in that post until 1602 giving the fabbrica of St. Peter's an important continuity. No major construction was undertaken during Gregory XIII's pontificate, but Della Porta directed maintenance and consolidation work, and had time to acquaint himself with the building and plan for the completion of the dome. During this time Della Porta probably had Michelangelo's wooden model altered to study his new dome profile. The reason for altering the dome design was probably to make it more visible from the piazza in front. Michelangelo had enough influence to overrule the clerics and retain the Greek cross plan, but his successors did not. Extensions to the nave were discussed during Gregory XIII's pontificate, and although the extension of the nave did not occur until after Della Porta's death, he may have anticipated the reduced visibility of the dome with an extended nave. As Fig. 1 shows Della Porta's taller dome is just barely visible over the extended nave. Michelangelo's lower dome would have hardly been visible from the piazza with such an extended nave.

Della Porta's plans for the dome finally came to fruition with the election of Pope Sixtus V in 1585. The newly elected Pope had ambitious plans for the city of Rome, and cut several new streets through the city fabric to accommodate pilgrims. In the area of the Vatican the obelisk currently centered in St. Peter's Square was transported there by Domenico Fontana, and work was restarted on the cupola in 1588 after the long hiatus. Sixtus V was anxious to have St. Peter's completed, and work proceeded rapidly, in some cases laborers working around the clock. By May 1590 the final stone was placed in the dome, and stucco work and the lead covering of the dome were completed by late 1591.

Because Della Porta redesigned the dome after the supporting drum was already completed it comes as no surprise that Michelangelo's design and Della Porta's are similar. Both designs employed 16 radial ribs connected by an inner and outer shell. On the exterior, Della Porta's dome is similar to Michelangelo's, Della Porta having slightly pointed the dome profile and raised the springing of the dome 4.8 meters higher than Michelangelo's[2]. However, Michelangelo's ribs are thicker, and project more strongly above the surface of the dome. Aesthetically Michelangelo's design is bolder, and more plastically articulated, while Della Porta's dome is more tightly drawn and thinly articulated.

In order to better understand the difference between Michelangelo's and Della Porta's versions of St. Peter's dome I conducted a finite element analysis of the two designs using the ANSYS analysis code. The work of analysis is still in progress, as to date only axisymmetric models have been investigated. However, some basic conclusions can be made regarding the structure and the design aims of the two architects. The discretized model of the Della Porta dome used dome profiles published by Poleni[6] and Di Stefano[2], controlled with actual measurements. The axisymmetric model with static gravity loads used plane stress elements with defined thickness for the ribs, and the dome was considered pinned at the level of the nave vault and restricted from lateral motion in the plane of the nave vault. This model does not analyze cracking in the dome nor differential settlement in its support, but is useful for qualitative comparison. A check against the detailed structural investigation undertaken in 1742 by Giovanni Poleni[6] indicates a good modeling of dome behavior. In his report Poleni published detailed elevations showing cracking and deflections in the dome structure. Comparing these results with the drawings shows a close correlation between analysis results and dome behavior. Therefore, despite the simplicity of the model the results are accurate enough to make some general conclusions regarding the dome structure.

The heavy lantern causes the crown of the dome to deflect downward, and tensile hoop stresses are present in the haunches of the dome (Fig. 3). Local areas of high principle stresses are found immediately under the lantern, as the inner and outer shells tend to shear past one another. The 1742 Vanvitelli measured drawings of the dome published by Poleni confirm the analysis in that they show cracking of the ribs in this area (Fig. 2). Repairs have been made to the rib cracks, but the stresses have been relieved by cracking at the junction of the outer shell and the rib. According to the capo degli operai this cracking has remained stable in recent history. Efforts to patch the crack result in re-cracking, but the fissure does not propogate further into the dome. Another significant area of principal stress in the drum counterforts. This area also contains significant cracking in the 1742 drawings. These counterforts are too small to provide significant resistance to the lateral spreading of the dome at the springing and are pushed aside and fractured by the movement. Their structural contribution to the dome is negligible, and they had to be extensively repaired in the 1920's [2] and 1940's[8].

The most significant area of stress in terms of dome performance is the region of tensile hoop stresses in the haunches of the dome. In masonry construction the object is to eliminate tension within the structure because of the low strength of masonry in tension, usually about 1/10th of its compressive strength. This preliminary analysis indicates that Della Porta's dome has a maximum tensile hoop stress of approximately 1.3 kg/cm^2, higher than my earlier reported figure[7]. This level of stress is below Masson's reported strength of Medieval lime mortar of 2 kg/cm^2,[4] and since accounts in the Archivio della Reverenda Fabbrica di San Pietro mention shipments of both lime and pozzolan it is probable that the mortar used in St. Peter's was of greater strength than that used in Medieval France. Despite this low level of stress, Mark and Hutchinson [3] have suggested that local tensile stresses in unreinforced masonry will, given time, eventually produce cracking. This low level of tensile stress eventually caused cracking in the St. Peter's dome, until by the 1740's major renovation was necessary. Della Porta provided for these tensile stresses by placing large iron hoops about the haunches of the dome (labeled P in Poleni's section, Fig. 2). Poleni only records 2 chains about the dome, but the account books in the Archivio della Reverenda Fabbrica di San Pietro, I, Ser. Arm, Arm. 25, Pacco 120 list deliveries of chains for the 'terzo cerchio' in October of 1589. At the time of Poleni's restoration both chains he knew about had broken (perhaps the cause for the deterioration of the dome which prompted the repairs), and he repaired these and added 5 more chains. This reinforcement has eliminated vertical cracks in the dome (with the exception of a vertical crack in the outer shell in the sector facing the Sistine Chapel) so that the present uncracked dome may act in a similar manner to the axisymmetric computer model.

A major difficulty remains in determining the exact form of Michelangelo's design for the dome. In an early study, Lille 93, Michelangelo began by sketching in a pointed profile for the dome but later sketched in a hemispherical outline. Drawings indicate that Michelangelo wavered back and forth between a pointed profile patterned after the Florentine dome of his patria and a hemispherical solution, but the large wooden model built just before Michelangelo's death originally had a hemispherical profile[5]. This wooden model was later altered to conform to Della Porta's design, removing Michelangelo's record of the exterior dome profile and his lantern. However, Dupérac's engraving of the project contains several discrepancies which make analysis of the project difficult.

In addition to vaulting shape, another important factor in determining dome stresses--and therefore stability--is the thickness of the dome shells. Della Porta's dome has tapering shells which become thinner towards the crown of the vault reducing the dead load and tensile hoop stresses by approximately 20% over an untapered dome. In an earlier comparison of Della Porta's and Michelangelo's domes using dome profiles by Di Stefano, Michelangelo's design had tensile hoop stresses significantly higher than Della Porta's dome, partly because of the heaviness and lack of significant tapering in the dome shells[7]. However, the dome profile published by Di Stefano does not match with the wooden model nor the Dupérac engraving.

The Dupérac engravings, made from the wooden model before its alteration, are an important source of information on Michelangelo's original project. However, the springing of the outer dome in section oversails the drum by a significant amount--probably an error in switching from measurements of the built drum to measurements of the wooden model. Di Stefano corrected this error in his dome profile, but the dome shells are thicker than those reported by Vasari, and thicker than measurements of the original Michelangelo model by Dupérac and Dosio. Vasari stated that the vault thickness was 4 1/2 palmi (1 palmo = 0.264 meters) or 1.19 meters. Likewise Dupérac in his sketch of Michelangelo's model (Met. Mus. Art 49.92.92) records a vault thickness of 4 1/2 palmi for the outer shell, and measured the inner shell at the springing as 3 oncie 3 minuti, or 1.19 meters ((3 3/5)/12 palmi times the scale factor of 15). Michelangelo's shells tapered only slightly towards the crown, and although Dosio records a vault thickness of 3 1/2 palmi at the crown of the outer shell (Casa Buonarroti, Florence, 35A) Dupérac records a measurement from the model at that point of 3 1/2 oncie, or 1.155 meters. Since the Dupérac measurement was taken directly from the model, it is chosen for analysis purposes.

The Michelangelo design shows a similar hoop stress pattern in the cross section through a rib, with a peak magnitude of about 1.5 kg/cm^2 (Fig. 3). Although the hoop stresses are similar in magnitude, the distribution of the stress is wider, resulting in a total force to be resisted about 60% greater than Della Porta's design--in other words more chains would have been necessary to prevent cracking in the Michelangelo dome. Michelangelo also used the strongly projecting ribs structurally as well as aesthetically. The deep ribs bear directly upon the counterforts placing a significant amount of compressive force upon them.   High principal stresses in the counterforts suggest that they may have cracked and failed as they did on Della Porta's dome, but a more detailed model is necessary to investigate this issue.

Studying the analysis results, it is apparent that the two designers conceived of their domes in slightly different terms.   Michelangelo designed a system of deep massive ribs which bore directly onto the counterforts of the drum.   The inner dome shell was deeply carved by inset panels so that it became proportionately very thin compared to the heavy ribs.   Della Porta on the other hand used thinner ribs and tapered vaults with an attenuated profile which allowed him to raise the crown of the dome by over 6 meters and still reduce the hoop forces from the levels in Michelangelo's lower design.   Future refinement of the analysis will likely change the quantitative value of the present study, but it is evident from the analysis that both designers had a good intuitive feel for dome behavior, and both men responded aesthetically to their conception of the dome structure.

References

[1]   Brandi, Cesare. La Curva della Cupola di San Pietro, Quaderno, Accademia Nazionale dei Lincei, No. 123, pp. 1-17, 1968.

[2]   Di Stefano, Roberto. La cupola di S. Pietro, Rome, 1980.

[3]   Mark, Robert and Hutchinson, Paul. On the Structure of the Roman Pantheon, Art Bulletin, LXVIII, pp. 24-34, 1986.

[4]   Masson, Henri. Le Rationalisme dans l'Architecture du Moyen Age, Bulletin Monumental, LXXVI, 1912.

[5]   Millon, Henry A., and Smyth, Craig Hugh. Michelangelo Architect. Milan, 1988.

[6]   Poleni, Giovanni. Memorie Istoriche della Gran Cupola del Tempio Vaticano, e dei Danni di Essa, e dei Ristoramenti loro, divise in libri cinque, Padova, 1748.

[7]   Robison, Elwin. St. Peter's Dome, Vatican: The Michelangelo and Della Porta Designs, in Domes From Antiquity to the Present, pp. 253-260, Proceedings of the IASS-MSU International Symposium, Istanbul, Turkey, 1988.

[8]   Wittkower, Rudolf. La Cupola di San Pietro di Michelangelo: Riesame critico delle testimonianze contemporanee, Florence, 1964.

Figure 1. Exterior view of Della Porta's dome for St. Peter's.

Figure 2. Section of Della Porta's dome for St. Peter's, from Poleni, Memorie istoriche...

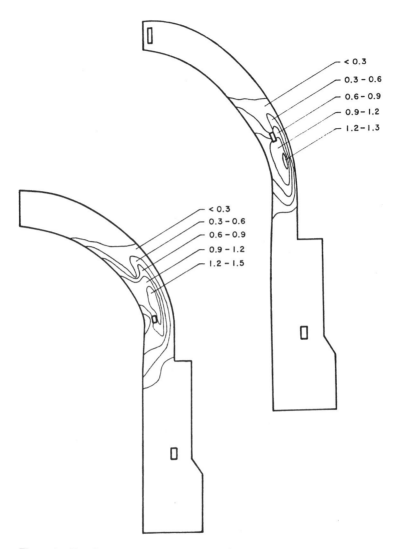

Figure 3. Tensile hoop stresses in kg/cm² on cross section through rib
for Michelangelo's dome proposal (left) and Della Porta's built dome (right).

Cracks and Chains. Unpublished Documents for a History of the Projected Restorations on the Cupola of Santa Maria del Fiore. In appendix: Leonardo and the Cracks on Brunelleschi's Dome.

F.P. Di Teodoro

The Armand Hammer Center for Leonardo Studies at UCLA, College of Fine Arts, University of California, Los Angeles, USA

ABSTRACT

The purpose of this study is to explain some still obscure or not well-known aspects of the vicissitudes of the cupola of Florence Cathedral and its cracks in the XVII and XVIII centuries. A considerable amount of unpublished material from some Italian libraries and archives – National Library, Riccardiana Library, Opera di Santa Maria del Fiore Archives in Florence, Marciana Library in Venice, Vatican Library – sheds light on some new aspects of the chains which at the end of 1695 the Survey Commission decided to apply to the cupola to prevent its collapse. This paper makes known the weight, size, number and conformation of the chains and studies the still unpublished documents which Poleni in 1748 drew upon in chapter XVIII of his "Memorie istoriche della Gran Cupola del Tempio Vaticano". It also studies and interprets documents yielding new information on the activities of the 1695 Commission. Alessandro Cecchini's writings published in 1753 by G.B. Clemente Nelli and an intuition of Carlo Pedretti lead to a hypothesis on Leonardo's late studies on arches and cupolas. The suggestion is put forward that these studies have a bearing on Baccio d'Agnolo's gallery begun in 1507–8 on the tambour of the cupola.

INTRODUCTION

I do not mean here to treat the numerous questions concerning the debate started at the end of the seventeenth century on the cracks of the dome of Santa Maria del Fiore and on the decision whether to furnish it with strong chains or not: on this subject reference can be made to the essays by Paolo Galluzzi (7), Salvatore Di Pasquale (1), Luciano Barbi and Francesco Di Teodoro (6) as well as to the book by Howard Saalman (4). I would like, instead, to present here information provided by unpublished and almost unknown documents which, in my opinion, have been neglected whereas they can clarify some still obscure aspects of that diverse and difficult debate. These documents will be dealt with more extensively on another occasion.

THE CRACKS

On 4th January 1694/5, Viviani's pupil and friend, Giovan Battista Nelli, presented Cosimo III, Grand Duke of Tuscany, with a report on the "difetti essenziali" verified in the dome of Florence Cathedral. His report showed such a serious situation that a special investigation commission appointed by the Grand Duke started to work only four days later. This unpublished report (14) (ff.31r-33r) includes the following:
- a description of the cracking phenomena in the base of the dome and in the adjoining areas;
- a description of the progress, conformation and dimension of the cracks on the North-East wind and Sirocco sides as well as in the vaulting cells of the dome, in the tambour and the two sacristies of the Priests and the Canons;
- an attempt at dating the cracks by considering that they were one soldo wide in the masonry, whereas they were only one quattrino of a Florentine braccio wide in the fresco by Vasari and Zuccari;
- a description of two phenomena which denoted the persisting progress of the cracks in the dome: 1) on the North-East wind side the mortar used to place some new tiles over the crack in September 1693, split along the crack itself in the nearest part to the ground; 2) the new pavement in the gallery by Baccio d'Agnolo, finished in November 1694, already presented some cracks in December of the same year;
- the first census-taking of the cracks in the various elements of the structure of the double dome and remarks on the state of Brunelleschi's wooden chain.

Some of these considerations would later be found in the report that the deputies drew up and signed at the end of 1695, on 6th December (2).

The first remark in Nelli's report seems to me extremely important; therefore I estimate that it would be worth quoting it in full: Nelle quattro cappelle contigue ai piloni delle sagrestie, i pavimenti allato ad essi appariscono essere di molto tempo fa avvallati e nei muri di testa delle cappelle, vari screpoli pendenti verso detti piloni; e gli archi delle medesime sottoposti alle finestre che alluminano le tribune, notabilmente aperti, dei quali sono calate alquanto, verso terra, parte delle pietre che gli compongono. Ma i muri delle sagrestie si vedono in tutte le lor parti saldi et in quella verso scirocco osservasi un arcone perfettamente a piano, di lunghezza quanta è la larghezza della sagrestia, largo braccia 3 2/5 e grosso b.2 incirca, il quale, con tutto che sia composto di molti pezi, pare d'uno solo: solamente nei voltoni posti sopra ad esse ed impostati intorno all'altezza di quegli delle cappelle e centinati di sesto acutissimo, vedesi appena, nelle congiunzioni dei sesti, qualche ben piccola apertura".

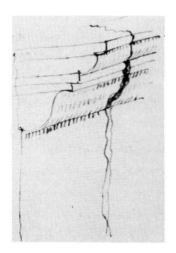

Fig. 1, Crack in the "Cornice del Brunellesco", Florence, N. L., II _ 21, f.52r

The sinking of the pavements of the four chapels adjoining the pillars in the directions of North-East wind and Sirocco, the existence of cracks slanting towards the pillars make me think of a probable combined effect of both a sinking of the foundations and of the beginning of the dome ring.

Nelli's document is the only official evidence from this time where such a detailed survey is described. All these considerations strangely did not appear in the report of December 1695 (2), when it was proposed to hoop the dome with four chains to contain its thrust. Unfortunately, we do not know the reason of that silence on the part of the members of the commission. On the other hand, it is well-known that the sinking of the foundations as a reason for the cracks was the most frequent justification in the works written by those who were against chaining.

On the contrary, Francesco Fontana, who had been asked to give his opinion, or perhaps had been sent by his father Carlo to present it in his stead, was very sententious in the opening of his report, drawn up on 13th June 1696:"Si riconobbe, in primo loco, tutto il basamento del piede di tutti i piloni della nominata cupola non avere patito cessione veruna".Actually, this may well have been a sort of answer to an anonymous work written by Alessandro Cecchini (9) where he objected to the decision of the commission. Cecchini did not hesitate, subsequently, to contest even Fontana's considerations (10).

The further remarks of Bartolomeo Vanni (17) and Leonardo Ximenes (11) allow us to follow the evolution of the cracking situation and evaluate the serious damage caused in the three tribunes and in the bays of the aisles adjoining the base of the dome.

Vanni informs us about the restoration carried out in 1713 in the half-domes of the three tribunes which had shown two "larghe crepature" in each of them since that year. Vanni himself reports in 1723 that "sorgono da terra le uguali crepature che, piegando verso i pilastroni della cupola passano nel tamburo: che sono segni manifesti dell'insensibile cedimento delle gran fondamenta" in the external walls of the bays of the aisles next to the base of the dome. He affirmed that even if in 1720, a few years before, he had ascertained that the cracks in the dome had been provoked (12,18) "da qualche tremoto o da più d'un tremoto". He had personally checked the level of the pavement of the two sacristies, that of the space underneath the dome and of the nearby areas, and had found it "perfettamente orizzontale sicché si vede che da basso non c'è seguito mal nessuno". But in 1696 even Cecchini (10) had already reported to have "ritrovato una parte di questo Edifizio al piano del suo ultimo cornicione per di dentro, a dove imposta la cupola più bassa dell'altra".

Thanks to the accurate surveying made by Ximenes in 1755 and published in 1757 we are given a description of the condition of the ogive arches that lead to the fifteen chapels of the tribunes.(Besides, Ximenes noticed a mouvement "in fuori con direzione riguardante a Scirocco"in the "vasto pilone

frapposto fra la tribuna di S.Antonio e quella di San Zanobi".)
The only parts which have not undergone the detaching of
stone-material or any cracking are: the arch in the chapel of
San Zanobi in the tribune bearing the same name, the arches in
two small chapels in the tribune of the Holy Cross next to the
pillar with the opening towards the left aisle and the arch in
the chapel of the tribune of S.Antonio, also called tribune of
the Cenception, which is next to the pillar with the opening
towards the right aisle.

It is not possible, in my opinion, to determine whether the
extent of the cracking phenomena from 1694 to 1755 was due to a
situation which had worsened over the years or whether, instead,
it was only the result of a more accurate investigation.

THE CHAINS

Some of Nelli's unpublished works in the National Library in
Florence (14), almost all of them autographed, supply us with new
information concerning the chains: location, weight, dimensions,
conformation.

It was Filippo Sengher (f.143r), one of the members of the
commission, who suggested, in June 1695, to hoop the dome with
four iron chains the dimensions of which (braccia
264,240,240,216 for a total of 960 braccia) make me think that
it was Sengher's intention to place them all in the space
between the two domes, i.e., to be more precise: one in the first
corridor (the present level 8), two in the second (the present
level 7), and one between the second and the third (the present
level 6).

The discussions which followed probably lead to a different
solution that was very similar to the final one mentioned in the
report of December 1695. As a matter of fact, Nelli wrote down
(f.145r): "Per rimediare al continuo moto della Cupola di
S.Maria del Fiore, il comun parere è di circondarla di presente
con quattro ordini di catene di ferro (...)delle quali una nel
tamburo, la seconda sopra le morse, la terza sopra le docce e la
quarta fra le due volte nel secondo corridore perché in detti
luoghi si possono accomodare con facilità, più che in altri, e
sono assai prossime a dove di esse è il maggior bisogno (...)".
The global length of the chains was measured as being 1096
braccia.

By comparison the commission evaluated the dimensions of the section: 3x1½ soldi (about 8,75x4,375 cm.). As to the weight,(f.146r), a portion of a chain one Florentine braccio long (58,3626 cm), would weigh 54 libbre, 10 once, 6 denari, 20 grani and 4/7 grano that is, around 18,6263 Kg.

The documents in the National Library of Florence provide the only and still unpublished drawings of the link between the various elements. I will deal with these drawings further on. At this point of my paper I consider it important to specify that a considerable number of documents (a summary is given of the most important) kept in the Archives of the Opera of Santa Maria del Fiore (13), which were known to Galluzzi (7) but were never published, provide all the available information on the construction of the chain:
- 23rd September 1695. Operaio Giulio Mozzi transmits the writ of the Grand Duke to Marquis Fabio Feroni, Soprintendente della Magona del Ferro, charging him with the construction of the chains in the Magona of Leghorn;
- 21st February 1695/6. A few wooden models are sent to Leghorn. They concern the "maglie", the "paletti" and the "biette", together with the elements of the angular chain to be placed on the eight corners of the extrados of the internal dome;
- 10th April 1696. Matteo Prini, Provveditore delle Fortezze e Fabbriche, is informed that the Opera of Santa Maria del Fiore has just received "otto pezzi di catena angolari e sei maglie di ferro";
- 2nd June 1696. Matteo Prini is told that "quarantotto maglie delle più piccole, quarantotto paletti e altrettante biette" should be constructed;
- 28th September 1696. "sedici pezzi del modello d'una delle catene per questa cupola contrassegnati ciascuno con numeri" are sent to the Magona;
- 20th October 1696. The 48 "maglie", the 48 "paletti" and the 48 "biette" have already reached the Opera;
- 5th January 1696/7. Matteo Prini is informed that the Opera has already received the 16 pieces of iron chain together with the 16 wooden models;
- 7th April 1698. Giuseppe Verdi, cashier of the Magona, is given " scudi quattromila quattrocento settanta di moneta, lire sei e soldi 13 predetti" as payment for the construction of the pieces of the chains.

The documents go on providing information on this subject until 28th September 1708 when the remaining iron that was kept

at Leghorn was requested by Nelli for the casting of a new major
bell in the campanile of Florence Cathedral.

On the whole, every chain — or rather the one chain
because, as it is well-known, only one chain was made but never

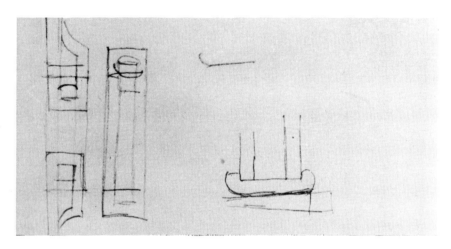

Figs. 2, 3, Elements of the chain designed for the dome,
Florence, N.L., II_ 22, f.175v; II_21, f.149v.

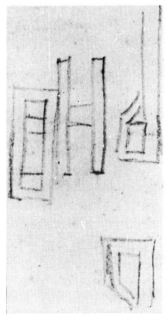

applied — consisted of eight angular
pieces and sixteen straight ones (two
for each face of the octagon). Their
link was obtained with the 48 "maglie",
the 48 "paletti" and the 48 "biette":
two "maglie", two "paletti" and two
"biette" every two "occhi" to be
linked.

The above-mentioned drawings in
the National Library of Florence show
what Viviani (16) (f.139r) had called
"stupenda invenzione che si vedde sul
modello in legno portato dal predetto
Sig. Sengher", that is:1) the way in
which the "occhi" of the chain were
linked; 2) their particular form
created by bending the extremities of
the bars; 3) the conformation of the

"biette" and the "paletti". The former ones were shaped in such a way to slide during the setting of the "paletti". Moreover, both presented a bent connecting surface to facilitate the penetration.

Because of the position chosen for the setting and the conformation of the various elements composing the chain, it was the commission's greatest worry and care to avoid any tampering and damage to the masonries of the dome, although proper adjustments had previously been made to position them. As a matter of fact, Bartolomeo Vanni (17) writes in 1723 that the "traccia già fatta nel corpo interno della cupola per inserirvi la prima catena" had not been restored yet. At the time the chains and the necessary iron parts to link the various elements were heaped in the warehouse of the Opera. And there they could also be seen by Domenico Maria Manni who was carrying out a research for Giovanni Poleni, in 1744 (19) (ff.10r–10v):"(...) a tal'effetto si vedono alcune di dette verghe di lunghezza braccia 14 piegate in mezzo, formando un angolo corrispondente a quello della cupola (...), nell'estremità di queste verghe piegate nel mezzo vi sono li suoi occhi formati dall'istessa verga rivoltata come ⌐⌐◯ perché in detti occhi vi si dovevano collegare con biette le altre verghe dritte ancor esse nella loro estremità occhiute (...)".

We do not know what came of the built chain. The inaction of the members of the commission, clearly indicates the situation of Florentine technical and scientific culture at that time; it also points out the distance between the building practice and Galilean mechanics. On the other hand we have to take into account that through the nineteenth century Vignola's well-known saying: "Ma le fabbriche bene intese vogliono reggersi per se stesse e non stare attaccate colle stringhe" has always had more weight than the scientific theories provided by architects and engineers.

LEONARDO

The eighth part of the gallery was built after the deliberation act of 8th November 1507 following a design presented by Baccio d'Agnolo, Simone del Pollaiolo and Giuliano da Sangallo and was shown publicly on 24th June 1515 but, as it is known from historical sources, Michelangelo's sharp criticism ("una gabbia da grilli", a cricket's cage) caused the work to be interrupted.

As pointed out by Carlo Pedretti (3) Michelangelo's reaction would be better understood if we were sure that Leonardo had given the idea or even designed the gallery. This conclusion can be drawn by considering the stylistic element and taking into account that Baccio d'Agnolo used to carry out other masters' designs. It would not be surprising if Leonardo - who was preparing a treatise "on the causes of cracking of walls" and on the corresponding "remedies" and who had given advice on the construction of the campanile of San Miniato (assigned to Baccio d'Agnolo) - had been asked to design and give suggestions as to the dome gallery even by Giuliano da Sangallo and Simone del Pollaiolo,called Cronaca. These two architects were working together with Leonardo when, between 1500 and 1506, he was consulted as to the foundations of San Salvatore. It seems to me that the way the structure of the gallery was conceived supports the hypothesis of a direct intervention on the part of Leonardo. The gallery was begun with one of the most damaged sides of the tambour (6). This was not by chance: it aimed at making the "ghirlanda" function as a chain.

The Codex Hammer (1506-1508) presents Leonardo's idea of buttressing or hooping the ring at the beginning of some domes to contain their thrust (ff.12B:12v and 12B:25r). This is explained in those passages where he deals with air bubbles on the surface of water and with their form. It was Leonardo's opinion that the static behaviour of the ephemeral architecture of an air bubble on the surface of water is based on the same mechanical principles of that of an actual dome: "The half-sphere of air clothed by water breaks in the third part of its curve; this is proved with the arches of walls (...)" (5).

The flanks and "a ring of smaller bubbles to act as buttresses" are the building principles at the basis of the domes in Leonardo's drawings: for example, in some of the drawings concerning the "tiburio" of Milan Cathedral in the Codex Trivulzianus, in Paris Ms.B and in the Codex Atlanticus.

In the Codex Arundel, f.158v, he also shows how a "more than a half-circle" arch breaks in the same way as the "more than a half-sphere" air bubble which is described in the Codex Hammer. As non-hemispherical bubbles do not need buttresses or flanks, so "the stability of the arch built by an architect lies in the tie or in its flanks".

The abortive gallery project dates from 1507 to 1515. As a gallery was meant by Brunelleschi himself to circle the octagonal tambour, the one by Baccio d'Agnolo was begun on the damaged side of the octagon thus reflecting Leonardo's views on the stability of arches and domes.

Among the folios of the Codex Arundel that form the homogeneus group of notes for a treatise "on the causes of the cracking of walls", f.141v reports Leonardo's views on the causes of the cracking of domes. Both the date assigned to the folio (1500-6) (8) - approximately in the same years when a few designs for the "ghirlanda" "ex parte exteriori dicte testudinis vel cupole" were being studied - and the detailed explanation of the typology of the cracks (a suitable description for the cracks in the Florentine dome) can be considered as the conclusions of a study of the cracking of Brunelleschi's "grande macchina".

That note, illustrated by two sketches, states: "When a dome or a half-dome is crushed from above by an excess of weight, its vaults will form a crack which diminishes towards the top and is wide below the inner side and wide outside; as it happens with the outer husk of an orange, divided into many parts lengthwise; if this is pressed on the opposite sides, the part of the joints that will open most is the most distant from the points of pressure; and for that reason never should the arches of the vaults of any apse be more loaded than the arches of the principal building. Because what weighs most also presses most on the parts below so that they sink into its foundations; but this cannot happen to lighter structures like the said apses".

In the first part of the note Leonardo estimates "an excess of weight" pressing on the top to be the cause of cracks in domes. In the second part we understand that a reason of cracking lies in the sinking of the local foundations. As we have already seen, these same causes were subsequently pointed out by Fontana, Cecchini and Vanni as the reasons for the "screpoli" (cracks) in the dome of Santa Maria del Fiore. Their explanation was positively or negatively received according to circumstances.

REFERENCES

Books

1. Di Pasquale,S. L'uso dei modelli nella costruzione della cupola di S.Maria del Fiore, Atti del Dipartimento di Costruzioni, Florence, 1984.

2. Guasti, C. La cupola di Santa Maria del Fiore illustrata con i documenti dell'archivio dell'Opera secolare, Barbera, Florence, 1857.

3. Pedretti,C. Leonardo Architetto, Electa, Milan, 1978.

4. Saalman, H. Filippo Brunelleschi. The Cupola of Santa Maria del Fiore, Zwemmer, London, 1980.

5. The Codex Hammer of Leonardo da Vinci Translated into English and Annotated by Carlo Pedretti, Giunti Barbera, Florence, 1987.

Papers in journals

6. Barbi,L. and Di Teodoro, F. Le lesioni della cupola di Santa Maria del Fiore: una proposta di datazione, Bollettino degli Ingegneri, XXXI, n.9, pp.13-18, 1983.

7. Galluzzi, P. Le colonne "fesse" degli Uffizi e gli "screpoli" della cupola. Il contributo di Vincenzo Viviani al dibattito sulla stabilità della Cupola del Brunelleschi (1694-1697), Annali dell'Istituto e Museo di Storia della Scienza di Firenze, II, fasc.1, pp.70-111, 1977.

8. Pedretti, C. Saggio di una cronologia dei fogli del Codice Arundel di Leonardo da Vinci, Bibliothèque d'Humanisme et Renaissance, XXII, pp.172-177, 1960.

Chapters in books

9.   Cecchini, A. Opinioni Intorno lo Stato della gran Cupola del Duomo di Firenze, in Nelli,G.B.C., Discorsi di Architettura del Senatore Giovan Battista Nelli..., pp.77-90, Eredi Paperini, Florence, 1753.

10.   Id. Che le crepature della Cupola del Duomo di Firenze non siano cagionate dal peso di sua Lanterna: ma sì bene dall'aver ceduto in qualche parte i suoi fondamenti, in Nelli,G.B.C., op. cit., pp.91-103.

11.   Ximenes, L. Del Vecchio E Nuovo Gnomone Fiorentino e delle Osservazioni astronomiche fisiche ed architettoniche fatte nel verificarne la costruzione, II, chapters V-VI, pp.141-173, Stamperia Imperiale, Florence, 1757.

Manuscripts

Città del Vaticano, Vatican Library, ms.:
12.   Cicognara, V, 3849, n.7, ff.1r-22r.

Florence, Opera di Santa Maria del Fiore Archives,mss.:
13.   IV-1-16; IV-1-17; IV-2-69; IV-2-76; IV-2-78.

Florence, National Library, mss.:
14.   II—21.
15.   II—22.
16.   Galileiano 222.

Florence, Riccardiana Library, ms.:
17.   Riccardiano 2141, ff.46r-62r.

Venice, Marciana Library, mss.:
18.   It., IV.646, now n.5507, ff.56r-77v.
19.   It., IV.669, now n.5530.

The Source of the Problem: the "Mathematical" Nature of Historical Buildings and their Restitution. The Works of Lelio Orsi.

F. Manenti Valli

Architects and Engineers, 5, Via Farini, 42100 Reggia Emilio, Italy

INTRODUCTION

When buildings of historical interest survive to our age, they have almost always undergone alterations with respect to their original configuration and therefore the creator's initial concept is not always evident and neither are the problems presented by the context which gave rise to the buildings themselves.

In order to restore prominent architectural works appropriately while respecting their intrinsic values, it is necessary to understand the original configuration regardless of the amount of work to be carried out on them. It is possible to acquire this knowledge through in depth study of the structure, comparisons with other buildings designed by the same artist or through parallel studies of analogous restoration of buildings in the same cultural area or of the same era. However, this information is not always available, as in the case of the example discussed here, where the architectural structure in question is the only existing piece of work of a late fifteenth century Emilian Master. The absence of other points of reference and the incompleteness of the work itself - to be described further on - , as well as alterations to the existing part constitute a very complex problem and make restoration extremely difficult.

RESEARCH METHODOLOGY

At this point a method for study, graphic restoration and subsequent practical application, assumes fundamental importance: the **metric-proportional research** method through which it is often possible to arrive at the exact composition grid which was essential to the original plan.

The organisation of space from an exclusively visual approach, typical of the figurative examples of Renaissance architecture, presupposed the presence of a geometric substratum which, subtended to the original plan, allowed its modular transposition. This was not an improvised reference but rather a precise scheme at a plano-volumetric level which allowed such works their true poetic expression in three dimensions. The individual architectural fields conformed to the scheme – plans, sections, elevations including the smallest details – in one single plan on which the creator based the dimensions of the entire structure.

The metric proportions, which were usually only interpreted in a manner limited to aesthetic perception, were also essential to static dimensions: a Science of Construction from the past which anticipated the calculus of building construction.

Careful and responsible restoration today cannot ignore the recovery of the composition grid nor deny a research method which constitutes a scientific (and therefore rigorously controlled) base for a philological interpretation which renders to the building the identity of its elements. This method, above all, makes it possible to follow the original creative process and at the same time check the carrying structures using the system employed by the original builders.

This does not imply, however, that through metric-proportional research it is possible to arrive at the exact formula of dimensions used by the artist – given that geometric combinations as a consequence of the modular constructions are expressed in different ways – but rather that it is possible to verify the results of the initial configuration.

The graphic and analytical method is strictly connected to the creation of a construction which has parameters that impose conditions on both measurements and numbers. It may appear, at first, that changed systems of measurements may result in a distorted interpretation and therefore affect restoration. On the other hand, whatever unit of measurement is used – perch, ell or the brick itself intended as a repeated measurement – it is equally possible to arrive at the underlying geometric layout of the building, given that the proportional ratio to be found between the parts and the layout is expressed as a pure number and is not altered whatever the measurement system proposed.

Graphic research is accompanied constantly by parallel analytical examination. Since the proportional plan is based on geometric figures – circles, squares, hexagons, pentagons – and the relations between their elements, there will always be irrational ratios in the analytical transposition: the numerical terms which appear in the formulas are to be understood as substantially approximate in excess or in defect to the second decimal place.

The constant repitition of measurements which has been revealed by other studies on historical buildings has implied the preparation of the coordination using a **tabular system** which proceeds alongside the research. A table has been compiled of the most important measurements which are noted each time in the structural system. According to logical combinations these figures are distributed over a number of columns where the geometrically progressive terms are established by the ratio inherent in the figure which forms the basis of the development of the plan. Not all the measurements appearing in the table correspond exactly to the architecture: however, at the moment in which the table is prepared, references and information which were previously unknown emerge: confirmation and suggestions arise from this for the restoration to the original of parts which have been altered or have disappeared all together and which were not evident in the structure of the building itself.

In the same way the discovery of the metric grid of some buildings has facilitated the interpretation of others and therefore has led to the identification of existing parts as well as those extraneous to the original context making a significant contribution to the work of restoration.

Consequently, by employing the latest computerised systems it is possible to work on numerical models of reality produced through photogrammetrical findings and to arrive at computer processing and parallel videographic restoration or by means of a plotter. In fact research into this method is being carried out today even though the results are not substantial enough yet to be reported here.

Geometric schemes and analytical tables establish, therefore, a **code of interpretation** which allows the exegesis of the works and supplies their graphic restoration and, therefore, the structural and typological knowledge necessary for accurate restoration.

This methodology has been further defined by the writer through years of research. It has been applied in the restoration of numerous buildings in Emilia from the Medieval [1] period but above all and with particularly satisfying results, with Renaissance buildings [2]. The example in question dates back to the second half of the fifteenth century.

THE MATHEMATICAL MATRIX IN VARIOUS DISCIPLINES

Laws of composition, which draw upon geometry for their formulas and modes of being and are integral to architectural works as far as these same instruments of measurements have been used, are also present in pictorial expression. In the Renaissance, in particular, every art form involved mathematical processes: both in the realisation of Humanist anthropomorphic concepts, geometric formulas were transferred to the field of graphic art where, in the "constructed" three dimensionality of space, they replaced the two dimensional "perspective" of the plane of the painting. A scientific matrix can also, therefore, be recognised in painting as in architecture; however it never substituted the artist's interior thought nor limited the initial creative process but was a componenet of the language of the "form" as colour, line and stroke. Once more there is the use of metric proportions by the ancient masters.

The need to organise space according to a mathematical order, is not only demonstrated at the level of building but also involves the larger dimension of whole towns. The imperfections of the real town give rise to the myth of the ideal town of the Renaissance. It is possible to hypothesise abstract urban models where the supporting geometric plan refers to exact proportional systems. When it is not possible to create new settlements, more restricted programmes of examination of the environment in existing context are applied: the interrelation between built-up and empty space, between houses and streets are also referred to metric plans. In the same way planning methodology is also fundamental to urbanistic experimentation. This emphasises once more the interdependence of the arts and the single methodology for the processing of the artistic product and the consequent possibility of its objective interpretation.

The Renaissance masters were often versatile in several disciplines: perhaps due to their ability to use the same planning procedure at the beginning of different art forms.

THE APPLICATION OF THE METHOD TO THE WORKS OF LELIO ORSI

It is significant, therefore, that we are considering here several works of one single master, **Lelio Orsi**, all dating from the same period but of different extractions: the drawing of the Madonna della Ghiara created for the Basilica of the same name in Reggio Emilia and the collegiate Church of St. Stefano designed for the small Po valley plane town of Novellara in whose planning Orsi was involved.

The analogy of the metric layout between graphics, architecture and, implicitly, the urban context to which it has been applied, underlines the presence of the same composition matrices: their identification has permitted a deeper criticism of the sketch, the restoration of the church's origianl plan and the interpretation of the relationship between the church and the city.

In December 1978 an exhibition of Orsi's pictorial work was held in Reggio Emilia [3]. However his role as architect at the small but illuminated Court of the Gonzagas had still to be considered. The destruction of his buildings, the alteration to those that remain, the lack of documents relating to his work and the continuing debate regarding the areas of competence between the artist and patron make a critical review of building works extremely difficult. The architectural themes often present in his drawing and painting as background to figurative action demonstrate a keen interest for architecture just as the respect for linguistic schemes and for rules of order indicate the hand of one who is also used to resolving problems of construction.

The proportional themes used by the artist in both types of work draws from the geometry of the square: a particularly significant figure for its implied symbolic content in the development of religious themes. This does not resolve the metrical problem by simple repetition of units but dialectically puts forward different combinations by the application of the $\sqrt{2}$ relationship established between the side and the diagonal or, equivalently, between the diameters of the inscribed and circumscribed circles: irrational relationships which cannot be defined with exactness at an analytical level but can be graphically realised and equally rapidly traced on the ground.

The theory of the square as a means of proportioning had already been formulated by Vitruvius: the visualisation of the harmonic themes indicated in the fifteenth century edition of Cesariano [4].

The significant "altitudes" in Orsi's works and the planimetric dimensions which are decisive for the construction of the system correspond to the graphic indications proposed by the fifteenth century writer for the selection of heights which eurhythmically refer to the exedrae minoris area. In this sense the graphic schemes proposed here must be understood as examples. They have been traced using analogous symbols in order to be able to compare the graphic and architectural works. The focal points where the geometric lines converge are marked by the same letters used in the Cesariano figure to underline the parallel.

Drawing of the Blessed Virgin of the Ghiara
Orsi's sketch dates back to 1569 and was used for the fresco by Bertone in the seventeenth century part of the Basilica.

A rigorously geometric plan based on the correlation between square and circle subtends the iconography of the drawing and implicitly the poetry of the content: the two figures which, in Medieval symbolism represented the symbolic meaning of the human and the divine, later adopted by the Renaissance culture, illustrate here the dual nature of the infant Christ.

The mixtilinear frame, curved at the top and straight on the other three sides, which encloses the figures of the Mother and Child indicates the metric key of the composition. The figure of the Virgin is perfectly centered on the vertical axis of the composition which passes through the face and the foot: the geometric axis which substantiates the ideological theme of the work. In a Cartesian system of coordianates, if we identify this axis with the ordinate Y, the abscissa X passes through the fibula and the ring clasping the cloak at the right shoulder: this is the point of origin of the system which gives rise to the mixtilinear frame and which the artist wanted to visualise clearly. Until today the significance was not understood. The figure of the Child tenderly held out to the Mother creates, with respect to her, a precise geometrical lying posture which is obtained graphically from the progression of cicles and squares inscribed in the upper left quadrant. The vertical on which she is imposed passes once more through the face and the foot: a theme of composition which Orsi frequently repeated in his work to illustrate the perpendicularity of the human body both seated and in movement.

The Mother's tender gaze into the Child's eyes is also modulated on the same rhythmic cadence: the left eyes of both figures are alligned in the same direction and along which the Child's arm is also extended The Child's right hand is open in a blessing symbolising, using a roman gesture, the eighth day, the day of the Lord.

The allegory is clearly demonstrated once again by the Child's eye reflected in the Mother's face which intermediates the passage between the centre of gravity of the composition and the symbol of the sun which, like the symbol of the moon, lies outside the frame because of the symmetrical position at the edges of the sheet, but is still precisely correlated to the scheme.

The Church of St. Stefano at Novellara

The same metric scheme has lent much to the plan of the church of St. Stefano which was probably never completely finished even if according to contemporary documents the foundations were completed in 1567. This has emerged not so much from the structure itself, which corresponds only to the finished part, as from the restitution of the original drawing as it has come to be defined through the recovery of the geometric substratum and whose authenticity has been demonstrated by the discovery of traces on the walls behind the facade. The hypothesis could be confirmed by sounding the ground at the level of the foundations.

The most recent critics limit the east facing front, the entrance, to the central part and exclude the front chapels which are attributed to the seventeenth century. On the other hand these have only been altered internally with the raising of the level of the roof. The argument is also based on the fact that they are followed, on the sides of the nave, by areas of different structure and use. The metric study, on the other hand, has established that the original plan involved the entire width including the adjacent areas even if they are now not pertinent to the organisation of the church and that the front chapels were present at the beginning and should have been followed by others as far as the transept and beyond. The transept, which is now very short, would necessarily have had to have been deeper than at present: this has been ascertained, if it is true that at various times the back walls were painted depicting a semicircular architectural form to lengthen the perspective of the space. The non completion of the work meant that curtain walls were built on the already existing perimetral foundations and they underwent further alteration on their sides which should have rather continued the internal division with the ideal profile.

Figure 2 illustrates the findings regarding the present state of the church; figure 3 illustrates its restitution to the original drawing.

At present, the limits of the nave are limited by shallow recesses which uinfluence the line of passage both visually and spatially: it represents a contradiction to the contemporary typological schemes which preferred straight paths uninterrupted by distractions. On the contrary, in the project they constituted only the separating wall divisions between nave and chapels. Their connotation is proved by traces found on the floor below the roof coinciding with the roof of the south-east chapel. Here, in fact, on the back wall of the facade there is an offset with a gentle inclination of 6% which shows the presence of a gutter for the waters of a stratum parallel to the front.   Above it, external painting shows that in the beginning the wall was exposed and the roof was lower. On the wall orthogonal to the first one corresponding to the outside of the central nave, more traces indicate a saddle roof corresponding to the chapel below; the above mentioned stratum belonged to this wall.

As the facade is the primary element in the establishment of a spacial relationship on an urban scale, it required the immediate construction of the two adjacent chapels. For some reason beyond our knowledge the work was stopped and the construction was limited to the present form.

We believe there is a significant typological reference for St. Stefano project in Carpi cathedral whose designs were supplied by Baldassarre Peruzzi some decades earlier and whose original image was handed to us by engravings dating back to the seventeenth century which portray a wooden model existing at that time [5] . The side chapels are evident; they are covered by saddle roofs outstretched orthogonally to the nave and built just below the half-moon windows. The roofs of the side chapels in the church of Novellara should have been built in the same way below the lunette windows as demonstated by traces on the outer sides. The closeness of the two small Po valley towns justifies the analogy between the two churches.

We can assume that the typological plan of Carpi cathedral derives from St. Peter's in Rome. There Peruzzi had worked first with Bramante, and later with Raffaello. Peruzzi seems to have referred to Raffaello's basilica scheme which modified the central plan project by Bramante. Through a complex artistic itinerary, St. Stefano is in a certain way debtor to St. Peter's cathedral which Orsi must also have studied very carefully during his long stay in Rome.

Metric-Proportional Research The dimensional concept of St. Stefano undoubtedly arose from the prospect. A square with the side AB = 16.69 m gives dimension to the facade central part specifying, in width, the external distance between the dados of the pedestals of the coupled pilaster strips and, in height, the level of projection of the pediment in respect to ground level. This is the key figure of the composition grid whose proportional scansions and successive inter-relation give dimension to the whole architectural structure through side-diagonal relation.

Knowledge of the proportional prospect scheme has led to the discovery of the original drawing of the plan and elevations thus making it possible to re-compose the spatial unity of the church plan. The traces that have been found on the floors below the roof confirm the validity of the restituition.

The metrical relations - analitycally verified – have been reported with a double sequence of images showing the elaboration of the project both in plan and elevation (see drawings 4 and 5). They are to be intended as explanatory schemes which give a graphic visualisation of the research and demonstrate the interdependence of the parts. The study, however, has been carried out on surveys on a 1:100 scale for the plan, prospect, side and transverse sections   in correspondence to the nave and transept, longitudinal section; and on surveys on a 1:20 scale for the portal, facade coupled pilaster strips and an inside bay. During the study, some anomalies among specular parts arose because of the partial realisation of the work and the modifications it has undergone. When this has taken place, the levels have been averaged in order to obtain a measurement closer to the project. The most significant values are reported in Table I.

A	B	C	D	measurements in perches	E
	0.86				
0.51		2.09	1.73		3.82
	1.23				
0.72		2.95	2.45		5.40
	1.73				
1.01		4.18	3.46		7.64
	2.45				
1.43		5.90	4.89	<- 1.5 p	10.80
	3.46				
2.02		8.35	6.91		15.26
	4.89				
2.86		11.80	9.78	<- 3 p	21.58
	6.91				
4.04		16.69	13.83		30.51
	9.78				
5.72		23.60	19.56	<- 6 p	43.16
	13.83				
8.08		33.37	27.65		61.02
	19.56				
11.43		47.20	39.10	<- 12 p	86.30
	27.65				

Table 1 Analytical table of the interrelation the most significant measurements of the architectural plan of the church of St. Stefano at Novellara.

The values of each column are in geometric progression to the ratio of $\sqrt{2}$; the irrationality of the ratio obliges an approximation to the nearest greater or lesser whole number to the second decimal place. The values in column A, added in groups of two, give the values of column B. The values in column B added in groups of two give the values in column C. The values in column D repeat staggered those from column B and, added to those of column C give the values of column E. The measurements in perches are referred to column D.

It is evident that to allow tracing on the ground, some of the values had to correspond with the local unit of measurement, while others obtained from the irrational ratio $\sqrt{2}$ reach an acceptable degree of approximation. We asked ourselves what could have been the unit of measurement peculiar to Novellara for land and building as it is well known that these units vary from place to place. Our research was fruitless. However, while working on the metrical study one unit of measurement was often repeated: we deduced that it was related to the local perch for which a unit value of 3.26 metres was established. The overall length of the church resulted as 15 perches. Later it was confirmed that the perch was also the unit of measurement used in the town of Guastalla which, at that time, came under the dominion of a branch of the Gonzaga family. The common family extraction of the two small capitals could confirm the hypothesis.

The prospect is the plan most explicitly related to the context of the environment: in this sense it necessarily represented a symbolic and metrical paradigm of reference on the main square of a town whose model was developing towards the "ideal" shape suggested by contemporary writers. The emergence of the prospect in relation to the square of which it formed the scenic background, the correspondence with the neighbouring houses on either side as straight wings and its function, should all have provided character and dimensions strictly related to the urban fabric. A further processing of the drawing of the prospect has led to the identification of existing relations and the precise spatial relationship established between the church and the township.

Conclusion Orsi is all of these: painter, architect, town planner and in all of these activities employed the same metrical themes. In the case of his painting these themes are used as a rigorous grid for the harmonious organization of the figurative context; in his building work they are applied as parameters of proportional elaboration and the static dimensioning of the construction plan; in the case of the urban context they become essential planning elements. The recovery of these themes implies the possibility of an in depth critical review of a piece of work from any discipline; in the field of architecture it allows us to arrive at the restitution of the original plan and consequently a more accurate restoration.

1.   Manenti Valli, F. Il Querciolese e la valle del Tresinaro. Chapter 12,
     Tipologia di chiese antiche nella media montagna reggiana. Vol. 2, pp
     293-308, Reggio E., 1982; La metrica di Lanfranco nelle fabbrica
     della Cattedrale di Modena, lecture to the Accademia Nazionale delle
     Scienze, Modena, 1984; Architettura e terremoti: il caso di Parma.
     Chapter, La Cattedrale di Parma: metrica di un impianto medioevale,
     pp 189 - 201, Parma, 1985.

2.   Manenti Valli, F. Annali della Scuola Normale Superiore di Pisa.
     Chapter, Architettura reggiana del Rinascimento: casa Ruini. Studio
     metrico di un edificio come termine di ricerca filologica e
     strumento negli interventi di restauro conservativo, S.III,V.III,2, pp
     515-580; Il palazzo dei Principi a Correggio, Chapter 2, Il palazzo
     nei valori architettonici e formali, pp 33-65, Milan, 1976; Il palazzo
     da Mosto e la fondazione Manodori, Chapter 2, Un'architettura tra due
     secoli, pp 41-109, Milan, 1980.

3.   Clerici Bagozzi, N., Frisoni, F., Monducci, E. and Piron-dini, M., Lelio
     Orsi, Milano, 1987 (for bibliographical reference to Orsi).

4.   Cesariano, C., Di Lucio Vitruvio Pollione de Architec-ture, liber
     sextus, c.LXXXVIII r., Como, 1521

5.   Pelloni, R., Un tempio degno di Roma. Chapter, La presenza di
     Baldassarre Peruzzi nel progetto per la Cattedrale, pp 35-48,
     Modena, 1987 (for the engraving and Cathedral plan, see pp 42 and
     39).

Fig. 1. Drawing of the Blessed Virgin of the Ghiara, 1569.

Proportional metrical study. It should be verified how the most significant points coincide with those of the design of the church of St. Stefano (See figures 4 and 5).

+	source point of the cartesian coordinate system	line m	vertical limit of the Child's head
		line n	vertical limit of the Mother's head
A-B	distance between the vertical passing through the Child's left eye and the Mother's figure on coordinate Y	line p	lower limit of the Mother's head = the lower limit of the transept of St.Stefano's
E	Child's left eye	line q	upper limit of the Mother's head = the upper limit of the transept of St. Stefano's
I	Mother's left eye		
S	the Child's right foot		
T	the Child's left foot	line r	directrix alligning the Child's and Mother's eyes
V	the Mother's right foot		

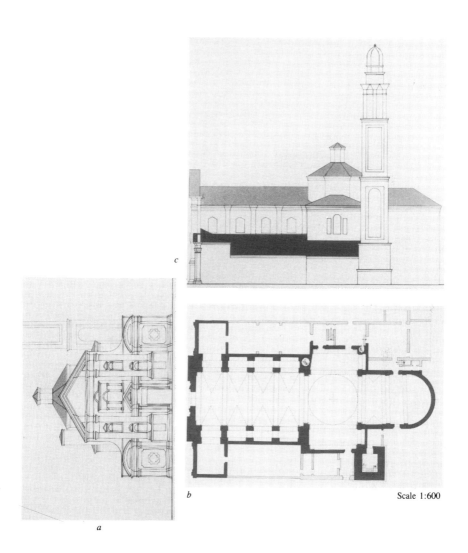

c

b   Scale 1:600

a

Figure 2. Church of St. Stefano at Novellara
Survey of the present state : a, prospect; b, plan; c, north side.

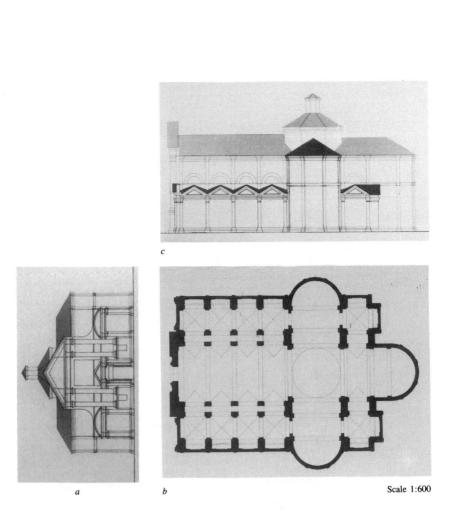

c

a   *b*   Scale 1:600

Figure 3. Church of St. Stefano at Novellara
    Graphic restitution of the original project: a, prospect; b, plan; c, north side.

4.1 – a square with side AB = 16.69 m dimensions the central part of the facade.

4.2 – the diagonals of the square, rotated on the ground line, determine the total width O*N* = 30.51 m of the church plan; rotated on the vertical lines from the base they determine the level of conclusion of the lantern AN = BO = AB√2 = 23.60 m and the fronton ridge in the facade at the cross over point.

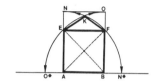

4.3 – the values O*A = BN* = AB (√2-1) = 6.91 m dimension the side chapels; rotated on the central part of the facade they determine the width of the portal which corresponds to the width of the octagonal lantern.

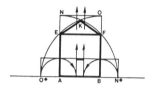

4.4 – according to the side-diagonal-side relation, the proportional subdivision of the facade central part horizontally dimensions the symmetrical fascia corresponding to the coupled pilaster strips and vertically the height of the chapels up to the top of the curved tympanum. The centre line of the square built on the global width corresponds to the springer level of the roof.

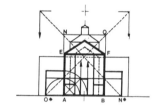

4.5 – the values AN = BO of the level of springer rotated on the outside of the church plan, respectively by points A and B, determine the position of the houses parallel to the sides of the church. The width of the chapels creates the same values of the empty spaces of the roads and the central part of the facade: AB; AB (√2-1); AB; AB (√2-1); AB.

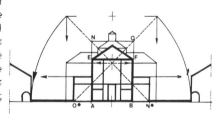

Figure 4. The church of St. Stefano at Novellara: sequence of restitution for the geometrical elaboration of the **prospect**

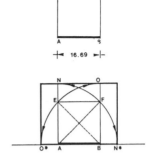

5.1 - a segment AB = 16.69 determines the central part of the facade; the relative square is built on it.

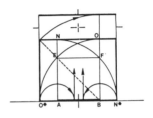

5.2 - the diagonals of the square, rotated on the horizontal line determine the global width $O* N* = 30.51$ m of the church plan; rotated on the vertical line from the foot determine the beginning of the transept: $AN = BO = AB \sqrt{2} = 23.60$ m .

5.3 - the values $O* A = BN* = AB (\sqrt{2}-1) = 6.91$ m dimension the side chapels; rotated on the central part of the facade create the width of the portal. The diagonals of the squares (side $O*B = AN*$), rotated on the verticals from the base, determine the limit of the transept at a distance from the beginning of the transept of twice the value AB.

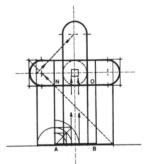

5.4 - The diameter of the dome is obtained from the width of the transept while the width of the lantern is determined by the width of the portal. Further geometrical elaboration gives the position of the transept apses and of the main apse.

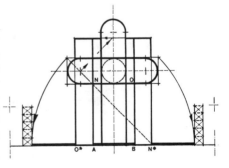

5.5 - The values $AN = BO$ of the limit of the transept, rotated respectively from the bases A and B, on the outside of the church plan, determine the position of the houses parallel to the sides of the church. The width of the chapels creates the same values of the empty spaces of the streets and of the central part of the facade: AB; $AB (\sqrt{2}-1)$; AB; $AB (\sqrt{2}-1)$; AB.

Figure 5. The church of St. Stefano at Novellara: sequence of restitution for the geometric elaboration of the **plan.**

Assessment Techniques Utilized with Historic American High Rises

S. Kelley, D. Slaton and C. Paulson
Wiss, Janney, Elstner Associates, Inc., Chicago, Illinois, USA

ABSTRACT

This paper provides an overview of the development of high rise construction in the United States, with a summary of investigative techniques utilized with historic high rises. Special conditions encountered with this class of structure are highlighted. Three case studies are presented to examine applications of investigative techniques to historic high rise structures.

INTRODUCTION

In Europe, historic buildings and structures may be hundreds or even thousands of years old. In the United States, however, buildings constructed in the late nineteenth and early twentieth centuries are considered historic landmarks. Materials such as terra cotta and iron, and construction techniques such as skeletal steel framing, are an important part of the American architectural heritage.

The purpose of investigating an historic high rise is to learn about its original construction and existing condition; to determine and evaluate the nature, causes, and extent of deterioration; and to monitor conditions over time. Information gathered through the investigation is utilized in the development of a repair or restoration scheme.

High rise construction materials and systems are sophisticated, and require special investigative techniques. An understanding of the behavior of high rise structural systems and the way in which they respond to external and internal forces is necessary before undertaking the investigation. The compatibility of structural and cladding systems, and the behavior of failure mechanisms, must also be taken into consideration in selecting and applying investigative techniques.

HISTORICAL BACKGROUND

Throughout the nineteenth and early twentieth centuries, innovations in architecture, engineering and construction fostered the development of high rise construction in the United States. The invention of the elevator, which first appeared in 1851 in a hotel in New York, made the use of taller buildings practical. By the 1880s, construction sites could be enclosed, heated with steam and illuminated by electric light, greatly speeding up the construction process as work could continue at night and through the winter.

Foundations

Prior to the development of the high rise structure in the 1870s, foundations for structures were usually empirically designed, simple spread footings. Conventions of practice gave no regard to the loads imposed by the footings to the soil. As the height of load-bearing structures increased, differential settlement became a consideration. In 1873, Frederick Baumann of Chicago promulgated the first rational technique for foundation design. This methodology consisted of performing wall or column load calculations, proportioning the footing according to the results, and designing footings with concentric loads.

The earliest isolated footings were tapered piers constructed of rubble or dimension stone that consumed considerable space in the basements of structures. Development of the iron rail grillage footing as an alternative to the stone pier is attributed to Burnham and Root, and was first employed in their Montauk Block (Chicago, 1882). The grillage footing uses layers of steel rails so that the same bearing area can be achieved with considerably less footing thickness. As rolled steel sections become more economical, rail grillages gave way to I-beam grillages and were completely supplanted by about 1890.

As buildings became higher, greater loads were imposed on foundations. Local soil conditions limited the capacity of the isolated footing in many areas of the country. Other forms of foundation systems such as the long (point-bearing) pile were developed. The concrete pier to strong bearing strata was developed as an alternative to the driven long pile. These piers were constructed as circular wells which were filled with concrete. The first building entirely supported by concrete piers was constructed in 1899, and by 1905 nearly every high rise in Chicago was so constructed.

In the nineteenth century, engineers first utilized metal frame construction in bridges, factories, and warehouses, and cast and wrought iron were the major metals used in construction. The invention of the Bessemer process in England in 1856 made it possible to produce large quantities of steel affordably. In the United States, steel production on a large scale was realized in the 1870s. The transition from iron to steel was gradual, with iron still used in building construction as late as the 1890s.

The first metal skeleton-framed high rise was the 11-story Home Insurance Building (Chicago, 1885). In this structure, column loads were transferred to stone pier footings via the metal frame without load-bearing masonry walls. Each level of the exterior wall was supported on a shelf angle fixed to the spandrel girder. At that time, high rise buildings were designed without wind bracing, under the assumption that the heavy masonry cladding provided sufficient rigidity for the whole structure.

As skeletal framing came into common use, masonry bearing wall construction reached its practical limit. Burnham and Root's 16-story Monadnock Block (Chicago, 1891) utilized traditional load-bearing masonry walls which at ground-floor level were 6 feet thick. This building also utilized the first rigid frame for lateral stiffness. At the same time, Burnham and Root developed a complete steel frame for the Rand McNally Building (Chicago, 1890). They also developed a steel frame laterally stiffened with a diagonal bracing system in the 20-story Masonic Temple (Chicago, 1892).

Several years later, the structural innovations of the Chicago school were taken further by D.H. Burnham & Company in the Reliance Building (Chicago, 1895). The exterior bays were designed as rigid steel frames, and two-story columns erected with staggered joints further increased frame rigidity. The exterior cladding is minimized with large window openings, in an early expression of the curtain wall.

Steel and concrete skeletal frame construction soon became universally accepted for high rise structures. The skeletal frame and exterior curtain wall suggested further innovations in building construction techniques. Thereafter, improvements of known design methods encouraged the construction of increasingly taller buildings.

METHODOLOGY

Investigative techniques utilized with historic high rises range from basic to sophisticated. Basic methods such as research, review of documents, and visual inspection are generally non-intrusive to the historic building fabric. These methods are selected for the first phase of investigation and may indicate that more complex techniques are needed. Sophisticated investigative techniques may be non-intrusive or may require opening or removal of building fabric. These methods include sample removal, field and laboratory testing and analysis, structural analysis, and instrumentation.

Research and Review of Documentation
Research and review of archival documents and photographs should be undertaken as a first step. Because high rise structures are complex, the details of construction are of primary importance. Original drawings and specifications may not accurately reflect the details of as-built construction; therefore, shop drawings which give accurate technical data are very valuable. Accurate information can also eliminate the need for extraneous inspection openings.

Visual Examination

Visual examination conducted from the ground or swing stages reveals cracks, deflections, misalignment, water staining or rusting, all of which are indications of possible distress. The location, size and patterns of distress suggest hidden conditions. Sources of water entry into the building fabric and evidence corrosion require special attention.

Field and Laboratory Testing

Removal of finishes in distressed areas may be warranted to examine internal conditions. Locations for inspection openings and sample removal should be as non-intrusive as possible to the historic fabric. A sufficient number of material samples, structural members and connections must be examined to afford a representative study.

Laboratory testing is utilized to determine the nature of the material and the causes and types of deterioration in order to define an appropriate repair. For structural metals, analysis of small samples provides information about the yield strength, yield point, tensile strength, elongation, modulus of elasticity, and compressive strength of the metal. Laboratory tests for masonry are used to determine compressive strength, modulus of rupture, and modulus of elasticity.

Structural Analysis

Research, visual examination, and testing may indicate the need for quantitative structural analysis of all or part of the building. In the historic high rise, this evaluation occasionally takes the form of computer analysis techniques. Quantitative information about the structural system may be obtained from field-checked historic documentation or from field measurement.

Load Testing

Load testing is especially useful where capacities are not readily obtainable through structural analytical methods, or where analysis is not persuasive. Tests may be conducted in the laboratory on components removed from the building, or in the field on a representative portion of the actual structure.

Instrumentation

Instrumentation can provide information about the reaction of the structure to temperature, humidity, gravity and wind, and about large and small scale movements of the building and its components. Short-term instrumentation may be monitored by personnel at the site, while long-term monitoring is facilitated by programmed recording devices.

APPLICATIONS: THREE CASE STUDIES

The case studies addressed below illustrate the application of a variety of elementary and sophisticated investigative techniques to different types of high rise construction. The Tribune Tower, an example of skeletal frame construction with masonry cladding, was evaluated primarily with basic methods. The Rookery, which combines masonry bearing walls and skeletal framing, was investigated with both elementary and sophisticated methods. Cape Hatteras Lighthouse was constructed with load-bearing masonry walls and no skeletal framing. It was evaluated using elementary and sophisticated methods, including lasers and other instrumentation that may be increasingly utilized in historic high rise analysis.

Tribune Tower

The Tribune Tower (Chicago, 1925) is a National Historic Landmark designed by New York architects Raymond Hood and John Mead Howells for the Chicago Tribune Competition of 1922. The Tribune has an especially elaborate framing system for a skyscraper of its day. The tower portion of the building including the buttresses is 34 stories or 450 feet in height and is clad in ornately carved buff-colored limestone. The structural steel frame utilizes a conventional column and girder system up to the twenty-fifth floor. At the top of the building, an ornamental octagonal tower is surrounded by a two-story, free-standing tracery wall and flying buttresses, supported by a dense grillage of transfer girders and beams at the twenty-fifth level. The steel structural columns of the tower below cantilever upward and support the tracery wall.

Numerous cracks were observed in the tracery wall and buttresses of the tower. These cracks are indicative of water-induced corrosion of the embedded structural frame, the most common form of distress in the historic high rise. Complete original contract documents and shop drawings were available, permitting the investigation to be carried out primarily using non-intrusive methods.

Crack Mapping   Crack mapping of the interior and exterior of the screen wall was carried out from scaffolding and swing stages. The locations of vertical cracks in pier elements, lateral displacement of limestone panels, spalling, loose stone, and points of water intrusion were documented on detailed elevation sheets developed from the limestone shop drawings. Patterns of distress were also identified and were found to correlate with the location of the steel frame as indicated on the original steel shop drawings and as confirmed by use of a metal detector.

Inspection Openings   In order to limit intrusion into the historic fabric, inspection openings were made only in mortar joints. By utilizing a borescope, voids within the wall could be examined through a one-half inch diameter opening. Corrosion of embedded steel was documented. In areas where there are no voids, larger openings were made by disassembling the limestone cladding and masonry back-up. Inspection openings were created in areas where the limestone panels exhibited distress, thus avoiding damage to intact panels. The condition of representative steel connections was evaluated, providing information for the development of repair and restoration documents.

Instrumentation   At this writing, instrumentation has been proposed to document and quantify movements of the tracery wall in response to wind and thermal loads. Techniques will include application of lasers, extensometers and accelerometers. The tracery walls are unique architectural elements with atypical structural systems. Movements are difficult to predict using conventional structural analysis techniques. The instrumentation program will verify whether movement is a factor in the observed cracking of the tracery wall.

Rookery Building

The 11-story Rookery Building (Chicago, 1888) is a National Historic Landmark designed by the firm of Burnham and Root. Many of the factors critical to the development of high rise construction are present in the Rookery, including characteristic foundation and framing systems. A rail grillage foundation system with footings no deeper than 13 feet below grade was used. The exterior wall structure combines granite, brick and terra cotta load-bearing elements on the street facades, and cast and wrought iron structural framing and masonry on the alley facades. The interior light well is constructed with a cast and wrought iron frame clad in glazed brick and terra cotta. The skeletal frame of the light well was constructed slightly shorter than that of the masonry bearing walls to allow for differential settlement.

Inside the building, rows of cast iron columns are spanned by wrought iron beams. The floor framing consists of wrought iron beams spaced at seven feet on center, with hollow, flat-arched structural clay tile spanning between the beams. All structural metal in the Rookery is encased in fireproof clay tile.

A general structural evaluation of the Rookery Building was carried out because a proposed restoration and renovation program entailed increasing loads on some parts of the structure. Analytical and materials investigations were conducted on a variety of structural components including cast iron columns, structural clay tile floor arches, load-bearing and face masonry, wrought iron floor beams, and rail grillage footings. Available original drawings included wrought iron floor framing plans and some masonry facade drawings. Original documentation of columns, foundations and load-bearing masonry was not available, thus requiring field examination of these items.

Field Investigations and Laboratory Tests   The cast iron columns were examined physically to determine their shape, size, and thickness; section properties were computed for subsequent use in column capacity analyses. Prism samples were removed from load-bearing clay brick masonry for determination of actual masonry strength. Tensile test coupons were removed from wrought iron floor beams for determination of yield and ultimate strengths. At five locations, the basement floor was removed and soil was excavated to expose the rail grillage footings; sizes of the exposed footings were measured and in-situ soil tests were conducted to determine shear and bearing strengths.

The masonry and structural framing of the light well walls were constructed integrally; therefore foreshortening of the frame and expansion of the masonry might have induced masonry stresses above acceptable levels. Strain gauges were installed on the light well walls; the mortar joints above and below each gauge were ground out; and the quantity of strain relief was measured. Samples of the brick were tested in the laboratory to determine the modulus of elasticity and compressive strength.   It was found that the frame did indeed induce stresses on the masonry but the stresses were within acceptable levels.

Structural Analysis   A review of building codes and cast iron column test data indicated that design practices regarding cast iron columns during the 1870s and 1880s were not conservative in many instances. Test data provided a rational basis for determination of column capacities.   Analysis indicated that several columns had reduced factors of safety, but none sufficiently reduced to warrant immediate repair of the columns.   However, either strengthening of the columns by concrete encasement or reduction of dead loads was recommended to increase the serviceability of the structure.

For the load-bearing masonry, test strength was lower than expected; however, comparison of pier capacity with calculated loads indicated an acceptable factor of safety.   For the wrought-iron floor beams, it was found that, except for a few minor instances, the beams had adequate capacity to support dead loads and current code-required live loads.   For the foundations, it was concluded that additional load could be sustained without excessive differential settlement.

The Rookery Building was not designed with an explicit lateral load-carrying system.   The original designers probably assumed that the massive exterior bearing walls provided sufficient lateral stability. These walls along the perimeter of the building are discontinuous at the lowest levels on the two alley facades, with the transmission of lateral forces between the masonry walls and the foundations interrupted by a structural iron frame wall.   Analysis of the lateral load resistance system was thus warranted.

Four stacks of load-bearing masonry vaults, symmetrically located in the building, rise full-height through the structure.   Structural analyses indicated that these vaults provide sufficient lateral stiffness to the entire structure without becoming overstressed.   It was determined that additional lateral bracing elements were not needed unless these vaults were removed.

Load Tests of Structural Clay Tile Arch   It was proposed that the reduction in dead load of the structure be accomplished through the removal of non-structural components (filler tile, concrete fill, wood sleepers, and flooring) from the structural clay tile arch.   The proposed new finish floor is an access system comprised of square panels supported by a grid of pedestals.

Behavior of the clay tile arch under concentrated loads such as those imposed by the pedestals was not predictable using conventional analysis techniques, therefore a concentrated load test was conducted. In a limited area of the building, the non-structural components were removed from the arch and a prototype access floor system was installed.   Lead ingots were placed on the floor system, directly above a pedestal which in turn rested on the structural clay tile arch. Deflection of the arch under this load was small and recovered immediately upon removal of the load, indicating satisfactory behavior of the arch under the concentrated pedestal load.

Cape Hatteras Lighthouse

Cape Hatteras Lighthouse (Buxton, North Carolina, 1869) is a National Historic Landmark and the country's tallest lighthouse. The 200-foot-tall structure rests on a raft of 6 inch x 12 inch pine timbers laid about ten feet below grade. The octagonal granite base is surmounted by a double-walled brick masonry shaft, with an iron and glass gallery and lantern. A cast and wrought iron spiral stairway extends the full height of the tower.

The study of Cape Hatteras Lighthouse was initiated because of concerns about the structural stability and physical integrity of the Lighthouse. Deterioration of the exterior cast iron had been noted for some time. The exterior masonry walls exhibited areas of peeling paint, and the interior walls revealed several long vertical cracks of unknown origin. Finally, erosion of the nearby shoreline, which had been of intermittent concern over the life of the structure, once again threatened its very foundations. A preservation and restoration program including a comprehensive technical investigation was initiated in response to these observed conditions.

Field Monitoring and Instrumentation Surveys were performed to assess the verticality of the Lighthouse and to establish baselines for verifying its location, elevation, and verticality in the future. A series of permanent targets was installed on the north and west faces for use in detecting any future lateral deflection or lean.

The tower was instrumented with an anemometer, pyranometer, laser, and low- and high-speed strip recorders to measure its short- and long-term response to wind and solar radiation. An electro-optical device was used to measure the horizontal deflection of the tower relative to its base. The detector sensed the tracking of a 50-watt Halogen light source installed near the top of the tower 150 feet above. By interpreting frequency and damping, a baseline "signature" of the structure and its movements was created.

The monitoring system for wind-induced movement was triggered at wind speeds of greater than 37 miles per hour. The tower was found to move only slightly with the wind; a deflection fluctuation of less than 0.04 inches occurred at the top of the tower. It was also discovered that horizontal deflections of the tower relative to its base correlated positively with thermal drift. The tower turned with the sun as portions of its exterior masonry walls warmed and expanded.

The width of a long, vertical crack on the interior masonry wall was instrumented with an extensometer (linear potentiometer). The crack was found to open and close about .006 inch during each diurnal cycle. While movement of the crack during the observation period did not appear to be significant, flexible material will be used in its repair to accommodate future change.

Field Testing   Subsurface exploration and geotechnical analysis of the existing foundation of the Lighthouse was conducted.   Several well points were installed at the site to monitor the depth of the water table over time, as preservation of the wood foundation depends upon its immersion in water.

Laboratory Analysis   Samples of iron were removed from various locations in the Lighthouse, including areas which had been exposed to weather and salt spray from the ocean.   Analysis determined the composition and characteristics of the iron and the nature and extent of corrosion.   The ultimate tensile strength, modulus of elasticity, and coefficient of thermal expansion were identified for the cast iron and wrought iron.   Crevice corrosion, typical of exposure to changing wet and dry environmental conditions, and galvanic graphite corrosion were identified.

When this study was undertaken, erosion of the nearby shoreline had reached a critical level.   At this writing, consideration is being given to moving the Lighthouse further from shore.   Initiation of the preservation program awaits this decision.

CONCLUSION

The case studies presented herein emphasize the importance of assessment techniques in long-term preservation.   By conducting a careful investigation, monitoring conditions over time, and designing a program for future testing, the continued conservation of the historic structure is assured, and its serviceability may be predicted and extended.

As high rises have become taller and more complex, special considerations have developed.   Newer structures are less rigid and less redundant because of non-load bearing curtain walls, greater heights, longer spans, and reduced dead loads.   Structural systems exposed to the environment expand and contract in response to temperature changes.   Cladding materials are attached to buildings differently than in the past, and new and different materials have come into use.

Investigative techniques such as those described above are already being applied to buildings less than 20 years of age, some of which may become our next generation of historic high rises.   The investigation of these structures demands a greater understanding of compatibility of materials and of means to monitor lateral movement of structures.   The high rises being constructed today will challenge future investigators.

REFERENCES

Chin, I.R., and Kelley, S.J., "Inspection of the Limestone Screen Wall at the Top of the Tribune Tower Building," WJE No. 871897, Wiss, Janney, Elstner Associates, Inc., Chicago, Illinois, January 13, 1988, unpublished report.

Chin, I.R., and Morden, M.R., "Inspection of the Stone Buttresses at the Top of the Tower Portion of the Chicago Tribune Building," WJE No. 851549, Wiss, Janney, Elstner Associates, Inc., Northbrook, Illinois, January 20, 1986, unpublished report.

Janney, J.R., *Guide to Investigation of Structural Failures*, American Society of Civil Engineers, New York, 1979.

National Institute of Building Sciences, *Structural Assessment*, APT Foundation, Washington, D.C., 1986.

Peck, R., "History of Building Foundations in Chicago," *University of Illinois Bulletin*, Vol.45, No.29, January 2, 1948.

Schueller, W., *High-Rise Building Structures*, John Wiley & Sons, New York, 1977.

Slaton, D., Hunderman, H.J., and Stockbridge, J.G., "The Cape Hatteras Lighthouse: Diagnostics and Preservation," *APT Bulletin*, Vol.XIX, No.2, 1987, pp.52-60.

Meinheit, D.F., and Paulson, C., "A Structural Evaluation of the Rookery Building, Chicago, Illinois," WJE No. 831183, Wiss, Janney, Elstner Associates, Inc., Northbrook, Illinois, November 16, 1984, unpublished report.

Meinheit, D.F., Paulson, C., and Kelley, S.J., Wiss, Janney, Elstner Associates Inc. Report, "Supplementary Engineering Studies on the Rookery Building," WJE No. 851018, Wiss, Janney, Elstner Associates, Inc., Northbrook, Illinois, January 6, 1986, unpublished report.

Ancient Babylonian Bricks: Their Technological Characterization and Simulation

R. Al-Kass*, M. Hadi*, N. Khalil* and F. Ali**

Building Research Centre

**The State Organization of Antiquities and Heritage, Baghdad, Iraq.*

ABSTRACT

The possibility of producing bricks close in colour, texture, appearance and other properties to those of the ancient archaeological Babylonian bricks was investigated. The various properties of the ancient bricks were obtained, through this it was possible to approximately identify the raw materials, forming method and firing temperature. Results of this investigation indicated that ancient bricks were made from calcareous soil similar to the type of soil now available near the archaeological city. X-Ray diffraction, differential thermal analysis, and scanning electron microscopy pointed out that the firing temperature of those bricks was in the range 750 – 800°C approximately.

Based on the obtained results, full size brick specimens were then formed (using the raw materials available near the ancient site) and fired at the pre-established firing temperature. The various properties of the produced bricks were obtained, evaluated and discussed.

INTRODUCTION

Brickmaking was one of the earliest industries of mankind. The process of firing to make brick hard, durable and esthetically attractive was developed about 6000 years ago by the people located in Mesopotamia; which is now a part of Iraq [1].

Because of the flat alluvial nature of most of the Iraqi lands bricks of clay have there continued to be the universal building material . During the last century, there has been an unceasing effort by both archaeologists and engineers to uncover the monuments and texts which reveal the history and civilization of the region. Recently a major project for the archaeological revival of Babylon has been adopted by the State Organization of Antiquities and Heritage. However, these preservation and reconstruction projects are often faced with the obstacle of finding building materials which are not far in colour, texture, appearance and other proper- ties to those of the ancient ones [2].

Many procedures were utilized to characterize mineralogical composition, firing characteristics of the clays used in ancient ceramics and to obtain the firing condition of such ceramics. Some of the techniques employed were scanning electron microscopy [3,4], X-Ray diffraction [3,4], differen- tial thermal analysis [5,6], pore structure [7], colour [8], petrography [9], measurements of thermal changes [10] and Mossbauer spectrography [11].

An attempt has been made, at the Building Research Centre, to study the type of soil, additives, forming technique and fir- ing conditions of soils and bricks from several archeological sites in Iraq in order to produce bricks of approximately similar properties. This paper is a part of the project and covers the ancient bricks of Babylon.

EXPERIMENTAL WORK

Brick samples from Babylon site were collected during several visits to the ancient city. Sample selection was made, in the presence of an archaeologist specialist in such a way as to repre- sent the majority of the site bricks taking into consideration colour, appearance, dimensions and minimum exposure to weathering conditions. Adobe bricks were also collected from Babylon structures for soil analysis and identification of the additives used. A visit was also made to a nearby brick fac- tory currently used to manufacture extruded bricks for the conservation operation at the site. The produced bricks were far different in appearance and properties from those of the ancient bricks. Soil quantity representing the brick factory soil deposit was also obtained to be used for brick manufac- ture.

To obtain the approximate firing temperature of the archaeo- logical bricks, fragments of Babylon bricks were refired in an electric furnace to 700, 750, 800, 850, and 900°C at heating up rate of 100°C/hr with one hour soaking at each peak tem- perature. Specimens before and after refiring were then exa- mined using differential thermal analysis, X-ray diffraction and scanning electron microscopy.

Chemical, mineralogical, and physical properties of the ancient bricks, adobe brick and the soil were obtained and evaluated. Based on the results gained, two soil mixes were prepared from Babylon soil; one without additive and the other with the addition of 2% (by weight) animal dung. Full size specimens were then formed using two techniques: hand forming in a wooden mould, and pressing by a manual press. The formed bricks and those which were brought from the brick factory (extruded green bricks) were dried first at room temperature then followed by oven drying at 110°C. The dried samples were fired in an electrical furnace (at heating up rate of 50°C/hr) to temperatures : 750, 800 and 850°C with 6 hours soaking time at peak temperatures. All physical and mechanical tests were carried out on at least 16 cores (50 mm in diameter and height) obtained from each type of brick-group and for each firing temperature.

RESULTS AND DISCUSSION

Properties of Ancient Bricks

The neobabylonian bricks (⌣600 BC), were generally pale red-brown in colour of two main sizes measuring 32 x32 x8 cm. and 32 x 16 x 8 cm. Sections in the ancient bricks revealed the presence of organic fibers which left their clear marks on the burned bricks. Such fibers were also identified in the un-burned bricks (adobe bricks) and were most likely [1]   some form of animal dung which was probably used to reduce drying cracks and also to act as a source of energy during burning of the bricks.

Chemical and mineralogical analysis of the ancient bricks, shown in Table (1), indicated that those bricks were   made from a soil of high calcite content, and that its composition is closely similar to the soil of the ancient city nearby.

Table 1. Chemical, mineralogical and physical properties of Babylon bricks

physical properties	group 1	group 2	chemical analysis	
			oxides	(%)
density (kg/m³)	1634	1343		
			SiO_2	50.38
water absorption (%)	19.7	29.6	Al_2O_3	13.79
			Fe_2O_3	4.14
apparent porosity (%)	32.2	39.8	CaO	17.64
			MgO	4.08
suction rate (kg/m². min)	1.2	3.4	SO_3	1.07
			L.0.I	6.95
compressive strength (N/mm²)	9.1	3.2	total	98.05
			main minerals	
efflorescence	nil to slight	nil to slight	quartz feldspar	
colour	pale red brown		calcite	

On obtaining the physical and mechanical properties of the ancient bricks variations among their results were noticed, therefore, the samples were categorized into two groups based on density variations (Table 1). Bricks of high density ($\sim$ 1600 Kg/m^3) showed relatively low water absorption ($\sim$ 20%), and high compressive strength ($\sim$ 9 N/mm^2), whereas, bricks of lower density ($\sim$ 1300 kg/m^3) showed much higher water absorption and lower strength. The main reason behind the variation in properties is postulated to be due to differences in the concentration of additives, variations in moulding moisture content and firing temperature.

Determination of Ancient Bricks Firing Temperature

X-ray diffraction patterns of the refired Babylonian bricks are shown in Fig.(1). As seen from this figure, the as received bricks indicated peaks corresponding to some clay minerals, present in the fired product. This behaviour is normally encountered with low fired clay articles : clays fired at temperature below 800°C gradually became hydrated and very slowly regain their original structures [6,7]. Thus it could be expected that the bricks were fired at about or below 800°C. The above contingent is further supported by noticing the large X-ray calcite peak in the as received sample, and which was also reflected by a large endothermic DTA peak at 880°C. Furthermore, and on observing the XRD patterns of the bricks in their as received state and after refiring, it could be observed that quartz peaks remained unchanged on refiring the brick fragments to 700 and 750°C, and that at this temperature range no new crystalline phases were formed. However, raising firing to 800°C and above, quartz began to decrease significantly due to its reaction with the decomposed constituents of clay and CaCO$_3$ to form new crystalline phases of wollastonite and anorthite. SEM examination of the microstructure of the fractured brick surfaces, before and after refiring indicated that an open cellular structure was produced on refiring the fragments at about 850°C, whereas, refiring at 800°C and below did not affect the brick structure significantly. From the evidence given above, it could be concluded that the approximate firing temperature of the bricks was in the temperature range of 750 - 800°C approximately.

Properties of Raw Materials and Laboratory Produced Bricks

Physical properties of the soil used for specimen preparation (brick-factory soil), and the chemical and mineralogical analysis of this soil and that of the ancient adobe bricks are shown in Table (2) and Fig. (2). It seems evident from the table and figure that the two soils were almost alike in their chemical and mineralogical properties : both soils were calcareous of approximately similar oxide content. Therefore, the brick factory soil could be used to produce bricks close in properties to the ancient ones on choosing a suitable forming technique and controlling firing conditions.

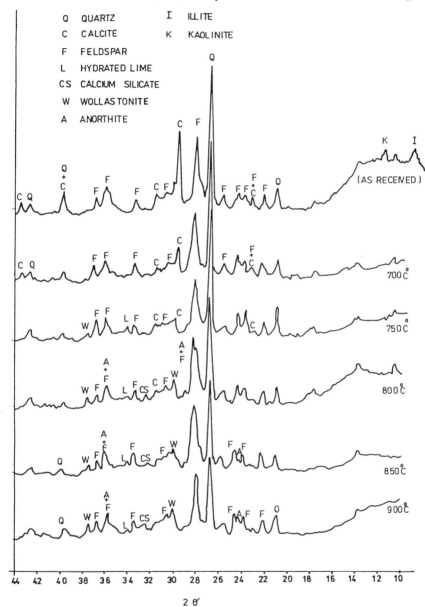

Figure 1. X-ray diffraction patterns of Babylon bricks fired at different temperatures.

Table 2. Physical, chemical and mineralogical   properties of
         Babylon soils

physical properties		chemical analysis			
			soil	adobe brick	main minerals
grain size (mm)	(%)	oxides	oxide content (%)	oxide content (%)	of both soils
sand (>0.02)	27	SiO_2	41.20	45.81	calcite
		Al_2O_3	16.41	14.88	quartz
silt (0.02-0.002)	41	Fe_2O_3	3.00	3.00	montmor-
		CaO	16.27	15.15	illonite
clay (<0.002)	32	MgO	5.36	4.05	illite
		SO_3	1.16	1.46	kaolinite
plasticity index (%)	29.0	L.O.I	15.04	12.83	feldspar
sp.gravity	2.7	total	98.44	97.18	
vol.drying shrinkage(%)	18.6				

A comparison between physical properties of unfired brick samples
formed by different methods is shown in Table (3).   Forming
moisture content and drying shrinkage were maximum for handmoulded samples, and minimum for pressed specimens, hence, drying
density varied accordingly.

Table 3. Comparison between physical properties of unfired brick
         samples formed by different methods

property	extr-usion	hand moulding		pressing	
		no add-itions	animal's dung 2%	no add-itions	animal's dung 2%
forming water content(%)	28	35	35	20	20
bulk density (kg/m³)	2042	1852	1707	1944	1828
linear shrink-age(%)	7.8	9.5	8.0	5.9	4.9

It is interesting to note the effect of fiber   additions (animal
dung) on reducing the drying shrinkage and bulk density of the
samples, and this might be one of the reasons why ancient people
added such material to their brick making soil.

The bricks fired in the temperature range 750 - 800°C yielded, in
general, a similar colour to that of the ancient bricks.   A close
similarity was also observed in appearance,   texture and internal

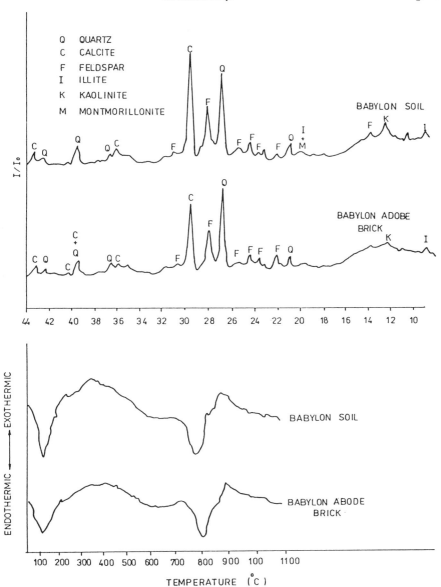

Figure 2. X-ray diffraction patterns and differential thermal curves for Babylon soil, adobe brick.

structure of the hand moulded samples and those of the ancient bricks. Tables (4-6) summarize the physical properties of the produced bricks at the three firing temperatures (750, 800 and 850°C). All properties varied considerably depending on forming methods, the additive added and the effect of firing temperature. Extruded samples exhibited maximum density and strength, and minimum water absorption and suction rate, whereas, hand moulded and pressed specimens, with or without animal dung, showed lower mechanical resistance and they were analogous in properties.

Table 4. Comparison between physical properties of brick samples formed by different methods, fired at 750°C

| property | extr-usion | hand moulding | | pressing | |
		no add-itions	animal's dung 2%	no add-itions	animal's dung 2%
linear change(%)	-0.2	-0.2	-1.4	-0.5	-0.3
bulk density (kg/m^3)	1710	1632	1432	1661	1560
water absorp-tion (%)	21.0	21.8	25.8	21.3	24.5
apparent porosity (%)	35.9	35.5	37.0	35.4	38.2
suction rate (kg/m^2.min)	1.2	1.7	2.9	2.2	2.8
compressive strength (N/mm^2)	17.9	8.4	2.9	7.8	4.7
efflore-scence	nil	nil	nil	nil	nil

On comparing appearance and other properties of the handmoulded specimens which were fired at about 750 - 800°C (Tables 4,5), with those of the Babylonian bricks (Table 3), a fair correlation could be noticed: the density varied between 1630 - 1340 kg/m^3, depending on the amount of organic fibers added, and accordingly varied other physical properties of both brick groups.

The handmade brick look could now be achieved commercially with an automatic casting machine [12] with a capacity of about 100,000 brick/shift per day. This portable equipment could easily be used to produce bricks at the sites where preservation work is needed.

Table 5. Comparison between physical properties of brick samples formed by different methods, fired at 800°C

property	extr-usion	hand moulding		pressing	
		no add-itions	animal's dung 2%	no add-itions	animal's dung 2%
linear change(%)	-0.3	0.2	0.3	0.3	-0.3
bulk density (kg/m^3)	1672	1540	1401	1640	1459
water absorp-tion (%)	21.0	24.2	28.6	23.3	29.2
apparent porosity (%)	35.1	37.3	40.1	38.2	42.6
suction rate $(kg/m^2.min)$	1.8	2.2	3.2	2.4	4.0
compressive strength (N/mm^2)	19.2	11.9	3.8	10.2	4.7
efflore-scence	nil	nil	nil	nil	nil

Table 6. Comparison between physical properties of brick samples formed by different methods, fired at 850°C

property	extr-usion	hand moulding		pressing	
		no add-itions	animal's dung 2%	no add-itions	animal's dung 2%
linear change(%)	0.4	1.1	1.0	1.0	0.6
bulk density (kg/m^3)	1711	1533	1379	1552	1467
water absorp-tion (%)	21.0	24.2	29.2	25.4	29
apparent porosity (%)	35.9	37.1	40.2	39.4	42.5
suction rate $(kg/m^2.min)$	1.3	2.8	3.4	3.0	4.5
compressive strength (N/mm^2)	18.6	13.3	3.6	8.5	4.4
efflore-scence	nil	nil	nil	nil	nil

CONCLUSIONS AND RECOMMENDATIONS

From the results obtained the following could be concluded:
1. Ancient Babylonian bricks were made from a calcareous soil of properties approximately similar to the soil now available near the ancient city.
2. Organic fibers, probably animal dung, was used in the ancient brick to control drying shrinkage and also to act as an energy source
3. The firing temperature of the ancient brick was in the temperature range of about 750 - 800°C.
4. Bricks similar in properties, texture and appearance to the Babylonian bricks could be produced by hand moulding the soil located near   Babylon, and firing to a temp. of 750-800°C.
5. The use of portable automatic casting machine to form bricks for conservation is recommended.

REFERENCES

1. Llyode S., Building in Brick and Stone, Singer Ch., Holmyard E.J., and Hall A.R. eds, Oxford, p. 456., 1954.
2. Damerji, M.S., On the Dimensions of the Archaeological Revival of Babylon Project, Sumer, Vol.35, No.1-2, p. 44, 1979.
3. Tite, M.S., Maniatis Y., Meeks N.D., Bimson M., Hughes M.J. and Leppard S.C., Technological Studies of Ancient Ceramics for the Near East, Aegean and Southeast Europe, Proceeding of Seminar on Early Pyrotechnology of Skithsonian Institution, Washington DC, pp. 61-77, 1979.
4. Maniatis Y. and Tite M.S., Technological Examination of Neolithic - Bronze Age Pottery from Central and Southeast Europe and from the Near East, Journal of Archaeological Science, 8, pp. 59-76, 1981.
5. Enriquez C.R., Danon J. and Beltrao M., Differential Thermal Analysis of Some Amazonian Archaeological Pottery, Archaeometry, 21, 2, pp. 183-186, 1979.
6. Kingery W.D., A Note on the Differential Thermal Analysis of Archaeological Ceramics, Archaeometry, 16, pp. 109-112, 1974.
7. Sanders H.P., Pore Size Distribution Determination in Neolithic, Iron Age, Roman and other Pottery, Archaeometry 15, 1, pp. 159-161, 1973.
8. Maston F.R., A Study of Temperature Used in Firing Ancient Mesopotamian Pottery, In R.H. Brill (edt.) Science and Archaeology, M.I.T. Press Cambridge, Mass., pp. 65-79, 1971.
9. Hays T.R., and Hessan F.A., Mineralogical Analysis of Sudanese Neolithic Ceramics, Archaeometry, 16, 1, pp. 71-79, 1974.
10. Tites M.S., Determination of the Firing Temperature of Ancient Ceramics by Measurement of Thermal Expansion, Nature, Vol.222, p. 81, 1969.
11. Janot Ch. and Delcroix P., Mossbauer Study of Ancient French Ceramics, Journal of Physics (Paris) Colloque, 35, 6, pp. 557-561, 1974.
12. Brick and Clay Record, 183, 5, p. 27, 1983.

SECTION 2 - MASONRY AND OTHER MATERIAL PROBLEMS

On the State of Structural Repair of Masonry

Fritz Wenzel
Institute of Bearing Structures, University of Karlsruhe,
D-7500 Karlsruhe, Federal Republic of Germany

INTRODUCTION

Grout injection and stitching as well as prestressing of old masonry has been practised for a long time. This technique of restoration helps to save the monumental value of historically important buildings more than taking down and rebuilding them and, as a rule, is distinctly less costly. The Special Research Programme "Preservation of historically important buildings" at the University of Karlsruhe has collected quite a few results regarding the effectiveness as well as the durability of such securing measures (Wenzel, Maus [1], Ullrich [2,3]). These results were achieved on buildings whose restoration and securing can be traced back to the twenties. The experience gained shall be summarized and presented in its practical meaning. The corresponding rules of dimensioning and execution which were developed at the University of Karlsruhe over the last few years (Dahmann [4], Haller [5]) are to be found in the 1987 yearbook of the Special Research Programme. There they are illustrated by sketches and examples of use. The application of these rules in practice presupposes that they are coordinated with the particular conditions of the respective old building.

Special questions of drilling technique and execution of construction (dry or wet drilling, sinkage, pre- or intermediate grouting, cleaning of the drill-hole, cement injection or mortar grouting) will be dealt with in the 1988 yearbook.

GROUT INJECTION

The purpose of grouting

Old masonry is grouted to increase its supporting capacity, to close cracks and cavities, to strengthen loose masonry and mortar, to replace missing mortar, to introduce new, larger forces into the masonry at local points, to involve the inner filling of multi leaf walls and pillars in the supporting structure, to link reinforcement bars and prestressed anchor ties to the masonry and protect them against corrosion(Pieper, Hempel [8], Hempel [9]). Where these or similar problems do not occur, grout injection does not need to be performed.

Fig. 1 Grout injection after surrounding and protecting an anchor bar against corrosion

Injection material

All types of cement customary in the trade and those with trass added are suitable as injection materials. Clay and expanding cement are not suitable. Very important are cements with a high sulfate resistance (HS-cement), which normally help to prevent damage due to expansion of old mortar containing gypsum (Dahmann[4], Pieper [7], Pieper, Hempel [8]). The disadvantage of these cements is their dark colour; if they leave the masonry they can easily cause stains on the surface which is why particular caution is advisable. Although super-hydraulic limes may be injected too these do not reach high enough strength in the masonry and tend to expand because of their C_3A-content. For cement injection water-cement factors from 0,8 to 1,0 and pressures up to 6 bar are used.

Synthetic resin as material for injections is expensive, there are unanswered questions concerning the compatibility and aging characteristics, furthermore synthetic resin is an alien material to masonry.

Experiences from the subsequent examinations
In most of the examined cases the objective of grout injection was achieved. Where this was not the case, deficiencies in planning, execution and supervision were important factors.

The success of grouting injection depends, among other things, on a sufficiently high water-cement factor of the material that is injected, otherwise it will "die of thirst". For this reason pre-moisturizing of the drill-holes is important and should be executed together with cleaning the holes of drill-dust. In addition the pressure must be maintained long enough, otherwise the material will not penetrate the old mortar or the cement paste will not find its way to cavities that are located further back.

Special Problems

Expanding caused by formation of minerals   There is great danger that mortar containing gypsum is present in old masonry. Even if several specimens of mortar are taken and examined and no gypsum is found, one cannot be sure that this result is relevant for the whole building including original parts, repaired parts and added parts. The usage of HS-cement as injection material seems to be obvious. As a rule it helps to avoid expansion in consequence of the formation of ettringite and thaumasit. This applies especially if the masonry is dry or can be dried out. Short moisturizing, e.g. heavy rain, is harmless if the masonry can dry out afterwards. According to today's knowledge (Hempel [9], Pieper, Hempel [8]) even if HS-cement is used expansion can not be excluded with absolute certainty.

Besides cement with a high sulfate resistance as an injection material in recent years, there are also special mortars for use in masonry containing gypsum (Ludwig [10]) which are obviously sulfate resistant but may only be applied over 5^0 C and have to be treated with moisture subsequently, a task difficult with old masonry. As the strength of these mortars is less than that of ordinary cement mortar and they do not provide sufficient corrosion protection, so that it is necessary to use anchors of rustproof steel, there are also losses in the static-constructive efficiency.

Efflorescences The moisture that gets into the masonry during the injection may contact salts that are included or sedimented in the stonework and then crystallize by drying. This can lead to efflorescences, destruction of paint layers and plaster surfaces and also to erosion of sandstone (Hilsdorf [11], Althaus [12]). It is therefore advisable to take specimens not only to determine the share of gypsum in old masonry but also to carry out mineralogical and material technological examinations with regard to possible efflorescences. Then at least one knows in advance what to expect after injecting and it is possible to think the concept of rehabilitation over if necessary. To what extent remedy is possible e.g. by harmonization of the injection material with the conditions on site has to be decided according to the special case.

STITCHING

The purpose of stitching

In general Stitching as subsequent reinforcement happens where tension or thrust occurs which the masonry cannot withstand. Examples can be found with Dahmann [4] and Pieper [7]. Stitching is always connected with grout injection to form the bond between steel and masonry as well as to provide corrosion protection.

In multi leaf masonry Here the reinforcement bars connect the two outer leaves through the inner filling which is strengthened by injection. As the outer leaves are only one stone thick mostly, special attention must be paid to the anchorage of the bars. (Fig. 2)

Reinforcement bars
As a rule bars made of ribbed reinforcement steel 420/500 with a diameter of 8 to 20 mm, mainly 12 to 16 mm, with anchorage by bond are used. Also steel with through rolled thread ribs, so called Gewi-steel, has proved useful. With long anchor bars a sleeve joint may be developed, with short anchor lengths an additional end anchorage with washer and nut or with a special end piece. When the danger of corrosion is regarded as extreme, rustproof steel is sometimes used, for example for strongly moisturized structural elements. Steel with a smooth unprofiled surface should not be used as the grip is weak.

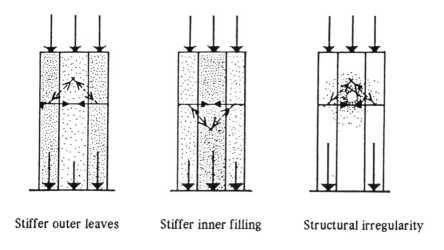

Stiffer outer leaves   Stiffer inner filling   Structural irregularity

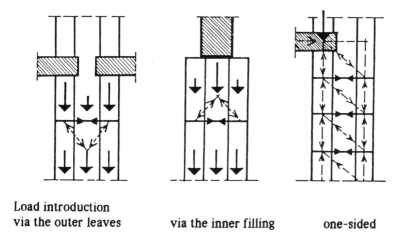

Load introduction
via the outer leaves   via the inner filling   one-sided

Fig. 2 Stitching in multi leaf masonry adjusting uneven force flow

Experiences from subsequent examinations

With 20 mm coverage of the reinforcement bar by cement in the drill-hole, corrosion protection is guaranteed. To ensure that the material that is injected covers the anchor uniformly, spacers must be attached to the bar. Sufficient protection of 25 to 30 mm coverage at the ends of the anchor must also be ensured. With shorter cement plugs there exists danger of corrosion, longer ones mostly cause too much loss in bond length in the outer leaves of multi leaf masonry.

Rules for dimensioning and executing stitching of multi leaf masonry

This refers to the 1987 yearbook of the Special Research Programme. It discusses the following: appraisal of allowable pressure of the existing, unimproved masonry; load assumptions for the reinforcement bars; choosing of the anchor grid; corrosion protection and bond.

PRESTRESSING

The purpose of prestressing

Old masonry is grouted and prestressed if strongly torn walls and pillars must be joined to regain their compression strength and thrust strength and in addition to withstand tensile stress; if the masonry is to be self supporting and span openings without auxiliary constructions of steel or reinforced concrete; if masonry buildings because of irregular subsoil are to act as stiff structures to force even settlements. When the causes for the cracks are removed e.g. by improvement of the subsoil or by reinforcement of the foundation, a loose armouring can be sufficient for further securing. As a rule prestressing is only applied in the case of severe damage of the masonry. With the help of prestressing the force flow may be corrected in old masonry constructions, in exceptional cases it may even change its direction. (Fig. 3)

Prestressed anchor ties

The most frequently used stressing tendons are steel rods with through rolled thread ribs on both sides, diameter 15 to 36 mm, steel quality about 850/1050 to 1100/1350. Such steel rods allow shortening at the construction site with a separator and joining with a thread sleeve so that they can be added to long pretensioning anchors. If the design stress is only used between two thirds and three fourths there are reserves left in case the anchor force should increase over the force of prestress e.g. because of changes of load or movements in the subsoil. In addition to that there is no stress corrosion cracking at this point because of the decreased utilization factor.

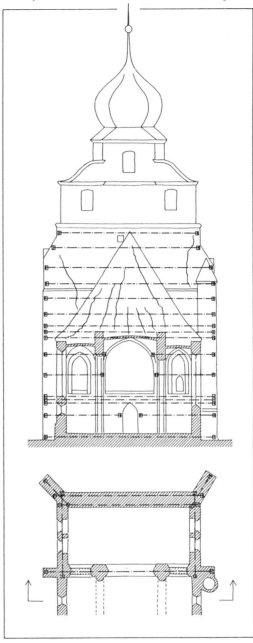

Fig. 3   Prestressing at the Westwerk of the collegiate church in Herrenberg

Performing long drillings up to 30 meters and more in masonry with a drift of less than 0,3 % is not extraordinary for specialized companies. The anchor heads are manufactured of reinforced concrete or steel (Wenzel [6]).

Rustproof steel with low design stress is not as qualified for prestressed anchor ties. A larger diameter is needed which causes a larger interference in the old substance. Recently rustproof steel with higher strength is available as well.

The subsequent bond by grout injection in the anchor canals gives additional security. When prestressing without bonding, a periodical supervision of the anchor ties is necessary. For this reason, and for subsequent stressing, access to the elements must be provided. One will have to limit prestressing without bond to cases where one is forced to provide the possibility of subsequent stressing.

Prestressing the old, torn masonry without any sort of force carrying filling in cracks and cavities (grout injection) can only be carried out with low forces, depending on the wall bond, superimposed load and friction and must therefore be regarded as unpromising.   Because the wall bond may relax, the prestressing forces can deteriorate later.

Extensive examinations are presently being carried out in the Special Research Programme, concerning both prestressing without bond and prestressing without or with minimized use of injection material.

Experiences from subsequent examinations
Concerning corrosion protection the statements on stitching bars also apply to prestressed anchor ties. By guiding the anchor in the masonry spacers are necessary to guarantee a coverage with cement of 20 mm around the steel and of at least 10 mm around the sleeves. Attention must also be paid to the corrosion protection of the anchor heads. As to anchors that lie outside the masonry, there are 60 years of positive experiences concerning protection by coating or embedding in cement mortar.

Periodic controlling measurements of the stress forces in newer anchors have been carried out by the University of Karlsruhe for 12 years. The anchor forces stay quite stable in the different buildings; the losses of stress move between 3 % and 12 % , depending on the special condition of the building. In special cases losses of stress up to one third were measured e.g. when subsequent underpinning was carried out or when constructive charge was subsequently reloaded on a new pile foundation.

Measurements were also carried out on older prestressed anchor ties. The results must still be evaluated. Up to now it can only be said that the examined anchors obviously now as before fulfill their function entirely.

Rules for dimensioning and executing prestressing of masonry
This again refers to the 1987 yearbook. It will provide information on the following: necessary examinations of specific structural circumstances; dimension of the stress force; influence of the load independent deformations of the masonry on the stress force; influence of creeping on the stress force; spontaneous plastic deformations of the masonry; stress force losses as a reaction to elastic and plastic initial deformations of the masonry; allowable design stress; diameter of the drill-hole; anchorage of prestressed rods with anchor bodies; partial surface pressure perpendicular to the horizontal joint; partial surface pressure parallel to the horizontal joint; anchorage of prestressed rods by bond; buckling of the masonry; buckling of multi leaf walls perpendicular to the plane of the wall; buckling upwards and necessary superimposed load; forces and design pressures in the transverse bars; additional end anchorage.

OUTLOOK

In the Special Research Programme examinations are presently carried out among which are the following, which will also support improvement and further development of grout injection, stitching and prestressing of the masonry of historical buildings:

Grout injection
Mineralogical and material technological analysis of the old masonry, especially the historic mortar. The development of repair and replacement mortar for grout injection as well as for jointing with the goal of the best coordination possible of old and new building materials. Differentiated inquiries on the reasons for damage to the church buildings in Lower Saxony which were restored with cement injection and prestressing and are damaged again. Examinations to reduce and to limit the injection material, also for the extended use of the technique of grout injection on masonry with valuable plaster and stucco or with delicate paintings and panels.

Stitching
Experiments with pulling out anchor bars

Prestressing

Prestressing without bonding providing the possibility to stress the anchor
subsequently or to remove the anchor. Strain measurements on anchors that
were installed longer ago.

Further examinations

Under the theme "Grout injection, stitching and prestressing," the engineer-
like inventories of buildings that were restored some time ago,including the
collecting of data on the building as well as of execution and planning records, and inspection and focused examinations, with interventions in the
buildings substance to examine the success or failure of the applied securing
techniques are going to be continued.

In connection with the theme of this contribution there are also low destructive examinations concerning the determination of strength and deformation values of old masonry, investigations dealing with the values of old
bricks or natural stones and surveys related to the behaviour of strength in
unimproved multi leaf walls and pillars. A systematic test on low and non
destructive examination procedures to determine the inner constitution of
masonry of historic buildings has also started.

It was possible to plan many of the above mentioned examinations for a
longer period of time - an advantage of the continous promotion of the Special Research Programme by the Deutsche Forschungsgemeinschaft (German
Research Community). Results can therefore not be expected at once, but
step by step.

References

[1] Wenzel, F. and Maus, H. Nachuntersuchungen an ingenieurmäßig sanierten Mauerwerksbauten. Erster Zwischenbericht, Erhalten historisch bedeutsamer Bauwerke, Jahrbuch des Sonderforschungsbereiches 315, 1986, pp. 211 - 221, Ernst & Sohn, Berlin, 1987

[2] Ullrich, M. Ingenieurmäßige Bestandsuntersuchungen an sanierten Bauwerken. Forschungsbericht der Arbeitsgruppe an der Fachhochschule Münster, Erhalten historisch bedeutsamer Bauwerke, Jahrbuch des Sonderforschungsbereiches 315, 1986, pp. 222 - 230, Ernst & Sohn, Berlin, 1987

[3] Ullrich, M. Ingenieurmäßige Bestandsuntersuchungen an sanierten Bauwerken. Zweiter Zwischenbericht der Arbeitsgruppe an der Fachhochschule Münster, Erhalten historisch bedeutsamer Bauwerke, Jahrbuch des Sonderforschungsbereiches 315, 1987, pp. 89 - 100, Ernst & Sohn, Berlin, 1988

[4] Dahmann, W. Untersuchungen zum Verbessern von mehrschaligem Mauerwerk durch Vernadeln und Injizieren, Diss. Univ. Karlsruhe 1983, Aus Forschung und Lehre, Institut für Tragkonstruktionen, Universität Karlsruhe, Heft 19, Karlsruhe, 1985

[5] Haller, J. Untersuchungen zum Vorspannen von Mauerwerk historischer Bauten, Diss. Univ. Karlsruhe 1981, Aus Forschung und Lehre, Institut für Tragkonstruktionen, Universität Karlsruhe, Heft 9, Karlsruhe, 1982

[6] Wenzel, F. Verpressen, Vernadeln und Vorspannen von Mauerwerk historischer Bauten. Stand der Forschung, Regeln für die Praxis, Erhalten historisch bedeutsamer Bauwerke, Jahrbuch des Sonderforschungsbereiches 315, 1987, pp. 53 - 72, Ernst & Sohn, Berlin, 1988

[7] Pieper, K. Sicherung historischer Bauten, Ernst & Sohn, Berlin and Munich, 1983

[8] Pieper, K. and Hempel, R. Schäden und Sicherungsmaßnahmen an Bauten mit Gipsmörtel, Erhalten historisch bedeutsamer Bauwerke, Jahrbuch des Sonderforschungsbereiches 315, 1987, pp. 73 - 88, Ernst & Sohn, Berlin, 1988

[9] Hempel, R. Untersuchungen über Treiberscheinungen beim Injizieren von Zementmörtel in historisches Gipsmauerwerk und über die Tragfähigkeit kurz verankerter Stahlnadeln, Diss. Univ. Braunschweig 1986

[10] Ludwig, U., Mehr, S. and Moldan, D. Schäden am Turmmauerwerk von Kirchen und Vorschläge für eine Konzeption von Mörteln für Sanierungsarbeiten, in Kolloquium über Steinkonservierung, Westfälisches Amt für Denkmalpflege, Münster 1984 (Ed. Oel, H.J.), pp. 289 - 310, Institut für Werkstoffwissenschaften, Glas und Keramik, Erlangen, 1984

[11] Hilsdorf, H.K., Kropp, J. and Garrecht, H. Ursachen und Wege der Feuchtigkeit in Baukonstruktionen, Erhalten historisch bedeutsamer Bauwerke, Jahrbuch des Sonderforschungsbereiches 315, 1986, pp. 249 - 271, Ernst & Sohn, Berlin, 1987

[12] Althaus, E., Faller, A. and Karotke, E. Putz- und Mauerwerksschäden durch Salze, Erhalten historisch bedeutsamer Bauwerke, Jahrbuch des Sonderforschungsbereiches 315, 1986, pp. 272 - 283, Ernst & Sohn, Berlin, 1987

[13] Bruggemann, B. Die Ermittlung der aufnehmbaren Kräfte von in das Mauerwerk eingebauten Nadelankern aus Betonstahl. Lehrstuhl für Hochbaustatik, Prof. Dr.-Ing. K. Pieper, Technische Universität Braunschweig, 1976

Mechanical Properties of Stone Masonry Walls

D. Anicic, Z. Soric, D. Moric and H. Macan
Institute of Civil Engineering, Faculty of Civil Engineering Sciences, University of Zagreb, Zagreb, Yugoslavia

SUMMARY

The results obtained by testing stone masonry walls built with cement-lime mortar have been reviewed. Thirteen wall specimens have been tested, out of which 7 were bilaterally reinforced with reinforced concrete (gunite). The walls were subjected to normal centric loads, to a compressive force along the diagonal in order to establish tensile strength, and to cyclic loads with a constant vertical and variable horizontal load.

The paper reviews the results obtained by testing the mechanical properties of all components (cement, lime, aggregate, mortar and stone) and by wall testing.

The obtained numerical values can be used as the basis for the design of earthquake strengthening of old stone buildings.

INTRODUCTION

A twenty-year program of reconstruction of cultural monuments damaged by the 1979 earthquake is currently under way in Dubrovnik. A number of residential and public buildings built from the 13th to the 18th centuries are being reconstructed. The load-bearing structures of these buildings involve stone walls and wooden floors; stone walls, arches and columns are also found frequently.

The Dubrovnik area is one of the strongest seismic regions in Yugoslavia: for a return period of 500 years its seismicity amounts to IX° on the MCS-64 scale, and for a return period of 1000 years to X° with a 63% probability (Aničić et al.[1]).

Earthquake strengthening of stone buildings is governed by the general principles of construction in seismic areas with due respect for conservation requirements and of the possibilities offered by the architectural concept of the building (Aničić et al.[3]). The design and the checking of the strength of the load-bearing structure call for knowledge of the following:

1) basic mechanical properites of existing walls; and
2) properties of the new stone walls to be built.

The first goal is **achieved** by wall testing in situ (Aničić et al.[3]). The second set of data has not been available for the case under consideration - apart from information reported abroad - because no studies of local materials have been undertaken to date.

This paper reviews the results obtained by testing a series of thirteen 100x100x60 cm stone walls built with cement-lime mortar and roughly dressed stone (Figure 1). Albeit limited in scope, the study has provided enough data to be used by the desinger in the design of new stone walls, improving the load-bearing capacity of existing old stone buildings.

STUDY PROGRAM

The study has involved the determination of the properties of materials used to build wall specimens, and wall testing. The mechanical properties of cement, lime, stone, aggregate and mortar, and of concrete and reinforcement, have been determined. Data on materials has been determined by methods conforming to Yugoslav standards (JUS) and are listed under the heading Test Results.

Wall specimens have been tested for the following types of loads (Figure 1):

- vertical centric load in order to determine the modulus of elasticity, compressive strength and the working diagram (4 specimens);
- diagonal load in order to determine the reference tensile strength of the wall (7 specimens);
- simultaneous action of constant vertical and cyclic horizontal load (2 specimens).

Half of these specimens were bilaterally reinforced by a 7 cm gunite lining (Figure 1). The lining was reinforced with a cold drawn steel wire mesh, made up of 8 mm horizontal and vertical wires spaced 100 mm in each direction. The two linings were connected by four ϕ 8 mm steel ties run through the mortar joints in the wall.

TEST RESULTS

Material testing

Standard tests of stone, limestone and dolomite in terms of composition, produced the following figures: compressive strength 120 MPa; tensile strength 6.6 MPa; water absorption after 24 hours 3.4%. Cement of declared strength 45 MPa - Portland cement with 20% slag - produced in standard specimens a compressive strength of 42 MPa and a bending strength of 8 MPa. Hydrated lime presented a compressive strength of 0.92, and a bending strength of 0.56 MPa. Mortar was prepared with a 7 to 3 volume mix of crushed 0-4 mm aggregate and 0-1 mm natural sand. The design strength of cement-lime mortar was 5.0 MPa for a cement : lime : aggregate ratio of 1 : 1 : 10. Mortar was prepared by volume batching of the components. The testing of several series of

mortar specimens at an age equal to the age of the walls on the day of
testing (30 months) produced the following data:

mean value of mortar compressive strength   7.0 MPa
standard deviation   1.45 MPa
coefficient of variation   0.20
mortar compressive strength, MM 7.0-1.3x1.45   5.1 MPa

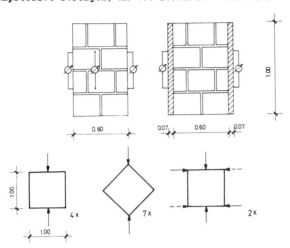

Figure 1. Load types and specimens shape

Accordingly, mortar strength matched the design value. Gunite
compressive strength, determined on cylinders 50 mm in diameter and
obtained from special made slabs, amounted to 26 MPa. The f_y/f_u grade of
the welded reinforcement mesh was 609/660 MPa and elongation at fracture
8.7 percent.

Wall Testing

Centric load   The test was run by gradually increasing the longitudinal
forces up to specimen failure or to the maximum capacity of the testing
facility. The force was increased in 100 kN steps. Wall deformation
along the sense of force action was measured on a 400 mm base in the
central section of the wall at 6 points. Figure 2 illustrates the normal
stress versus the mean value of relative deformation. The mean values
reviewed in Table 1 have been obtained from the measurements.

Because of the indequate capacity of the testing facility,
specimen failure was not achieved. The magnitudes of the moduli of
elasticity for gunite reinforced walls were determined by measurements
on the gunite surface (Figure 1).

<u>Diagonal test</u>   The reference tensile strength of the walls was determined by the diagonal tensile test. The specimen was placed into special steel shoes, supported at the two corners and tested for compression along the diagonal. The force was increased in 100 kN steps. Failure occurred along the compressed diagonal when the wall tensile strength was reached. The reference tensile strength is calculated from the expression

$$\sigma_n = 0.45 \ N/A \qquad (MPa) \tag{1}$$

where
N - logitudinal (vertical) force at failure
A - mortar joint cross section

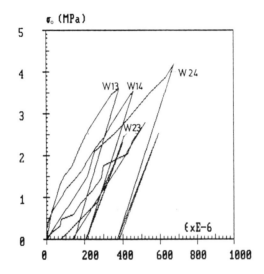

Figure 2.   Normal stress vs. strain

The increase of the failure force between the composite wall and the nonreinforced wall was on average three times. This is more important than the comparison between the tensile stresses. Relative wall deformation was measured in the central part of the compressed diagonal along a 400 mm base. Figure 3 illustrates the reference tensile stress calculated according to formula (1) versus relative compressive deformation along the diagonal. For composite specimens wall area (A) is equal to the actual area, i.e., there were no corrections due to differences of material (stone wall – concrete). All the results are reviewed in Table 2.

Cyclic loading   This test was run on two specimens, a stone wall and a wall with a gunite lining. The walls were tested in a unit with sliding teflon bearings permitting the simultaneous action of constant vertical and alternately variable horizontal loads along the top wall edge. The time course of testing is illustrated in Figure 4.

Table 1.   Moduli of elasticity for stone walls and gunite reinforced walls

Wall type	Initial tangential modulus of elasticity E_0 (MPa)	Secant modulus at 30% strength $E_{0.30\,\sigma_n}$ (MPa)	Estimated compressive strength σ_u (MPa)
Stone wall with cement-lime mortar	8750	6430	≈ 6.2
Stone wall with cement-lime mortar and bilateral gunite lining	29820	10790	$>>6.2$

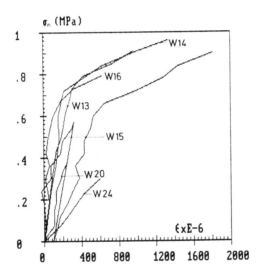

Figure 3. Reference tensile stress vs. strain

Table 2.   Reference tensile strength, σ_n, and ultimate
           bearing capacity, P^u, of diagonally loaded
           specimens

Specimen designation	Wall type	σ_n (MPa)	P^u (kN)	Guniting effect
19	stone	0.410	550	
20	"	0.405	540	1.00
24	"	0.345	460	
13	stone+gunite	0.970	1600	
14	"	1.020	1680	3.00
15	"	1.960	1600	
16	"	0.790	1300	

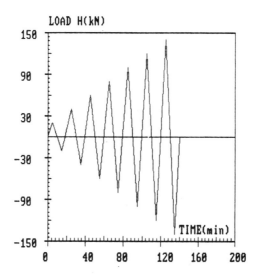

Figure 4. Load - time history for cyclic loading

        Figure 5 presents the hysteresis loops obtained by testing the
wall with a gunite lining. No failure was achieved in either sample
tested under cyclic loading. When the resultant of the vertical and
horizontal force reached the edge of the wall, the wall rotated as a
rigid body about the compression edge. Because of the high strength of
the stone and lining, no failure occurred due to bending or compression
of the compressed part of the cross section. The calculations also
showed that no failure along the diagonal need have occurred, the
tensile stresses for the applied combination of vertical and horizontal
force being lower than the tensile strength of the wall. Wall rotation
about the compressed edge could be reduced by increasing the

longitudinal force in the wall; in this case, however, normal stress would exceed the value found in real buildings (0.3-0.6 MPa). Energy absorption as established by cyclic loading was found to be satisfactory. Hysteresis loops show no pinching characteristic for slip in the joints. The degradation of rigidity is gradual, and the obtained ductility high (about 3.2). The bilinear working diagram can be considered satisfactory for mathematical modelling.

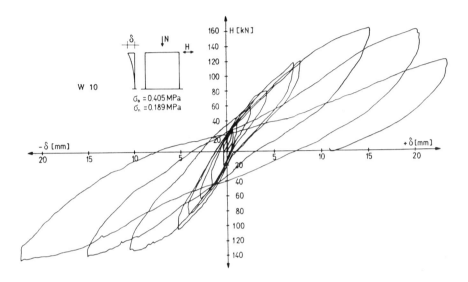

Figure 5. Hysteresis loops at cyclic loading

CONCLUSION

The tests have provided data which can be used in the design of new load-bearing stone walls and for the strengthening of existing walls by gunite. The numerical values established by testing should be understood as mean values and reduced by the estimated scatter of results which could be established by testing a considerably larger specimen series.

ACKNOWLEDGEMENT

This study has been financially supported by the Institute for the Reconstruction of Dubrovnik and by the Self-Managing Community of Interest for Science of the Socialist Republic of Croatia, to which the authors express their gratitude.

REFERENCES

1. Aničić D., Earthquake Strengthening of Historical Monuments in Dubrovnik, Yugoslavia, VIIth European Conference on Earthquake Engineering, Athens, Sep. 20-25, 1982, Vol. 5, pp. 313-320

2. Aničić D., Morić, D., Zaninović,V., Ultimate Tensile Strength in Stone Masonry and Brick Masonry Walls, 1st DGKH Congress, Plitv. Jezera, 18-19.10.1984, Vol. 1, pp. 257 - 264

3. Aničić D., Mihailov V., Velkov D., Reconstruction, Seismic and Structural Strenghthening of Historical Monuments in Dubrovnik, Institute for the Reconstruction of Dubrovnik, Monograph, Dubrovnik,1988.

Assessment of Old Masonry by Means of Partially Destructive Methods.

F. Berger

Institute of Bearing Structures, University of Karlsruhe, D-7500 Karslsruhe, Federal Republic of Germany

Abstract

Walls, columns, pillars and foundations of masonry make up the bulk of historical buildings. The bearing capacity of old masonry has to be determined before any redesigning takes place or before a new use introduces new loads to the building.

The usual procedure is to examine bricks or stone and mortar samples individually and then to calculate from the results the load bearing capacity of masonry with the help of several empirical formulas. Another procedure is to test small, full-scale specimens extracted from the masonry. These methods are either inaccurate or too destructive.

First results of the research carried out at the Institute of Bearing Structures at the University of Karlsruhe have shown that procedures can be developed (based on recent theoretical considerations), to estimate the material strength of masonry, which provide more information and are less destructive.

The bearing capacity of masonry can be calculated by multiplying two different values: the strength of the specimens, which is also an upper limit of the masonry strength, and a reduction factor, which mainly depends on the deformation behaviour of brick or stone and mortar.

The strength of stones is determined by means of compressive tests on small samples (20 to 30 mm in diameter).

The factor of reduction can be determined in two different ways:
- Comparison of the tensile strength values coming out of splitting tests on fine stone or brick specimens, and specimens with mortared bed joints;
- Calculation using the dynamic E-moduli of unit and mortar. These can be defined by in-situ ultra-sonic measurement of the sound velocity in brick or stone and mortar.

1   Introduction

With all in-situ testing methods we have to consider whether they are incompatible with the value of the historic building. The demand of the monument conservationists that one take care of the ancient monument forces one to develop less destructive methods.

The reported research was carried out on single leaf masonry with new bricks. Tests on masonry with ancient bricks will follow.

2   Conventional Testing Methods

2.1   Direct determination of bearing capacity

The bearing capacity can be tested on masonry specimens, which are sawed or broken off the building. Thereby the test results are influenced by the partial destruction of the specimen structure, however, the test specimens must have minimum dimensions and one needs to test a great number of them. Because of these problems, this testing method is applied less frequently.

2.2   Indirect determination of bearing capacity

The compressive strengths of brick $\beta_{D,Zi}$ and mortar $\beta_{D,m}$ are determined separately. With these results the compressive strength of masonry $\beta_{D,M}$ is calculated with the aid of one of the numerous well known empirical formulas. These were obtained with the results of many different test-series on masonry using different mathematical arrangements.

This procedure of determination of the bearing capacity needs less expenditure of work and is less destructive than that of testing small specimens. Their results however show more scattering, but they are nevertheless frequently applied.

2.2.1   Determination of compressive strength of bricks $(\beta_{D,Zi})$

The compressive strength of bricks has to be determined on complete bricks (DIN 105) or on bored cores. The extraction of these specimens out of the masonry causes rather less destruction, although the results of these tests are useful.

They are used when the reliable determination of the compressive strength of brick by means of testing other mechanical properties (i.e. ultra-sonic velocity or rebound-hammer) is not possible.

2.2.2   Determination of the compressive strength of mortar $(\beta_{D,m})$

This procedure is considerably more difficult than the one using the bricks, and in a lot of cases it is impossible.

Extracting small specimens of mortar out of the bed joints often badly disturbs the structure, therefore the result of the following compression test is rather falsified. It is difficult to extrapolate the results to larger structures.

Other non-destructive testing methods, (i.e. chemical analysis, testing of micro-hardness, ultra-sonic-velocity), are not sufficiently developed for the accurate determination of the compressive strength of mortar.

In all cases it must be taken into consideration that the hardening of the mortar in the joints between the brick differs substantially from that of mortar samples in steel forms, which were used in all former masonry researches.

3   Determination of Masonry Compressive Strength Using Bed Joint Cores.

3.1   The Theoretical Basis of the Method

Thirty years ago a theoretical explanation of the failure behaviour of centrally pressed masonry was found, [Refs. 1-4.] According to this, the interaction between the different lateral deformations of mortar and bricks under vertical pressure loading affects lateral compression and tensile stresses in mortar and bricks. The heights of these lateral stresses are set by the deformability of brick and mortar and their mutual interaction. The compressive strength of the brick in the vertical direction is diminished according to the increase of its lateral tensile stress. Therefore the deformability accounts for the available compressive strength of the bricks in the masonry.

Until today there has been no success in formulating these interrelations into a good mathematical equation.

The first aim of our research was to find a testing method, which took into account this interaction between bricks and mortar.

Our starting point was the compressive strength of brick $(\beta_{D,Zi})$, which is theoretically the upper limit of the compressive strength of masonry $(\beta_{D,M})$ and can be determined with sufficient precision without harming the structure. But the main question to ask is, how far is the compressive strength of bricks in the masonry reduced to the compression strength of masonry, in other words, what is the value of ratio $K_M = \beta_{D,M} / \beta_{D,Zi}$ (factor of reduction)?

The testing method that we found, is the splitting tensile test of cylindrical bed joint cores (Figure 8).

A bed joint divides this core into two symmetrical brick segments. Due to the usual geometry of ancient masonry, its diameter is ten centimetres. According to our tests, samples can easily be bored out without any damage, provided that:
- the mortar compressive strength is below $0.55 \, N/mm^2$ and
- the operating speed of the diamond-armed core bit and the pressure of the cooling water are appropriately measured.

There is a sufficient amount of reliable and practical research into splitting tensile tests (Figure 1) of homogeneous materials, i.e. concrete and brick [5, 6].

Bed joint cores tested to failure in the splitting test show equivalent results, but they have a lower failure load than homogeneous brick samples of the same size. This reduction depends on the characteristics of deformability of the brick and mortar and their interaction.

In order to explain this reduction qualitatively one has to start with a bed joint core with mortar, that has the same characteristics as brick. The shear and transverse stresses (Figure 2) in a splitting test are equal for the case of homogeneous materials.

Augmenting the deformability, i.e. diminishing the modulus of elasticity of the mortar, it shows an increasing tendency towards being squeezed out of the bed joint. The static friction between brick and mortar hinders this deformation. This produces an additional shear and transverse tensile stress in the brick (Figure 2, middle). The resultant stress gives the real stress distribution in a bed joint, depicted at the bottom of Figure 2. Depending on the deformability of the mortar, the transverse tensile stress may change to transverse compressive stress. Near the edge between brick and mortar the transverse tensile stress in the brick is increasing. The earlier the transverse tensile stress limit in the brick is exceeded, the more deformable the mortar.

3.2   Modelling with an F.E. Computer Program

We verified these qualitative correlations by using F.E. calculations. The finite element program that was used, took into account linear stress-strain behaviours of the materials. In order to arrange the element mesh, we cut a quarter segment along the x- and y- axes out of the full circle of the sample. The calculation was made for the plane strain case.

The results of the F.E. calculations for three different material combinations are shown in Figures 4, 5; i.e.:
- homogeneous sample: brick only
- heterogeneous sample: brick and stiff mortar
- bed joint core: brick and soft mortar.
The material characteristics of the brick and the load (1 kN) are the same in all three cases.

The calculated transverse tensile and compressive stresses are depicted in Figure 4. The increase of the transverse tensile stress in the brick resulting from the diminution of the modulus of elasticity of the mortar is evident.

Figure 5 shows the distribution of the calculated shear stress along the joint between brick and mortar. In the case of "brick only" the tension points inwards and protects the brick against splitting. In the cases of both "brick and stiff mortar" and "brick and soft mortar" the tension diminishes and points outwards at the edge. The reason is the shear stress, which is caused by the hindered transverse deformation of the mortar.

The results of these calculations validate the soundness of the qualitative description of the mechanical process which was explained earlier.

3.3   Experiments

We produced bed joint cores and masonry pillars and subjected them to splitting tensile tests and compression tests. For the time being, we used new brick and mortar, because there was no other material available.

3.3.1 Mortar

We made five different kinds of mortar (A to E), varying the mix ratio sand : binder. Out of each kind of mortar a large quantity of specimens were produced in plastic forms covered for three days with moist cloths and then stored with the samples of masonry. At regular intervals during the three weeks, four specimens were subjected to compressive and bending tensile tests. (German standards DIN 18555/3).

The deformations in transverse and longitudinal direction were measured on cylinders with a length of 250 mm and a diameter of 100 mm, under continually increasing pressure in the longitudinal direction. The modulus of elasticity was defined in the range from zero to one third of the failure stress.

The average data on the mechanical properties of the mortars is shown in Table 1.

3.3.2 Brick

For the tests we used four grades of new normal size well baked brick (240/115/71 mm). There was no new material available with a pressure strength below 20 N/mm^2 which would have equalled the ancient material. In each case the bricks stem from one mixture and one baking. Grade I is badly mixed and weakly baked. Obviously some damaged bricks were picked out, but nevertheless the quality range of the grade varied widely. Grade IV is a double baked klinker, which is not comparable to a weakly baked brick. The average data of compressive strength (DIN 105) is given in Table 2.

Then, we bored numerous cores (diameters of 32, 44 and 52 mm) in the direction of the various axes of the bricks. We then determined the compressive strength, splitting tensile strength and the moduli of elasticity. The results of these tests are shown in Table 3.

Compressive strength:

The compressive strength of cores perpendicular to the bed joint amount on average to 89% of the brick compressive strength according to DIN 105. The corresponding compressive strengths parallel to the bed joint in the longitudinal and transverse axes of the brick amount to 58% of the strength perpendicular to the bed joint (grades I to III), or 51.6% of the strength according to DIN 105. The intensively baked klinker (grade IV) does not show any difference in strength along the different axes. Probably the sintering during the baking has made them isotropic.

Splitting tensile strength:

The relationship between splitting tensile strength of the cores in the transverse axis of the brick and the compressive strength of the cores perpendicular to the bed joint can be specified in function of regressional lines. These results agree with those given in [6].

Modulus of elasticity:

We measured the longitudinal and transverse deformation of the cores perpendicular to the bed joint by strain gauges and drafted the stress strain lines accordingly. From this we determined the moduli of elasticity in the range from zero to one third of the failure tension. We noticed the interesting fact, that the moduli of grade I and II are equal. This may be the reason why the compressive strength of masonry made of the more durable brick grade II does not essentially exceed the compressive strength of masonry made of brick grade I.

3.3.3   Pressure Tests on Masonry Pillars

Combining the mortar A to E with the brick grades I to IV we produced 20 different kinds of masonry. In order to test the compression strength we built at least seven small pillars of each kind of masonry (Figure 7). One such small pillar consists of five stacked bricks. The bed joints were 12 mm thick. To make certain of this, we used thin upright stripes as a pattern. The results of the compression tests are shown in Table 3. In addition we built three RILEM-masonry blocks out of most types of masonry, in order to extrapolate our results better into those for the compressive strength of huge masonry samples.

3.3.4   Splitting Tensile Tests on Bed Joint Cores

Simultaneously with the small pillars we built sets of two kinds with 12 mm joints, twenty out of brick grade I, 10 each out of grades II - IV (Figure 7). Four weeks later we bored bed joint cores with a diameter of 103 mm. When we did so about 3% of the cores broke. This was mostly due to fissures in the brick. After having dried the cores sufficiently we applied hard felt stripes to them and tested the splitting-tensile strength. With the exception of a few samples of brick grade I, which had some fissures, all samples split perpendicularly. (Figures 8 and 9).

There were no gaping fissures or protruding mortar just before the moment the sample broke. We observed this with the aid of lacquer (which permits the detection of cracks). The failure loads of the bed joint cores are summarised in Table 4. The deviations are still within the range of the compressive strength of masonry pillars data.

3.3.5   Comparison Between Splitting Tensile Strength of the Bed Joint Cores and Compressive Strength of the Masonry Pillars

With the results of the compression and splitting tensile tests we made further detailed examinations of the correlations. As we expected, there was no satisfactory correlation between the data on the compressive strength of masonry, brick and mortar.

The most important influence on the value of the failure load was the transverse strain capacity of both materials. We called this Q_{Zi} and Qm. It can be calculated with the following equation:

$Q = $ E-Modulus / Poisson's ratio (in the notation Zi refers to brick, and m to mortar).

In Figures 10 and 11 the compressive strength of masonry and failure load of the splitting tensile tests are computed in accordance with the above equation. The correlations show evident similarities. The regressional lines of these distributions have the equations:

compressive strength of pillars:
$$\beta_{D,M} = 6.81 + 0.317 \text{ x } 10^{-8} \text{ x } Q_{zi} \text{ x } Q_m (N/mm^2)$$

failure load of bed joint cores in splitting test:
$$F_{FK} (N_{mm}) = 139 + 4.442 \text{ x } 10^{-8} \text{ x } Q_{Zi} \text{ x } Q_m$$

The regressional lines are determined with $R^2 = 0.92$ or 0.8. This proves the evident correlation between the failure loads of both testing methods for the same parameters: Q_{Zi} x Q_m.

If we could verify in further experiments these similarities of dependence (not only of the compressive strength of masonry, but also of the splitting tensile strength of bed joint cores), there could be a way to use these correlations for *a posteriori* determination of the strength of ancient masonry.

The reduction factor of the experiments has to be determined by the following relationships:

Masonry in compression test:
ratio $K_M = \beta_{D,M} / \beta_{Z,i}$
          $\beta_{D,M}$ = compressive strength of masonry
          $\beta_{D,Zi}$ = compressive strength of masonry
Cores in splitting test:
ratio $K_F = F_{FK} / F_{Zi}$
          F_{FK} = failure load of bed joint cores
          F_{Zi} = failure load of homogeneous cores;
          same material, same diameter.

The relationships between these two ratios drawn in one diagram, (Figure 12), show linear correlation for each particular brick grade. These regressional lines ($R^2 = 0.75$ until 0.95) correspond well with the results of the tests. The lines for the brick grades I and II are near the line $K_m = K_{fk}$.

Further investigations of ancient brick, which must have a lower compressive strength than brick grade I or II, will, we hope, complete our present studies. Increasing the compressive strength of the brick (grade III and IV) the lines in Figure 12 level off. The reason is the normal stress level, which is generally different in both testing methods. The normal stress in the splitting tensile test amounts to 15% or less of the normal tension of the brick compressive strength along one axis. With this low tension the mortar stays within the stress range of its modulus of elasticity, even for very hard brick material. On the other hand, the corresponding tension of a brick pillar under load amounts to 30% of the brick compressive strength along one axis. Hence in conjunction with the harder bricks there is a process of plastification in the mortar. This produces additional transverse stress and diminishes the reduction factor K_M.

3.3.6   Conclusion

The investigations above prove the simultaneous influence of the transverse strain of brick and mortar on the reduction factors in the compression test of masonry pillars (K_m) as well as in the splitting tensile test with bed joint cores (K_F). The reduction factors with soft brick are approximately the same. These correlations can be used for the determination of the bearing capacity of ancient masonry. The procedure for this can be roughly subdivided into the following steps:

a) determination of brick compressive strength in cores. One has to reckon here with the differences between the data of cores parallel and perpendicular to the bed joints.
b) determination of splitting tensile strength (F_{Zi}) of the bricks on cores parallel to the joint (d = 50 - 70 mm).
c) determination of the reduction factor of the sample (ratio K_F) in boring out the cores with a horizontal symmetrical bed joint and testing them in a splitting test (F_{Fk}).

Calculating the ratio $K_F = F_{FK} / F_{Zi}$.

d) determination of masonry compressive strength:

With the simplifying premise $K_m = K_F$ the compressive strength can be calculated by multiplying the brick compresssive strength with the reduction factor:

$$\beta_{D,M} = \beta_{D,Zi} \times K_m$$

Generally several tests have to be carried out. The question of how many tests are necessary depends on the type of masonry. The statistical deviation of quality of the brick test with an impact hammer (Schmidt) can give a hint of this direction. For the present the described correlations are applicable to joints, that are 10 - 15 mm thick. This procedure will fail in the case of very soft mortar, because the joints break during boring. Until now the proposed procedure was tested on masonry with new bricks only and does not claim to be generally accepted. At present additional investigations are being carried out in section C2 of the SFB 315 at the University of Karlsruhe. One issue is the question of deviations, and another the thickness of the joints.

4   Additional Ultrasonic Measurement

The described method of bed joint cores for the examination of the factor of reduction is not suitable for brick masonry with very soft mortar, or thick bed joints, or for any masonry made of natural stone. While trying to remove this drawback we experimented with the measurement of the ultrasonic pulse velocities (V_s) of brick and mortar.

The velocity depends primarily upon the elastic properties of the material [Ref. 7, 8]. As described in Section 3.1, the available compressive strength of the bricks (or stones) in the masonry is set by the characteristics of deformability of its materials. Hence by measuring the ultrasonic velocities of bricks or stones and mortar, the determination of the factor of reduction is as practicable as when using the bed-joint core method.

The tests were performed on the masonry specimens taken from bricks I, II and mortar C, E, F. (See Section 3.) Supplementary specimens were made from a fifth grade of brick with:

$(\overline{V} : \beta_{D,Zi} = 38.3 \, N/mm^2 (V = 16\%); E-\text{modulus} = 15873 \, N/mm^2; \text{Poisson's ratio} = 0.19)$

and with two additional kinds of mortar of the following properties:

$M5 : \beta_{D,m} = 0.9 \, N/mm^2 (V = 5.7\%); \text{E-modulus} = 3030.3 \, N/mm^2; \text{Poisson's ratio} = 0.24/M \, 7 : \beta_{D,m} \, 3.2. \, N/mm^2 \, (V = 5.9\%); \text{E-modulus} = 4.783 \, N/mm^2; \text{(Poissons ratio} = 0.16)$.

The compressive strength of the new masonry pillars were determined as:

$$V / M \, 5 = 7.5 \, N/mm^2$$
$$V / M \, 7 = 11.9 \, N/mm^2$$

The ultrasonic test equipment we used was a Krautkrämer USL 33. The transmitter and receiver had a frequency of 50 kH. Up till the present we have measured only the velocity of the compressive wave. The testing arrangement for the brick is shown in

Figure 14. The velocity of mortar was determined indirectly by measuring the time for the wave propagation through a brick-mortar sandwich (Figure 15) and measuring the sound velocity in the bricks and the geometrical dimensions of the bricks and the mortar joint. With the results of this test, the dynamic moduli of elasticity of bricks and mortars were calculated by the equation:

$$E_{DYN} = V_s^2 . \zeta . \frac{(1+n)(1-2n)}{1-n} \ (kN/mm^2)$$

ζ = density $(kh \ / \ m^3)$
V_s = pulse velocity (km / sec).

Test results are shown in Table 5.

Using a similar procedure to that perfected in section 3.3.5, we have defined the transverse strain of the materials by the product Q_{Zi} x Q_m, but in this case Q was calculated by $Q = E_{DYN}$ / Poisson's ratio. In Figure 13 the compressive strengths of masonry are plotted correspondingly to the results of this equation, showing evident similarities to Figures 10 and 11. This correlation demonstrates that the assumption that the factor of reduction can be determined by ultrasonic velocity measurement is correct.

We are testing a larger number of specimens from different kinds of masonry. From these we will aim to improve the accuracy of the ultrasonic measurement, the measurement of shear waves for the determination of dynamic Poisson's ratio and the in-situ measurement between different boreholes in a masonry wall.

References

1. Hilsdorf; H.K.: Untersuchungen über die Grundlagen der Mauerwerksfestigkeit, Materialprüfungsamt für das Bauwesen, Bericht Nr. 40, TH München 1965.

2. Hilsdorf, H. K.: Investigation into the Failure Mechanism of Brick Masonry Loaded in Axial Compression, Proceedings of International comference of Masonry Structural Systems, Texas, November 1967.

3. Morsy, E.H.: An Investigation of Mortar Properties Influencing Brickwork Strength, PhD Thesis, University of Edinburgh, 1968.

4. Khoo, C.L. and Hendry, A.W.: Ein Burchkriterium für zentrisch belastetes Ziegelmauerwerk, 3. Internationale Mauerwerkskonferenz, Dokumentation S. 139-145, Essen 1973.

5. Bonzel, J.: Über die Spaltzugfestigkeit des Betons. In: Beton 3/1964.

6. Schubert, P. and Friede, H.: Spaltzugfestigkeit von Mauersteinen. In: Die Bautechnik 1980.

7. Krautkrämer, J. and H.: Wersstoffprüfung mit Ultraschall, 5. Auflage, Springer-Verlag 1986.

8. Bungey, J.H.: The testing of concrete in structures, Surrey University Press, ISBN 0-903384-29-9, 1982.

9. Hennicke, H.W. and Leers, K.J.: Die Bestimmung elastischer Konstanten mit dynamischen Methoden, Tonindustrie-Zeitung 89, Nr. 23/24, 1965.

Figures

Figure 1 - Splitting test on a homogeneous boring cylinder and the stress-distribution on the principal axes.

Figure 2 - Splitting test on a core with mortar joint: distribution of the lateral stress and shear stress at the mortar joint.

Figure 3 - Modeling by means of F.E. computer program: element mesh, support conditions and loading of the considered segment.

Figure 4 - Results of the F.E. calculation: Distribution of the x-stress along the y-axis.

Figure 5 - Results of the F.E. calculation: Distribution of the shear stress $_{x,y}$ along the mortar joint.

Figure 6 - Cores drilled from brick, which will be tested later.

Figure 7 - Masonry prism and brick specimen from which a core has been extracted.

Figure 8 - Splitting test on a core with mortar joint.

Figure 9 - Failure of a core with mortar joint, which has been subjected to a splitting test.

Figure 10 - Compressive strength $\beta_{D,M}$ of the masonry prisms in relation to the product $Q_{Zi} \times Q_m$ of the material parameters (Q = E-modulus / Poisson's ratio: Zi = brick, m = mortar).

Figure 11 - Unit failure load F_{FK} of the core when subjected to splitting test in relation to the product $Q_{Zi} \times Q_m$ (see Figure 10).

Figure 12 - Relation between the ratio $K_M = \beta_{D,M} / \beta_{D,Zi}$ (of the masonry prism subjected to compression) and the ratio $K_F = F_{FK} / F_{Zi}$ (of the core subjected to splitting).

Figure 13 - Compressive strength $\beta_{D,M}$ of the masonry prisms in relation to the product $(Q_{Zi} \times Q_m)_{DYN}$ of the material parameters (Q = Dynamic modulus of elasticity / Poisson's ratio).

Figure 14 - Measurement of ultrasonic pulse velocity of bricks.

Figure 15 - Measurement of ultrasonic pulse velocity of mortar (by testing a brick-sample with a bed joint).

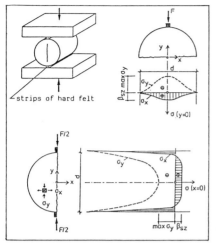

Fig. 1

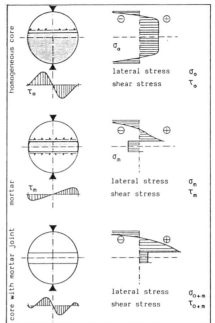

Fig. 2

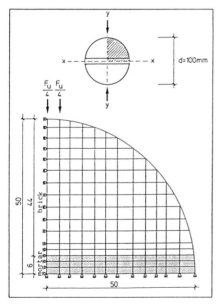

Fig. 3

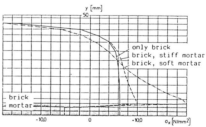

Fig. 4

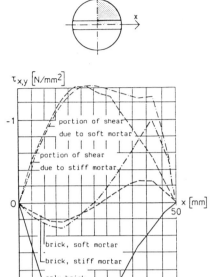

Fig. 5

Fig. 6

Fig. 7

Fig. 8

Fig. 9

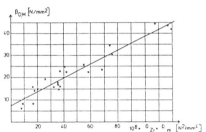

Fig. 10

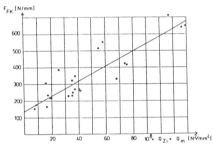

Fig. 11

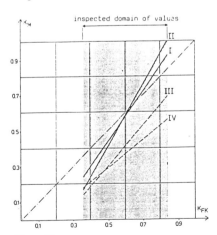

Fig. 12

	A	B	C	D	E
mix ration sand:binder (in volume)	10:1	5:1	3,8:1	2,9:1	1,8:1
compressive strength (N/mm^2)	1,59	3,8	10,7	15,3	23,7
variation coefficient (%)	9,4	7,9	7,2	7,5	8,5
E-modulus (N/mm^2)	2254,3	6071,2	9927,7	13030,2	13750,0
poisson's ration	0,15	0,18	0,16	0,18	0,19

Table 1: Mechanical properties of the mortars

	I	II	III	IV
compressive strength according to DIN 105 (N/mm^2)	28,1	45,1	55,9	124,3
variation coefficient (%)	27,8	5,2	8,3	10,9
compressive strength of cores (Ø 32mm, ⊥ bed joint) (N/mm^2)	27,6	37,3	50,6	107,0
variation coefficient (%)	26,8	16,8	13,0	12,7
splitting strength of cores (Ø 52mm) along the width of the bricks (N/mm^2)	2,9	3,12	3,91	7,33
variation coefficient (%)	28,5	18,7	14,1	15,9
E-modulus (N/mm^2)	9874,0	9141,0	19140,0	32899,0
variation coefficient (%)	44,0	14,6	9,7	7,0
poisson's ration	0,20	0,16	0,18	0,20

Table 2: Mechanical properties of the bricks

mortar \ brick		I	II	III	IV
A		6,16	7,9	15,6	19,1
	V	(21,6)	(10,1)	(21,2)	(13,7)
B		7,9	13,8	16,9	25,8
	V	(17,5)	(21,0)	(14,8)	(9,4)
C		15,3	15,7	23,4	44,9
	V	(20,3)	(5,1)	(14,4)	(9,5)
D		14,3	22,1	30,2	41,6
	V	(13,6)	(12,7)	(7,7)	(8,4)
E		17,3	24,4	34,3	43,7
	V	(20,4)	(22,4)	(9,4)	(6,3)

Table 3: Mean failure stress (N/mm^2) and variation coefficient V (%) of masonry prisms subjected to compression

mortar \ brick		I	II	III	IV
A		16,3	19,7	34,6	44,3
	V	(25,1)	(12,1)	(16,0)	(13,3)
B		17,3	24,3?	36,8	59,0
	V	(8,3)	(19,9)	(17,8)	(22,9)
C		24,4	30,4	37,7	82,0
	V	(25,0)	(17,3)	(17,3)	(22,0)
D		26,8	29,2	47,5	74,8
	V	(24,7)	(17,4)	(15,6)	(20,3)
E		25,0	30,2	48,0	73,6
	V	(28,3)	(17,6)	(9,3)	(19,6)
only brick (calculated)		50,6	57,1	72,1	136,4

Table 4: Mean failure loads (kN) and variation coefficient V (%) of cores with mortar joints subjected to splitting test

	bricks			mortar				
	I	II	V	C	E	F	M5	M7
ultra-sonic pulse velocity (compressive wave) (m/sec)	2747	2366	3294	2891	2874	2185	1579	1906
variation coefficient (%)	19,8	5,1	4,5	—	—	—	8,9	7,5
dynamic modulus of elasticity (N/mm^2)	10839	9461	17181	13970	14120	7419	3560	6082

Table 5: ultra-sonic pulse velocity (V_s) and dynamic modulus of elasticity (E_{dyn}) of materials
$$E_{dyn} = V_s^2 \, \varrho \, \frac{(1+\mu)(1-2\mu)}{1-\mu}$$

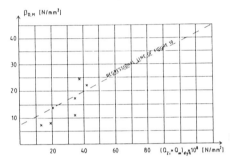

Fig. 13

Fig. 14

Fig. 15

Analysis and Structural Behaviour of Masonry Cross Vaults

R. Barthel

Institut für Tragkonstruktionen, Universität Karlsruhe

ABSTRACT

This paper introduces a research project dealing with the structural performance of various types of historic cross vaults giving special consideration to the shell effect and folded-plate action. Linear and non-linear calculations of arches and basic types of cross vaults have been conducted. The load cases considered are those of self weight and spreading of the abutments. The effect of different structural details has been examined in parameter studies. The results have been checked by comparing them with the actual damage surveyed. As well, typical damages can be explained theoretically by this kind of analysis. The objective is to compile a basic compendium of structural knowledge to keep destructive repair measures to a minimum and to give them better direction.

INTRODUCTION

In practice there are many sources of uncertainty when examining and analysing historic vault structures. The application of conventional calculating methods is complicated due to the three-dimensional shapes which are often doubly curved, to the material properties of the masonry and to the boundary conditions. This often leads to expensive remedial measures, which are often unnecessarily extensive and which alter and, to some extent, destroy the historic building substance.

The Deutsche Forschungsgemeinschaft has therefore financially supported a research project which consists of the following four steps.

1) The most important types of cross vaults are to be compiled and classified according to their shape, structure and material. The objective is to determine a few idealized basic types from the endless variety existing in order to make them accessible for analysis.

2) Typical sorts of damage occurring to vaults are to be described considering the vault shape, structure and the loading case. Records of damage surveys and completed repair operations are to be compiled and evaluated.

3) Analysis is to be conducted by means of the finite-element method, examining the influence of various parameters. The theoretical results are to be compared with the actual damage in the vaults; also a theoretical explanation may be given.

4) The work will be concluded by giving advice for the analysis and repair in practice. Which simplifications can be made when calculating? Which parameters are to be considered?

This work has not been completed but first results are presented in the following.

CHARACTERISTICS OF THE VAULTS

Geometry

Examinations will be focused on quadripartite cross vaults on a rectangular base. The side ratio of the rectangular base may have different values. The transverse, diagonal and wall arches are usually composed of segments of circles. The webs between them show a single or double curvature. Photogrammetrical surveys to determine the exact course of the contour lines have been conducted only rarely. A rough classification of the most common types of cross vaults is shown in Figure 1. Historical development and context have been omitted.

1) Circular cylindrical cross vaults formed by the intersection of two semicircular barrels with the same radius.
2) Cross vaults with pointed tranverse, cross and wall arches with equally or similarily high vertexes. The height of the vaults results from the cross arches which are generally semicircular. This also determines the radius of the pointed transverse and wall arches. The webs are translational surfaces and slightly twisted depending on the radii of the arches.
3) Pointed cross vaults with dome-like doubly curved webs.
4) Dome-like cross vaults. The vertexes of the transverse and wall arches are lower than those of the cross arches. The webs are doubly curved and in a certain case the four webs may form a spherical sector (pendentive dome).

Beyond those, there are numerous variations and combinations which can be regarded as alterations of one basic type. All types may occur with or without ribs. The thickness of the vaults ranges from about 10 to 60cm.

Structure and material

Of influence on the structural behaviour are among others the type of masonry and the type of masonry bond, the height and type of the fill in the vault spandrels, the connection between the ribs and the webs and the connection between the webs and the wall of the nave as well as the neighbouring vaults. As an especially important example the principal types of connections between the ribs and webs are shown in Figure 2. A specific interdependence cannot be determined between the vault shape, the structure and the material.

TYPICAL FORMS OF DAMAGE

The patterns of damage depend in the first place on the vault shape and the loading case. The case of spreading of the abutments is of special importance. Even small displacements force the vaults to separate into various parts since the material has no tensile strength. A mechanism of

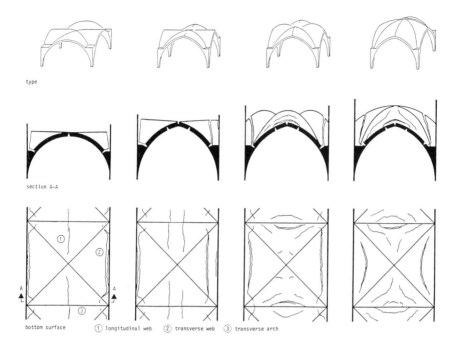

type

section A-A

bottom surface   ① longitudinal web   ② transverse web   ③ transverse arch

Fig.1   Some basic types of cross vaults and typical crack patterns
caused by spreading of the abutments

movement is created. Two types of cracks occur:
a) bending tensile cracks due to the great eccentricity of the line of
thrust. The cracks open only either on the top or bottom surface of the
vault. Since they are signs of rotation these spots can be considered as
hinges or hinge lines.
b) cracks due to tensile forces. These extend through the entire
material thickness of the webs.

In circular cylindrical cross vaults hinge lines are marked by
cracks on the bottom surface following the crown of the longitudinal
webs and on the top surface near the springer of the vault. Cracks
through the entire thickness of the web occur in the transverse webs
parallel to the nave walls and/or directly at the connection to the nave
wall. The result is the structural performance of a three-pinned arch.

In cross vaults with pointed arches of equal height two parallel
cracks occur on the bottom surface near the crown of the longitudinal
webs and one crack at the crown on the top side. In relation to the
height of the vault the hinges near the springers are lower than those
in circular cylindrical cross vaults.

The webs of the other types are very stiff due to the double curvature. Displacements of the abutments therefore often lead to the separation of the webs from the transverse arches. The webs are also dismembered into individual arches. The separation of the web and the transverse arch is the result of the different rises. A flat arch subsides more than a steep arch does when the abutments move horizontally.

Additionally, in all vault types, cracks often appear between cross ribs and the web masonry. Ribs with bonding to the web masonry are partially separated. Especially the keystones of the diagonal ribs are often torn from the web masonry. Ribs often show spalling and longitudinal cracks which are signs of high edge pressure.

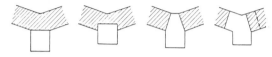

Fig.2   Structural connection between rib and web

ANALYSIS

Computer programs and basic assumptions

The FE-Program "ADINA" was applied with "PATRAN" acting as pre- and post-processor. Linear calculations have been carried out using the isoparametric shell element available in ADINA. The material property is linear elastic, isotropic or orthotropic. Cracks due to tensile forces can be simulated iteratively by opening the finite-element mesh and repeating the calculation.

Non-linear calculations of two-dimensional arches have been conducted with two-dimensional solid elements and of three-dimensional vaults with three-dimensional solid elements. By applying these elements linear strain distribution is not required. The material model for concrete is transferred to masonry which makes possible the simulation of cracks caused by tensile bending. The assumptions are the following:

1) non-linear stress-strain relationship in compression. The stress-strain curve begins with an initial tangent modulus and goes up to a peak value followed by a falling branch. Under low compression the material behaviour is approximately linear-elastic with an E-modulus of 3000 MN/m^2 and ν =0.25.
2) biaxial or triaxial respectively compressive failure envelope
3) no tensile strength
4) orthotropic post-tensile cracking behaviour. The stiffness perpendicular to the cracking plane diminishes; the stiffness parallel to the plane remains.

In all calculation procedures carried out to date the deformations have been small. Therefore effects of second-order theory are not considered.

Arch
In a masonry circular arch a chain of three hinges is created when the
abutments move horizontally. Heyman (1) transfered the plastic theory
of steel structures to arch structures. The location of the hinges as
well as both the maximum and minimum horizontal force can be determined
from the steepest and flattest possible line of thrust. More refined
calculations were conducted by Sawko and Rouf (2). They analysed arches
with single imposed loads and took the plasticising of material at the
hinges into account.

We were concerned with non-linear analysis of arches under self
weight and displacements of the abutments. An important fact is that
even very small displacements of the abutments cause cracking. In the
examples shown in Figure 3 hinges were created after movements of only a
few millimeters and the horizontal thrust approached the minimal and
maximal ultimate value. The range of elastic behaviour without cracking
is very small. As a result of the calculated displacements the cross
section cracked to an extent of up to 80%. Nevertheless, the pressure in
the remaining cross section reached values of only one quarter to one
third of the failure compression stress. For small displacements these
may therefore be regarded as "elastic" hinges rather than "plastic"
hinges.

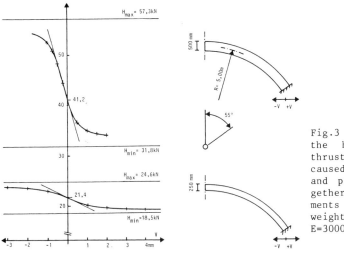

Fig.3 Change of
the horizontal
thrust of an arch
caused by spreading
and pressing to-
gether of the abut-
ments (width: 1m,
weight: 20kN/m³,
E=3000MN/m²)

Two arches lying upon each other.
The way, in which two arches lying upon each other interact, was
examined to obtain indications of how ribs and webs without shear
connection behave or how double - layered transverse arches work. A
contact surface was defined between both arches of two-dimensional solid
elements. Pressure can be transferred perpendicularly to the contact
surface but no tensile forces at all. Initially, friction was not
considered.

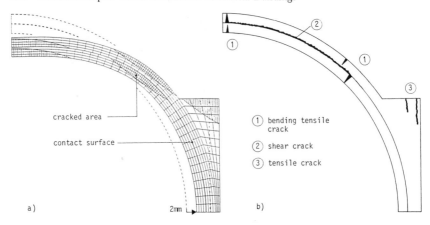

<table>
</table>

cracked area

contact surface

① bending tensile crack
② shear crack
③ tensile crack

a)   2mm   b)

Fig.4   Two arches with contact surface between. a) deformed element
        mesh with cracked areas b) crack pattern.

There is little interaction between both arches when self weight and
small horizontal displacements of the abutments are taken into account
only. They separate a little at the crown as well as near the fill.
There are, though, shifting movements along the contact surface. Figure
4 shows the crack pattern common in many thick transverse arches and
between cross ribs and the webs. It corresponds with the analysis.

Circular cylindrical cross vault under self weight

Ungewitter and Mohrmann showed the application of the thrust-line method
to vaults in 1901 (3). The web is divided into two-dimensional arches
following the fall-lines and the lines of thrust are determined. The
forces concentrate in the diagonal rib or in the groin. Pieper used the
same method to analyse a circular cylindrical cross vault but he assumed
a hinge near the springer (4). The height of the hinge was assumed by
experience as being o.4R . Heyman used the shell theory in 1966 to
determine the resulting forces (1). Nethertheless all authors give
different values for the resulting forces (Table 1). The values are
often used in practice and they are often even applied to other types of
vaults without further calculations.

	$H/g \cdot R^2$	h/R
Ungewitter/ Mohrmann 1901	0,46 [1]) -0,52	0,20 [1]) -0,30
Heyman 1966	1,00	0,47
Pieper 1983	o,88	0,40

$W = 1,14 \ g \ R^2$ (without fill)
$x = 0,47 \ R$ (without fill)
g ... weight per square unit
R ... radius

1) depending on the fill

Table 1: Resulting forces at a quarter of a circular cylindrical cross
         vault according to Ungewitter/Mohrmann, Heyman, Pieper

Several parameter studies were conducted on a cross vault with a
radius of 5m and a thickness of 25cm. It was assumed that the vault has
a stiff masonry fill of about one-half of its total height, thus
obtaining a rigid support there. A condition of symmetry was assumed
along the transverse arch due to the neighbouring vault whereas a horizontal support resulting from the nave wall was assumed along the wall
arch.

– Isotropic Material. The external forces are approximately as large as
those Heyman had determined. The internal flow of forces does not follow
the fall-lines but takes a more direct path to the abutments. In the
bottom two third of the vault a biaxial stress state prevails. The webs
in this area press themselves against the nave wall and the neighbouring
vaults. In the upper parts near the vertexes of the transverse and wall
arches tensile stress occurs in horizontal direction. It causes cracking
from the vertex on downward along the edges for about 22 degrees. Those
cracks along the nave wall – regarded as typical – exist even without
movements of the abutments. Bending tensile stress does not occur. The
compressive stress remains far below the failure value. It is therefore
possible to apply linear calculation. The greatest stress occurs in the
bottom section of the groin.

– Orthotropic Material A masonry bond with horizontal courses was
assumed. Therefore the stiffness in horizontal direction is smaller than
in the vertical direction. There is not great influence. The flow of
forces change only slightly.

– Isotropic Material plus Diagonal Ribs Additional beam elements along
the groin simulate a diagonal rib which is connected stiffly with the
webs. Figure 5c shows the stress trajectories in a vault with a very
stiff rib. (E = 10000 MN/m^2, A =0.2 m^2, these values correspond to a rib
consisting of sandstone and with a cross-section of 45 by 45cm) The rib

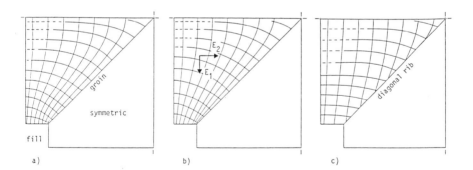

Fig.5   Stress trajectories at a quarter of the circular cylindrical
        cross vault under self weight. a) isotropic material b) ortho-
        tropic E$_1$/E$_2$ = 1/0,7 c) isotropic with additional diagonal rib

attracts the forces but not very strongly. Even in the case of an (unrealistic) stiff rib the stress trajectories do not follow the fall-lines as assumed using the thrust-line method. At the support 57% of the entire weight of the webs is transferred through the cross rib. Using the thrust-line method the result would be 68%.

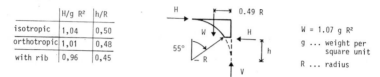

	H/g R²	h/R
isotropic	1,04	0,50
orthotropic	1,01	0,48
with rib	0,96	0,45

W = 1.07 g R²

g ... weight per square unit

R ... radius

Table 2: Resultant forces at a quarter of a circular cylindrical cross vault with isotropic and orthotropic material and with a additional diagonal rib

Circular cylindrical cross vaults under self weight plus spreading of the abutments.

The circular cylindrical cross vault with the same dimensions as above was analysed when subjected to displacements of the abutments using the three-dimensional solid element and using non-linear material properties. The slightest displacements of the supports change the external forces and create a totally different flow of forces in the webs (Figure 6). Since the nave wall does not act as a lateral abutment the thrust-line is steeper and the effective span is smaller. The horizontal thrust

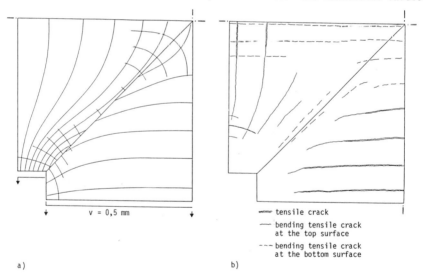

v = 0,5 mm

==== tensile crack

— bending tensile crack at the top surface

--- bending tensile crack at the bottom surface

a)   b)

Fig.6   Circular cylindrical cross vault subjected to displacements of the abutments   a) stress trajectories b) crack pattern

is reduced 20% to $0.83gR^2$. The cracks parallel to the nave wall become wider and move towards the abutment. In the plan the cracks are straight and parallel. This indicates a one-dimensional stress state in arches parallel to the nave wall. The bending tensile cracks in the longitudinal web following the crown and near the abutment correspond to the mechanism of the three-pinned arch. Bending tensile cracks also occur in the groin at the bottom surface and on both sides of the groin at the top surface. They are results of the different deformability of the webs and the stiffer groin.

Cross vault with pointed arches and straight contour-lines under self weight

Various vaults with a thickness of again 25 cm, a span of 10 m and varying width were also analysed by means of shell elements and a linear material model. Again they were supported rigidly at about one-half of the entire height (Figure 7, 8). The external forces related to the base area do not vary to the extent expected (Table 3). Once again there is no bending tensile stress. Cracks caused by tensile forces only occur at the wall arches, not at the transverse arches. The course of stress trajectories do not follow the fall-lines. Near the keystone the transverse web participates in the arch action across the large span.

CONCLUSIONS

For the analysis of cross vaults subjected only to self weight linear calculations are appropriate. The non-linear calculations using the above mentioned program and material model are very expensive, and a great effort is required to obtain reliable results and to check them.

The results show that cross vaults are real shell structures with a biaxial state of stress. Even a very small spreading of the abutments may cause the typical crack patterns in the vaults. The cracked state can therefore be considered as the normal service-state.

The other types of vaults will be assessed using the described methods and comparing the results. The influence of the vault thickness, the height of the fill and the interaction between diagonal ribs and the webs will be further examined and evaluated.

REFERENCES

1. Heyman, J. The Stone Skeleton. Int. J. Solids Structures, 1966, Vol.2, pp. 249 to 279.
2. Sawko, F.; Rouf, M.A. A Numerical Model for Masonry. Proc. of the 7th IBMaC, 1985, Vol.1, pp. 519 - 526.
3. Ungewitter, G.; Mohrmann, K. Lehrbuch der gotischen Konstruktionen, Leipzig 1901.
4. Pieper, K. Sanierung historischer Bauten, Berlin 1983.

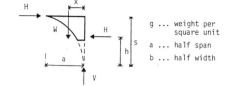

a/b	s/a	x/a	V/g·a·b	H/g·a·b	h/s
1/1	1,41	0,49	1,12	0,73	0,46
1/0,625	1,18	0,45	1,15	0,85	0,48
1/0,5	1,12	0,41	1,19	0,90	0,52

g ... weight per
    square unit
a ... half span
b ... half width

Table 3: Resultant forces at a quarter of a cross vault with a span of
10 m but different width

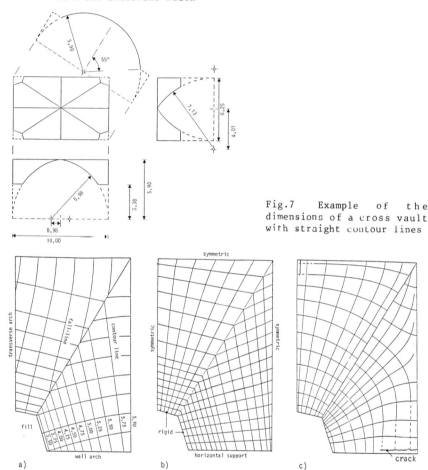

Fig.7   Example   of   the
dimensions of a cross vault
with straight contour lines

Fig.8   A quarter of a cross vault with straight contour   lines
a) contour and fall-lines   b) finite-element mesh   c) stress
trajectories and cracks

Monumental Buildings: Mathematical Simulation

G. Menditto and R. Capozucca

Department of Structural Engineering, University of Ancona, Ancona, Italy

ABSTRACT

The typical problems related to the restoration of monumental buildings involve the analysis of mathematical simulation. The authors report on several simulations which can be used for masonry elements or structures such as panels, columns, arches, vaults and towers.

INTRODUCTION

The typical problems connected with the restoration and seismic adjustment of monumental buildings depend on the stress field, the overall stability and local stability of some main members, i.e. panels, columns, arches, vaults and towers. On this subjected the following is reported.

MASONRY PANELS

Restoring masonry panels requires a knowledge of the stress field; Fig. 1 illustrates a proposed model [4] which is resolved in an approximate way [7], [8].

On the basis of the following expressions:

$$\sigma_x = \begin{cases} 0 & \text{for} \quad 0 \leq y \leq v \\ p(1+B(x)\eta)\, e^{-\alpha\eta} - p & \text{for} \quad 0 \leq \eta \leq u \end{cases} \tag{1}$$

where $\eta = y - v$ and $\alpha = 1/L$, being:

$$v = v(x) \tag{2}$$

a function describing the separation curve between the cracked section and the integral section;

$$u = u(x) \tag{3}$$

distance of each point of the separation curve from the top edge;

$$B = B(x) \tag{4}$$

being the unknown function so that $B(x) \leq 0$.

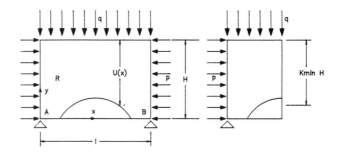

Fig. 1 - Masonry panel method.

These analyses give:

i)   the σ_x distribution connected to the amplitude of the cracked section for different geometries of the panel;

ii) the estimation of the K_{min} value for each section of the panel corresponding to the balance;

iii) the greatest height of the cracked area as $15 \div 20\%H$;

iv) an almost linear stress-distribution for panels with $\beta = H/L < 1.5$ for which the K values exceed 0.85;

v)   the possibility of following the trend of the separation curve between cracked and uncracked areas and of checking the stress field for each condition of balance with partially cracked sections. The finite element codes [8] which consider an increasing load and a rigidity matrix panel which changes for each step corresponding to the tight mesh-element, is used (Fig. 2);

vi) the amplitude of the cracked area for the typical panels ($\nu < 0.4$) is $15\%H$ for $\beta < 1.3$;

vii) the considerable influence of Poisson's ratio on the separation curve (Fig. 3);

viii)the σ_x distribution related to the sizes of the panels.

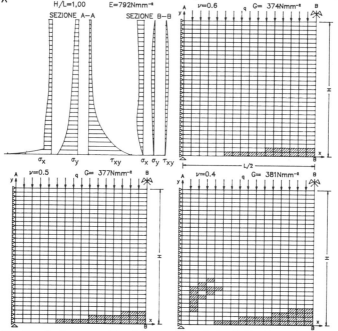

Fig. 2 - Analyses results of masonry panels by finite element method.

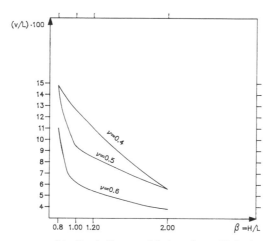

Fig. 3 - Influence of Poisson's coefficient.

Frequently in historical centres there are buildings which are jointed to each other by panels. Therefore whenever a partial demolition of one of these occurs the problem of panel stability arises even in the presence of dead load only. This fact strongly conditions the choice of method and technology of restoration. In these cases the whole wall and the single panel are analysed on the basis of the homogeneous, isotropic, linear-elastic masonry behaviour. Generally this situation appears different from reality; the masonry is an ansiotropic continuum and non-linear, especially if in a precarious state (Fig. 4-5). Using an ideal model can nevertheless be significant when the results obtained provide inadmissible conditions in an ideal situation, which will consequently be unacceptable in a real situation.

If y is the lateral displacement, the following equation resolves the problem of stability of a slender panel according to the simulation illustrated in Fig. 4:

$$EJ \frac{d^3y(z)}{dz^3} = -q(H-z) \frac{dy(z)}{dz} \tag{5}$$

from which

$$Q_{CR} = 7.837 \frac{EJ}{H^2} \quad ; \quad L_{CR} = 1.986 \sqrt[3]{EJ/q} \tag{6}$$

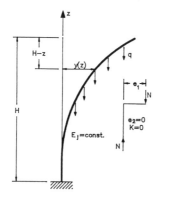

Fig. 4 -Model for stability analysis.

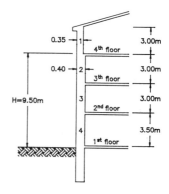

Fig. 5 - Vertical section of reference building.

The yield load of the panel depends on the yield resistance

$$N_U = \varphi(b \cdot s \cdot \sigma_R) \tag{7}$$

where

$$\varphi = \varphi(h/s \sqrt{1.5} \cdot \varepsilon_R , H/i, e_1/e_2) \tag{8}$$

and

$$e = M/N + H/300 \qquad (cm) \qquad (9)$$

where M is the bending moment and N is the axial force.

The safety load is calculated as follows:

$$\overline{N} = N_u/\gamma \qquad (10)$$

where γ : coefficient of safety. For example in Fig. 5 the values of the buckling loads (Table 1) in the two cases of degraded and consolidated masonry respectively, are obtained. In addition the safety load N obtained by a limit resistance analysis is shown in Table 1. The model in Fig. 6 was employed to evaluate the anchorage between the panels and the floors.

Table 1 - Calculation results.

$R'_{mK} = 1 \, N \cdot mm^{-2}$	$R'_{mK} = 3 \, N \cdot mm^{-2}$	$N = 91.8 \;\; kN$
$E_m = 700 \, N \cdot mm^{-2}$	$E_m = 3000 \, N \cdot mm^{-2}$	$M = 0.945 \; kN \cdot m$
$Q_{CR}^{(1)} = 187 \, kN$	$Q_{CM}^{(2)} = 802 \, kN$	$e = 1 + 3.16 = cm$
$H_{CR}^{(1)} = 15.5 \, m$	$H_{CR}^{(2)} = 25.23 \, m$	$\overline{N} = 120 \, kN$ for $\gamma = 6$

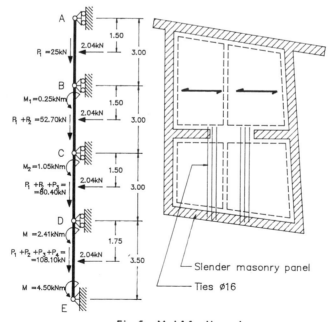

Fig. 6 - Model for tie-rods.

COLUMNS

Anti-seismic resistance is conferred to the bearing columns by means of inclined bored holes ($\emptyset$ 3 ÷ $\emptyset$ 4 cm) located on the lower side, the insertion of threaded brass rods ($\emptyset$ 8) and sealing with epoxy resin (Fig. 7).

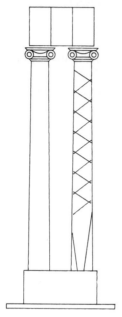 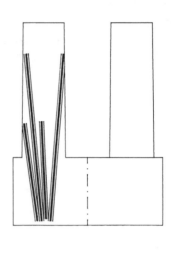

Fig. 7

The perforations should reach the bearing plinth so as to confer a fixed end to the columns. This fact explains the use of a simple model for the column dynamics. The model is a simple oscillator characterised by a natural period T_0 so as to evaluate the spectral acceleration S_a which when amplified makes it possible to evaluate the greatest bending moment and shear force at the column base.

The following mathematical expression is used in dynamic analysis:

$$m_0 = m(1 + 0,24\,\mu l/m) \tag{11}$$

where

μl : total column mass;
m : dead load masses;

$$T_0 = 2\pi \sqrt{m_0/K} \tag{12}$$

$$S^*_a = S_a(1 + 0.12\,\beta) \tag{13}$$

where K is flexural rigidity and $\beta = \mu l/m$;

$$T_{max} = m'g\ S^*_a\ (1 + 0.39\ \beta)\qquad(14)$$

$$M_{max} = m'g\ S^*_a\ (1 + 0.28\ \beta)\qquad(15)$$

where m' is mass considering the dead and accidental loads.

TOWERS

Generally the tower foundations are almost superficial. Therefore restoration work concerns the elevation and the deep homogeneous foundations. The latter reach the formation soil so as to obtain an efficient fixed end.

It is then possible to make use of the models shown in Figs. 8(a) and 8(b) which reproduced the situation before and after restoration works.

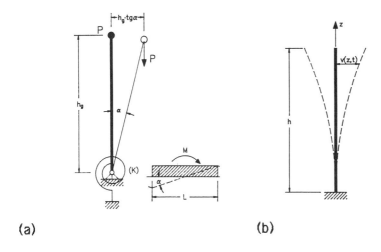

(a)   (b)

Fig. 8 (a) Model for stability analysis in static phase.
(b) Model for stability analysis in dynamic phase.

For Fig. 8 (a) reference is made to the following expressions:

$$K = \frac{L^3 \cdot E_t}{(1-v^2)\ I_\alpha}\qquad(16)$$

E_t : elasticity module of soil ;

v : Poisson's coefficient;

I_α : influence coefficient.

For Fig. 8 (b) reference is made to the following expressions:

$$v(z,t) = q(t) (z/H)^2 \tag{17}$$

$$\lceil^* = 1,41 \; \frac{H^2}{\rho} \; \sqrt{\frac{\gamma}{E \cdot g}} \tag{18}$$

$$\alpha^* = \gamma \cdot A \cdot \int_0^H (z/H)^2 \, dz \tag{19}$$

$$m^* = \gamma \cdot A \cdot \int_0^H (z/H)^4 \, dz \tag{20}$$

$$M_{max} = \int_0^H \frac{x^*}{m^*} \cdot \gamma \cdot A \cdot S_a \, (z/H)^2 \cdot z \, dz \tag{21}$$

where:

A : section area of tower;
γ : specific weight of masonry;
H : height of tower;
z : vertical axis;
ρ : inertia radius of the tower section;
S_a/g : known by Italian Regulations.

ARCHES, VAULTS, DOMES

The models employed in the past for arches, vaults, domes were limited only to balance. Recently continuum discretization techniques such as finite difference method (FDM), finite element method (FEM), boundary element method (BEM) have been used on the basis of an improved knowledge of the constitutive masonry law.

In this way a model with deformable joints connected by rigid bars was suggested for the cylindrical masonry vaults (Fig. 9). The joint is made by two deformable external layers connected to a membrane stress field.

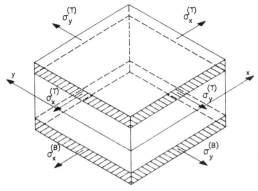

Fig. 9 - Typical node.

Using the displacement method it is possible to know the stress and deformation field in a finite number of joints located on the surface (Fig. 10).

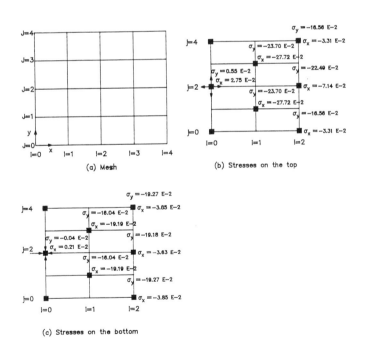

(a) Mesh

(b) Stresses on the top

(c) Stresses on the bottom

Fig. 10 - Cylindrical shell 6 cm thick -only dead load 1.00 KN/m^2- stress in daN/cm^2.

REFERENCES

1. Heyman, J., The Stone Skeleton, Int. J. Solids and Struct., vol.2, pp. 249-279, 1966.
2. Belluzzi, O., Scienza delle Costruzioni, Zanichelli, Bologna, Italia, 1978.
3. Di Pasquale, S., Distorsioni Fittizie per Problemi di Strutture a Vincoli Unilaterali, pp. 183-188, Congresso AIMETA, Palermo, Italia, 1980.
4. Villaggio, P., Stress Diffusion in Masonry Walls, J. Struct. Mech., vol. 9, pp. 439-450, 1981.
5. Di Pasquale, S., Questioni di Meccanica dei Solidi non Reagenti a Trazione, pp. 251-263, Atti Congresso AIMETA, Genova, Italia, 1982.
6. Sparacio, R., Murature; Analisi Tensionale di Murature: Verifica agli Elementi Finiti, P. Lavegna Ed., Salerno, Italia, 1983.
7. Capozucca, R., An Approximate Method for Analysis of Stress Distribution in Masonry Walls, Masonry International, vol. 1, pp. 22-27, 1984.
8. Capozucca, R. and Pace, C., Analisi dello Stato Limite di Fessurazione di Pannelli Murari, l'Industria delle Costruzioni, n. 152, pp. 58-61, 1984.
9. Capozucca, R. and Menditto, G., Metodologie di Indagine per la Definizione dell'Assetto Strutturale di alcuni Teatri d'Epoca delle Marche, Atti Convegno ASS.I.R.C.CO., Catania, Italia, 1988.

Structural Survey of Istanbul City-Walls with Special Emphasis on Preservation and Strengthening of Walls and Towers

İ. Aka, M. Yorulmaz and F. Çili

Istanbul Technical University, Teknik Üniversitesi 80191 Taksim, Istanbul, Turkey

ABSTRACT

Today the 7 km long land walls of Istanbul are in a ruinous state. Relatively well preserved parts of the wall are confined to a very limited area. There are serious cracks in the towers. Earthquakes and subsidence have caused structural damage. In some parts, the original wall and towers are represented only by a fragment of the original construction. The Municipality of Istanbul started a project for the conservation of the City Walls. This included the reconstruction of the Belgrade Gate along with a total of four flanking towers. The reconstruction project was prepared by TAÇ (Turkey's Trust for Preservation of Monuments, Sites and Tourism Assets). During the excavation conducted around Belgrade Gate, the section of the walls under the present ground level was discovered to be intact. Therefore, the reconstructed upper parts were built on top of the older one, after the addition of a horizontal bond beam made of reinforced concrete. The second part of the project was to investigate and propose preventive measures to stop further damage and consolidate the parts of the fortification which were under threat. This included the analysis of the damage types and proposals for repair. Our team did a survey of the present state of the walls and proposed different types of intervention. For sections where the cracks and distortions could not be stabilized, taking down the dangerous parts of the walls and the towers seemed to be the best solution. For sections of the walls and towers to be preserved by consolidation, the proposed modes of intervention were:
. construction of concrete or reinforced concrete buttresses,
. insertion of bond beams.

INTRODUCTION

The land walls of Istanbul, extending for about 7 kms from Yedikule (Seven Towers) on the shore of the Marmara Sea to Ayvansaray on the Golden Horn, Figure 1, served the Ottomans for a short period after 1453. As they lost their function as a result of developing warfare techniques, they were abandoned to their fate.

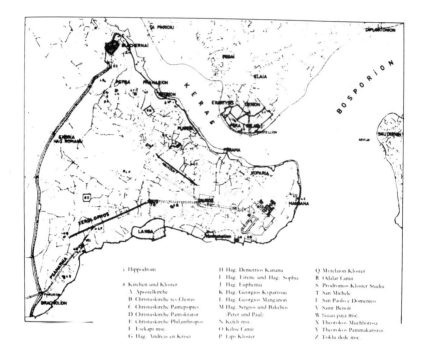

The following reference list appears within the figure:

¿ Hippodrom	H Hag. Demetrios Kananu	Q Myrelaion-Kloster
4 Kirchen und Kloster	I Hag. Eirene und Hag. Sophia	R Odalar Camii
A Apostelkirche	J Hag. Euphemia	S Prodromos-Kloster Studiu
B Christuskirche tes Choras	K Hag. Georgios Kyparissiu	T San Michele
C Christuskirche Pantepoptes	L Hag. Georgios Manganon	U San Paolo e Domenico
D Christuskirche Pantokrator	M Hag. Sergios und Bakchos	V Saint Benoit
E Christuskirche Philanthropos	(Peter und Pauli)	W Sinan paşa msc.
F Isekapi msc.	N Kefeli msc.	X Theotokos Muchliotissa
G Hag. Andreas en Krisei	O Kilise Camii	Y Theotokos Pammakaristos
	P Lips Kloster	Z Toklu dede mse.

Fig. 1.   General outline of the Istanbul Land Walls (W.Müller-Wiener)

The land walls, comprising the moat, the outer walls and the inner walls with their towers were repaired while they were in use, but after they ceased to be functional, they suffered considerable damage and destruction under the effect of various natural events, especially earthquakes and by the people living in their vicinity, [1].

In recent years, especially during the construction of the main highways leading into the city, some sections of the walls were demolished and the towers flanking the highways were repaired. In 1986 work was started on the preparation of a repair and strengthening project for the land walls.

This paper aims to give information about proposals and implementation projects related to the structural systems of the gates, inner and outer walls and towers which according to the restoration project, will be either preserved as they are, or repaired, strengthened or reconstructed.

WORK PROCEDURE

A thorough survey of the walls from the structural view point was made during 1987 and important structural damage was determined, [2], [3], [4] . On the basis of the information and documents thus obtained, the walls, especially the towers were grouped according to the type and degree of damage. Among these groups, those with damage likely to progress and those presenting structural danger were singled out, and appropriate methods and types of strengthening were proposed. It is believed that, with the exception of the Belgrade Gate with its four flanking towers and the walls in between which would be restored to give an idea of how they looked during the Byzantine period, the walls, gates and towers would be preserved in their present state as archaeo-logical remains. The restoration project would aim at strengthening the remains so as to prevent further deterioration under the influence of various factors. The authors believe that to do the opposite, i.e. to demolish the existing structure and to use modern means and materials to build something which will have an appearance similar to the original would be an easy solution, but not suitable to the purpose.

TYPES OF DAMAGE PATTERNS AND PRINCIPLES OF REPAIR

The moat
A large section of the ditch outside the wall had been filled with rubble, debris and earth. Visible sections can be restored with small repairs. If it is wished to restore the moat in a certain area, it is necessary to excavate the fill and to expose the walls. Excavations show that the sections of the walls currently uncovered are generally in good condition and they require only minor repairs.

The Outer Walls and their Towers
An important section of the outer walls was either destroyed or covered with earth. Although they appear to have suffered various types of damage, they are generally in a stable state and will very probably remain so for a long time; therefore no urgent intervention is needed. If desired, they can be repaired by filling the cavities or by dis-mantling the unstable parts and reconstructing them with the use of the same materials.

The Inner Walls
These are thick masonry walls which do not present any special feature from the view point of their structural systems. Some sections do not require any structural intervention but there are other sections where the parts of the walls above the ground level have cracked or fallen into decay to the point of complete destruction.

At places where cracks and cavities appear to be dangerous, it is possible to repair and strengthen the walls by removing the unstable sections and by filling the cavities with stones, or preferably with concrete. If the concrete filling is thick enough, the outer faces of the walls can be refaced with stone.

Fig. 2.   Recently Repaired Tower (Tower 65)

Fig. 3.   Slightly Damaged Tower (Tower 70)

Fig. 4.   The Tower which had Large Cracks (Tower 19)

Fig. 5.   A Leaning Tower (Tower 58)

Fig. 6. Partly Collapsed Tower (Tower 14)

Fig. 7. An Unstable Tower (Tower 92)

The Inner Wall Towers

The towers are the most important components of the land walls both
from the visual aspect and from the viewpoint of damage patterns. Nearly
all of the towers, except   those which underwent repairs during the
last decades, are damaged to different degrees, Figure 2, 3, 4, 5, 6, 7.
This is especially true for the towers which were constructed during
the reign of Theodosious. As indicated below, these towers have been
classified into groups according to the degree of damage they have
suffered. After determining the restoration principles for the whole
project, it is necessary to prepare a special strengthening project,
for each tower. This will be done by taking into consideration the condition of each tower and the repairs it has undergone at different
periods. Because this wide-scoped restoration project will take a long
time to complete, it is necessary to take provisional measures until
the project is implemented.

In many towers, the lower part of the rear wall is an integral
part of the curtain wall. The other three walls of the tower are
separated from the curtain wall with a joint. Above the level of the
curtain wall, the towers are built as a solid prismatic body, with
the fourth wall supported on the curtain wall. Because of this special
detail of construction, the walls which are over the curtain wall have
suffered considerable damage or were destroyed above the level of the
curtain wall. Defects and serious cracks have been noticed at the joints
of the curtain wall and the towers.

The towers can be grouped as follows according to the degree of the
damage they have suffered:
a) Towers in good condition, these have been repaired recently, Figure 2.
b) Towers with slight damage ; damaged stone facings, small cracks at
the corners of the openings or at the sides of the previously repaired
sections which were not properly tied to the original structure, Figure 3.
c) Towers with large cracks. These cracks are larger and more dangerous
than those mentioned under (b), Figure 4.
d) Leaning; probably caused by soil conditions, can affect the tower
completely or at one specific section separated by large cracks from the
tower, Figure 5.
e) Collapse. Sometimes the collapse of a corner and the resulting collapse of the adjoining walls leaves the tower with only two walls, or
even with only one standing, Figure 6.
f) The supports of some towers have been seriously damaged or disappeared completely. Some parts of the walls are likely to break off or
overturn at any time, Figure 7.
g) Some towers have no visible trace above the ground level; only the
remains of the foundations can be seen. At damaged towers, a single type
or a combination of damage patterns can be noticed.

Repair Procedures

It was considered necessary to take temporary measures until the end of
the period of time necessary for the preparation and implementation of
the projects for the restoration and strengthening of the 7 km long land
walls. The following procedure is proposed for the temporary repair and
strengthening of the towers and the curtain wall.

I. The walls and vaults which have large cavities or gaps will be filled with stones or preferably with concrete.

II. For walls which have lost their stability in the lateral direction, stability will be ensured by reconstructing one or two walls instead of the missing walls. The additional walls can be at different heights.

III. The sections which are leaning or have cavities underneath, will be reinforced with concrete supports.

IV. In towers with large cracks, horizontal steel ties will be used to prevent the cracks from becoming larger. The steel ties will be placed parallel to the inner face of the cracked walls and anchored by vertical elements at the exterior faces of the perpendicular walls.

V. In cases referred to in paragraph IV, it is possible to use reinforced concrete ties placed within the wall, instead of using steel ties.

VI. When the conditions of the wall are suitable, prestressing can be applied to the ties referred to in paragraph IV.

VII. When the danger of collapse can not be avoided and the measures mentioned above or similar ones cannot be implemented, it is proposed to dismantle the dangerous sections and store the material for use in later restorations.

In all these restorations, it has been decided as a principle that loose, unstable stones will be taken out to reach the sections in sound condition, that new repairs should be tied to the existing structure and in cases when the loose, unstable sections are too large and difficult to dismantle, they should be strengthened by the injection of grout.

PROJECT FOR THE BELGRADE GATE AND THE NEIGHBOURING WALLS

As mentioned in "Work Procedure" it was planned to restore the Belgrade Gate and its four flanking towers. The project aimed to give this section of the land walls the appearance it had during the Byzantine period.

The weights of the walls and towers and earthquake effects were calculated, the foundations and various other sections were checked. Measures were taken to ensure safety.

The earthquake effect was calculated on the basis of lateral force. $F = C.W$ and calculations were based on $C = 0.18$, taking into consideration Istanbul's earthquake risk and the rigidity and importance of the walls.

The maximum soil stress under the foundation was calculated as 40 t/m^2 and the soil has an allowable load carrying capacity of a similar level at the base of the foundation.

Towers

The walls, vaults and arches of the towers were completed. A project was prepared for the construction of certain intermediate floors in timber and the top floors in reinforced concrete. The dimensions and design earthquake loads of Tower 23, and Tower 24 are given in Figure 8.

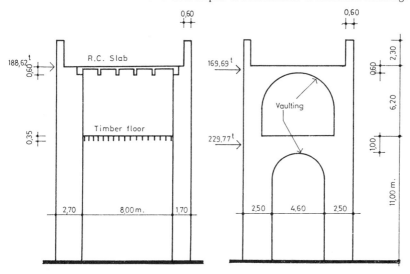

Fig. 8. Sections of the Tower 23 and Tower 24

It was determined that allowable compressive and shear stresses could be taken as 8 kg/cm^2 and 1.5 kg/cm^2 respectively. The maximum calculated stresses were always found to be less then half of these values.

The Inner Walls

In order to reveal the sections of the walls covered with earth, an excavation was made to a depth of 5-6 m. It was seen that the lower sections had been well protected and were in very good condition. After the faces of the walls were cleaned, no other operation was necessary.

In the walls above the current ground level, deteriorations were generally on the surface. Wall sections which had become loose or had cracks under the effect of external factors were dismantled. In accordance with the restoration project, it was sufficient to build new sections above the existing wall or to fill the cavities with concrete. Reinforced concrete bond beams of 40 cm depth were cast over the walls after removing the earth accumulated on the upper levels of the walls. Insertion of bond beams will cause an increase in the duration of the 4.70 m thick walls, Figure 9.

There are supporting vaults over the entrances to the towers and under the stairs. Missing parts of the vaults were completed by the construction of brick masonry using lime-cement mortar with an allowable compressive stress of 8 kg/cm^2. The maximum normal stresses, calculated at various sections of the vaults, were between 4.06-7.25 kg/cm^2. The lateral displacements of the vaults is prevented by the thick and heavy walls supporting them and the thrust takes its full value.

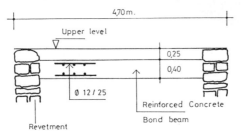

Fig. 9.   Detail of the Bond Beam

It was preferred to repair the vaults which were partly damaged or
cracked by using bricks having the same dimension and resistance as the
original ones and the same cross-sections even if they were more than
necessary according to the calculations.

CONCLUSION

A thorough survey of the Istanbul land walls was made during 1987 and
structural damage patterns were determined. The walls and especially
the towers were grouped according to the type and degree of damage.
Appropriate methods and types of strengthening were proposed for the
different kinds of damage patterns. The restoration project had an
aim at strengthening the remains so as to prevent further deterioration
under the influence of various factors.

Secondly, a restoration project was prepared for the Belgrade Gate
and its four flanking towers. Stability and earthquake load capacity of
the towers and neighbouring walls were verified against the vertical and
lateral loads.

REFERENCES

1.   Ahunbay, M. Report on the Conservation of Istanbul Land Walls and
     Moats and Environmental Development Project. Architectural Appraisal
     and Conservation Proposals: A Historical Survey of the Land Walls,
     Istanbul 1987 (In Turkish, unpublished report).

2.   Aka,İ., Yorulmaz, M., Çılı, F. Present State of the Load Bearing
     Capacity of Land Walls of Istanbul. Strengthening Propositions for
     Sections Requiring Immediate Interventions, Istanbul, 1987 (In
     Turkish, unpublished report).

3.   Aka, İ., Yorulmaz, M., Çılı, F. Structural Report on the Stabiliza-
     tion and Restoration Project of Istanbul Land Walls: Belgrade Gate
     and the Neighbouring Towers and Outer Wall Sections, Istanbul, 1987
     (In Turkish, unpublished report).

4.   Aka, İ., Yorulmaz, M., Çılı, F. Istanbul Land Walls, Structural
     Report on the Stabilization and Restoration Project of Inner Walls,
     Istanbul, 1987 (In Turkish, unpublished report).

Nondestructive Evaluation of a 19th Century Smokehouse in Colonial Williamsburg, Virginia

G.R. Kingsley[1], R.A. Livingston[2], T.H. Taylor, Jr.,[3], and J.L. Noland[4],

[1] Atkinson- Noland & Assoc., Boulder, Colorado
[2] Dept. of Geology, University of Maryland
[3] Colonial Williamsburg Foundation
[4] Atkinson-Noland & Assoc,. Boulder, Colorado

ABSTRACT

The nondestructive evaluation of the Benjamin Powell brick smokehouse in Colonial Williamsburg is described. The smokehouse suffers from severe deterioration, apparently due to salt crystallization. Because of the unusual pattern and high rate of the deterioration of the brick masonry, novel techniques have been employed to evaluate the nature and extent of the problem. This paper describes the use of a mechanical pulse technique in which stress waves are induced in the masonry by a hammer blow, and the pulse received on the opposite side of the wall is analyzed in terms of arrival time, attenuation, and frequency content. The test results are related to material properties and structural condition of the masonry, particularly the presence of voids or discontinuities in the wall interior.

The results of the mechanical pulse tests are compared to those of other nondestructive tests, published elsewhere, which have been used to map the salt and moisture profiles within the brick walls. These techniques include x-ray analysis and prompt neutron-gamma analysis.

INTRODUCTION

The brick masonry smokehouse adjacent to the Benjamin Powell House in Colonial Williamsburg, Virginia, has suffered severe deterioration of both brick and mortar due, apparently, to salt crystallization. Because of the unusual pattern and high rate of the deterioration, novel techniques have been employed to evaluate the nature and extent of the problem. Among these techniques have been the neutron probe (analysis of elemental composition in-situ), Livingston [1,3], and X-ray analyses of elemental composition and mineralogy of core samples, Livingston [2]. These techniques have been implemented to map the salt and moisture profiles in the walls to identify possible sources of deterioration. This report describes another evaluation of the smokehouse using nondestructive wave transmission techniques to investigate the physical (as opposed to chemical or elemental) nature of the unobservable interior wythes of masonry. The primary function of the wave transmission techniques is to locate discontinuities such as air voids or cracks in the material.

The nondestructive evaluation (NDE) of the smokehouse was performed from June 22 - June 24 1988. The Benjamin Powell House and surrounding structures were open to the public throughout the testing period -- there was no interruption in building use. There was no disturbance to the visitors or staff other than the visibility of "non-period" electronic equipment at the site.

DESCRIPTION OF THE STRUCTURE

The North elevation of the Benjamin Powell Smokehouse is shown in Figure 1. The structure is roughly square, and is topped by a pyramid shaped roof. The walls are made of handmolded brick masonry. The West wall is solid, and the North and South walls are penetrated only by three small ports along the top of the walls. The single door is centered on the East wall. The walls are approximately 16 inches (406 mm) thick, however this dimension is variable due to the extensive deterioration at some locations.

The bricks in the smokehouse are based on a nominal 8 inch (204 mm) module. The exterior wythes (a.k.a. "leaves") are laid in a Flemish bond, and the interior wythes are laid in American bond. The bond patterns and the dimensions of the bricks suggest that the walls are composed of four wythes with a possible discontinuity between the interior and exterior wythes, since the two bonding patterns may not intermesh.

The brick and mortar on portions of both the interior and exterior of the smokehouse are decaying rapidly, presumably because of salt crystallization. The pattern of the deterioration is unusual, not following typical patterns of moisture penetration or rising moisture. The deterioration is most pronounced in the upper two-thirds of the North and South walls. The mortar in the deteriorating portions of the wall requires repointing every one or two years, and consists of a sand lime mixture without portland cement. In the lower portions of the walls, the mortar is a harder cement mortar that is not deteriorating visibly, and even retains delicate tooling marks. The bricks in the lower portions are also more sound than those above. In Figure 1 a bold line marks the division between the sound masonry below

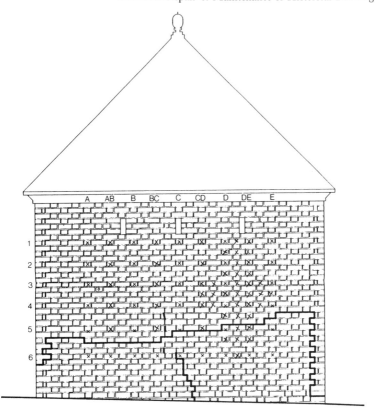

Figure 1.   North elevation of the smokehouse, showing the grid of test points, a vertical crack, and the demarcation between sound masonry (lower wall) and decaying masonry (upper wall)

and the deteriorationg masonry above.   (The vertical bold line shows the position of a crack).

The historical function of the smokehouse was for curing and preservation of salt-cured meats.   Records show that the smokehouse underwent extensive repairs (of unknown form) in the late 19th century, after which the masonry was covered with a plaster coating.   The smokehouse was restored in the late 1950's and early 1960's, at which time the plaster coating was removed by hand to expose the brick.

A small scale exploration, performed previously, of the foundation at the center of the South wall exterior showed that the smokehouse is founded in a narrow trench, with approximately six courses of masonry below grade. The trench is located in a dense clay soil with poor drainage, Taylor, [5]. This concurs with the measurement of rising ground water via the Neutron probe.

NDE METHODS AND EQUIPMENT

The NDE methods used to evaluate the smokehouse are wave transmission techniques which utilize the properties of propagating waves to infer information about material density and the location of voids or any interruption of the stress-wave path. The two methods applied -- ultrasonic and mechanical pulse -- are differentiated chiefly by the frequency and amplitude of the input signal. The ultrasonic pulse is an electro- acoustically generated pulse of low amplitude and a frequency of approximately 54 kHz. The ultrasonic test equipment used was the V-meter manufactured by James Instruments, Inc.

The mechanical pulse is introduced by a simple hammer blow which, depending on the type of hammer head employed, generates a signal in the range of 5 - 10 kHz with an amplitude that depends on the vigor of the hammer blow. The mechanical pulse hammer and accelerometers are manufactured by PCB Electronics. The hammer is 3 lb, with a 2 in. diameter rubber head. The signal is received by a piezoelectric accelerometer. The signal is recorded using a BBC Metrawatt Goerz SE561 Digital Transient Recorder. The sample interval was 1 μsec (sample rate = 1,000,000 samples per second)

APPROACH

The wave propagation tests on the smokehouse were of the direct or through-wall type, meaning that the input was generated on the exterior of the wall, and the signal was received on the interior of the wall directly opposite the input. To accomplish this, a grid was established over a 5x8 foot (1.5x2.4 meter) area on the interior and exterior of the North and South walls as shown in Figure 1. On the North wall, the upper 5 rows and 9 columns on one-foot centers correspond precisely to the grid used in the neutron probe analysis, Livingston [1].

TEST RESULTS

The ultrasonic pulse test was attempted but abandoned for evaluation of the smokehouse. The large wall thickness, low material density, and possible hidden voids in the masonry proved impenetrable for the low-amplitude, relatively high frequency ultrasonic pulse.

Through-wall mechanical pulse tests were successfully run on all grid points of both North and South walls. The results from the North wall are summarized in Figure 2 in the form of a contour map of the grid area. The contour map represents transmission quality in the North wall based on an analysis of amplitude, frequency content and arrival time. The numbers associated with the contours do not represent direct measurements but rather qualitatively assigned levels of "transmission quality", where level 1 (dark shading) represents crisp, high amplitude signals with visible high frequencies, and contour level 5 (light shading) represents signals with low amplitude, low velocity, and low frequency. Examples of typical wave forms are shown in Figure 2. The analysis of "transmission quality" is an effort to represent the full range of information contained in the received pulse in the absence of a valid numerical approach.

INTERPRETATION OF RESULTS

Ideally, the proper interpretation of NDE test results requires the calibration of nondestructive measurements with a limited number of destructive tests from the same structure, Noland [4]. Destructive tests usually involve the removal of a specimen from the wall in the form of a core or a prism which is then taken to a laboratory for analysis. In the case of the smokehouse, this was not an acceptable proposition, so results must be interpreted in the absence of verifiable data. Some information was available from a description of two 1/2" cores taken from the North wall for X-ray analysis, Livingston [2]. One of these cores indicated the presence of a void in a lower part of the North wall. The location of this void is consistent with missing material along the central collar joint at 8" depth, although the uncertainty is +/- 1.5 inches

The North wall was the most extensively investigated wall in this study. Transmission quality for the North wall is shown in Figure 2. The quality of transmission is indicated by shading. Lighter shading represents a poorer quality of transmission. A fairly regular decline in quality is evident from the mid-height of the wall down towards the base across the entire wall width. In the top half of the wall, several points ("hills" on the contour map) indicate regions with distinct, isolated flaws.

The increasingly poor quality transmission through the lower part of the North wall contradicts the appearance of the wall on both interior and exterior. On the interior and exterior of the wall, both the brick and the mortar in the lowest part of the wall appear to be of the highest quality and show the least amount of deterioration, (see Figure 1), just the opposite of the transmission quality contour. This indicates that the variation in transmission quality due to the surface deterioration of the brick and mortar is small relative to the variation due to changes in the character of the interior wythes.

Two things may have caused the decrease in transmission quality: (1) the interior wythes of the lower portion of the wall are made with an inferior grade of brick or rubble, or (2) there is an increase in the number and density of air spaces in the lower wall.   The second possibility may be due either to poor workmanship resulting in incomplete filling of collar joints with mortar, or subsequent delamination of the collar joint from the brick material over a large area of the wall.   Experience with controlled laboratory specimens suggests large air spaces between the interior and exterior wythes at contour levels 4 and 5. This theory is supported by the results of the 1/2" core drilled from this section of the wall, which showed the presence of a void in the interior of the wall.

Although the neutron probe measurements were intended primarily to measure the distribution of contaminants in the walls, the data can also yield insights into structural problems. Gamma rays generated within the neutron source are attenuated during transmission through the wall. The attenuation varies with the mean density along the path-length from source to detector. In this situation, the mean density can vary as a function of volume of air space in the wall, as well as with the amount of water present.

The map of intensity of the 1.461 MeV gamma ray peak is shown in Figure 3 for the North wall. The darker the shading, the higher the transmission and hence the lower the attenuation. There is a distinct region of low attenuation in the right-hand side at about 4.5 feet (1.4 m). This suggests the presence of voids, which is consistent with results of the mechanical pulse measurements. To better compare the two sets of data, an indicator variable was computed. This variable takes the value of one at a measurement point when the mechanical pulse quality was $\geq$ 4 and the gamma intensity was $\geq$ 80 percentile, (in other words, when the mechanical pulse transmission was poorest and the mean density the lowest). The resulting map, Figure 4, shows a well defined region where missing mortar is likely.   In terms of the structure as a whole, this region is located above the horizontal line in Figure 1.

However, there are other regions where the gamma ray and mechanical pulse transmission do not appear to agree, such as along the lowest part of the map, where the mechanical pulse transmission quality is also poor but the mean density according to gamma ray attenuation is high. This may be explained by the presence of rising groundwater at

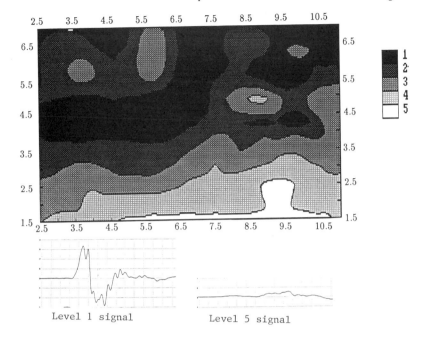

Figure 2.   Contour Map of Quality of Mechanical Pulse
Transmission, North Wall, Powell Smokehouse

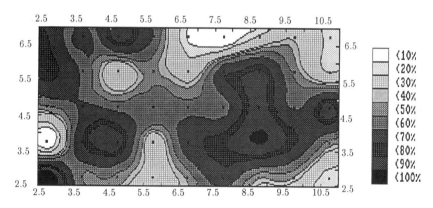

Figure 3.   Contour Map of Gamma Ray Transmission, North
Wall, Powell Smokehouse

this level, as indicated in the H elemental map presented in Figure 5. In this case, the highest H signal is represented by the darkest shading. In this region, there seems to be good agreement between increased water and increased density. Both maps show a vertical feature in the center of the wall that is in the same position as the vertical crack in Figure 1. This suggests that rising groundwater may be causing further extension of the crack through freeze-thaw cycles.

Further processing of the neutron probe data is now being done to remove this moisture effect on the gamma ray transmission data and thus to obtain a more accurate picture of void distribution. Also, maps of Fe, Ca Si are being developed in order to more directly determine the brick to mortar ratio along the wall. This can then be compared against the mechanical pulse transmission results to investigate further the relationship between transmission quality and absence of mortar.

So far, it appears that the highest measured chloride levels are associated with those upper areas of the masonry wall with the most solidly filled collar joints. A variety of other evidence strongly suggests that this upper part of the wall may have been rebuilt at some time in the past. Hence, it is possible that the chlorides may have been introduced at that time in the material used to fill the joints.

CONCLUSIONS

A combination of NDE techniques has provided several insights into the condition and causes of damage of the Benjamin Powell smokehouse, some of which go against conventional wisdom. The observed surface deterioration of the brick due to salt action does not seem related to rising ground water. Thus installing a barrier against ground water will not halt the deterioration due to salt, although it may reduce cracking associated with freeze-thaw cycles. The source of the salts that have caused the deterioration is in the upper portion of the walls. More specifically, the surface deterioration coincides with those areas where the interior wythes are the most solid and the collar joints appear to be complete. If this represents a reconstruction of the upper part of the building in the past, the material used for the interior wythes and collar joints of the walls may be the source of the salts.

The mechanical pulse wave transmission technique used to evaluate the masonry smokehouse was effective, and the results were verified in part by the results of the neutron probe analysis. Because the results from each type of anal-

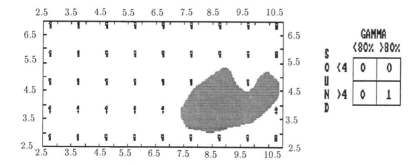

Figure 4. Map of Transmission Indicator Variable, Combining Sound and Gamma Transmission, North Wall, Powell Smokehouse

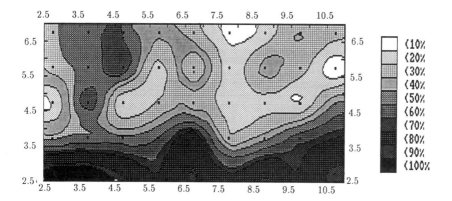

Figure 5: Contour Map of Hydrogen Gamma Ray Intensity, North Wall, Powell Smokehouse

ysis are complimentary, the two nondestructive methods are most effective when used together.

ACKNOWLEDGEMENTS

This work was funded as part of a National Science foundation grant (No. ECE-8315924) for field evaluation of NDE techniques for masonry structures. The grant is under the direction of Dr. John B. Scalzi.

REFERENCES

1.   Livingston, R.A., Evans, L.G., Taylor, T.H., Trombka, J.I., "Diagnosis of Building Condition by Neutron/Gamma Technique",   Building   Performance: Function, Preservation and Rehabilitation , ASTM STP 901, G. Davis Ed., American Society for Testing and Materials, Philadelphia, 1986, pp. 165-180.

2.   Livingston, R.A., "X-ray Analysis of Brick Cores from the Powell-Waller Smokehouse, Colonial Williamsburg," Proceedings   of   the   Third   North   American   Masonry Conference, Arlington Texas, June, 1985.

3.   Livingston, R.A., Chang, L., Evans, L.S., Trombka, J.I., "The Application of the Neutron Probe to the Nondestructive   Examination   of   Architectural   and Archaeological Materials",in E.V. Sayre et al. (ed) Materials Issues in Art and Archaeology, Materials Research Society Symposium Proceedings Volume 123, Materials Research Society, Pittsburgh, 1988, pp 59-65.

4.   Noland,   J.L.,   Atkinson,   R.H.,   Kingsley,   G.R., "Nondestructive   Methods   for   Evaluating   Masonry Structures",   Proceedings   of   the   International Conference on Structural Faults and Repair, London, July 1987.

5.   Taylor, T.H., "Conservation of Original Brickwork at Colonial Williamsburg", Proceedings of the Material Science and Restoration Conference, Esslingen, West Germany, Sept., 1983.

SECTION 3 - MATERIALS AND REPAIRS

Pozzolanic Mortars for Repair of Masonry Structures

G. Penelis, J. Papayianni and M. Karaveziroglou
Department of Civil Engineering, Aristotle University of Thessaloniki, 540 06 Thessaloniki, Greece

ABSTRACT

In this paper mechanical properties of pozzolanic mortars that can be used for structural restoration of monuments are presented. The selection of materials and proportions of mortars under consideration were based on composition and strength data resulting from the analysis of old mortars from various historical buildings of Thessaloniki(4th to 15th centuries A.D.). Hydrated lime, pozzolana of different origin and pozzolanic activity, as well as cement were used as binding agents while brick powder, sand(fine and coarse) and crushed full bricks were used as aggregates. Laboratory tests were made to determine the strength properties (compressive strength, tensile strength and modulus of elasticity) of these mortars in order to show the contribution of each of their constituents to strength development.

INTRODUCTION

In the restoration of masonry structures it is recommended that the new mortars be, as far as possible, similar to the original ones. This concept leads to the necessity of determining the physical-chemical and mechanical properties of the old mortars.

The aim of this research is to find the composition and proportions of the new mortars which will be "equal" to the old ones as far as their mechanical properties are concerned. Therefore, laboratory tests as well as "in situ" tests regarding the monuments of Thessaloniki region have been carried out. They cover a period of more than 1000 years. The analysis of the old mortars is the subject of a whole research on building materials used in ancient years. All the results of this research are not given in this paper. So, it must be said that the choice of the proper materials for the composition of the new mortars was made with reference to them.

Old mortars
To analyse old mortars, samples of the existing ones were taken from the following monuments:
 - Roman part of Rotunda (4th century A.D.)

- Christian part of Rotunda (4th-5th century A.D.)
- Acheiropoietus (7th century A.D.)
- Hagia Sophia (8th century A.D.)
- Panagia Chalkeon (11th century A.D.)
- St.Panteleimon (12th century A.D.)
- Bey Hamanu (15th century A.D.)

According to their analysis all these mortars contain sand and lime; additionally, in some of them fragments and powder of bricks have been found, which give them a light red hue. A quantity of each mortar was carefully crumbled by hand and then sieved in order to find out the gradation of their grains; the max size of grain was different in each mortar. For example, in Panagia Chalkeon the max size was up to 25mm and in Christian part of Rotunda it was up to 6mm.

In relation to the mechanical properties of the old mortars, some of them with lime and sand present lower compressive strength than other ones, such as those of Hagia Sophia(Penelis[1]) and Rotunda(Penelis, et al.[2]). The ancient mortars of "high" compressive strength, which range from $2.9N/mm^2$ in Roman part of Rotunda to $4.5N/mm^2$ in Hagia Sophia, have compounds with hydraulic activity(pozzolana) as has been seen after X-ray analysis. But the use of natural pozzolana as binding agent in new mortars gives mixtures which develop lower strength than that of the old ones. So, when an "increased" strength new mortar is needed for restoration it is necessary to add cement.

New mortars. Materials and mix proportions
In order to prepare mortars for repair with the same properties as the old ones it has been thought useful to look for materials which have the same origin as these of the ancient structures. Under this consideration "traditional" materials, which are easily found in Greece, have been used in the new mortars. These materials are lime, pozzolana(from Santorin and from Skydra), natural sand and crushed bricks. For the reason mentioned above, in several mixtures a part of pozzolana has been replaced by cement.

Taking into account the analysis of old mortars, the new ones were prepared with different grain gradation(Table 1). The mixing proportions of the mixtures with grain max size up to 6mm were based on the analyses of old mortars(Penelis,et al.[2]) and they tested according to the current specifications for mortars(DIN 1053[3]). The amount of water was assessed for each mortar to be that required for a fluidity 17±0.1cm(DIN 18555[4]). Mixtures with aggregate up to 25mm, which are not included in this paper, have been also tested according to the current specifications for concrete.

Test results
The mechanical strength of the new mortars was determined on 4x4x16cm specimens; the dynamic modulus of elasticity was determined by ultrasonic measurements on the same specimens before testing for flexural strength. The results are given in Table 2.

The elastic modulus of elasticity is calculated taking into account the compressive strength of the mortars and their dynamic modulus of ela-

sticity E_d(Penelis,et al.[2]). The density of the mortars is given immediately after mixing(Table 1) as well as after 28 days curing(Table 2).

DISCUSSION OF RESULTS

Mortars with Santorin pozzolana
Based on the results in Table 2(Mortars K1 to K17) the following can
be   said : In mortars with sand as K1, K4 and K5 the mechanical strength
increases with the grain size of sand. So, the strength of K4 and K5 is
higher   than   that   of K1. Mortar K4 presented lower compressive strength
σ_D and higher flexural one σ_z than that of K5; K4 has a different sand
gradation than that of K5. The influence of the aggregate gradation on
the mechanical strength should be further investigated.

Ceramic material improves the strength of mortars with sand. This
comes out by comparing the mortars K2 and K3 to K1, the K19 to K9 and the
K8 to K7, in which a part of sand has been replaced by crushed bricks.
Mortars K6 and K3 have the same mix proportions but in the first mixture
the fine part of crushed bricks up to 2mm was included. The flexural and
compressive strengths of K3 are higher that those of K6(Table 2). So, it
can be assumed that it is the fine part of the whole ceramic quantity
that contributes to hydraulic activity. It is also of interest the diagram   in Fig.1, which illustrates the influence of water/binder ratio on
the compressive strength of mortars; the values of water/lime+pozzolana+
+cement ratio given in Table 1(W/L+P+C) must be reduced because of the
contribution of the ceramic component to hydraulic activity;this reduction
(points marked with dotted line) is 60% for mortar mixtures K10, K11,K12,
K13, 75% for K2, K3, K8 and 85% for K6(see mixing proportions in Table 1).
The influence of cement content on the strength of mortars is indicated
in Fig.2. In this figure one can also see the improvement of strength due
to ceramic content.

The dynamic modulus of elasticity E_D, generally rises when the compressive strength σ_D of the mortars increases(Fig.3). The static modulus
of elasticity of the new mortars(Table 2) is higher than that of the ancient mortars with the same strength. For example, the modulus of elasticity of the Roman part of Rotunda(average compressive strength 2.9N/mm²)
is 1350N/mm² and that of the Christian part(average compressive strength
3.8N/mm²) is 2100N/mm² according to in situ measurements of the dynamic
modulus of elasticity. This must be taken into account when comparison
is to be made with test results in Table 2.

Mortars with Skydra pozzolana
Considering the mechanical characteristics of mortars K18 to K22 we can
say the following: The compressive strength of mortars with sand increases with the grain size of sand(mortar K19 compared with K18). The comparison of compressive strength between the mortars K18 with K1 and K19
with K5 indicates that this pozzolana is of lower activity compared to
Santorin earth. But the strength of mortars with Skydra earth goes up to
that of mortars with Santorin earth when a part of pozzolana has been
replaced by Portland cement in mortars with ceramic material (mortars
K21, K22, K10, K13).

In addition, it must be noted that hardened mortars with Skydra pozzolana have a lighter coloured greyish hue than that of mortars with Santorin pozzolana which matches better to old structures.

CONCLUSIONS

The factors which increase the mechanical strength of lime-pozzolana mortars seem to be:
(a) The appropriate aggregate gradation.
(b) The addition of ceramic material especially of that of grain max size up to 2mm.
(c) The cement content of the mortars.

Skydra pozzolana should be further investigated. Mixtures with Skydra pozzolana and cement showed mechanical strength quite close to that of Santorin. So, the Skydra earth may replace the Santorin pozzolana in mortars used for repair. This is very interesting especially for monuments in North Greece where Skydra earth is produced.

ACKNOWLEDGEMENTS

We thank the 9th Ephorate of Byzantine Antiquities of Thessaloniki for its contribution.

REFERENCES

1. Penelis. G. Seismic behaviour of masonry Roman and Byzantine monuments, pp.280-326, Proceedings of the Int.Symposium on Restoration of Byzantine Monuments, Thessaloniki, Greece, 1985. 9th Ephorate Byzantine Antiquities, Thessaloniki, 1986.

2. Penelis, G., et al. Restoration and Strengthening of Rotunda, Thessaloniki, 1980.

3. DIN 1053 Mauerwerk, Berechnung und Ausfürung Ausgabe November 1974.

4. DIN 18555 Prüfung von Mörtel mit mineralischen Bindermittel Ausgabe September 1982.

Table 1. Mixing proportions of the mortars

origin		Mortar No	Lime	Pozzolana	Cement	Sand max size 2mm	Sand max size 6mm	Crushed bricks max 2mm	Crushed bricks size 6mm	Water	Density kg/dm³	Water L+R+C
Pozzolana origin	Santorin	K 1	1	1	-	6	-	-	-	2.24	1.86	1.120
		K 2	1	1	-	3	-	3	-	2.70	1.88	1.350
		K 3	1	1	-	3	-	-	3	2.42	1.87	1.210
		K 4	1	1	-	-	6	-	-	1.92	1.94	0.960
		K 5	1	1	-	-	6	-	-	1.86	1.93	0.930
		K 6	1	'1	-	3	-	-	3	2.20	1.84	1.100
		K 7	1	1	-	-	5	-	1	1.97	1.90	0.985
		K 8	1	1	-	-	3	-	3	2.24	1.86	1.120
		K 9	1	0.8	0.2	6	-	-	-	2.16	1.90	1.080
		K10	1	0.8	0.2	3	-	-	3	2.14	1.90	1.070
		K11	1	0.6	0.4	3	-	-	3	2.45	1.89	1.225
		K12	1	0.4	0.6	3	-	-	3	2.33	1.90	1.165
		K13	1	0.2	0.8	3	-	-	3	2.25	1.82	1.125
		K14	1	0.8	0.2	-	6	-	-	1.83	1.95	0.915
		K15	1	0.6	0.4	-	6	-	-	1.78	1.98	0.890
		K16	1	0.4	0.6	-	6	-	-	1.62	2.07	0.810
		K17	1	0.2	0.6	-	6	-	-	1.53	2.08	0.765
	Skydra	K18	1	1	-	6	-	-	-	2.17	1.94	1.085
		K19	1	1	-	-	6	-	-	1.67	2.02	0.835
		K20	1	0.8	0.2	6	-	-	-	2.17	1.84	1.085
		K21	1	0.8	0.2	3	-	-	3	2.08	1.93	1.040
		K22	1	0.2	0.8	3	-	-	3	2.25	1.92	1.125

Table 2. Test results(28 days)

Mortar No	Density kg/dm³	Strength		Modulus of elasticity	
		Flexural N/mm²	Compressive N/mm²	Dynamic N/mm²	Static N/mm²
K 1	1.59	0.166	0.410	1118	553
K 2	1.47	0.234	0.859	1244	634
K 3	1.51	0.261	1.318	1807	940
K 4	1.68	0.421	0.697	1505	760
K 5	1.59	0.258	0.928	2390	1231
K 6	1.54	0.214	0.770	1900	965
K 7	1.63	0.194	0.784	1820	917
K 8	1.51	0.269	1.249	2446	1272
K 9	1.55	0.311	1.438	2431	1288
K10	1.48	0.519	2.605	3038	1686
K11	1.62	0.433	3.581	4846	2791
K12	1.62	9.859	4.589	5747	3460
K13	1.65	1.810	5.573	6912	4341
K14	1.65	0.264	1.270	2774	1442
K15	1.72	0.487	1.678	4184	2238
K16	1.76	0.638	2.035	4703	2540
K17	1.83	0.839	3.771	7300	4271
K18	1.60	0.193	0.336	1541	709
K19	1.74	0.142	0.652	1640	823
K20	1.50	0.303	0.520	2103	1051
K21	1.56	0.816	3.066	3461	1973
K22	1.61	1.409	5.018	6853	4215

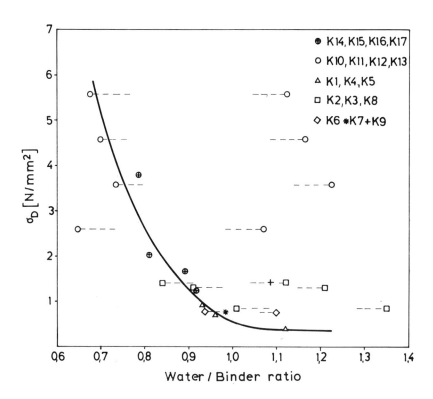

Fig.1 Effect of water/binder ratio on compressive strength of mortars with Santorin earth.

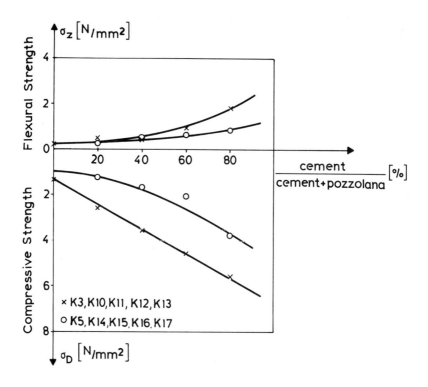

Fig.2 Influence of cement content on the strength of mortars.

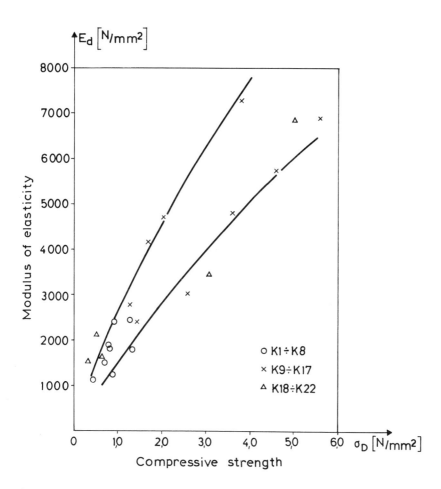

Fig.3 Experimental results for the relationship between compressive
strength and dynamic modulus of elasticity.

Application of Cement Grouting to Historic Buildings

R. Zepnik and W. Schönbrodt-Rühl

*VEB Denkmalpflege Dresden, Projektierungsatelier,
Friedrichstrasse 33, Dresden, 8010, DDR*

ABSTRACT

This article deals with the application of cement grouting
to four historic buildings in the district of Dresden. The
stabilization of masonry at the Dresden palace "Palais im
Großen Garten" will be reported on as our first example. The
prevention of further settlements at the castle "Albrechtsburg" in Meißen and at the castle "Ortenburg" in Bautzen by
subsurface grouting are the next examples to be dealt with.
Finally we tell about the renovation of the fountain "Mosaikbrunnen" in Dresden. The foundation and the fountain basin
were reconstructed by cement grouting.

STABILIZATION OF MASONRY AT THE "Palais im Großen Garten"

At the end of World War II the palace was severely damaged by
bombs. The situation at the north side was especially dangerous. The thrust of a wide-spanned vault caused the wall to
rotate outwards. The masonry was bowed some 25 cm. Two pillars
made of quartzitic sandstone are situated in the centre of the
wall (see fig. 1). Each of them is loaded with about 1,8oo kN
from the dead weight of the building. The original cross -

Figure 1: Dresden palace "Palais im Großen Garten",
          north front

sectional area of one pillar amounted to 1.37 m². It had
been reduced to 50 per cent due to fire. In the early fif-
ties the arches beside the pillars were filled with masonry
to prevent the building from collapsing. The pillars were to
be replaced by new ones but the essential problem was to assure the stability of the wall as a whole. It was decided to
grout the voids by cement-clay-water-mixture before changing the pillars. The joints were filled by cement-lime-mortar
to a depth of 80 mm. 154 holes were drilled by a wet type
rock drill. In the ground floor reinforcing rods of 14 mm
diameter were inserted into the holes as anchorage to connect
the wall and the vault. About 3.4 tons Portland cement
(PZ 1/475) were used. The work was carried out in 1984. Until today there have not been any clues yet that the cement
stone and the old masonry would not be compatible. As there
is no heating in the building and the palace is to be used
only in summertime we do not expect crystalisation of sulphate at the sandstone facing.

SUBSURFACE GROUTING AT THE CASTLE   "Albrechtsburg" IN MEISSEN

The castle "Albrechtsburg" in Meißen near Dresden is a
unique historic monument. It was built at the end of the 15th
century. The retaining pillar at the south-west gable-front
(see figure 2) was erected in 1864 because the stability of
this wall had been endangered even at this time. But this
method is generally not suited for this purpose because settlements occur under the new pillar foundation and the weight
of the pillar additionally loads the wall. The formation of
cracks went on slowly. Since 1984 a considerable increase in
the crack widths between the end-wall and the ceilings has
been observed. At the beginning of the analysis we supposed
that thermal stresses had caused the displacements. In the
architectonic description the depth of this foundation was
said to be about 6 m. An exploration of the pillar support
was carried out. The digging point (see figure 3) showed
that the foundation was absolutely insufficent. A leaking
water-pipe was the real cause for the deterioration during
the last years. The fine grain of the soil had been washed away.

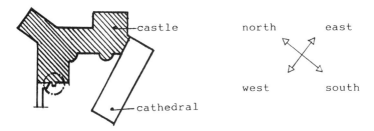

Figure 2. Plan Albrechtsburg

The foundation was reconstructed by cement grouting. Investigations were carried out before. The concentration of sulphate
in the masonry amounted to 0.33% and the pH-value was 8.4 .

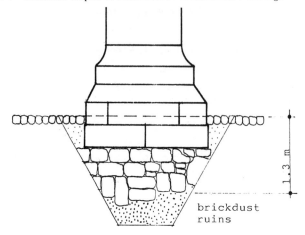

brickdust
ruins

Figure 3: Pillar foundation

The mixture consisted of cement, fine sand, clay and water.
Four drill holes of 55 mm diameter at an angle of 30 degrees
to the vertical were made until the maximum depth of 4 m.
Fourteen grouting lances of 33.5 mm diameter were driven in
by pile-hammer until the depth of 5 m (see fig. 4). 16.4 t
cement and 5.2 t fine sand were used. After hardening of the
cement two further holes were drilled and two lances were
rammed to check the effect of grouting. The advance rates of

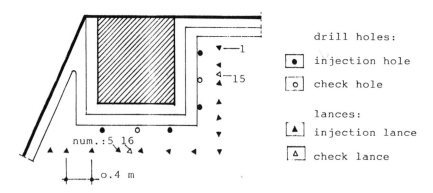

drill holes:

⬤ injection hole

◯ check hole

lances:

▲ injection lance

△ check lance

Figure 4. Plan of the pillar foundation,
          Location of drill holes and injection lances

Table 1. Advance rates of the pile-hammer before and after
        grouting

DEPTH FROM - TO (metre)	TIME (second)			
	before grouting lance number		after grouting lance number	
	1	5	15	16
0 - 1.0	7	5	7	7
1.0 - 2.0	11	10	18	16
2.0 - 3.0	12	14	90	95
3.0 - 4.0	42	48	-	-
4.0 -	61	122	-	-
MAXIMUM DEPTH (metre) no further advance	4.7	5.0	2.2	2.9

the pile-hammer showed that the soil resistance after grouting was much higher than before (see table 1). This proof was
necessary to demonstrate that the grouting mixture did not
pour into distant big cavities but actually stiffened the soil.
This renovation was finished in 1988.

SUBSURFACE GROUTING AT THE CASTLE "Ortenburg" in bautzen

The north-eastern part of the castle has displaced as a consequence of water influence. The walls were damaged to such
a degree that in this part of the building the security of

visitors could not be guaranteed (see figure 5). In
preparation of the cement injection the geological situation
under the foundation was explored by experts. Tests were

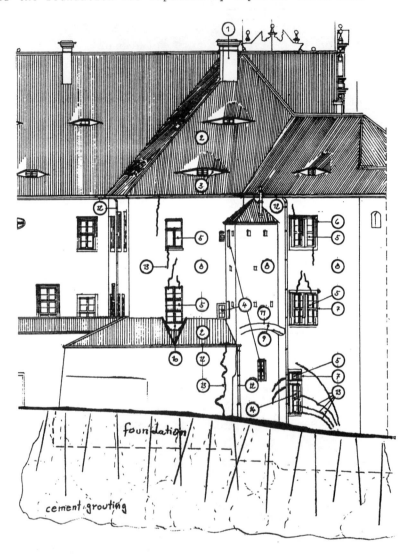

Figure 5. Ortenburg,elevation of the north-eastern part

carried out to investigate the concentration of sulphate in
the ground and the pH-value of the soil. The subsurface
grouting was carried out in 1987 to prevent further settlements. 83 holes of 45 mm diameter were made by pile-hammer
(total length 410 m) and rock drill (total length 35 m). The
greatest depth amounted to 7 m. The composition of mixture
was as follows (volume parts): 10 parts cement, 1 part fine
sand (0 ... 0.8 mm) , 1 part clay and 8 parts water. The total volume of grouting mixture was 198 m^3. The work proved
to be successful. No further settlements were observed.

CEMENT GROUTING AT THE FOUNTAIN "Mosaikbrunnen im Großen
Garten" in Dresden

On the occasion of the great horticultural show in Dresden in
1926 several fountains were built. They were temporary constructions and should be used for some months only. However,
one of them remained working until 1980. The fountain basin
is covered with mosaics of coloured glass. This architectonic gem is to be preserved although the structure is dilapidated. The fountain basin is standing on eleven single footings. There were many cracks in the basin consisting of a
5 to 8 cm thick reinforced concrete shell and a 2 cm thick
mortar layer in which the mosaics were pasted. Many reinforcing rods are rusty because they are not covered by concrete.
While erecting the fountain the coarse basin shape was made
of loamy sand and the concrete directly placed on it. Settlements occured resulting in a 2 cm high cavity under the
whole shell which now became a load-bearing element. The renovation of the foundation and of the basin itself was carried out in 1988. The soil under the foundation level and a-
round the single footings was stiffened by grouting of cement
suspension. Eleven injection lances of 33.5 mm diameter were
rammed until the depth of 2.3 m. The cement consumption a-
mounted to 1.4 tons. The cavities under the concrete shell

were also filled with cement suspension. 43 pipe nozzles were
put into drill holes of 25 mm and were fixed by cement mortar
(see figure 6 and 7). The impermeability to water and the
load-bearing capacity are restored. However, the remaining
service life is limited because it was not possible to insert
supplementary reinforcing rods.

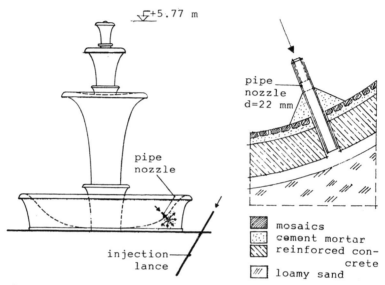

Fig. 6 Fountain "Mosaik-
       brunnen"

Fig. 7   Reinforced concrete
         shell of the basin

SUMMARY

The four examples showed to which kind of tasks we are able
to apply the method of cement grouting. As any other method
was more expensive or even there was not any other alternative of injection technique this method is very important
for our work.

Grouts for Repairing and Strengthening Old Masonry Structures

G. Penelis, M. Karaveziroglou, J. Papayianni

Department of Civil Engineering, Aristotle University of Thessaloniki, 540 06 Thessaloniki, Greece

ABSTRACT

The main problems anticipated in grouting old masonry structures are related to flow properties, segregation and rate of strength development.
It is also desirable that the proportioning of these grouts be based on
constituents of existing mortars of old structures which are to be grouted. In this work flow curves, time-bleeding % and time-strength development curves are presented for a number of grouts made from various
combinations of their main constituents(hydrated lime, pozzolana, cement,
brick powder and sand). In addition the grading analysis of the solid
part of each grout is given.

INTRODUCTION

The choice of a suitable grout for repairing old structures is not only
dependent on the properties of set grout(strength, flexibility, porosity)
but on these of fresh grout which determine how effective it will be in
situ. For example, the grading of constituents of the solid part of the
grout (especially the max. size of their grains) determines the smallest
size passage into which it can be injected. The fluidity after mixing is an
important factor in repair work as it is known that dense and stiff grouts
cannot be pumped. The bleeding can result in poor adhesion between grout
and upper faces of cracks as channels or spaces are left at the top of
grouted voids. This, of course is closely related to the porosity of the
strengthened structure. The rate of increase in strength is a means of
comparing different grouts under the same curing conditions. In most cases a slow rate of strength development is advantageous but it is desirable to know the early mechanical strengths and modulus of elasticity.

Bearing all these in mind, it is suggested the above referred properties are taken into account when performance type criteria for
grouts are considered.

EXPERIMENTAL WORK

Three series of mixtures were prepared(Table 1). In the first series E1
up to E6 as well as E11 and E13, the activity of pozzolana Santorin earth

was examined in different proportions and in combination with cement, sand and brick powder. In the second series E7 up to E10 the activity of another pozzolana from Skydra(Skydra Earth) was investigated. In the third series E12 and E15 up to E18 some of the previous mixtures were repeated with the addition of an expanding and lignin based water reducing agent in order to estimate the effect of this agent on grout mixtures.

To find the rate of strength development twelve specimens(4x4x16)mm for each mixture were prepared, cured and tested according to DIN 4227 Teil 5 at age of 8, 14, 21 and 28 days. The results are shown in Table 3.

Parallel to the strength test;the density, the water retention, the time of efflux immediately after mixing and one and two hours later, as well as the rate of bleeding of the same mixtures were measured according to ASTM C185-81, C941-81 and C940-81 respectively. The test results are given in Table 2.

The selection of "traditional" materials such as hydrated lime,pozzolana, brick powder and sand was based on the existing experience of our Laboratory(Penelis, et al.[1]). The two pozzolanic materials used (Santorin Earth and Skydra Earth) as well as the brick powder passed a sieve opening of 0.25mm while the sand used has a max size of grain<1mm. The Santorin Earth had a finer gradation than Skydra Earth. Brick powder was produced from bricks fired at 900°C. All the constituents of the mixtures were measured by weight. Data referring to chemical composition and physical properties of the constituents is also available.

The grading analysis of the solid part of each grout mixture is also given in Table 4.

DISCUSSION OF RESULTS

Rate of strength development
Based on test results of Table 3 we can see in Fig.1,2 and 3 that the cement content determines the rate of strength development. The greater the proportion of cement the higher the rate of strength development. We can distinguish two areas in strength-time diagrams; area II of high strength and area I of low strength. Mixtures with high proportion of pozzolana fall into the lower limits of areas I in Fig.1 and 2. Comparing grouts E6 and E7, it seems that when a high proportion of pozzolana is used Santorin Earth is more active than Skydra Earth. This may be due to its fineness as well as to its chemical composition. But when the proportion of pozzolanic material in the mix is lower(for example 0.6 or 0.2) there is no difference in strength and Skydra Earth seems to cooperate better (see pairs of grouts E3-E9, E4-E10, E5-E8). The mixtures with lime:pozzolana ratio 1:2 presented better strength as it is indicated by comparison of E12 and E13 with E2 grouts.

The addition of sand as an aggregate contributes to strength especially when the mixture is poor in cement(compare E2 with E4 in Table 3).

The brick powder seems to play an active role in strength development. When pairs E4-E5, E8-E10 are compared it is obvious that brick powder contributes to strength mainly after the age of 14 days. It is also noted that mixtures with brick powder retained more water and the mixture had higher ratios Water/Lime+Pozz.+Cement. This was in agreement with grading analysis of these mixtures(see Table 4)which showed that the addition of brick powder in grouts enriches the finer fragments of solid constituents especially those of 150μ and 75μ. The grout E11 in which brick powder was only used as aggregate showed relatively high strength. This leads to the thought that brick powder is not only a filler but takes part in strength development as an active constituent.

The addition of the mentioned expanding agent had a positive effect in strength development. The strength-time curves of grouts E12,E15,E16, E17 and E18 were more regular. These mixtures also presented a greater water retention, good fluidity and remarkable increase in their cohesiveness.

Fluidity of grouts
As far as the fluidity of the grouts is concerned we can see that the main factor which influence the fluidity is the ratio Water/Lime+Pozz.+ +Cement. As it is indicated in Fig.4 the grouts can be grouped in three teams. One with W/L+P+C 0.50 up to 0.70 another with W/L+P+C 0.70 up to 0.85 and a third with the higher W/L+P+C ratio. Grouts in which part of the sand was replaced by brick powder showed better fluidity with time while grouts with sand presented a stiffness. For example, E4 was impossible to flow one hour later. The time of efflux of grouts with expanding agent remained low two hours after mixing. A thixotropic behaviour was noticed with some grouts with high brick powder content.

Bleeding
In Fig.5 we can see that grouts with Skydra Earth showed a lower rate of bleeding. This can be explained as Skydra Earth has a lower density than that of Santorin Earth and the solid material in grouts suspends better. There is also a difference in bleeding rate between grouts with sand and those with brick powder which is also due to their density. The low density brick powder bleeds slowly while grouts with sand bleed very soon. This means that there is reason to fear an early segregation in these grouts. The higher bleeding of grouts with brick powder is due to their higher W/L+P+C ratio. The density, the specific surface of the constituents as well as the W/L+P+C ratio seem to be the main factors which influence the rate of bleeding. We suggest that these factors be further investigated.

CONCLUSIONS

In grouts made from hydrated lime, pozzolana, cement, sand and brick powder the rate of strength development is analogous to cement content. Their time of efflux depends on the W/L+P+C ratio.

The sand addition seems to contribute to strength especially with mixtures low in cement, but grouts with sand tend to segregate earlier and to lose their fluidity.

The brick powder seems to be a very important constituent of grouts which plays an active role in strength development. It also improves the fluidity and decreases the segregation rate.

Santorin Earth seems to be more active than Skydra Earth but in grouts with low cement content, which also contain sand or brick powder, Skydra Earth cooperates better. Therefore there is no reason to use Santorin Earth instead of Skydra to repair monuments in North Greece where Skydra Earth is produced.

REFERENCES

1. Penelis, G., et al. Restoration and Strengthening of Rotonda, Thessaloniki, 1980.

2. ASTM Vol 04,02. Concrete and Mineral Aggregates, 1983.

3. DIN 4227 Spannbeton, Bauteile aus Normalbeton mit beschränketer oder voller Vorspannung.

Table 1. Mix Proportions of tested grouts

No	Lime (L)	Santorin earth (P)	Skydra earth (P)	Portland cement (C)	Sand max size<1mm	Brick powder max size<25mm	Water	Expanding agent	$\dfrac{W}{L+R+C}$	Time of sinking DIN 4227 Teil 5 sec
				C o n s t i t u e n t s						
E1	1	0.2	–	0.8	–	–	1.515	–	0.75	34
E2	1	0.6	–	0.4	–	–	1.417	–	0.70	31
E3	1	0.2	–	0.8	2	–	1.750	–	0.87	33
E4	1	0.6	–	0.4	2	–	1.563	–	0.78	34
E5	1	0.6	–	0.4	1	1	1.875	–	0.93	35
E6	1	0.8	–	0.2	1	1	1.869	–	0.93	39
E7	1	–	0.8	0.2	1	1	1.875	–	0.93	34
E8	1	–	0.6	0.4	1	1	1.875	–	0.93	37
E9	1	–	0.2	0.8	2	–	1.637	–	0.81	33
E10	1	–	0.6	0.4	2	2	1.530	–	0.76	35
E11	1	0.6	–	0.4	–	2	2.187	–	1.09	32
E12	1	2	–	0.4	–	–	1.720	0.034	0.50	34
E13	1	2	–	0.4	–	–	1.788	–	0.52	35
E15	1	0.8	–	0.2	1	1	1.670	0.02	0.83	35
E16	1	–	0.8	0.2	1	1	1.610	0.02	0.80	33
E17	1	0.6	–	0.4	1	1	1.660	0.02	0.83	37
E18	1	–	0.6	0.4	1	1	1.690	0.02	0.84	35

Table 2. Properties of grout mixtures

No	Density kg/m³	Water retention (ASTM C 941-81) sec	Time of efflux after mixing (ASTM C939-81) in sec			Final bleeding (ASTM C940-81) $(V_w/V_i) \times 100$
			after 2min	after 60min	after 120min	
E1	1.510	59	31	49	68	2.0
E2	1.494	79	65	95	115	2.1
E3	1.784	90	17	22	25	3.1
E4	1.798	-	230	impossible flow	impossible flow	2.0
E5	1.666	85	25	30	34	2.3
E6	1.670	92	24	28	32	2.6
E7	1.569	88	20	25	25	2.5
E8	1.740	81	23	26	28	2.3
E9	1.767	138	26	38	41	1.3
E10	1.760	152	30	58	65	2.4
E11	1.640	93	35	40	47	3.5
E12	1.596	187	75	110	120	3.9
E13	1.588	104	90	120	140	3.0
E15	1.682	136	44	54	55	4.0
E16	1.634	128	40	62	74	2.7
E17	1.742	157	46	60	62	2.6
E18	1.746	209	47	65	67	2.4

Table 3. Strength of grouts at different ages

No	Age days	Tensile strength N/mm²	Compressive strength N/mm²	Age days	Tensile strength N/mm²	Compressive strength N/mm²	Age days	Tensile strength N/mm²	Compressive strength N/mm²	Age days	Tensile strength N/mm²	Compressive strength N/mm²
E1	8	0.51	1.05	14	0.25	1.45	22	0.58	2.25	27	0.57	2.45
E2	8	0.16	0.34	14	0.20	0.42	22	0.37	0.80	27	0.28	0.96
E3	10	0.16	1.01	13	0.23	1.16	21	0.37	1.68	28	0.67	2.25
E4	10	0.39	0.50	13	0.25	0.58	21	0.33	0.85	28	0.44	1.10
E5	9	0.20	0.43	17	0.22	0.71	21	0.43	0.94	28	0.52	1.30
E6	8	0.10	0.21	16	0.11	0.34	21	0.16	0.64	29	0.22	0.72
E7	8	0.12	0.25	16	0.10	0.35	21	0.20	0.42	28	0.26	0.61
E8	7	0.20	0.44	13	0.37	0.75	21	0.45	0.98	28	0.66	1.55
E9	7	0.40	0.92	15	0.49	1.60	21	0.98	2.28	28	1.14	3.22
E10	7	0.12	0.38	13	0.39	0.67	21	0.37	0.81	28	0.34	1.18
E11	9	0.34	0.42	14	0.45	0.97	21	0.64	1.91	29	0.50	2.65
E12	9	0.07	0.28	14	0.20	0.53	21	0.40	0.90	29	0.42	1.30
E13	8	0.09	0.32	14	0.23	0.52	21	0.44	1.00	28	0.53	1.44
E15	8	0.04	0.20	14	0.25	0.44	21	0.48	1.06	28	0.44	1.39
E16	8	0.05	0.24	14	0.29	0.49	21	0.37	0.88	27	0.39	1.20
E17	8	0.23	0.62	14	0.59	1.44	21	0.66	2.07	27	0.83	2.42
E18	8	0.21	0.57	14	0.53	1.18	21	0.55	1.54	27	0.92	2.10

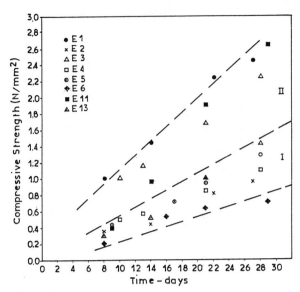

Fig.1 Rate of strength development of grouts with Santorin Earth.

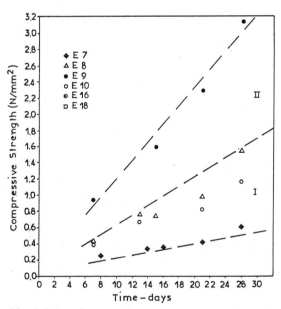

Fig.2 Rate of strength development of grouts with Skydra Earth

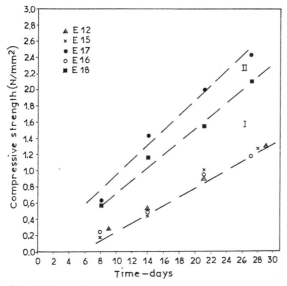

Fig.3 Rate of strength development of grouts with expanding agent.

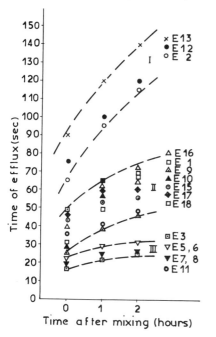

Fig.4 Change in fluidity of grouts.

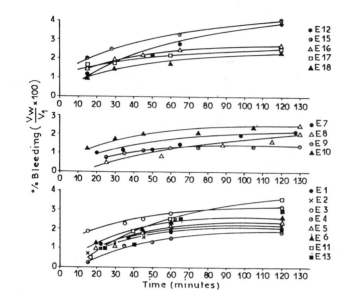

Fig.5 Rate of bleeding of grouts.

Table 4. Gradation of the solid phase of tested grouts

NO	Percentage passing through sieve openings						
	1mm	600µ	300µ	150µ	75µ	45µ	pan
	99.9	99.1	97.6	94.4	71.2	83.7	0
E2	99.9	97.2	92.7	85.4	66.3	18.2	0
E3	99.9	90.9	66.7	49.5	39.5	11.4	0
E4	99.9	90.2	62.3	45.0	36.7	16.7	0
E5 and E17	99.9	94.0	81.0	64.5	47.0	16.5	0
E6 and E15	99.9	93.5	77.5	60.5	41.9	13.5	0
E7 and E16	99.9	93.2	77.0	55.7	38.8	14.0	0
E8 and E18	99.9	93.4	77.3	59.6	42.5	13.8	0
E9	99.9	89.5	63.1	47.4	38.4	13.0	0
E10	99.9	90.6	63.2	43.0	33.8	15.0	0
E11	99.9	91.1	65.9	44.9	33.4	10.5	0
E12 and E13	99.9	94.7	86.1	72.0	50.8	14.5	0

The Use of Synthetic Fibre Material for Prevention and Repair of Damage to Historical Buildings

G. Croci*, M.L. Polichetti** and M. Cerone*.
*Department of Structural and Geotechnical Engineering, University La Sapienza, 00184 Rome, Italy.
**Superintendent of Environment and Architectonic Properties, 60100 Ancona, Italy.

Introduction

This paper supplies some results of experimental research on masonry walls reinforced with synthetic fibres.

The use of non-ferrous materials was studied with two basic aims:
1) To study the problem of durability common to ferrous material.
2) To determine the possible advantages of synthetic fibres and their behaviour during seismic action.

Laboratory Tests on Synthetic Fibres

The materials used are made up of a polymer mixture based on propylene, specially treated so that the binding between polymer and water of the cement paste is optimized. Each thread has an equivalent cross section, equal to the ratio between the linear weight and the material's specific weight ($0.00093 Kg/cm^2$).

The following tests were performed (Figure 1):
1) static tensile tests
2) cyclical tensile tests (30 cycles between 50 and 350 Kg)
3) relaxation tests (114 hours under constant load = 30% breaking load).

The static tensile test diagrams (Figure 2) show a low elastic modulus for the first part of the curve. This is due to some experimental adjustments. It is suggested that a small amount of prestressing takes place in the threads. From then on the behaviour is characterised by a larger elastic modulus ($E = 20.000 Kg/cm^2$) which remains partially constant until collapse occurs.

The synthetic fibre threads behave as a fragile material. Only one of the groups of fibres that made up the thread is involved in the failure mechanism. The break point tensile stress values are variable with a minimum of $1600Kg/cm^2$ and a maximum of $3200Kg/cm^2$ or even more. This last value is relative to the simultaneous breaking of all the fibres, while the minimum value refers to the failure of only a few of them. This latter case can hardly be expected in reality because the injections of cement mixture ensure the collaboration of all the fibres; moreover the threads used in the tests were made by craftsmen and were not controlled by any quality assurance system.

Cyclical tests were made on three samples similar to those used in static tests. Varying the load between 50 and $350Kg$ the collapse load was measured and it was respectively 790, 884 and 956 Kg. Figure 3 shows the load- displacement diagram.

The graphic indicates a very small hysteresis and a tendency towards stabilization along a nearly linear and strain-hardening path. During the cyclical part of the tests the elastic modulus is about $34.000Kg/cm^2$ and it is greater than the elastic modulus measured during the last part of the curve. This is due to the rearrangement of the fibres. One can observe here the increase of the elastic modulus in comparison with that measured in a static test $(20.000Kg/cm^2)$.

Figure 4 shows the behaviour of the threads under the application of a static load of 30% break-point, versus time. The viscous elongation $(\Delta\ell_{f,\infty})$ reaches 50% of the initial elastic one, and almost all of it occurs within the first few hours. (After 0.5 hours $\Delta\ell_{f,0.5} = 33\%\Delta\ell_{f,\infty}$, and after 5 hours $\Delta\ell_{f,5} = 50\%\Delta\ell_{f,\infty}$). This phenomenon, which is not relevant under actions which last for a short time (like seismic ones), makes a re-traction of prestressed threads necessary after a certain period.

Regarding the effect of thermal variations, in spite of the fact that the synthetic fibre's thermal coefficient is about ten times greater $(\alpha = 0.8 \text{ x } E - 4 \quad °C)$ than that of the masonry, during practical application they have resulted in only small variations of stresses $(50Kg/cm^2$ per $\Delta T = 30° C)$.

Experimental Tests on Reinforced Masonry ELements and Numerical Simulation

After the test on the actual material, some samples of reinforced shear wall masonry were tested. The samples are 0.4 x 1.00 x 2.00m., and in order to reproduce the conditions of some real historical buildings, they are made with sandstone bricks and cement mortar, and reinforced in several different ways. The load is given by a jack held in place by an appropriate steel frame; the deformations are measured by means of dial gauges (see Figures 5, 6, 7, 8).

The first sample is a control one consisting of a non-reinforced masonry element, stressed in shear and bending moment and used to determine normal conditions. It is subjected to two loading-unloading cycles; the maximum load reached is about two tons (see Figure 9). The second sample (see Figure 10) is made up of masonry bricks reinforced with rectilinear synthetic fibre threads placed where there are tensile stresses. One can observe a great increase in the bearing capacity (five, six tons) and a high ductility.

The third sample is reinforced by means of fibres placed in a snakelike fashion; the inclination is 45 degrees (see Figure 11). It is interesting to make a comparison between the behaviour of this sample and samples 7 and 8 which are reinforced in the traditional way using inclined steel bars. Sample 7 is made up of normal steel, while the other is made of steel treated with products which protect against corrosion. These diagrams show that with equal reinforced areas of steel or synthetic fibres, the same levels of resistance are obtained; but using the threads the behaviour is undoubtedly more ductile. This ductility, obtained in the presence of a material characterized by fragile behaviour, is due to the major fibres' capacity to be deformed, and to its ability to take advantage of micro-cracks and anelastic deformations of masonry without losing the mutual exchange of stresses, as would happen in the case of steel.

The deterioration of the bearing capacity in the case of steel bars treated with protective products is shown in Figure 12. This is probably due to a further loss of adhesion and to the progressive unthreading of bars from the masonry.

The fourth sample is reinforced with inclined fibres so as to supply a better shear-resistance (see Figure 13). In this case the final load is five tons, slightly inferior to the previous one, but above all, the ductility is much lower.

Sample 5 has the reinforcing cables placed along the rectilinear path and it is loaded orthogonally to the medium plane (Figure 14). The breaking point load is about two tons; the ratio between this load and the one measured in the case of a panel loaded in plane is about 2.5, i.e. the same ratio as that between the respective heights.

In the last few months further tests have been carried out on shear-wall masonry reinforced with synthetic fibres. The masonry used in this set of tests is of poorer quality in terms of stiffness and resistance and it has been reinforced with a smaller amount of synthetic material than the first set, but they have the same topology. At the same time other types were made, consisting of shear-wall masonry reinforced with synthetic fibres and concrete multi-layer plaster. Although the tests on these walls are still in progress, some results are available and are worth mentioning. The sample reinforced with synthetic fibre thread (see Figure 15) shows a good ductile behaviour and a reduction of the breaking load compared to the results obtained in the first set of tests. As to the masonry shear-wall reinforced with multi-layer plaster, its ductility is not as good (see Figure 16) but the breaking load is a third higher.

The experimental test described above has been numerically simulated, by discretizing the shear-wall into finite elements. The finite element method is based on assemblages of mono-dimensional members, described in more detail in [2]; the individual finite element is simulated by six truss-members located on the sides and diagonals of a rectangle.

Figures 17 and 18 show the results of a simple masonry shear-wall, and of a masonry shear-wall reinforced by synthetic fibre threads laid on the strained side. Both cases agree with the experimental tests, both in terms of stiffness and ductility and in failure-load terms.

These studies, although, at the moment, not supplying exhaustive answers, show new perspectives for the use of synthetic fibres for existing masonry, and in particular for strengthening it against seismic damage, thanks to the high ductility shown by all the different tests.

Fig. 1 Static tensile test on synthetic fibre rope.

References

1. Croci, G., Cerone, M.; The onset of arching effect in masonry walls, Geodynamic Meeting of the National Research Council, Report n° 263, Rome, 1979.

2. Andreaus, U., Ceradini, G., D'Asdia, P.; A simple model for the dynamic analysis of deteriorating structures; Proceedings of the Seventh International Conference on Structural Mechanics in Reactor Technology. Vol. L, pp. 591-598, Chicago, USA, August 22-26; 1983.

3. Andreaus, U., Ceradini, G., Cerone, M., D'Asdia, P.; Masonry columns under horizontal loads: a comparison between finite element modelling and experimental results. Proceedings of the Seventh International Brick Masonry Comference. Melbourne, Australia, 17-20 February 1985.

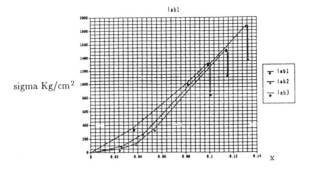

Fig. 2 Tension-failure test

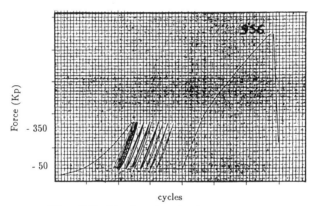

cycles

Fig. 3 Cyclic tension test

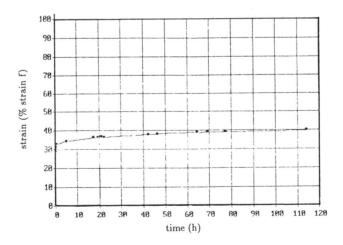

time (h)

Fig. 4 Relaxation test

Fig. 5

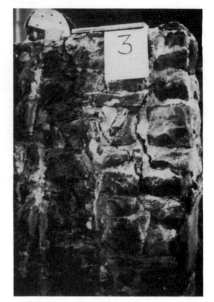

Fig. 6

Fig. 7

Fig. 8

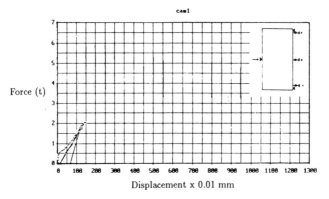

Fig. 9
Masonry shear-wall

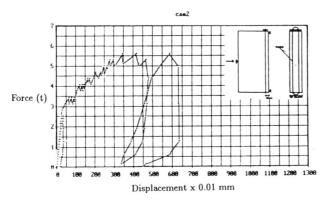

Fig. 10
Masonry shear-wall reinforced with synthetic fibres

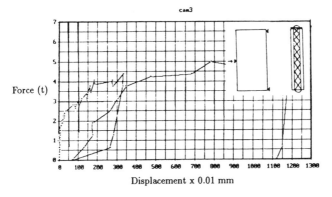

Fig. 11
Masonry shear-wall reinforced with synthetic fibres

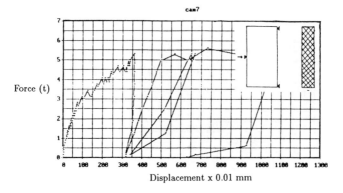

Fig. 12
Steel reinforced masonry shear-wall

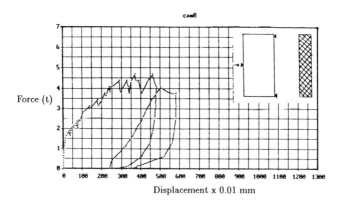

Fig. 13
Steel reinforced masonry shear-wall

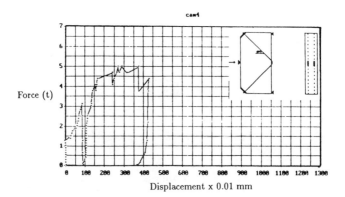

Fig. 14
Masonry shear-wall reinforced with synthetic fibres

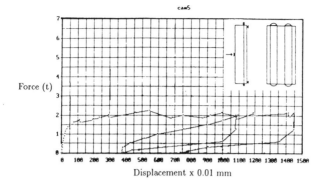

Fig. 15
Masonry shear-wall reinforced with synthetic
fibres

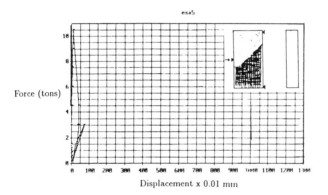

Fig. 16
Masonry shear-wall reinforced with synthetic
fibres

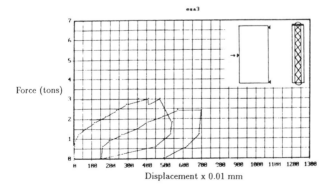

Fig. 17
Masonry shear-wall reinforced with synthethic
fibres

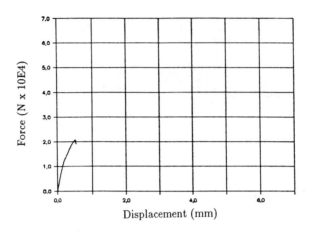

Fig. 18 Masonry shear-wall

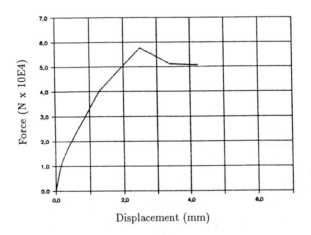

Fig. 19 Masonry shear-wall reinforced

SECTION 4 - STUDIES OF DOMES

A Study of the Sinan's Domed Structures

E. Karaesmen

Middle East Technical University, Ankara, Turkey

ABSTRACT

The great masterbuilder Sinan's domed edifices are known as built with structural ingenuity. Finite element technique is applied to investigate their structural response under both gravity and seismic actions. Findings are discussed.

INTRODUCTION

Advantages of vaulted structures have been known even in the very early ages of history, but more interesting features related to domes have become apparent only in the later periods. There is evidence that the first constructions of domed components in various regions of the world have started independently. Istanbul needs a special mention here as the worlds's center of dome and cupola tradition, dating back to the Byzantines, with reference to the majestic presence of Haghia Sophia. As the Turks brought their ancestral cupola experience from pre-Ottoman ages to the Anatolian lands, these two different traditions merged in such a perfect way that Istanbul became a museum of dome collections during the golden age of the Ottoman Empire, e.g.Rumpler[1]. The great masterbuilder Sinan whose name should be mentioned with veneration was at the very origin of the spectacular developments of the building art of his time.

Interpretations of the evaluation of the building art of the Byzantine-Ottoman eras were generally focused on the architectural aspects of the subject considering the structural properties as associates to the architectural features. However, structural solutions are sometimes so strikingly successful that functional, economical and aesthetic aspects could all be interpreted in terms of the engineering features. The basic philosophy of Sinan's domed buildings is mainly based on a meaningful balance and alliance of the architecture with the structure. Indeed, it is why we consider it worthwhile to study closely the evaluative steps in Sinan's masonry domed edifices by series of observations from both architectural and engineering

views.   On   the   other   hand,   historical   buildings   are
incessantly subject to restoring and redesigning work,   which
should   be   based   on comprehensive and exact   knowledge   of
their structural behaviour.   Some graduate work based on   the
structural   modelling of Sinan's major edifices for   computer
analysis   techniques   was   recentlycarriedoutundertheguidance
of the author,e.g.Karaesmen[2][4];   Ünay [2][3].   The present
text is prepared to describe the aim,   philosophy and adopted
mathematical   approach in these studies and to summarize   all
recent important findings.

DOME: AN ENIGMATIC PHENOMENON

Engineering Aspect Versus Spiritual Understanding
Domed   structures   are   not ordinary edifices.   They   have   a
solemn character and they do reflect an intense   spirituality
originated   from   overwhelming   fulfilment   of   sharing   an
uncommon   and special feeling.   The classical art   philosophy
identifies   the dome,   essentially as a device for simulating
the sky and thus the engineering aspect is easily shadowed by
such brilliant   interpretations on the spiritual   and   symbolic
particularities   of   its   spatial   effects.   Indeed,   one's
sensitivity   is very strongly stimulated while standing under
the   psychologically captivating pressure of   the   apparently
infinite   dome   of   Haghia Sophia which is   an   architectural
summit.   But,   it   should   be also remembered that   the   same
Haghia Sophia had largely swayed,cracked, partially collapsed
and been repaired several times during the   history.   Despite
the   external,   massive   and   inelegant   looking   buttresses
constructed   later   to prevent   excessive   deformations,   the
edifice is still the object of the risk of further damage   as
stated   by various recent   studies,   e.g.Mungan[5];   Mark[6].
These   facts   reflect the engineering reality concerning   the
domed structures which is somehow considered as an   enigmatic
phenomenon.   Indeed, the main dome is both a ritual center and
the   element of engineering prestige in such edifices and the
control   of the well known thrust action in and   around   this
dome requires already a particular care.   However, the enigma
is   not only due to happenings in and immediately around   the
main   dome.   The overall mechanism of load transmission in   a
typical   Ottoman mosque from the top of the main dome to   the
foundations   of inner piers and outer walls through   drums,
pendentives,   cupolas,   arches   and   auxiliary   cupolas   is
subjected to irregularities and complexities for both gravity
effects   and   seismic actions. These flows of   forces   whose
general   orientation is schematically outlined as in   Figure
1,   are   likely   to be more complicated than in the   case   of
vaulted   Gothic   cathedrals where large and   frequent   flying
buttresses   would   greatly   ease   the   creation   of   a   more
controlled load distribution pattern, e.g.Heyman[7].

Sinan's Insight Into Domed Structures
The   Seljuks   first   and Ottomans later   brought   their   dome
experience   from   Central Asia to the Anatolian   lands   where

several public buildings with domes were constructed during the fourteenth and fifteenth centuries. These early Ottoman edifices were based either on the concept of a unique large dome covering the whole inner space or on the series of small domes one neighbouring the other at the same level. Both, thrust action and lateral seismic actions would thus be transmitted to massive exterior piers or walls. The progress in the late fifteenth and early sixteenth centuries brought secondary and partial domes surrounding the main dome at an inferior level to resist thrust action. The control of this action is not sufficient to ensure the overall stability of the edifices formed by unusually sophisticated components, such as pendentives, plain or bow string-arches, all subject also to highly complex seismic forces.

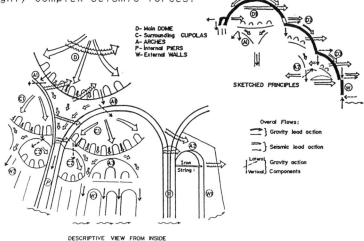

DESCRIPTIVE VIEW FROM INSIDE

Figure 1. Schematical load transmission in Ottoman domes

On the other hand, building techniques of Ottomans were also greatly improved during the sixteenth century allowing the construction of masonry components in any curved, sophisticated geometry. Within the social context, mosques with large domes were considered as the prestige buildings. Domed structures had become, thus, engineering summits and social targets to be reached.

Sinan(1490-1588) developed his structural ingenuity first as a military engineer. He later served, for almost half a century, as the chief architect of the Empire during which he was involved directly or indirectly in the construction of nearly five hundred works including mosques, bridges, hydraulic infrastructures, hospitals, palaces, schools, etc. His first prestige mosque of large dimensions was built in the name and to the memory of the dead and beloved Şehzade (Prince) Mehmet in Istanbul around the years

1534-1548. The structural system is based on a mixture of perfectly developed arches, pendentives and a series of surrounding partial domes which altogether horizontally integrate with the central dome in a way to balance and control its thrust and seismic action. This integrated system is supported by four internal pillars.

A higher level of structural challenge is reached in the Süleymaniye Mosque in Istanbul, built to the name of Süleyman the Magnificent, where there is only bi-axial symmetry. Consequently the load transmission mechanism is still more complex and daring especially with regard to the seismic conditions of Istanbul. A further development came with Mihrimah Sultan Mosque known as the largest structure of its kind, with a single large dome supported on only four corner pillars connected by externally visible elegant arches. The edifice is commonly referred to as possessing a unique structural grace, e.g.Kuran[8].

The structural achievement in the Selimiye Mosque at Edirne completed by 1575 gives the impression of being out of the limits of human imagination. Eight elegant, slender columns are symmetrically located as inner piers. Thus, there are eight zones through which the mechanism of flow of horizontal and vertical load actions would take place (Figure-2). The main dome of the edifice is known as having the largest span width for a masonry structure i.e., 31.28 m. All structural elements are constructed without any radial symmetry and located in a way to satisfy to a great extent the requirements of lightning, ventilation, acoustics and psychological fulfilment.

Figure 2. Selimiye Mosque-Plan and representative section

Original documents on Great Sinan's outstanding activities, found in the Ottoman archives are only related to the worksite planning and material supply at the Süleymaniye Mosque construction. No engineering-architectural design documents are available so far to verify the half mythological sayings on Sinan's incomparable creativity: whether it was based on structural intuition or also backed somehow by mathematical and physical knowledge? Observational findings would indicate that the great master probably knew or felt strongly the basic rules of graphical statics, and that he also was aware of the structural response against seismic effect. He realized the conceptual and practical importance of creation of continuum media and developed a mortar of superior binding quality as well as making highly ingenious use of iron bars as bow strings at just the required locations. Computer analysis facilities of our time would contribute to investigate all these considerations as described in the following sections of the text.

STRUCTURAL INVESTIGATIONS

Philosophy of Structural Analysis
Masonry domes constitute the most classical type of shell. In the past, the dimensioning of domes was carried out intuitively. Although masonry domes were mostly considered as overdesigned, some of them had challenging dimensions combined with beautiful appearance. Some unfortunate accidents such as the collapse of Beauvais Cathedral, and the partial collapse and uncontrollable deformations in the Haghia Sophia led the builders to develop more careful design considerations. The stability of masonry domes is closely related to the curve of thrust and to the formation of inelastic hinges on the structure. The concept of the hinges is theoretically based on assumptions such as that the compressive stresses should be low enough so that the crushing strength of the masonry can be taken effectively as infinite. Also the tensile strength of mortar is ignored, and sliding of one masonry unit on other is considered as not possible. On the other hand, masonry brickwork was mostly preferred to stone in domes and cupolas for the sake of construction flexibility. The quality of this work had been greatly improved in Sinan's edifices by the use of a particular mortar obtained by adding the white of an egg to the mixture.

To evaluate the minimum thickness of the domes, within the framework of the design process, the engineering attention should be focused on the limit case when a collapse mechanism is just formed. But our interest at this stage is centered on an exact and detailed understanding of the load transmission and of overall behaviour of the structure. Therefore preliminary analysis of finite element application has been carried out with elastic behaviour assumptions related to checking of some critical sections. It should be remembered that in Finite Element Method, the actual continuum, a geometrically complex domain, is replaced by an equivalent idealized structural model which could be formed by a collection of geometrically simpler subdomains called finite elements such as bars, beams, plate and shell elements, etc.. The complex geometry of domed structures requires generally mixed models having all types of components as in the two case studies described in the following sections.

Case Study-1: Şehzade (Prince) Mosque
Şehzade (Prince) Mehmet Mosque is referred to as forming the
turning point between apprenticeship and masterly period in
Sinan's edifices. It exhibits all aspects of Sinan's
unsurpassable ingenuity in building art. Piers, walls and
arches were built of stone masonry and curved space elements
with shallow brick, particular mortar were used everywhere.
There is perfect three dimensional spherical symmetry in this
skeleton making its load transmission mechanism less
complicated than in some other major edifices (Figure 3). The
upper tier of the building consists of the main dome, 19.00m.
in diameter resting on a stone ring which is supported by
eight external buttresses and twenty-four columns located
between the elegant windows of the dome region. The ring is
connected to a bottom drum with these buttresses and columns,
altogether resting on the four main arches of the second
tier. The arches are neighboured circumferentially by four
partial domes each surrounded by two partial smaller cupolas
resting on thick exterior walls. At the corners of the second
tier, there are also four pendentives highly complex three
dimensional, transition elements connecting the main dome to
surrounding partial domes and supporting main arches. The
first tier of the skeleton consists of four large interior
piers, massive exterior walls and eight small bow string
arches connecting the piers to the exterior walls in the
prolongation of four central main arches, at a lower level.

    Following initial steps in investigation two
representitive models were considered. One was based on the
main dome and its immediately neighbouring elements only and
the second one considering the whole skeleton from top of the
main dome to the base of the building. Structural
computations were based on the assumption of an elastic
continuum to get the basic understanding of the response of
the whole building formed by a complex mixture of linear,
planar and space components. The finite element model
corresponding to the study of the skeleton as a whole which
is sketched in Figure 4 comprised 378 nodes, 200 frame
elements and 240 shell elements. The system was analysed
under action of both gravity loads and seismic effect. The
vertical load of the whole system was evaluated as 160000 kN
including the self weight of masonry, weights of lead covers
and snow. Lateral effect investigation was approached by
spectral analysis logic. But, the system being revealed too
stiff, the solution was completed by considering the
application of equivalent lateral loads at all components
proportional to their weights. The total equivalent lateral
load representing the seismic action was estimated as
16000 kN (%10 of the gravity loads).

    All deflected shapes are both graphically and
numerically obtained. Figure 5 shows the lateral
displacements of the arches under action of gravity loads. The
displacements of the connection joints of the arch and the

piers are computed as 0.2 mm. outward in both x and y directions, whereas the crown of arch moves inward by 0.04 mm This distorted deformation is obviously due to the four surrounding partial domes reacting to thrust forces and tending to create a horizontal inward displacement. It also shows the existence of a torsional moment in the cross-section of arches. On the other hand, main arches stay fully in compression media, the maximum stress being computed at the crowns as 0.862 N/mm². As for load transmission patterns they are fully evaluated for both gravity loads and seismic actions as summarized in Figure 6 and stresses in all elements are automatically obtained. Some of the meaningful findings could be summarized and commented as follows.

Main dome: The average thickness was taken as 50 cm. in the main central dome. The maximum compressive stress in the shell element is found to be about 0.3 N/mm² and in the crown. The meridional stresses are nearly equal to a constant value of 0.13 N/mm² which is a low value with regard to the thickness. The bending moment variation fits the perfect geometry of the dome, making thrust lines stay in centerline zones.

On the other hand, the previously mentioned 24 short columns are highly operational in dealing with seismic effect. At the upper tier of the edifice a large percentage of the lateral forces reacting to thrust and to seismic actions of the main dome were concentrated on these short columns. Differences in support conditions are such that the columns connected directly to the huge main arches contribute more actively to seismic resistance than the others supported by pendentives, flexible components. Thus, maximum shear stresses were evaluated in these columns under seismic action as 0.3N/mm² which is rather close to the allowable limit. The dimensioning of short columns, especially directly supported ones by main arches, was daring and a more perfect architectural arrangement could be hardly obtained for this refined portion of the edifice.

Secondary Arches: Iron bow strings had been used in the eight secondary arches connecting the four inner piers to massive exterior walls at the bottom level of the second tier. These strings revealed important contributions in the seismic response since about 28% of the total seismic action in the building was transmitted through these elements.

Inner Piers: Though they look huge and over designed, the four central piers are estimated by some experts as having regularly shaped stonework only at the skin and their internal holes are filled by a loose mixture of unmortared brick and stone pieces. Combined effect for seismic action and gravity loads is evaluated creating a flexural moment of 24800 kN.m at the base of these piers. For hollow sections of masonry the compressive stresses were then computed as

3.8 N/mm² which is an indication of no overdesigning at all, as far as engineering sense is concerned.

Partial cupolas: Surrounding cupolas that cover gracefully additional large inner spaces show primary importance for overall stability of the structural system, too. Their contribution to load transmission mechanism in the whole skeleton was computed as 17% for seismic action, which is a remarkable result.

Case Study 2: Mihrimah Sultan Mosque
Two mosques which were erected by Sinan in the name of Mihrimah, talented artist and beloved daughter of the Süleyman the Magnificent are of an architectural character likely reflecting the refined personality of this extraordinary lady to whom they were dedicated. The second Mihrimah Mosque has also an engineering challenge with a single large dome of diameter 20.80 m. resting directly on four external arches supported by slender corner piers (Figure 7). Smaller domes visible near to exterior walls are located at a lower level and they do not interact with the main skeleton.

In the structural investigation, a finite element network formed by 150 shell elements and 148 frame elements with 226 nodes was used. The system was analyzed first for the gravity loads of 89000 kN in total. As for the total lateral load due to seismic effect, two alternatives were studied: In a first scheme, lateral load was estimated as 10% of the gravity loads as a result of Turkey's present seismic code considerations. An alternative of 15% was tried, too in order to cover poor zonal soil conditions. Both cases were studied applying, eigenvalue analysis to depict modal behaviour and evaluate corresponding period values of the structural system. Periods computed being too small (between 0.15-0.25 seconds) and system revealed too stiff, dynamic analysis was not fully followed and equivalent lateral load method was used, instead. Load transmission mechanism was evaluated as schematically represented in Figure 8. The arches with strong iron ties were highly governing all mechanisms of load transmission and action flow. Four corner columns rather slender for a large edifice, were taking each nearly 25000 kN.m of seismic moments yielding in a 4.2 N/mm² of stress. Computer outputs showed that the columns were not presenting perfect cantilever behaviour under seismic effect because of the bow string arches controlling and restraining free lateral motion. Indeed, the building had once slightly cracked during one of the past earthquakes and been repaired: but, observational traces are not apparent presently.

CONCLUDING REMARKS

Sinan's mosques represent the apogee of the searches for greatness in domed buildings. Perfection in both planar and structural arrangements is reached. Dimensioning of the

structural   component   is   ingeniously made   and   the   systems
cannot   be   qualified as   poorly   designed even   in   the   light   of
contemporary   knowledge.   Findings of   the   investigations   on   two
major   mosques   were   interesting,   highly   instructive   and
encouraging   for   future   studies.

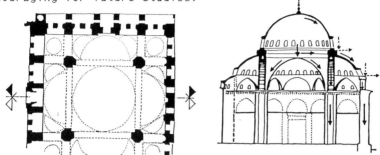

Figure .3. Şehzade Mehmet Mosque-Plan and section with sketched principle of action flow

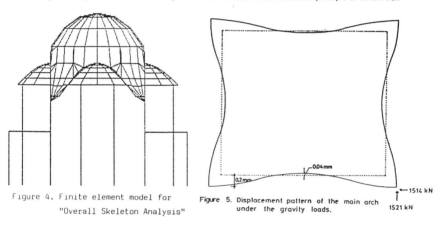

Figure 4. Finite element model for
"Overall Skeleton Analysis"

Figure 5. Displacement pattern of the main arch
under the gravity loads.

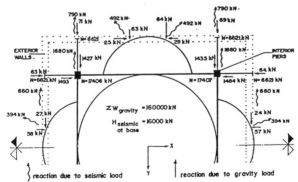

Figure 6. Şehzade (Prince) Mosque - Support reactions due to gravity and seismic loads

Figure 7. Mihrimah Mosque - Outside view

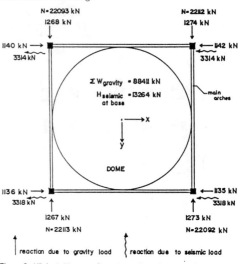

Figure 8. Mihrimah Mosque - Support reactions due to gravity and seismic loads

REFERENCES

1. Rumpler, M. La Coupole dans l'Architecture Byzantine et Musulman, Edition Le Tilleul, Strasbourg, 1956.

2. Karaesmen, E., Ünay, A.i. A Study of Structural Aspects of Domed Buildings, Proceedings of the IASS-MSU International Symposium on Domes, Istanbul, 1988.

3. Ünay, A.i. A Study of Structural Behaviour of the Şehzade Mehmet Mosque, M.S. thesis dissertation M.E.T.U., Ankara, 1988.

4. Karaesmen, E. Domed Buildings in Ottoman Architecture, lecture notes, Stanford University, Ankara-Palo Alto, 1988.

5. Mungan, i. On the Structural Development of the Ottoman Dome, Proceedings of the IASS-MSU International Symposium on Domes, Istanbul, 1988.

6. Mark, R., Westagard, A. The First Dome of Hagia Sofia: Myth Vs. Technology, Proceedings of the IASS-MSU International Symposium on Domes, Istanbul, 1988.

7. Heyman, J. On Shell Solution for Masonry Domes, International Journal of Solid Structures, Vol.3, pp.227-241, 1967.

8. Kuran, A. Sinan, the Great Old Master of Ottoman Architecture, Ada Press Publishers, Istanbul, 1987.

Structural Stability and Profile in the Dome of Santa Maria del Fiore, Florence

T. Aoki[1], K. Hidaka[2] and S. Kato[3]

[1] *Department of Structural Engineering, Nagasaki University, Bunkyo-machi 1-14, Nagasaki 852, Japan*
[2] *Institute of Art and Design, University of Tsukuba, Tsukuba, Ibaraki 305 Japan*
[3] *Department of Architecture and Regional Planning, Toyohashi University of Technology, Tempaku, Toyohashi 440, Japan*

ABSTRACT

The dome of Santa Maria del Fiore in Florence has a profile of the pointed-fifth curvature in its inner angles. To clarify the structural rationality of this dome, we have analyzed relationships between sectional profiles of dome(round, pointed-fourth, pointed-fifth, pointed-seventh) and the structural stability on the basis of FEM analysis models with elasto-plastic joint elements.

INTRODUCTION

The dome of Santa Maria del Fiore in Florence was built by Brunelleschi from 1420 to 1436(Photo.1). One of the most important problems in this enterprise should have been to determine the curvature of the dome. The profile of dome is fundamentally correlated to the structural stability as well as the aesthetical effect of the structure. The first item of the building program sanctioned in 1420 prescribes that the curvature should be pointed-fifth in the inner angles, that is, the corner arc has its center on the point dividing the diameter with ratio 1:4(Fig.1).

This profile was not introduced immediately before the drafting of the cupola program. In fact, a document written by Giovanni di Gherardo da Prato in the end of 1425 mentions that the pointed-fifth curvature had been decided "decades ago", and we know that the curvature had been continuously approved before it was finally specified in the cupola program of 1420.

Generally speaking, it is obvious that a pointed dome is structurally stronger than a semi-spherical dome of the same diameter. However, no attempt has been made to clarify the rationality of the pointed shape in the particular case of the Florentine dome. Applying numerical analysis models with elasto-plastic joint elements on FEM, we have analyzed relationships between sectional profiles of the dome and the structural stability.

ANALYTICAL MODELS

We have supposed four different profiles of dome: 1)round, 2)pointed-fourth, 3)pointed-fifth and 4)pointed-seventh(Fig.1). To make two-dimensional analytical models with elasto-plastic joint elements, we take one-eighth vertical part of the structure from the ground level to the uppermost oculus of the dome. It is inevitable to allow some ambiguity in estimating the structural influence upon the dome exerted by the supporting structure. In consideration of the structural effect of the 'tribuna morte', we have prepared two kinds of models: one without it(A) and the other with 'tribuna morte' incorporated with the supporting structure(B)(Fig.1). The actual state of the supporting structure as a whole may be within the limit confined by these two models. Thus, we have analyzed eight models in all, two(A and B) to each four profiles. The elasto-plastic joint elements are distributed radially to the center of the dome. Compressive or tensile forces working in the hoop direction through vertical boundary planes are properly taken into consideration by adding a series of horizontal elasto-plastic members. These members link a hypothetical supporting point on the central axis of the dome and a finite element in the inner layer of the shell. One of these members has a different stress-strain

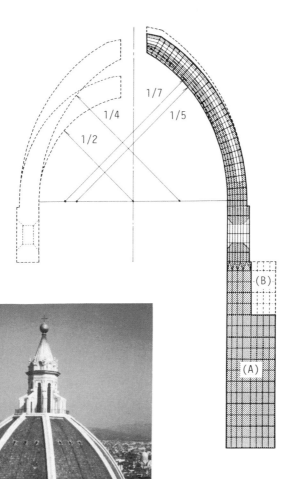

Fig.1 Numerical analysis model with elasto-plastic joint elements. Four different profiles are supposed.

Photo.1 The dome of Santa Maria del Fiore. External view.

relation, corresponding to the wooden ring embedded at the base of the dome. Table 1 lists the material properties of the dome. Table 2 specifies the characteristic values of the elasto-plastic joint element applied to determine the yielding condition.

RESULTS OF THE ANALYSIS

The results of the analysis are shown in Figures 2, 3, 4, and 5. In Figure 2-a, where the profile of the dome is supposed to be semi-circular, the horizontal thrust and displacement at the base of the dome would be large enough to threaten the stability of the structure. Compared with pointed domes, as is shown in Fig.3, the stress of the wooden ring is larger and cracks proceed at an earlier stage of loading. If we ignore the existence of the 'tribuna morte'(Fig.2-a, A), the structure will be weakest and the horizontal outward thrust at the base of the dome will be largest. When the load parameter λ reaches 1.6, the semi-spherical dome without 'tribuna morte' will collapse on the level of the wooden ring. With 'tribuna morte' taken into account(Fig.2-a, B), the structure becomes less yielding but the displacement is still critical enough.

The situation is changed for the better in the case of pointed domes. Horizontal outward thrust at the base of the dome diminishes as the dome grows more pointed, though the difference among three types is not remarkably large.

In the dome of pointed-fourth curvature without 'tribuna morte' (Fig.2-b, A), displacement at the base of the dome is relatively large and there is an outward displacement at the base of the drum(the uppermost part of the supporting structure) as well. Figure 2-b-B shows the same mode of deformation as Figure 2-b-A. The displacement, however, is considerably less than that of Figure 2-b-A.

In the case of the dome of pointed-fifth curvature, horizontal outward thrust and displacement at the base of the dome does not diminish noticeably. Here, however, the decentered dead load of the dome, heavier than the pointed-fourth one, causes another structural effect to counteract advantageously the outward thrust and to lessen the displacement at the base of the drum. This decentered load effect appears more markedly in case(A) than in case(B) where the higher supporting structure is subject to the horizontal outward thrust(Fig.2-c).

A much heavier dome of pointed-seventh curvature may exert greater decentered load against the supporting structure. In fact, the pointed-seventh dome supported by the lower supporting structure(Fig.2-d-A) presents a relatively large inward displacement at the base of the drum. The same kind of displacement is less perceptible in the pointed-fifth dome, and naturally far less in the pointed-fourth one. However, Figure 2-d-B shows that the higher supporting structure, being subject to outward thrusts, deforms outward at the base of the drum. The decentered load effect is canceled in this case.

In Figure 2, we can see the difference between model(A) and model(B), which confirms the structural efficiency of the 'tribuna morte'. In case(A), the displacement at the dome base is greater, the mode of deformation is more salient and consequently cracked area, indicated by dark shading, spreads higher. This holds good whether the profile is semi-circular or pointed. Correspondingly, Figure 3 gives another explanation to the structural meaning of the 'tribuna morte'. As the load parameter λ increases, the stress of the wooden ring increases linearly up to a certain point. And then, the gradient changes suddenly, which attests the occurrence and development of cracks. The linear relationship between the load parameter λ and the stress of the wooden ring σ_w can be regarded as a sort of stiffness index of the structure. In Figure 3, the gradients corresponding to the model(A) are gentler than the ones corresponding to the model(B). Thus, due to the existence of the 'tribuna morte', model(B) is more rigid than model(A).

CONCLUSION

From the structural point of view, a steeply pointed dome is superior in respect of the displacement at the dome base where the deformation is largest. The horizontal thrust and displacement at the base of the round dome would be large enough to threaten the stability of the structure. On the other hand, if we compare the analytical results of the pointed-seventh dome with those of the actual pointed-fifth profile, the advantage of the former in structural rationality is not decisive as the advantage of the latter in construction and building economy(Table 3). In this respect, as is shown in Figure 5, the pointed-fourth dome lies, as it were, on the border of safer pointed domes which present a marked contrast to the group of weaker domes represented here by semi-circular and pointed-third domes. Thus, according to our FEM analysis, the profile of the existing pointed-fifth dome of Santa Maria del Fiore may be judged ideal.

REFERENCES

1. H. Saalman : Filippo Brunelleschi, The Cupola of Santa Maria del Fiore, London, 1980.

2. P. A. Rossi : Le Cupole del Brunelleschi, Bologna, 1982.

3. S. Di Pasquale : The Dome of Santa Maria del Fiore, An Opportunity to State a Theory of Masonry Structure, Proceedings of the IASS Symp., Madrid Spain, pp.8.43-8.62., 1979.

4. A. Chiarugi : La Cupola del Brunelleschi, Problemi di Tracciamento e Costruzione, Il Modello dell'ACMAR, La Cupola del Brunelleschi, Il Convegno di Ravenna, pp.31-37, 1984.

5. S. Kato, K. Hidaka, and T. Aoki : Analytical Studies of the Historical Masonry Structure - The Florentine Dome of Santa Maria del Fiore, Proceedings of the IASS Symp., Osaka Japan, vol.1, pp.225-232, 1986.

6. S. Kato, K. Hidaka, and T. Aoki : A Study on the Formulation of a Elastic-plastic Joint Element by Truss Elements - An Application of the Theory of Effective Strength, Trans. of A.I.J., No.370, pp.50-59, 1986.

7. S. Kato, K. Hidaka, and T. Aoki : Structural Role of the wooden Ring of the Dome of Santa Maria del Fiore in Florence, Proceedings of the IASS Symp., Istanbul Turkey, pp.327-336.

Table 1 Material constants of the dome and the lower supporting structure

Brick
Young's modulus=1.0×10^5 kgf/cm^2 Poisson's ratio=1/6 Weight per unit volume: dome=1.7tf/m^3 lower structure=2.0tf/m^3
Mortar
Young's modulus=1.0×10^5 kgf/cm^2 Poisson's ratio=1/6 Strength(kgf/cm^2): compressive(σ_c)=200   tensile(σ_t)= 2
Wooden ring
Young's modulus=1.0×10^5 kgf/cm^2 Cross section =30cm x 30cm

Table 2 Material constants used in the finite element analysis

Joint element for mortar

Angle(ϕ_0)   =45^0
Height(h)   =1.0cm
Young's modulus(kgf/cm^2):
   diag. member=8.62×10^4
   vert. member=5.95×10^4
Compressive strength(kgf/cm^2):
   diag. member= 50
   vert. member=150
Tensile strength(kgf/cm^2):
   diag. member=1.89
   vert. member=1.16

Joint element of the key-stone without the diagonal member

Thickness(t)   = 86.29cm
Height(h)   =284.55cm
Young's modulus=1.0×10^5 kgf/cm^2
Strength(kgf/cm^2):
compressive(σ_c)=200
    tensile(σ_t)= 2
     strain(ε_c)=-0.0025

Member

Young's modulus=1.0×10^5 kgf/cm^2
Strength(kgf/cm^2):
compressive(σ_c)=200
    tensile(σ_t)= 2
     strain(ε_c)=-0.0025

Wooden ring
Young's modulus=1.0×10^5 kgf/cm^2 Strength(kgf/cm^2): compressive(σ_c)=300   tensile(σ_t)=300

Table 3 Ratio of the weight of the dome

Curvature	Dome	Dome+Drum
1/2	2738 ton (0.825)	5469 ton (0.894)
1/4	3230 ton (0.973)	6017 ton (0.984)
1/5	3319 ton (1.000)	6117 ton (1.000)
1/7	3418 ton (1.030)	6228 ton (1.018)

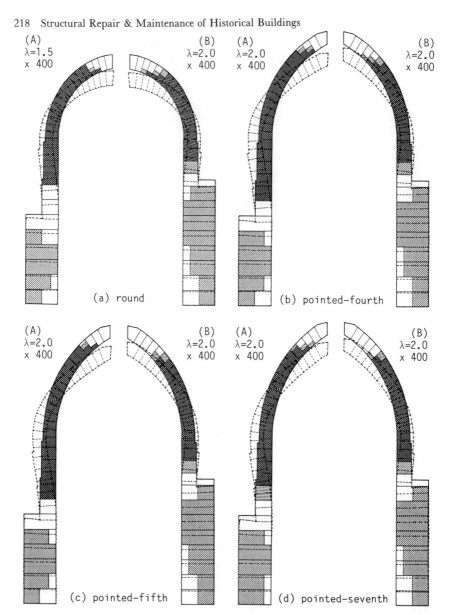

Fig.2 Deformation (shown by broken lines) and tensile force in the hoop direction. Light shading indicates tensile stress in the hoop direction, dark shading indicates longitudinal cracks. λ is load parameter(λ=1.0 corresponds to the structure under its dead weight).

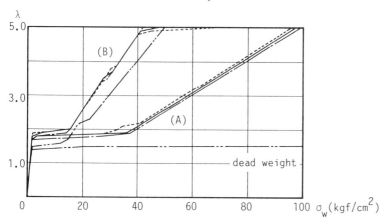

Fig.3 Relationship between load parameter λ and stress of the wooden ring σ$_w$.

————··———— semi-circular
————·——— pointed-fourth
——————— pointed-fifth
———————— pointed-seventh

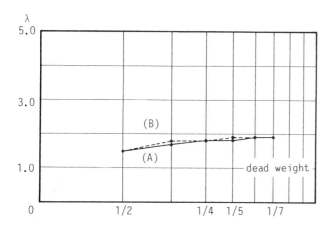

Fig.4 Relationship between load parameter λ and profile of dome at the moment when the first cracks occur.
Solid line: model(A)
Broken line: model(B)

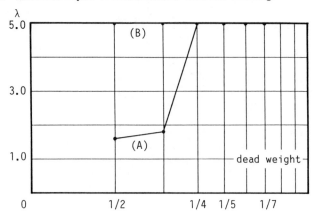

Fig.5 Relationship between load parameter λ and   profile of
dome at the final state.
                    Solid line: model(A)
                    Broken line: model(B)

Analysis and Mathematical Simulation of the Urbino Cathedral Dome

G. Menditto, I. Betti

Institute of Structural Engineering, University of Ancona, 60100 Ancona, Italy

ABSTRACT

A complete analysis of the dome of the Urbino Cathedral has been carried out using the analytical and F.E. methods. The limitations of the traditional calculation methods in interpreting the present state of cracks, the importance of thermal loads and the influence of the drum on the static behaviour of the dome are emphasized.

Introduction

The Cathedral of Urbino, built where the church of S. Maria in Castello originally stood from 1474 onwards, was only completed in 1604 with the construction of the dome (with octahedral base) by Muzio Oddi. The violent earthquake in 1781 and the incorrect building methods were fatal for the Dome which collapsed in 1789.

G. Valadier was given the task of repairing the Cathedral and of completely reconstructing the Dome, the drum and the four arches at its base. The architect built a massive drum made up of eight buttresses interconnected by masonry arches, and placed on it a simple canopy dome. This last addition has a thickness ranging from 115cm at the base to 50cm at the top, an internal diameter of 13m and a height from the base of the dome of 8.30m (Fig. 1). From the extrados eight ribs jut outwards, which are 30cm long. They are positioned to correspond with the eight buttresses of the drum. At the intrados there is a plaster lacunar, anchored to the canopy with iron hooks.

Over the whole surface of the intrados there are meridian cracks positioned to correspond with the places where the parallel rings join the meridian ribs of the lacunar (Fig. 2).

An initial static analysis has been carried out by using the analytical method evaluating the effects of the dome's self-weight, of the lantern weight and of the hoop at the base, but it has been verified that one cannot attribute the state of failure to any of these load conditions. Therefore, one needs to use the F.E. method. With this method one is able to follow the real geometry of the structure considering the presence of elements such

fig.1

fig.2

as ribs, and to evaluate the effects of all the possible load types, including the thermal loads. The results obtained with the analytical method have not been wasted, as they have been used to verify the reliability of the F.E. model.

Analytical Method

We have examined the individual dome (without the drum) and have considered it to be thick. Analyses have been carried out using the approximate elastic treatment of Geckeler. We have considered an equivalent spherical dome without the hole at the top having elastic modulus $E = 0.5E + 07KPa$, Poissons ratio $v = 0.2$, masonry specific weight $\tau m = 18 \ KNm - 3$, equivalent radius $R = 6.90m$ and medium equivalent thickness $h = 0.70m$ (calculated considering the weight of the spherical equivalent canopy to be equal to the one of the real dome, opened at the top).

The angle of the wave length is $88.12°$. For this reason the bending stresses influence the whole dome (this confirms that the dome is thick), even though they are only significant in an area of about $40°$ (further values are smaller than 4% of of the maximum ones). The results obtained are to be considered acceptable only for the first $45° - 60°$ from the base upwards because the hole at the top has been omitted.

Static schemes

We have considered the following constraint conditions for the dome:
    a - dome with rollers at the base
    b - dome with slides at the base
The real constraint is in between these two limit conditions.

Loading conditions

We have considered the following loading conditions:
    a - the masonry self-weight (total weight $W = 3869.04 \ KN$)
    b - the reference weight of the lantern $P = 235.6 \ KN$ (real weight $Q = 1.472P$)
    c - the effect of the hoop no° 1, positioned at the level of the base and stretched to 100 KN (reference stretch).

Results

When examining tables 1 and 2 we find that there are no appreciable differences between the two static schemes referring to the tensional and deforming state caused by the self weight and by the lantern weight. Hoop n° 1, however, produces different results in the two cases.

F.E. Method

The twenty years experience of CRIS and the results obtained by Chiarugi, Fanelli and Giuseppetti [1] in the case of the Brunelleschi Dome in Florence, represent an indisputable guarantee of the validity of the F.E. method in simulation of the behaviour of large-scale structures. For this reason we have applied such a method to the Urbino Cathedral using the calculation code FIESTA [2].

Mathematical models

Reference has been made to an ideal dome obtained by regularizing the geometry of the real one. The ovalization present was overlooked and the lacunars have been considered non structural elements. The external ribs, suitably regularized, have been considered. The perfect symmetry of the geometry and of the loading conditions has allowed us to limit the study to an eighth of the dome (one could also consider only one sixteenth of the structure). To this section ideal mechanical features have been attributed, such as: the solid is elastic, homogeneous, and isotropic without cracks. We have assumed the elastic modulus $E = 0.5 - E + 07 \, KPa$, Poisson's ratio $v = 0.2$, thermal expansion coefficient $\alpha = 0.8E - 05$ and density $dm = 1.8tm^{-3}$. Two different F.E. mathematical models have been studied: the simplified and the complete model.

The simplified model is limited to the dome (Fig. 5), it includes 130 elements of the hexahedron and pentahedron type and has 901 nodes. Along the two vertical planes at $45°$ which determine the eighth of the dome constraints are placed which respect the conditions of symmetry (horizontal displacements zero in the direction normal to the vertical plane). Rollers are put at the base in each node which, impeding the vertical movements and leaving free the horizontal ones, work globally as radial slides.

The complete model includes, apart from the dome itself, the drum, which is made up of a top ring inserted in eight vertical buttresses fixed at the base and connected with masonry arches. In this way, a more refined mesh is defined (Fig. 6) including 216 elements, of the hexahedron and pentahedron types, which have 1435 nodes. The constraints applied to it are perfect joint supports at the nodes of the buttress base, (in addition to those which respect the conditions of symmetry along each one of the two vertical planes at $45°$ defining the eighth of the structure analysed.)

Loading Conditions

On both models, thought to be non cracked, the effects of the following loading conditions have been studied:

a - SELF WEIGHT - not considering the weight of the lacunars and of the plaster coat we have a total weight of 483.63 KN for the first model and 1181.5KN for the second one. If we want to consider the weight of the plaster coat and the lute which forms the lacunars we may, in the first approximation, multiply the results obtained by the ratio 1.113;

b - LANTERN WEIGHT - a reference weight has been introduced which is 1.472 times inferior to the real one, corresponding to a uniform vertical pressure of 100 KPa;

c - FOUR HOOPS - to each hoop (table 3), considered to be working on its own, a reference stretch force of 100 KN has been applied. Hoop n° 1 is stretched at 240 KN and, therefore, the results relative to it are to be multiplied by 2.4. But with regard to the other hoops, it is not possible to know the "in situ" stretch in advance;

d - THERMAL LOADS - a "winter-type" thermal load has been applied, choosing an extrados temperature of $-2°C$ and an intrados temperature of $+18°C$, and assuming a linear variation through the thickness of the masonry mass. This thermal distribution is realistic enough for the dome, considering its modest thickness, but is less true for the massive drum. Therefore we can only consider the order of the results obtained to be

TAB.1: Analytic method - dome with rollers
```
-----------------------------------------------------------------------------
```

		Sm (KN/m)	Sp (KN/m)	Qm (KN/m)	S (KN/m)	Mm (KNm/m)	Mp (KNm/m)	X (m)	α (rad)
∅=27	s.w.	-46.17	-30.59	---	-40.77	---	---	-1.97E-05	2.57E-05
	l.w.	-24.66	24.66	---	-21.77	---	---	2.74E-05	----
	h.1	-0.22	0.40	0.12	-0.25	0.28	0.14	3.71E-07	2.06E-06
∅=47	s.w.	-52.09	-6.09	---	-34.85	---	---	6.33E-06	4.06E-05
	l.w.	-9.84	9.84	---	-6.58	---	---	1.73E-05	----
	h.1	0.74	5.85	-0.82	1.10	-0.17	0.08	8.57E-06	5.85E-06
∅=67	s.w.	-62.51	28.54	---	-24.43	---	---	7.43E-05	5.03E-05
	l.w.	-6.41	6.41	---	-2.51	---	---	1.40E-05	----
	h.1	1.27	1.63	-3.00	3.26	-4.72	-1.17	2.96E-06	-2.48E-05
∅=87	s.w.	-82.62	78.07	---	-4.32	---	---	1.86E-05	5.46E-05
	l.w.	-5.45	5.45	---	-0.28	---	---	1.29E-05	----
	h.1	-0.47	-93.48	8.94	-8.95	-4.19	-0.99	-1.84E-04	-1.33E-04

TAB.2: Analytic method - dome with slides
```
-----------------------------------------------------------------------------
```

		Sm (KN/m)	Sp (KN/m)	Qm (KN/m)	S (KN/m)	Mm (KNm/m)	Mp (KNm/m)	X (m)	α (rad)
∅=27	s.w.	-46.29	-30.78	-0.06	-40.91	0.07	0.02	-1.99E-05	2.58E-05
	l.w.	-24.66	24.66	---	-21.77	---	---	2.74E-05	----
	h.1	0.09	0.88	-0.05	0.10	0.10	0.08	8.15E-07	1.59E-06
∅=47	s.w.	-52.05	-4.77	-0.41	-34.80	0.20	0.09	8.26E-06	4.33E-05
	l.w.	-9.84	9.84	---	-6.58	---	---	1.73E-05	----
	h.1	0.64	2.50	-0.71	0.96	-0.69	-0.16	3.67E-06	-9.88E-07
∅=67	s.w.	-62.05	33.37	-1.10	-23.23	-0.86	-0.17	8.31E-05	5.11E-05
	l.w.	-6.41	6.41	---	-2.51	---	---	1.40E-05	----
	h.1	0.08	-10.63	-0.20	0.22	-2.53	0.75	-1.93E-05	-2.66E-05
∅=87	s.w.	-82.56	63.68	-0.98	-3.34	-4.62	-0.97	1.57E-04	1.16E-05
	l.w.	-5.45	5.45	---	-0.28	---	---	1.29E-05	----
	h.1	-0.60	-56.91	11.45	-11.45	7.549	1.48	-1.12E-04	-2.38E-05

Sm - Sp = meridian - parallel extensional force (positive if of traction)
Qm   = transverse shear force
Mm - Mp = meridian - parallel bending moment (positive if streches the internal fibres)
X   = radial displacement (positive if centrifugal)
α   = rotation (positive if streches the internal fibres)

TAB.3
```
------------------------------------------------------
```

	x(m)	z(m)	∅	
hoop 1	7.60	0.05	90°	strands (240KN)
hoop 2	6.70	2.90	67°	square iron hoop 45x45
hoop 3	6.00	4.46	54°	flat iron hoop 80x20
hoop 4	4.88	5.88	41°	flat iron hoop 80x20

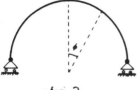

fig. 3

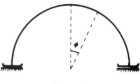

fig. 4

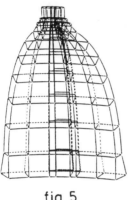

fig. 5

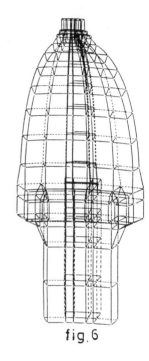

fig. 6

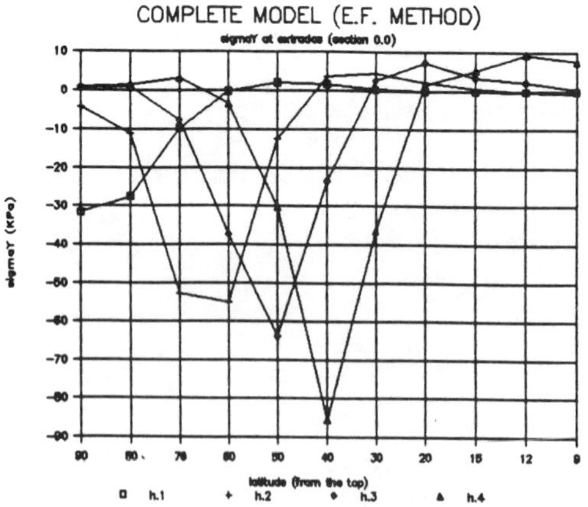

COMPLETE MODEL (E.F. METHOD)
sigmaY at extrados (section 0.0)
sigmaY (KPa)
10
0
-10
-20
-30
-40
-50
-60
-70
-80
-90
90
80
70
60
50
40
30
20
15
12
9
latitude (from the top)
h.1
h.2
h.3
h.4

fig. 7

correct.

Results

We can distinguish those relative to the displacements and those relative to the stresses.

Displacements

It is necessary to say first that the values obtained with the elastic linear analysis are certainly inferior to the real ones, because of the non linear behaviour of the masonry and of viscosity. Under the self-weight the dome dilates in the area of $50^o < \theta < 90^o$ which corresponds to the zone where, according to membrane theory, parallel traction exists. The simplified model presents (table 4) radial displacements at the base, three times larger than those of the complete model, without taking into consideration the "hoop effect" of the drum. As we go towards the top the differences decrease, diminishing the local effect of the different constraints. The base section presents a clock-wise rotation of $0.286E - 05$ rad (evaluated for $\theta = 19.5^o$ in the complete model). The lantern, instead, produces effects which are practically identical in the two models: the local effect of the different constraint damps in the first 20° from the base. Hoop no^o 1, because of its position, causes different effects in the two models up to half way up the dome, while hoops no^o 2-3-4 provide essentially the same ones (table 5). Finally the thermal variations cause effects in both of the models which are nearly one order superior to those produced by the other load conditions. The result, even though inaccurate, considering the approximation of the thermal distribution through the masonry, must anyway make us reflect on the importance of the thermal loads, which are often completely neglected by designers.

Stresses

With reference to the only complete model the following stresses (positive if in traction and expressed in KPa) have been calculated for various loading combinations (tables 6,7,8):
- σ_z, representative of the meridian state of stress, in the meridian sections 0.0^o and 8.5^o;
- σ_y, representative of the parallel state of stress, in meridian section 0.0.

In this way we have deduced that:

- as evident from the analytical method, the effect of the hoops does not dump very quickly (Fig. 7);
- comparing the σ_z in the points of the meridian section 0.0^o, which is found on the key of the arches of the drum, with those in the corresponding points of the meridian section 8.5^o, placed on the buttress (left side), they join at the base of the first minor values. This fact indicates that a natural arch effect (not measurable with traditional methods) begins above the arches of the drum;
- the lantern is harmful for the global static behaviour, causing some parallel tractions over the whole surface of the extrados;
- in winter there are parallel and meridian traction stresses over the whole extrados surface the first 2-3 times greater than the second one. If one extrapolates that the same happens in summer on the surface of the intrados, the causes of the cracking of the internal lacunars can soon be found. With future studies in which a thermal "summer load"

TAB.4: E.F. method - radial displacements (m)

		s.w.	l.w.	h.1
θ = 15°	E.F.c	-0.279353E-04	0.222876E-05	0.117914E-07
	E.F.s	-0.279733E-04	0.223097E-05	-0.108682E-07
θ = 30°	E.F.c	-0.247853E-04	0.225255E-04	0.654407E-06
	E.F.s	-0.262637E-04	0.224459E-04	0.140404E-05
θ = 50°	E.F.c	0.143004E-04	0.185792E-04	0.750644E-06
	E.F.s	0.126888E-04	0.183760E-04	0.257590E-05
θ = 70°	E.F.c	0.431216E-04	0.935474E-05	-0.167000E-04
	E.F.s	0.779059E-04	0.111406E-04	-0.356831E-04
θ = 90°	E.F.c	0.325651E-04	0.355994E-05	-0.330150E-04
	E.F.s	0.106533E-03	0.925618E-05	-0.881391E-04

TAB.5: E.F. method - radial displacements (m)

		hoop 2	hoop 3	hoop 4	T.load
Xmin	E.F.c	-0.60895E-04	-0.62950E-04	-0.64526E-04	-0.51842E-03
	E.F.s	-0.59760E-04	-0.62871E-04	-0.64558E-04	-0.58521E-03
Xmax	E.F.c	0.27927E-05	0.39657E-05	0.41826E-05	0.19902E-03
	E.F.s	0.27670E-05	0.39623E-05	0.41857E-05	0.27125E-04

TAB.6: E.F. method - σz (KPa) in section θ = 0.0° of complete model

		s.w.	l.w.	h.1	h.2	h.3	h.4	T.1	S1	S1t	S2	S2t	S3	S3t
θ = 15°	extr.	-8	-17	0	0	0	2	63	-34	29	-35	29	-35	28
	intr.	-6	-30	0	0	-1	-8	-156	-52	-208	-51	-208	-51	-207
θ = 30°	extr.	-27	0	0	0	4	13	164	-30	134	-30	133	-30	134
	intr.	-23	-26	0	-2	-7	-5	-199	-64	-262	-63	-262	-69	-267
θ = 50°	extr.	-44	-5	2	11	-17	-5	306	-56	250	-52	254	-25	282
	intr.	-51	-11	-3	-9	34	-19	-360	-72	-432	-79	-439	-102	-462
θ = 70°	extr.	-43	-6	6	-57	19	9	451	-57	393	-43	408	-182	269
	intr.	-102	-8	-5	43	-17	-8	-528	-126	-654	-137	-666	-32	-561
θ = 90°	extr.	-32	-3	-22	9	2	0	291	-39	252	-92	200	-69	222
	intr.	-43	-2	16	-11	-2	0	-229	-51	-281	-13	-243	-39	-269

TAB.7: E.F. method - σz (KPa) in section θ = 8.5° of complete model

		s.w.	l.w.	h.1	h.2	h.3	h.4	T.1	S1	S1t	S2	S2t	S3	S3t
θ = 15°	extr.	-9	-18	0	0	0	2	68	-37	32	-37	32	-37	31
	intr.	-6	-30	0	0	-2	-8	-155	-51	-206	-51	-206	-50	-205
θ = 30°	extr.	-26	0	0	0	4	11	156	-29	128	-29	127	-29	128
	intr.	-24	-26	0	-2	-7	-3	-192	-64	-256	-64	-256	-70	-262
θ = 50°	extr.	-44	-5	2	11	-16	-5	299	-56	242	-52	247	-26	272
	intr.	-51	-11	-3	-9	33	-19	-361	-73	-434	-80	-441	-101	-462
θ = 70°	extr.	-48	-7	6	-53	17	9	444	-63	381	-49	395	-179	265
	intr.	-105	-8	-4	42	-16	-8	-536	-129	-664	-139	-675	-37	-573
θ = 90°	extr.	-47	-3	-21	9	2	0	280	-57	223	-106	174	-86	195
	intr.	-57	-3	16	-11	-3	0	-353	-67	-420	-29	-381	-56	-409

TAB.8: E.F. method - ʃy (KPa) in section θ = 0.0° of complete model

		s.w.	l.w.	h.1	h.2	h.3	h.4	T.1	S1	S1t	S2	S2t	S3	S3t
θ = 15°	extr.	-59	-44	0	1	3	5	427	-130	297	-130	297	-129	298
	intr.	-82	-9	0	3	6	-11	-489	-104	-593	-104	-593	-95	-585
θ = 30°	extr.	-58	21	0	4	3	-36	556	-33	523	-32	524	-21	535
	intr.	-45	17	1	1	-16	-60	-581	-25	-606	-22	-603	-19	-599
θ = 50°	extr.	-6	15	2	-13	-64	-30	533	15	548	20	553	-11	522
	intr.	-3	15	-1	-25	-43	-29	-575	18	-557	16	-558	-44	-619
θ = 70°	extr.	23	6	-10	-53	-8	3	601	34	635	10	612	-118	484
	intr.	-2	5	-14	-23	-16	-2	-488	6	-482	-29	-517	-86	-573
θ = 90°	extr.	6	1	-32	-4	1	1	678	9	687	-67	611	-78	600
	intr.	-8	1	-21	-10	-1	1	-575	-7	-582	-57	-632	-82	-657

S1 = 1.113s.w.+1.472l.w.   S1t = S1 + T.1   S2 = S1 + 2.4h.1   S2t = S2 + d.T
S3 = S2 + 2.43h.2   S3t = S3 + T.1

TAB.9: Sm (KN/m)

		E.F.c	E.F.s		Analytic-r.		Analytic - s.		
		val.	val.	E.F.c%	val	E.F.c%	val	E.F.c%	E.F.s%
θ = 27°	s.w.	-25.31	-25.25	-0.23%	-46.17	82.42%	-46.29	82.90%	83.32%
	l.w.	-13.35	-13.35	-0.03%	-24.65	84.68%	-24.65	84.68%	84.74%
	h.1	-0.03	-0.08	148.39%	-0.22	612.90%	0.09	-396.77%	-219.48%
θ = 47°	s.w.	-35.89	-36.52	1.77%	-52.09	45.14%	-52.05	45.04%	42.51%
	l.w.	-7.59	-7.62	0.38%	-9.84	29.58%	-9.84	29.58%	29.09%
	h.1	0.11	0.24	108.77%	0.74	546.49%	0.64	464.91%	170.59%
θ = 67°	s.w.	-48.41	-51.43	6.24%	-62.51	29.13%	-62.05	28.16%	20.64%
	l.w.	-5.18	-5.33	2.80%	-6.41	23.73%	-6.41	23.73%	20.36%
	h.1	-0.44	-0.77	75.34%	1.27	-390.41%	0.09	-119.41%	-111.07%
θ = 87°	s.w.	-50.24	-76.37	52.01%	-82.62	64.43%	-82.56	64.33%	8.10%
	l.w.	-3.63	-4.83	32.88%	-5.45	49.94%	-5.45	49.94%	12.84%
	h.1	-0.84	0.84	-199.76%	-0.47	-43.90%	-0.60	-28.35%	-171.82%

TAB.10: Sp (KN/m)

		E.F.c	E.F.s		Analytic-r.		Analytic- s.		
		val.	val.	E.F.c%	val	E.F.c%	val	E.F.c%	E.F.s%
θ = 27°	s.w.	-22.12	-22.89	3.45%	-30.59	38.28%	-30.78	39.13%	34.49%
	l.w.	8.22	8.18	-0.50%	24.65	200.01%	24.65	200.01%	200.52%
	h.1	0.34	0.73	113.37%	0.40	16.57%	0.88	156.10%	20.03%
θ = 47°	s.w.	-4.04	-4.67	15.31%	-6.09	50.56%	-4.77	17.98%	2.32%
	l.w.	8.46	8.37	-1.02%	9.84	16.34%	9.84	16.34%	17.54%
	h.1	0.46	1.43	206.67%	5.85	1158.28%	2.50	438.28%	75.53%
θ = 67°	s.w.	7.38	22.53	205.35%	28.54	286.88%	33.38	352.37%	48.15%
	l.w.	4.04	4.80	18.80%	6.41	58.82%	6.41	58.82%	33.69%
	h.1	-5.81	-12.24	110.71%	1.63	-128.05%	-10.63	83.06%	-13.12%
θ = 87°	s.w.	-5.61	59.27	-1156.69%	78.07	-1491.80%	63.68	-1235.25%	7.43%
	l.w.	1.24	5.62	353.31%	5.45	339.44%	5.45	339.44%	-3.06%
	h.1	-24.24	-61.86	155.21%	-93.48	285.70%	-56.91	134.81%	-7.99%

will be directly considered and the correct values of boundary temperature taken, we will be able to simulate the real behaviour of the dome and it will be possible to calibrate the model itself by measuring the size of the cracks.
- the hoops cannot significantly reduce the traction caused by the variations in temperature if they are working separately. On the other hand a beneficial effect can be achieved by the first three hoops working together. An excessive stretch (pretensioning technique) of the hoops could, however, produce undesirable effects in normal thermal conditions.

Comparisons

In tables 9 and 10, the values of Sm and Sp evaluated with the different methods are indicated.

From the comparison one can see that considering the self-weight:
- the static scheme with rollers at the base is less precise than the one with slides, which, in turn, gives results of the same order as those furnished by the F.E. method (simplified model);
- the simplified model (F.E. method) gives results which are similar to those of the complete model (F.E. method), except at the base of the dome where the effects of the different degree of constraint has no room to be cancelled by the dumping action of the parallel rings.

Regarding the lantern weight:
- the two analytical methods give the same results when the constraints on the present loading condition are considered. These results coincide with those of the F.E. method for the simplified model;
- the F.E. method for the simplified model provides results which are practically identical to those of the corresponding method for the complete model, except in the proximity to the base for the reasons which have already been mentioned.

Regarding hoop no^o 1, the different methods provide very different values, while still satisfying the above mentioned order of precision.

Conclusions

From the static analysis carried out it has been possible to prove that:
- thermal loads represent a load condition which is very important for domes of this type. In fact the different summer temperature between intrados and extrados surfaces, causing parallel traction stresses 2-3 times greater than those of the meridian, is the principal cause of the present meridian cracks. So it is not correct to neglect their effects as this results in values comparable to the other loading conditions commonly considered, such as the self-weight of the canopy, the lantern weight and the differential subsidence;
- the simplified calculus scheme, which leaves out the effect of the drum, is correct above the parallel placed at 20° from the base regarding the case of self-weight, the lantern weight, hoops no^o 2-3-4 and the thermal loads, while it gives only results of a similar order when the effect of hoop no^o 1 is considered;
- the analytical method with slides at the base proves to be reliable enough regarding the simplified F.E. model in the first 60° from the base, that is, the whole area where the effect of the hole at the top is not felt;
- the analytical method with rollers at the base proves to be less reliable than that with slides at the base.

We may conclude that the analytical method, even if it provides valid help in obtaining the right order of values, is not as accurate as the complete F.E. method, if one wishes to calculate the effects of particular loading conditions (e.g. thermal loads), and of special elements such as "eyes", ribs, buttresses and arches, which were usual in the architectural works of the past.

References

1. A. Chiarugi, M. Fanelli, G. Giusieppetti, Analysis of Brunelleshi- type dome including thermal loads, IABSE Symposium: Strengthening of Building Structures, Venezia, September 29-30, 1983.

2. FIESTA is an heirarchical F.E. code by ISMES (Bergamo).

3. I. Betti, Cupole in muratura: metodologie di calcolo confronti e proposte, graduation thesis, University of Ancona, 1988.

An Analytical Model for Axisymmetric Structures using the Finite Element Method

C. Ignatakis and E. Stavrakakis

Department of Civil Engineering, Aristotle University of Thessaloniki, 540 06 Thessaloniki, Greece

ABSTRACT

An analytical model is presented for the calculation of the stress-strain distribution and the creation and propagation of cracking in meridian levels of axisymmetric structures under axisymmetric loading. The model includes triangular finite elements whose behavior may be governed by either of the following linearly elastic constitutive laws: (a)Axisymmetric isotropic. (b)Axisymmetric anisotropic stratified. (c)Plain stress isotropic. (d)Uniaxially stressed material. In this way the following structural elements can be represented accordingly: (a)Shell. (b)Embedded tierods. (c) Piers or elements of the types (a) and (b) meridionally cracked. (d)Non embedded external tierods. Finally comparative results of analyses of a Byzantine dome are given. In these results the influence of the cracking criterion adopted is apparent.

INTRODUCTION

The main characteristic of the response of axisymmetric structures under axisymmetric loading is that any radial displacement u_r automatically induces a strain in the circumferential direction $\varepsilon_\theta = u_r/r$ and, as the stresses in this direction are certainly non-zero, this fourth component of strain and of the associated stress has to be considered. The problem is well known and the finite element method has been successfully used to solve it (Zienkiewicz[1]).

Masonry domes and drums are typical axisymmetric structural forms which usually have the following morphological and mechanical characteristics:
(a) A ring of windows cuts away the structure forming inclined or vertical isolated piers located at the vertices of a regular polygon.
(b) Wooden or metal tierods run across the windows having embedded ends in the masonry and connecting adjacent piers to each other, forming a ring.
(c) Circumferential tension is developed in the lower parts and compression is developed in the higher parts of the dome.
(d) The tensile strength of the masonry is small(almost non tension material).
(e) Cracking often appears in the lower parts of the dome in meridian levels due to dead loads in combination (or not) with seismic loads.

(f) Compression stresses, relatively small compared to the strength of the masonry, are developed under service loads, so that the assumption of linear behavior of the material is almost accurate.
(g) Beyond the filling of the cracks with mortar injections, addition of an external metal tierod appropriately prestressed at the appropriate level is a usual strengthening method.

An analytical model representing successfully the above mentioned characteristics of the domed structures is indispensable for the interpretation of the damage and for the dimensioning of any interventions.

PRESENTATION OF THE ANALYTICAL MODEL

The model does not have the scope to represent the microscopic behavior of the masonry but it aims to determine the stress-strain distribution and the cracking propagation in meridian levels of a complete axisymmetric structure, using the finite element method. The uncracked masonry is considered to be a homogeneous and isotropic material with average linearly elastic behavior.

Geometry of the model
The model   consists   of triangular ring finite elements. The element grid is automatically created given the equations of the inner and outer generatrix curves defining the structure(see example,Fig.2). The addition of new nodes or elements is possible in any position. An automatic renumbering of the nodes and the unknowns is then performed.

Loading
The model can accept concentrated loads at the nodes. Mass (self-weight) loads are automatically transformed to concentrated loads given the density of the material. Roof cover loads are also automatically transformed to concentrated loads, given the density of the material and the equation of the outer generatrix curve defining the roof.

Elements library-Constitutive laws
The elements library of the model includes four types of ring triangular axisymmetric finite elements to represent as closely as possible the specific characteristics of each member of the structure.

Axisymmetric isotropic material
It is used for the uncracked regions of the masonry. It has the following constitutive law:

$$\bar{\sigma} = \bar{D} \cdot \bar{\varepsilon} \tag{1a}$$

$$
\begin{vmatrix} \sigma_z \\ \sigma_r \\ \sigma_\theta \\ \tau_{zr} \end{vmatrix}
= \frac{E(1-v)}{(1+v)(1-2v)} *
\begin{vmatrix}
1 & v/(1-v) & v(1-v) & \emptyset \\
 & 1 & v(1-v) & \emptyset \\
\text{symmetric} & & 1 & \emptyset \\
 & & & (1-2v)/(1-v)/2
\end{vmatrix}
*
\begin{vmatrix} \varepsilon_z \\ \varepsilon_r \\ \varepsilon_\theta \\ v_{zr} \end{vmatrix}
\tag{1b}
$$

Axisymmetric anisotropic (stratified) material
It is used for the representation of wooden tierods with meridian level of stratification. In the

constitutive law the modulus of the elasticity and the Poisson's ratio have different values in the circumferential and the meridian directions (Zienkiewicz[1]).

Plain stress isotropic material   It is used to represent the cracked regions of the masonry and the cut off or corroded embedded tierods. It has the following constitutive law:

$$
\begin{vmatrix} \sigma_z \\ \sigma_r \\ \sigma_\theta \\ \tau_{zr} \end{vmatrix} = \frac{E}{1-v^2} * \begin{vmatrix} 1 & v & \emptyset & \emptyset \\ & 1 & \emptyset & \emptyset \\ \text{symmetric} & & \emptyset & \emptyset \\ & & & (1-v)/2 \end{vmatrix} * \begin{vmatrix} \varepsilon_z \\ \varepsilon_r \\ \varepsilon_\theta \\ V_{zr} \end{vmatrix} \tag{2}
$$

The zero values of the third column and row indicate the inability of the material to resist circumferential stresses.

This type of element can also simulate the openings between piers. The piers are actually almost under plane stress in meridian levels. Consequently the piers can be represented by an axisymmetric drum of an equivalent thickness. The thickness can be calculated from the equation of the stiffnes of an individual pier with the stiffness of the adjacent part of the drum(Fig.2). An appropriate modification of the material density is also required in order to equate the self-weight of the model with the self-weight of the actual structure. Using the procedure described above, a macroscopic behavior of the pier can be derived. Integrating the stresses across the adjacent part of the drum, the total internal forces can be calculated in any level but the stress distribution in the cross-section is actually unknown.

Uniaxially stressed material   It is used to simulate non-embedded external tierods. It has the following constitutive law:

$$
\begin{vmatrix} \sigma_z \\ \sigma_r \\ \sigma_\theta \\ \tau_{zr} \end{vmatrix} = E * \begin{vmatrix} \emptyset & \emptyset & \emptyset & \emptyset \\ & \emptyset & \emptyset & \emptyset \\ \text{symmetric} & & 1 & \emptyset \\ & & & \emptyset \end{vmatrix} * \begin{vmatrix} \varepsilon_z \\ \varepsilon_r \\ \varepsilon_\theta \\ V_{zr} \end{vmatrix} \tag{3}
$$

It is obvious that this type of elements permits only normal circumferential stress to be developed.

Computational procedure-Meridional cracks
Loading A simple cracking criterion has been adopted in meridional level based on the circumferential tensile stress of the material. Application of the step-by-step loading technique is not necessary since a linear constitutive lawgoverns the stress-strain distribution. The procedure of determination and propagation of the cracks is the following:
i. The analysis of the structure is carried out under the total load and the stress distribution is determined.
ii. The value of the circumferential stress of each element of the types (a) and (b) is compared with the assumed tensile strength of the material.

If the stress developed is greater, the element is modified to type (c) cracked element.
iii. The cracked elements are stored in a file.

Steps i, ii and iii are repeated until no further crack occurs. Any instability in the computational procedure indicates tendency of the structure to collapse. The successive cracking cycles can give a picture of the cracking evolution.

Unloading In some cases an unloading stage, usually concerning the removal of the roof cover, is an intermediate stage of an intervention procedure. For this reason a criterion for crack closure has been adopted based on the value of the radial displacement. The computational procedure is the following:
i. The analysis of the cracked structure is carried out under the loads remaining after the unloading. The stress-strain distribution and the radial displacements of all the elements are determined. It is obvious that circumferential stress can not be developed in the cracked elements but, in general, a non-zero radial displacement appears.
ii. All the cracked elements which have negative radial displacements are assumed to reveal a tendency to close the cracks. From these elements only a few are selected, having the greater negative radial displacements, and are modified to type (a) uncracked elements. These elements are assumed to have a zero circumferential tensile strength ever since.
iii. The modified elements are stored in a file.

Steps i, ii and iii are repeated until no further cracking closure occurs. The successive cracking closure cycles give a picture of the closure evolution. It is worth to be stated that an attempt to modify all the cracked elements strikes against the fact that in some of them cracking occurs again during the next cycles.

A CASE STUDY

Comparative results of analyses of the central dome of St.Panteleimon church in Thessaloniki are presented. It is a small church built about seven centuries ago. The dome has a diameter of 5.80m, a total height of 4.80m, a drum height of 2.30m and it consists of an ellipsoid shell resting on piers at the vertices of a regular octagon(Fig.1)(9th Ephorate of Byzantine Antiquities[2]). A wooden tierod runs across the windows, intersecting the masonry piers and connecting them to each other. The tierod, having an original cross-section of almost 12x12cm, is today practically inactive because of heavy corrosion. The dome has a thickness of about 30cm and a roof cover of byzantine ceramic tiles lying on a mortar bed.

Model of the dome
In Fig.2 the finite element model and the general geometrical characteristics of the dome are shown. In table 1 the structural elements, the corresponding finite elements and the material properties are shown.

Pier simulation As mentioned above, the piers can be simulated by an axisymmetric drum of an equivalent thickness. Taking into account the cross-section of an individual pier shown in Fig.2 and equating its stiffness

Table 1. Structural and finite elements-Material properties

Structural element	Finite element type	$E_z=E_r$ GPa	E_θ GPa	$v_z=v_r$	v_θ	γ KN/m³
Shell	(a) Isotropic axisymmetric	1.5	1.5	0.19	0.19	18.0
Wooden tierod	(b) Stratified axisymmetric	1.0	10.0	0.20	0.20	6.0
Piers	(c) Isotropic plain stress	1.5	∅	0.19	∅	12.4
Meridionally cracked shell	-"-	1.5	∅	0.19	∅	18.0
Corroded wooden tierod	-"-	1.0	∅	0.20	∅	6.0

with the stiffness of one eighth of a drum, an equivalent thickness of 59cm has been derived.

Inner and outer generatrix curves of the dome   Using curve fitting and re-gression analysis techniques it was proved that the ellipsoid curves shown in Fig.2 are good estimations of the generatrix curves of the dome. The shell was divided in five zones of equal thickness and twenty zones of equal epicentral angle of 4.5°. The drum was divided in eight zones in the thickness direction and twenty zones in the height direction. The mo-del consists of 309 nodes and 520 triangular elements.

Analyses
In table 2 some results of the analyses are shown. Three analyses were carried out using different assumptions. In the first analysis no crack-ing criterion was adopted. It was also accepted that the wooden tierod is active. In the second analysis a cracking criterion was adopted. It was assumed that the masonry has zero circumferential tensile strength (non tension material). It was also accepted that the wooden tierod is still active. In the third analysis, in addition to the cracking criterion, it was assumed that the wooden tierod is inactive because of corrosion.

In Fig.3 the mean stresses distribution and the maximum radial dis-placement of the first analysis are shown. In Fig.4 and 5, in addition to mean stresses distribution and displacements, the successive cracking stages of the second and third analyses are shown. In general the results are in good agreement with the typical response of domed structures (see also Heyman[3] and Mainstone[4]).

From Fig.4 and from line 2 of table 2 it can be concluded that, if a cracking criterion is adopted, the tension zone, the radial displacements and the wooden tierod stress increase considerably. From Fig.5 and from line 3 of table 2 it can be concluded that, if the wooden tierod fails,

Table 2. Results of the analyses

Analysis	Tension zone epicentral angle	Cracking stages required	Number of cracked elements	Maximum radial displacements(mm)	Stress of wooden tierods(MPa)	Total horizontal thrust(KN)
1	25.5°	-	-	0.0871	0.28	33.4
2	42.7°	5	57,26,9,3,∅	0.1742	0.48	39.6
3	64.0°	4	16,7,2,∅	0.2821	-	76.0

the tension zone and the radial displacements become greater.

In Fig.3,4,5 the distribution of the vertical normal stresses of the piers base cross-section are shown. The more the cracking is intense the more the relevant resultant moves outwards.

CONCLUSIONS

The model presented is a simple, flexible and effective analytical tool for the analysis and the interpretation of the response of axisymmetric structures under axisymmetric loading. Crack pattern and stress distribution can also be determined. Cracked regions, embedded or external tierods and drums cut off by windows can be simulated. The linear elastic constitutive law is a realistic assumption for masonry structures because of the relatively small stresses developed under service loads.

REFERENCES

1. Zienkiewicz,O.C. The Finite Element Method in Engineering Science, McGraw-Hill, London, 1971.

2. 9th Ephorate of Byzantine Antiquities. Architectural and Structural Documentation of St.Panteleimon Church. 9th Ephorate of Byzantine Antiquities Archives, Thessaloniki, Greece.

3. Heyman,J. Statical Aspects of Masonry Vaults and Domes, pp.229-235, Proceedings of the Int.Symposium on Restoration of Byzantine and Post-Byzantine Monuments, Thessaloniki, Greece, 1985. 9th Ephorate of Byzantine Antiquities, Thessaloniki, 1986.

4. Mainstone,R.J. Masonry Vaulted and Domed Structures, with Special Reference to the Monuments of Thessaloniki, pp.237-248, Proceedings of the Int.Symposium on Restoration of Byzantine and Post-Byzantine Monuments, Thessaloniki, Greece, 1985. 9th Ephorate of Byzantine Antiquities, Thessaloniki, 1986.

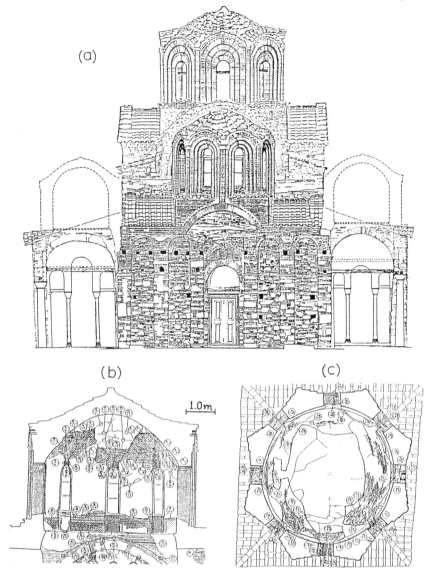

Figure 1.   Church of St. Panteleimon: (a) Western view. (b) Central Dome
elevation.   (c) Central Dome plan.

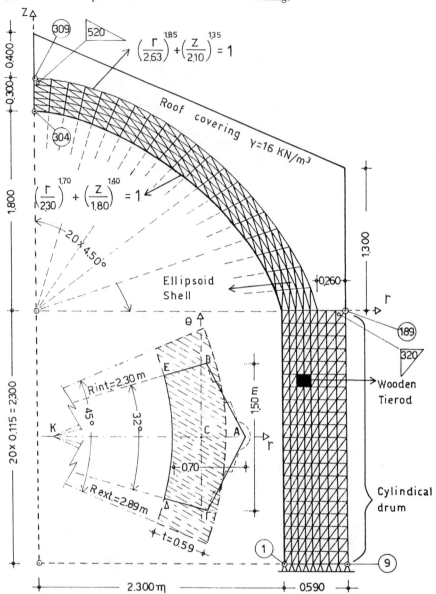

Figure 2.   Finite element model of the Central Dome.

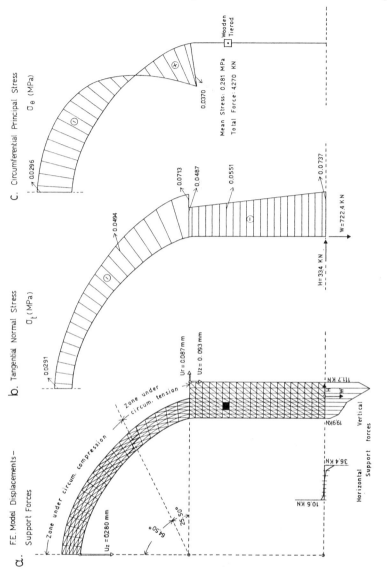

Figure 3. First Analysis: No cracking criterion adopted.

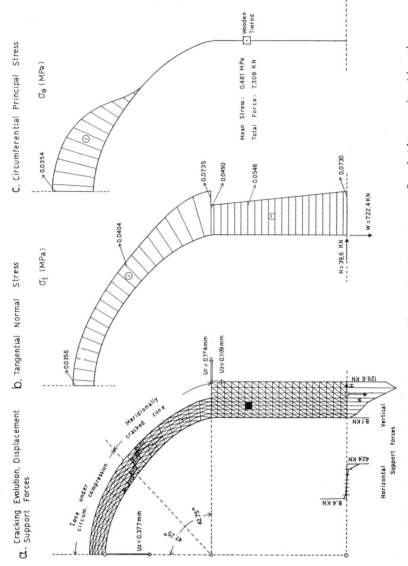

Figure 4.   Second Analysis: Cracking criterion: $\sigma_{\theta u} = \emptyset$. Active wooden tierod.

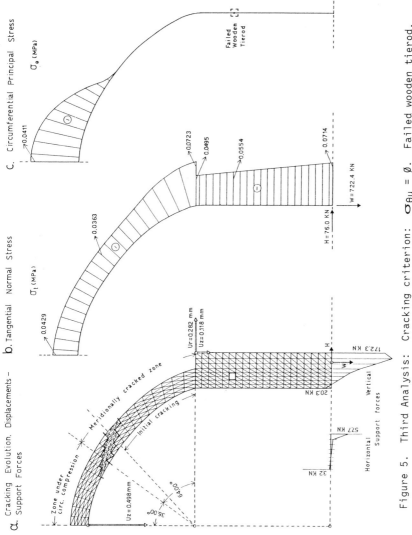

a. Cracking Evolution. Displacements – Support Forces

b. Tangential Normal Stress

c. Circumferential Principal Stress

Figure 5.   Third Analysis: Cracking criterion: $\sigma_{\theta u} = \emptyset$.   Failed wooden tierod.

Numerical Models for the Original Structure of the "Mole Antonelliana"

R. Arrigoni*, V. Nascè*, G. Pistone*, P.P. Strona**
*Dipartimento di Ingegneria Strutturale, Politecnico di
Torino, 10126 Torino, Italy
**Centro Ricerche FIAT, 10043 Orbassano, Italy

ABSTRACT

The Mole Antonelliana is one of most interesting historical buildings in
Turin particularly from its structural design point of view. It was built
during the second half of the 19th century. Some unexpected displacements
and cracks in the masonry, originated a large debate on its safety for se
veral years: lastly heavy concrete reinforcement was inserted about fifty
years ago. In view of the Antonelli Centenary Celebration (1989), we would
like to try to answer this question: if the fears concerning the structural safety expressed by eminent engineers were justified or not. With
this aim, the Mole's structure has been analyzed and a corresponding who
le FEM Model has been defined. In the paper, after the general overview
of the problems concerning the Mole Antonelliana structure and its histo
ry, the analysis models are explained and the most important obtained re
sults are shown.

INTRODUCTION

The Mole Antonelliana is one of most interesting historical buildings in
Turin particularly from the viewpoint of its structural design. It has a
square dome, whose structure is readily seen to be very thin, topped by
a spire, and it is the tallest masonry building in the world.
It was built during the second half of the 19th century.
The methods used at that time for the assessment of a building's safety
- with but a few exceptions in the case of steel constructions - were em
pirical and largely based on the similarity between the new building and
a previous one which had proved satisfactory and had served as an example.
In the extremely rare case of a totally new work, with no previous example or rule to go by, the assessment of safety could not be founded on
any objective criterion: the only warranty being the expertise, experien

ce and stature of the architect.

The same applied to the construction of the Mole Antonelliana until 1870, when some unexpected displacements and cracks in the masonry, probably due to the high level of the dome thrust and to unequal settlements of the pillars, happened during the construction and originated a large debate on its safety[1,2].

This debate went on for decades and saw the participation, both in Turin and in Milan, of some of the best known structural engineers of the time, including Curioni and Clericetti, Tatti, Mazzucchetti, Guidi, Panetti, Colonnetti, Giberti, Danusso, Albenga.

Lastly, about 50 years ago, reinforced concrete was lavishly added to the structure in order to strengthen it, and the issue of safety was settled once and for all.

However, there is no historical evidence of any static analysis and overall calculation of the structure having been performed, not even in our century and not even by those who designed the reinforcing structure, probably due to the complexity of the building.

As a result, there is one basic question still awaiting an answer: were the fears and the outcry about the safety of the original structure really justified? was it really necessary to provide such a large and suffocating concrete reinforcement?

Therefore, in view of the Antonelli Centenary Celebration (1989), we would like to try to answer the question.

ANALYTICAL MODEL

Model construction was preceded by an accurate survey of the Mole Antonelliana by F. Rosso which made it possible to identify the components affecting the building's structural behaviour. Based on this preliminary study, the position, structural type, material, dimensions and weight of all the load-bearing elements, or at any rate of all elements of significance in terms of weight, were recorded[3]. In order to obtain a picture in close keeping with the actual structure it was deemed necessary to perform additional measurements and observations, especially as to the size and type of some elements and the way they had been placed (workmanship, mutual connections, restraints, etc.).

Then a 3D Finite Element Model was defined in order to analyse the behaviour of the Mole Antonelliana from a statical point of view[4]. Only a quarter of the building was analysed by means of beam and shell elements and the required symmetry constraints were defined. As far as the properties of the materials were concerned, the $\sigma - \varepsilon$ curve was assumed to be linear and no-tension effects in the wall were neglected.

The foregoing approximations might seem considerable for a masonry building, but we believe that when dealing with a highly complex structure, such as the Mole Antonelliana, linear analysis should be viewed as the most suitable initial approach to gain an

insight into the fundamental aspects of structural behaviour. As a further
confirmation of this choice, it should be pointed out that:
- the prevailing stresses in the various building elements are compressive;
- various uncertainties still remain as to:
  . the morphology of the original structure, now largely concealed by
    the strenghtening structure of r.c.;
  . the construction methods and the damages to the building which oc-
    curred at the earliest stages;
  . the performance of constituent materials and the efficiency of the
    iron tie rods;
- linear analysis can serve as a starting point for subsequent, more so
  phisticated numerical models aimed mostly at clarifying local conditions.

The analysis performed on the basis of shell and beam elements made it
possible to work out a structural model in close keeping with Antonelli's original concept. Antonelli's intention, in fact, was to produce a
masonry building which might vie with the most daring contemporary at-
tainments in the field of steel constructions, then in full swing. This
is why, instead of the traditional continuous wall construction, Antonelli introduced veritable space frames of masonry, completed, where ne
cessary, by extremely thin ribbed shell structures (figs. 1 and 2).
In greater detail, the "Mole Antonelliana" can be subdivided into three
main parts:
- the bottom area, up to 25.65 m above ground, consisting of one-dimensional vertical members joined together by arches so as to obtain a
  dual-symmetry space frame, with panels formed at the various storeys
  and around the perimeter by vaults and walls, respectively. This portion has been analysed by means of beams reproducing the space frame;
- the dome proper, consisting of two 12 cm thick ribbed and mutually con
  nected shells, and culminating, at +81.27 above ground, in "the granite chamber" and the spire; this uppermost portion has been analysed
  by means of shells reproducing the two actual surfaces and respective
  connections;
- a central portion, the "tambour" conceived by Antonelli so that it
  would produce an impression of amazing lightness of the suspended "vol
  to" - the dome - in the eyes of a viewer looking up from the women's
  gallery (fig. 3); in this extremely complex portion, continuous surfaces and one-dimensional members play equally important roles: therefore it has been modelled by means of beams and shells.
Moreover, the model reproduces a number of peculiar items that are part
of the building, such as, for instance, metal tie rods with their connections to one another and to the structure, the huge granite corbels
at the dome's impost, etc.

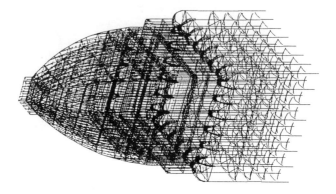

Fig. 2 - Analytical Model

Fig. 1 - A view of "Mole"

As for the software tools used, the analysis and the handling of model data and results were carried out with the aid of the general purpose Finite Element Code MSC-NASTRAN and the interactive pre/post-processor Code PATRAN.

The Quarter "Mole" mesh holds 4810 nodes, corresponding to approx. 28,000 degrees of freedom, and 2512 beam elements, alongside 4349 3/4 node shell elements.

Gravity load conditions have been analysed . Moreover, the effects due to a unit displacement imposed at the foot of the columns in the inter nal circle have been studied.

Alongside the main model, a few smaller models corresponding to diffe- rent construction stages, were also taken into account.

The FEM computations were performed at the CRAY X MP/48 of CINECA in Bologna: CPU time requested for each run was about 3.5 minutes.

The pre/post-processing phase was performed at the VAX 8700 of FIAT Re- search-Centre.

RESULTS

Since the primary aim of this investigation is to arrive at a sound histo rical judgement on the controversy on the stability of the Mole and the subsequent, much criticized, consolidation works, it is essential to a- nalyse the results obtained from the numerical model vis-à-vis the actual displacements and cracks which occurred during the building's life.

With this end in view, an examination of historical sources was carried out first of all, collecting a wealth of interesting information. These studies revealed important aspects of the actual behaviour of the struc- ture (e.g. through an examination of the temporal succession of the main damages observed and of contemporary debates on their origin and extent) and made it possible to identify factors which had a significant bearing on the overall static balance of the building (such as the decade long - 1869-1878 - interruption in the construction process).

Though in the presence of divided views as to the origin and seriousness, or the very existence, of some phenomena, historical research made it pos sible to ascertain a number of indisputable facts with good accuracy, thus laying the foundations for model checking.

It should also be pointed out that the functional behaviour of the "Mole" was substantially satisfactory: though it suffered from damages, until 1930 the building survived - with no consolidation works - despite the fact that in 1887 it had been affected by a rather severe earthquake.

Hence, the damages mentioned above should be viewed as signs of adapta- tion of the structure in the post-elastic field - noticeable ones, su- rely, but still within a context of overall equilibrium.

The most important instances were:
- the formation of cracks in the parabolic arches (+25.65 above ground);
- the noticeable bulging out of the dome at the impost;

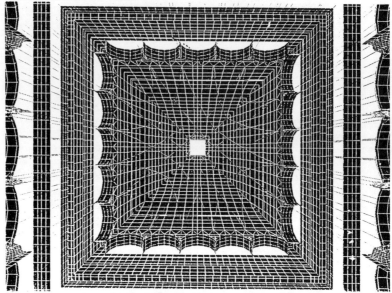

Fig. 3 - A view of the "volto" from women's gallery

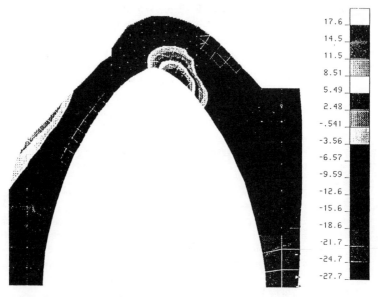

Fig. 5 - Stresses in a parabolic arch

- the slant of the columns connecting the parabolic arches to the dome;
- the cracks in the dome in the corner areas of the lower part.

Moreover, to provide an answer to questions arising from the initial re
sults obtained from the numerical model, we carried out additional checks
and measurements aimed at supplementing the data contained in the histo
rical sources; these concerned, in particular, the unrecoverable displa
cements that can at present be observed in the building's plan section
starting from +25 m above ground up to the level at which work was interrupted in 1869 (+70 m above ground).

Model analysis results made it possible to work out a description of the
overall behaviour of the structure and to obtain more detailed information on the stress paths in some structural elements of special importance within the context of the building's design concept.

Fig. 4 shows a view of the displacements in the Mole's cross section.
The following comments can be made:

- the displacements in the bottom area, beneath the parabolic arches (up
  to 25 m above ground level) are governed by the differential deformations between the columns making up the inner circle and the exterior
  columns; the former, being subjected to a state of stress over one and
  a half times higher than that affecting the latter, undergo considerable vertical deformations (about 3 cm). On the other hand, no considerable horizontal displacements are found to occur, owing to the marked
  stiffening effects of the vaults;
- the differential deformations in the columns result in a rigid rotation of the sturdy parabolic arches which are supported by them: as a
  result, in the areas immediately above, the model indicates the presence of inward horizontal displacements, which have been confirmed
  by our observations;
- the displacements of the dome and tambour are governed by horizontal
  thrusts of the dome and are particularly visible at the bottom in the
  central portions of the shells; these outward displacements, of considerable magnitude (eight to ten times greater than those mentioned in
  the previous paragraph) are also observed in the lower structures down
  to the flex point of the deformed shape, which is at any rate close to
  the extrados of the parabolic arches.

An analysis of the state of stress proved particularly interesting in the
case of the parabolic arches since in these elements considerable tensile stres
ses were seen to occur in areas where cracking had already been observed a century ago (Fig. 5).

Furthermore, an examination of the stresses in the horizontal corridors
at the base of the dome revealed a frame behaviour with tension peaks
in the inner corner areas, precisely where large vertical cracks appeared and can still be observed.

An analysis by means of partial models, simulating the succession of e-
vents occurring during the construction stages, has been found to be

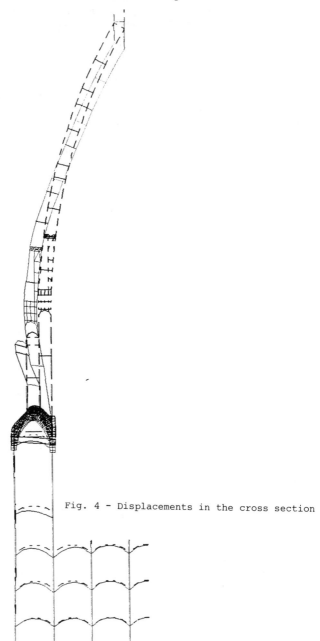

Fig. 4 - Displacements in the cross section

especially valuable to gain an understanding of the problems raised when construction was temporarily halted (1869-1878; a model that extends upwards to 70 m above ground).
The magnitude of the inward displacements in the upper portion of the dome (which is revealed by the structural analysis) demonstrates the fundamental role played by the propping (which Antonelli always denied).

CONCLUSIONS

The linear 3D FEM numerical model described in this report provides useful indications on the main displacements and lesions of the building and therefore can provide a correct interpretation of the fundamental aspects of the structure's overall behaviour, as recorded by the historical sources.
The information collected so far has made it possible to identify a number of interesting phenomena, which were not recognized before, such as: the initial displacements of the dome dating back to the early construction stage (before 1869); the differential displacement of the two columns at the impost of the parabolic arches (even apart from the concomitant settling of the foundation) and its considerable repercussions on the overall displacement of the building; the lack of congruence between the displacements actually observed in the dome at the impost and the corresponding state of stress in the tie rods.
The results obtained have also pointed out the possibility of carrying out more detailed analyses on specific aspects and portions of the building: e.g. accurate descriptions of the materials and geometrical models reproducing the actual structures as faithfully as possible.

REFERENCES

1. Roberto Gabetti, Problematica antonelliana, Atti e Rassegna Tecnica della Società degli Ingegneri ed Architetti in Torino, n. 6, 1962.

2. Franco Rosso, Alessandro Antonelli e la Mole di Torino, Stampatori, Torino, 1977.

3. Stefano Aimone Prina, Indagine statica sulla struttura originaria del Tempio Israelitico di Torino, Tesi di Laurea A.A. 1986-1987, Politecnico di Torino, Torino.

4. Roberta Arrigoni, Analisi numerica della struttura originaria della Mole Antonelliana, Tesi di Laurea A.A. 1987-1988, Politecnico di Torino, Torino.

Design of Interventions in Domes. The Importance of Consideration of Cracking

C. Ignatakis, K. Stylianidis and E. Stavrakakis
Department of Civil Engineering, Aristotle University of Thessaloniki, 540 06 Thessaloniki, Greece

ABSTRACT

The main morphological and structural characteristics of the Byzantine Domes are described in brief. Their behavior and typical damages under vertical and seismic loads are also presented. The usual repair and strengthening techniques are summarised. Two comparative analyses of the intervention procedure in the central dome of St.Panteleimon Church in Thessaloniki are finally discussed. It is confirmed that a phase by phase analysis, following the corresponding intervention sequence, is needed. Cracking consideration seems to be the most significant factor affecting the results. If the cracking is ignored,considerable alterations appear in the stress-strain distribution.

INTRODUCTION-THE BYZANTINE DOME

The most significant monuments of the Byzantine Architecture existing to-day are the Churches and the Defence Walls. The Churches,especially, have great interest not only for the Archaeologists and the Architects but for the Structural Engineers as well. Many structural forms have been developed in this period beginning from the imposing low domed Hagia Sophia, Konstantinoples and terminating to the small and elegant churches of the Period of Paleologi. These churches are characterized by their specific dome shape, usually called "byzantine".

Morphological characteristics

The byzantine dome is characterized by a high cylindrical shell usually cut away by eight windows forming an equal number of strong piers at the vertices of a regular octagon(Fig.1). A wooden tierod usually runs across the upper part of the openings, intersecting and connecting the piers to each other and forming a wooden ring. The drum supports a thick hemispherical-like dome. The heavy roof covering usually consists of ceramic tiles on a lime mortar bed.

Material characteristics

Masonry consists of shallow solid bricks (4 to 5cm thick) and crushed-tile lime mortar forming joints of the same order of magnitude thickness as the bricks. The tensile strength of the masonry is very small(2-5% of the compressive strength). Consequently the material can be considered as non tension material(Heyman [1]). The compressive stresses developed under service loads are low -one or two orders of magnitude lower- compared with the compressive strength of the masonry. Consequently the assumption of a linear constitutive law is a realistic consideration.

Behavior and typical damages under vertical loading
Under the thrusts of the shell the piers move outwards inducing circumferential tensile stresses at the lower parts of the shell. Cracks usually appear in meridional levels at the keys of the small arches at the upper sill of the openings(see Fig.1, cracks I). This cracking pattern is a typical characteristic of the byzantine domes. Tierods, if any, are usually capable of limiting the piers' movements and the resultant cracking.

Corrosion of timber or sliding of the embedded ends of the tierods in the piers causes additional cracking(see Fig.1, cracks II). The dome is still stable but it tends to function as a ring of arches all having the uncracked crown region of the shell as a common keystone(Mainstone [2]). In some cases horizontal cracking at the inner part of their bases also appears(see Fig.1, cracks III). The supporting system, usually consisting of arches and vaults resting on piers, inevitably moves away. Cracking becomes more intense and small hinge rotations appear at the top cross-sections of the piers(Heyman [1]).

Behavior and typical damages under seismic loading
If the cracking is limited, the shell behaves under seismic loads as a diaphragm because of its great stiffness, tending to equate the displacements of the tops of the piers. Bending moments at the piers are relatively small. Under these circumstances the dome reacts as effectively as possible.

If on the contrary the cracking is intense, the heavily cracked shell can not fully respond as a diaphragm because of considerable stiffness loss. Deformations are relatively large, out of phase response of piers is probable and bending moments at the piers bases become significant as they tend to behave like a free standing member. Hinging failures at the base cross-sections of the piers and local collapses of the shell are probable.

REMEDIES IN DOMES

Interventions in structures can be classified in two main categories:interventions of active and passive type. When an active type intervention is applied, forces are imposed on the structure to diminish or to reverse an undesirable stress-strain distribution. Prestressing is a typical example. This type of intervention is used to strengthen, rather than to repair a structure. On the contrary, passive types of intervention are usually used in almost non stressed but sometimes highly strained regions, such as cracked elements, aiming to improve a future response or to ensure a material continuity. As no forces are imposed and a local dismantling is a prerequisite for the recovery, these regions can be considered as zero stressed regions. The passive type interventions will be activated under future loading, usually seismic in regions of high seismicity. Mortar injections and timber replacements are typical examples of passive type interventions.

In a heavily damaged dome, a combination of passive and active type interventions seems to be preferable. Mortar injections can offer a material continuity, repair or replacement of corroded wooden tierod can offer an aesthetic restoration but both of them are unreliable, regarding the strengthening of the dome. Concrete skins are not recommended as a normal procedure. Addition of external, active type, reversible, corrosion resistant ties is an effective strengthening measure under these circumstances.

The optimum level for the placing of ties is the region around the base of the shell and the top of the drum where maximum circumferential tensile stresses are developed. Sometimes the cross-sectional shape of the piers can not permit the placing of ties at the top of the drum without local visible dismantling(Fig.2). In these cases the ties must be placed at the lowest possible level of the shell base. For the assessment of tie forces, the intervention procedure must be taken into account. Cracking consideration also significantly affects the magnitude of the forces to be imposed. A comparative example is presented in the next chapter.

INTERVENTIONS IN THE CENTRAL DOME OF ST.PANTELEIMON CHURCH OF THESSALONIKI

General characteristics of the church and the central dome

The St.Panteleimon Byzantine Church of Thessaloniki is a small and elegant church built during the early Period of Paleologi about seven centuries ago. In its initial form it had one central dome, one dome on the narthex and two more domes on the gallery. Today only the central dome and the dome on the narthex exist. The greatest part of the gallery, including the two domes, has already collapsed. The dome is at present heavily damaged. The damages have been intensified by the 1978 earthquake sequence.

The central dome is 4.80m high with a 5.80m diameter and it consists of an ellipsoid shell 0.30m thick, resting on piers at the vertices of a regular octagon(Fig.2). A wooden tierod runs across the upper part of the openings, intersecting and connecting the piers to each other and forming a wooden ring. Today the tierod is heavily corroded and can be considered as inactive. The heavy roof covering consists of ceramic tiles on a lime mortar bed.

In Fig.1 (9th Ephorate of Byzantine Antiquities[3]) the main internal cracks existing today in the dome are shown. The classification of the preceding chapter has been used to characterize the cracks.

Intervention phases in the dome

The intervention measures in their sequence of application are the following:
a) Roof covering removal. Roof covering loads account for almost 40% of the total load of the dome. The roof removal is a prerequisite for the application of the mortar injections and the placing of metal ties.
b) Mortar injections application and replacement of the corroded wooden tierod by a new one, also wooden. The quality of timber joints is open to doubt and consequently activation of the new timber members under future loading is not to be considered.

c) Placing of metal ties and prestressing. Each tie forms a ring at the lowest possible level on the external surface of the shell(Fig.2).Titanium ties are used, as titanium is a highly corrosion resistant metal.
d) Reconstruction of roof covering.

ANALYTICAL PROCEDURE

Two comparative analyses of the intervention procedure in the dome are presented. In both analyses the intervention sequence described in the preceding chapter is taken into account. In the first analysis (Case I) under self-weight loads no cracking criterion was adopted. In the second analysis(Case II) it was assumed that the masonry has an ultimate circum-ferential tensile strength $\sigma_{\theta u}$=0.04MPa. Cracks developed in meridian levels are taken into account and tne model is appropriately modified. The ana-lytical model is presented in an other paper in this conference(Ignatakis -Stavrakakis[4]). In table 1 the structural elements, the corresponding finite elements and the material properties are shown.

Table 1. Structural and finite elements-Material properties

Structural element	Finite element type	$E_z=E_r$ GPa	E_θ GPa	$v_z=v_r$	v_θ	γ KN/m³
Shell	(a) Isotropic axisymmetric	1.5	1.5	0.19	0.19	18.0
Wooden tierod	(b) Stratified axisymmetric	1.0	10.0	0.20	0.20	6.0
Piers	(c) Isotropic plain stress	1.5	Ø	0.19	Ø	12.4
Meridionally cracked shell	-"-	1.5	Ø	0.19	Ø	18.0
Corroded wooden tierod	-"-	1.0	Ø	0.20	Ø	6.0
Titanium tierod	(d) Uniaxially stressed	Ø	105.0	Ø	0.20	45.1

E: Modulus of elasticity, v: Poisson's ratio, γ: Density

Case I. No cracking consideration
(a_I). As no cracking had to be considered, under a linearly elastic con-stitutive law there is no reason to take into account the historical background. An analysis was carried out under self-weight loads represent-ing the roof covering removal. The wooden tierod was considered to be in-active because it is heavily corroded and consequently it can not resist any thrusts. The analytical model and the representation of the piers with a cylindrical axisymmetric drum are shown in Fig.2. The mean values of the principal circumferential stresses σ_θ and the normal stresses σ_t in the

tangential direction are shown in Fig.4a. This is considered to be the stress distribution after the roof covering removal.

(b).A second analysis was carried out under an arbitrarily chosen prestressing load of 20KN imposed through the tierods. The mean values of σ_θ and σ_t are shown in Fig.5a. Then a rough estimation of the required cross-sectional area of the tierods was performed. The criterion used for this purpose was that a compressive circumferential stress of 0.3MPa at the base of the shell should be developed under total service loads. This specific value was adopted because compressive stresses of the same order of magnitude were calculated in the compression zone near the keystone of the shell under service loads at its initial construction stage and it was assumed that this value can represent the physical reaction of the shell under realistic loading. Taking into account that the yield stress of titanium is f_y=300MPa and a safety coefficient of n=1.75 is sufficient, a cross-sectional area of 4cm² was calculated corresponding to two rods of 16mm in diameter.

(c).A third analysis was carried out under the loads corresponding to roof reconstruction. This time, additional finite elements of type (d)(see table 1) were used to represent the additional titanium tierods(see Fig.2, right half-dome). The mean values of σ_θ and σ_t are shown in Fig.5b. In the same figure the additional stresses developed in the tierods are also shown. It is easily concluded that the tierods stresses are very small. This can be explained by the fact that the axial stiffness of the tierods is very small relative to the axial stiffness of the shell and, in addition, the level at which they have been put is a level of almost zero radial displacement.

(d).Having in mind that the final circumferential compressive stress in the base of the shell must be equal to 0.3MPa, a combbination of the analyses above gives a value of N_I=58.1KN for the prestressing force.

Case II. Cracking consideration

(a_{II}).In this case the analytical procedure is more complicated. It must not only consider the intervention sequence but it must also take into account the historical background and the cracking patterns created progressively due to time-depended failures. At first, at the initial stage of construction, a cracking pattern was considered to be created in meridian levels due to circumferential tensile stresses exceeding the assumed tensile strength of the material $\sigma_{\theta u}$=0.04MPa. At this stage of analysis the wooden tierod was considered to be active. A progressive failure of the wooden tierod due to time-depended corrosion resulted in further cracking. In Fig.3 the progressive cracking pattern and the relevant stresses finally developed are shown. As the first intervention measure is the roof covering removal, the unloading procedure, incorporated in the finite element program used, was then activated to define any cracking closure, but no closure resulted. In Fig.4b the mean stresses σ_θ and σ_t are shown representing the stress state after the roof removal.

(b).The second intervention measure is the mortar injection procedure. After the completion of this procedure, the material continuity is reestablished and compressive stresses can be developed under future loads. The cracked model resulted from the analyses of stage(a_{II}) is appropriately modified to the relevant model of stage(b) of case I. Consequently the stresses already shown in Fig.5a represent again the influence of prestressing load.

(c).As in stage(b), the roof reconstruction results in the stress distribution already shown in Fig.5b.
(d).A combination of the analyses above gives a value of N_{II}=37.0KN using
the criterion adopted in the corresponding stage of case I. In Fig.6b the
mean stresses σ_θ and σ_t are shown.

CONCLUDING REMARKS

The analysis of domes, including future interventions is a highly nonlinear
procedure mainly because of the strucutral alterations due to progressive
cracking, mortar injections and new members placing. A phase by phase analysis, following the corresponding structural alterations and the future
intervention sequence, can lead to more reliable results compared with the
results of a conventional analysis. In the comparative analysis presented
above the differences observed are significant. For example the prestressing force of a phase by phase analysis was found to be 36.3% less than
the relevant force of a conventional analysis, although the criterion used
to determine the forces was identical for both of them. The circumferential stress distribution is also different, both in shape and magnitude.

REFERENCES

1. Heyman,J. Statical Aspects of Masonry Vaults and Domes, pp.229-235,
    Proceedings of the Int.Symposium on Restoration of Byzantine and Post-
    Byzantine Monumnets, Thessaloniki,Greece, 1985. 9th Ephorate of Byza-
    ntine Antiquities, Thessaloniki, 1986.

2. Mainstone,R.J. Masonry Vaulted and Domed Structures, with Special Re-
    ference to the Monuments of Thessaloniki, pp.237-248, Proceedings of
    the Int.Symposium on Restoration of Byzantine and Post-Byzantine Mo-
    numents, Thessaloniki, Greece, 1985. 9th Ephorate of Byzantine Anti-
    quities, Thessaloniki, 1986.

3. 9th Ephorate of Byzantine Antiquities. Architectural and Strucutral
    Documentation of St.Panteleimon Church. 9th Ephorate of Byzantine
    Antiquities Archives, Thessaloniki, Greece.

4. Ignatakis,C.-Stavrakakis,E. An Analytical Model for Axisummetric
    Strucutres Using the Finite Element Method, Proceedings of the Int.
    Conference on Structural Studies, Repairs and Maintenance of Histo-
    rical Buildings (STREMMA 89), Florence, Italy, 1989.

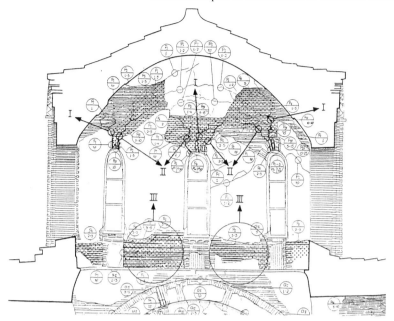

Figure 1.   Central Dome of St. Panteleimon Church.   Crack Pattern.

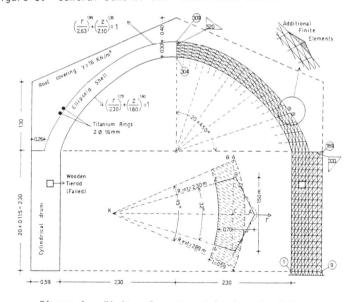

Figure 2.   Finite element model of central Dome.

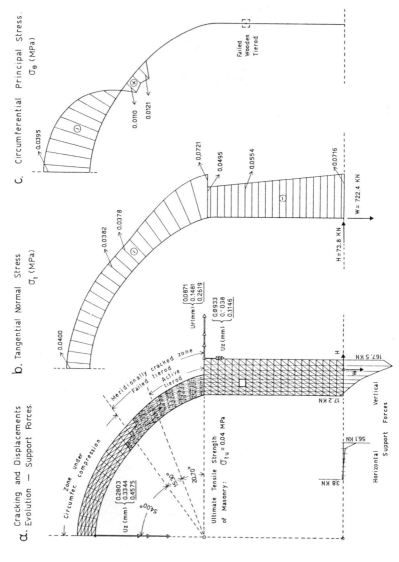

Figure 3.   Case II: Cracking criterion: $\sigma_{\theta u}$ = 0.04 MPa, failed wooden tierod. Stress distribution under total dead weight.

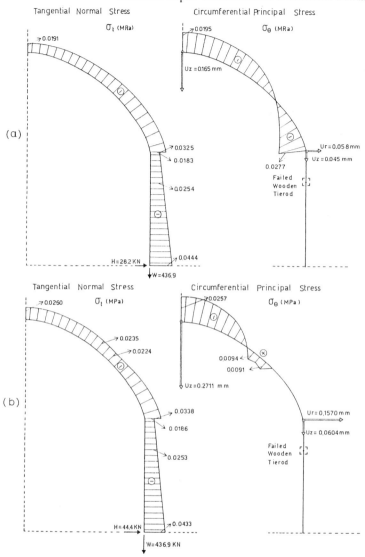

Figure 4.   Stress distribution under self-weight.
          (a) Case I: No cracking criterion adopted.
          (b) Case II: Cracking criterion: $\sigma_{\theta u}$ = 0.04 MPa

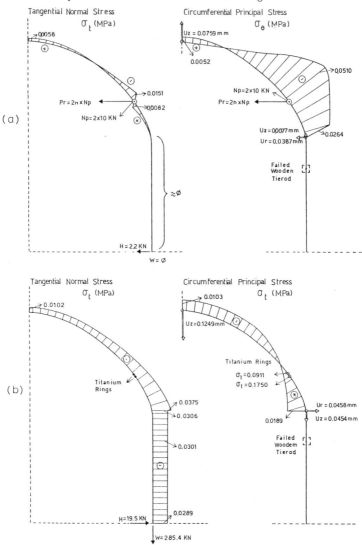

Figure 5.   Stress distibution under:
          (a) Prestressing force N=20KN. (b) Roof cover weight.

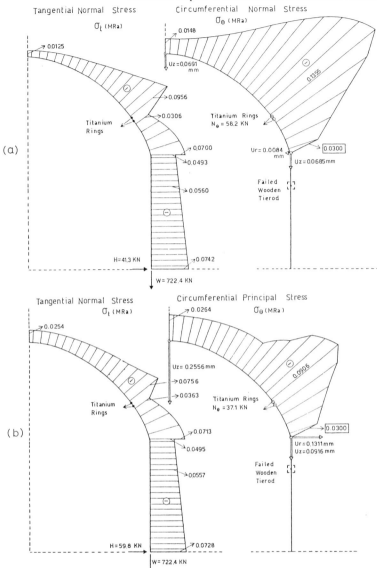

Figure 6.   Final stress distr. after the interventions under total dead weight.
(a) Case I: No cracking criterion adopted.
(b) Case II: Cracking criterion: $\sigma_{\theta u}$ = 0.04 MPa

Structural Stability and Profile in the Dome of Hagia Sophia, Istanbul

K. Hidaka*, T. Aoki** and S. Kato***

Institute of Art and Design, Univesity of Tsukuba, Tsukuba, Ibaraki 305, Japan
**Department of Structural Engineering, Nagasaki University, Bunkyo- machi 1-14, Nagasaki 852, Japan*
***Department of Architecture and regional Planning, Toyohashi University of Technology, Tempaku, Toyohashi 440, Japan*

ABSTRACT

It is interesting to compare structural characteristics of the first dome of Hagia Sophia with those of the rebuilt second dome. We have analyzed these two domes applying FEM numerical analysis with elasto-plastic joint elements to confirm the structural superiority of the latter.

INTRODUCTION

The first dome of Justinian's church of Hagia Sophia collapsed on 7 May 558. The collapse was probably caused by an earthquake which struck Constantinople in December 557. Contemporary Byzantine chroniclers, Agathius and Malalas, never failed to record disaster. Their description of the stupendous event also informs us of the reconstruction work, started immediately, and carried on to a new and higher profile.

Agathius wrote as follows: "Through the earthquake the church had lost the most central portion of its roof, that part which was higher than the rest. The Emperor restored it, strengthened it and gave it greater height. Although Anthemius was then dead, Isidorus the younger

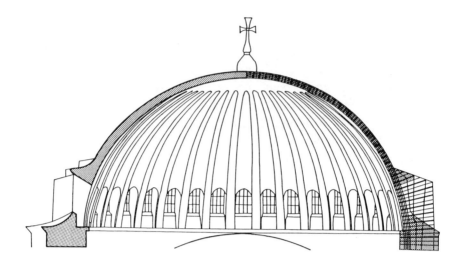

Fig.1 The dome of Hagia Sophia

Photo.1 The dome of Hagia Sophia. External view.

and the other architects considered the previous design, and by that which remained they judged of what had fallen, made out its structure and its weakness. ... Then they rebuilt the crowning middle part — orb, hemisphere, or what you will — and this became more nearly perfect, well turned, and everywhere true to line, narrower and steep in profile. It did not astonish the observers as before, but it was much more securely set."[Reference 1, p.90].

According to the account given by another contemporary chronicler Malalas, the increase in height of the rebuilt dome was 20 Byzantine feet, that is, about 6.24 m (1 Byzantine foot = 0.312 m). On the other hand, Theophanes, writing in the early ninth-century, gave the measure as "more than 20 feet". An eleventh-century writer Cedrenus, probably under the influence of Theophanes, states that the rebuilt dome was made "more than 20 feet higher than the previous structure".

Efforts have been made to restore the first dome of Hagia Sophia, shallower than the actual one by 20 Byzantine feet. Admittedly, the collapse of 558 was due to this shallow profile of the dome, not fully resistant against seismic forces. Though the structural deficiency of the first dome is apparent, no attempt has been made to compare structural characteristics of the first dome with those of the second one and to clarify the structural superiority of the latter.

FEM ANALYSIS OF THE FIRST AND SECOND DOME OF HAGIA SOPHIA

In order to understand the first and second dome of Hagia Sophia from the structural point of view, we have executed a series of FEM analyses based on numerical analysis models with elasto-plastic joint elements(Fig.2). The church as it stands today presents many deformations some of which are not insignificant. The piers supporting the main arches lean backwards and the semidome arches linking them are out of their center towards the inside. The dome base is not a circle nor does it lie on a single plane. According to the detailed survey carried out by Van Nice and others, the internal diameter of the dome base is 30.87 m on the axis from east to west and 31.90 m on the axis from north to south. In the western part of the dome, rebuilt between 989 and 994/5 by the Armenian architect Trdat, the cornice is about 0.5 m higher than in the sixth-century section at north and south.

If we take into consideration these deformations and irregularities, the analysis would be too complicated to bring any concrete results. Therefore, in order to frame models for the numerical analysis, we have to idealize the structure to such a extent that we can take advantage of symmetry of the structure with respect to the central axis of the dome. This assumption enables us to take one fortieth of the dome to be framed into a model.

It is essential in framing models to assume distributive patterns of joint elements. In the following analysis, they are distributed in the normal direction to the hemi-sphere of the dome, with the exception of the lower portion of the first dome. Here, from the dome base up to the drum-like wall where windows are opened, joint elements are distributed radially to the center of the dome.

We have another problem due to the relationship between the dome and the lower supporting structure. At north and south the dome is carried by the great massive arches, while at east and west it is a relatively thin semidome arch that supports the corresponding part of the dome. Regarding our purpose to clarify the structural superiority of the second dome, we assumed that the first dome should be analyzed on the model corresponding to the north-south section and the second dome on the model corresponding to the east-west section. In other words, the model representing the first dome is on the safer side, while the model representing the second dome is on the risky side.

The profile of the first dome has been studied since the voluminous work of Antoniades issued in the early years of this century. Without entering into a difficult work to reconstruct the initial profile of the dome, we have derived it from the extraordinary contribution of Mainstone published in 1988. On the assumption that the radius of curvature of the dome could not have been much different from that of the pendentives, Prof. Mainstone restored the profile of the first dome as a partial sphere with a radius of 75 Byzantine feet, lifted 8 Byzantine feet above by a low drum with windows to allow passage on the cornice.

In our numerical analyses, we also tried to understand the structural role and efficiency (or inefficiency) of the iron tie-rings inserted by Fossati brothers in the years 1847-49. The restoration work of Fossati in Hagia Sophia was recorded to have involved a reinforcement of the dome with two sets of iron chains, one on the level of the cornice and the other on the level of the square dome base. A hypothetical elasto-plastic member is added to express the Fossati-ring embedded in the cornice. Though no one has identified the rings since they were installed (hence even the existence of the rings is to be questioned), we assumed that the ring in the cornice consisted of doubled iron bars with a section of 5 x 5 cm square. The assumption, however, is not at all essential even if in our series of analyses the stiffness of the supporting structure is indexed according to the stiffness of the Fossati-ring. The material properties of the dome used in the analyses are listed in Table 1. Table 2 specifies the characteristic values of the elasto-plastic joint element applied to determine the yielding condition.

RESULTS OF THE ANALYSIS

As is shown in Figure 3, horizontal outward thrust and displacement at the base of the first dome is far greater than that of the second dome. In addition, the mode of deformation given by broken lines is different: the deformed first dome presents slight undulation but the profile of the second dome is roughly preserved even after deformation. This is because the load of the second dome is transmitted downward within the shell of masonry, while the shallow first dome is inevitably subject to bending moment caused by the dead load.

The shaded area in Figure 3 shows that the lower part of both domes is subject to tensile stress in the hoop direction. But there is a difference between the two. In the first dome, the shaded part extends well above the window openings, causing longitudinal cracks. In the second dome, on the other hand, the shaded part does not exceed the upper fringe of the openings. We may conclude that the window openings at the base of the dome may affect the structural stability of the shallow first dome, while the second dome is sufficiently stable in spite of the existence of the openings which are indispensable for the aesthetical effect of the church.

In the range from 10 to 100 on abscissa in Figures 4 and 5, the line representing the second dome has a steeper inclination than the one representing the first dome. This means that the profile of the second dome is more rational and resistant from the structural point of view. With respect to the Fossati-ring, these figures show that the dome equipped with the ring differs little in the structural stability. Hence we may safely conclude that it is inefficient.

In Figures 4 and 5, the lines are almost horizontal up to 10 on abscissa. In other words, the strength of the two domes does not vary in this range of considerably low stiffness of the supporting structure. The value of λ corresponding to the second dome is 2, while the value to the first dome is 1. From this result, we can deduce that the first dome will easily collapse if the stiffness of the supporting structure is somehow exceptionally weakened. And the assumption may be made real by a strong earthquake or progressive development of deformations. In this respect, especially in the first dome, it was decisively important to compose a circular structure which would function as a sort of tension ring at the base of the dome. In contrast, due to the rational profile, the need for such a structural device is less vital in the second dome.

CONCLUSION

On the basis of FEM analysis with joint elements, we have clarified the structural superiority of the second dome of Hagia Sophia in comparison with the first dome. Both displacement and deformation are less in the former. The deformation mode of the latter presents a threatening influence of bending moment caused by the dead load, of which the former is independent.

REFERENCES

1. R. J. Mainstone : Hagia Sophia, Thames and Hudson, Hungary, 1988.

2. S. Kato, K. Hidaka, and T. Aoki : A Study on the Formulation of a Elastic-plastic Joint Element by Truss Elements - An Application of the Theory of Effective Strength, Trans. of A.I.J., No.370, pp.50-59, 1986.

3. R. L. Van Nice :   St Sophia in Istanbul - An Architectural Survey, Washington, 1st instalment 1965, 2nd instalment due 1986. (The fundamental record of the present state of the structure.)

4. R. J. Mainstone : Justinian's Church of St Sophia, Istanbul - Recent Studies of its Construction and First Partial Reconstruction, AH, vol.12, pp.39-49, 1969.

5. R. J. Mainstone : The structure of the church of St Sophia, Istanbul, Transactions of the Newcomen Society, vol.38, pp.23-49, 1965-66.

6. W. Emerson and R. L. Van Nice : Hagia Sophia - The Collapse of the First Dome, Archaeology, vol.4, pp.94-103, 1951.

7. W. Emerson and R. L. Van Nice : Hagia Sophia - The Construction of the Second Dome and its Later Repairs, Archaeology, vol.4, pp.162-171, 1951.

8. W. Emerson and R. L. Van Nice : Hagia Sophia, Istanbul - Preliminary Report of a Recent Examination of the Structure, AJA, vol.47, pp.403-436, 1943.

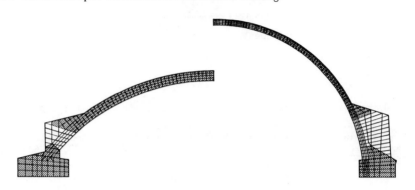

Fig.2 Numerical analysis models with elasto-plastic joint elements.
The first dome(N-S section, left) and the second dome(E-W section,
right) of Hagia Sophia.

Table 1 Material constants of the dome

Brick
Young's modulus=1.0×10^5 kgf/cm² Poisson's ratio=1/6 Weight per unit volume: dome-1.7tf/m³

Mortar
Young's modulus=1.0×10^5 kgf/cm² Poisson's ratio=1/6 Strength(kgf/cm²): compressive(σ_c)=200 tensile(σ_t)= 2

Iron chains
Young's modulus=2.1×10^6 kgf/cm² Sectional area =50cm²

Table 2 Material constants used in the finite element analysis

Joint element for mortar
Angle(ϕ_0)   =45⁰ Height(h)   =1.0cm Young's modulus(kgf/cm²): diag. member=8.62×10^4 vert. member=5.95×10^4 Compressive strength(kgf/cm²): diag. member= 50 vert. member=150 Tensile strength(kgf/cm²): diag. member=1.89 vert. member=1.16

Member
Young's modulus=1.0×10^5 kgf/cm² Strength(kgf/cm²): compressive(σ_c)=200 tensile(σ_t)= 2 strain(ε_c)=-0.0025

Iron chains
Young's modulus=2.1×10^6 kgf/cm² Strength(kgf/cm²): compressive(σ_c)=1000 tensile(σ_t)=1000

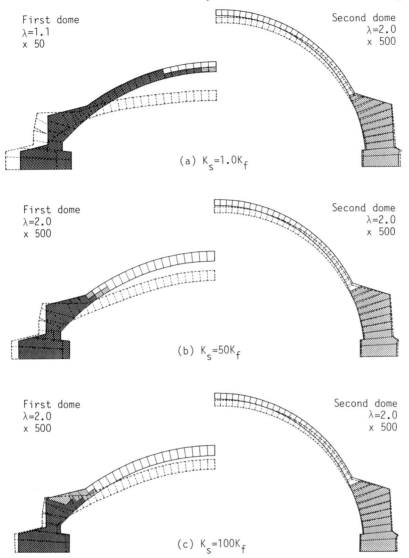

First dome
λ=1.1
x 50

Second dome
λ=2.0
x 500

(a) K$_s$=1.0K$_f$

First dome
λ=2.0
x 500

Second dome
λ=2.0
x 500

(b) K$_s$=50K$_f$

First dome
λ=2.0
x 500

Second dome
λ=2.0
x 500

(c) K$_s$=100K$_f$

Fig.3 Deformation (shown by broken lines) and tensile force in the hoop direction. Light shading indicates tensile stress in the hoop direction, dark shading indicates longitudinal cracks. λ is load parameter(λ=1.0 corresponds the structure under its dead weight). K$_s$ is stiffness of the lower supporting structure and K$_f$ is stiffness of the Fossati's ring.

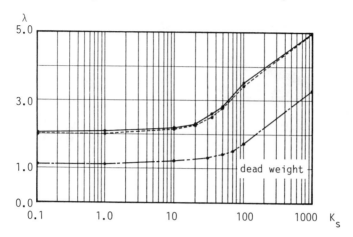

Fig.4 Relationship between load parameter λ and stiffness of the lower supporting structure on the moment when the first cracks occur.
———·—— first dome
——————— second dome with Fossati's ring
———————— second dome without Fossati's ring

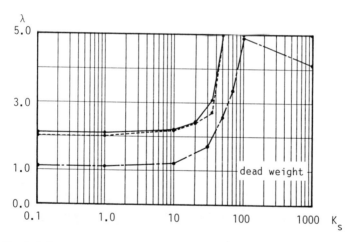

Fig.5 Relationship between load parameter λ and stiffness of the lower supporting structure at the final state.
———·—— first dome
——————— second dome with Fossati's ring
———————— second dome without Fossati's ring

Simulation of Ancient Structures Using Boundary Elements
The Case of Santa Maria del Fiore

C.A. Brebbia and J.M.W. Baynham

Computational Mechanics Institute Wessex Institute of Technology, Southampton, UK.

1 Introduction

While many architects and designers are nowadays conversant with the new powerful computer tools available for drafting and visualization, most of them find analysis codes difficult to use. This is because the development in computer graphics which has produced a whole new generation of user friendly systems has not been matched by a corresponding improvement in the structural analysis codes. The popular finite element technique is cumbersome to use and largely out of date, having originated a generation ago when computers were just starting to made an impact in engineering analysis.

Fortunately there is no need at present to be restricted to using finite elements for the analysis of structural components, particularly three dimensional solids which are difficult to model using that technique. A new method called boundary elements was developed in 1978 [1], which, contrary to finite elements, requires only the discretization of the surface of the structural piece, and hence it lends itself to being easily combined with the graphics packages now widely available for architectural use.

Boundary elements have also emerged as a powerful alternative to finite elements particularly in cases where better accuracy is required due to problems such as stress concentration. The most important advantage of boundary elements, however, is, as mentioned above, that it only requires discretization of the surface rather than the volume. Hence boundary element codes are easier to use with existing Computer Aided Engineering Systems. The process is simplified even further by the use of discontinuous elements which are available in boundary elements but incompatible with finite element theory. The mesh shown in Figure 1 illustrates these boundary elements. The figure represents the surface discretization of one eighth of a problem, i.e. a cylinder with a perforation. Notice that the use of elements which sometimes do not meet at the edges and can be arbitrarily graded, facilitates the meshing. In addition, there is no need to use elements on the planes of symmetry.

Figure 2 shows a mechanical component, i.e. part of a crankshaft which has been discretized using discontinuous boundary elements. These views can be easily rotated to check that elements on the surface are not missing. Figure 3 shows the surface stresses (von Mises' effective stresses) which the designer can use to find out the parts of the structural component which are under large stresses. The next step may be the redesigning of the component which involves altering its dimensions and changing the number of elements required for the analysis. At this stage the use of discontinuous boundary elements is specially attractive as it is easy to vary the mesh during the design process. Such variations create difficulties with finite elements as some of them may become distorted or have bad dimensional ratios. It is evident from these examples, and the application presented in this paper, that the Boundary Element Method is an ideal tool for CAD, mainly because it is easy to generate the data required to run a problem and carry out the necessary modifications to achieve an optimum design. More important, boundary element codes are easy to use and can shorten the 'turn around' time taken by the analysis and design, bringing forward the completion date of the project.

Most of the advantages of BEM are related to its more complex mathematical formulation, which provides a high degree of versatility and accuracy. The reader interested in this feature is referred to [2], where the mathematical theory of the method and its applications are discussed at length. Reference [2] includes some simple codes for stress analysis and temperature problems which can be run on any PC compatible. For a more complete treatment of the theory which includes non-linear problems and time dependent studies, the reader is referred to [3].

It is also important to point out that the advantages of boundary elements are only achieved by well written codes, as the technique is more susceptible to errors if the correct numerical techniques are not used. The results presented in this paper were all obtained using the BEASY (Boundary Element Analysis System) code developed at the Wessex Institute of Technology, in the UK. This system is used in over 250 installations all around the world, most of them related to mechanical and aeronautical applications. It is the aim of this paper to bring the technique to the attention of architects who will find it much easier to use than existing finite element codes.

Another important consideration for having selected boundary elements in this paper is the high accuracy of the technique when dealing with stress concentration problems. This is particularly important when trying to analyse structural defects such as cracks and take remedial action. The case of Brunelleschi's cupola at Santa Maria del Fiore has been taken as a typical application. The study has concentrated on trying to understand the process by which the cracks occurred in the dome.

2   The Case of the Cupola of Santa Maria del Fiore

The cupola of the Church of Santa Maria del Fiore in Florence has been the subject of several major investigations due to the presence of cracks which propagate from the octagonal base towards the lantern at the top, (Figure 4). These cracks occur on the segments that are supported by walls rather than on those which are open. The dimensions of the octagonal base and the cupola itself have been taken from reference [4]. Figure 5 shows two different computer drawn views of the cupola, also from [4], where the beam-type supports and the eight circular windows are described. Figure 6 presents the dimensions considered in the analysis.

Although the cupola consists of two different shells, one interior and the other on the outside, it was decided as a first approximation to have a solid section with an equivalent modulus for the material. This model can be easily improved in subsequent investigations as it is comparatively simple to prepare the boundary element data from our knowledge of the geometry of the structure.

First the boundary element code BEASY was used to analyse the stiffness of the octagonal beams at the base of the cupola. The problem can be considered two dimensional, and because of symmetry only one half of each portion of the beams needs to be analysed. Figure 7 depicts the mesh used for the supporting beam. Notice that the right hand side represents half the beam resting on the supporting wall, and the left hand side represents part of the opening. Although this beam is an idealization of the real situation it helps us to understand the different stiffnesses of the two portions of the base. The stiffnesses have been found by assuming unit forces acting at different points on the top of the beam. It was found that the behaviour of the beam could be modelled using vertical springs whose stiffness varied in the ratio 1 to 3 from the centre of the opening to the wall. A further reduction of the spring constant at the opening in the case of the portion supported by the wall was also found, given a relative stiffness of approximately two there. Consideration of these relative values is very important in order to understand the behaviour of the cupola and how the cracks are produced. It is recommended that further studies investigate this problem in more detail using fully three dimensional models and a better representation of the actual geometry and properties of the masonry at the base. It is interesting to notice the different ways in which the vertical direct stresses in the supporting beam transmit load from various application points to the supports, which are clearly shown in Figure 8.

Once the stiffness of the beam was modelled the spring coefficients were introduced as boundary conditions in the model of the shell. One eighth of the cupola has been discretized using 178 boundary elements as shown in Figure 9, and the model was then subjected to gravity load. The boundary element code BEASY then gives the designer the complete state of displacements, stresses or strains. In this particular case, the study centred on trying to understand the formation of the cracks and hence the graphical output in Figure 10 shows the normal stresses along the plane of symmetry where the shell is fractured. It can be seen that circumferential tensile stresses develop near the outer surface of the shell at the bottom and that their effect extends further than half the height of the cupola. This stress distribution explains the formation of cracks in the part of the shell supporting the walls. They are basically due to the different stiffnesses of the two types of support at the base.

Although this is only a preliminary study it shows the advantages of using boundary elements. Further improvements can be achieved by better modelling of the two shells and the supporting structure. While in finite elements modelling of this type will require considerable effort, particularly during the discretization process, the BEASY code can easily deal with the geometry of the structure as it always applies elements only on the surface.

3   Conclusions

Boundary element codes have numerous advantages when modelling structural components. The analysis mesh needs to be defined only on the surface without the cumbersome and artificial internal subdivision characteristic of older techniques such as finite elements. The geometrical definitions of the structure can then easily be used for the analysis. In addition, the meshes do not need to obey the stringent requirements of continuity which are typical of finite elements. Furthermore it is simple to modify a mesh if the designer wishes to focus on a particular region of interest.

Simulation using boundary elements gives very accurate results and allows the architect or engineer to obtain a better understanding of the structural problems comparatively quickly. Using boundary elements it is possible to model quickly and accurately study structures such as the cupola of Santa Maria del Fiore and, if required, investigate a series of remedial actions.

References

1. Brebbia, C.A.; The Boundary Element Method for Engineers, Pentech Press, London, Computational Mechanics Publications, Boston, 1978.

2. Brebbia, C.A. and Dominguez, J.; Boundary Elements, An Introductory Course, Computational Mechanics Publications and McGraw Hill, Southampton and NY, 1989.

3. Brebbia, C.A., Telles, J. and Wrobel, L.; Boundary Element Techniques - Theory and Applications in Engineering, Springer-Verlag, Berlin and NY, 1984.

4. Di Pasquale, S., Bandini, P.L. and Tempesta, G.; Rappresentazione Analitica e Grafica della cupola di Santa Maria Del Fiore, Cooperativa Libraria, Unaversitatis Studii Florentini, Firenze.

5. BEASY Users' Manual, Computational Mechanics Publications, Southampton and Boston, 1989.

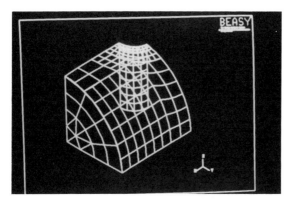

Figure 1 Cylinder with cylindrical perforation; representing one eighth of the problem.

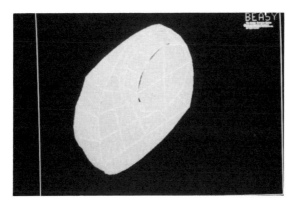

Figure 2 Boundary element discretization of a mechanical component.

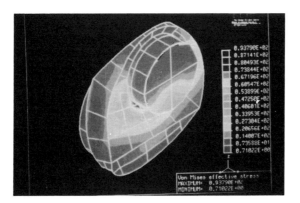

Figure 3 Distribution of effective stresses over the component.

Figure 4 View of the Cupola
of Santa Maria del Fiore.

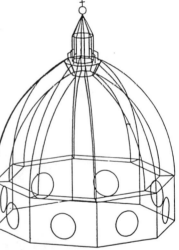

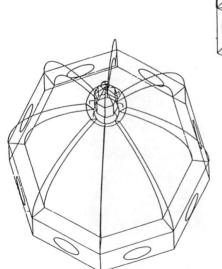

Figure 5 Two different computer
views of the cupola (from [4]).

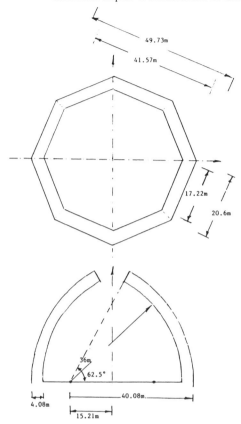

Figure 6 Dimensions of the cupola of Santa Maria del Fiore.

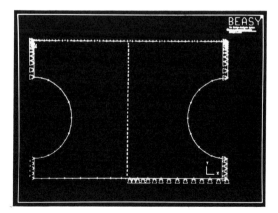

Figure 7 Discretization of the beam using two dimensional boundary elements, with boundary conditions showing position of the support.

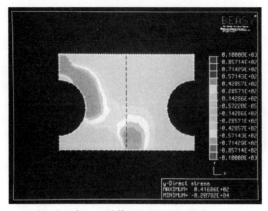

8a: Load at middle of unsupported span.

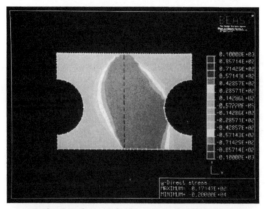

8b: Load at end of unsupported span.

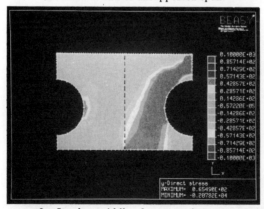

8c: Load at middle of supported span.

Figure 8 Contour bands of vertical direct stress resulting from unit load at three different positions on the beam.

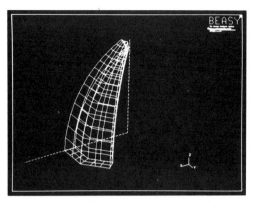

9a: Orthogonal view of the mesh.

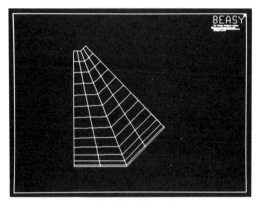

9b: View from above.

Figure 9 Three dimensional boundary element mesh used to model one eighth of the cupola.

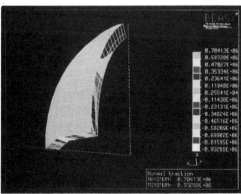

Figure 10 Contour bands of normal direct stress: non-zero on the plane of symmetry and on the base. Showing tensile circumferential direct stress near the outer surface of the shell in a position immediately above the middle of the supporting wall.

SECTION 5 - SEISMIC BEHAVIOUR AND VIBRATIONS

Probabilistic Approach to Generate the Reference Motion for the Protection of Historical Monuments Against Earthquakes

N. Theofanopoulos, T. Hanazato and M. Watabe

Architectural Department, University of Tokyo Metropolitan, 2-1-1 Fukazawa, Setagaya-ku, Tokyo 158, Japan

ABSTRACT

In this paper, we discuss the input earthquake motion required to examine the earthquake resistant capacity of Parthenon. Radical alterations and minor damage have occurred during the 25 centuries of the monument's history, which impose the necessity of structural strengthening and restoration. The expected response spectra for return periods of 100 and 1000 years were obtained based on probabilistic analyses of Greek earthquake records for the period between 1900 and 1986. Earthquake motions compatible to those response spectra were generated. Those motions correspond to the base of the hill where Parthenon is constructed. The amplified motions at the top of the hill were calculated taking into account the topography and the geology of Acropolis hill.

INTRODUCTION

The various historical monuments constructed in seismic regions have been subjected to a number of destructive or damaging earthquakes during their history and they have survived due to their excellent design and construction or by chance due to the characteristics of the earthquakes that hit them. Of course, the monuments that exist today at seismic areas represent a small fraction of the originally constructed ones. The rest of them, have been destroyed principally by earthquakes. The inherent structural complexity, variability of building and foundation materials, as well as their final state of repair, makes each historical monument a special case of study. It is simply impossible to devise rules of thumb or general recommendations for the protection of monuments against earthquakes, that will be generally applicable or effective without adapting them to local conditions, which may vary even within the same structure.

In this study our attention will be focused on Parthenon which is one of the main historical monuments of Greece. Parthenon's behavior under seismic actions for 25 centuries was completely satisfactory. However, during the various phases of the monuments history, radical alterations have occurred concerning the general geometric configuration, the interconnection of structural members and the state of materials, which all impose the necessity

of   considering   its earthquake capacity. The scope of this research is to
study the possibility of the monument in this existing state,   safely
withstanding the earthquake loads, probabilistically derived from seismological
data of the region.

SEISMIC RISK ANALYSIS

The determination of design earthquakes corresponding to particular levels
of seismic risk, can be reasonably based on statistical seismicity methods
under the condition that sufficient earthquake data is   available for
analysis. Data may be divided into two categories. The instrumental data, which
is considered to be complete, accurate and well suited for statistical
analysis and the pre-instrumental data, which is regarded as inaccurate and
incomplete, in terms of magnitude estimation or epicenter placement. The main
advantage of pre-instrumental records is that they represent a time period many
times longer than that of the instrumental ones. The existing instrumental
records cover a relatively short period to allow for accurate estimates of
seismic risk. Instrumental measurements are mostly limited to 30 years in
Greece, while felt earthquake records, often of questionable quality and
completeness, span about 100 years.

In this study the earthquake motions at the base of Acropolis hill where
Parthenon is located were represented as acceleration response spectra with
damping 5% of critical. Although seismic hazard has usually been evaluated in
terms of some peak amplitude of ground motion, such as, peak acceleration etc.,
this type of seismic hazard analysis fails to furnish information about the
frequency characteristics of the earthquake motions, which are extremely
important in accomplishing dynamic response analysis of structures.

Another significant task is the selection of acceptable levels of risk.
Some of the most critical facilities, i.e., nuclear power plants, high-rise
buildings, large dams and hospitals are easier to deal with, in a sense that
regulations or recommendations have already defined acceptable levels of risk.
On a specific project, such as the Parthenon strengthening, lack of seismic code
restraints, acceptable levels of risk should be determined. It is usual to
define the parameter under consideration for two levels of seismic risk. The
structural strengthening of Parthenon should be directed;

(1) to   prevent   structural and most architectural damage   given   those
    earthquakes reasonably expected to occur several times during the life of
    the monument (level 1) and
(2) to prevent total collapse, given the worst earthquake expected to occur
    (level 2).

The first criterion requires definition of the term "several times" during
the life of the monument. In this study a return period of 100 years was
adopted to represent the earthquake motions of level 1. This time period, is of
the same level as the usually prescribed one, for level 2 design of high-rise
buildings in Japan, but it was adopted due to the difference in the length of
the useful life of a monument and a high-rise building. The second criterion,
is practically satisfied by examining maximum credible earthquakes, the most
critical of them often occurs on a relatively close fault. Return period of
1000 years was assumed to represent the earthquake motions of level 2. This

return period was adopted due to the uniqueness of Parthenon and it should not be considered too long, because it represents approximately   one third of the monument's life.

The development of seismic risk models is well reported in the   literature [1] to [6] and will not be repeated here.

Analytical model
   A data base of earthquake records with magnitude greater than   5.0 which occurred in the area of Greece during the period between 1900 and   1986,   was composed by considering the earthquake catalogues prepared by Makropoulos and Burton [7] and by Comninakis and Papazachos [8]. Those historical records   are composed of earthquake magnitude, epicenter location, focal depth   and occurrence time.

   In the analysis, the area source model was chosen to   represent   seismic sources around the site, [1]. The region of Greece was divided into 19 seismic zones, as Papazachos [9] did, on the basis of seismotectonic criteria, such as, seismic rates, focal mechanisms etc. The earthquake epicenters, as well as the seismic zones in the area of Greece used in this study are shown in figure 1.

   The attenuation equation for spectral acceleration proposed by Kawashima et al. [10] was adopted in this study,

$$S_A(M, \Delta, T) = a(t)10^{b(T)M}(\Delta + 30)^{-1.178} \tag{1}$$

where M is the earthquake magnitude, Δ is the epicentral distance and T is the natural period. To consider the uncertainties of the normalized response spectra among the ground motions whose magnitudes and epicentral distances were the same, the coefficient of variation was assumed as 0.3 for all periods between 0.1 and 3.0 seconds, as Itoh et al. [11] did.

   The algorithm of analysis is explained by Theofanopoulos in reference [12] and the flow chart of analysis is summarized in figure 2. The same analysis was repeated ten times equal to the number of control natural periods of the acceleration response spectra given by equation 1. Seismic hazard curves for the control natural periods of the expected acceleration response spectrum at the base of Acropolis hill, are shown in figure 3. The hazard curves are greatly affected by the different attenuation law that is valid for each natural period.

   The response spectra for return periods of 50, 100 and 1000 years are shown in figure 4. The spectral values at the predominant period range, for return period of 1000 years are approximately twice the corresponding ones for return period of 100 years.

Simulation of earthquake motions compatible with the expected spectra
   Earthquake motions compatible with the expected acceleration response spectra for return periods of 100 and 1000 years, were generated by the following method. First, stationary earthquake motions were composed by superposition of sinusoidal waves with a set of phase angles uniformly

distributed in the interval between 0 and 2π. These stationary waves were multiplied by the fourth type of envelope function, proposed by Theofanopoulos et al. [13]. These envelope functions correspond to earthquake magnitudes and distances, relative to active faults in the vicinity of Athens with potential to generate earthquake motions of level 1 or of level 2, respectively.

The resulting earthquake motions for return periods of 100 and 1000 years, along with the target and the response spectra of the generated motions are shown in figures 5 and 6, respectively. One can observe a good fit of the target and the response spectra of the simulated motions. The maximum acceleration for return period of 100 years was 200 gals and for return period of 1000 years it was 460 gals. These motions can be considered as realistic for the area of Athens, having in mind, the historical earthquakes occurred in the vicinity of the city and the seismotectonic formation of the area.

EFFECTS OF TOPOGRAPHY ON GROUND EARTHQUAKE MOTIONS

The earthquake ground motions recorded at a site are function of numerous parameters and variables acting at the source, along the transmission path and the local receiver site. In designing any important structure, accurate input ground motion predictions are required. The accuracy of the ground motion prediction depends on the degree to which the numerous interacting phenomena have been understood and accounted for, in the prediction procedure. One of the main factors that affect the ground motion is the topography around a recording station.

In order to take into account the topographical effects, the Acropolis hill where Parthenon is located was modeled as a linearly elastic shear beam with an exponentially varying cross-section. Since the height-to-width ratio of the hill is small, it may be postulated that the primary response of the hill due to earthquake motions at its base will be principally in shear; therefore, the effect of bending on response will be negligible. The same assumptions were adopted by Mostaghel and Nowroozi [14] to estimate satisfactorily the amplification factors of the maximum base acceleration at Kagel mountain, California, during the 1971, San Fernando earthquake. Theofanopoulos and Dan [15], by modeling in the same way the mountain where Elaiochori village is located, calculated a reliable earthquake motion at the village due to 1986, Kalamata-Greece earthquake and by the use of that motion they easily explained the extensive damage. Taking into account the effectiveness of the assumptions on the modeling of a hill, in the cases afore-mentioned, the same method was followed in the case of Acropolis hill, as well.

The differential equation governing the motion of a beam with varying cross-section in pure shear with consideration of damping [14] is,

$$\ddot{u}(\xi,t) = \frac{KG}{L^2\rho}[u''(\xi,t)+2a u'(\xi,t)]-\frac{C}{\rho}\dot{u}(\xi,t)-\ddot{u}_g(t) \qquad (2)$$

and the corresponding boundary conditions are,

$$u(0,t) = 0 \qquad (3)$$

$$\acute{u}(1,t) = 0 \tag{4}$$

where

$$\dot{} = \frac{\partial}{\partial t} \quad and \quad \acute{} = \frac{\partial}{\partial x}$$

$$\xi = \frac{X}{L} \tag{5}$$

where L is the height of the hill, x is the height of a point between the base and the top $(0 \leqslant x \leqslant L)$ as shown in figure 7, k is a factor depending on the cross-sectional shape, G is the shear modulus of elasticity, ρ is the density of hill's material, $\ddot{u}(x,t)$ is the acceleration at a height x relative to the base, C is the damping coefficient of the hill, $\ddot{u}_g(t)$ is the ground acceleration at the base and α is given by;

$$\alpha = \frac{1}{2}\ln\frac{A(L)}{A(0)} \tag{6}$$

where A(0) and A(L) are the cross sections of the hill at the base and the top, respectively. This equation fulfills the assumption of an exponentially decaying slope [14], which is valid for Acropolis hill slopes.

The algorithm to solve equation 2 is explained in reference [14]. The absolute acceleration time history at any height of the hill $\ddot{u}_a(\xi,t)$ is given by;

$$\ddot{u}_a(\xi,t) = \ddot{u}_g(t) + \sum_{n=1}^{\infty}A_n\varphi_n(\xi)\left[-\ddot{u}_g(t) + 2h\omega_n\int_0^t\ddot{u}_g(\tau)e^{-h\omega_n(t-\tau)}\cos\omega_{nd}(t-\tau)d\tau + \right.$$

$$\left. (1-2h^2)\omega_{nd}\int_0^t\ddot{u}_g(\tau)e^{-h\omega_n(t-\tau)}\sin\omega_{nd}(t-\tau)d\tau\right] \tag{7}$$

where n declares the n-th mode of vibration,

$$A_n = \frac{\int_0^1\varphi_n(\xi)d\xi}{\int_0^1\varphi_n^2(\xi)d\xi} \tag{8}$$

with,

$$\varphi_n(\xi) = e^{-\alpha\xi}\sin(\xi\sqrt{\lambda_n^2-\alpha^2}) \tag{9}$$

where λ_n is the non-dimensional frequency calculated from the equation;

$$\frac{\tan(\sqrt{\lambda_n^2-\alpha^2})}{\sqrt{\lambda_n^2-\alpha^2}} = \frac{1}{\alpha} \tag{10}$$

ω_n is the circular frequency of the n-th mode given by;

$$\omega_n = \sqrt{\frac{K}{L}} \, V_s \lambda_n$$

$$\omega_{nd} = \omega_n \sqrt{1 - h^2} \qquad\qquad (11)$$

where h is the damping ratio of the n-th mode;

$$h = \frac{C}{2\rho\omega_n} \qquad\qquad (12)$$

Application and results

In the case of Acropolis hill, the ratio of the area of the top to the area of the base cross section was taken equal to 0.25, the height to the top of the hill L=70 m, the damping ratio h=0.05, the shear wave velocity v_s =2000 m/sec, and the shape factor k was assumed equal to the unity. The analysis was based on the contribution of the first eight modes of vibration.

The resulting motions at the top of the hill for return periods of 100 and 1000 years, along with the motions at the base of the hill plotted in the same scale, are shown in figures 8 and 9, respectively. In addition to the amplification of the motion, a noticeable difference in the strong motion duration can be observed. This result is compatible with the observed earthquake motions at Kagel mountain during an aftershock of 1971, San Fernando earthquake [16]. Comparisons between the acceleration response spectra at the base and the top of Acropolis hill, for each return period, are shown in figures 10 and 11, respectively. The spectral amplitudes at the top, are about 1.4 to more than 5 times greater than those at the base, in the period range between 0.04 and 0.2 sec. For periods greater than 0.3 sec. the effect of topography is negligible. Taking into account that the shear wave velocity is 2000 m/sec and using the period of 0.1 sec. (the period where the peak amplification occurs), a wavelength of 200 m is obtained and it is comparable with the half length of the Acropolis hill. Thus, it seams feasible for the shear waves of the motion at the base, with period of about 0.1 sec. to cause resonance, because their wavelengths are comparable to the dimensions of the hill.

CONCLUSIONS

Reliable input earthquake motions for the response analysis of Parthenon's columns were generated, analyzing statistically the earthquake records obtained in the area of Greece for a period of 100 years and considering the amplification due to the hill where the monument is located.

The period of Acropolis hill for the first mode of vibration was about 0.10 sec.. Taking into account that the natural period of Parthenon's columns for the first mode of vibration is greater than 0.236 sec., as pointed out by Hanazato et al. [17], it can be concluded that the topography does not influence periods corresponding to the first mode, but those corresponding to higher modes with low participation factors. This result is compatible to the behavior of the monument against earthquakes through the centuries. It can be also concluded that the integrity of Parthenon may be owed to the fact that the frequency characteristics of the earthquake motions at the top of Acropolis hill did not coincide with those of the monument columns.

REFERENCES

1. Cornell, C. A. Engineering Seismic Risk Analysis. Bull. Seism. Soc. Am., Vol. 58, 1583-1606, 1968.
2. Cornell, C. A. and E. H. Vanmarcke. The Major Influences of Seismic Risk. Proc. 4WCEE , Santiago, Chile, Vol.1, 69-83, 1969.
3. Kallberg, K. T. and C. A. Cornell. Seismic Risk in Southern California. Report R 69-31 Dept. of Civil Engineering, MIT, 1969.
4. Kiureghian, A. D. and A. H. S. Ang. A Fault Rapture Model for Seismic Risk Analysis. Bull. Seism. Soc. Am., Vol.67, No.4, 1173-1194, 1977.
5. Oliveira C. Seismic Risk Analysis. EERC Report No.74-1, University of California Berkeley, 1-102, 1974.
6. Shaw, H. C., C. P. Mortgat, A. Kiremidjian and T. C. Zsutty. A Study of Seismic Risk for Nicaragua, Report No.11, John Blume Earthq. Eng. Center, Stanford Univ., 1975.
7. Makropoulos K. C. and P. W. Burton. A Catalogue of Seismicity in Greece and Adjacent Area. Geophys. J. R. Astr. Soc., 65, 741-762, 1981.
8. Comninakis P. E. and B. C. Papazachos. A Catalogue of Earthquakes in Greece and the Surrounding Area for the Period 1901-1985. Publication of the Geophysical Lab. No.1, University of Thessaloniki, 1986.
9. Papazachos B. C. Seismicity Rates and Long Term Earthquake Prediction in the Aegean Area. Quaterniones Geodaesiae, 3, 171-190, 1980.
10. Kawashima, K.,K. Aizawa and K. Takahashi. Attenuation of Peak Ground Motions and Absolute Acceleration Response Spectra. Report of Public Works Research Institute, Japan, Vol. 166, 1985.
11. Itoh T., K. Ishii, Y. Ishikawa and T. Okumura. Development of Seismic Hazard Curves Based on Different Analytical Models. Proc. of 4th International Conf. on Structural Safety and Reliability, Kobe, Japan,1985.
12. Theofanopoulos, N.. Input Earthquake Motions for the Response Analysis of Various Important Structures. Doctoral Thesis, University of Tokyo Metropolitan, 86-101, 1989.
13. Theofanopoulos, N., M. Watabe and K. Matsukawa. Strong Motion Duration and Intensity Function. 9th SMiRT, Lausanne, K1/31-36, 1987.
14. Mostaghel N. and A. A. Nowroozi. Earthquake Response of Hills. Bull. Seism. Soc. Am., Vol. 65, No.6, 1733-1742, 1975.
15. Theofanopoulos, N. and K. Dan. Simulation of the Ground Motion at Kalamata-city Greece. Proc. of 9WCEE, Tokyo, Japan, 1988.
16. Davis, L. L. and L. R. West. Observed Effects of Topography on Ground Motion. Bull. Seism. Soc. Am., Vol. 63, 283-298.
17. Hanazato, T., N. Theofanopoulos and M. Watabe. Seismic Response Analysis of Parthenon Columns. Proceedings of 1st International Conf. on Structural Studies, Repairs and Maintenance of Historical Buildings, Florence, Italy, 1989.

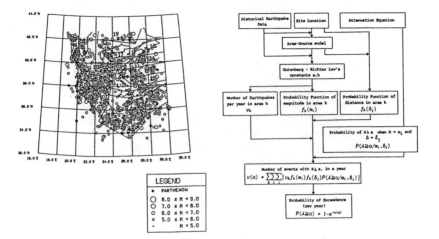

Fig. 1. Plot of earthquake epicenters in the area of Greece for the period 1900-1986, and the seismic zones adopted in this study.

Fig. 2. Flow chart of the seismic risk analysis adopted in this study.

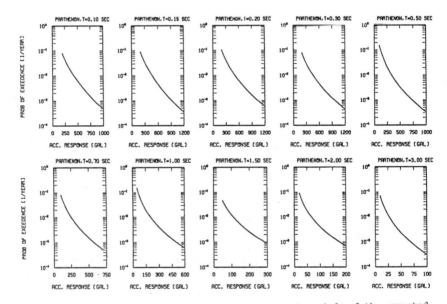

Fig. 3. Seismic hazard curves for the control natural periods of the expected acceleration response spectra.

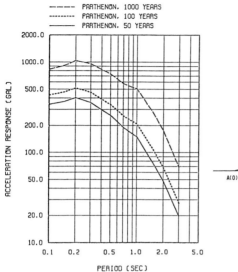

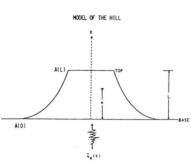

Fig. 4. Expected response spectra at the base of Acropolis hill for return periods of 50, 100 and 1000 years.

Fig. 7. The model of the hill.

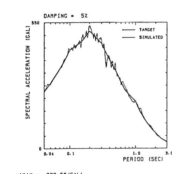

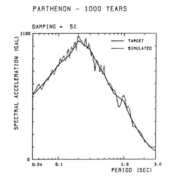

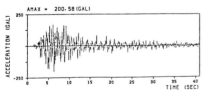

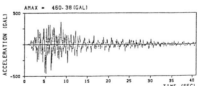

Fig. 5. Simulated earthquake motion for return period of 100 years, along with the target and the calculated spectra.

Fig. 6. Simulated earthquake motion for return period of 1000 years, along with the target and the calculated spectra.

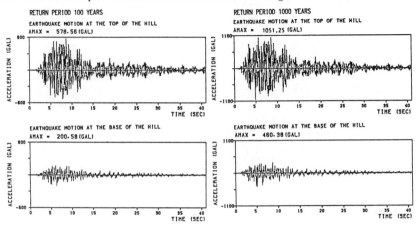

Fig. 8. Comparison between the motions at the base and at the top of Acropolis hill for return period of 100 years.

Fig. 9. Comparison between the motions at the base and at the top of Acropolis hill for return period of 1000 years.

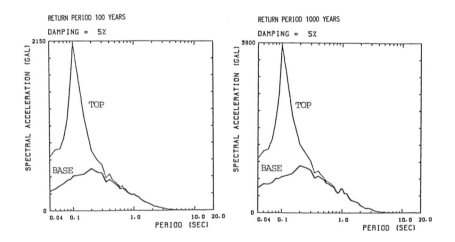

Fig. 10. Comparison between the acceleration response spectra of the motions at the base and at the top of Acropolis hill for return period of 100 years.

Fig. 11. Comparison between the acceleration response spectra of the motions at the base and at the top of Acropolis hill for return period of 1000 years.

Seismic Vulnerability via Knowledge Based Expert Systems

F. Casciati and L. Faravelli

Department of Structural Mechanics, University of Pavia, Via Abbiategrasso 211, I 27100 Pavia, Italy

ABSTRACT

Italy has a unique experience in preserving, from seismic damage, ancient villages, historical town centres and monumental areas. At the beginning of the Eighties different studies of seismic prevention were developed in different regions of that country. They led to a form, to be filled building by building, by which a census of the local vulnerability is obtained. This paper illustrates the main features of an expert system prototype which assists the operator in filling the form. Attention is focused on the use of the "confidence measure" in the treatment of uncertainty.

INTRODUCTION

Consider a historical building which has survived large seismic damage during the centuries. One can conclude that either it is located in a site of insignificant seismic hazard or it is designed to support horizontal forces. Recent Italian seismic experiences showed the falseness of this apparently logic belief.

For example, the village of Gemona lost, during the Friuli seismic event of 1976, a beautiful complex of old buildings, including a nice church. A similar result was recorded in S.Angelo dei Lombardi during the Southern Italy earthquake of 1980.
As a consequence the political authority decided that ancient villages, historical town centres and monumental areas should be preserved from the seismic risk.

A check of the scientific and technical background in the field led to conclude that:
i) the recent developments in seismology, wave propagation and signal analysis enable the engineer to estimate the seismic hazard at the site with confidence.

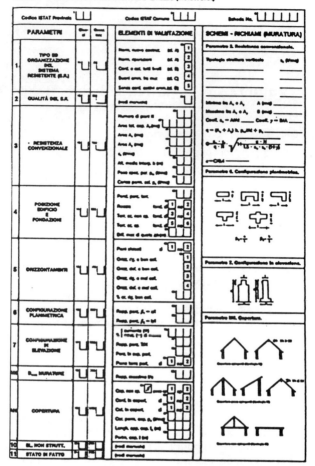

Figure 1 - Form for Level 2 Vulnerability assessment of masonry buildings, from [6]. The eleven items are: 1) building quality; 2) resistant system quality; 3) conventional resistance; 4) building site; 5) horizontal element features; 6) plan configuration; 7) vertical configuration; 8) interwall distance; 9) roof type; 10) nonstructural elements; 11) actual state (maintenance conditions).

For example, stochastic models, e.g. Faravelli [1], or seismological idealizations, e.g. Faravelli-Kiremidjian-Suzuki [2], can be used to generate likely ground-motion time-histories.

ii) earthquake engineering is presently a mature subject, e.g. Augusti-Baratta-Casciati [3] and Clough-Penzien [4] among others. Further developments are required for some types of structural components of common use in historical buildings, such as masonry or timber elements. However, the earthquake engineer possesses the appropriate knowledge for strengthening inadequate buildings.

Unlimited financial resources could therefore permit each local government to repair and strengthen the whole historical core of the municipality. Obviously, this is not the general case. Before strengthening monumental sites, it is necessary to assess the actual structural vulnerability of their components. The knowledge of the liability of the different buildings to suffer damage, in fact, makes it possible to establish the priorities and to prepare a long-term economical plan of prevention and mitigation. Details on this subject can be found in the "Programma Quadro delle Ricerche" (Research Framework) [5] edited by the Italian Ministry of Cultural Goods.

Such a situation led to prepare, for masonry structures, the form represented in figure 1. It is taken from the GNDT (National Group of Earthquake Prevention) document [6] and was originally proposed by Benedetti and Petrini [7]. A different form has to be filled for each building of interest. A vulnerability index can be reached by assigning a weight to each answer class (A, B, C, D) and a weight to each of the eleven items the form requires, e.g. Benedetti - Benzoni - Parisi [8]. New forms for other kinds of buildings, more valuable from an architectural point of view, are presently in progress.

The special aspect investigated by the authors was the possibility of making less expensive and more reliable the collection of the data. For this purpose an expert system prototype was prepared by Faravelli [9]. This paper gives an overview of this expert system and discusses the features of the way the uncertainty is treated.

SOME BASIC ASPECTS

The understanding of the developments in progress at the University of Pavia requires the reader be informed of two aspects: i) the contents of the Level 2 (Masonry) Vulnerability form in figure 1 and ii) the specific "artifical intelligence" (AI) approach one adopted. The first point has been widely explained in reports written in Italian and, hence, a short synopsis is given in the next sub-Section. The reader is referred to Faravelli [9] for details on the second aspect. Just the material required by the successive Section is summarized in the sub-Section on the expert system prototype below.

The vulnerability form

The method of classifying masonry buildings in seismic areas proposed by Benedetti and Petrini [7] makes use of a numerical value, called the "vulnerability index". It represents the seismic quality of each building and is obtained as a weighted sum of the numerical values expressing the seismic quality of the structural and non-structural elements of interest. They were reduced to eleven as summarized in the form in figure 1. The elements can be of a descriptive nature, as the "resistant system quality" (item 2 in figure 1), the morphological "configurations" (item 6 and 7 in figure 1), the structural typology (items 5 and 9 in figure 1) and the status descriptions (items 10 and 11 in figure 1). Some of them, however, have an evaluative nature as the "building quality" (item 1 in figure 1) since specific reference is made to the code requirements, the "conventional resistance" ("total shear strength", i.e. item 3 in figure 1) which is estimated by the approximate formula at the top of the right column of figure 1, the "building site" (item 4 in figure 1) where the soil slope has to be assessed and the "interwall distance" (item 8 in figure 1).

For evaluating all these elements, appropriate field investigations are planned. The operators must follow detailed rules and instructions prepared in order to minimize the discrepancies among surveyors. For this purpose the operator must provide answers to some questions which are regarded as "evaluation elements" (second column from right in figure 1). The answers are then combined to assign the item under discussion to a class. Class A indicates situations that are in agreement with the prescriptions of the Italian seismic code. Class D characterizes the unsafe configurations.

For instance, the operator trying to estimate the quality of the resistant system (item 2 in figure 1) must assign his building to one of the 18 classes listed in the manual. Then:

Class A contains homogeneous masonry of good quality bricks or well squared stones (or tufa). The homogeneous sandwich masonry is included when good interconnections are manifest.

Class B is analogous to class A, but homogeneity is no longer required.

Class C contains masonry of roughly squared stones or bad quality bricks. The sandwich masonry without interconnections belongs to class C when it shows regularity.

Class D groups together the remaining classes.

It is obvious from this short overview that:
i) algorithmic computer codes are unable to account for the descriptive (qualitative) elements. Non-algorithmic (linguistic) procedures (expert systems) are therefore required in order to implement a "Level 2 Vulnerability Assistant" into a (portable) computer;
ii) the presence of algorithmic steps (see the approximate formula of item 3 in figure 1) makes unsatisfactory the first generation of expert systems. They, in fact, were not able to alternate qualitative and quantitative steps, e.g. Casciati - Faravelli [10] and Gavarini and Pagnoni [11].

A "Vulnerability Assistant" expert system

In order to build a knowledge based expert system, the best approach is to select a commercial "shell". It already includes: 1) the inference engine; 2) the text editor and 3) the consultant. The inference engine processes the answers to some questions it poses in order to reach a conclusion over the topic on which it was consulted. The knowledge base can be made available to the inference engine by compiling a text, i.e. a sequence of rules, prepared by the expert by means of the editor. An operator, then, starts the logic process by activating the consultant. He also provides the answers the inference engine needs during its deductive path (either backward or forward chaining).

A particular shell of the second generation running also over (portable) personal computers is the INSIGHT 2+ [12]. It was used by Faravelli [9] for building her "Vulnerability Assistant" expert system. There are three main advantages this shell presents, see Casciati-Faravelli [13]:
1) Local calculations are allowed. For instance, when the plan configuration (item 6 in figure 1) is approached, three length measures must be provided. However, the assignment to class A rather than B or C or D depends on the ratios of the second and third length with the first one. The "shell" computes by itself these ratios (since special rules are written for this purpose by the "expert") and avoids the execution of calculations by the operator. The capabilities of the shell covers algebraic operators, logarithmic and exponential functions, as well as direct and inverse trigonometric functions.
2) External algorithmic codes can be used without interrupting the decision process. For instance, when the conventional resistance (item 3 in figure 1) is calculated, a set of elements are first collected by the inference engine. It has then to apply the approximate formula previously

discussed. This formula was implemented in a FORTRAN code, called "CALC", which reads the data in a file, say COLLEG, and writes the output in the same file. The shell offers the possibility of specifying in a rule that CALC must be activated, COLLEG being the connection disk. A list of the parameters to be put in COLLEG and to be sent to CALC can also be specified. Also in this case the use of the present device made in [9] is limited. However,nothing prevents CALC from being a complex finite-element structural code. The potentialities in the assessment of the structural resistance can then be easily imagined.

3) A "confidence measure" is available. When the operator is required to provide an answer to a question, YES or NO (TRUE or FALSE) are generally two extreme situations. It is much more likely that the answer the operator can provide is "almost surely true (or false)" or "may be true (or false)". The shell permits the operator to cover all the range between 0 (FALSE) and 100 (true). Moreover, this confidence measure can be used in the computations. For instance, one of the parameters to be provided to the approximate formula in item 3 of figure 1 depends on how old the masonry is. Therefore, the "confidence measure" can be used, in the corresponding rule, to decrease the value of that parameter as the confidence in the masonry age increases.

UNCERTAINTY TREATMENT

The expert system prototype which was presented in [9] provides two kinds of results: the resulting classification (first column from the left in figure 1) for the item under investigation and the quality of the information (second column) which led to this classification. This quality is expressed by the resulting confidence measure. A number in the range (0,100) is substituted for the naive concept codified in [6] of four different degrees of confidence. They are: E (high quality), M (average), B (low quality) and A (operator's guess).

However, this "confidence measure"is also the weak point of the shell INSIGHT2+. The reason is that the confidence calculations are driven directly by the inference engine. In other words the expert who builds the knowledge base is unable to dominate these calculations. For instance, a conclusion is reached when the confidence in it is greater than a value fixed by the expert, but no mention is made of the alternative events. Even with a low confidence in their occurrence, these events can, in fact,influence significantly the deductive process. Moreover, the limit value fixed by the expert cannot be too low or too high, otherwise the conclusion comes out to be too optimistic or too pessimistic, respectively.

The authors decided to prevent unsatisfactory conclusions by building into the knowledge base a logic treatment of uncertainty accounting for the elements listed above and other minor aspects. This, of course, is made by additional rules which condition the inference engine process. As a consequence, the expert system prototype proposed in [9] was modified to provide for each item the possibility of belonging to class A, B, C or D. Here probability has not any frequentist meaning: it is regarded as degree of belief. At the end of the consultation, therefore, one obtains also the probability mass function of the vulnerability index and some central measures are computed.

Further developments are in progress making use of other uncertainty measures. It is known, in fact, that linguistic influence is well matched by the theory of possibility. As an ultimate objective of the research, however, the whole uncertainty treatment should be framed in the more general "theory of evidence" [14], unifying all the different approaches which presently are formulated as alternatives.

CONCLUSIONS

This paper illustrates the developments in progress in Italy in the field of vulnerability assessment. The adoption of expert system shells of the second generation, in particular, opens the way to a large variety of improvements using more sophisticated models of the structural behaviour. This second generation, in fact, makes the expert system capable of interacting with external algorithmic codes. Therefore, finite element structural analysis codes can be run during the process. This permits the analyst to identify the strength of the building under investigation, provided the structural scheme and the material constitutive law are available.

These properties, as well as many of the parameters to be estimated and/or investigated, are uncertain quantities due to the building technology which characterized the past centuries. Unfortunately, the way of treating the uncertainty of commercial second generation shells is still elementary. This paper suggests to obviate the inconvenience by building a more sophisticated scheme of uncertainty treatment by means of additional rules without shell modifications. However, one cannot exclude that the production of an "ad hoc" shell, even elementary in its inference process, may prove more efficient in preventing the seismic damage of historical buildings. This point must be carefully checked in the future research activity.

ACKNOWLEDGEMENT

This paper is part of   research funded by the National Group
of Earthquake prevention (GNDT) of the Italian Research
Council (CNR). It is coordinated by Prof. A. Corsanego, as
chairman of the national research group on Vulnerability.

REFERENCES

1.   Faravelli, L. Source-to-Site Seismic Models in Structural
      Dynamics. Proc. 3rd Int. Conf. on Recent Advances in
      Structural Dynamics, Southampton, Vol. 2, pp. 1021-1032,
      1988.

2.   Faravelli, L., Kiremidjian, A. and Suzuki, S., A
      Stochastic Seismological Model in Earthquake Engineering.
      Proc. 5th ASCE Specialty Conf. on Probabilistic Methods
      in Civil Engineering, Blacksburg (VA), pp.241-244, 1988.

3.   Augusti, G., Baratta, A. and Casciati, F. Probabilistic
      Methods in Structural Engineering. Chapman & Hall, 1984.

4.   Clough, R.W. and Penzien, J. Dynamics of Structures. Mc
      Graw Hill, 1975.

5.   Ministero Beni Culturali. Programma Quadro delle Ricerche
      del Comitato Nazionale per la Prevenzione del Patrimonio
      Culturale dal Rischio Sismico. (In Italian), 1987.

6.   GNDT - CNR. Istruzioni per la Compilazione della Scheda
      di Rilevamento Esposizione e Vulnerabilita' Sismica degli
      Edifici. (In Italian), September 1986.

7.   Benedetti, D., and Petrini, V. Sulla Vulnerabilita'
      Sismica di Edifici in Muratura: Proposta di un Metodo di
      Valutazione. (In Italian), Industria Costruzioni, Vol.
      18, 1984

8.   Benedetti, D., Benzoni, G., and Parisi, M.A., Seismic
      Vulnerability and Risk Evaluation for Old Urban Nuclei.
      Earthquake Engineering and Structural Dynamics, Vol. 16,
      pp. 183-201, 1988

9.   Faravelli, L., Expert System for Fragility Assessment of
      Monumental Sites. Int. Symp. on Earthquake
      Countermeasures, Beijing, 1988.

10.   Casciati, F., and Faravelli, L., L'Impiego di Sistemi
      Esperti in Ingegneria Sismica. (In Italian), Proc. 3rd
      Conf. "L'Ingegneria Sismica in Italia", Roma, pp.199-210,
      1987.

11. Gavarini, C. and Pagnoni, T., Amadeus. Un Sistema Esperto per la Valutazione d'Urgenza dell'Agibilita' degli Edifici dopo il Terremoto. (In Italian), Dept. of Structural Eng. and Geotech., Univ. "La Sapienza", Roma, 1988.

12. INSIGHT: Insight Knowledge System, Level Five Research. Melbourne Beach, Florida, U.S.A.

13. Casciati, F. and Faravelli, L., Individuazione di Problemi di Meccanica dei Solidi Suscettibili di Inquadramento in Sistemi Esperti. (In Italian). Proc. 9th Nat. Conf. AIMETA, Bari, pp. 553-556, 1988.

14. Shafer, G., A Mathematical Theory of Evidence, Princeton University Press, 1976

Application of a Numerical Method to the Study of Masonry Panels with Various Geometry under Seismic Loads

Sandro Chiostrini and Andrea Vignoli

Department of Civil Engineering, University of Florence Via di S. Marta, 3 50139 Florence, Italy

ABSTRACT

A non-linear finite element procedure was applied to masonry structures. Special contact elements were used in the analytical model to simulate the mortar. A realistic representation of masonry characteristics was obtained by a suitable distribution of the conventional and contact elements and by the appropriate setting of the free parameters in such a way that the numerical model effectively represents both the actual material and the restrains. Several structural elements were tested with horizontal loads to simulate seismic conditions. An experimental test was reproduced by the analytical procedure obtaining a good agreement between computed and laboratory results.

Introduction

Many structural studies and experimental tests on masonry buildings have been performed in the last ten years, due to the need to repair damage caused by earthquakes and to learn how to reinforce other buildings in the event of seismic loading. In particular, attention has been focused, (at the Dept. of Civil Engineering of the University of Florence), on the problems associated with the repair, maintenance and reinforcement of ancient monumental masonry buildings. [1-4].

Even today masonry is commonly used despite the difficulties associated with evaluating the actual behaviour of the material when subjected to severe loading. The response of many structures under working loads can in fact be predicted by linear theories, if the constitutive relations can be treated as linear which usually does not introduce appreciable errors. On the other hand the small traction strength of mortars, the problems related to crack openings, and other such complex problems, make the real behaviour of masonry very difficult to represent by analytical models when the loadings are severe.

The aim of the present paper is to show that it is posssible to correctly simulate experimental tests performed on masonry elements using a new finite element model [3-4]. A special interface finite element, which was first developed for heat-transfer applications

[5], was introduced to model the small traction strength of mortar in a masonry building. This technique provided good results, especially for the study of "block masonry," and under certain conditions, for "brick masonry" modelling as well. In this latter case experimental tests were adequately simulated numerically.

Analytical Approaches in Evaluating the Structural Behaviour of Masonry.

As stated above, most numerical solutions for the structural analysis of masonry buildings are performed by linear analysis. Though simple and quick, this approach cannot represent the real non-linear behaviour of masonry. In order to evaluate the ultimate strength of a building, other methods must be considered.

To this end, two types of approach have been developed, i.e.; continuum "exact" solutions and "approximate" numerical models. The first approach has only a few practical applications mainly because: (i) the masonry buildings' components present a complex geometry, often including openings (windows, doors, etc.) which makes exact solutions impossible to find; (ii) it is difficult to adequately respect the masonry material constitutive law, and to represent phenomena such as crack openings and the small traction strength of mortar.

It is clear that it is necessary to use numerical approaches for an effective representation of real problems. In this way an approximate solution for the structural behaviour can be obtained.

Before introducing the approach adopted by the authors, it must be pointed out that the masonry collapse-mechanism mainly depends on the relative strength of the mortar and bricks (or any other components of masonry). Therefore a collapse situation can be achieved in different ways: (i) - sliding along the mortar horizontal bed joints planes. (This tends to happen when the mortar-brick adherence is small and the structure is subjected to horizontal loads); (ii) - sliding along vertical mortar joints (under the same conditions as (i) and under vertical loading); (iii) - if the mortar collapses, with cracks along the direction of the bed joints; (iv) - if the mortar-brick bond collapses with cracks crossing both elements.

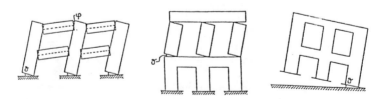

Frame mechanism   Floor mechanism   Rocking mechanism
Fig. 1: Como-Grimaldi collapse mechanisms

Because of the uncertainty in determining the correct fracture mechanism of masonry material, it is sometimes better to evaluate the solution, abandoning the idea of studying the real "microscopic" behaviour of the masonry in order to examine only the "global" collapse mechanisms. The most interesting approach, which follows the above idea, is the Como-Grimaldi method [6]. It considers, from the point of view of the limit analysis, three different collapse-mechanisms (see Figure 1), which depend on the load intensity and the relative element stiffness.

A Finite Element Approach to the Study of Masonry Elements

An iterative non-linear finite element calculation procedure was adopted by the authors. A particular element [5, 7], called a "gap" contact element, is used to represent numerically the traction strength of masonry. As the load increases, the cracking evolution of the panel is represented by the progressive opening of these gap-elements. Since the global tangent stiffness matrix changes, both due to the effects of varying geometry (geometrical non-linearity), and because of the the gap conditions (open or closed - material non-linearity), an iterative procedure was adopted in the numerical solution. Using this scheme, it was possible to represent the masonry characteristics and, with suitable arrangements of gap-positioning and free-parameters setting, to simulate experimental results with a good degree of approximation.

Obviously, when gap-elements are positioned in a fixed direction, the collapse mechanism is biased. Models such as these correspond to the real situation only when considering "block-masonry." When the case of "brick-masonry" is considered, the modelling pattern of the real stucture strongly influences the collapse mechanism and the simulation results. In the case of "brick- masonry" this approach can be seen as an interesting way of reproducing experimental tests or evaluating the collapse load corresponding to a known fracture mechanism. When this method is used to predict the structural behaviour of brick masonry strucures, special attention must be paid to accurate evaluation of the influence of gap-positioning and free-parameters setting.

Panel Modelling

In the first phase of the study, a micro-model was adopted. All the bricks and the mortar planes of the real structure were introduced in the numerical representation of the panel using two - dimensional finite elements. Bricks were represented by an isotropic four-node element, while mortar bed joints were introduced using gap-elements. The model described above corresponds to the conditions indicated at points (i), (ii) and (iii) above. The adopted hypothesis, that cracks can happen only in the mortar bed joints, excludes collapse mechanisms involving a complete brick-mortar collaboration. It is important to note that this choice is not necessarily the best: in fact, different models can be created simply by assuming diverse relative positions between "gap" and "conventional" finite elements.

Two possible arrangements for gap-positioning are presented in Figure 2. The second choice was preferred, despite the increased number of elements, because in this case the gap-constants (i.e. element stiffness in the nodel direction - k - and friction coefficient for interface sliding - f -) [8] have an effective physical meaning.

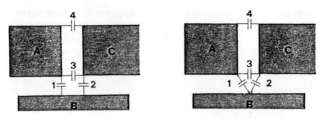

Fig. 2: Two possible solutions for gap-positioning

A Real Experimental Test Simulation

An example of the type of simulations that can be performed by the above model is shown in Figure 3. Data and results were derived from reference [8].

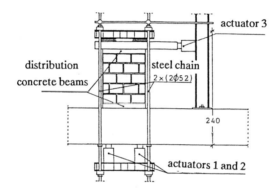

Fig. 3: Experimetal test scheme

The principle characteristics of the model were: (i) - the vertical pre-stress was performed by hydraulic jacks 1 and 2 and by four steel chains; (ii) - the horizontal testing load was performed by jack 3; (iii) - two concrete distribution beams were built to contain the masonry panel and transmit vertical pre-stressing. Other representations of the same model are shown in Figure 4.

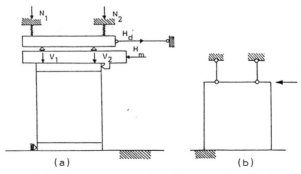

Fig. 4: Simpler representations of the experimental scheme

The characteristics of the numerical model were [3]: (i) - steel chains were represented by "equivalent" trusses elements (see Figure 6) with physical constants (E) of steel. The trusses' area was determined by assuming an equivalent stiffness for the real chains; (ii) - concrete distribution beams were introduced adopting isotropic four-node elements with the physical properties of concrete; (iii) - the load was applied in two steps: a vertical pre-stress load was applied first, and then the horizontal testing load was applied to the panel in several steps of 8 Kn each step. Iterations were carried out to achieve the equilibrium position before increasing the load.

Problems concerning free-parameters setting are treated in reference [7]. It is important to note that, with suitable values of finite elements physical constants, it was possible to reproduce with perfect agreement not only the global experimental test results of Figure 5, but also the collapse mechanism shown in Figure 6.

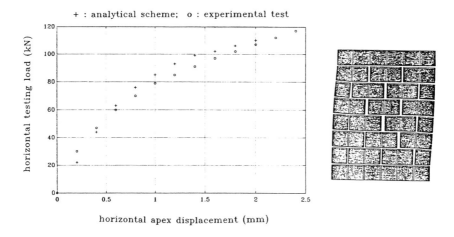

Fig. 5: Load displacement curve   Fig. 6: Collapse mechanism

The Modelling of Masonry Walls

The small scale model described above cannot be used to study an entire building or a large structural element. In fact, while crack openings can still be represented by adequate gap-elements, it is practically impossible to introduce into the numerical model all the bricks actually contained in the structure.

In the present study the so-called "macro-brick" element [8] was used to obtain a reasonable representation of large structures.

Comparison of the Adopted Approach with the Como-Grimaldi Approach.

The Como-Grimaldi limit analysis method for masonry structures hypothesizes an elastic unidimensional constitutive relationship. The fracture mechanisms shown in Figure 1 are specified following the reasoning described in reference [6].

It is possible to simulate the Como-Grimaldi hypothesis with the adopted procedure by providing suitable gap elements and macro-bricks. Three different schemes, under the same load conditions, were considered, as shown in Figure 7. The vertical load was fixed while the horizontal one was applied progressively as was stated earlier.

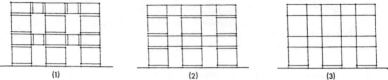

Fig. 7: Different analytical schemes

The different gap elements in the three schemes were chosen to simulate the different strength conditions postulated in the Como-Grimaldi hypothesis between horizontal and vertical masonry elements. Results obtained by the present analysis are shown in Table 1. The corresponding collapse mechanisms are presented in Figures 8-11.

Tab. 1

Fracture Mechanism	Scheme	Vertical Load (kN)	Ultimate Shear Value (kN)	
			Present an.	C-G analysis3
Frame	1	460	160	190
Floor	1	460	440	460
Floor	2	460	480	460
Rocking	3	460	520	520

Fig. 8: Frame mechanism by scheme 1   Fig. 9: Floor mechanism by scheme 1

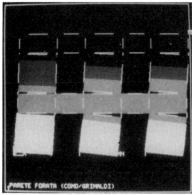 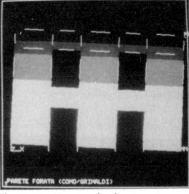

Fig. 10: Floor mechanism by scheme 2   Fig. 11: Rocking mechanism by scheme 3

Evolutionary Analysis of a Masonry Wall

The same structural shapes used for the Como-Grimaldi analysis were represented using finite elements and subjected to increasing loads, until collapse was reached. The different settings for macro-bricks and gap elements permitted displacements and crack openings in the zones where traction stresses occurred.

In particular, the analysis was performed with the scheme shown in Figure 12, where the dark zones represent concrete distribution beams to sustain vertical loads.

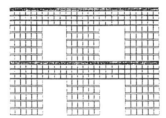

Fig. 12: Evolutionary analysis analitical scheme

The physical parameters corresponded to those determined for the panel. The collapse displacements are shown in Figures 13 and 14.

The collapse cracking pattern and the relative load level obtained in the evolutionary analysis corresponded approximately to those obtained by the Como-Grimaldi frame mechanism. It is also shown in Figure 12 that the gap-planes, represented by the double lines, were positioned so as to permit crack-openings where traction stresses were expected.

It is also appropriate to point out that, in modelling large structural elements using the concept of "brick masonry", it is often necessary to use a large number of gap and conventional finite elements to avoid a strong influence of the gap-positioning on the analytical response.

For this reason, it is important to investigate the modelling problem in more detail, and try to reach the most practical analytical scheme with which to achieve convergence quickly.

Fig. 13: X-displacements collapse situation   Fig. 14: Y-displacements collapse situation

Conclusions and Suggestions for Further Research

A finite element procedure was applied using a particular interface-element previously adopted for heat-transfer applications. The procedure proved to be particularly indicated for simulating block-masonry behaviour, where the contact region is easy to define. The approach is also of interest in the study of brick-masonry problems.

An experimental test on a masonry panel was simulated using finite elements. These obtained a good representation of the collapse mechanism and the load-displacements curve. A comparison between the present procedure and a limit-analysis method demonstrated good agreement between the ultimate load value and the collapse mechanism. Results show that the adopted method can be utilized for the study of masonry structures even if, at the present, some uncertainties concerning the most convenient ways to model real brick-masonry structures still remain. In fact, the analytical response of the model is strongly influenced by the positioning of the elements. Further researches to improve the structural modelling and to extend the range of simulations performed with this approach will be carried out in the future.

References

1. Blasi, C., Vignoli, A.: Dynamic test controls of antiseismic upgrading on the Colosseum at Rome. Proc of the 8th Europ. Conf. Earthquake Engrg., Vol.5, pp. 11.2/7 - 11.2/23, Lisbon, 1986.

2. Blasi, C., Spinelli, P., Vignoli, A.: A dynamic behaviour and monitoring of monumental buildings - Proc. IABSE Coll. on "Monitoring of Large Structrues and Assessment of their Safety", pp. 311-324, Bergamo, Italy, 1987.

3. Gonelloni, Luca: Modelli numerici per l'interpretazione del comportamento sperimentale di pannelli in muratura. Grad. thesis, Dept. of Civil Engrg., Univ. of Florence. (Tutors: Chiarugi, A., Vignoli, A.)

4. Senesi, Claudio: Analisi delle Costruzioni in muratura: procedure per lo studio al discreto in campo non-lineare. Grad. thesis, Dept. of Civil Engnrg., Univ. of Florence. (Tutors: Chiarugi, A., Vignoli, A.)

5. AAVV:ANSYS: Engineering Analysis System, User's Manual. Swanson Analysis Systems Inc., Houston, Pen. 1986.

6. Como, M. Grimaldi, A. An unilateral model for the limit analysis of masonry walls; Proc. "Unilateral Problems in Structural Anlysis", Ravello 22-24 September, 1983.

7. Chiostrini, S., Foraboschi, P., Sorace, S.: Problems connected with the application of a non-linear finite element method to the analysis of masonty structures. Proc. STREMA, Florence, 5-7 April 1989.

8. Bernardini, A., Modena, C., Vescove, U.: Ricerca sperimentale sui parametri di resistenza e deformabilita'di murature in laterizio armato e alveolato. J. "Costruire," n. 109, 1978; n. 114, 1979.

Analysis of Microtremor Records at Zeus-Olympeion Athens and Assessment of its Safety by Employing Dynamic Response Analysis

N. Theofanopoulos, T. Hanazato, K. Matsukawa and M. Watabe

Architectural Department, University of Tokyo Metropolitan, 2-1-1 Fukazawa, Setagaya-ku, Tokyo 158, Japan

ABSTRACT

In the present research, microtremor records at Zeus Olympeion, Athens were first analyzed in order to calculate the fundamental period of its columns. Then, seismic hazard analysis to determine the response of the columns due to earthquake motions of various return periods, was conducted. Finally, dynamic response analysis was employed to verify the validity of the seismic hazard analysis results and to examine the earthquake resistant capacity of Olympeion's columns against earthquake motions that correspond to return periods of 100 and 1000 years. The results of dynamic analysis in the case of return period of 1000 years, show that the columns may resist the shear forces induced by these earthquakes along their height, except the upper two drums, but they may not undertake the imposed overturning moments at any level along their height.

INTRODUCTION

In a spacious, rectangular walled precinct to the south-east of Acropolis hill, near the center of Athens, fifteen huge Corinthian columns of Zeus Olympeion still tower up today. The number of the temple columns when it was complete was 104. The dimensions of the temple's stylobate are 107.89m length and 41.11m width. A double row of columns was to surround the elongated cella, in front of either end of which three parallel rows, each of eight columns, would form a veritable forest of columns [1]. The plan of Olympeion is shown in figure 1. The columns still standing, were painted with black color. The construction of the temple was started, perhaps under the tyrant Pisistratus about 520 B.C. and left so unfinished that only the platform was kept for the much later building. The construction of the temple was restarted after an interval of three centuries in 174 B.C. and finally completed 305 years later by the Roman emperor Hadrian.

Thirteen columns of the south-east corner, still standing as a coherent group and other two isolated in the south pteroma are the sole remains of the former glory. Another isolated column in the south pteroma was brought down by a hurricane in 1852,[1].The rest of the columns are believed to have been demolished intentionally in 1759, to use the fragments as building materials or for making lime, [2]. This means that the monuments present state is not attributable to earthquakes that hit the area during its history. Therefore, the behavior of the remaining part of the monument in the case of a future destructive earthquake is doubtful considering the material alterations and the already weakened interconnections of structural members. The cultural importance of the monument imposes the necessity of examining its earthquake resistant capacity and the methods adopted in this study may constitute a base for the anti-seismic protection of the numerous similar historical monuments in the earthquake stricken countries around the Mediterranean sea.

STRUCTURAL CONDITION OF OLYMPEION

The columns of Olympeion are composed of 18 drums, have height equal to 16.89m and aspect ratio (height/diameter) equal to 9.3, which is approximately twice that of Parthenon's columns aspect ratio. The diameter of the drums ranges between about 2m at the base and about 1.7m at the top. The average height of drums is about 0.98m. The drum to drum contact was assumed to be perfect and the applied shear force at the drums' interface was considered to be undertaken by the friction force. Due to the lack of information concerning the use of wooden or metallic pivots as in the case of Parthenon, their contribution to the shearing resistance of Olympeion's columns was neglected. Figure 2 shows a typical column of Zeus Olympeion along with the cross sections at three levels. It seems to be a rather slender column, liable to easy destruction by earthquake motions. The fact that Olympeion's columns remain untouched by earthquakes may not be correlated with the absence of destructive earthquakes in the area of Athens, but may be attributed to the structural perfection of the monument.

ANALYSIS OF MICROTREMOR RECORDS

Three microtremor records have been obtained, two of them at the top along the east-west and north-south directions, and the other one at the base of a column. The places where the microtremors were recorded are shown as 1, 2 and 3 in triangle frames in figure 2. These records were available in analog form and in order to be analyzed they were digitized by the use of a high accuracy digitizer with a sampling rate of more than 300 points per second. The digitized at unequal time intervals records, were equispaced with time increment of 0.02 sec, base line corrected and filtered using cosine taper filter with cut-off frequencies 0.05 and 25 Hz, respectively. The resulting velocity, as well as, the integrated displacement time histories of each microtremor record are shown in figures 3 to 5, respectively. The maximum velocities and displacements at the top are about 3.5 times greater than those at the base of the column.

Moreover, the Fourier and power spectra of the digitized records were calculated. Figures 6 to 8 show the normalized to their peak values Fourier and power spectra for each microtremor record, respectively. The maximum spectral values were obtained, for the first record at period 0.553 and for the other two records at periods 0.101 and 0.102 sec, respectively. At the second and third record another peak at period 0.55 sec was also observed. In order to estimate the fundamental period of Olympeion's columns, the Fourier spectral ratios of the records obtained at the top to that of the records obtained at the base of the column were calculated. Those spectral ratios are shown in figures 9 and 10. They attain their peak values at periods 0.525 and 0.499 sec, respectively. In both cases the spectral ratio was about 15 to 18 for the predominant periods, about 1.8 for the period range between 0.04 and 0.3 sec and more than 2 in the long period range. These results lead us to the conclusion that the natural period of Olympeion's columns should be about 0.525 sec for the first mode of vibration and about 0.101 sec for the second one.

SEISMIC HAZARD ANALYSIS

Probabilistic seismic hazard analysis for the site where Olympeion is located was conducted, based on historical earthquake records in the area of Greece covering a period of about 100 years. The results of the seismic hazard analysis are presented in terms of acceleration response spectra with damping 5% of critical, following the procedure explained by Theofanopoulos, [3]. The resulted acceleration response spectra for return periods of 50, 100 and 1000 years are shown in figure 11. Under the assumptions, that the contribution of higher than the first modes is negligible and that the column of Olympeion can be satisfactorily modeled as a single-degree of freedom oscillator, the expected maximum relative displacements at the top of the columns can be obtained by multiplying the response acceleration values of the calculated response spectra for the fundamental period of the column by the square of fundamental circular frequency. For fundamental period of the column equal to 0.525 sec and for return periods of 50, 100 and 1000 years, the maximum displacements at the top will be 1.04, 1.33 and 2.65cm, respectively. Since, the real behavior of Olympeion's columns and that of a single-degree of freedom oscillator are different, the obtained results will give us only an indication about the order of the expected relative displacements at the top of the columns. In order to examine the validity of these results, dynamic response analysis of a single column due to earthquake motions generated by Theofanopoulos, [3], for return periods of 100 and 1000 years, was conducted.

DYNAMIC RESPONSE ANALYSIS

Linear response analysis of 18 lumped masses system, accounting for both translational and rotational modes at each level of drums' separation were performed. The influence of the beam was not considered in the modeling procedure. The rotational spring constants KR, at each level were calculated by the following equation;

$$KR = a.\sqrt{\sigma_v}.r^4 \tag{1}$$

where σ_v is the vertical compressive stress at each level, r is the radius of the drums' interface and a is the proportionality index. This proportionality index a, was estimated through modal analysis of Olympeion's columns having in mind to obtain fundamental period of the model equal to the estimated one by microtremor analysis. Moreover, the translational spring constants were evaluated from the elastic deformation characteristics of the drums, by assuming that the shear forces at drums' interfaces are undertaken by the friction in the range of linear response. Table 1 shows the parameters of Olympeion's columns used in the dynamic response analysis. Mode superposition method was applied to solve the differential equation of the problem as explained by Hanazato et al., [4]. The first five modes of vibration were considered in the analysis. The natural periods of these modes were 0.531,

0.101, 0.039, 0.021 and 0.013 sec, respectively. This result reveals that, the natural periods obtained for the first two modes of vibration for the assumed model are identical to those estimated by analysis of microtremor records.

Figure 12 shows the time histories of acceleration, velocity and displacement response at the top of the column, for return periods of 100 and 1000 years, respectively. The amplification factor of peak velocity is about 4, which is comparable with the amplification factors observed in microtremor records. The peak relative displacement at the top of the column was equal to 1.80 and 3.78cm for return periods of 100 and 1000 years, respectively. These values exceed somewhat the estimated ones by the seismic hazard analysis, but the resulting values for both methods are of the same order.

Figure 13 shows the distributions of the resulting maximum shear coefficients along the height of the column, for return periods of 100 and 1000 years. These maximum shear coefficients attain relatively small values, except the upper two drums where their values for return period of 1000 years exceed the unity. The friction coefficient between the drums' interface is unknown, but if it is assumed to be equal to that of Parthenon's drums, i.e., 0.8, the upper two drums could not undertake the seismic loads for return period of 1000 years. Therefore, a possible higher value of friction coefficient or the existence of shear resisting pivots between the drums' interface, may contribute in undertaking the excess shear force at the upper two drums. In the case of columns with beam resting on their top, the values of maximum shear coefficient will be reduced considerably, and the response of Olympeion's columns in shear, during earthquakes of the considered level, may be satisfactory. However, the resulting overturning moments at the base for both return periods were 181 and 356 ton.m, respectively. The restoring moment due to the columns weight is considerably smaller, equal to 130 ton.m. Similar observations were made at each level of drums' separation. This means that the Olympeion's columns may withstand safely the shear forces induced by earthquake motions, but they should be strengthened to undertake the excess overturning moment.

CONCLUSIONS

A methodology to evaluate the fundamental period of Zeus Olympeion columns was presented. By the use of the obtained fundamental period and the results of seismic hazard analysis, approximate values of the maximum displacement response at the top of Olympeion columns were evaluated. Finally, dynamic response analysis of a single column was conducted and the results lead us to the conclusion that Olympeion's columns should be strengthened to undertake the excess overturning moment at each level and the excess shear force at the upper two drums for earthquakes with return period of 1000 years. For earthquakes with return period of 100 years, it is only required to strengthen the first 14 drums from the base to withstand the excess overturning moment.

ACKNOWLEDGMENTS

The authors wish to express their gratitude to professor P. Karydis of National Technical University of Athens for his permission to use the microtremor records.

REFERENCES

1. Berve, H., G. Gruben. Greek Temples, Theaters and Shrines. Thames and Hudson, London, 394-397, 1963.

2. Ambraseys, N. On the Protection of Monuments in Seismic Areas. Proceedings of the 2nd International Meeting for the Restoration of Acropolis Monuments, Athens, 207-228, 1983.

3. Theofanopoulos, N., T. Hanazato and M. Watabe. Probabilistic Approach to Generate the Reference Motion for the Protection of Historical Monuments Against Earthquakes. Proceedings of 1st International Conf. on Structural Studies, Repairs and Maintenance of Historical Buildings, Florence, Italy, 1989.

4. Hanazato, T., N. Theofanopoulos and M. Watabe. Seismic Response Analysis of Parthenon Columns. Proceedings of 1st International Conf. on Structural Studies, Repairs and Maintenance of Historical Buildings, Florence, Italy, 1989.

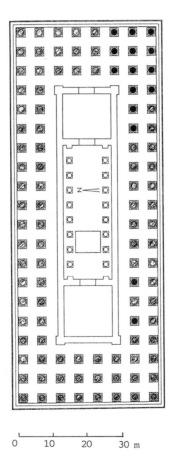

Fig. 1. Plan of Zeus Olympeion. The columns still standing are painted with black color, (this figure was taken from [1]).

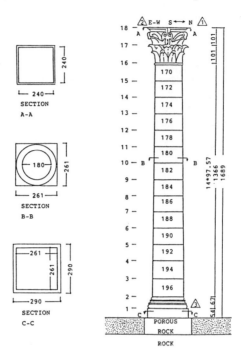

Fig. 2. A typical column of Zeus Olympeion.

DRUM	MASS (ton)	HEIGHT (m)	MOMENT OF INERTIA (ton.m)	K_R ($\times 10^5$tonf.m)	K_H ($\times 10^6$tonf.m)
18	10.70	1.01	4.22	3.10	9.90
17	7.61	1.01	2.31	2.27	6.72
16	6.02	0.98	1.57	2.72	7.14
15	6.16	0.98	1.62	3.14	7.29
14	6.31	0.08	1.69	3.59	7.45
13	6.45	0.98	1.76	4.01	7.63
12	6.60	0.98	1.83	4.47	7.82
11	6.75	0.98	1.90	4.90	7.98
10	6.90	0.98	1.98	5.37	8.17
9	7.05	0.98	2.05	5.86	8.35
8	7.20	0.98	2.13	6.36	8.54
7	7.36	0.98	2.20	6.87	8.73
6	7.52	0.98	2.29	7.36	8.91
5	7.68	0.98	2.37	7.95	9.10
4	7.84	0.98	2.46	8.50	9.28
3	8.01	0.98	2.55	9.08	9.47
2	6.02	0.67	2.02	16.80	20.44
1	10.01	0.54	5.92	32.32	38.21

Table 1. Parameters of Zeus Olympeion's columns.

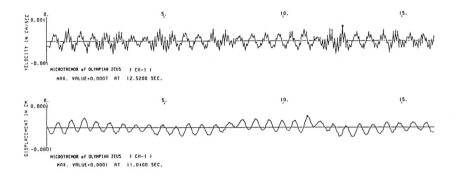

Fig. 3. Corrected microtremor record and integrated displacement at recording point 1 (top).

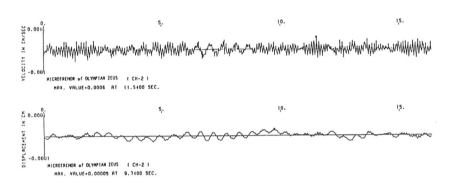

Fig. 4. Corrected microtremor record and integrated displacement at recording point 2 (top).

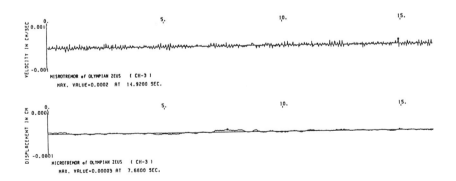

Fig. 5. Corrected microtremor record and integrated displacement at recording point 3 (base).

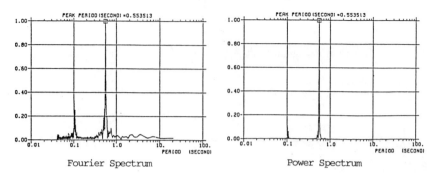

Fig.6. Normalized Fourier and Power Spectra corresponding to recording point 1.

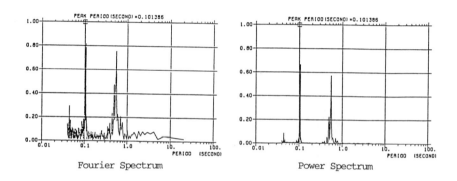

Fig.7. Normalized Fourier and Power Spectra corresponding to recording point 2.

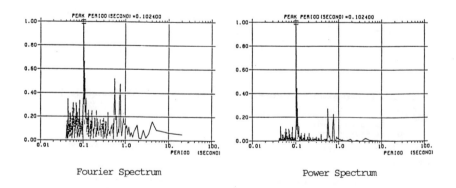

Fig.8. Normalized Fourier and Power Spectra corresponding to recording point 3.

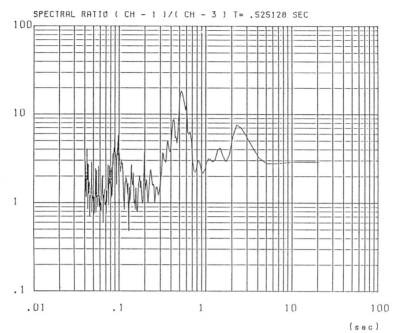

Fig. 9. Fourier spectral ratio between recording points 1 and 3.

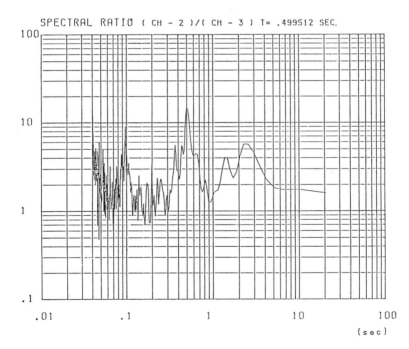

Fig. 10. Fourier spectral ratio between recording points 2 and 3.

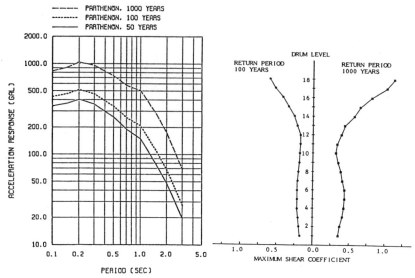

Fig. 11. Expected response spectra at the base of Acropolis hill for return periods of 50, 100 and 1000 years.

Fig. 13. Distribution of maximum shear coefficients due to earthquakes with return periods of 100 and 1000 years.

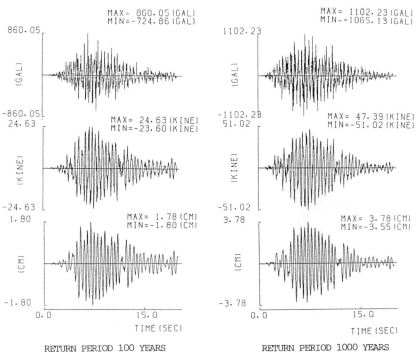

Fig. 12. Responses at the top of the column due to earthquake motions for return periods of 100 and 1000 years.

Seismic Isolation Retrofitting of the Salt Lake City and County Building

J. Bailey, E. Allen
E.W. Allen and Associates, Consulting Structural Engineers, Salt Lake City, Utah, USA

ABSTRACT

The City and County Building, a massive unreinforced masonry structure completed in 1894, has been seismically retrofitted using base isolation. The isolation system consists of 443 lead-rubber isolators installed underneath the building on top of existing spread footings. The building is isolated from the surrounding ground by a perimeter moat wall, permitting lateral movement to take place during an earthquake.

It is believed that this is the first historic structure in the world to be retrofitted against possible seismic damage using base isolation.

INTRODUCTION

Construction on the Salt Lake City and County Building began in 1890, and the building was dedicated and occupied in 1894. The building is a five story unreinforced masonry and stone bearing wall structure with a 76 meter high central clocktower. Plan dimensions are 40 meters by 80 meters. The style of architecture is Richardsonian/Romanesque Revival.

The building was, for many years, Utah's tallest. Even today, because of its ornamental architectural style and prominent location in the center of a city park, the building is a highly visible landmark (Figure 1).

STRUCTURAL HISTORY

At the time the building was designed and built, earthquake engineering was a non-existent science. The possible susceptibility of the structure to earthquake damage was likely not even considered.

Occupants became aware of the problem in later years when occasional minor earthquakes would produce cracks in walls and over doorways, loosen stonework, produce visible swaying in the clocktower structure, and set decorative statues askew.

The largest earthquake experienced by the building occurred in 1934, which prompted the removal of the 4 statues over the main building entrances and the statue atop the clocktower. The March 12, 1934, Hansel Valley earthquake had an approximate Richter magnitude of 6.1. Hansel Valley is about 80 miles from Salt Lake. Accelerations felt by the building at its base were likely not greater than .05 G. Although not reported in the local paper, folklore claims that the clockworks were shaken loose and crashed down through the tower floors and fifth level skylight, finally coming to rest on the fourth floor. Miscellaneous wall cracks have continued to appear through the years, with some attributed to settlement, some to earthquakes, but with no documentation or records kept.

Figure 1. City and County Building, Salt Lake City, Utah, USA.

Eventually the condition of the building became the subject of official concern, and in the early 1970's, a modest study of the building was funded by the City and County. The structural portion of the study concluded that the building was, for the most part, structurally sound, and would likely meet all requirements of the 1940 Uniform Building Code without modification. However, the building was woefully inadequate, seismically, and would require extensive modification to be brought up to code.

The clocktower, because of its height, weight, and configuration, was the most obvious seismic hazard. A study of the tower concluded that a steel space truss within the tower was the best solution, primarily because it would not add significant weight to a building which had already shown some signs of settlement distress.

During the following decade a certain amount of construction work was undertaken as funds were budgeted by the City and County. Small construction packages were bid that allowed the restoration of most of the exterior of the East Entrance, and the implementation of the first sections of the planned stabilization of the Clocktower. But the continued deterioration of the building and the inescapable effects of inflation eventually forced a reconsideration of this approach to the building's restoration, and the City decided to have a comprehensive study made of the structure to determine whether the building should, or could, be restored and seismically retrofitted, how the space could best be utilized, and the costs involved with the different approaches.

This study strongly recommended that the building be saved, primarily due to its historical significance and unique architecture. However, costs involved to seismically retrofit the building, using a conventional Uniform Building Code (UBC) approach, appeared to be prohibitively high. In order to bring the building up to Zone 3 standards, it would be necessary to totally gut and replace the interior structure, and construct a new building within the original exterior ornamental facade.

TESTING AND DETERMINATION OF AS-BUILT CONDITIONS

Field tests of existing materials were conducted to determine the reliable degree of strength of the as-built structure. The tests included in-place shear, compression prism, core compression, stone compression, and footing concrete compression tests. Significant findings were that the sand-lime mortar used in the masonry, and the footing concrete, were of generally poor quality, stone used for foundations was of a very high quality, and the laying of brick between wythes through the various wall thicknesses was generally quite good.

Original architectural plans were available for preliminary studies and the development of working drawings. Although inaccurate in many respects, these drawings provided a good starting point in determining many of the as-built conditions.

STRUCTURAL ANALYSIS AND DESIGN

The first challenge in this preliminary phase was to refine the structural study and explore ways of reducing the anticipated cost of seismic retrofit.

Preliminary analyses were done to arrive at seismic retrofit schemes using the UBC, Base Isolation (BI), and the ABK Method, a relatively new methodology being tried in California for seismic hazard mitigation of existing unreinforced masonry buildings. Common to all three schemes were the following:

1. A steel space truss within the clocktower to stabilize it and transfer seismic forces down into the main building. Conservatively, it was decided to use results of the conventional, non-isolated analysis for sizing of tower steel members and tower wall anchorage for all three solutions because of the significance of the tower as a seismic hazard.

2. A structural plywood diaphragm in the fifth floor attic spaces in order to stabilize the top of exterior masonry walls.

3. Lightweight reinforced concrete topping over portions of existing floor diaphragms to increase their stiffness and strength.

4. Anchorage of exterior masonry walls to floor and attic diaphragms.

5. Plywood shear walls within attic spaces to laterally stabilize the main building roof structure.

6. Anchorage of seismic hazards, such as chimneys, statues, gables, dormers, gargoyles, and balustrades, around the exterior of the building.

7. Diaphragm anchorage to interior masonry walls, for shear transfer and to provide a tension tie through the walls.

The original base isolation scheme consisted of approximately 500 isolators, to be installed on new footings a couple of meters below the bottom of existing footings. Directly above the isolators, and below the existing footings, would be a series of reinforced concrete beams to carry the weight of the structure between isolators. These beams would all be rigidly interconnected by struts to tie the system together.

Preliminary calculations indicated a dramatic reduction in force levels. Shotcreting of existing walls would not be necessary, and existing floor diaphragms would require only minimal strengthening around their perimeters. It would be necessary, however, to entirely remove the first floor to provide working space for the foundation work.

In essence, the BI solution shifted the focus of the structural work from the shear walls above to the foundation, reducing much of the seismic retrofit work to a massive underpinning project.

Preliminary cost estimates indicated the ABK Method as the most economical solution, although it was questioned whether the method could be extrapolated to a building of this monumental size. In terms of damage control and disruption in the historic fabric of the building, the ABK solution was felt to be inferior to the BI solution. Although the BI solution exceeded the ABK solution in cost by over $1 million, based on rough schematic estimates, it was still considerably less expensive and architecturally disruptive than the UBC solution, which would require total demolition and reconstruction of the interior of the building. Calculations also indicated that the base isolated building stayed well within the elastic range (.08 G, vs. .55 G for a non-isolated building), so that predicted damage would be minimized for the design earthquake.

These findings were presented to the Mayor and City Council, with a recommendation to proceed with base isolation. It was decided to conduct a detailed analytical study, which would include dynamic time history analyses on a detailed building computer model.

BASE ISOLATION CONCEPT

Although no seismograph records for major earthquakes in Salt Lake exist, earthquake records in other areas, with geology similar to Salt Lake, indicated that the City and County Building might be subjected to amplified force levels as high as .55 G. Resisting these forces using such approaches as the UBC and ABK methodologies would require significant construction throughout the building. This work would have great impact on existing architectural finishes, such as moldings, wainscots, door frames, and floor tile. This conventional type of seismic retrofit work would primarily serve to prevent building collapse, but non-catastrophic damage would still be extensive due to seismic energy being absorbed through inelastic deformation of building components.

Base isolators are very stiff in the vertical direction in order to transfer gravity loads, but are flexible in the horizontal direction, thus isolating the building from the horizontal components of seismic forces. Base isolation would shift the fundamental period of vibration of the structure to a range outside of the predominant energy content of the design earthquake. In simple terms, the structure would tend to vibrate at a different frequency than the ground below it, thus avoiding resonance and significantly reducing the level of force experienced by the building. (The concept works in much the same way as shock absorbers do in an automobile, isolating the car and its occupants from road vibrations.)

A typical bearing used on this project is approximately 43 cm. square by 38 cm. tall (Figure 2). It consists of a sandwich of alternating steel and rubber layers with a lead core. The purpose of the lead core is two-fold: it acts as a fuse, preventing building motion due to wind loads, but yielding and providing inelastic viscous damping to absorb energy during a seismic event. This damping also helps to control horizontal deflections. The steel plates, which are bonded to the rubber, prevent the rubber from spreading outward under vertical loading, thus making the bearings very stiff in the vertical direction.

In order for the bearings to work properly, it is necessary to isolate the perimeter of the building from the ground horizontally so that the building could translate relative to the ground during an earthquake. To do this a retaining wall would need to be constructed around the building's exterior with a 30 cm. seismic gap. Computer runs indicated that the maximum deflection that the building would experience relative to the ground during the design earthquake was about 12 cm. The additional clearance was provided as a factor of safety. A bumper restraint system was also installed in the moat to act as a backup safety device.

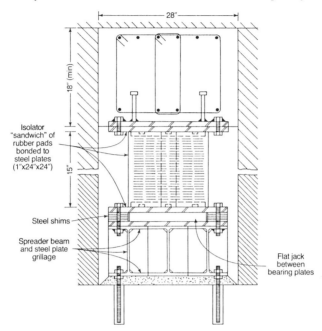

Figure 2. Typical installed base isolator.

BASE ISOLATION DESIGN

Shortly after the approval of the base isolation schematics, exploratory trenches dug around the foundation revealed significant variance between the original drawings and the as-built conditions. It was discovered that footings beneath the building were roughly 50% wider and thicker than shown on the original plans, with a massive concrete mat, 23 meters square by 1.4 meters thick, underneath the 4 main tower piers. The original base isolation scheme of placing isolators below existing foundations had to be abandoned.

The structural design team revised the scheme so that isolators would be installed on top of the existing footings. However, because of isolator installation clearances, it became necessary to raise the new 1st floor 36 cm.

Although a significant amount of tunneling and undermining work was eliminated by the decision to install the isolators above the existing footings, it was now necessary to cut hundreds of slots through existing walls above the footings in order to install the isolators. Also, a considerable amount of notching into existing walls for side beams was necessary. Tests had indicated that the stonework at the base of existing walls was extremely hard (1,500 kg./sq.cm. compressive strength), and it would be difficult to cut into it or through it. Also of concern were the types of tools that would be permitted for foundation work. The sand-lime mortar appeared to be of extremely poor quality at many locations, and it was felt that an impact hammer of any significant size would vibrate much of the mortar loose. Because of this concern, it was specified in the contract documents that only non-impact methods of stone removal would be permitted.

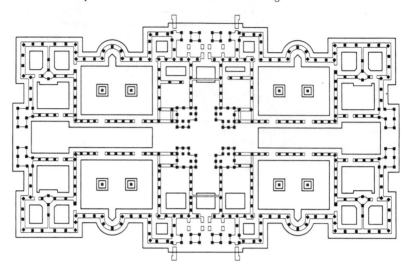

Figure 3. Plan view showing isolator layout.

The final design, on which construction documents were based and construction has proceeded, consisted of 443 bearings (Figure 3) placed on top of the original spread footings, with a new concrete structural system built above the bearings to distribute loads to the isolators. This new structure contains the following elements:

1. New concrete side-beams are poured on each side of all masonry walls. The walls are notched in 10 cm. on each side to receive these beams. Post-tensioning rods are drilled through the walls and tightened to clinch the masonry material between the new beams (Figure 4).

2. At isolator locations, all wall material is removed to accommodate the bearings themselves and a new concrete cross beam is poured over the top of the isolator and connected to the two side beams. The cross beam acts as a double cantilever in transferring the wall load from the side beams onto the isolator.

3. Below the isolators, several small steel beams are welded together to form a grillage to distribute vertical loads from the isolator onto the existing footing (Figure 2).

4. A new concrete 1st floor diaphragm is built, linking all of the isolators so that they will act together as a system.

5. After the 4 steps above are completed, the mortar joints directly below the new side beams are removed, thus transferring the building weight onto the isolators and completing the isolation process.

All isolators were made the same size to cut down on fabrication costs and simplify installation details. The different types of isolators were reduced to 2, those with lead plugs and those without. At one time, all isolators had lead plugs, but computer analyses had indicated unacceptably high tower shear for certain earthquake records. The isolators with lead plugs, approximately half of the total, were located around the perimeter of the building to cut down on torsional response.

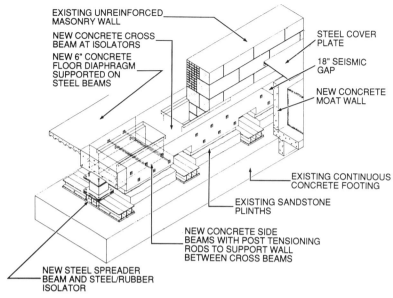

EXISTING UNREINFORCED
MASONRY WALL

NEW CONCRETE CROSS
BEAM AT ISOLATORS

NEW 6" CONCRETE
FLOOR DIAPHRAGM
SUPPORTED ON
STEEL BEAMS

STEEL COVER
PLATE

18" SEISMIC
GAP

NEW CONCRETE
MOAT WALL

EXISTING CONTINUOUS
CONCRETE FOOTING

EXISTING SANDSTONE
PLINTHS

NEW CONCRETE SIDE
BEAMS WITH POST TENSIONING
RODS TO SUPPORT WALL
BETWEEN CROSS BEAMS

NEW STEEL SPREADER
BEAM AND STEEL/RUBBER
ISOLATOR

Figure 4. Isometric showing how isolators are installed at exterior walls.

CONSTRUCTION

Prior to bidding the final contract, several different methods were tried by prospective contractors in an effort to determine the most efficient means of stone removal using non-impact tools. Two methods thought to be promising were line drilling, that is drilling a series of holes close enough to each other to form a single cut, and high pressure water jet cutting. Both methods worked, but neither proved to be cost effective.

As this job was truly unique, with no real precedent, it was difficult to obtain a reliable cost estimate. Experts in stone and concrete coring and cutting were consulted and shown the schemes, to get a general idea of the cost, as well as the stone removal methods likely to be employed. Fortunately, as things turned out, the local bidding climate was very favorable and this portion of the work was well within the budget.

The method chosen by the low bidder, and used for a large portion of the stone cutting, was a wire saw. The saw, manufactured in Spain, consists of a 1.27 cm. diameter diamond embedded steel wire, guided by a series of pulleys that can be adapted to each cutting situation. A control panel and device mounted on a track maintains tension on the wire. The wire is kept cool with a steady stream of water. Large diamond blade rotary saws, up to 1.22 meters in diameter, were also used to make the vertical cuts. Overcutting at corners could not be permitted, so this method left a considerable amount of partially cut stone within the holes that had to be broken out later. Both line drilling and wire saw cutting were used to make the horizontal cuts across the top of the slots.

Every effort was made, in preparing the bid documents, to have the contractor account for minor variations in existing footing elevations in his bid. A difference of plus or minus 7.62 cm. from the average elevation shown on the drawings was to be accounted for by adjusting grout thickness, cross beam depth, etc. Since the first floor was not to be removed prior to bidding, the average footing elevation was determined by studying the existing drawings, and checking actual footing elevations where possible in a very limited number of locations. Preliminary data seemed to indicate that the 7.62 cm. tolerance would be adequate. It had been recommended that, perhaps, the first floor should be removed as a separate contract so that existing footing and plinth conditions could be verified, and information thus obtained could be incorporated in the bid documents. This suggestion was denied as it would delay the overall project completion date.

Upon removal of the 1st floor, however, it became apparent that almost the entire south half of the building foundation was up to 15.24 cm. higher than shown on the bid documents. The north half, where footing elevation measurements had been taken previously, was almost entirely at the assumed elevation. Another problem not anticipated was that the stone used for plinths varied greatly in thickness, both along their length, and from side to side. Uniform stone thicknesses and widths had been shown on the original drawings, and verified in only a few accessible isolated locations prior to bidding and subsequent floor removal.

As luck would have it, the contractor began work on the south end of the foundation, where almost all of the problems were encountered. In order to stay ahead of the contractor, and answer the myriad questions generated by varying foundation conditions, it became necessary for the writer to stay full time at the job site for about 6 weeks. An additional structural engineer was assigned to the project for 4 months to help solve the steady stream of problems created by unforeseen existing conditions.

Also at the site were two engineers employed by the City and assigned to the project full time. This greatly eased the burden on the project engineer, as these people were on site to spot potential structural problems as they turned up, and to alert the project engineer. A full time field engineer is a must on any job of this size and complexity.

Another major concern was the possibility of building settlement and potential cracking at time of mortar joint removal. The isolators were pre-loaded to take up any slack in the isolator assemblage before cutting the mortar joints between isolators. The isolator vertical stiffness is considerable (535,000 kg./cm.). It was decided to pre-load to 2/3 of the estimated dead load, rather than the entire dead load; this would lower the risk of cracking the walls above, which might occur if too much pre-load were applied.

Pre-loading was accomplished using Freyssinet flat jacks in a shim space provided for this purpose below each isolator. The particular flat jack used is 41 cm. diameter by 3.18 cm. thick, with a rated load of 172,000 kg. Two workmen could easily pre-load 3 isolators in an hour. The procedure used is as follows:

1. Place flat jack with circular shims in space between isolator and spreader beam. The shims are fabricated to fit in the two dished areas located in the center of each side of the flat jack.

2. The flat jack comes with 2 valve stems. Epoxy is pumped into one of the stems until all air is bled off through the 2nd stem, at which time it is locked off. As pressure increases, the central dished out area of the flat jack expands as it fills with epoxy and presses against the 2 nested shims.

3. The hydraulic jack for pumping the epoxy is a double-acting type, where the hydraulic fluid, gauge, and assorted hoses are kept separate from the epoxy, thus allowing the hydraulic jack to be re-used. A solvent is used to clean the fittings and the top cylinder which comes in contact with the epoxy. When the gauge reading indicates the desired pre-load, the flat jack valve stem is locked off.

4. The remaining space between the two 61 cm. square plates not occupied by the flat jack is shimmed tight with steel shim plates, and the 4 corner bolts are tightened down.

5. Once the epoxy has cured, temporary safety screw jacks are removed and used elsewhere on the job.

Installing individual isolators under the 8 cast-iron columns posed special problems. A special column clamping device was designed and fabricated to grip the column in friction as well as bolt double-shear. The clamping device, in turn, bolted to the needle beams fabricated from channel sections which were used to jack against in order to pick up the load. An additional collar was installed below the clamping collar to support the new 1st floor beams. These beams were installed first to provide lateral bracing for the column during the underpinning procedure. Once it was verified by surveying instruments that the load was picked up, the bottom of the column and cast iron base plate were cut off, removed, and replaced with a base isolator. After isolator pre-loading, the needle beams, jacks, and clamping device could be removed and re-used on the next column. This method worked well for all but one column, which cracked and had to be repaired.

CONSTRUCTION STAGING

Of critical importance was the staging of mortar joint removal once all isolators were in place and pre-loaded. It would be unwise to allow the contractor to proceed at will with mortar joint removal, since parts of the building might be cut loose while other parts are still rigidly attached to the ground, making the building susceptible to even small tremors. The contractor had to meet the following requirements:

1. The new 1st floor diaphragm had to be substantially in place before any mortar joints were cut.

2. All mortar joints must be removed in as short a time as possible.

3. A specific joint cutting sequence must be followed so that one part of the building does not become isolated for an extended period of time while another part is still tied down.

It must be realized that the building is in greater seismic danger during the whole isolator installation process, as significant portions of wall must be removed to install the isolators. An earthquake of any significant size during isolator installation could be catastrophic to the building.

In regions seismically more active than Utah, the added degree of risk during the installation process would need to be studied carefully, as the potential for a significant earthquake during the isolator installation time window would be much greater. Perhaps isolator locking mechanisms could be employed during isolator installation in areas of high seismicity where the degree of risk during construction is judged to be unacceptably high.

CONCLUSIONS

The experience of designing and constructing a seismic isolation system for the Salt Lake City and County Building has indicated the feasibility of this method for retrofitting existing buildings. It is an approach that offers the possibility of preserving as much of the original architectural fabric as possible, and, at the same time, providing a greater degree of protection from non-structural damage than conventional strengthening.

But not all existing buildings are equally candidates for base isolation. To be economically retrofitted with such a system, a building must substantially meet the following criteria:

1. The building's shape must be suitable. The plans and elevations must be reasonably regular. The structure's height should be less than its width so uplift is not a major problem. Short, heavy buildings are more suitable than high-rises, as their non-isolated period is in the range most likely to benefit from base isolation.

2. The site must allow the building to move relative to the ground without interference from adjacent structures.

3. The building should have interiors worth preserving. Alternative strengthening techniques require demolition of many interior surfaces and alteration of spaces.

4. The anticipated difficulty or expense of repairing non-structural damage in an unisolated condition should be substantial, to justify the additional cost of an isolated structure.

Finally, the difficulty of documentation and construction, and the complexity of engineering an isolated structure, make base isolation a technically challenging solution that should not be undertaken casually. For the foreseeable future it will remain an experimental technique that will require resources beyond those typically found on small restoration projects. But, with time and experience, base isolation is likely to find its place as an accepted procedure that can be considered on its own merits and used where appropriate.

Seismic Response Analyses of Parthenon Columns

T. Hanazato, N. Theofanopoulos and M. Watabe
Architectural Department, University of Tokyo Metropolitan, 2-1-1 Fukazawa, Setagaya-ku, Tokyo 158, Japan

ABSTRACT

Dynamic analyses of Parthenon's columns have been conducted to study their feasibility to withstand seismic loads safely. Using lumped mass systems and considering both rotational and translational modes, dynamic characteristics of Parthenon columns, such as natural period, were estimated. Moreover, linear response analyses were performed utilizing synthetic earthquake ground motions for return periods of 100 and 1000 years. Furthermore, non-linear response analyses using an equivalent translational system were carried out.

INTRODUCTION

Parthenon is one of the main historical monuments in Greece, gathering a lot of sightseers from all over the world (See Photo.1). The masonry building was constructed on the Acropolis hill in 5th century B.C., where seismic activity is considered to be high. The behavior of Parthenon under seismic loads for 25 centuries was satisfactory. However, during the various phases of the monument's history, radical alterations have occurred, concerning the general geometric configuration, the interconnection of structural members and the state of the materials. For example, the recent earthquake which occurred in the vicinity of Athens in 1981 was reported to cause damage to some of the columns - slight translational displacements between drums (See Photo.2). It is considered that the wooden pivots inserted between drums could not withstand the seismic loads due to the material weathering.

The aspects mentioned in the previous paragraph impose the necessity to consider about Parthenon's earthquake resistant capacity. It was reported that Parthenon has been partially strengthened, but at that moment earthquake resistant design has not been accomplished. The scope of this research is to study the feasibility of the monument, in this existing state, to withstand earthquake loads safely. Dynamic response analyses of the columns, linear and non-linear ones, have been conducted utilizing the synthetic earthquake ground motions for return periods of 100 and 1000 years generated by Theofanopoulos et al. [1].

STRUCTURAL CONDITIONS OF PARTHENON

The columns have a height of about 9.6m including their capitals, having a mean aspect ratio (height/diameter) equal to about 5.6 (See Fig.1). The column is composed of 11 drums and a capital. The diameter of the drums ranges from about 1.9m at the base to about 1.5m at the top, while the average height of the drums is about 0.87m. The material used for the construction of the building is white Pentelic marble. The condition at the interconnection between the drums is the following [2]. The drum to drum contact after the construction of the monument was perfect, because the drums after their placement were caused to revolve around a central pivot, until they rested absolutely in contact on the drum beneath, by the attrition of sand inserted for the purpose (See Fig.2). The shear force mobilized between two drums is considered to be sustained by the friction ,as well as, by the dowel action of the pivot composed of a wooden pin inserted into two wooden blocks (See Fig.2). In the present state, the most of the columns have beams and pediments on their capitals, while some of them have not. This condition was also taken into account in the response analyses.

ANALYTICAL METHOD OF LINEAR RESPONSE

Analytical model
Linear response analyses were performed for three different models, as shown in Fig.3. Thirteen or twelve lumped mass systems were assumed, and rotational and translational modes at each level of drums' separation were considered. Model (A) represents a column with a beam and a pediment on its capital, which is subjected to seismic loads perpendicular to the longitudinal direction of the beam. Model (B) is similar to Model (A), and it is subjected to seismic loads in the longitudinal direction of the beam. On the other hand, Model (C) represents a column without any member on its capital. Rotation of the top mass was considered in the case of Models (A) and (C), while it was neglected in the case of Model (B).

Parameters used for analysis
Dynamic characteristics of Parthenon such as natural period of its columns were not available. Considering the microtremor records at Zeus Olympeion and the difference in the dimensions between Parthenon and Olympeion, the natural period of Parthenon's columns, as well as, other parameters for the linear response analysis were estimated. The fundamental period of Olympeion's column composed of 18 drums was equal to 0.53sec. according to Reference [3]. Then, the rotational spring constant K_R at each interface was estimated on the assumption that K_R is proportional to the square root of the vertical compressive stress (σ_V) and the fourth power of the interface's radius (r), i.e.,

$$K_R = \alpha \sqrt{\sigma_V} \ r^4 \tag{1}$$

Here, (α) denotes the proportionality index assumed to be the same for each of the three models. This proportionality index (α) was evaluated through eigenvalue analysis of a single column of Olympeion in order to obtain fundamental period equal to the estimated one by microtremor analysis. Using the estimated value of (α), the rotational spring constants at drums' interfaces of Parthenon's columns were evaluated. Moreover, the translational spring constants (K_H) were evaluated from the elastic deformation characteristics of the drums, because the shear forces between two drums were assumed to be sustained by the friction in the range of linear response and consequently the translational displacements can be neglected at the interfaces. Table 1 shows the parameters adopted for the linear response analyses.

Formulation of equations of motions

The equation of motion of the assumed MDOF system subjected to earthquake ground motions was derived from the equilibrium of rotational moment and shear force mobilized at the drums interfaces.

$$[M]\{\ddot{\delta}\} + [C]\{\dot{\delta}\} + [K]\{\delta\} = -\{M'\}\ddot{y}_0 \tag{2}$$

Here, $[M]$: Mass matrix composed of mass, height of drum, and moment of inertia

$[C]$: Damping matrix which can be obtain by combining the result of the eigenvalue analysis and the assumed damping ratio

In this study, the damping ratio is equal to 5%

$[K]$: Stiffness matrix composed of rotational spring constant and translational spring constant

$-\{M'\}\ddot{y}_0$: Externally applied load vector

$\ddot{y}_0$ expresses input ground motions

$\{\delta\}$: Displacement vector composed of rotational angle and translational displacement

Step by step integration procedure using linear acceleration method, as well as, mode superposition procedure were applied to solve this differential equation. In the former procedure, the time increment for the calculation was 1/10000 sec, and in the latter one, the first three modes of vibration were considered with the time increment equal to 1/500 sec.

ANALYTICAL METHOD OF NON-LINEAR RESPONSE

Non-linear response analysis using lumped mass system with only translational mode was carried out, in cases that the maximum shear coefficient obtained by the linear response analysis exceeded the assumed friction coefficient. In this analysis, the spring constants in the elastic range were determined following the assumption that the natural periods and the modal shapes of a column should coincide with those obtained by the linear response analysis in the previous section. To represent non-linear characteristics, bi-linear type of load-deformation relationship was used, as shown in Fig.4. The shear force at the reduction point was assumed to be equal to the maximum friction resistance, whose value was obtained by multiplying the friction coefficient and the weight of the overlaying drums at each level.

INPUT EARTHQUAKE GROUND MOTIONS

The input ground motions for the dynamic response analysis were generated probabilistically for the return period of 100 and 1000 years, considering the amplification effect of Acropolis hill (Theofanopoulos et al. [1]). The maximum acceleration of the synthetic input motions was equal to 580 gals for return period of 100 years and 1050 gals for 1000 years, respectively.

RESULTS OF LINEAR RESPONSE ANALYSIS

Natural periods and vibration modes

Fig.5 shows the estimated vibration modes and natural periods of the three models of Parthenon's column (See Fig.3). In each case, the first three modes were considered. It can be recognized that the rotational condition at the top, as well as, the weight of the additional members at the top influence considerably the modal shapes and natural periods.

Results of response analysis

In Fig.6 are compared the results of the calculated maximum displacements at each level using step by step integration and mode superposition procedures. It is found that the results obtained by mode superposition procedure considering the first three modes are in good agreement with that obtained by step by step integration procedure. This result indicates that it is sufficient to take into account the first three modes in the mode superposition procedure. Hence, only the results of mode superposition procedure considering the first three modes of vibration will be presented in the rest of this study.

Fig.7 shows the time histories of the input ground motions, as well as, the response at the top of each model. Moreover, the distributions of maximum response values along the height of columns are presented in Fig.8. Representative results of the response analysis for the three models are also summarized in Table 2. Differences among the responses of the three models can be recognized, and they are considered to be caused due to the difference in natural periods and vibration modes of the three models. The maximum response acceleration in the case of Model (C) yields to greater values than the other models, because the fundamental period of that model is close to the predominant period of the input earthquake motions [1]. The weight of top mass, as well as, the direction of input ground motions influence the response characteristics of the columns.

Fig.9 and Fig.10 show the distributions of the maximum shear coefficient and the maximum rotational moment mobilized at drums' interface along the height of the columns. In these figures, remarkable differences among the results of the three models can be observed. The shear coefficient of Model (C) which represents the column without beam on its capital attains very high values relative to those obtained by the other models. Assuming that the friction coefficient is equal to 0.8, the mobilized shear coefficient of Model (C) exceeds that value from the base to the top of the column for return period of 1000 years, and from the middle to the top for return period of 100 years. In the case when the pivots at the interfaces between drums have already weathered and they can not resist seismic loads, translational displacements may occur due to earthquake ground motions. This result is consistent with the fact that the differential displacements were caused by the 1981, Corinth Earthquake at the drums' interfaces of some columns, as shown in Photo.2. On the other hand, the shear coefficients of Model (A) and Model (B) subjected to the synthetic ground motions were estimated to be smaller than the assumed friction coefficient, except in the case of Model (A) and input earthquake motion with return period of 1000 years, where the shear coefficient near the top slightly exceeds the friction coefficient. Comparing the shear coefficient of Model (A) with that of Model (B), the effect of the beam, i.e., constraint of rotation of the top mass , can be recognized. Since the shear coefficient of

the   Model (B) is smaller than the friction coefficient, it is considered that
the structure is relatively safe against seismic translational loads subjected
in the longitudinal direction of the beam.

Considering the analytical results of this research and the observed
damage due to the recent earthquake, it can be concluded that it is necessary
to   strengthen Parthenon's columns against seismic loads, especially for the
columns which have no beam on their capitals.

RESULTS OF NON-LINEAR RESPONSE ANALYSIS

As presented in the previous section, the resulted shear coefficient due to the
synthetic earthquake ground motions exceed the assumed friction resistance at
the drums' interfaces in the case of Model (C). Non-linear response analysis
using an equivalent translational system and the synthetic input ground motions
for return periods of 100 years and 1000 years was employed. Fig.11 shows the
distributions of the maximum response displacement and the maximum shear
coefficient along the height of the column. In this analysis, two cases were
considered. In the first case, the effect of pivots between drums was
considered (Case 1), and in the second case, the pivots made of titanium alloy
were placed to strengthen the columns (Case 2). It is found in Fig.11 that the
model in Case 1 may be unstable, but that the model in Case 2 may be stable,
because the pivots undertake the excess seismic loads. Substitution of the old
wooden pivots by new ones made of hard shear resisting materials can be
considered effective in strengthening Parthenon's columns against seismic
loads.

CONCLUSIONS

It can be concluded that Parthenon in the existing state is not safe against
earthquake ground motions derived probabilistically for return periods of 100
and 1000 years. In the case that the pivots at drums' interfaces became
ineffective due to weathering, the seismic loads may cause translational
displacements between drums. Moreover, the existence of beams and pediments on
the capitals of the columns, as well as, the direction of input ground motions
influence the response characteristics of Parthenon's columns. It is necessary
to strengthen Parthenon's columns against seismic loads, especially in the
case of columns without beam on their capitals.

REFERENCES

1.Theofanopoulos,N., Hanazato,T. and Watabe,M. Probabilistic Approach   to
   Generate the Reference Motion for the Protection of Historical Monuments
   against Earthquakes, Proc. of 1st International Conf. on Structural Studies,
   Repairs and Maintenance of Historical Buildings, Florence, Italy, 1989.
2.Penrose, C.K.   An Investigation of the Principles of Athenian Architecture,
   Mc Growth Publishing Company, Washington, D.C., 1973.
3.Theofanopoulos,N., Hanazato,T., Matsukawa, K. and Watabe, M.   Analysis of
   Microtremor Records at Zeus-Olympeion Athens and Assessment of its Safety by
   Employing Dynamic Response Analysis, Proc. of 1st International Conf. on
   Structural Studies, Repairs and Maintenance of Historical Buildings,Florence,
   Italy, 1989.

Photo.1 An exterior view of Parthenon

Photo.2 Observed damage to Parthenon's
column due to the recent earthquake

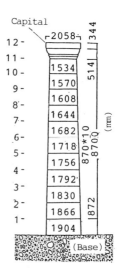

Fig.1 Parthenon's column

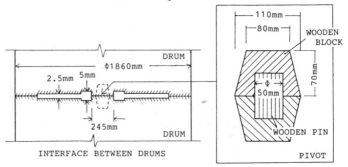

Fig.2 Drums' interface and pivot (after Penrose,C.K.(1973)[2])

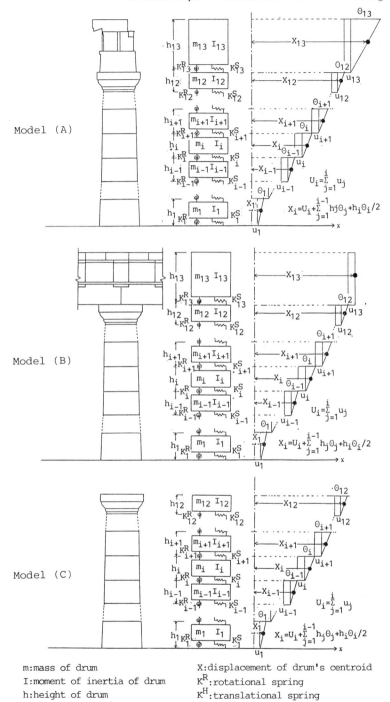

Model (A)

Model (B)

Model (C)

m:mass of drum   X:displacement of drum's centroid
I:moment of inertia of drum K^R:rotational spring
h:height of drum K^H:translational spring

Fig.3 Models for linear response analysis of Parthenon's column

Table1 Parameters used for linear response analysis

DRUM	MASS (ton)	HEIGHT (m)	MOMENT OF INERTIA (ton·m)	K_R (x10⁵tonf·m)	K_H (x10⁶tonf/m)
13	60.77	3.15	143.80	8.86	7.31
12	6.63	1.02	1.72	3.14 (2.12)	5.37
11	4.36	0.87	0.92	3.48 (2.47)	6.59
10	4.58	0.87	0.99	3.85 (2.78)	6.90
9	4.80	0.87	1.08	4.27 (3.13)	7.25
8	5.02	0.87	1.17	4.69 (3.51)	7.56
7	5.26	0.87	1.28	5.17 (3.91)	7.91
6	5.47	0.87	1.36	5.68 (4.38)	8.29
5	5.73	0.87	1.47	6.22 (4.87)	8.61
4	5.97	0.87	1.58	6.83 (5.40)	8.96
3	6.22	0.87	1.70	7.43 (5.97)	9.34
2	6.47	0.87	1.81	8.12 (6.58)	9.72
1	6.75	0.87	1.96	8.84 (7.23)	10.08

( ):Model (C)

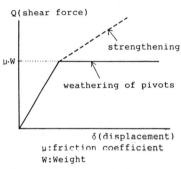

Fig.4 Assumed characteristics between load and deformation for Non-linear response analysis

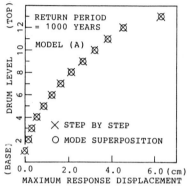

Fig.6 Maximum relative response displacement calculated by 2 kinds of procedures (Linear response analysis)

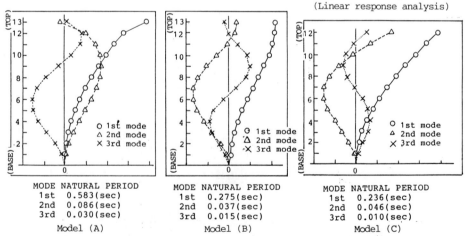

MODE	NATURAL PERIOD
1st	0.583(sec)
2nd	0.086(sec)
3rd	0.030(sec)

Model (A)

MODE	NATURAL PERIOD
1st	0.275(sec)
2nd	0.037(sec)
3rd	0.015(sec)

Model (B)

MODE	NATURAL PERIOD
1st	0.236(sec)
2nd	0.046(sec)
3rd	0.010(sec)

Model (C)

Fig.5 Vibration modes and natural periods of the three models shown in Fig.3

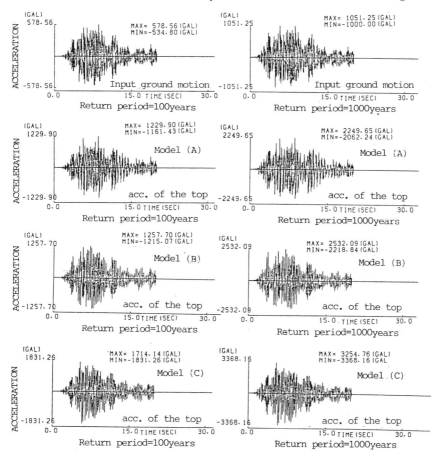

Fig.7 Time histories of input ground motions and resulted response at the top's centroid of each model shown in Fig.3 by linear response analysis

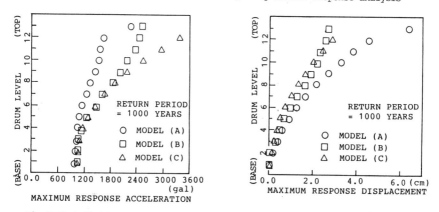

Fig.8 Distributions of maximum response values along height of columns obtained by linear response analysis for return period of 1000 years

Table2 Maximum values of input ground motions and responses at top's centroid of each model

RETURN PERIOD OF INPUT MOTION(years)	100			1000		
MAX.ACC. OF INPUT MOTION($\ddot{y}_0$max)(gal)	579			1050		
MODEL	(A)	(B)	(C)	(A)	(B)	(C)
MAX.ACC. OF MOTION AT TOP'S CENTROID ($\ddot{X}$max)　(gal)	1230	1258	1831	2250	2532	3368
AMPLIFICATION FACTOR ($\ddot{X}$max/$\ddot{y}_0$max)	2.12	2.17	3.16	2.14	2.41	3.21
MAX.RELATIVE DISP. OF MOTION AT TOP'S CENTROID (cm)	2.96	1.30	1.51	6.34	2.62	2.84
MAX.RELATIVE VEL. OF MOTION AT TOP'S CENTROID (kine)	37.4	31.1	41.1	77.7	61.6	81.9

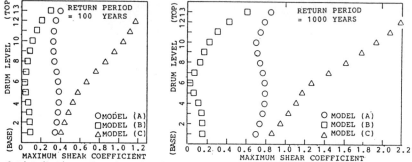

Fig.9 Distributions of maximum drum's interface shear coefficient along height of column obtained by linear response analysis

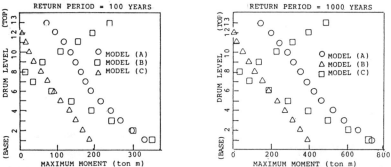

Fig.10 Distributions of maximum rotational moment at drum's interface along height of column obtained by linear response analysis

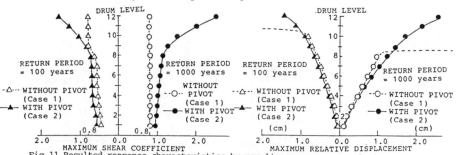

Fig.11 Resulted response characteristics by non-linear response analysis (distributions of maximum relative disp. and shear coefficient)

Dynamic Behaviour and Numerical Simulation of Old Bell Towers

H. Wimmer, J. Majer, G. Niederwanger

Institut fur Festigkeitslehre und Flachentragwerke, Universitat Innsbruck, Austria

ABSTRACT

Analysis of the structure with the aid of numerical simulation should be undertaken for the design and successful implementation of structural restoration measures on old damaged churches and bell towers. The latter needs sufficient quantitative measurements and serves as a basis for parametric studies to find out the most efficient restoration method. This paper deals with the problem of dynamically stressed bell towers.

INTRODUCTION

Damage to old bell towers appears in most cases in the form of cracks. Without discussing the cause of the occurrence of the initial crack there is no doubt that dynamic effects from ringing bells, vibrations caused by traffic and earthquakes participate to a high degree in the starting and propagation of cracks.

For structural repairs the measurements of the dynamic behavior of the system tower-nave and its numerical simulation are an important basis. By analyzing the system and parametric studies the best way of repair can be found. (Majer [7,9]). The named numerical investigations certainly require some measurement of the dynamic behavior of the tower and the attached vaults to gain a realistic insight into the structural behavior. Since the influence of swinging bells is the predominant effect we will deal with it in the following.

DYNAMIC LOADING OF THE TOWER BY SWINGING BELLS

The mechanical idealization of a swinging bell is the physical pendulum with the mass of the clapper integrated within the mass m of the bell. As the displacement of the bell supports is

usually small this support can be considered fixed in the
numerical calculation. If the movement of the
belfry and consequently the displacements of the suspension
point are large instability phenomena of the oscillations in
time domain – typical for nonlinear vibrations – may occur. In
that case the horizontal displacement of the suspension point
snaps through from the same phase into the counter phase
(Contri [4]) relative to the movement of the bell's centre of
gravity.

Accepting a rigid point of suspension the equations for the
horizontal and vertical reaction forces depend on the angle ϕ
and are given by

$$H(\phi) = -m.g.\delta.(3.\sin \phi .\cos \phi - 2.\sin \phi .\cos \phi_o) \qquad (1)$$

$$V(\phi) = m.g.\left[1 + \delta.(3.\cos^2\phi - 2.\cos \phi_o.\cos \phi - 1)\right] \qquad (2)$$

with $\delta = \dfrac{m.l_s^2}{J_A}$ as defined in Figure 1.

Where H(t) and V(t) can be expressed in terms of Fourier
series

$$H(t) = m.g.\delta.\sum_{n=0}^{\infty} a_{2n+1}(\phi_o).\sin\left[(2n+1)\frac{2\pi}{T}.t\right] \qquad (3)$$

$$V(t)= m.g.\left\{1 + \delta.\sum_{n=0}^{\infty} b_{2n+2}(\phi_o).\cos\left[(2n+2)\frac{2\pi}{T}.t\right]\right\} \qquad (4)$$

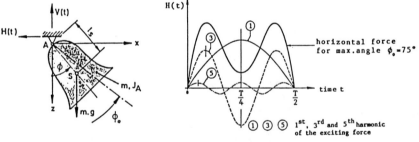

T ... period of the bell	H(t) ... horizontal force
ϕ_o ... max.angle	V(t) ... vertical force
m.g ... weight of the bell	A ... point of suspension
J_A ... moment of inertia	S ... centre of gravity

Figure 1. Reaction forces of a swinging bell.

The Fourier coefficients which depend on the maximum angle ϕ_o
can be found in the literature (Baumgart [3], Lurenbaum [6]).
Since the amplitude of the angle ϕ_o of electrically driven bells
is usually smaller than 90° but greater than 75° the predominant
portion of H(t) is given by the third harmonic term.

EXPERIMENTAL MEASUREMENTS

The measurement of the dynamic response of the tower and the belfry was carried out in different levels of the tower and in the attached vaults of the nave by piezoelectric transducers in order to obtain sufficient data for the subsequent computing. Most of the bell towers in Austria are connected with the nave in a nonsymmetrical manner. Because of this the bells are excentrically suspended and hence the towers are excited not only into bending oscillations but also into torsional movements, so that it is necessary to measure not only in the swinging direction of the bells but also perpendicular to it. When the tower is already separated from the nave by cracks the relative movements between tower and nave can be measured by inductive transducers too. The signals of the piezoelectric transducers are proportional to the acceleration. The results from these transducers are automatically integrated to give displacements. These and the signals of the inductive transducers are recorded synchronously on tape and YT-recorder. Evaluation of the results is carried out by using a spectrum analyzer (Fast Fourier Transformation).

Figure 2 shows a typical frequency spectrum of the horizontal displacements of a tower (in the direction of bell swinging) measured in the level of the bells. The predominance of the third harmonic can be recognized distinctly. If the vertical component of the dynamic reaction of the bell is acting excentrically to the axis of the tower there will also be even-numbered peaks in the frequency spectrum in addition to the odd-numbered multiples of the pendulum frequency of the bell. The above situation can also cause oscillations acting transverse to the swinging direction of the bells (Majer [10]). An analogic effect with even harmonics in the horizontal vibration (pendulum direction) is produced if large horizontal displacements of the suspension point of the bells take place, for instance when having a very flexible belfry (Andres [1]).

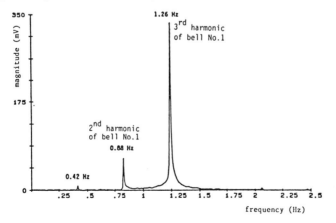

Figure 2. Spectral analysis of bell tower oscillation

The tower was excited for determining the fundamental natural frequency of the building, to horizontal vibrations by impact using a timber beam between a slightly swinging bell and the tower wall. The decay of measured amplitudes in the time domain also indicates a global rate of damping. Another method of determining natural frequencies, namely the use of an oscillator with excentrically rotating masses (shaker), brings up difficulties because of the fact that the mass-forces in the range of lower frequencies are very small as they depend quadratically upon the speed of revolution. Further the narrowness of the bell chamber and the difficulties of fastening the oscillator to the often poor masonry are important obstacles for putting this method into practice. A possibility for finding out the first natural frequency of the tower is given if this frequency is situated in the range of the variability of the pendulum frequency of the bell, because the bell represents a nonlinear oscillator and its period of swinging becomes larger with increasing amplitude ϕ . In this case the bell is used as a means of exciting the tower to horizontal oscillation mostly in the triple frequency of the bell's variable pendulum frequency. If the first natural frequency of the tower lies between the third and the fifth harmonic of the ensemble of all bells it is possible to find the dynamic magnification factor and with it the resonance peak, the natural frequency and the global damping of the tower by determining the portion of each harmonic of the measured response. For simplification the tower is supposed as a SDOF-System with damping proportional to the displacement velocity (viscous damping) (see Niederwanger [11], Majer et al [8]).

For the numerical modelling of the dynamic system the stiffness of the belfry - often wooden - supporting structure in the tower is needed. For that purpose deflection measurements were made under horizontal loading upon the belfry. The test structure was anchored in the masonry of the tower and the maximum horizontal force was chosen comparable to the maximum reaction force of the bell. The largest deflection was about 15mm. After stopping the test a permanent deformation remained indicating some clearance in the joints of the wooden belfry.

NUMERICAL SIMULATION

Assumptions
The modelling of damaged bell towers would suggest the application of 2D or 3D finite elements when considering the cracks. Since the constitutive model of stress transfer and the complete geometry of cracks in general are not known a beam model including the shear force deformation seems to be sufficient. The distribution of the parameters of the cross-section and the mass are derived from geometric measurements of the building. The global Young's modulus of the masonry, the boundary conditions for the foundation and the nave as well as the mechanical properties of the belfry are determined for

the numerical simulation. These parameters, namely the global
Young's modulus, damping and boundary condition parameters
can be evaluated from the measured natural frequency, using the
response under excitation of impulsive loading and bell ringing.

The belfry generally consisting of a truss-like structure was
modelled as a beam with mechanically equivalent properties and
fixed in the tower wall. The influence of the elastic
foundation of the tower must not be neglected (Lohse [5],
Schroder [13]). This effect of flexibility was taken into
account by a linear-elastic spring.

Method of Calculation

For the following numerical studies the parish church of the
village of Altenmarkt (Salzburg) was selected (Majer [10]),
erected in 1400, partially destroyed in 1762 and then rebuilt.

The beam elements used take into account the axial deformation,
bending moment and shear force. The influence of the latter
should not be neglected when dealing with towers of small
slenderness. The dynamic response of the system was evaluated
by means of direct time integration (Newmark method). The
eigenvalue analysis was performed using the subspace iteration
(Bathe [12]). Figure 5 shows the discretisation of the tower
(separated by cracks from the nave) and the belfry as a beam
model. The applied program system (ADINA) uses a so-called
lumped mass model and assigns three degrees of kinematic
freedom (one rotation, two displacements) to each of the element
nodes. The damping forces which were necessary to eliminate the
transient portion of the dynamic response were taken into
account by the following assumption

$$\mathbb{C} = \alpha.\mathbb{M} + \beta.\mathbb{K} \qquad (6)$$

in which $\mathbb{C}$, $\mathbb{M}$, and $\mathbb{K}$ mean the damping-, mass- and stiffness
matrix of the system. The coefficients α and β will be
evaluated with the help of the equation

$$\alpha + \beta.\omega_i = 2.\omega_i.D \qquad (7)$$

and by analyzing the damping of two characteristic frequencies
ω_i of the dynamic system. In the case under consideration the
measurements only yield the global damping ratio D according
to Lehr but no information about the structural damping $\beta.\mathbb{K}$.
Therefore β was set to zero and α became

$$\alpha = 2.\omega_1.D = 4\pi.f_1.D \qquad (8)$$

Figure 3 shows the vibration modes of the system tower-belfry
for the lowest natural frequencies. The first natural
frequency is exactly equal to the measured value $f_1 = 1.37$ Hz.
The influence of the degree of flexibility of the clamped
support in the soil is to be seen distinctly in this figure.
Between the third and the fifth mode of transversal vibration
there is a longitudinal mode with the frequency of 5,10 Hz.

Figure 4 presents the calculated response of the damped system tower—belfry when the heaviest bell is swinging in steady state and the time dependent decay of amplitudes after setting the horizontal reaction force H(t) to zero.   This means in reality two different states.   The first state is comparable with the steadily swinging bell.   The decaying part of the response shown in fig.4 only ought to be compared with the state of free vibration of the tower which was measured by the above mentioned shock test.   The latter offered a possibility of calibrating the damping ratio   in the numerical model by relating the logarithmic decrements for a SDOF-system with viscous damping of the model.

Parametric Studies

These are carried out in order to estimate the efficiency of different systems of structural repair, ie:

a)   Stabilization by strengthening the masonry of the tower by injection and reinforcement with the consequence of raising the natural frequencies and therefore varying the frequency ratio results inevitably in change in the dynamic tuning.

b)   Reduction of the dynamic effect of the bell's reaction force upon the tower by variation of the stiffness of the belfry as well as by variation of its mass and the level where it is fixed to the tower wall.   (Other methods which reduce the horizontal bell force directly and their consequences will not be discussed here (see Majer [10]).)

c)   Variation in particular, of the frequency ratios of bells and tower (dynamic tuning).

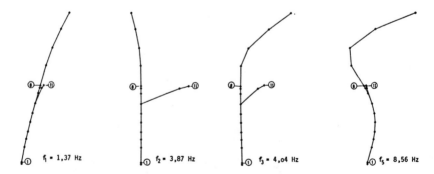

Figure 3. Natural modes of the system tower-belfry.

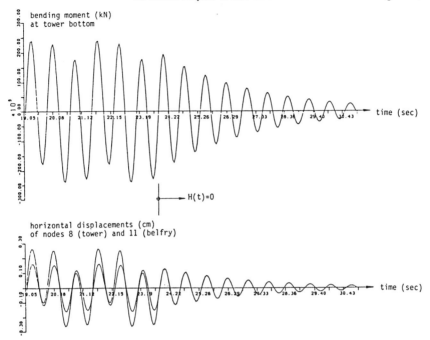

Figure 4. Calculated response of tower and belfry points under dynamic bell loading and free vibration.

At first the influence of the flexural rigidity of a common belfry on the fixing moment of the tower and the horizontal displacements in the altitude of the bell chamber were investigated. The results indicate that too flexible but still realistic belfries may increase the bending moment of the tower by up to 20 percent.

The next study concerned the effect on the maximum bending moment at the tower bottom of the location at which the belfry is fixed to the tower. The foot of the belfry was positioned at successively lower levels and the discretisation was improved by intermediate nodes. The astonishing result was that the decrease of bending moments was very small with a maximum of about 14 percent. The deflection can be reduced to about 18 percent as further investigation has shown (see fig.5). But it has to be emphasized that the mentioned analysis was carried out for a flexible supported tower bottom. The more the bell tower system approaches to a clamped end cantilever the larger is the effect of setting the foot of the belfry at a lower level. Notice that these results cannot be compared with those by Schmidt [12], because in his investigation only the level of the suspension point of the bell has been varied. In every case our studies further show that in general the stress situation for the tower

becomes worse the more flexible and heavy the belfry. Very
long and heavy belfries can theoretically reach resonance with
the fifth of the harmonic portion of bell's reaction force and
hence produce the opposite effect to the one we are trying to
achieve.

Further analysis was carried out on the influence of varying the
ratio of the first natural tower frequency to the next harmonic
of the horizontal bell force (tuning), that is generally the
third harmonic. The increase of stiffness due to restoration
work was simulated by varying only the Young's modulus of the
tower whereas the bell's frequency is a given quantity with a
small range of variation. Fig.6 shows the dynamic magnification
factor depending on the frequency ratio for the horizontal
displacement of the tower for three values of damping.
Concerning the greatest bending moment of the tower the curves
show nearly complete affinity (Majer [10]).

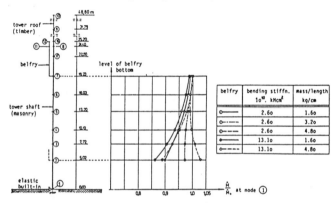

Figure 5.   Influence of the altitude of the belfry bottom on the
maximum bending moment of the tower.

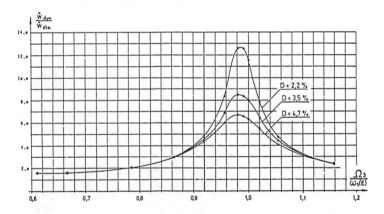

Figure 6. Magnification factor concerning the horizontal displacement of node (8) of tower under different damping and modulus of elasticity E.

CONCLUSION

For the investigation of typical methods for the reduction of the stresses in bell towers, caused by the force of swinging bells it is necessary to measure the dynamic behavior and to build up a numerical simulation model based on these measurements. Some results of parametric studies are:

a) A more favourable state of the belfry can be expected if it is stiff but light and the bell forces are introduced into the lower part of the tower.

b) The effect described above can be intensified if the structure is stiff by having a built-in support of the tower.

c) The most important effect on the stresses of a bell tower is the ratio of the natural frequency of the tower-belfry system to the frequency of the nearest harmonic portion of the horizontal component of the swinging bell (which is generally the third one).

d) Work described in points a) and b) as well as the structural strengthening of the damaged masonry of the tower alter the natural frequencies. It is important to be certain that any changes in the frequency ratio mentioned in c) will not bring the frequency of the system too close to the resonance frequency of the system.

ACKNOWLEDGEMENT

Partial support of this research by Jubilaumsfonds der Nationalbank, Vienna, Project Nr. 2268, is gratefully acknowledged.

REFERENCES

1. Andres, W. Dynamisch beanspruchte Glockenturme bei großen Drehungen und Verschiebungen, Dissertation Universitat Wuppertal, 1983.

2. Bathe, K.J. Finite Element Procedures in Engineering Analysis, Prentice-Hall, New Jersey 1982.

3. Baumgart, F. Ermittlung der Erregerkrafte bei Glockenturmen Der Bauingenieur, Vol.45, pp.444-446, 1970.

4. Contri, L. Analisi numerica di un fenomeno di interesi oscillatoria, Cattedra II di scienca delle construzioni della facolta di ingegneria dell'universita di Padova, 1968.

5. Lohse, G. Das dynamische Verhalten von elastisch eingespannten Bauwerken, VDI-Berichte, Vol.4, pp.57-60, 1955.

6. Lurenbaum, K. Schwingungen von Glockenturmen, VDI-Berichte, Vol.48, pp.95-99, 1961.

7. Majer, J. Statische und dynamische Probleme bei der Instand-setzung historischer Kirchen, Bautenschutz-Bausanierung, Vol.10, pp.44-52, 1987.

8. Majer, J, Niederwanger, G. Dynamische Messungen an schadhaften historischen Glockenturmen und darauf beruhende Sanierungsmaßnahmen, VDI-Berichte Vol.631, pp.215-231, 1987.

9. Majer, J. Anwendung von Stahl- u. Spannbeton beim Sanieren historischer Bauten, Zement und Beton, Vol.2, pp.57-65, 1986.

10. Majer J.(Ed.) Zusammenwirken von Turm und Glockenstuhl als Ursache schwerer Schaden an Kirchturmen, Forschungsbericht Inst. fur Festigkeitslehre u. Flachentragwerke, Universitat Innsbruck, 1988.

11. Niederwanger, G. Dynamische Messungen an Bauwerken und deren Auswertung, Osterr. Ingenieur- u. Architekten-Zeitschrift, Vol. 2, pp.52-54, 1985.

12. Schmidt, G. Abhangigkeit der Massenkrafte des Glockenturmes von der Hohenlage des Glockenstuhls, Die Bautechnik, Vol. 10, pp.355-359, 1967.

13. Schroder, F.H. Das Schwingungsverhalten elastisch gelagerter Turme mit uber die Hohe veranderlicher Steifigkeit und Massenbelegung, Der Bauingenieur, Vol.45, pp.207-213, 1970.

SECTION 6 - REPAIRS AND STRENGTHENING

Structural Consolidation of El Nazar Church, Cappadocia, Turkey

M. Yorulmaz, F. Çili and Z Ahunbay
Department of Architecture, Istanbul Technical University,
Teknik Üniversite 80191 Tadsim, Istanbul, Turkey

ABSTRACT

El Nazar is a medieval rock-hewn church situated at the Göreme valley of Cappadocia in Central Anatolia. Deeply concerned with the continuing deterioration of the monument due to climatic, hydrogeological factors, the Turkish Ministry of Culture and Tourism asked the Technical University of Istanbul to determine the measures for the preservation and consolidation of the structure. The results of the investigation and the proposed interventions are presented in this paper.

INTRODUCTION

In modern usage, Cappadocia is the name given to the part of central Anatolia which covers the provinces of Kayseri, Niğde and Nevşehir, Figure 1. Geographically, this is a high plateau surrounded by three volcanoes, Erciyes (Argaeus), Hasandağ (Argos) and Melendiz which have been active in the past, covering the area with several hundred meters of sedimentation. The erosion of this deposit in the course of thousands of years has resulted in the creation of an extraordinary landscape. The charm and excitement of the area is hightened by the intervention of mankind. During the Byzantine period, several churches and monasteries were carved in the soft rock which lent   itself easily to free forms. The architecture of these structures is similar to the types of regular churches built elsewhere at the same period. The churches are richly decorated with frescoes which are usually post Iconoclastic period, dating from the tenth century and later.

Today Cappadocia is a natural and archaeological site under protection. There is an international campaign initiated by the joint effort of UNESCO and the Turkish Ministry of Culture and Tourism to protect the landscape and the monuments from further damage.

The church of El Nazar, which is the subject of this paper, is one of these religious buildings. It is carved into an isolated conical rock, Figure 2, 3. Besides the church, there are two more levels; the lower being below ground level is entered by a separate door on the southern

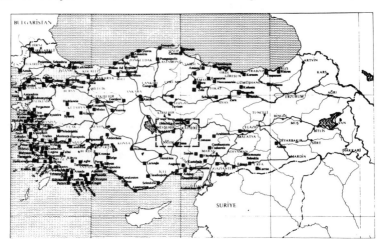

Figure 1.   Map of Turkey with Cappadocia at the center (E.Akurgal)

face of the rock. The upper level is a single chamber which can only be
reached by means of a ladder from the western side. Access to the church
suits the functional topology of the building; the ground level on the
western side of the rock is about 60 cm lower than the floor of the
church, thus providing direct access to the interior. The naos is a domed
cross with equal arms, except the eastern one which has a horseshoe plan
ending with an apse, Figure 4, 5. The apse is flanked by two small rooms,
each with a rounded end. Being slightly rectangular in plan (5.15 m x
6.05 m) the central area is covered by an elliptical dome. The arms of
the cross are vaulted. The main arches supporting the dome are lower
than the vaults, separating the arms from the central space distinctly.

The church is dated to the end of the tenth century by M.Restle, [6] ,
who has done a survey of the frescoes which cover the interior surfaces
of the naos. Scenes from the Bible and the life of Jesus Christ are
depicted along with the busts of prophets, saints and martyrs inscribed
in medallions.

The present condition of the monument calls for urgent action. Parts
of the outer wall have fallen down at the west and the east, subjecting
the interior to all types of weather conditions, Figure 2. Advanced
structural problems threaten the stability of the monument. The northwest
pillar has collapsed, producing serious cracks in the rock above. The
southeast pillar has cracked and is nearing collapse. There is urgent
need for intervention in order to prevent further losses. This fact has
been verified by several experts and the monument is given priority in
the action plan of the Ministry of Culture and Tourism for the conservation of the Göreme valley.

Figure 2.   General view of El-Nazar   Figure 3.   General view of El-Nazar
            from the west   from the north

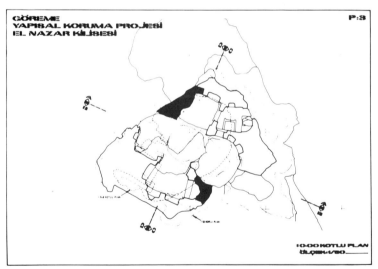

Figure 4.   Plan of El-Nazar with proposed additional masonry

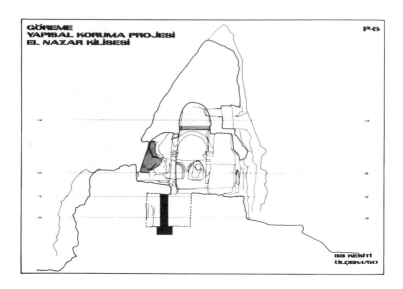

Figure 5.   Cross-section of El Nazar

GEOLOGY OF THE EL NAZAR SITE

According to Professor Dr.Kemal Erguvanlı and Dr.Mustafa Erdoğan who
have collaborated with the authors in the El Nazar Structural Consolidation project, [1], the geological character of the El Nazar site can be
summarized as follows:

     The site is covered by volcanic deposits which are the result of
volcanic activity in Central Anatolia during the Upper Miocene. As a
result of repeated eruptions, an approximately 400 m thick layer of
volcanic sediment was deposited over the site. Volcanic rocks with
dasitic, rhyolitic and andesitic character have settled in the lakes
which have appeared in the area after the Oligocene. This deposit is
called "the Ürgüp Formation" and has tuffaceous layers at its base,
lahar and ignimbrite layers at the top. The church of El Nazar is carved
into the tuffaceous and the lahar levels. The tuff layer rises up to
the church level.

     Severe continental climate is effective in the region. The weather
is hot and dry during spring, summer and autumn; cold and rainy during
winter. The surface water which erodes and causes the alteration of the

volcanic rocks around the El Nazar church enters the site from the
north, east and south and is directed towards the brook at the west by
the irrigation channels dug for agricultural purposes. The rocks around
the church do not permit the surface water to penetrate into the ground
and move freely under the surface. This phenomenon is verified by the
poor underground water potential of the region. Although the permeability of the volcanic tuffs is low, their water absorption capacity
is high. Water penetrating into the surface is absorbed by the clay and
caught in the pores. Due to the absence of discontinuities like joints
and cracks and the inactivity of pores, after saturating the tuff, water
is inactive. There is no free flowing underground water in the region.

PROPERTIES OF THE EL NAZAR ROCK

The physico-mechanical properties of the El Nazar rock have been determined by experiments done in the Engineering Geology and Rock Mechanics
Laboratory of the Mining Faculty of Istanbul Technical University.

Physical properties
Dry density is 1.59 gr/cm^3, when saturated density is increased to
1.94 gr/cm^3. Average water absorption is 27.62 % by weight, 35.93 % by
volume. Average porosity is 31.28 %. Thermal expansion was found to be
5.34 x 10^{-6}/C^o.

Mechanical properties
Mechanical experiments were carried out on dry and saturated specimens
by using an automatic deformation controlled testing machine. The
results are given in Table 1.

Table 1. Mechanical Properties of the Rock

	Dry	Saturated
Uniaxial compressive strength	74.0 kg/cm^2	21.0 kg/cm^2
Tensile strength	7.6 "	3.3 "
Tensile strength in bending	5.0 "	–
Static Young modulus	28250.0 "	10880.0 kg/cm^2

These results show that the rock material loses its mechanical
properties by 50-70 % after water intake. When saturated the rock shows
a plasto-viscous behaviour and its yield stress drops considerably.

DECAY MECHANISMS ACTING UPON THE EL NAZAR CHURCH

Erosion
As is shown by the results of the experiments conducted on rock specimens, the tuff surface is sensitive to water. The surface water from

the surrounding area is collected by irrigation channels which are directed towards the fields surrounding El Nazar rock. Surface water flows freely around the monument, removing the softened surface layers of the eastern and western facades and the ground level of the rock, Figure 3. By the action of surface water, coving occurs; the lower parts of the rock are eroded, leaving the upper sections suspended, without any support. Rising damp weakens the lower sections and erosion goes on.

As rainfall hits the rock surface, it has an erosive effect forming channels, which gaining direction get deeper and wider in time, causing further losses from the exterior and interior surfaces of the church.

Cracks
When it rains, water penetrates the exterior surface of the rock and is trapped there. When exposed to frost, the weakened structure of the rock is fractured. This type of crack can be seen all over the exterior surface of El Nazar rock, Figure 6.

A second group of cracks, the origin of which can be associated with the previous cracks are reflected in the inner surface of the church, on the floor, walls, the southeast pillar, vaults and the dome, Figure 7.

Collapsed part of the floor
The floor of the church has collapsed partially, leading most of the existing floor areas to act like cantilever slabs, Figure 8. It is easy to predict that these pieces will also fall down in time. There are cracks in this part of the floor. Due to the collapse of the floor the southeast pillar has cracked horizontally, leaving the superstructure without support. The movements in the floor area have lead to crack formations on the surrounding walls.

Figure 6. South wall with cracks

Detachment of surface crusts and thin wall sections

Cracks of different origin cause detachment from the main rock. An interesting example of crack pattern is observed on the southern facade of the rock. There is a crust like section which is weakly held on to the main rock; it may fall down after heavy rainfall or by frost action. Thin wall sections have fallen down from the eastern and western facades. The most important and problematical loss from the El Nazar rock is on the western wall. Some say that it fell down after being attacked by lightning. On an old photograph of El Nazar which is published by Jerphanion, [2], the west facade can be seen before the collapse occurred, Figure 9. Although this gap on the western facade is being used as a symbol for the valley in some of the touristic publications about Göreme, considering the future life of the monument, it is necessary to take measures against losses. This gap in the exterior wall has caused crack formation on the surrounding walls, vaults and the rock mass.

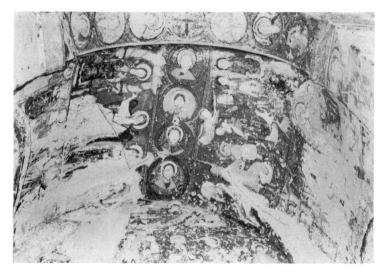

Figure 7. Vault over the southern cross-arm

PROPOSED MEASURES AND THE STRUCTURAL REINFORCEMENT

Environmental measures

Surface water should be directed elsewhere before it reaches the church. In order to stop erosion of the rock around the base of the El Nazar rock by the action of water dripping from the cone the surrounding area should be reinforced with a protective layer.

The foundation of the church should be protected from underground water in case it appears. For this purpose the church should be made impervious to water from the surrounding area; an open channel lining the base of the church at the north side can help to collect and drain the surface water approaching the monument from this side.

Figure 8.   Cantilever floor and southeast pillar with cracks

Interventions to the Monument (Treatment of major defects)

Erosion problems The undercutting at the north and west faces of the church and the south wall should be stabilized by means of new masonry walls using the local stone and a mortar made of lime and the crushed rock aggregate of Göreme. In order to render the structure safe against water, the foundations of these walls will be made of reinforced concrete and damp-proofed, Figure 4, 5.

Cracks The thermal cracks on the exterior of the rock can be grouted by a mixture made of epoxy resin which is thermically stable and the powder of Göreme rock.

For this purpose, the micro injection method recommended by the ICCROM group can be used, [3]. The same mortar and technique can be applied for the repair of cracks at the southeast pillar, the floor, walls, vaults and the dome. Since the walls, the vaults and the dome are covered by frescoes, the grouting operation should be carried out with utmost care, in order not to spoil the decoration.

Collapsed floor It will be appropriate to construct a masonry wall with a concrete foundation to support the floor which will still be in a dangerous state even after the repair of its cracks, Figure 5. The new

wall will be similar in construction to the masonry fillings applied
to the eroded parts of the ground plan and the outer face of the rock.
Instead of reconstructing the missing section of the church floor it is
proposed to use a temporary timber platform which will keep people from
falling into the crypt.

Semi-detached surface crusts and missing sections The missing parts
of the walls or the weakened sections may be strengtnened by the insertion of masonry supports or fillings. The big open area at the western
facade presents a serious problem, the solution of which deserves
consideration. In the solutions proposed by ICCROM and ISMES experts,
[3], [4], an attempt has been made to leave the broken wall as it is
after controlling the bearing capacity of the supporting system. In our
calculations for testing the adequacy of the present cross sections, it
was assumed that a new arch had formed (span: about 8 meters) between
the northeast and the southwest pillars. The stresses in this system
were found to be within acceptable limits. If the west facade is considered as a cantilevered wall hung on to this arch, it is essential
that the tensile stresses produced by the suspended section should not
exceed the bearing capacity of the rock. The calculations have revealed
that these stresses might reach the danger limit in saturated conditions.

Consequently, even if it might raise some criticism, we propose to
construct a masonry wall, similar to the original seen on the photograph
published by Jerphanion, [2], Figure 9, 10.

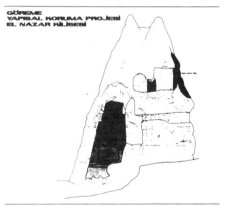

Figure 9. West façade of El Nazar   Figure 10. Proposal for the west
           at the beginning of the   facade
           20th century (G.de
           Jerphanion)

Protection of the outer surface from atmospheric conditions After completion of all repair and consolidation procedures, it will be appropriate to protect the surfaces exposed to rain by means of a protective covering. If the water repellants and stone consolidants proposed by the Institute Royal du Patrimoine Artistique Bruxelles,[7], are applied according to the prerequisities of the project, we hope that the decay processes originating from weather conditions can be minimized.

CONCLUSION

In all of the interventions to the structural system, use of steel was deliberately avoided. This was due to the maintenance problems as well as the negative effects which the difference between the coefficients of expansion of the rock and steel may cause.
It was aimed to propose interventions which are,
. discernible; can easily be differentiated from the original structure,
. reversible so that they can be removed without causing any damage to the original structure when a more appropriate material and/or technique is available.

The project and proposals have been presented to the Turkish Ministry of Culture and Tourism. At present the construction of the supporting walls under the church floor has started.

REFERENCES

1. Erguvanlı, K., Yorulmaz, M., Çılı, F., Ahunbay, Z., Erdoğan, M. Göreme Yapısal Koruma ve Sağlamlaştırma Projesi-El Nazar Kilisesi, İstanbul, 1987 (Unpublished report).

2. Jerphanion, G. de. Les Eglises Rupestres de Cappadoce, Planches Premier Album, Librairie Orientaliste Paul Geuthner, Paris, 1925.

3. Lızzi, F. et al. Göreme Structural Consolidation, ICCROM Mission, 8-10, September 1985 (Unpublished report).

4. Malliet, V., Rossi, P. Göreme Structural Consolidation Mission Report, July 28 - August 2, 1986.

5. Madraw, E. et al (ed.). The Rock-cut Churches of Göreme, a photo-grammetrical Survey, Middle East Technical University, Ankara, 1986.

6. Restle, M. Die Byzantinische Wandmalerei in Kleinasien, Verlag Aurel Bongers Recklinghausen, 1967.

7. De Vitte, E. et al. Investigation of the Conservation of the Göreme Rock, Institut Royal du Patrimoine Artistique, Brussels, 1987 (Unpublished report).

8. Bowen, R. The future of the past at Göreme in Turkey (Ed. Marinos, P. G., Koukis, G.C.), pp. 731-737, Proceedings of an Int. Sym. organized by the Greek National Group of IAEG, The Engineering Geology of Ancient Works, Monuments and Historical Sites, Athens, Greece, 1988, Balkema, Rotterdam, 1988.

Consolidation of the Tower of St. Mary's Basilica at Tongeren, Belgium. Preliminary Investigation and Design.

D. Van Gemert

Department of Civil Engineering, Katholieke Universiteit Leuven B-3030 Heverlee, Belgium

ABSTRACT

The geo-electric sounding technique is described as a tool for designing and controlling the consolidation of the tower of St. Mary's Basilica at Tongeren, Belgium. The principles of consolidation of masonry by injection of hydraulic or polymeric grout are explained, as well as the principles of the geo-electric sounding technique. The application of the methods at the preliminary research program on the tower is explained, and the conclusions drawn from the tests are discussed. The combination of consolidation injections and geo-electric controls offers a reliable and economical method of structural restoration of monuments and structures.

INTRODUCTION

The construction of the St. Mary's Basilica at Tongeren started in 1240 (Derricks[1]). The new church had to replace the old Romanesque church, which was burned at the storming of the tower by the army of Duke Henry of Brabant. The tower of the old church was kept in use until ± 1500. In 1442 the construction of the new Gothic tower was started, and it was finished in 1582 with a wooden spire. In 1598 this spire was struck a first time by lightning and completely destroyed by fire. After a complete restoration at the beginning of the 17th century, the church was again destroyed by the army of King Louis XIV of France in 1677. In 1687 the necessity of consolidation work on the tower has been mentioned for the first time. The works were executed at the beginning of the 18th century. In 1845 the church-fathers ordered a new and urgent restoration of the tower, because the 18th century consolidation had proved to be insufficient. This work was executed between 1848 and 1858. Finally in 1871 it was decided to replace the wooden spire by a supplementary storey on the tower. Its construction was started in 1877 and was ended in 1882. That situation still exists today, Fig. 1.

Figure 1. St. Mary's Tower today.

Until 1877 and with the wooden spire the tower had a height of 73 m of which 47.5 is stone masonry. After the renovation of 1882 the tower reaches a height of 52.5 m, completely in stone. But the renovation would not be the end of the problems. On the contrary, it was the cause of new damage .

The original stone used was the local marl stone. It is a soft stone, with a strength of 2.5 to 4.5 N/mm², and a density of 1400 kg/m³. For the construction of the upper storey with a height of 9 m the Gobertange limestone was used, with a density of 2300 kg/m³. Although in the construction project the lower part of the tower was partly strengthened to take up the loads from the new upper storey, severe cracking of the tower walls occurred, so that the church-fathers were forced already in 1905 to call for a new restoration. These calls were finally put into a new restoration project in 1951, and the work could start in 1972, under the direction of the architect G. Janssen. But already during the restoration work of the buttress important cracking occurred in the newly restored parts, Fig. 2.

Figure 2. Cracks in buttress of SW pillar of tower.

Crumbling of stone and the appearance of new cracks showed that the
tower structure was still moving. Therefore the architect called for
the assistance of the Engineering Office Groep Swartenbroeckx n.v. at
Hasselt.   In   collaboration   with   the   Reyntjens   Laboratory   of
K.U.Leuven the office has set up a research program to evaluate the
actual security situation of the tower, to determine the causes of
cracking and to make proposals for an appropriate consolidation
treatment. The experiments have run from December 1987 to June 1988,
and were conducted by the Reyntjens Laboratory, in collaboration
with Geosurvey n.v. for the geo-electric measurements and De Neef
Engineering n.v. for the execution of the consolidation injection
experiments. The program was supported by the church-fathers of St.
Mary's Basilica, the city council of Tongeren and the Ministry of
Publics Works of the Flemish Government.

RESEARCH PROGRAM

Based on the positive experiments in a previous research program (Van
Gemert[2]) on consolidation of ancient masonry by means of injection of
hydraulic and polymeric grouts, it was decided to study the
possibility of strengthening and stabilizing the tower by injections.
For that purpose the following program was set up and executed.
1. Geo-electric sounding of the masonry before injection;
2. Taking cylindrical corings from the masonry to calibrate the
   measured resistivity maps;
3. Test injection with hydraulic and polymeric grouts;
4. Geo-electric sounding and physico-mechanical testing of injected
   masonry.

Injection of hydraulic or polymeric grout is frequently used nowadays for the consolidation of degraded historic masonry. The principle of consolidation by means of grouting is quite simple (Van Gemert[3]). Masonry is a composite material made of bricks or stones and mortar. The bearing capacity of the masonry is due to the strength of the stones and mortar, and to the adhesion between mortar and stones. The adhesion forces enable the masonry to resist the splitting forces which arise in the masonry at loading. By injection of a polymeric or hydraulic grout in the pore structure of the masonry one can diminish the splitting forces and at the same time increase the adhesion between stones and mortar. This will result in a strong increase of the compression strength and the durability of the masonry.

The grouting work will only be effective if the grout is uniformly distributed over the masonry mass. Moreover, the grouting work will only be economically executable if it can be designed and estimated on before. The control of the distribution of the grout and the difficulties encountered in estimating the job still are important obstacles, which prevent a wide diffusion of the grouting technique.

The geo-electric sounding technique is a non-destructive technique, which gives a clear picture of the internal situation in the masonry. The electrical resistance of the masonry is influenced by the material composition, the porosity and void content, the humidity, the presence of salts. The same elements also determine the bearing capacity and the durability of the masonry. By taking cylindrical corings from the masonry in those regions where the resistivities show important differences or variations, it is possible to calibrate the resistivity measurements with respect to the desired parameter : composition, void content, distribution of grout, strength.

GEO-ELECTRIC SOUNDING OF MASONRY

The geo-electric method is based on the measurement of the electrical resistance of the stone mass. The method is derived from the sounding techniques, used in geology for the examination of soil stratification. The basic equations are the laws of Ohm and Pouillet about the electrical resistance

$$V = R.I,$$

where V = electric potential (Volt)
  I = current intensity (Ampère)
  R = resistance (Ohm)

$$j = E/\rho^e,$$

where j = current density (Ampère/m²)
  ρ^e = specific resistance (Ohm.m)
  E = field intensity (Volt/m)

The equations are adapted for the three dimensional situation.   In this three dimensional technique the current density is measured per unit volume (Ampère/m^3), and the specific resistance is determined as a function of the volume of masonry involved and of the distance L between the current electrode S1 and the potential measuring electrodes P1 and P2 (see fig. 3).

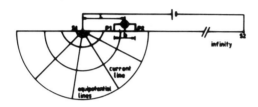

Figure 3. Geo-electric measuring scheme.

The perfect contact between the masonry and the electrodes is obtained by dipping the electrodes in a CuSO$_4$ solution.   A spherical tension field is created around the current electrode S1 as around a point source.   By changing the distance L between the measuring electrodes P1 and P2 and the current electrode S1 the evolution of the resistance of a masonry volume with dimensions L along the depth in the wall and b along the surface is measured.   At the cross-points of a mesh, spread out over the masonry surface, the evolution of the resistance with the distance or depth L is measured.   Two typical curves are shown in figure 4.   In each measuring point the left end of the curve corresponds to the resistance of the buttress.   The curve for measuring station 1 in figure 4 shows that the resistance of the buttress is high.   The resistance of the following layers of material is lower because the measured mean value for the total masonry volume involved is decreasing.   The rising curve in measuring point 4 indicates the presence of large voids just behind the buttress.   At greater depths the resistance is decreasing again, which results in a descending curve of the resistivity.

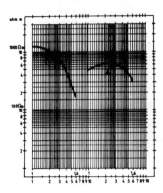

Figure 4. Evolution of resistance with depth in points 1 and 4

From the resistivity curves, which in fact are the mean values of the resistance of a growing slice of masonry, the resistivities are calculated as a function of the depth in the masonry.

APPLICATION OF GEO-ELECTRIC SOUNDING IN MASONRY EVALUATION

A typical cross-section of the tower structure is shown in figure 5. A view of the southside of the interior of the tower is shown in figure 6. The specific resistance (Ohm.m) or resistivity distributions are calculated from the resistance curves (Fig. 4), and plotted in contour maps. An example is shown in figure 7, for the resistivities in the pillar NE.

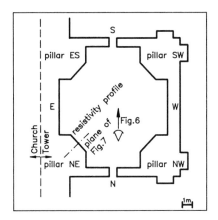

Figure 5. Cross-section of tower.

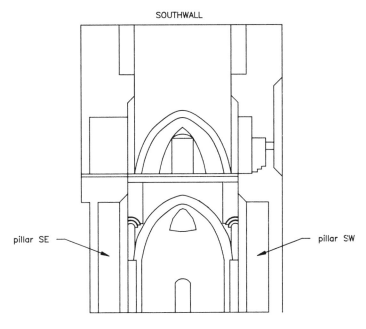

Figure 6. Southwall of tower.

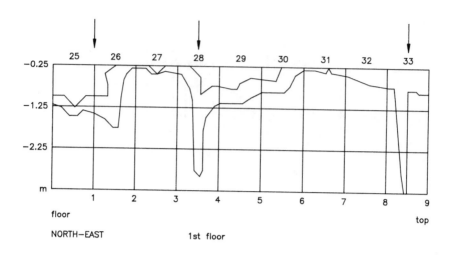

Figure 7. Resistivity contour lines in pillar NE.

In drawing the contour lines the resistivity of the interior buttress with a thickness of 0.25 m has been subtracted. For example in this NE-pillar the calibration corings have been taken at the heights of 1 m, 3.5 m and 8.5 m above floor level, as indicated in figure 7.   The corings are taken in those locations where the resistivity curves indicate changes in the properties.   In this way the number of corings can be significantly reduced, and the corings are made in the right locations.

    The corings are taken with a diamond tool, cooled with water. To avoid the wash-out of the lime mortar a preliminary injection of polyurethane resin is executed at the location of coring.   At hardening this resin forms a foam which packs up all the loose stone and mortar particles, and protects them against the water flow.   Now it is possible to take a consistent core, as shown in figure 8.

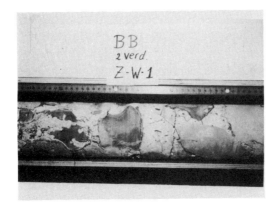

Figure 8. Masonry core, held together by polyurethane foam.

From such cores the test samples are taken to measure all the masonry properties : composition, porosity and void content, strength.

An important element to determine is the grout comsumption. The grout consumption also depends on the nature of the grout. The comsumption of hydraulic grout is calculated as the volume of voids, not including the pores in the stone and the mortar. The penetration of hydraulic grouts in the pores of the material is found to be negligible. The determination of the volume of voids in the pores is hindered by the polyurethane foam of the preliminary injection. However, the foam can easily be removed by calcination at 400°C. At this temperature the polyurethane foam is burned, whereas the transformation of limestone ($CaCO_3$) into lime (CaO) and CO_2 is negligible. If an epoxy resin is used as consolidation grout, we must account for a penetration of resin in the material pores. For epoxy resin this penetration rate is found to be about 20 % of the pore volume.

From the geo-electric measurements, calibrated with only four corings, it could be concluded that no big cracks were present in the pillars, and that still a good bond was present between the buttress of marl stone and the interior core of rubble masonry. The composition of the core is very heterogeneous. It is an incoherent mixture of big (up to 0.5 m) and small pieces of hard and soft stone, rubble and soft lime mortar, the whole crossed by a network of fine cracks. To explain the severe cracking of the buttress on the inside as well as on the outside of the tower, the mechanical properties of the core and buttress were measured. The results are collected in Table 1.

	marl stone	core masonry
Strength N/mm²	2 - 4.5	1 - 2
E-modulus N/mm²	500 - 1500	2200
Rupture strain %	< 1	2 - 3

Table 1. Mechanical properties of materials.

Due to their different composition, the strength of the marl stone is greater than the strength of the core, but its deformability is lower.   This leads to a constant transfer of the loads between the marl buttress and the rubble core.   Every restoration activity disturbs the equilibrium reached at that moment, and gives rise to a renewed load distribution, and to new cracks, especially in the marl stone with its lower rupture strain.   This explains the cracking, experienced since 1972 and shown in figure 2.

APPLICATION OF GEO-ELECTRIC SOUNDING IN GROUTING SURVEY

If the resistance of the masonry is measured after an injection with cement or polymer grouts, it becomes possible to relate the changes of the resistivity with the changes in porosity and thus with the grout consumption and grout distribution in the masonry mass.   A test zone with a width of 1 m and a height of 2 m was injected for this purpose.   The resistivity profile after both injections is shown in Fig. 9.   The shaded part shows the zones where the injection grouts have penetrated.

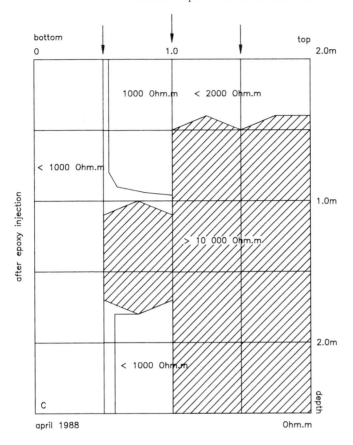

Figure 9. Resistivity profile after injection.

The coring, taken in the zone with only cement injection, is incoherent (Fig. 10, core 1) whereas the corings with combined cement and epoxy injection and with epoxy injection are very coherent (Fig. 10, core 2).

Figure 10. Corings after injection
           (core 1 : incoherent; core 2 : coherent).

The corings were cut into test samples, which were analysed to
determine strength and grout consumption.   The cement grout
consumption had been predicted to be 5,8 % by volume, and the epoxy
consumption 10,2 %, based on the core analyses before injection. The
cement injection was very irregular, due to the fact that the dry
lime mortar extracted the water from the grout.   The dry grout then
blocked the cracks and no further injection flow was possible.   The
epoxy grout consumption was measured to be 12,6 vol. %, which
corresponded very well to the predicted consumption rate.   The
distribution of the grout was very homogeneous throughout the zones,
indicated by the geo-electrical measurements. Even with this limited
grout consumption an increase of the strengths from 1 N/mm² to 3,5
N/mm² was achieved.

CONCLUSIONS

The consolidation of ancient masonry by means of injection of
hydraulic or polymeric grouts is a soft, monument friendly technique.
The altered materials are improved to meet the mechanical and
physical requirements. The geo-electric sounding is found to be a
reliable control method, which enables a thorough control of the
distribution of the injection grout. A direct relation between the
value of the resistivity and the porosity or void content and the
mechanical properties of the masonry is not yet found. However, the
maps of contour lines are extremely valuable for the determination of
the locations of the calibrating corings and of the necessary number
of corings. In the consolidation project on the tower of St. Mary's
Basilica at Tongeren, the technique has been used to evaluate the
masonry composition in order to design the necessary consolidation
procedures and products.   It was also used to evaluate the
effectiveness of the grouting. With the geo-electric technique a
thorough design and control of consolidation work by means of
injections becomes possible.

REFERENCES

1. Derricks, P. O.L.V. Basiliek te Tongeren, Toren.   Historiek. Unpublished, 1986 (in Dutch).
2. Van Gemert, D. and Van Mechelen, D. Geo-electric control of consolidation injections in ancient masonry.   Proceedings of International Symposium "The Engineering Geology of Ancient Works, Monuments and Historical Sites" (Ed. P. Marinos and G. Koukis), Athens 1988, A.A. Balkema, Rotterdam, 1988, pp. 1027-1033.
3. Van Gemert, D. The use of grouting for the consolidation of historic masonry constructions.   Stable-Unstable (Ed. R. Lemaire and K. Van Balen), Leuven University Press, 1988, pp. 265-276.

Criteria for the Substition of Wooden Tierods in Byzantine Churches; St Panteleimon Church of Thessaloniki

C. Ignatakis and K. Stylianidis

Department of Civil Engineering, Aristotle University of Thessaloniki, 540 06 Thessaloniki, Greece

ABSTRACT

In most Byzantine and post-Byzantine Churches there are wooden or metal tierods resisting the horizontal thrusts from the arches and the vaults. These tierods have been proved to be the most sensitive, perhaps, structural members because of their gradual failure, caused either by the corrosion of the material or by the sliding of their supports in the masonry. The contribution of the tierods to the structural stability is shown by comparing analyses of arches with and without tierods. Wherever there are clear indications of defective functioning of the tierods, their substitution by new ones seems to be inevitable. This paper presents the criteria used for the substitution of the wooden tierods of the four arches which support the central dome of the St. Panteleimon Byzantine Church of Thessaloniki. It is pointed out that these criteria are of some general validity and can be applied in similar cases.

INTRODUCTION

It has long been recognised that arched and vaulted structures have a tendency to spread under vertical loads. Tieing is an effective method, known many centuries ago, to restrain outward movements. Ties of timber or iron are usually found in byzantine churches spanning between the springings of arches and vaults at one or two levels. In this latter case, one of the two ties may be acting more as a strut in relation to an arch that springs at its level from the opposite side of the column. It will then be found to be of timber even when the true ties are of iron (WG F of UNIDO/UNDP Project RER/79/015 [1]). Ties are also found arround the bases of domes or across the window openings of drums beneath domes.

An example is given in Fig.1 to show the contribution of the tierods to the structural stability. It is a comparative analysis of the western arch of St. Panteleimon church in

Thessaloniki under total dead weight loads. In case (a) it was assumed that the existing wooden tierods remain effective since in case (b) it was assumed that the ties have completely failed. It has to be pointed out that in the corresponding analytical models the supporting system, consisting of piers, columns, foundation beams and soil springs, has been taken into account, although they are not sketched in Fig.1. Some conclusions can be drawn. In case (a) of effective ties, the axial forces acting on the cross-section are much greater, especially at the keystone region, since the bending moments are smaller. The combination of bending moments and axial forces gives a thrust line lying inside the cross-sections across the whole length of the 45cm thick arch. On the contrary, in case (b) the thrust line is lying outside the cross-sections almost across the whole length of the arch. As a consequence, much more damage must be expected in an arch in cases where ties do not exist or they have failed. In addition, the outward displacement of the springing level is ten times greater in case (b) than in case (a). On the contrary, at the piers, axial forces and bending moments do not differ substantially. Consequently, the absence or failure of ties is expected to affect the soft arches rather than the stiff piers (Penelis [2]) with a single exception related to the significant shear developing at the piers. Combined normal and shear stresses can create inclined sliding surfaces, especially when the piers are tunnelled by vaults in both directions. Sliding surfaces of this type are very dangerous as they can lead to brittle type failures.

The designers and masons of old small churches could not of course imagine that their structures could ever be characterized as creations of architectural, artistic or historical importance. On the other hand, they had to deal with rather poor materials and techniques. Design concepts, like long-life or "durable" design, had no significant meaning at that time. Under these circumstances, design and construction mistakes were unavoidable. Failures of ties were very often in the past, as they are today, a result of design and installation mistakes, decay of timber, rusting of iron and inadequacy of end anchorages (WG F of UNIDO/UNDP Project RER/79/015 [1]). In some cases ties were cut-off after some years of function.

Addition of new ties is an effective remedial measure to substitute failed tierods recommended by many authors (Mainstone [3],Wenzel [4]) and adopted by many constructors (Beckmann [5]). It is a rather "clear" intervention, having the great advantage of being reversible (Mainstone [3]). On the other hand, relatively new technology, such as drilling of thick masonry and access to high strength and corrosion resistant metal ties, can ensure an easy to handle, durable and reversible intervention. During the design procedure, some questions arise concerning the selection of the position, the material, the anchorage types, the prestressing process in relation to other intervention measures, the magnitude of the forces to be imposed and the cross-sections of the ties. Some criteria must be established for these selections. In the following section the criteria used for the substitution of the wooden tierods of the St. Panteleimon Byzantine Church of Thessaloniki, with special reference to the ties of the four main arches supporting the central dome, will be discussed.

CRITERIA FOR THE SUBSTITUTION OF WOODEN TIERODS

The specific problem of St. Panteleimon concerning wooden ties is that at the narthex, the initially existing tierods were cut-off. At the chapels, which are remainders of the old gallery, tierods exist but they are out of function and at the main arches the effectiveness of the existing tierods is open to doubt.

Selection of position
Free spanning additional ties have the drawback that they are necessarily visible and aesthetically unacceptable. But there is a long tradition of using wooden or iron cross-sections of considerable size in byzantine churches at visible positions. As a result, additional ties at also visible positions must not be ruled out. The best position for ties is slightly above the springing level of the arches or vaults (WG F of UNIDO /UNDP Project RER/79/015 [6]). In St. Panteleimon church this is exactly the position where the original ties have been installed. In the case of the narthex it was decided to add new ties at the same position as the previously existing ones. In the case of the chapels it was decided to put them at the same level near the existing or the previously existing ones. In the four main arches, where the effectiveness of the existing ties is open to doubt, placing of new ties at any level near the level of the existing ones would induce undesirable local shear stresses in the piers supporting the arches. On the other hand, drilling of the heavily damaged masonry just above the marble columns was considered to be dangerous. As a consequence, it was decided to install new ties at the same levels, near the existing ones, just at the faces of the above mentioned masonry.

Selection of material
Wooden tierods would be preferable to replace extant wooden ones. But they have the drawbacks that timber can hardly be considered as corrosion resistant material and prestressing procedure is almost unfeasible. On the contrary, metal ties are easy to handle and many different steels are available, varying in cost, corrosion resistance and strength (WG F of UNIDO/UNDP Project RER/79/015 [6]). Taking into account the cost in relation to the importance of the monument and the reversibility of the intervention, austenitic stainless steel alloyed with chromium, nickel and molybdenum was proposed. It is worth mentioning that steel prestressing bars can improve the ductility of the structure (WG F of UNIDO/UNDP Project RER/79/015 [7], Case study of Rotunda, Thessaloniki).

Selection of the type of anchorage

Many anchorage types are also available, such as expanding anchor bolts or resin bolts, each one having advantages or disadvantages (Beckmann [5]). In the case of St. Panteleimon, using as criterion the reversibility and the distribution of the anchorage stresses in a wide region, the placing of a metal anchorage plate on a concrete pad at the outer surface of the origin of the arches was proposed (Fig.2). The anchorage plates are visible and easily reversible. It must be mentioned that anchorage plates were used in Panagia Chalkeon at Thessaloniki some decades ago.

Selection of the prestressing process

This selection is connected to the sequence of the application of the other strengthening measures at the arches, as well as at the whole structure. Using as criterion the optimal final stress-strain distribution, the step-by-step prestressing of the tierods was proposed. Half of the force to be imposed must be applied before the application of the mortar injections in the arches.

Selection of the magnitude of the applied forces

The following criteria were used:

i. The applied forces must be lower than the axial load of the wooden tierods under service loading, assuming that they function completely. In this way the overstressing of the bearing structure is avoided.

ii. During all the steps of the application of forces, the wooden tierods must remain in tension (compression must be avoided). In this way, inverse sliding of anchorage ends does not take place.

iii. During all the phases of intervention, the serviceability criterion (acceptance of limited cracking) and the strength criterion (preventing of formation of plastic hinges) under design loads must be fulfilled.

Selection of the cross-sections of the metal tierods

The following criteria were used:

i. The working stresses must be kept low, so that any possible corrosion under tension is avoided (Tassios [8]) and the possibility of further retensioning in future is secured.

ii. The axial stiffness of the new metal tierods must be of the same order of magnitude as the axial stiffness of the existing wooden tierods. In this way the intense disturbance of the structure, caused by the development of large displacements during any possible gradual or sudden failure of the existing tierods, is avoided.

Based on these criteria, cross-sections of considerable size were found to be necessary. As a result, the ultimate strength of a tie was found to be greater than the ultimate strength of the masonry under the anchorage forces. To prevent an anchorage failure, a local reduction of the cross-section of the ties was decided. In this way, the axial stiffness of the ties is not considerably affected while

yielding of the ties is ensured before an anchorage failure.
This reduction was made at the region of connection to each
other of the members constituting a tie, at the middle of its
length (Fig.3).

RESULTS

Under the intervention criteria presented, the cross-sectional axial forces and bending moments of the western arch of
St. Panteleimon church are shown in Fig.4. It can be concluded that, whatever the effectiveness of the original wooden
tierods might be, the results are similar. Comparing Fig.4a
with Fig.1a it can be also concluded that the intervention
has just the aim to substitute the initially effective wooden
ties by metal, reversible and corrosion resistant steel ties.

REFERENCES

1. WG F of UNIDO/UNDP Project RER/79/015 Building Construction under Seismic Conditions in the Balkan Region. Vol.6,
   Repair and Strengthening of Historical Monuments and Buildings in Urban Nuclei. Chapter 3, Typical Structural Forms
   and their Seismic Behaviour, pp.17-77, UNIDO, Vienna,1984.

2. Penelis, G. Seismic Behaviour of Masonry Roman and Byzantine Monuments, pp. 279-326, Proceedings of the Int. Symposium on Restoration of Byzantine and Post-Byzantine Monuments, Thessaloniki, Greece, 1985. 9th Ephorate of Byzantine Antiquities, Thessaloniki, 1986.

3. Mainstone, R.J. Masonry Vaulted and Domed Structures with
   Special Reference to the Monuments of Thessaloniki, pp.
   237 -248, Proceedings of the Int. Symposium on Restoration
   of Byzantine and Post-Byzantine Monuments, Thessaloniki,
   Greece, 1985. 9th Ephorate of Byzantine Antiquities,
   Thessaloniki, 1986.

4. Wenzel, F. Diagnosis and Therapy of Domed and Vaulted
   Masonry Structures, pp. 259-265, Proceedings of the Int.
   Symposium on Restoration of Byzantine and Post-Byzantine
   Monuments, Thessaloniki, Greece, 1985. 9th Ephorate of
   Byzantine Antiquities, Thessaloniki, 1986.

5. Beckmann, P. Repair and Strengthening of Masonry Structu-
   res, pp. 267-277, Proceedings of the Int. Symposium on
   Restoration of Byzantine and Post-Byzantine Monuments,
   Thessaloniki, Greece, 1985. 9th Ephorate of Byzantine
   Antiquities, Thessaloniki, 1986.

6. WG F of UNIDO/UNDP Project RER/79/015 Building Construction under Seismic Conditions in the Balkan Region. Vol.6,
   Repair and Strengthening of Historical Monuments and Buildings in Urban Nuclei. Chapter 5, Methods of Emergency Intervention, Repair and Strengthening, pp. 97-139 ,UNIDO,
   Vienna, 1984.

7. WG F of UNIDO/UNDP Pro)ict RER/79/015 Building Construction under Seismic Conditions in the Balkan Region. Vol.6,
   Repair and Strengthening of Historical Monuments and Buildings in Urban Nuclei. Chapter 8, Case Study: The Rotunda,
   Thessaloniki, pp. 165-187, UNIDO, Vienna, 1984.

8. Tassios, T.P. On Selection of "Modern" Techniques and
   Materials in Structural Restoration of Monuments, pp. 357-
   384, Proceedings of the Int. Symposium on Restoration of
   Byzantine and Post-Byzantine Monuments, Thessaloniki,
   Greece, 1985. 9th Ephorate of Byzantine Antiquities,
   Thessaloniki, 1986.

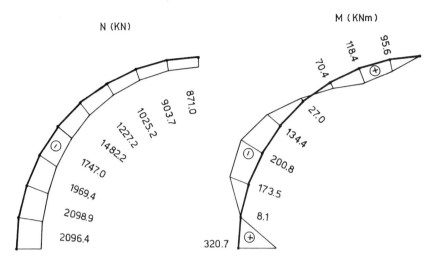

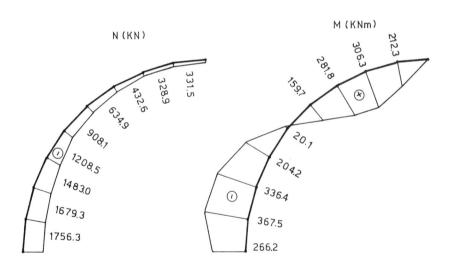

Fig.1 Axial forces (N) and bending moments (M) acting on the western arch of St. Panteleimon. (a) Completely effective wooden ties. (b) No ties considered.

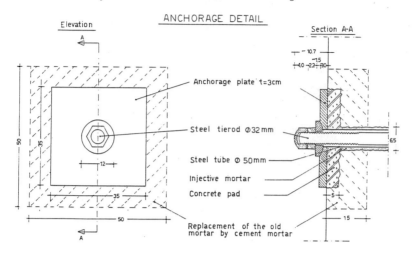

Fig.2. Anchorage at the outer surface of the wall (in cm).

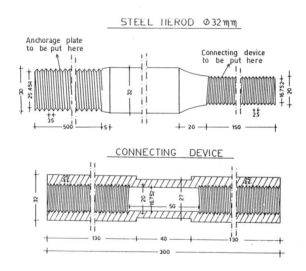

Fig.3. Reduction of cross-section of a steel tie (in mm).

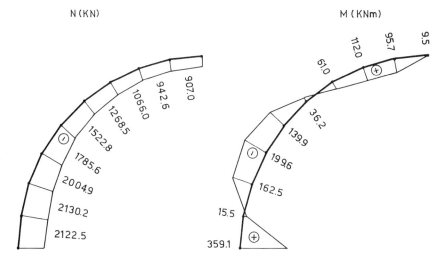

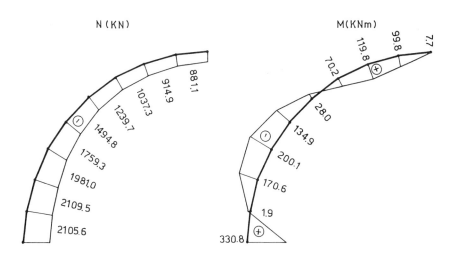

Fig.4. Axial forces (N) and bending moments (M) acting on the western arch of St. Panteleimon after the application of the prestressing force. (a) Completely effective wooden ties. (b) No ties considered.

SECTION 7 - RESTORATION

Deterioration and Restoration of Historic Concrete Structures

Carolyn L. Searls and Sven E. Thomasen

Wiss, Janney, Esltner Associates, Inc., Emeryville, California, USA

ABSTRACT

Concrete has been one of the most widely used building materials of the last 100 years. It has been used extensively in bridges, buildings, and civil engineering structures. Many early concrete structures are now beginning to require extensive restoration and strengthening. The deterioration has commonly been caused by a combination of environmental factors, inferior materials and detailing, and inadequate maintenance.

Preservation of historic concrete structures often requires intensive investigation and careful analysis supplemented by testing to establish the causes of deterioration and to ensure that the repair materials and construction procedures are compatible and sympathetic to the existing historic fabric. The preservation technologist must evaluate the structure for safety, performance, aesthetics, and for future service life.

Case studies of two structures in California, a large bridge with multiple arches and a city hall with concrete facade, are used to illustrate the concepts of investigation and restoration of historic concrete structures.

INTRODUCTION

Types of Deterioration Problems
The common symptoms of concrete deterioration in historic structures are surface erosion, spalling and delamination, cracking, and corrosion of embedded metal and reinforcing steel. These problems result from a number of factors and identification of the causes of deterioration is essential to successful repair and restoration.

Surface Erosion Surface erosion is the weathering of the concrete surface by sun, water, or wind-borne sand. Erosion will attack the softer cement paste, first at the surface layer which exposes the aggregate and then the paste between the aggregate.

Spalling and Delamination Spalling is the loss of surface material in patches of varying sizes. Spalling is commonly associated with corrosion of embedded metal. Delamination occurs in structures where the concrete has a rendering finish and it is sometimes found over an entire wall surface.

<u>Cracking</u>   Cracks are common in all concrete structures.   They vary in width from microscopic to wide and in depth from surface crazing to full section.   Cracks can be either dormant or active.   Active cracks can be progressive or they can have daily or seasonal changes.   All cracks are unsightly and while small cracks might be structurally harmless, larger cracks increase the potential for water infiltration and further deterioration.

<u>Corrosion</u>   damage to embedded metal and reinforcing steel and the resulting spalling of material are the most commonly observed failure modes in historic concrete structures.   The considerable expansive pressure of the formation of corrosion products will cause cracking and spalling of the concrete cover.   The load carrying capacity of the structure can be diminished by spalling of the concrete and by loss of reinforcing steel area.

<u>Causes of Concrete Deterioration</u>
The causes of deterioration are often interrelated and progressive in nature.

<u>Water Related Deterioration</u>   Moisture is by far the environmental agent that is most harmful to concrete.   Water exerts pressure when it freezes, supports biological growth, and is a carrier for chemicals and salts.

Frost damage appears as cracking and delamination of the surface.   The damage depends on the number of cycles and speed of temperature variations around the freezing point, the amount of surface cracking, permeability, and degree of saturation of the concrete.

The presence of biological organisms such as algae, moss, lichen, and plants, prevents the concrete from drying out, and the chemical products of their metabolism disintegrate the cement binder.   The formation of biological growth in a crack can exert considerable pressure which ultimately fractures the concrete.

Infiltrated water is a carrier of chemicals, which dissolve cementitious binders as the water permeates through the concrete.   As the water evaporates, salt particles expand and cause erosion and surface delamination.   Chloride ions from salts combine with moisture to produce an electrolyte, which corrodes embedded steel.

<u>Environmental Deterioration</u>   Carbonation occurs when carbon dioxide in the air and in the rain reacts chemically with the cement paste at the concrete surface.   The reaction neutralizes the alkalinity of concrete and reduces the protection of embedded metal, permitting corrosion of reinforcing steel.

<u>Expansion and Contraction Failures</u>   Volume changes can be one-way or cyclic and they often cause distress when the structure has no provisions for differential movement.   Creep and shrinkage of concrete and thermal expansion and contraction can result in cracking and crushing.

<u>Materials and Workmanship</u> Early concrete structures were often constructed with soft aggregates such as cinders or dimensionally unstable aggregate such as crushed bricks which expand when wet. Early concrete was also poorly consolidated when placed in the forms, and this tended to leave voids at congested areas and 'honeycombs'--aggregate without cement paste--at the surface. Problems of workmanship, some of which are not unknown in modern concrete construction, are cold joints where one layer of deposited concrete is allowed to harden before the next layer is poured, and insufficient cover over reinforcing steel.

<u>Condition Assessment</u>
The objective of the assessment is to gather information about design, construction, past history, and present condition of the structure in order to evaluate the safety, present performance, risk of future distress, and need for strengthening or rehabilitation. The scope of the assessment varies but it always includes obtaining information on the history and background of the structure as well as performing a visual inspection. Historical records such as old drawings, photographs or journals often show the original design. The important information to be gathered from the background search includes details of the internal reinforcing and the type and location of anchors.

Visual observations are made of the materials and the structural elements and signs of distress, such as cracks, spalling, rust spots, or evidence of leakage are recorded on drawings and documented with photographs. Close-up examinations from hydraulic lifts or scaffolding are made at ornamental sections and at cornice and slab soffits where fractures might be difficult to observe from a distance and where failure often represents a considerable hazard.

The location of reinforcing steel is found with a calibrated metal detector. The copper-copper sulphate half-cell test detects the potential for active corrosion of the embedded steel by measuring the voltage drop between steel and the surface of the concrete. Ultrasonic testing is used to detect cracks, flaws, or delamination in the concrete and the measurements can be done manually or continuously from a moving vehicle.

Laboratory tests are performed on concrete samples removed from the structure to analyze material composition, the cause of observed distress, chloride content, depth of carbonation, and the expected durability of the structure.

<u>Concrete Restoration</u>
Repair and restoration of historic concrete may consist of either replacement with new material or patching the historic material. Duplication of original material and detailing should be as exact as possible to assure a repair that is functionally and aesthetically acceptable. Repair procedures should be tested on small concrete sections before treating the entire structure. The test procedures should be as close as possible to the actual repair conditions and patching and coatings should be allowed to weather before final selection is made.

The concepts of investigation, assessment, and restoration of historic concrete structures are illustrated by the following two case studies.

CASE STUDY - THE COLORADO STREET BRIDGE

Introduction

The Colorado Street Bridge in Pasadena near Los Angeles, California, is an open spandrel, eleven-span arched reinforced concrete structure built in 1912-13. At 447 m (1467 ft.) long and 46 m (150 ft.) above the bed of the arroyo, it was the longest and highest bridge of its time built in the United States. The bridge features extensive decorative detailing and picturesque refuge bays set into the side railings on each pier. The bridge was designed by Joseph Alexander Low Waddell, one of the nation's foremost bridge engineers, and built by John Drake Mercereau, a well known California builder. Figure 1 shows a view of the bridge and Figure 2 identifies elements of a typical bridge span.

Fig. 1. View of the Colorado St. Bridge

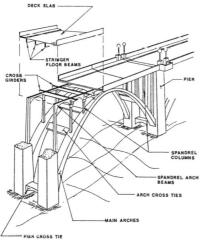

Fig. 2 Elements of a bridge span

The two-lane bridge served the major connection between Pasadena and Los Angeles until the 1950s, when an adjacent bridge was built. Since then only minimal maintenance has been provided for the old bridge. Approximately ten years ago, the State of California Department of Transportation observed serious deterioration of the bridge and undertook a series of studies [1] to evaluate its condition and make recommendations for its repair.

Evidence of Distress and Deterioration

Top of Slab   Cracking of the asphalt overlay was extensive. Sidewalks and railings had considerable cracking and spalling. Some expansion joints were inoperable and differential displacement across joints occurred, as shown in Figure 3.

Drains were easily clogged, and ponding conditions occurred at several spans. Water had penetrated through cracks and open joints and this falling water had caused extensive deterioration at the slab soffit, underdeck support members, piers, and arches.

<u>Bottom of Slab</u>   Severe cracking with efflorescent residue was found on the underdeck area of several spans and on the sidewalk soffit of all spans.

<u>Underdeck Support Members</u>   At three piers, the stringer floor beams had lost 50% of their bearing area as water penetrating through expansion joints had disintegrated the concrete.   Shear cracks were observed in many cross girders, indicating inadequacy of the existing reinforcement.

Fig. 3. Distress at bridge deck and railing

<u>Piers and Arches</u>   Concrete cracking, spalling, and delamination occurred throughout the structure, particularly in areas where the concrete had been exposed to constant leakage.   Reinforcing steel was exposed in many locations where corrosion had caused the concrete to spall, as seen in Figure 4.   However, only minimal steel section loss had occurred.

<u>Foundation Blocks and Ties</u>   Corrosion of reinforcement and spalling of the concrete had occurred, but not to the extent found in the piers and arches.

<u>Investigation</u>

<u>Visual Inspection</u>   A complete close-up visual inspection was performed of the top and the underside of the deck using a truck-mounted "snooper vehicle."   A crane was used for inspection of selected piers and arches. Remaining piers and arches were surveyed using binoculars from the ground.

<u>Delamination Survey</u>   The bridge deck was inspected using a vehicle-mounted sound recording device to detect subsurface deterioration.   This instrument recorded delaminations between the asphalt overlay and concrete deck and within the concrete slab at the level of the top reinforcing mat.   The levels of delamination, ranged from 33% to 93% of the surveyed deck area.

Fig. 4. Distress at Arches

<u>Copper-Copper Sulphate Half-Cell Test</u>   This field test was used to determine if the reinforcing steel was actively corroding. The electrical potential was measured at 10-foot intervals on the bridge deck slab.   In every span, electrical potential gradients above 0.35 volts were measured, indicating greater than 90% probability that corrosion was occurring.

<u>Carbonation Test</u>   Concrete cores were removed from the structure and treated with the chemical phenolphthalein to test for carbonation.   The chemical turns red on highly alkaline concrete and remains colorless on carbonated concrete.   The observed carbonation depth of cores from the bridge was from 50 to 75 mm, a depth greater than the typical concrete cover over the reinforcing steel.

<u>Compression Strength</u>   Compression strength tests were made of selected concrete cores and results were correlated with Schmidt Hammer tests conducted in the field.   Compressive strengths were well above the required strengths.

<u>Chloride Content</u>   Chemical analyses were made of cores to determine chloride content.   The chloride content measured was well below the threshold limit established by the Federal Highway Administration and the Transportation Research Board for removal of contaminated concrete.

<u>Structural Analysis</u>   A structural analysis of the bridge was performed by DeLeuw Cather Company.   It was found that the deck, the spandrel columns and the underdeck cross girders did not meet current code requirements for highway traffic and seismic capacity.

<u>Concrete Restoration</u>
The historic value of the bridge made it desirable to retain the structure if the load capacity could be brought up to modern highway standards.   The selected rehabilitation scheme, shown in Figure 5, retains the arches, piers, and foundation ties, while replacing members above the arches with strengthened sections matching the appearance of the original bridge design.   This approach results in a structure that will meet AASHTO HS-20 loading and current seismic load standards.

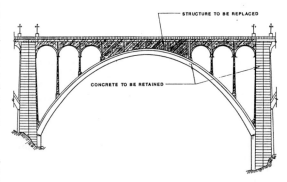

<u>Repair of Arches, Piers, and Foundation Ties</u>   The existing concrete is carbonated to a depth below the reinforcing steel and no longer

Fig. 5. Schematic view of Concrete Restoration

protects the steel from corrosion.   Rather than replacing this concrete cover, the restoration will rely on the ability of a water repellent to prevent water from reaching the reinforcing steel.   The water repellent treatment will not affect the appearance of the concrete.

A considerable amount of spalled or delaminated concrete will be removed and replaced.   The exposed reinforcing steel will be coated and secured with drilled-in anchors.   The appearance of the original construction will be matched by controlling the concrete mix, by using formwork that duplicates the existing form lines and by light sandblasting of the concrete patches to simulate the effect of years of surface erosion on the existing concrete surfaces.

CASE STUDY - PASADENA CITY HALL

Introduction
The City Hall in Pasadena, California, is one of the most distinctive public buildings in the United States.   The architects for the 1926 U-shaped building, Bakewell and Brown, also designed the San Francisco City Hall.   The three-story building, as seen in Figure 6, has a central wing with a gigantic open barrel vault topped by a massive circular tower.   The tower is pierced by a series of Roman arches topped by a belfry.   Above it rises the dome and the lantern, a column-supported cupola.   Walking through the barrel vault, the visitor emerges into a patio filled with greenery and fountains.   Stylistically the City Hall has an exaggerated Spanish Baroque flavor with numerous towers and lanterns in the enclosed court.

Fig. 6. Pasadena City Hall

The entire structure was built of reinforced concrete.   The cast-in-place concrete was covered with a thin layer of integral colored stucco. The many decorative elements were precast concrete sections--also called 'cast stone'-- which were set into the cast-in-place structure.   The cast stone elements, which included balustrades, the large pediment over the entrance arch, and cartouches and finials at the four stair towers, had typically been cast against a plaster mold and with a shell thickness up to 5 cm.   The concrete mix, one part white cement and three parts white siliceous sand, was pressed into the molds and reinforced with galvanized wire mesh.   The edges and the webs of the cast stone elements had embedded steel anchors which were solidly grouted into the cast-in-place building construction.

Evidence of Distress and Deterioration

Cast-in-Place Vertical Walls   The cast-in-place concrete walls have a two-layer stucco finish of 5 to 10 mm thickness.   The original integral colored stucco had been coated with paint in 1959.   The coating was generally in good condition except in some areas where water infiltration had caused peeling.   Visual inspection showed no evidence of extensive cracking, spalling, staining, or other deterioration, but acoustic tapping of the walls detected that large sections of the stucco had delaminated from the substrate. Petrographic examination of cores indicated that the concrete surface in many areas was still smooth and shiny due to a failure of the stucco rendering to contact it when it was installed. The poor bonding of the stucco to the concrete had been aggravated by water intrusion into the voids.

Cast-in-Place Ornamental Sections
The stucco at these sections was similar to the finish at the vertical walls but distress and deterioration in form of cracks, stucco spalling, and paint peeling was much more common. Laboratory examination of concrete cores found that the problem of debonding of stucco was more severe and widespread than first revealed by the visual survey. Most damage was found below horizontal ledges and at leaking rainwater gutters where water had infiltrated the concrete and the stucco, as seen in Figure 7.

Fig. 7. Spalling at Roof Cornice

Precast Cast Stone Sections Visual inspections and laboratory analysis of the core samples from the cast stone sections showed that the concrete was in excellent condition with a solid cement paste and a sharp angular sand aggregate. Apparently a consolidant type coating had been applied at one time to the concrete surface. The coating was found to be a void-filling material rather than a binder and while it was ineffective it was also harmless.

A number of the cast stone elements were cracked or the concrete had spalled, as seen on the finials in Figure 8. It was found that the damage had been caused by corrosion of embedded steel anchors resulting from water infiltration at defective joints and horizontal surfaces.

Fig. 8. Cracked Finial

Concrete Restoration

The restoration treatment was selected after extensive testing of repair methods and materials and it was first applied to a small building section before it was approved for general application.

The typical repair for debonded vertical wall areas consisted of spot-gluing the stucco with epoxy injections at 200 mm on center, as seen in Figure 9. Spalled or badly delaminated stucco was replaced with new construction.

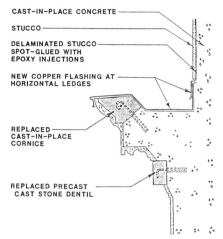

Fig. 9. Typical restoration
procedures

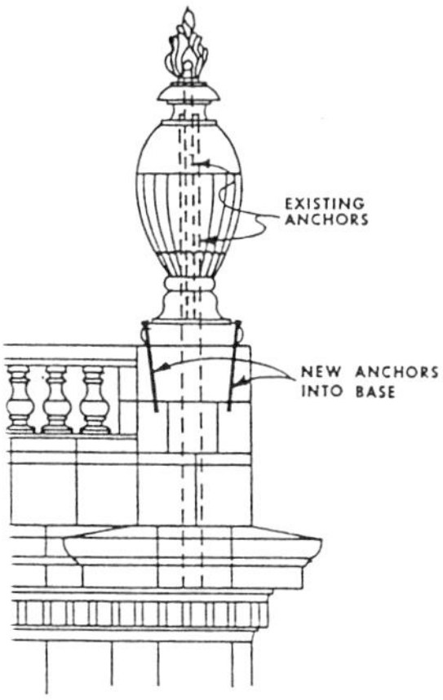

Fig. 10. Retrofit of Finial

Damaged cast stone sections were repaired by patching with concrete that matched the original mix in terms of color and aggregate gradation. Cracks were filled by epoxy injection and exposed elements such as Urns and Finials were anchored with drilled-in reinforcing, as seen in Figure 10.

REFERENCE

1. DeLeuw, Cather & Company, Colorado Street Bridge Inspection Findings and Rehabilitation Report, January 1984.

Anastylosis of the Arch of Demetrius-Apollonius in Perge

M. Yorulmaz[1], G. Tanyeli[1] and Ü İzmirligil[2]

[1] *Faculty of Architecture, Istanbul Technical University, Taksim 80191 Istanbul, Turkey*

[2] *Central Laboratory of Restoration and Conservation, Sultanahmet, 34400 Istanbul, Turkey*

INTRODUCTION

Perge was one of the most important cities of the Mediterranean coast of Asia Minor which was called Pamphylia in Antiquity (Fig. 1). In the excavations that were carried on in the last forty years, the colonnaded north-west street and the main public buildings of the city were studied. The triumphal arch which is the subject matter of this paper was disclosed in the excavations of 1973 and 1974 by late Prof.Dr.A.M.Mansel [1].It is situated on the junction of the two colonnaded streets of the city and gives the east-west street access through its only arch (fig. 2). The lower parts of the piers of the structure were discovered in situ and the remaining blocks of stones were found scattered around them. After the preliminary studies, Ministry of Culture and Tourism, General Directorate of Antiquities and Museums decided to reconstruct the architecturally unique arch, which holds the longest Greek inscription in Pamphylia, under the guidance of Istanbul University, Faculty of Letters, Archaeological Research Station of the Region of Antalya.

HISTORICAL STUDIES AND THE RESTITUTION

After the excavations the fragments of the inscription were re-arranged, then the inscription, which is almost the same text on the two facades of the arch, was translated by late Prof.G.Bean. According to the translation of the inscription, it was written on the west facade of the arch that the building was built "by brothers Apollonius and Demetrius, in the time of prefect Gaius Caristanius Phronton and was dedicated to Artemis Pergaia and Apollo Epekoos"; and on the east facade it was recorded that it was constructed by "Domitianus (81-96 A.D.) after deified Vespasianus and Titus". But a part of the east inscription was scraped after the completion of the building to erase the memory of the emperor Domitianus . The inscription was evaluated in 1975 by Prof.Dr.J.İnan [2] and the structure was renamed the "Arch of Demetrius-Apollonius" and dated to the 1st century A.D.

The studies that were carried out to reveal the architectural peculiarities of the structure were continued up to the year 1979. During

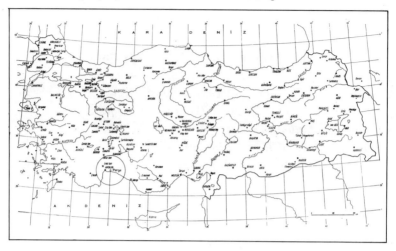

Fig. 1.   Map of Turkey and the location of Perge

the research it was considered, at first, that the building originally
consisted of two Doric piers (pylons) and an arch which stands upon the
truncated pediments. Above the arch, there was an Ionic style attic.
The exact places of the blocks of the attic could be easily determined
by the scholars because of the inscription on it. However, the pylons
posed an important problem that was discussed much by the scholars
whether there was a missing row of stones on the pylons or not.
Although numerous small fragments of stones were found in the excavations, no fragment was identified as one that originally belonged to this
row.Nevertheless,the existence of a missing row of stones was proven by
the architrave of the colonnaded street which was articulated to the
triumphal arch. The socket of the architrave of the colonnade and the
architrave itself were identified, and the original height of the
architrave was estimated almost precisely. This evidence made
scholars sure that the arch has to comprise a missing row of stones
(Fig. 3).

THE MATERIALS AND TECHNIQUES OF CONSTRUCTION

According to the consequences of the physico-mechanical tests done in the
Engineering Geology and Rock Mechanics Laboratory of the Mining Faculty
of Istanbul Technical University, the main building material of the arch
is an extremely dense type of travertine. Its physical and mechanical
properties are as follows:

Density	:	2.52 gr/cm^3
Water absorption by weight	:	1 %
Uniaxial compression	:	1050 kg/cm^2
Tensile strength	:	30 kg/cm^2

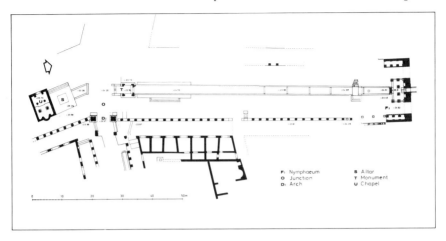

Fig. 2.   Main colonnaded streets of the city and the Arch of Demetrius-
          Apollonius. Plan (From Ü.İzmirligil and A.Şakar)

Dynamic Young modulus	:	4.2×10^5 kg/cm^2
Static Young modulus	:	4.4×10^4 kg/cm^2
		(0-20 kg/cm^2 for stresses)
		2.1×10^5 kg/cm^2
		(>20 kg/cm^2 for stresses)

The Arch of Demetrius-Apollonius was built of 151 blocks of stone
which were organized in 22 rows and of 151 blocks only 11 are missing.
The building was a pseudo-isodomus masonry construction. Each block of
stone was fastened to the adjacent block with two iron clamps. But,
there was no clamp on the row of the stylobate. Between the row of the
pedestal and the stylobate, there was a layer of mortar which makes
one think that other rows of stones were also bound to each other vertically
with mortar. The technique which was applied in the dressing of the
stone blocks was anathyrosis. This means that only the front face and
the edges of a block were hewn sharply and precisely and the rest were
chiseled roughly just to shape the rectangular block .

The blocks of the attic of the arch were marked to determine their
places on the building with the letters of the Greek alphabet. This
system of marking defines the exact places of the blocks from the north
to the south and from the top to the bottom of the building (Fig. 4).
The application marks were also looked for on the other blocks of the
building, but, what were found on the voussoirs were insufficient to
suppose that this system was employed in the construction process of
the building as a whole. It can be claimed that marks were not used on
the blocks of the pylons at all.

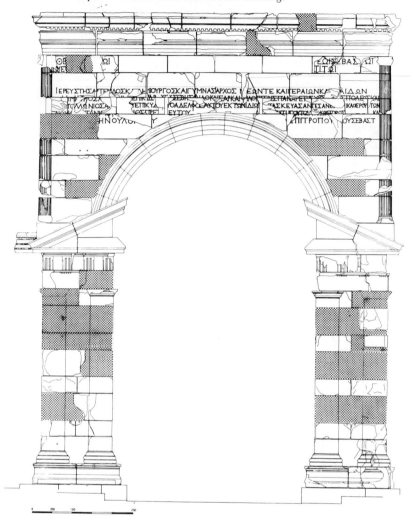

Fig. 3.   The restitution of the east facade of the arch. The missing
          blocks shaded (Ü.İzmirligil, F.Arman, G.Tanyeli)

THE TECHNICAL PROBLEMS AND THE CONSTRUCTION

The approach to the problems of the restoration in this building is to
solve the individual problems of the elements of the structure, sin-
gly,   in a process which is defined independently for each of them.
In this case, this method became an unavoidable necessity, because the

building could not be rebuilt with the same technique as   was
applied in its original construction. This means that an important
structural problem had to be solved here. All the architectural problems
concerning the restoration process would be solved according to the

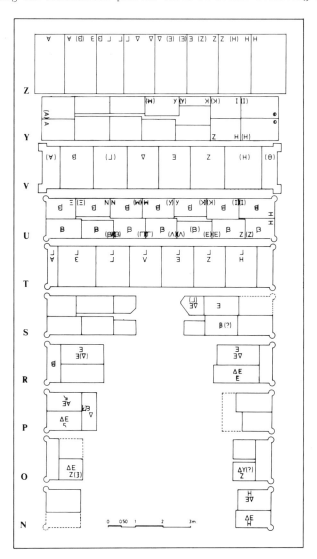

Fig. 4.   The application marks on the blocks of the attic. Plan
(G.Tanyeli)

structural solution of the system in which the restorer-architect
could only play a secondary role behind that of the engineer.

When the project started at first, it was thought to rebuild the
arch with the same techniques of construction of the original building.
For this purpose, the behaviour of the original building a. under
vertical loadings, b. under the earthquake loads which effect the
structure in two directions, separately, were taken into account.
It was concluded, consequently, that the building could safely resist
against the vertical loading and against the earthquake loads which
effected the building along its longitudinal axis. However, an
earthquake which effects the structure along its transversal axis can
create tensile and shear stresses that can result in the damage of
the building. This defect makes the intervention to the structural
system an unavoidable necessity,so two proposals were prepared: a. to
build, within the masonry construction of the building, a reinforced
concrete frame which can behave satisfactorily under all kinds of
loadings. b. to apply prestressing for overcoming the tension and
shear stresses with the aid of friction forces at the most problematic
parts of the pylons in which high tension and shear stresses have
occured. The original material of the arch, a sort of travertine,
makes prestressing possible because of its high compressive strength.

Both proposals were developed as complete projects and the second
proposal (prestressing) was preferred as being more advantageous. It
minimizes the intervention to the original structure. The prestressing
is applied on the pylons only and the rest of the structure was left to
be built with the original clamped masonry technique (Fig. 5).

After the structural solution of the system the building process
of the arch began. At first, the missing blocks were produced with
an artificial material which was made of cement and aggregate of
travertine. The partially broken blocks were also reintegrated with the
same material. In the reintegration process, stainless steel pins and
an epoxy resin mortar were used. On the other hand, blocks were fastened to
each other with two stainless steel clamps for each block as those in
the original structure. Besides clamps, rows of stones were stiffened
with vertical pins, and both contacting faces of the blocks, horizontal
and vertical, were bonded with the epoxy resin mortar which was made
of epoxy resin plus silica and travertine powder. The important cracks
on the stones were also repaired with the same method.

The reconstruction process of the arch began in 1983. In this
year the in situ parts of the pylons were dismantled and the area on
which the foundations would be built was excavated. During the excavation, one of the main canals of the water maintenance system of the city
was found and a decision for preserving it was made, because the canal
is still in use, unintentionally, as a drainage outlet for the once
urban area. Therefore, what had to be done was to alter the reconstruction project according to this unexpected problem. After the alteration,
the foundation and the projected prestressed concrete inner cores of
the pylons were built and then, up to the summer of 1987, 5 rows of the

Fig. 5.   The reconstruction project showing the foundation and the
prestressing system. (M.Yorulmaz, S.Önkol, G.Tanyeli).

stone blocks were placed around these cores. Reconstruction will continue at a rather slow pace in the future due to financial problems,
and authors hope to see it completed.

REFERENCES

1.   Mansel, A.M., Perge Kazısı 1973 Çalışmaları, Belleten Vol. 38,
     p. 542, 1974 and Mansel, A.M., 1974 Perge Kazısı, Belleten, Vol. 39,
     p. 551, 1975.

2.   İnan, J., Demetrios und Apollonios Bogen in Perge, p. 128,
     Proceedings of the XI.International Congress of Classical Archaeo-
     logy, London, 3-9 September, 1978.

The Rock House: Preserving the Ruins of an Eighteenth Century Vernacular Stone Residence in Piedmont, North Carolina, USA

J Edwin Hendricks

Wake Forest University, Winston-Salem, North Carolina, USA

INTRODUCTION

Captain Jack Martin's Rock House in Stokes County, North Carolina poses unique preservation problems. This substantial residence, completed in the 1790s, stands as a ruin, its roof destroyed in the 1890s. The house is of vernacular design, with strong English features. The English influence is somewhat surprising considering the presence of a strong Moravian settlement with German architectural styles only thirty miles away. The house was constructed with field stone using red clay mortar and plastered with a cementous material. Exposed for almost one hundred years to the elements and to vandals in search of construction stone, many of its walls have deteriorated. Weathering has removed most of the stucco covering. Much of the structure remains stable, however, and it appears that the ruin will survive into the twenty-first century unless disturbed by some outside force.

The structure was allowed to deteriorate until recently when the Stokes County Historical Society acquired it and asked for assistance from the Preservation Program at Wake Forest University under the direction of Dr. J. Edwin Hendricks, Ph.D., Director of the Preservation Program and Professor of History. Four summer field schools have attempted to arrest the deterioration of the building through providing a concrete cap for the stable walls, installing bracing for unstable walls, replacing arches and re-installing window and door frames.

The students have prepared proposals for roofing the structure--seeking to preserve the ruin rather than to restore or reconstruct it. A variety of plans are under consideration, their implementation hampered by the extreme rural location of the structure, an absence of preservation legislation in the host county, a lack of funding, and a divergence of opinion in the historical society which controls the property.

STOKES COUNTY HISTORY

Stokes County is located on the northern boundary of North Carolina, some three hundred miles from the Atlantic Ocean, just south of Virginia. Stokes' 459 square miles are dominated by the Sauratown Mountains, entirely contained within the county and once home to the Saura Indians.

The county was formed in 1789 and is predominately rural. There are 37,000 inhabitants of whom 90 percent live in rural areas. Fifty percent of the rural population engages in agriculture and the remainder work in business and industry. Many farms are operated by families where one or more of the adults work off the farm as well. Seventy percent of all land is in farms but this includes vast areas which are forested. The average size of farms is 70 acres. The median family income is $17,000, significantly smaller than the average income in North Carolina or in Forsyth, the only adjoining county with a substantial urban population.

The Dan River snakes diagonally across the county from the northwest to the southeast and its unpolluted waters make bathing, canoeing, and tubeing popular sports. A state park and summer resorts from the turn of the century testify to the attractiveness of the region. On a plateau in the middle of the county, near a sharp bend of the Dan, the county seat of Danbury was established in 1849.

There are only two towns of more than one thousand inhabitants in the county, King (1164) and Walnut Cove (1164). Danbury, the county seat, has only 150 residents. Recent infusions of industry and residences in the southern part of the county bode well for the future and have brought marked improvements in the educational system and in other services available in the county. Among other things the county has a funded arts council, a recreation program, and an active historical society. However, the county remains largely poor and largely rural.

JOHN (CAPTAIN JACK) MARTIN

John Martin was born in Virginia in 1756 to parents of English ancestry. In 1768 young Jack moved to North Carolina, most likely with an elder brother. Tradition states that Martin began building his house in the early 1770s. In 1776 Martin was a militia lieutenant in action against the Cherokee Indians. He was an active patriot leader and fought against local Tories and in organized campaigns as the Revolutionary War came to an end.

In 1784 Martin married Nancy Shipp and presumably completed the second stage of construction on the Rock House. The Martins raised ten children, three girls and seven boys. Martin prospered as a piedmont North Carolina planter. He accumulated much land (six to eight thousand acres by the time of his death), much livestock (four horses, ten cows and calves, and a "stock of hogs"), and many slaves (thirty-two according to his estate inventory). In addition to serving as a militia leader, Martin represented Stokes County in the General Assembly on two occasions, 1798-1799 and 1811-1812. As magistrate in the Stokes County Court of Pleas and Quarter Sessions, Martin presided over the court with a rustic justice which gained him much notoriety.

Martin's land holdings and the prominence of his house (its white stucco was visible for some distance) further enhanced his position in the community. At his death over thirty people owed him money. The house was well furnished and some rooms were paneled with pecan. Martin possessed a desk, a book case, and more than eighty books. Mrs. Martin boasted a set of "fine English china."

Martin died April 5, 1822 while fighting a forest fire near the Rock House. His wife Nancy lived until 1841. Both are buried in a small family cemetery nearby, along with a son, William, who was killed by a slave overseer in 1859. Martin descendants dispersed over North Carolina, the south, and ultimately across the nation.

THE ROCK HOUSE

The ruins of the Rock House stand as a monument to Captain Jack Martin and the impact he had on the history of Stokes County. For the place and time it was an exceptionally large house. Its method of construction is rare in this region despite the ready availability of building materials. Its four stories included a full basement and an attic large enough to require a fireplace for heating. Its interior kitchen and fireplace for cooking were not common in the antebellum South. The basic rectangle of the house measures 35.6' x 24.4', with an enclosed north porch 17.6' x 8' and an open south porch 18' x 8'. Room height averages 9' and the distance from basement floor to chimney top is 43'.

An estimated 40,000 wheelbarrow loads of stone were required for construction and most of these had to be transported to the site from neighboring fields and quarries. Construction was accomplished by stacking the stone with a red clay mortar and then surfacing the entire building, inside and out, with a plaster or stucco finish. The building technique was known in neighboring areas especially among the German Moravians at Bethabara and Salem, about 25 miles to the south. The walls averaged twenty-two inches thick, thinning toward the top. The roof was likely made of shingles split on the site, some handmade bricks were used to line the fireplaces, and the stucco was made with lime from shells imported at considerable expense from the coast rather than local limestone. The thickness and stability of the walls and the size and location of setbacks and holes for timbers indicate a well framed and substantial structure. The skill of the rock masons is still evident in the surviving arches over windows and doors and in the two-thirds of the walls still standing after being exposed to the elements for about one hundred years.

Construction seems to have been accomplished in at least two phases. The stone work of the north portico is of a different nature than the remainder of the house and the porch is tied in with the upper but not the lower walls of the house. The south-facing porch is larger than the area between the two south basement windows, indicating a later addition. This fits with the story that Martin began the house before the

Revolution and finished it afterward. The lower floors may have been occupied early and the top floors finished after peace and Martin's marriage.

The design of the house is somewhat Medieval English and compares with Bacon's Castle and the Criss Cross House in Virginia. The basement and two main floors each contained two large rooms. One basement room had an earth floor, no fireplace, one small window to the south and only a vent hole to the north. Entrance was from the other basement room, a kitchen, and the area was probably used for cool dry storage. The kitchen floor was paved with stone and it had a fireplace "large enough to roast an ox." The kitchen windows north and south and was entered from outside the house through a doorway in the east wall. Little evidence exists for the four rooms on the next two floors except that each of them had a fireplace. Access between main floors was provided by stairs located within the enclosed north porch. The west end of the attic had a small fireplace as well and tradition states that children and household slaves shared this space. The two chimneys, one on the east and one on the west, each contained three separate flues. Near the top of the house the chinmneys narrowed and were flanked by large flat stones to form shoulders which shed water.

Although the building was located near well travelled paths during Martin's lifetime, by the time of the Civil War transportation patterns had shifted some miles away to the south side of the Sauratown Mountains. After the Civil War the house's isolation contributed to its decline so that its roof was not replaced when it either burned or was blown off by a storm about 1890. In the early 1930s plans were drawn to renovate and occupy the house but this did not occur, largely because of the isolated location. The house continued to deteriorate as time passed and the surrounding acres were largely devoted to growing corn and tobacco. With the roof missing the rains washed the mud mortar from the stones and the exterior and interior plaster began to fall off. Only a few remnants remain to show what the surface of the walls looked like. Stones on the top of the walls loosened and fell. The south wall, presumably more exposed to wind and rain, began to collapse.

PRESERVATON EFFORTS

Efforts to preserve the Rock House have involved many people over a long time. In 1931 the Daughters of the American Revolution erected a plaque marking the house as a historic site, hoping to discourage vandals. Instead, more stones and eventually the plaque itself disappeared. The house was part of an estate and abortive efforts to find a suitable use for the structure culminated in the transfer of the House to the Stokes County Historical Society in 1975. The Society worked diligently to prepare the site for a ceremony on 4 July 1976 the bicentennial of the nation's birth. The site was placed on the National Register of Historic Places. Workmen removed vines, fallen stones, and debris. After the bicentennial, the house remained a favorite site for history lovers, other lovers seeking a romantic setting, and those looking for a readily available source of stone. Society members prepared plans for a nature park and a nature trail but could not find funds to implement them. The house's isolated location added to its appeal and to its vulnerability. Uncertainty as to the best preservation and restoration techniques contributed to further delay and deterioration continued.

Over the next few years, portions of the south wall continued to collapse. Individuals carried away many loads of stone on the assumption that they would never be missed. The east wall began to deteriorate as well and stones from the tops of the walls continued to fall. In the spring of 1984, someone in search of building stone deliberately demolished the southeast corner of the house. This destroyed all remnants of the south wall more than a yard above the ground and caused major shifting and falling of portions of the east wall leaving it in a hazardous condition.

The Historical Society installed a chain to prohibit vehicular access, placed a mobile home on land just south of the house (the occupant of the home was given free rent in exchange for serving as a watchman), and installed lights to provide further security. The Society had already contracted for work to be done on the site that summer in an effort to arrest the deterioration.

In the summers of 1984, 1985 and again in 1988, Dr. J. Edwin Hendricks, Professor of History, Wake Forest University, directed Preservation Field Schools at the Rock House. Students again cleared debris and growth from the House. Each year an average of fifteen undergraduate students and a graduate assistant studied the techniques of preservation in the classroom and put them to work on the site. They placed a cement cap on the walls to lessen damage from seepage. They reinforced arches and reinstalled door and window frames. Students used timbers to brace the very unstable northeast corner, rebuilt doorways and some window arches, and replaced the lintel stone over the entrance into the basement.

Field School students sifted debris taken from the house in an effort to locate artifacts which might provide evidence of the contents of the house and demonstrate the lifestyles of those who lived there. Material from between the stones on both porches and the debris from the stone-floored kitchen and adjoining earthen-floored room provided many artifacts. Hand wrought nails, a broken arrowhead, an early glass marble, buttons, and many pieces of pottery and china (including fragments of what may well have been Nancy Martin's "fine English china,") all point to affluent occupants in the early nineteenth century giving way to less well-to-do inhabitants following the Civil War. This coincides with the historical record. Objects from more recent times demonstrate the continuing popularity of the site. Archaeological studies for the entire site are needed and should be conducted as soon as preservation is assured.

PRESERVATION OPTIONS

Preservation is indeed the first priority for Captain Jack Martin's Rock House. Experience with unused structures generally, and with this house in particular, shows that if left as it is the structure will continue to deteriorate. Although recent work has slowed the erosion of relatively stable sections of the walls, the east wall and northeast corners are in great danger of collapse. Vibrations from the fall could well cause damage to remaining stonework.

Although both chimneys appear stable, the east one could be damaged by falling walls, or continuing erosion of the clay binder. All the fireplaces show signs of deterioration due to water coming down existing chimney stacks. Both chimneys also show signs of bowing outward about midway between chimney-top and ground. Thorough investigation is needed to determine whether this is a pre-existing condition, if it is being caused by weathering, or if the foundation needs stabilizing.

Should reconstruction of any of the walls be attempted, whether for purposes of stabilizing the existing structure or for complete restoration, the condition of the existing walls and foundations must be determined. Experts in the evaluation of this type of construction are difficult to find, but engineer certification of the soundness of existing construction is absolutely necessary before decisions about future work can be made.

Preservation plans for the Rock House await decision and funding. Options range from complete reconstruction and use as a residence or a museum to allowing the ruins to continue to deteriorate until nothing is left but a heap of stones. The latter alternative is clearly unacceptable and the first is costly. Estimates for a complete restoration range from five hundred thousand to one million dollars. There is no evidence of a need for a museum in this isolated site nor any present plan for a suitable alternate use for the restored building. Destroying a magnificent ruin in a country and an area where ruins are few in order to create an approximation of what may have existed in the past is unjustifiable. The ghost of John Ruskin and the spirits of many present-day preservationists would be highly disturbed.

Since preservation funds from state and national governments in the United States are limited, isolated sites such as the Rock House must depend largely on private funds. Only in the last quarter century have governmental funds been available for preservation at any level. Certainly no funds, private or public, will be allocated to a project which has limited specific goals and no realistic long-range plan.

One possibility for preserving the building involves the construction of a dome or a canopy or even a second, larger building to cover the entire structure. A geodesic dome or an inflatable dome would protect the house but in so doing would completely destroy the esthetics of the site. The perspective of the house in the countryside would be lost and even the romance of the existing ruin would be destroyed. The United States National Park Service has erected modernistic canopies or roofs on poles over many Indian ruins in the American southwest. Casa Grande in Arizona is one such site; and, although the four-story stacked earth structure is being protected from the elements, it suffers from the intrusion of modern elements in a historic setting. Structures have been built to protect large ships, such as the Swedish warship **Wasa** in Stockholm, and even buildings, such as Augustus' **Ara Pacis** in Rome. These provide protection and a controlled climate, but often at great expense and with a loss of esthetic values.

An alternative for the Rock House could be a roof reproducing the lines of the house as nearly as possible. Such a roof might be supported by steel or alumnium framing which could also mark the location of missing walls, floors, and other portions of the structure. Wooden beams would accomplish the same function and create an impression of the building techniques of the period. The roof might be a reproduction of the original wooden shingles or it might be of some transparent or translucent material. An example of the latter is the aluminum skeleton covered with transparent plastic over the Piazza Armerina in Sicily. Some idea of the effectiveness of this technique of creating a shadow structure can be seen in the three-dimensional metal skeleton which delineates the Benjamin Franklin house in Philadelphia, Pennsylvania.

A roof, supplemented by engineering studies on the stability of foundations, chimneys and walls is the best option for the preservation of the Rock House. Once this is accomplished, unstable walls can be repaired and the most immediate dangers eleminated. In this way the image of the finished house will be suggested and the romance of the ruin preserved--all at minimum cost and with no future possibilities eliminated. And the Rock House will be preserved.

REFERENCES

Fitch, James Marston. Historic Preservation: the
    Curatorial Management of the Built world. New
    York: 1982.

Hendricks, J. Edwin. The Rock House: Report and
    Exhibit Design for the Stokes County Historical
    Society. Wake Forest University Field School
    Report. Winston-Salem, North Carolina: 1987.

MacKendrick, Paul. The Mute Stones Speak. New
    York: 1960.

Zook, Nicholas. Museum Villages USA. Barre,
    Massachusetts: 1971.

Restoration of Kuwait's First Courthouse

Abdul Hamid Darwish*, Dr. Sami M. Freig**, Ghazi Sultan***

*Kuwaiti Engineer's Office, Kuwait
**Construction Engineering and Management, Kuwait University, Kuwait
***Architect Planner, Kuwait

ABSTRACT

In this paper the experience gained through the renovation of the historical Kuwait's First Courthouse has been presented. The architectural solution of the problem is outlined, and the different engineering problems are identified. The procedure used to accomplish the work and methods adopted to solve the various problems on the job are introduced in detail.

INTRODUCTION AND HISTORICAL BACKGROUND

The original Kuwait Courts building was constructed in 1936 and a later court and additions added in the late 50's, with a third court added in the early 60's.

It had been used as an official government building since its creation, and was transferred to the use of a court house and later vacated.

According to government plans, it was deemed for demolition and fell to vacant possession and deterioration.

In 1984 the Kuwait Municipality decided that the building should be preserved for its historic value, and hired the architect to convert it into new offices for the Municipality's Urban Design Department. The architectural plans were drawn up and tendered in March and April 1986. Work on the project was completed by September 1987, with the building being occupied by October 1987.

This case study deals with both the architectural and structural concepts adopted for the restoration of Kuwait's First Courthouse.

1.   **The Architectural Concept**

The building was totally dilapidated and in a very bad condition when work commenced; basically consisting of 3 courtyards. The single storey facing the main street was the oldest (1936); the second, a two-storey structure, at the back on the left hand side was built in the 50's, and the third on the right hand side was built in the 60's. (Fig.1)

The 1936 building was built of mud walls 60cm wide and still in good condition, but the roof, the windows, the doors and floors were all in poor condition.

Early in construction it was decided to totally demolish the 60's structure, part of the 50's structure (the second floor) and remove the 1936 room. But structural problems were discovered, leading to total demolition of the 50's building.

The new plans created three courtyards, one around the '36 court, one around to 50's court (which was entirely duplicated after being demolished) and a new court was designed for the 60's area. Block wall construction was used for all new construction. (Fig.2)

The architectural concept was to create three skylight covered courtyards, each holding a different department of the Urban Design Department, looking down on the landscaped area in each court. (Fig.3)

It was initially decided to duplicate and retain, wherever possible, all the external elevations of the building, this was done - except for the entry gates and boundary walls on the main street where the architect introduced a new elevation. (Fig.4)

Of the original details the architect duplicated all the old windows and doors made in teakwood and used them in almost exactly the same way in the new project. (Fig.5)

While duplicating the old architectural features and avoiding new material, the external wall plastering was another challenge, accomplished by reinstating with durable plaster coats which would resist the adverse hot weather climate in Kuwait.

The external walls were initially prepared by chiselling all the old chipped plaster and washing away the mud joining the stones. Then 4mm galvanized rods were installed. (Fig.6)

The expanded metal was tied to the rods inserted between stone layers. A splatter-dash mix consisting of normal cement sand mortar was used for an even surface. A layer of fiber reinforced chips 5 to 7mm thick was trowelled to obtain a smooth surface. A primer and finally a trowelled rough textured paint, was used to echo the old character of Kuwait.

The only new design feature was the introduction of new terrazzo tile geometric tiles in three different colors, one for each court, and color trims were added to each window and doorway of the building to match the tiles of the courtyards. (Fig.7)

The major technical innovations besides structural ones were the removal of the wet areas to the newly constructed part of the building and the design of the HVAC system, to supply air to all rooms from the corridors and all the returning air (except in some of the larger rooms on the second floor) was directed through a return system located in the walls of the three courts. The result was that all the corridors and courts were now quite cool.

The combination of all these elements created Kuwait's first renovated building for the government in 1987, and one of the most popular buildings designed by the architect. (Fig.8)

2.   Structural Concept

2.1   Description of Old Structural Elements

The one and two storey historical Old Courthouse built 53 years ago, consists of stone masonry wall bearing, which is 60cm thick at ground floor level and is founded on a strip plain concrete footing which is 35cm thick and placed 70cm below ground level. The floor slabs were of a composite construction, timber joists spanning between wall bearing timber packing, overlaid by a clay layer and, on top, a reinforced concrete slab. The roof slab consisted of a metal deck supported on timber joists.

2.2   **Problems Encountered**

a)   Non conformity between the preliminary condition and the actual status.

b)   Non availability of old building records.

c)   Limited reserve capacity of the existing structural supporting elements, especially columns and foundations.

d)   User constraints on renovation process.

e)   Solutions for repair should be adapted to user convenience.

f)   Limited application of destructive or load testing due to the age of building.

g)   Continuous inspection during the construction process due to unforeseen conditions.

h)   Insurance Costs: due to lack of technical assessment for hidden items and proper evaluation of calculated risk, insurance companies exaggerate their offer for insurance policies.

i)   Specialist Sub-Contractors: though the renovation project is a highly technical one many amateurs try to apply themselves to the field.

2.3   **Preliminary Structural Survey**

In August 1983, a survey was conducted to assess both the structural integrity and safety of the existing building and to establish whether it was viable to replace the existing light-weight first floor by a reinforced concrete slab carrying wall portions to suit the usage of the building.

Visual inspection was carried out on three test pits which were 80cm deep, along the face of the wall, plus six concrete cores. One bore hole was taken outside the existing building to record the bearing capacity. The report concluded that the foundation of the existing building showed no signs of differential settlement. Certain areas were found to be structurally unsafe, and were regarded as unacceptable for any renovation; demolition and reconstruction using a reinforced concrete suspension system was recommended.

2.4   **Final Structural Survey**

In May 1986 a thorough field exploration program was carried out. It consisted of drilling three bore holes for sub-soil investigation to a depth of 10 meters. Standard penetration tests were recorded at one meter intervals to the bottom of the bore holes. Sampling was carried out using split barrel samplers and all relevant laboratory tests were conducted for soil classification, defining soil parameters required for foundation redesign, soil improvement and the design of a shoring protection system.

The sub-soil investigation revealed the existence of a top layer of man-made rubble-like concrete tiles, underlaid by blackish brown silty contaminated sand. The depth of the weak soil ranged between 2 to 4.5 meters where the organic material dissipated in sand layers. The soil bearing capacity at 1 to 2 meters depth had a value ranging from 50 to 120 KN/m^2.

The layers below showed a fairly homogeneous silty fine to coarse sand throughout the bore holes. Moreover there were no reinforced steel connections between columns and roof slab.

The roof slab on the ground floor, which consisted of clay and chandel wood overlaid by a reinforced concrete slab, which had to be retained after demolishing the upper floor, was seriously affected by the decay of supporting wooden joists and the corrosion of the top steel reinforcement. (Fig.9)

3.   **Solutions and Impact**

3.1   **Technical**

a)   **Shoring Protection for Adjacent and Neighbour Footing**

Due to the existence of weak soil layers and in order to keep the depth of new foundations the same as the old, it was necessary to go deeper and up-grade the soil by replacing the 60cm sand gravel structural fill.

The Municipality decided to protect the Kuwait Court's old foundations by excavating below the existing level. This was also done to protect the old and neighbouring foundation from any unexpected failures.

The shoring line location had been carefully chosen to be as close as possible to the old and neighbouring footing. (The neighbouring building is a two storey building with a light structure at the top).

The surcharge from the neighbouring building and the renovated old Kuwait Court were assumed, based on normal load assessment, data collected from the soil report, the layout of the shoring line, the boundary and site conditions submitted by the contractor and by the use of a shoring computer program, (seventeen different runs with variable steel H pile sections and spacings were executed to choose the most reliable steel section and spacing, taking into consideration the engineering and economic aspects). This showed the optimum solution to be a pre-bored cantilever broad flange H pile system concreted into augred holes and sheeting by wood lagging. (Fig.10)

b) **Eccentric Footing on Weak Soil**

As the eccentric footing is very sensitive to load and soil bearing pressure, and since the bearing capacity of contaminated, organic soil showed a very low bearing value, equivalent to one third of the one estimated for design, consequently eccentric loading conditions, from wall bearing supporting elements abutting the property line on low soil bearing capacity, uneconomic and impractical footing sizes would have been imposed to avoid tension in the soil for eccentricities outside the compression core. In such circumstances the designer had to resort to soil improvement as the sole solution. (Fig.11)

c) **Soil Replacement**

The eccentric loaded wall bearing on weak soil at the foundation formation level with designed dimensions was no longer valid, due to the need to increase the footing base area by three times the original design dimension, thus creating an uneconomic footing design and affecting the design of all other adjacent footings.

Two solutions were proposed:

1. Use of driven piles

2. Soil replacement

The first solution was impractical due to the cramped working area. Moreover, hammer driven pile vibrations may exacerbate the existing delicate situation of the neighbouring building, thus creating other failures. This was not recommended. Therefore, it was decided to go for the soil replacement solution.

After removing all debris and contaminated soil, remnants of old sewage lines and cesspools down to a firm soil strata, a clean sand gravel mix was placed in 15cm layers and compacted using the optimum moisture content. A maximum dry density ranging from 90% to 95% was achieved up to a height of 60cm.

Eight Plate Load Tests were carried out on the top layers at a depth of 1.4m from the existing grade. The purpose of this investigation was to determine whether the proposed design capacity of 150 KN/sq.m was reached after replacing the 60cm by structural fill and back filling it by the standard method.

The aim of testing is to assess a modulus of elasticity for the 60cm thick layer for further use in calculations when comparing different foundation width, bearing pressure and settlements. The interpolation for larger foundations of the resulting settlements compared with the results of a plate load having a 0.6m diameter circular plate may be too small and should be taken into account. To be on the safe side the calculated settlements should be doubled for the proposed structure.

3.2   Contractual

a)   Cost Implications

The demolition, removal of contaminated soil under formation level, shoring protection, soil improvement and redesign of footing foundations had generated an extra cost for the project of 15% of the assigned budget.

b)   Time Impact

The original contract period was estimated to be 180 days. However, the project completion time had been extended by an extra 60 days representing approximately 30% of the original contract duration.

SUMMARY AND CONCLUSION

The preliminary structural survey should be followed by a thorough final survey specifically for concealed sub- or super-structure supporting elements.

The architect/engineer should not only establish his design criteria from data collected before starting work but should inspect during the course of the work for unforeseen or over-looked items. Due to the lack of records for old buildings, the effect of unpredicted structural defects may have a significant impact on the original design, methods and means of restoration and finally on both the cost and time of the project.

REFERENCES

1.   Sherban Cantacuziono., Susan Brandt
     SAVING OF OLD BUILDINGS
     The American Society for Testing and Materials
     1916 Race St, Philadelphia, PA 1986

2.   Gerald Davis, ASTM, STP 901,
     BUILDING PERFORMANCE FUNCTION
     and REHABILITATION
     Architectural Press Ltd., London 1980

3.   Laurance E. Reiner.
     HOW TO RECYCLE BUILDINGS
     McGraw Hill, Inc 1979
     New York, USA

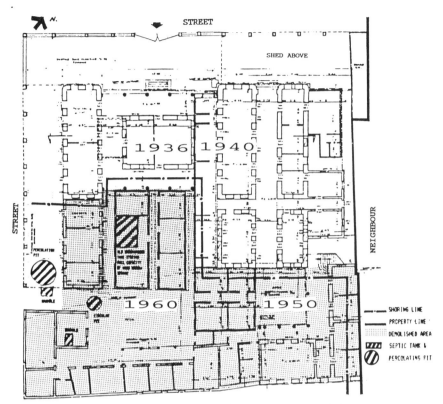

Fig.1   PLAN OF KUWAIT'S FIRST COURTHOUSE

Fig.4   NORTH ELEVATION BEFORE RENOVATION

BEFORE   RENOVATION

Fig.9   CHANDLE WOOD CEILING

Fig.6   INTERNAL ARCHES

AFTER   RENOVATION

Fig.7   INTERNAL ARCADE

Fig.2   INTERNAL COURT YARD

Fig.3 COURT YARD AND SKYLIGHT

Fig.5 EXTERNAL TEAK WINDOWS

Fig.8 NORTH ELEVATION AFTER RENOVATION

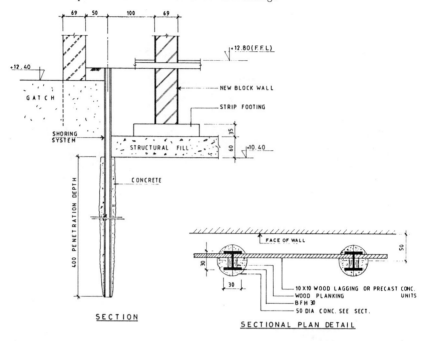

Fig.10   SHORING AND NEW ADJACENT FOOTING

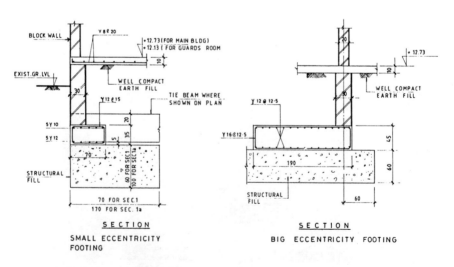

Fig.11   ECCENTRIC FOOTING ON WEAK SOIL

The Rehabilitation of the Seminario Conciliar

Arleen Pabón de Rocafort
School of Architecture, University of Puerto Rico

INTRODUCTION

By the year 1983, the Seminario Conciliar Building, a huge privately-owned historic building located in the San Juan of Puerto Rico Historic Zone, was doomed to an uncertain future -- leading to complete and pervasive deterioration. This notable building presented extremely important historical and architectural characteristics. That year sealed its fate. Dr Ricardo Alegría, one of Puerto Rico's leading historians and preservationists became interested in the building. At the same time, federal funds for the rehabilitation of historic buildings became available giving a much-needed boost of encouragement to preservation activities in Puerto Rico.

HISTORIC BACKGROUND

The city of San Juan, capital of the Island of Puerto Rico, was founded in 1521 when the capital of the Spanish colony was moved here. The growth of the new city was spasmodic, at best, but by the 17th century both the defensive city walls and the grid block urban setting were laid. One of these streets was the Calle del Cristo. The Seminario Conciliar Building, one of the finest examples of 19th century architecture in the Old San Juan zone, is located in this justly-famous road, also called "museum street." The street has received that name due to the many important historic buildings that lie there. The Seminario Conciliar sprawls over more than half of one of the historic city blocks, being an essential element of the spatial urban sequence of the Calle del Cristo.

The structure housed, since 1830, the first center of higher education in the island. Although many had hoped for such a center since the birth of the city, the construction of the Seminario Conciliar Building was not begun until the year 1827, under the combined efforts of Bishop don Pedro Gutiérrez de Cos and Captain-General don Miguel de la Torre. The building which cost around forty-one thousand pesos (in the currency of the time) was probably designed by Bishop Gutiérrez and Agustín Cantero. Cantero was the meister builder for the fortification works of the city. The Seminario Conciliar was dedicated to Saint Ildefonso and it was to house the first seminary of the island. The building was constructed on a lot adjacent to the Episcopal Palace and close to the Dominican Convent and the San José Church (the third oldest church in the Americas). The lot measured sixty two by forty six and a half varas (eg. Castro 1).

The original building was shaped as a block with an interior patio or cortile. This block has a severe main facade perforated by seven doors, perceived by the observer as windows, due to their height and to the fact that they are covered by wooden grillwork (rejas abalaustradas). The architectural design, created to suit the steep incline of the site, placed these doors on top of a podium-like structure that slowly metamorphoses into a basement level. In a masterful show of control in terms of the plastic experience, the architects contrasted the severe block-like structure to the sensuous forms of the balaustered grillwork. The architectural rhythm established by the fenestration is simple yet elegant and effective. The portal received special treatment, quite unusual for San Juan. A monumental unit is created by means of pilasters and a pediment. The portal also sports two coats-of-arms: one is the royal one and the other one belonged to Bishop Gutiérrez. By means of this portal the building became a showplace of both the Catholic Church and of the King of Spain. The classical elements are transformed into anthropomorphic icons which give nobility and dignity to the facade.

It was soon realized that the size of the building was not enough for the intense needs of the city. During the tenure of Bishop don Gil Esteve y Tomás, another lot was acquired on the west side of the original building, with the idea of expanding it. The new building was constructed to house more

Figure 1, Seminario Conciliar
by A. Pabon

seminaristas. However, it would also house some
students and an order of missionaries. The new
building was also fashioned in block form; both
blocks were connected by means of a corridor. The
blocks are speared in the center by interior patios
which aim to provide light and ventilation to the
interior of the buildings. The beauty of these
spaces is emphasized by means of the arcades that
arch elegantly around the patios, giving the areas
a graceful sense of proportion and elegance.
Morphologically-speaking there are fascinating
elements in this building that are unique examples
in the island. The refectory, for example, presents
an unique type of vault, unlike any other in Puerto
Rico. The chapel is developed as an octagon with
chamfered corners, crowned by a dome of imposing
height and painted with grisaille frescoes dating to
the late 19th century. It is one of the few 19th
century domes in Puerto Rico which rests on a drum.

The building was occupied by various religious
orders during its history, but it has always been
the property of the Catholic Church. In 1858, for
example, it was transferred to the Jesuits and

became a center for secondary level studies.   It has always been used as an educational center.   Because it was the most prestigious local center of studies, most of the leading political and intellectual figures of Puerto Rico were educated here during the 19th and 20th centuries.   This fact was a key one regarding the decision to rehabilitate the building as a new locus of academic endeavours.

REHABILITATION WORK

During 1983, President Reagan sponsored the 1984 Jobs Bill.   The main purpose of the bill was to directly create jobs in the construction field.   The bill channeled these efforts via historic buildings and thus, the National Park Service unit of the United States Department of the Interior. The impression many received was that the intention of the bill was aimed at the creation of construction-related jobs.   Some felt that this emphasis was, to a certain extent, misplaced.   The issue, some stated, was to stress to the public the viability of using public funds to develop healthy conservation programs.   Others felt that the provisions of the bill were too stringent.   After so many years without a government-sponsored program related to the conservation of historic buildings, it was unfair to put many constraints on the program.   In particular, the fact that only six months were granted to spend funds was seen as a blow below the belt for some states where climate conditions from January until April made it virtually impossible to carry out any kind of exterior work.   The strict and limited program, however, gave a boost to the preservation movement.

An initial sum of $125,000 was granted by the Puerto Rico State Historic Preservation Office to be used in the rehabilitation of the Seminario Conciliar Building.   The federal sum granted was to be matched by the grantee on a one to one basis.   The committee supervising the rehabilitation work of the Seminario provided the match with some cash and with substantial in-kind services and materials donated by individuals and private firms.   A clear idea of the difficulties involved in the project can be gained when it is realized that the building covers approximately 144,000 square feet of construction and that the conditions of part of the building were extremely ruinous when restoration was initiated.

Due in part to the limitation of funds, the

rehabilitation philosophy designed and approved by
the committee established the desire to preserve as
much as possible; maintaining modern interventions
at a minimum, whenever possible.

The building originally was built of masonry
(rubble) covered with limestone stucco. Structurally-
speaking, this material posed no immediate problem.
Sections of some walls, however, exhibited moisture-
related problems. It was determined that the
problems were mainly due to capillary action and, in
some particular cases, to rain penetration. Because
of this situation, the stucco had to be replaced in
the areas where it had lost its bonding capabilities
or where it was missing. The historical composition
of the original stucco was carefully taken into
consideration, in order to determine if the new
patches would act in a compatible manner with the
older sections. For that reason, the use of Portland
cement (never used historically in Old San Juan)
was kept to a minimum in order to guarantee the
correct relationship between the new stucco and the
historic rubble fabric.

Although the walls posed no major structural
problems, the ceilings were another matter altogether.
Traditional roofs in the Old San Juan Historic Zone
were created by a simple yet effective system.
Wooden beams ran in one direction (usually along the
shorter distance of the interior facade) and embedded
into the rubble wall. Over these beams, at right
angles, rested wooden slats (alfajías). On top of
these slats, flat terracotta bricks were laid in
layers. Finally, a cover (ususally some stucco
whitewash) was thrown on the exterior as a means of
waterproofing the ensemble. As expected, this type
of roof although easily constructed needs to be
carefully maintained if it is to provide support for
a long time. Maintainance on this building,
unfortunately, had been sadly remiss. In the first
place, the roof showed evidence of moisture problems.
In addition, in many cases, the embedded ends of the
beams had been affected by the moisture present in
the walls. This moisture, the result of capillary
action or descending vertical humidity, had a direct
result on the beams ends. When the roofs were
dismantled it was found, as expected, that many ends
had rotted, rendering whole sections of the roof
structurally unsafe. Many others were, for all
technical matters, non-existant.

Historians mention that in the construction of

this building, pitch pine wood (an English name
colloquially converted by Spanish-speaking locals
into pichipén) was imported and used for the roof
slats. It is one of the most important examples
in which we see Spanish architects accepting the use
of newly-imported (at the time) materials. Most of
slats, built of this material, had succumbed to
either humidity or termites or both -- the everlasting
plagues of the tropical environment. The structural
integrity of the slats had been so undermined that
they were no longer performing any structural task.
The roof, or what was left of it, was being supported
solely by the beams, many of which had rotted ends.
It was indeed amazing how the roof could still stand
in some places.

The slats, possessing a cross section of
approximately two to three inches by one inch were
not difficult to replace. The beams were another
matter altogether. These beams, as well as most
beams used in the San Juan Historic Zone, were shaped
out of ausubo trees (a local, precious wood, almost
extinct now). With sections of approximately six by
twelve inches and a length between fifteen and twenty
feet, they were almost impossible to replace.

Due to the scarcity of funds, it was impossible
to subject the existing rotted beams to a wood
consolidation process. There are no firms in the
island which offer such services; the cost of bringing
specialized foreign firms would have made the
rehabilitation process of the building an extremely
expensive undertaking. Because of this, it was
decided to experiment reinforcing the structural
system as a whole vis a vis each individual element.
A wooden beam, called a madrina, was attached to the
wall, running perpendicular to the direction that the
beams run. In some other cases, when the embedded
ends were only partially rotten, small wooden brackets
were also added to certain problematic beams as
structural supports. Both of these solutions were
not only very economical but also extremely respectful
of the integrity of the materials and the
architectural spaces. In addition, they were
"historic" solutions, having been used in some parts
of the building as well as in other buildings of the
area.

Fortunately, two other important historic
buildings were being restored in the vicinity by the

Figure 2, Seminario Conciliar
by A. Pabon

local government. Following unfortunate restoration
practices, all the <u>ausubo</u> beams were being replaced
by new, if inferior, ones -- in spite of the public
outcry. The beams so discarded were given to the
Seminario Conciliar. They were used to substitute
the beams which were structurally unsound. In
addition, historic marble tiles and many other
fragments were obtained and used to replace ruinous
parts of the Seminario.

Final detailing of the project is still going
on. Quite recently, all restoration work in the

chapel was finished. Structural studies revealed
that the impressive cracks in the dome and some
walls were due to settlement of the foundations. It
was concluded that no additional settlement was to
be expected and that the structure was stable.
Cracks were specially treated and grisaille work
restored to its original glory.

The rehabilitation process of the Seminario
Conciliar provided an extraordinary living workshop
for students of art and architecture who visited the
site many times to observe the ongoing labor of many
skilled craftsmen. It also stimulated the rebirth
of a number of long-lost architectural crafts. An
important example was the elaboration of all the
wooden balausters by hand by an old artisan living
in the interior of the island who had worked as a
very young man with this kind of technique. The
success of this project, on the other hand, has
kindled the interest of the state government which
has just recently started a macro scale rehabilitation project of the Ballajá sector, practically
adjacent to the Seminario Conciliar site.

The rehabilitation project of the Seminario
Conciliar has brought about the conservation of a
very important building, the rehabilitation of an
important historic structure and has initiated the
re-vitalization of an important urban district within
the historic zone. It is remarkable, however, to
observe that well under one million dollars have been
invested to achieve what is considered by many to be
one of the finest local rehabilitation projects in
recent times. The quality of the rehabilitation
work merited, among other distinctions, a special
citation from the National Trust for Historic
Preservation of the United States.

It is with pride that we can look at this
building again, as a center of studies. Modern
scholars, walking and working in this centuries-old
building, can still carry on the legacy of higher
education for the benefit of Puerto Rico and the
Caribbean basin.

REFERENCES

Buschiazzo, M.   Los monumentos históricos de Puerto
Rico.   Buenos Aires: Editorial, 1955.

Castro, M.A.   Arquitectura en San Juan de Puerto Rico
(siglo XIX).   San Juan, Puerto Rico: Editorial
Universitaria, 1980.

Col y Toste, C.   Historia de ʲᵃ instrucción públic⁻ en
Puerto Rico hasta el año 1898.   Bilbao: Editorial
Vasco-Americana, S.A., 1970.

de Hostos, A.   Historia de San Juan, ciudad murada.
San Juan, Puerto Rico: Instituto de Cultura Puertorri-
queña, 1966.

Underhill, C.   "The Rehabilitation of the Seminario
Conciliar."   The San Juan Star (San Juan, Puerto Rico)
22 June 1986.

Anastylosis of the Apollo Temple in Side/Antalya, Turkey

M. Yorulmaz, F. Çili and Z. Ahunbay
Faculty of Architecture, Istanbul Technical University, 80191 Taksim, Istanbul

ABSTRACT

Temple of Apollo in Side (Pamphylia) is a second century A.D. monument from which several architectural fragments existed, lying scattered on the site. A project was initiated by the International Friends of Side to raise some of the architectural pieces up into their original position in the building. The original structural system had to be modified in order to erect the broken vertical and horizontal members. This paper presents the method adopted for the purpose.

INTRODUCTION

Side is an ancient settlement on the southern shore of Turkey. In the chronicles of the historian Eusebius, the foundation date is given as 1405 B.C., however little is known about the early period of its development. The early inhabitants chose the name "Side" meaning 'pomegranate' in their language for the site.

Side was the most important coastal settlement of Pamphylia, the region which stretches 60 kilometers to the west and 30 kilometers to the east of Side and is bordered by the Taurus mountains at the north. It was a flourishing trade center which transacted business with the eastern Mediterranean countries.

The ancient city lies on a peninsula which is about 1 km long and 350-400 m wide (Fig. 1). It was enclosed by land and sea walls. Access to the city from the mainland was through the main gate at the north from which a colonnaded street led to the center of the city. This was the main architectural axis, connecting the land gate to the major buildings of the town; the theatre, the agora and the agora bath. The main street stretched further south after making a right angled turn near the theatre and terminated in an open space between the main temples of the city.

The archaeological excavations in Side started in 1947 under the leadership of the late professor A.M.Mansel from the Istanbul University. The main sacred buildings of the Roman city were concentrated at the southern end of the promontory. The first year of the excavations was

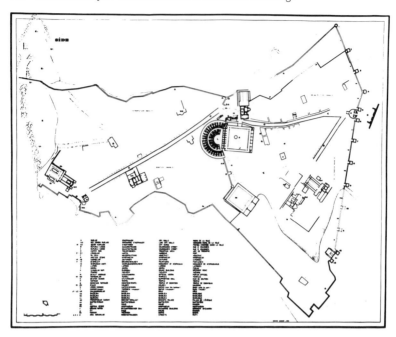

Fig. 1. Plan of Side (A.Şakar, 1976)

devoted to reveal these buildings. To the west of the open space which
marked the end of the colonnaded street, there were two temples in the
area denoted "N" by K.Lanckoronski [1] . During the sixth century, the
temples were enclosed within the atrium of a Christian basilica.
Excavations revealed in-situ stylobate and bases. The larger of the
temples (N_2) had been seriously damaged during the Byzantine era. The
smaller temple, on the other hand, was probably not disturbed during the
Byzantine period but after the total abandonment of the city during the
Middle Ages, was used as a quarry for obtaining marble and producing lime.
Both of the temples were peripteral in plan, with six columns on the short
and eleven columns on the longer sides (Fig. 2). Mansel [2] identified the
monuments as the temples of Athena (N_2) and of Apollo (N_1) and dated them
to the second half of the second century A.D. depending on stylistic and
numismatic evidence.

CONSERVATION WORK IN SIDE

After twenty years of excavation work (1947-1966), the main features of
the city were brought to light. All the sculpture and some of the valuable architectural fragments were deposited in the local museum and thus
protected from plundering and vandalism. Due to the insufficiency of the
funds, the rest of the archaeological finds was left exposed to the
action of man and nature.

There were a few attempts at restoring and presenting the finds in a better setting. Partial anastylosis of the colonnaded street was one of these. The agora bath was restored by the contribution of Devres family and now houses the local museum. Another project was the re-assembly of the Vespasianus monument. The architectural fragments belonging to the edifice were re-erected by Dr.A.Machatschek in 1962. In order to complete the missing parts, concrete was used in a very restricted and unobtrusive way. Partial anastylosis of the central hall of the state agora (M building) was undertaken in 1965 by the same architect. The eastern elevation of the interior was partially reconstituted using the fragments found at the site.

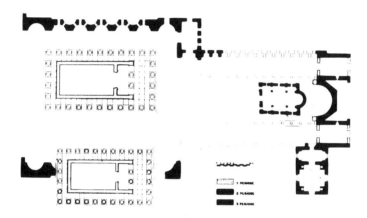

Fig. 2. Side, site plan of the temple area (L.Merey, 1947)

There is an amenity group - The International Friends of Side-which provides financial support to the archaeological research and conservation work in Side. In 1977 the president of the foundation at the time, late A.Friendly proposed Professor Jale İnan, the director of excavations in Side and chairman of the Classical Archaeology Department of Istanbul University, to start a project for the temple of Apollo. Professor İnan consulted the Technical University of Istanbul, Faculty of Architecture for expertise. The authors were responsible for preparing the anastylosis and the structural project for the re-erection of the northwest corner.

SOME CONSIDERATIONS REGARDING THE ANASTYLOSIS OF THE APOLLO TEMPLE

According to the Charter of Venice (Article 15) "Ruins must be maintained and measures necessary for the permanent conservation and protection of architectural features and of objects discovered must be taken. Furthermore, every means must be taken to facilitate the understanding of the monument and to reveal it without ever distorting its meaning.

All reconstruction work should, however, be ruled out a priori.
Only anastylosis, that is to say, the reassembling of existing but dismembered parts can be permitted. The material used for integration
should always be recognizable and its use should be the least that will
ensure the conservation of a monument and the reinstatement of its form".

The project for the anastylosis of the Apollo temple in Side was
prepared by taking the Charter of Venice as the guideline. The scope of
the project was restricted by the present state of the temple and the
quantity of the extant original material. The cella walls had disappeared
completely. After inventorying the architectural fragments belonging to
the temple, it was found out that there could be a chance for only a
partial re-erection of the western façade.

Side is an archaeological site where monuments like the theatre,
several baths, the nymphaeum and basilicas have been preserved in their
full height. Unfortunately, modern development has interfered in such a
way that, today the character of the archaeological site is threatened
seriously. Thus attempts for the re-erection of monuments which have
been disturbed in time is a positive effort to save the archaeological
remains in Side from perdition.

PROPOSAL FOR ANASTYLOSIS

After the excavations of 1947, the site of N_1 and N_2 was cleaned and the
architectural fragments were left in position as they were found. During
the excavations the architect in charge, L.Merey, produced measured
drawings of the temples and prepared detailed reconstitution drawings of
the east elevation of the Apollo temple (Fig. 3). These were published
by Mansel [3] with the preliminary report of 1947 excavations. Later in
his book Die Ruinen von Side Mansel [4] published a perspective drawing
prepared by architect M.Beken, which intended to show the temple as it
stood in the second century. Beken based his drawing on those produced
by Merey but added the missing features such as the acroteria to complete
the image.

None of the reconstitution drawings attempted to show the existing
pieces as they stood in the monument. This required a more detailed study
of the surviving fragments, for which time was not spared. Therefore,
at the beginning of studies for anastylosis, it was necessary to find
out the quantity and identity of the extant marble fragments. After a
quick survey of the site in May 1977, a detailed inventory of the existing
fragments was started. Excavations at the east and west ends of the temple
revealed fragments which had not been known to the previous authors. The
new finds resulted in the revision of the previous reconstitutions,
especially in the entablature zone.

A letter-code system of designation was devised for the identification of architectural elements belonging to different levels; A for bases,
B for columns, C for capitals, D for architraves, E for friezes, F for
horizontal and raking cornices, G for pediment blocks. The identification
code and number was painted on each marble piece. The majority of the

Fig. 3. Side, Temple of Apollo. Reconstitution
drawing of the east elevation (L.Merey,1947)

pieces belonging to the west façade had fallen towards the sea and had
not been moved during the 1947 excavation. A survey was made to show
the positions of the blocks on the site, after which it was possible to
reveal new pieces which were under blocks belonging to upper levels.

This thorough survey of the existing architectural pieces helped to
determine the extent of the project. The abundance of original material
belonging to the west elevation of the temple made it favourable for
this part of the building to be re-erected. The fact that none of the
columns belonging to the peripteros were preserved intact was another
factor which restricted the scope of the project. Finally, it was
decided to restore only half of the western and a small section of the
northern elevation of the temple (Fig. 4).

CHOICE OF THE STRUCTURAL SYSTEM FOR ANASTYLOSIS

In order to reassemble the broken members of the monument in a sound post
and lintel structure which could be able to stand by itself and resist
earthquakes, it was necessary to integrate and restructure the vertical
and the horizontal members. For this purpose, the missing parts of the
original blocks had to be completed by using either the original material
(white marble, probably from Proconnessus-Marmara Island) or concrete.
The second solution was preferred because it offered a more flexible
solution for jointing the original and the new. The concrete to be used
would contain white cement, crushed marble aggregate, marble powder and
sand. Several trials were made to determine the right mixture to match
the original stone chromatically and be strong enough to bear the compressive stresses. Experiments were made at the laboratory of the Oyma-
pınar Dam Construction Site on sample cubes. It was possible to attain

Fig. 4. Side, Temple of Apollo. Proposal for
the anastylosis of the west façade
(Z.Ahunbay, 1978)

compressive strength values of 150 kg/cm^2 at 7 days and 245 kg/cm^2 at
28 days. The size and grading of the aggregate and the amounts (by
volume) of the cement and the water in the mix are given below.

I. Marble aggregate	II. Marble powder	35%
1. Size 0 (0-5 mm) 35%	III. Sand (0-2 mm)	5%
2. Size 1 (5-8 mm) 15%	IV. White cement	300 kg/m^3
3. Size 2 (7-10 mm) 20%		
4. Size 3 (10-20 mm) 30%	V. Water	135 lt/m^3

Samples taken from the marble fragments belonging to the temple
were examined at the Engineering Geology and Rock Mechanics Laboratory
of the Mining Faculty of Istanbul Technical University. The physico -
mechanical properties of the marble were determined by tests on
cylindrical samples with a diameter of 5 cm. The results were as follows;

I.   Density   2.68 gr/cm^3
II. Uniaxial compressive strength   530 kg/cm^2
III. Young modulus

. E dynamic 5.8 x 10^4 kg/cm^2

. E static (1.7-5.0) x 10^4 kg/cm^2 at 0-25 kg/cm^2 stress range

. E static (1.3 x 10^5) kg/cm^2 at 200-400 kg/cm^2 stress range.

The results of the tests on the original stone and the concrete showed that they could be used together alternately in vertical or horizontal members.

Restoration work started in 1983 with the removal of the in-situ members at the northwest corner of the temple. In the original design, foundations had been built with conglomerate blocks. The stylobate blocks were bonded to the foundation by means of a mortar bed only. The new system needed a stronger bonding between the foundation and the upper levels. For this purpose, a reinforced concrete foundation in the form of a continuous beam was proposed (Fig. 5). The upper structure was assumed as a one-degree freedom system; a cantilever restrained by the foundation. In the dynamic design of the structure, maximum ground acceleration was assumed to be 0.065 g, depending on the risk value of the site.

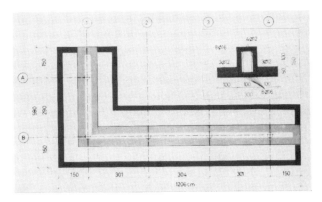

Fig. 5. Details of the continous foundation (M.Yorulmaz, F.Çılı, 1982)

In the original design, dowels were used to join the marble blocks vertically. Starting from the stylobate, they were present at all junctions; that is, the stylobate level was joined to the base, the base to the column, the column to the capital, the capital to the architrave, the architrave to the frieze, the frieze to the cornice and the cornice to the pediment and the pediment to the raking cornice levels by means of dowels. Due to the size and number of the dowels, this system of vertical bonding was not sufficient against earthquake loading. In the new structure, it was proposed to connect each member to the lower and the upper levels by means of stainless steel (DIN 1.4571) bars. At the base of the structure twelve stainless steel bars with a diameter of 26 mm were used to connect the foundation to the stylobate, the base and the column levels. Six bars of the same diameter were found to be adequate for the upper joints.

In the new system, each structural member retained its identity as an entity. For this purpose, they had to be completed or repaired. There were also problems related to the reconstruction of lost and badly damaged members. The missing stylobate blocks and bases were cast with concrete. The reinforced concrete foundation was bonded with the upper members by means of twelve deformed bars. When the original stylobate block existed, stainless steel was used for the purpose. The bars passed through the stylobate blocks and were anchored in the bases of the columns.

Originally the columns were made of 710 cm long monolithic marble blocks. Most of the surviving fragments belonged to the upper halves of the shafts (Fig. 6). It was proposed to cast the missing section in reinforced concrete (Fig. 7) and join it with the repaired original fragment by means of six 1 meter long stainless steel bars. Araldite (BY 154, HY 2995), a strong and comparatively thermo-stable epoxy resin was chosen for all fixing and binding purposes. Epoxy bond was used to achieve better adhesion between the marble and the concrete.

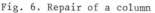

Fig. 6. Repair of a column   Fig. 7. A repaired column fragment
                                            is being lowered into position

There was only one capital which had been preserved almost intact. By making use of a siliconrubber mold, it was possible to complete the existing fragments. The missing sections were cast with the same concrete mix as in the bases and columns (Fig. 8, 9).

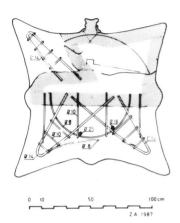

Fig. 8. Reinforcement for   Fig. 9. Capital C_7 ready for lifting
      capital C_7 into position

The broken or split architrave blocks had to be repaired and completed. Stainless steel bars were anchored into the original fragments and the missing parts were cast with concrete (Fig. 10).

Bronze cramps had been used in the original design to the adjacent blocks at different levels. The same means of joining was employed by using stainless steel cramps. In ancient technology, molten lead was poured to cover the metal and fill the cavities so that the cramp would be fixed in its position firmly and was protected from corrosion. During the restoration Araldite was used for the same purpose.

The work till 1988 has progressed up to the architrave level (Fig.11). The next years' work will be devoted to superposing the frieze and cornice blocks by using the same way of integration and jointing.

CONCLUSION

The structural engineers of the project believe that the system they proposed for this anastylosis has been successful in re-erecting the northwest corner of the Apollo temple with minimum intervention to the original members.

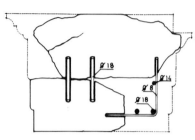

Fig. 10. Architrave (D 15)
reinforced with vertical
rods and additional
armature

Fig. 11. The first architrave (D 21)
block fitted into position
(July, 1988)

Within the modern landscape of Side, the anastylosis of the temple
evokes memories of the Roman city, recreating the relationship of the
ancient harbour and the sacred site where the temples of the beloved
gods of the city were situated. By the visual impact of the anastylosis,
the spirit of the place is revived.

REFERENCES

1. Lanckoronski, K.G., Städte Pamphyliens und Pisidiens, Vol. II, Vienna
   1982.

2. Mansel, A.M., Side 1947-1966 Yılları Kazıları ve Araştırmalarının Sonuç-
   ları, Türk Tarih Kurumu Basımevi, Ankara, 1978.

3. Mansel, A.M., 1947 Senesi Side Kazılarına Dair Önrapor (Vorlaeufiger
   Bericht über die in Side im Jahre 1947), Türk Tarih Kurumu Basımevi,
   Ankara, 1951.

4. Mansel, A.M., Die Ruinen von Side, Deutsches Archaeologisches Institut
   Abteilung Istanbul, Walter de Gruyter, Berlin, 1963.

Church of St. Mary the Virgin, Sandwich, Kent, England: the Repair of the Seventeenth Century Timber Roof

Ann E. Stocker and Leonard Bridge
Purcell Miller Tritton and Partners, Architects
Peter Ross, Arup Research and Development, Engineers

ABSTRACT

The timber roof spanning the 47'0" (1432 cm) wide nave of St. Mary's Church is of unusual construction for its seventeenth century date. As part of a general programme of repairs to the building the condition of the main trusses was checked and found to be considerably less than satisfactory. The paper describes the evaluation of the structure, and the options for repair. The aim had been to retain as much of the original structure as possible, and to maintain the existing form. This was achieved by means of a simple steel tie rod between the feet of the rafters.

INTRODUCTION

Sandwich is a small town, close to the east coast of Kent and one of the Cinque Ports. During Edward III's reign (1327-1377) the Cinque Ports, which actually numbered more than five, were obliged to provide ships and men for the King's service because he had no standing naval force. In return the King granted the towns certain privileges.

Sandwich had been built at the mouth of the River Stour, which gradually silted up so that the port became land-locked. As trade declined the town lost importance and remained almost static so preserving its original character.

In mediaeval times there were three churches in Sandwich, St.Mary's, St.Peter's and St.Clement's. Only St.Clement's is still in regular use as the parish church, St.Peter's and St.Mary's are both in the care of the Redundant Churches Fund.

St.Mary's church stands on the oldest site of Christian worship in the town, close to the bank of the River Stour and dates from the twelfth century. A few fragments of stonework such as the responds of the nave arcades indicate its earlier form which was a conventional narrow nave with north and south aisles, a chancel and a central tower. In 1579 the town was badly damaged by an earthquake and probably as a result in 1668 the central tower fell down demolishing most of the remainder of the church at the same time.

The building now consists of a wide nave, occupying the space of both the former nave and the south aisle, a north aisle, chancel and north porch. The former south porch has been used as the base of small timber framed bell tower which dates from 1718.

One of the most surprising and interesting features of the interior is the timber roof of the nave which spans 47'0" (1432 cm). This is an exceptionally wide span for a timber roof of this date in England especially when compared with other roofs of the same period in far more important buildings. The nave roof of York Minster for instance only spans 50'0" (1524 cm). A truss of similar design was used by Sir Christopher Wren, in the high roof of the west portico of St. Paul's Cathedral. In a small quiet town with several churches an easier solution might have been sought the most obvious of which would have been the introduction of intermediate supports along the line of the former south arcade.

For some reason it was decided to span the whole width and one end of the trusses bears on the masonry of the south wall, the other end is supported by a timber plate and columns which form the arcade to the aisle on the north side. The chancel roof is of similar construction but the span is only 37'0" (1127 cm) and the trusses bear onto masonry walls on both sides.

After the second World War the church became disused and neglected and by 1956 there was a proposal to demolish it in order to widen the road on the north side. A committee of "Friends of St.Mary's" was formed who averted the threat of demolition and arranged for repairs to be carried out. The plaster ceiling, which followed the shape of the lower members of the trusses, was removed exposing the roof timbers to view. The roof coverings were removed and a fibreboard ceiling was laid above the rafters before the re-tiling with hand-made clay tiles was done. Other repairs were also made and the church continued in use but with declining congregations.

During the summer of 1984 Purcell Miller Tritton & Partners were asked to inspect the church and provide the Redundant Churches Fund with a report on the condition of the building.

The Redundant Churches Fund (a registered charity) was set up by law in 1969 "to preserve churches no longer needed for worship but which are of architectural historial or archeological importance". Before agreeing to take over St. Mary's the Fund needed to know how much would have to be spent on repairing the church. The architects preliminary estimate was £60,000.

Their inspection was a general one and indicated that the usual range of repairs would be needed including replacing the defective copper in the long valley gutter between the nave and the north aisle with lead as well as overhauling the rainwater goods and surface water disposal system, work to the masonry, glazing and so on. It was also recommended that "the nave roof trusses should be examined in more detail as they appear to have spread outwards. There is considerable deflection in part of the south wallplate and the joints of the braces with the tie beams have opened up. Some restraint in the form of steel ties which are relatively unobtrusive may be needed. The roof timbers should be defrassed, treated with insecticide and the ironwork painted".

By an Order in Council dated March 1985 the building was vested in the Redundant Churches Fund "to be preserved in the interests of the nation and the Church of England". The repairs could now go ahead so a Specification and drawings for the work that was needed were prepared and the lowest tenderer E.H.Cardy appointed to carry out the work starting in October 1985.

During the work of taking up and renewing the valley gutter, between the nave and north aisle, scaffolding was erected inside the church along the line of the timber arcade. From the scaffolding the ends of the trusses could be seen at close quarters and some repairs were made. A certain amount of deflection in the timbers was noted in relation to the level of the scaffolding, which indicated movement in the roof.

From the scaffolding it was possible to see the roof trusses more clearly than from ground level and it was obvious that the decay and structural weakness was more extensive than previously envisaged.

A mobile platform was hired by the contractor and brought into the church in November 1985. Fortunately the floor of the nave is more or less level, and there is no fixed seating, so it was possible to move the platform around relatively quickly in a way that would have been very difficult and expensive in a church with raised pew platforms and fixed pews. However it was only possible to inspect the lower members of the trusses from the mobile platform, which could not safely reach the ridge.

The survey showed a number of serious defects in the structure. The king post of one of the trusses was completely disconnected from the tie beam, with a 3" (76 mm) gap at the lower end of the post. Apart from general decay in the timber many of the joints appeared to be weak and overstressed.

The original designers of the roof had met the challenge of spanning a exceptional width in an unusual way. They provided six trusses along a length of 73'0" (2225 cm) spacing the trusses at between 10'0" (304 cm) to 12'0" (365 cm) centres. Each truss is of king post form except that the tie beam is not at plate level but intersects the principal rafter about 5'0" (152 cm) above this level, measured vertically. This form may have been adopted to provide a ceiling in three different planes rather than a flat one, to reduce the length of the tie beams or to accommodate the window head at the west end.

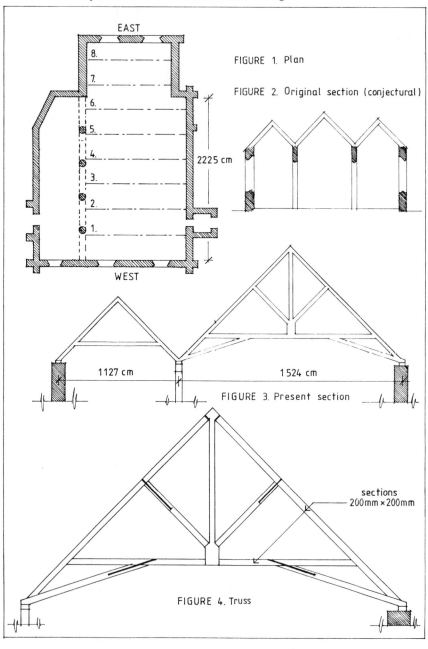

FIGURE 1. Plan

FIGURE 2. Original section (conjectural)

EAST

8.

7.

6.

5.

4.

3.

2.

1.

WEST

2225 cm

1127 cm

1524 cm

FIGURE 3. Present section

sections
200mm × 200mm

FIGURE 4. Truss

On the south side the ends of the trusses bear onto inner and outer timber plates supported on the external masonry wall. These plates were in poor condition and had been partially pushed out of position.

On the north side of the nave the ends of the trusses are supported on a timber plate carried on four timber columns each, braced to east and west, which form the north arcade. The use of timber columns to form an arcade is unusual but not without an earlier precedent in this area. At St. Mary's Church in Wingham 6 miles (10 km) away the nave arcade consists of six timber columns, five of chestnut, one of oak, which date from c.1574. The four timber columns at Sandwich do not support the ends of the trusses but are spaced evenly to provide a suitable appearance for the arcade. The foundations of the earlier stone columns may be seen below the timber floor and the timber columns rest on stone bases. The timber columns are octagonal in shape for about three quarters of their length upwards from the ground and then change to a rectangular shape. A strange projecting cap had been added, apparently recently, at the junction between the two shapes. Contrary to their appearance each of the columns is shaped from a single piece of timber, despite the work involved in achieving this.

The roof structure of the north aisle is also of timber and the six trusses are of simple triangular shape with a collar at mid-span of the rafters. The north ends of the trusses bear on the outer north wall while the south ends are carried on the same timber plate and columns as the nave roof trusses.

Between the trusses of both the nave and chancel is a series of staggered purlins carrying secondary rafters of smaller sections than the main rafters. The majority of these rafters and purlins were in fair condition and did not need extensive repairs.

Considerable thought was given to how to repair the nave roof trusses since it is hoped to use the church for occasional concerts and other public gatherings. As the roofs had been re-tiled about 15-20 years earlier it was important not to disturb the outer coverings and repairs would have to be made from the inside. The question of cost was also, of course, relevant.

One option that was considered at this stage was to insert a separate steel framework of trusses which would relieve the original timber trusses of their load. This idea was investigated and costed but was eventually rejected as being too visually intrusive.

As the timber was in much worse condition than originally envisaged it was then decided to carry out a more detailed survey in order to devise an acceptable method of repair.

AIMS and STRATEGY

The main aim of the repair work to the roof was to restore the missing structural integrity so that the church was safe to use but to retain as much of the original fabric as possible. To achieve this the strengthening would have to be added discreetly but it should be apparent that the work was of twentieth century date. The span of the trusses for their date made it important that the original form was maintained and could be clearly seen.

In work of this kind it is first necessary to understand the form of the structure, and then to determine its condition. With this information, an approximate analysis can be made, in order to get an idea of the overall factor of safety, and the mechanism of collapse. The assumptions of the model may have to be re-evaluated until it realistically represents the actual structure. It is also necessary to exercise judgement when using Codes of Practice to evaluate structures which have stood for several hundred years.

When the analysis has been done, then the remedial options can be evaluated.

The condition of the structure would also need analysing and checking mathematically to determine if there was a safety margin and if so, how great or small?

When all this information was available alternative solutions could be offered and the one that could best meet the difficult criteria would be selected.

FORM OF STRUCTURE

The original medieval roof was undoubtedly of exposed timber, although the details are unknown. It could perhaps have been framed from close coupled rafters with collars, or one of the other types which abound in Kent. However the C17 rebuilding took place at a time of emerging Classicism, when exposed frames were out of favour. Full classical ornament could not be expected in furthest Kent, but a ceiling was installed, with splays which gave much-needed height for this enormous width, and which in any case were necessary to avoid cutting off the tops of the windows at each end (Fig 3).

It was also a time of greater structural knowledge, and the rigidity of triangulation was now understood by theory, and not simply by intuition; the king-post truss emerged as the most direct solution for a roof frame, and, with queen-posts, dominated roof construction for the next two hundred years.

The trusses at Sandwich had to have extended rafters to clear the raised ceiling. Clearly they would be inadequate on their own, and were strengthened with raking ties, connected, not to a node, but to the mid-panel points of the bottom tie. Thus, although the structure was apparently triangulated, the bottom tie was put into significant bending.

Most of the timber is softwood, with occasional pieces of oak. The conifers which were used were not native trees but were imported from the Baltic; an increasing source of timber. The basic section is approximately 8" (200mm) square, although the lowest bay of the rafter is increased in width.

The joints are also typical of C17 work, with an increasing reliance on metal. Wrought iron straps and forelock bolts (tightened by driving an iron wedge into a slot in the shank) are used at tension joints, with the occasional later threaded bolt. Compression joints are connected by mortices and pegged tenons.

CONDITIONS AND ANALYSIS

There was much beetle attack of the sapwood, but the residual sections were basically sound. The principal defect was the bending deflection of the bottom tie (Fig.7), which varied from 50mm-200mm (2"-8"). The member of one truss had already been replaced, another was fractured and braced with steel straps (Photo 1). This has lead to a pronounced spread of the rafter feet, and bending of the rafter at B.

An elastic analysis was made of the critical condition: dead load (self-weight and tiles) and snow load, and the member stresses compared with the permissible stresses in BS 5268, the Code of Practice for design in timber. The results showed high, but not unacceptable, stresses in the timber, and an outward deflection of only 20mm (0.75"). Thus the assumption of elasticity was not justified, and so it is most likely that the trusses had been fabricated from green timber. This was often the case, as large timbers take years to dry out, and many frames in England sit happily with deformations which are well outside normal limits. The reason is that timber is a material which is prone to creep under load when subject to a change in moisture content. When the load is axial the effect is minimal, but bending deflection can be magnified by a factor of up to 3. The deflection of member BD would thus increase considerably if it were erected and loaded at an un-seasoned m.c. of around 60%, which then dropped to a cold roof equilibrium m.c. of 16-18%.

It was also evident that the two-bolt connection of the strap at C was overloaded and the trusses showed varying degrees of slip up to 100mm (4").

Both these factors increase the spread of rafter feet, and increase the bending movement in the rafter at B by up to threefold. Some of the timber joints at B, originally in compression, were now subject to tension, pulling the pegs out of the tenon (Photo 2), and needing the later addition of steel straps and bolts.

    In addition, on some trusses the end shear distance on the raking
tie (S,Fig 7) which restrained the rafter, was sub-standard, giving
the possibility of failure.

    The analysis now models the observed form of the trusses, and
indicates areas where the timber or the joints were substantially overstressed. While it could be understood that the trusses had not
collapsed, the factor of safety against failure was unacceptably low.

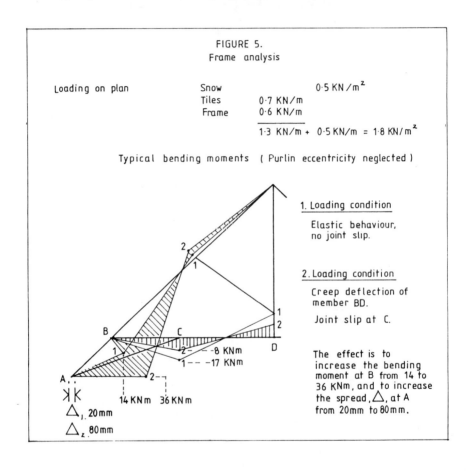

FIGURE 5.
Frame analysis

Loading on plan   Snow   0·5 KN/m²
                           Tiles   0·7 KN/m
                           Frame   0·6 KN/m

                                        1·3 KN/m + 0·5 KN/m = 1·8 KN/m²

        Typical bending moments   (Purlin eccentricity neglected)

1. Loading condition

    Elastic behaviour,
    no joint slip.

2. Loading condition

    Creep deflection of
    member BD.

    Joint slip at C.

    The effect is to
    increase the bending
    moment at B from 14 to
    36 KNm, and to increase
    the spread, △, at A
    from 20mm to 80mm.

2 – – -8 KNm
1 – – -17 KNm

14 KNm 36 KNm

△₁ 20mm

△₂ 80mm

REMEDIAL OPTIONS

The proposal to install a separate subframe in steel had already been rejected. The converse of this, to replace members on a large scale, and reinforce joints until the frame had an acceptable factor of safety would be both prohibitively expensive and ultimately, false.

The basic problem was the inadequacy of the tension connection between the feet of the rafters, both in strength and stiffness. Since the trusses were still standing, it would only be necessary to relieve a proportion of the load, and prevent further spread, as this would be the mechanism of collapse.

The ideal solution would be to buttress the supports. In our medieval churches generally, the ability of the arcade walls to resist lateral thrust has often contributed significantly to the life of the roof. In the context of St Mary's, however, the timber arcade and the aisle roof precluded this. The most straight forward solution was the introduction of a steel tie, linking the feet. This could be post-tensioned to give an active load, reducing the stresses in the lower part of the truss, and to provide a passive restraint to the increase in out thrust under snow load.

REPAIR WORK

The initial survey was carried out from a moveable tower scaffold, using a portable floodlight, and recording details with photographs. It is important to obtain enough information to establish the general condition, so that the scope of the remedial works is reasonably well defined. The second detailed survey can only be done when full access is provided by the builder.

With the contract awarded, the nave was completely scaffolded and boarded out just below eaves level. A tower could then be moved around on this level for inspection and remedial work within the pitch of the roof. The timbers were first 'defrassed', that is, scraped clean of any wood de-natured by beetle attack, and then systematically examined. A huge amount of 'frass' was removed - two lorry loads in fact.

After this inspection it was found necessary only to replace five members - two halves of bottom tie members, one king post, and two braces.

The original trusses were made of redwood, probably of Baltic origins. For the size that was needed the only replacement which is commercially available is Douglas Fir. There was of course a problem in fitting a new member into the position occupied by the previous, distorted member (Photo 1). Here, a template was made, and a curved member 200mm square was cut from a section 300 x 200mm. Even so, a small make-up piece was needed to extend the raking tie.

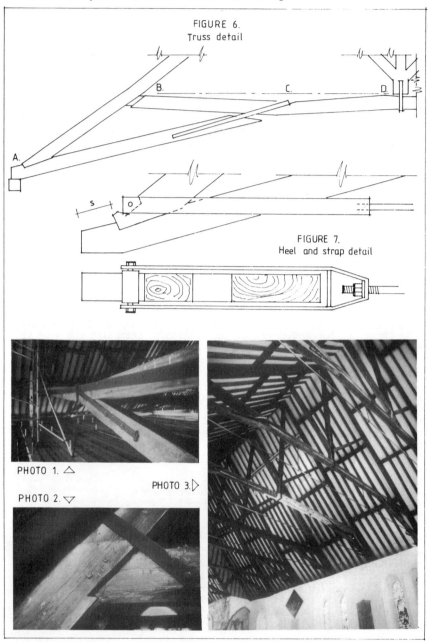

FIGURE 6.
Truss detail

FIGURE 7.
Heel and strap detail

PHOTO 1. △

PHOTO 3. ▷

PHOTO 2. ▽

The scaffolding was arranged with 'slots' in it, so that the new pieces could be lifted into position after removing temporary ties. The scaffolding layout was also related to the module of the trusses, so that a pair of frames could be used to prop the truss while a member was replaced.

When jointing the new section to the existing, no attempt was made to imitate original joints. A straight forward vertical half lap was used, with 30mm connecting bolts. The heads were recessed and plugged to increase the fire resistance.

With the repairs complete, all the timbers were given two coats of a "gel preservative" type of insecticide.

We were fortunate in the enthusiasm and interest shown in the work by the builder and John Martin (a Director of his company) worked on site as a carpenter with his men. It is still possible even today, to find contractors able and willing to continue the craft tradition.

Acknowledgments

      Client: The Redundant Churches Fund
                      St Andrew-by-the-Wardrobe
                      Queen Victoria Street
                      London EC4V 5DE

      Architects: Purcell Miller Tritton & Partners
                      9 London Road
                      Sevenoaks Kent TN13 1AH

      Engineers: Arup Research & Development
                      13 Fitzroy Street
                      London W1P 6BQ

      Quantity   The Wood & Weir Partnership
      Surveyors: 71 London Road
                      Sevenoaks Kent TN13 1AX

      Contractor: W W Martin (Thanet) Ltd
                      Dane Park Road
                      Ramsgate Kent CT11 7LT

Cost of timber repairs £36,422

Restoration of the Soldiers' Monument, Trinity Churchyard, New York City

Glenn Boornazian* and Norman R. Weiss**
Cathedral Stone Company of New York
**Graduate School of Archtitecture, Planning and
Preservation, Columbia University, New York, N.Y., USA*

SANDSTONE: HISTORY OF USE AND PRESERVATION

The Soldiers' Monument (ca. 1855) stands in the north yard of Trinity Church, in lower Manhattan, New York. Very little historical information exists in the Parish Archives concerning the construction of the Monument, but there is considerable documentation on the Church itself, which stands at the intersection of Broadway and Wall Street. The construction technology, building materials, post construction treatments, and repair histories of the Church (completed 1846) and the Monument are extremely similar. The following is a selection of relevant information from archival data assembled during an earlier investigation of the condition of the exterior stonework of the Church [1].

The building that survives to the present day is the third Trinity Church constructed on this site. The architect, Richard Upjohn, submitted plans for a new church in the English Perpendicular gothic style, on September 9, 1839. Of particular significance to our work is the question of the selection of stone, which was raised as early as September 18, when the architect submitted an estimate of construction cost based upon use of Connecticut brown sandstone, presumably from the quarries at Portland and Middletown, on the Connecticut River [2]. On the following day, the New York Commercial Advertizer commented on this preliminary concept.

> Why should the rich corporation of Old Trinity select the most perishable stone they can find when for a small addition to the expense those walls might be laid in everlasting granite.[3]

A broader investigation of possible sources of stone led to submissions from the owners of four quarries, including those in Little Falls, New Jersey, and Syracuse, New York, the latter producing the grey Onondaga limestone.

The Committee made every inquiry as to the fitness, quality and cost of the various kinds of stone for the proposed edifice, and of the supplies that could be had, from the different quarries within a convenient distance from the city, and selected the brown sandstone from Little Falls, New Jersey, as the most suitable in colour and durability...[4]

Upjohn visited the Little Falls sandstone quarries, and on December 4, 1839, the Standing Committee accepted a bid from William H. Harris, a builder, to supply the New Jersey stone. The Parish signed a contract with Harris and James Thom, a stonecutter, on March 6, 1840, with delivery scheduled

...so soon during the present ensuing spring as the opening of navigation on the Morris canal will permit.[5]

The third Trinity Church was completed in 1846; space limitations led to minor interior alterations in 1849-50 and 1864. It was perhaps the narrowness of the passage behind the altar that finally resulted in serious consideration of proposals to extend the Church to the west. Approval was given on June 27, 1876 for construction of a one-story extension designed by Frederick Clarke Withers in the late gothic Flamboyant style [6]. This project, executed between April 3 and June 27, 1877, was illustrated in an article in American Architect and Building News.

The addition is of stone, corresponding with the stone-work of the church which was built by Mr. R. Upjohn in 1846... The contractor for the addition was Philip Herrmann.[7]

The west and south elevations were published with the caption "Stonework a reddish brown Sandstone". Sandstone from the Little Falls quarries was probably used.

In May, 1910, a Special Committee recommended to the Vestry that a Chapel be constructed on the north side of the Church. Minutes of a meeting of May 25, 1910 specifically defined a structure "on the lines suggested by the plans by Mr. Thomas Nash...". The Vestry resolved on June 13, 1910, to undertake this project, at an expense not to exceed $25,000. Nash's plans, presumably more fully developed at this point, were recommended (by the Special Committee) for adoption by the Vestry in February, 1911, and on June 12, 1911, an appropriation of $60,000 was made for construction. Work was carried out in 1912-13, and the Chapel of All Saints was consecrated on November 30, 1913 [8]. Specifications for the Chapel described the exterior stonework as

...in color and general character agreeing with the Church of which it is to form a part". [9]

But the material was actually specified as "Long Meadow brown stone", rather then the New Jersey stone of Upjohn's work. The architect probably used the "Worcester" stone, a brown sandstone quarried by the Norcross brothers in East Longmeadow, Massachusetts. The most probable explanation for the selection of Massachusetts sandstone for All Saints' Chapel is the apparent collapse of the New Jersey sandstone industry at this time. In the 1908 Annual Report of the State Geologist (of New Jersey), J. Volney Lewis commented on the closing of the quarries.

Public taste has changed.   Brownstone houses and "fronts" are
no longer fashionable. The colors are too somber to suit the
popular taste for residences and are not adapted to the
prevailing styles of architecture. Fewer, large buildings of
a public or semi-public character are constructed of it, and even
the churches are adopting the lighter tints.[10]

The economic impact of this change of taste on the quarries that served the New York construction market can be documented by industry statistics. In 1909, New Jersey sandstone production in the catagory of dressed building stone was $39,090.   Five years later, in 1914, the figure was an insignificant $200 [11].

For Little Falls, the problem may have also been a technical one, forcing the closing of these quarries before those in Newark and Belleville, New Jersey.

Little Falls Brownstone: Old quarries on both sides of the
Passaic River just below the falls at this place were formerly
worked extensively.   The limit of economic operation was
apparently reached on the north side when the workings   came
under the thick overlaying sheet of trap rock. On the south side
the quarries extended far below the level of the river, involving
the   necessity of pumping. Further extension above this level
would necessitate the removal of the street at the top of the bluff.
Hence these   quarries are not likely again to become producers of
brownstone on a   larger scale.[12]

In 1878, Thomas Egleston, a professor at the School of Mines at Columbia University, first observed some deterioration of the exterior stonework.

In the year 1878, I   noticed that the stone of which Trinity
Church,   in this city,   is built, showed serious signs of decay.
In the year 1880 it became   necesssary to undertake a
thorough   investigation of the causes of this decay, in the hope of
learning   some means of checking it. The work was placed in my
hands.[13]

By his own description Egleston's investigation seems to have been a comprehensive one.

These studies of the stone in place, and of its decomposition,
lasted through several months. I examined the stone inside and
outside the   Church, as far as it was accessible, high up into the
steeple...[14]

In 1886, with the permission of the Corporation of Trinity Church, Egleston published in Transactions of the American Society of Civil Engineers a very considerable commentary on the decay of building stone in general,   and preservative treatments then in use [15].   He described the deteriorated stones as exhibiting deep pitting, flaking and crumbling, explaining variations in the extent and localization of these conditions in terms of mineralogy and construction detailing.

Egleston was responsible for a program of work carried out in the summer of 1884.

> When the report of the cause of decay was made to the
> corporation, it was thought necessary to redress the stone
> previous to treating it. The decomposition has gone nearly into
> the interior of the stone, six inches in some cases, and it was
> found that some of the stones were so rotten that it was not
> worthwhile to redress them, and they were removed and new
> stones put in their place.[16]

Although no waterproofing treatment of the exterior walls is described as having
been accomplished at the time of the presentation of his paper, Egleston's intention to
do so was quite clear. His early experiments were with oil.

> In the experiments made in the year 1861, I was successful in
> preventing the further decay of a building which has, up to this
> time, shown no signs of lamination or disintegration. This was
> done by the use of thoroughly boiled oil alone, applied with a
> brush during the warmest of our summer weather, when the
> stone was very hot. It was done twice at intervals of several
> years, and completely arrested the decay for the time being.
> [17]

By the 1880's he became interested in formulations of paraffin, oil, and sulfur,
omitting sulfur in the case of sandstones. His recommendation for Trinity Church was
such a material, applied hot, but he cautioned against attempting to heat the stone
prior to treatment.

> If the stone is heated from the outside, with the intent to bring
> the surface of the stone up to such a point that it will heat the
> paraffin, there is great danger that the stone will suffer more
> from the remedy than from the disease.[18]

The next observation of masonry problems at Trinity Church appears indirectly in a
1925 letter by H. deB. Parsons, who was for several years in the early part of this
century an engineering consultant to the Parish. On February 10, 1925, Parsons was
asked to prepare a report on the condition of the exterior masonry, and on possible
techniques of preventing further decay. He presented a summary of his findings in a
document dated March 18, 1926 [19]. Parsons' recommendations for treatment of the
stone, based in part upon some discussions with English engineers during a trip to
London in the previous year, was Sylvester's process (soap and alum solutions),
followed by hard paraffin wax, applied hot [20]. In general, Parsons commented that
no treatment was known to permanently arrest deterioration, and suggested that the
further advice of a chemist be sought.

Specifications entitled "Preservation of exterior stone work" were issued by Parsons
on June 9, 1926.

> 16. When the surface is dry, the stone work shall be heated in an
> approved manner to a temperature of 180 to 250 F, as may be
> found best, until the stones are completely heated. The heating
> shall be applied slowly and kept under control. The surfaces
> shall then be coated with hot melted paraffin until the stones will

not   absorb   any more into the pores and interstices.   The surface
shall then be rubbed off with clean cloths.[21]

This technique had been patented earlier by Robert M. Caffall.   A formulation "for
waterproofing and preserving building materials" composed of paraffin, creosote and
turpentine   was   described   in   his   patent   of 1880; Caffall's apparatus   for heating
masonry   walls   immediately   prior   to   application   of   the   molten   compound   was
illustrated in a second patent,   issued in 1882 [22].

PROJECT PLANNING

The decision on the part of the Parish of Trinity Church   to carry out a restoration
project on the Soldiers' Monument was based both on concern for the condition of the
monument itself, and on the opportunity that it presented to serve as a prototype for
the restoration of the Church. Because of the similar age, materials, and maintenance
histories of the two structures, the latter was a logical concept. Useful   information
ranging from stone repair techniques to cost analysis data was ultimately obtained
from the work completed last year on the Monument.

The authors (working at that time for the Center for Preservation Research, Columbia
University) were hired by the Parish, which acted as its own construction manager.
Qualified contractors were contacted to bid on the work, based on a simple scope-of-
work statement.   Appended to this was   a portion of the detailed technical study of the
sandstone of the Church   prepared a year earlier by one of the authors   (Weiss; see
reference 1).

Once the contractors were chosen and the pipe scaffolding was installed, the authors
conducted   a   hands-on   condition   survey   which   was   recorded   on   reproducible
photographic mylar sheets. (Elevation photographs were shot with a 4x5" view camera.)
The survey information allowed the authors to map the various types of deterioration
conditions, and to identify the locations in which each specific restoration technique
was required.   During the work the authors maintained a constant on-site presence,
supervising the craftsmen and recording the amounts of time and material required for
each task.

Stone Cleaning
The most noticable condition on the Monument which demanded attention was the
presence of paraffin wax, as had already been detected in analytical studies of
samples from the Church. An unwanted effect of the wax treatment was the heavy
soiling of the stone. Although   numerous historical photographs of the Church   through
1913 show it to be relatively clean,   uniform black soiling can be seen in several
photographs from the early to mid 1930's.

Preliminary cleaning tests were carried out on June 25, 1986. Acidic products
conventionally used for the cleaning of sandstone did not remove the soiling
effectively, presumably   because of the presence of the wax treatment that prevented
the cleaners from wetting the stone surface.   The most complete series of tests was
done to evaluate the possibility of alkaline de-greasing, followed by acidic cleaning.
This two-step approach has become more common in the United States in recent years.
Surface pH was measured prior to, and after testing to ascertain that complete
neutralization had taken place.

The materials selected for stone cleaning, based on these test results, were ProSoCo T-792 Alkaline Prewash, followed immediately by ProSoCo Restoration Cleaner [23]. The stone surface was pre-wetted with water for 2 to 3 minutes, and the Prewash brush applied.   After approximately 45 minutes, the material was flushed off with water at 500 psi using a broad fan nozzle (minimum flow rate of 6 gallons/minute). The Restoration Cleaner, which is acidic, was diluted at 2 parts cleaner to 1 part water. It was applied for 5 minutes, then re-applied, scrubbed manually and pressure rinsed.

A large catch basin was constructed at the stepped base of the Monument to collect chemical run-off.   This was accomplished by lining a wooden framework with a rubber roofing membrane which was flashed into the joint between the uppermost granite step and the lowest course of sandstone.

Cleaning was the first task completed; the results were visually dramatic. In this instance, cleaning was of more than cosmetic value. Thorough removal of the soiled wax layer constituted an important measure for the preservation of the stone, as it is expected to effectively reduce moisture entrapment. It was, moreover, necessary to eliminate this coating prior to impregnation with the consolidant.

Stone Repair
Stone repair was the second and largest task completed; the specific operations involved are outlined below.

Pinning   Stainless steel and threaded nylon pins were used for two types of repairs: the stitching together of fractured stone, and the re-assembly of pieces which had been completely detached from the monument.   The first step was the drilling of 3/8" holes in the stone, using carbide tipped masonry drill bits.   After a dry run of the repair was completed to insure a correct fit, the pins were set in a structural polyester adhesive (Akemi Marmorrkitt 1000, Transparent Special L, Knife Grade) [24].   Care was taken to prevent the adhesive and/or pin from coming to the exposed surface.   As a rule these materials were kept back 1/2" and a composite patching compound applied.

Patching   Patching formulations were developed to match the three most typical colors of stone. The final selection of mixes was based upon the appearance achieved by allowing experimental formulations to cure for 48 hours, then brushing them lightly with a solution of acetic acid to expose the aggregate as a simulation of weathering. Emphasis was placed on the selection of colored aggregates, which made it possible to minimize the quantities of pigments used. The binder was a mixture of white and grey portland cement and hydrated lime.   An example of one of the mixes is as follows: 1 part white portland cement; 1 part grey portland cement; 1 part hydrated lime; 8 parts reddish brown sand (passed through a # 30 screen); 1/4 part pigment (raw umber) [25].

In all areas that were to be patched, decayed or structurally failing stone was removed or repaired. Preparation work also included some undercutting, so as to dovetail the patch into the adjacent stone. This work was achieved with the use of grinders and hand tools.

If the areas to be patched were 1" or less in depth, keying was accomplished by drilling 1/4" diameter holes approximately every 2" apart and a minimum of 3/4" in depth. The masonry surface was cleaned of all debris, and prewet prior to trowel application of the compound. (It is extremely important to work the mortar into the holes.) The patch was then brought up to the level of the adjacent surface.

If the area to be patched was deeper then 1" or was in any way vulnerable to stress, an armature was constructed. This was done by drilling a system of holes 1/4" in diameter in which stainless steel wires could be placed. The wires were bent to span from one hole to another, and raised at least 3/4" off the masonry surface. They were set in the holes with Akemi.

After the adhesive was allowed to set (at least 24 hours), the masonry was prewetted to begin application of the patching compound. It was applied in layers of no more than 3/4" at a time. Each layer was scratched and then allowed to dry at least 24 hours prior to the application of the next layer. This process was repeated with an unpigmented mix until a level of no more than 1" from the surface was reached. The pigmented mix was used as the final layer. Where necessary, modelling was done to mimic the tooling of the original stone. This was carried out approximately 4 to 6 hours after application of the pigmented layer [26].

Retooling Retooling was only prescribed in highly visible areas where stone decay had resulted in the loss of significant surface ornament.   The approach was rather conservative; only primary design elements were treated. This process was executed with a combination of pneumatic and hand tools.

Replacement   Stone replacement was done in a few situations where structural integrity was in question, or where the completeness of a design element was considered to be significant. As there are no brownstone quarries active in the eastern United States it is extremely difficult to obtain replacement material [27]. The few pieces needed on the Soldiers' Monument were salvaged from the demolition of a local structure.

Repointing   Repointing of the Church is documented in 1926-28, 1944-45 and 1959-60, resulting in considerable variation in joint appearance today. This situation also exists on the Monument, where it was not possible to locate samples of original mortar. Examination of a small specimen of original material from the tower of the Church indicated that the mid-19th century mortar was composed of lime, pigmented in the range of color of the Little Falls sandstone. The mix used for work on the Monument was as follows: 1 part grey portland cement; 2 parts hydrated lime; 7 parts reddish brown sand (passed through a #30 screen); 1/4 part pigment (raw umber) [28].

Repointing was done locally as needed, or where there was considerable visual confusion. Removal of existing mortar was done to eliminate unsound or visually unacceptable material from the joints. A minimum depth of 3/4" was established as a standard for the work, to insure good adhesion. This was done with the utmost caution to avoid damage to the stone. In some locations this could be done by a skilled stone mason with a power grinder. Where the stonework was more intricate, hand tools were used.

Once the joints were prepared, the wall was prewetted. The repointing mix was pressed into the open joints with the use of custom made (narrow) pointing irons. The joints were finished slightly recessed from the stone surface [29].

Stone Consolidation

A preliminary review in 1983 of the condition of the stone by another consultant, Masonry Stabilization Services Corporation, resulted in the removal of three cores from two areas at the west end of the Church [30]. One set (that is, a core from each stone) was forwarded to Helmut Weber of Bayplan (Bayerische Bautenschutz und Fachplanung GmbH), Munich, West Germany. The other set was tested by James M. Dunlap of ProSoCo, Inc., Kansas City, Kansas. We were able to review the data that these laboratories produced, comparing it with historical (19th century) analyses, and with some additional laboratory work carried out in 1986.

The Bayplan study showed relatively similar water absorption characteristics for the two stones. The finer-grained material, almost certainly from the Upjohn portion of the Church, had a 24 hour absorbtion of 5.50%, the coarser-grained stone, 4.22% [31]. Both of the cores exhibited a (proportionally) very high 10 minute absorbtion, a feature that suggests considerable sensitivity to the effects of rain exposure. This is of particular significance in the light of the high acid solubility (for a sandstone) of the coarser-grained stone, for which a figure of 8.29% was reported. This value that is close to the high end of the range of data that we were able to recalculate from chemical analyses (by J.B. Mackintosh) reported in 1886 by Egleston [32]. Most acidity is observed in the early minutes of each rainfall; acid-soluble building materials with a pore structure that results in high early absorbtion of water are thus especially fragile if directly wetted by rain.

Dunlap measured the resistance of the two Trinity Church samples to sodium sulphate crystallization, somewhat as Charles G. Page had done on the Little Falls sandstone in 1847, but more severely stressing the material, and continuing the test to failure [33, 34]. Both were essentially destroyed after 6 cycles. Comparison was made with samples of the stone that Dunlap had treated with consolidants. Weber also reported treatment of some of the Trinity Church samples [35].

Consolidation is the re-establishing of cohesion by deposition of a durable, substitute binding material within the pore system of the stone. This process should also improve measurable engineering properties, and reduce water absorption [36].

Current literature on conservation methods contains many enthusiastic reports of the application of silicic acid esters to consolidate deteriorated stone [37]. Much of the developmental work was done in Germany, where the resulting products were used to consolidate sandstones. Recently, the stone consolidants most widely used in Germany have become available in the United States. They are marketed under the names of Conservare H and OH; the H product is formulated to provide water-repellency as well as consolidation.

Weber's data on treatment with Conservare consolidants can be compared to the results of some work done at Columbia University on brown Massillon (Ohio) sandstone. He reported absorbtion of 3.44% and 4.04% (by weight) of Conservare OH, and a final deposition of about 1.6%. The Massillon samples, with final consolident deposition of 1.5 to 2.8%, showed a dramatic improvement in compressive strength of 70 to 100 %. These results are based on a total of 60 samples, including some treated with Conservare H [38]. Weber reported a considerable reduction of water absorption after treatment with the hydrophobic Conservare H. 24 hour absorption was less than 0.46%, as compared with 4.22 to 5.50% prior to treatment.

Dunlap's data on sodium sulphate crystallization (DIN 52111) are excellent for samples treated with Conservare H, with or without pretreatment with the OH. All samples were intact, showing essentially no weight loss, after 10 cycles. Perhaps of greater significance in terms of field performance is his measurement of water vapor transmission rate (DIN 52615). Retention of permeability was reported as 80-82% for the fine-grained stone, and 77% for the coarser-grained stone. This ability to maintain a relatively open pore structure is an important characteristic of silicic acid ester consolidants.

Consolidation was the final step in the restoration program, as it was necessary to have already accomplished both the cleaning (that is, wax removal) and the elimination of flaking stone. Conservare H was chosen to reduce the risk of frost damage and acid dissolution of the sandstone. All dust and construction debris was removed from the surface by pressure rinsing. As the consolidant is carried in MEK, workers were required to wear protective clothing, and to avoid all operations which might create sparks. The product was applied with the use of hand pumped and hand held spray units, with fittings that could not be attacked by the MEK. In general, stone saturation was reached after the completion of two cycles (six applications). A penetration depth of approximately 3 to 4 inches was observed where there was subsequent opportunity for examination.

It is recommended by the manufacturer that within a half hour of reaching saturation the surface be wiped down with a cloth dampened with MEK, to prevent buildup of the cured material. In some areas too much time was allowed to pass before this was done. As a result a white film was created on the surface, causing much concern. Tests using a water rinse of 500 psi sucessfully removed this film, but consultation with the manufacturer's chemists suggested that it would eventually embrittle and be eliminated by weathering. At the present time (about a year later) most of the consolidant residue has disappeared as predicted.

REFERENCES

1. Weiss, Norman R. (for Center for Preservation Research, Columbia University), "Conservation study: exterior stonework, Trinity Church, New York, NY," prepared for Parish of Trinity Church, 2/17/87.

2. Matero, Frank G. and Jeanne M. Teutonico, "The use of architectural sandstone in New York City in the 19th century," Bulletin of the Association for Preservation Technology, XIV (2), 11-17 (1982).

3. New York Commercial Advertizer, September 19, 1839, cited in Upjohn, Hobart B., "Trinity Church, New York: a history of its building operations," typescript in Avery Library, Columbia University, with ms. notes by the author, 193?.

4. "Report of the Building Committee," January 11, 1847, reprinted in Berrian, William, An Historical Sketch of Trinity Church. New York: Stanford & Swords, 1847, pp. 343-348.

5. Original contact, dated March 6, 1840, cited in Upjohn, Everard M., Richard Upjohn, Architect and Churchman. New York: Columbia University Press, 1939, p.53.

6. Kowsky, Francis R., _The Architecture of Frederick Clarke Withers and the Progress of the Gothic Revival in America after 1850_. New York: Columbia University Press, 1980, pp. 122-127.

7. Anon., "The alterations in Trinity Church. New York. Mr. Frederick C. Withers, architect," _American Architect & Building News_, III (110), 42 and two engraved sheets of designs   (Feb. 2, 1878).

8. Vestry and Special Committee minutes are housed in the Trinity Parish Archives.

9. Trinity Parish Archives: "Specifications for A Memorial Chapel, Thomas Nash, Architect, 1170 Broadway, New York City, " 1911, p. 3.

10. Lewis, J. Volney, "Building stones of New Jersey," Part III in _New Jersey Geological Survry. Annual Report. 1908_. Trenton: MacCrellish & Quigley, 1909, p. 108.

11. Eckel, Edwin C., _Building Stone and Clays: Their Origin. Characters and Examination_. New York: John Wiley & Sons, 1912, Table 77, p. 147; also Bowles, Oliver, _Sandstone Quarrying in the United States_ (Bureau of Mines Bulletin 124). Washington: Government Printing Office, 1917, Table 6, p. 132.

12. Lewis, cited above, p.90.

13. Egleston, Thomas, "The cause and prevention of the decay of building stone," Transactions of the American Society of Civil Engineers, XV (341), 647-716 (Oct. 1886), p. 648.

14. Egleston, cited above, p. 649.

15. Egleston, cited above.

16. Egleston, cited above, p. 706; also footnote on p. 698: "All the decayed surfaces of the stone at Trinity Church were recut in the summer of 1884." Egleston's redressing of stones was also mentioned by Smock, John C., "Building stone in New York," Bulletin of the New York State Museum, 2 (10), 197-396 (Sept. 1890), p.297, "Trinity Church (1846) is a fine architectural example of the stone from Little Falls. The decay in some of the stones of the exterior walls necessitated a careful examination and redressing a few years ago."

17. Egleston, cited above, p. 702.

18. Egleston, cited above, p. 704.

19. Parsons, H.deB., "Report on preservation of exterior stone work, Trinity Church, New York, N.Y., " dated March 18, 1926, pp. 2-3.

20. For information on Sylvester's process, see Anon. , "Stone-preserving processes, Royal Institute of British Architects," The Builder, 19 (941), 103-105 (1861).

21. Trinity Parish Archives: Parsons, H.deB., "Preservation of exterior stone work, Trinity Church," specifications dated June 9, 1926, Part No. 2, pp. 3-4.

22. Caffall, Robert M., "Compound for waterproofing and preserving building materials," U.S. Patent No. 230,919, dated August 10, 1880; Caffall, Robert M., "Process of and apperatus for applying waterproofing material," U.S. Patent No. 253,505; dated February 14, 1882.

23. These cleaners are manufactured by ProSoCo, Inc., P.O. Box 1578, Kansas City, Kansas 66117.

24. Akemi adhesives are distributed in the United States by Wood and Stone Inc., Manassas, Virginia.

25. This mix conforms to Type S, ASTM C 270-86a, "Standard specification for mortar for unit masonry," in Volume 04.01, 1986 Annual Book of Standards. Philadelphia: American Society for Testing and Materials, 1986.

26. Techniques for the patching of sandstone have been described by Weiss, Norman R., et al., "Sandstone conservation study (draft typescript)," prepared for the New York Landmarks Conservancy, n.d. A pamphlet summarizing the findings of this study was written by Lynch, Michael F. and William J. Higgins, The Maintenance and Repair of Architectural Sandstone. New York: New York Landmarks Conservancy, 1982.

27. The East Longmeadow quarries were last open in the early 1970's, when some buildings at New York University were constructed of this stone. A brown sandstone is quarried in Ohio by the Briar Hill Stone Company, Glenmont, Ohio.

28. The repointing mix conforms to Type O, ASTM C 270-86a (see reference 25, above).

29. Mack, Robert C. and James S. Askins, "An introduction to repointing," Bulletin of the Association for Preservation Technology, XI (3), 44-60 (1979); also Ashurst, John, Mortars, Plasters and Renders in Conservation. London: Ecclesiastical Architects' and Surveyors' Association, 1983.

30. Boyer, David W. (for Masonry Stabilization Services Corporation), "Preliminary recommendations for the restorative cleaning, conservation and stabilization of decaying exterior masonries," report submitted to Henry L. Norde, dated February 4, 1983.

31. Weber, Helmut (for Bayplan), laboratory report, dated Munich, July 29, 1983.

32. Egleston, cited earlier, p. 697.

33. Dunlap, James M. (for ProSoCo, Inc.), laboratory report, dated December 13, 1983.

34. "Appendix, Note B," dated March 5, 1847, in Owen, Robert Dale, Hints on Public Architecture. New York: G.P. Putnam, 1849, reprinted New York: Da Capo Press, 1978. Page's data was also published by Merrill, George P., Stones for Building and Decoration. New York: John Wiley & Sons, 1903 (3rd ed.), p. 388.

35.   Weber, cited earlier.

36.   Clifton, James R., <u>Preliminary Performance Criteria for Stone Treatments for the United States Capitol</u> (NBSIR 87-3542).   Washington: U.S. Department of Commerce, 1987.

37.   Weiss, Norman R. and Carol A. Grissom, eds., "Alkoxysilanes in the conservation of art and architecture: 1861-1981," <u>Art and Archaeology Technical Abstracts, 18</u> (1), 150-202 (1981, supplement).   The terminology of organosilicon compounds used in the building industry has been reviewed by Roth, Michael, "Comparison of silicone resins, siliconates, silanes and siloxanes as water repellent treatments for masonry" (Technical Bulletin 983-1), available from ProSoCo, Inc., n.d.

38.   Zinsmeister, Klaus J.H., Norman R. Weiss and Frances R. Gale, "Laboratory evaluation of consolidation treatment of Massillon (Ohio) sandstone," <u>Bulletin of the Association for Preservation Technology, XX</u> (3), 35-39 (1988).

The Restoration of the Palm House, Kew

C.R. Jones

Posford Duvivier, Consulting Engineers, Peterborough

ABSTRACT

Details are given of the history of the Palm House, the Survey and the background to the various decisions made for repair and replacement of materials.

INTRODUCTION

The Palm House at Kew is a Grade 1 listed structure and one of the finest examples of a curvilinear glasshouse surviving. (See Fig.1) It was built between 1844 and 1848. The primary structural elements are curved arch ribs formed from rolled wrought iron. Secondary structural and decorative elements are largely in cast iron although there are some wrought iron members. Some basic statistics are as follows:-

Length	326 ft.	(99.4 metres)
Maximum height	66 ft.	(20.1 metres)
Complete length of glazing bar	10 miles	(16 kilometres)
Bay Centres	12 ft.6 in.	(3.81 metres)

HISTORICAL BACKGROUND

The design and construction of the Palm House has been well recorded by Edward J. Diestelkamp[1]. The following paragraphs have been largely extracted from his paper in order to serve as an historical introduction.

By the time that William Hooker was appointed as director in 1841 the existing Palm House was overcrowded and palms were growing through the roof. Hooker held discussions about preliminary designs for a new house with various people but the most prominent were Richard Turner and Decimus Burton.

Richard Turner (c.1798 - 1881) had a considerable background in iron-working. He had expanded his uncle's ironmongery business into new premises with a foundry in Dublin. Beginning with the production of curvilinear glasshouses in the 1830s, he had built the Dublin (Glasnevin) Palm House and the initial portion of the Belfast Palm House by the mid 1840s.

Decimus Burton also had experience with glasshouses. He was the "architect" of Paxton's Great Stove at Chatsworth. This was at the time the largest glasshouse in Europe, although Burton's precise role is not known. He was also Architect to the Royal Botanic Society, Regents Park.

Turner and Burton produced various schemes to which neither would agree. In an attempt to break the impasse, Turner sent for his foreman who was a "first rate practical man". Turner then proposed the use of arched iron ribs in order to reduce the number of columns in Burton's scheme. These were originally intended to be cast, but were later changed to wrought in order to take advantage of the recently patented deck beam. (Fig 2). This is thought to be the first use of a rolled I section in a building. Turner also patented his purlin system whereby the arches were tied together with a post tensioned rod which ran through purlin tubes.

Turner maintained that he lost £7,000 from the contract, the main reason being given as the rise in the cost of wrought iron. It is felt that the financial constraints upon him led directly to a very tight design in terms of weight of iron work.

The building was originally glazed with green tinted glass, and the floor was covered with iron grilles. The glass was changed very quickly to "clear" as there was insufficient light. The use of a grilled floor forced Kew staff to keep the palms in pots. This has changed over the years until about half the area was converted to beds.

Little is known of the subsequent history of the House except that there was a major refurbishment of the heating and basements (due to leakage) c.1870.

By 1950 the Palm House presented a very sorry, leaden appearance. Corrosion had been aggravated by the internal humidity and use of nicotine sprays to the extent that some of the arch ribs webs had been eaten through.

A major refurbishment was therefore carried out in the 1950s. Some measures that were taken helped to protect the building but, unfortunately, other items accelerated the effects of corrosion. The main ironwork was not dismantled as the plants were moved from wing to wing whilst the work was carried out, and this could not have helped the efficiency of the project.

In 1981 doubts were expressed over parts of the structure. Pieces of ironwork such as guttering had fallen from above. The building had been painted every 4 or 5 years but the difficulties, for example, in painting 10 miles of wet glazing bar were readily apparent. Due to the lack of access the painters were forced to hang on to the gutters etc. Because of the possible danger the painters refused to do further work on the building. Additionally there were some 600 broken panes of glass annually which cost around £20,000 to repair, not including the cost of heat loss. The glaziers continued for some years after the painting but then declared also their lack of willingness to proceed.

In 1981 Posford Duvivier were asked by the Property Services Agency to survey the building and report on the condition. As it happens, our work on the restoration of the nearby Temperate House had just been completed.

THE SURVEYS

We soon found that the drawings available did not match the existing structure. We therefore dismantled some small local areas in order to prepare a full set of drawings to a fair degree of detail.   Fig. 3 demonstrates the complexity of some of the ironwork.

Our task was made more difficult than usual by the mass of plant growth but also by the amount of all types of fillers that had been used over the years. It was not uncommon to examine an area of paintwork which appeared reasonable, only to find that putty covered a corroded area.

Limited samples of wrought and cast iron were taken for tensile testing and used to calibrate the remainder of the ironwork by hardness tests.   We also loaded a wrought iron purlin and a cast iron floor grille to destruction.

The surveys showed that the building was in urgent need of restoration. Removal of one of the windows, for example, led to the collapse of the adjacent clerestory pilaster.   The glazing bars were badly corroded, particularly at the ends.   Most of the secondary structural cast iron elements required replacement or repair.

THE BRIEF

The Property Services Agency decided to proceed with the restoration with Posford Duvivier as Lead Consultant responsible for structural, civil and mechanical and electrical design with the Property Services Agency providing in-house architectural services. The Quantity Surveyors were Ager & Stockwell.

After discussions with the Curator and his staff, the following outline brief was handed to us:-

. The collection of very important plants was to be rehoused during the project for a maximum of three years. Temporary structure to be provided.

. Investigate possibility of low maintenance glazing system using polycarbonate and/or aluminium glazing bar.

. Provide staff accommodation area in existing basement.

. Provide new basement for display of marine plants.

. Remove plant shelving and replace the floor grilles with plant beds.

. Investigate methods for future maintenance.

. Update the mechanical and electrical services including heating, ventilation and humidification.

STRUCTURAL ANALYSIS

The preliminary analysis was done by hand using assumed wind loadings. Because of the unique shape it was decided to test a 1:200 scale model in the BRE wind tunnel.   The results demonstrated that our assumptions were largely correct except that higher pressures were indicated local to the main doors.

A typical residual section after corrosion was established from the survey and used as a basis for a computerised two-dimensional analysis.   The results showed that a limited amount of strengthening was required to the main arch ribs, at heavily corroded areas.   This was to be accomplished by adding mild steel and ductile iron plates by welding.

In the central transept area, it was assumed that the gallery deck plates acted as a diaphragm to transfer the wind and out of balance loads from the half arches back to the main arches on grids 10 & 17, (see Fig. 4).   As it happened, the gallery plates were cast from the worst quality cast iron on the project, and it was therefore decided to strengthen the edge with a new ductile iron ring beam.   The main arches were formed from the same basic section as the standard arch ribs, with added cheek plates.   Drillings revealed the possibility of corrosion.   Structural analysis also highlighted inadequacy against buckling.   It was therefore decided to strip down the arches, check for corrosion, and add a top plate to help resist buckling.

The remainder of the elements, including columns and spandrel brackets, were shown to be adequate.

REPLACEMENT GLAZING

Polycarbonate was initially thought to be an ideal replacement for the glazing because of its resistance to impact and it is easy to bend.   After investigation doubts were expressed over colour fastness and resistance to scratching.   The flexibility was only of real value if one sheet could be used from dado to clerestory but the removal of the lapped panes would have affected the overall look of the building.   Moreover, because of the higher thermal expansion coefficient, it would have been necessary to use a new shape of glazing bar.

After contact with Pilkingtons, it was found that curved toughened glass could be obtained in large quantities for virtually the same price as curved annealed glass.   It was recognised that there would be extra costs inherent in the accuracy of fabrication of the glazing bars, and the necessity of providing templates for specials, but it was thought that these costs would be more than offset by the lack of breakage.   To reduce the need for external painting, white silicone sealant was specified to replace the putty.

Extensive research was undertaken to try to obtain wrought iron to repair or replace the glazing bars.   Although second hand iron was available, the only possible source for newly puddled iron was Ironbridge.   However, the Director of Ironbridge confirmed that new iron would not be available until after the anticipated completion of the restoration.   Also, although it was known that small sections (squares and rounds) were being rolled reasonably successfully from second hand iron, it was thought that the expertise was not available to cog down and roll a more complicated section.

Our experience on the Temperate House, where we designed a specially extruded aluminium glazing bar, led us to examine the possibilities of a similar system. It proved difficult, if not impossible, to match the existing bars in profile and for joint details. Following a large deflection analysis, an extruded aluminium bar of the same profile as the existing was found to give excessive deflection.

A lead was given from the restoration of the Belfast Palm House (also a Turner building) where extruded mild steel bars were used. It was decided that stainless steel would be more appropriate for the high humidity environment but the availability of the Belfast dies meant that we could readily experiment with the stainless steel and show samples to interested bodies. Subsequently rolling was also investigated as extrusion of stainless steel is done by one company only in the U.K. Although the budget prices for rolling varied by £2,000 per ton, the lowest was far cheaper than extrusion. In the event the Contractor has opted for extrusion because of ease of calling for material as and when required, however the threat of competition considerably lowered the cost.

The revised glazing detail is shown in Fig. 5.

REPLACEMENT/REPAIR OF CASTINGS

The building contains some 7,500 castings of which approximately one third are structural, the remainder being purely decorative. From the survey results an assessment was made as to the amount of replacement that would be required. For the structural elements this varied from 20% for the dado gutters to complete replacement for the clerestory components. The replacement of decorative items was limited to missing components. Repairs were to be by the Metalock stitching process.

Each different component was drawn up as accurately as possible so that meaningful estimates could be obtained from foundries. An example of the drawings is shown in Fig. 6. There was a temptation to re-detail some of the components, particularly gutter components, in order to reduce corrosion traps etc., but changes were very minor and limited to non-visible items in order to retain the original appearance. Some thicknesses were increased to give more protection.

It was originally intended that the worst affected structural members would be replaced in austenitic iron to give increased corrosion resistance. However, the fall in the value of the pound against the dollar led to a rapid jump in the cost differential against other irons (because of the cost of nickel etc.). It was therefore decided that all of the structural members would be replaced in ductile iron since it was hoped that the increased tensile strength would be more resistant to cracking after corrosion.

As quality of fit and control of supply were of paramount considerations, the Contractor was limited to a maximum of two foundries. We assessed five foundries who were capable of doing the work and their addresses were given in the document. It is a measure of buoyancy of the foundry business at that time that three of these firms stopped trading between the dates of printing and tender return.

As it was known that the grid dimensions varied by ±12mm, and thought desirable that castings be put back from whence they came, a coding system was devised, whereby each casting was tagged with its individual number before removal. New castings had the number stamped on.

CIVIL WORKS AND MARINE DISPLAY

The Client had requested that the rain water run-off be re-used in the humidification system to reduce the dependency on relatively expensive de-ionised water.   There was much discussion on the optimum size of storage tanks as it appeared that the rain water would be used at a faster rate than deposited. Eventually, however, it was decided to use two 50,000 gallon concrete tanks. The drainage system is valved so that the effluent from wash down can be directed into the foul drainage.

Since the two north and south existing basements were in poor condition and suffered from lack of headroom, it was found necessary to rebuild them completely with a lower floor.   Owing to the lack of space it was also necessary for the new walls to follow the lines of the existing, and sheet piling was provided to protect the existing foundations.

It had been Kew's intention to take on a marine biologist to design and set up the Marine Display in a new basement located between the existing North and South basements.   He did not appear until the design phase of the project was virtually complete.   This meant that the design team had to forecast his needs as best they might.   We therefore provided a basic concrete box accessed by two concrete helical staircases positioned below the iron spirals used to climb up to the gallery (See Fig. 7).   The central portion of the roof is domed.   Columns and ring beams are formed from abraded white concrete.   Permanent sheet piling is used to protect the adjacent foundations.

The arrival of the marine biologist has allowed the internal design to firm-up.   There will be a range of tanks visible by the public including a coral reef and a mangrove swamp.   Some of the tanks will be tidal.   About half of the total area is for non-public use only and will be used for Mechanical and electrical plant and propagation.

MAINTENANCE

External maintenance has been carried out from a series of curved aluminium ladders which rested on the glazing bars.   These had the distinct disadvantage of requiring personnel to stand on the glazing bars (perhaps hanging on to gutters) in order to move the top of the ladder.   Internal maintenance necessitated full scaffolding out from ground level.

We initially proposed the use of permanent walkways along all the lanterns, but the Client was reluctant to accept this for aesthetic reasons.   We then made a comprehensive survey of the cherry picker and moving gantry market.   The best machine for our use was the Danish "Spider" hydraulic platform which could cover the building externally up to gallery level, but could be folded down to go through the doors and give access comprehensively internally.   Rapid technical development may result in alternative platforms being available by Contract completion.

Above gallery level we have provided four moveable gantry ladders, one for each side, which are operated from gallery gutter level.

TEMPORARY HOUSE

Various types of temporary accommodation for the plants were investigated. These included fabric covered tent-like structures and/or inflatables as the User had in mind the future use after completion. It soon became clear that the most efficacious structure was the wide-span glasshouse, although a sophisticated heating system was incorporated to avoid damage to the plants. The roof had a maximum clear height of 8 metres, however larger plants were installed in a pit.

RBG Kew had spent the winter putting all of the plants into pots. The actual move then took a very efficient nine days only. Some of the cycads are extremely "bent" and we therefore designed lifting frames out of scaffolding to enable them to be relocated.

SERVICES

The survey of the mechanical and electrical services had shown that the boilers had reached the end of their useful life. Moreover, the existing heating system of pipes under the plant shelves was extremely inefficient and polythene protection was required on the glazing to prevent cold down draughts in the winter.

The restoration project includes for a complete new boiler system which heats radiators in the service trenches. Humidification will be provided by semi-automatic compressed air and water misting.

The ventilation of the house had originally been provided by the vents in the dado wall, opening clerestory windows, and sliding sashes. It is not known when the sliding sashes last worked, or if they ever did, but the windows have not been openable for many years.

The windows and dado vents are to be refurbished and motorised to allow ventilation at the touch of a button.

DISCUSSIONS WITH CONSERVATION BODIES

It soon became clear that any changes to the building would be critically assessed by various "watch-dogs" including the Historic Buildings and Monuments Commission and the Victorian Society. We therefore prepared a brochure which outlined our proposals in detail. This was presented to about twelve interested bodies at a reception at Kew, and followed by a similar presentation to the Royal Fine Arts Commission.

We had expected a reaction to the glazing proposals, particularly the use of stainless steel, but had not perhaps anticipated the strength of feeling which opposed changes to the internal layout, including the removal of the plant shelf, provision of plant beds, and access to the Marine Display from around a central tank.

After many meetings it was decided to keep the floor and shelf layout at the apse ends as the original. The small iron columns supporting the plant shelf (which were no longer the original slate but 1950's concrete) are to be used to line the beds with a capping of slate. None of the marine display is now to be visible from the ground floor.

TENDER DOCUMENTS

As in all restoration projects there were various types of documentation to consider. For this project it was felt that the survey and subsequent detailed drawings justified a lump sum bid. There would have been some advantages in having a two stage contract, i.e. a split into dismantling and re-erection but the time span given for the temporary housing of the plants did not allow for this. Furthermore, it was felt advisable to have the same contractor re-erect whatever he had dismantled.

As the budget exceeded £0.5 million the project was advertised in the EEC. There were 42 replies (none from outside the U.K.). Of these 19 were interviewed and whittled down to 9 tenderers.

SITE WORKS

One of the problems of working on the site is the lack of working area.The Contractor has only been allowed the area within the ivy hedge surrounding the building. Consequently all fabrication work was expected to be done off-site.

Work started in September 1985. The dismantling of the cast iron work progressed very well. There has been a tendency to repair more castings than envisaged, partly because of the comparatively high cost of some of the patterns and foundry work particularly in relation to those castings curved on plan or in elevation. This has led to welding repairs being used as well as metal stitching, although both types of repair are carried out in the same shop. The overall cost of repair/replacement, however, remains approximately as the tender figure.

The most significant change to the project has been the discovery that the welding of the outer Tee section to the arch ribs was of extremely poor quality, although it had looked adequate at the lower levels. The Tee itself was badly corroded in many areas and, when removed, often revealed a rib flange in a similar state. Many of the joints in ribs had laminated, and cracks had appeared between flanges and webs. The latter were difficult to track as it was difficult to see the difference between a crack and a rolling mark.

These discoveries led to extensive repairs including the replacement of the Tee with a mild steel flat, replacement of some flanges, the addition of web plates, and a consequent extension of the Contract by nearly six months.

There were few people (if any) who were experienced in the erection of structural ironwork. Consequently there was an extensive 'learning curve' during the initial stage of reconstruction but these difficulties were soon overcome.

The completed restoration was handed to the Client in November, 1988.

REFERENCE

1   Diestelkamp. E.J., The Design and Building of the Palm House, Royal Botanic Gardens, Kew.
    Journal of Garden History Vol. 2 No. 3 233-272.

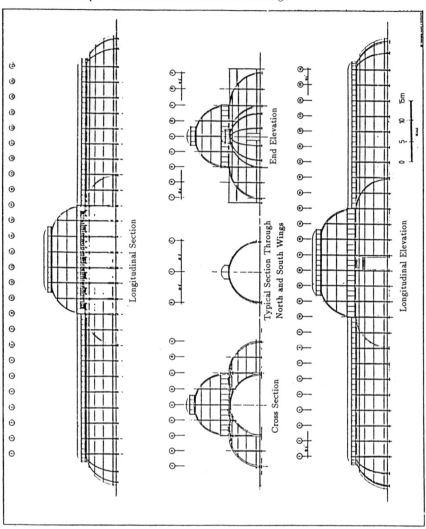

FIG.1

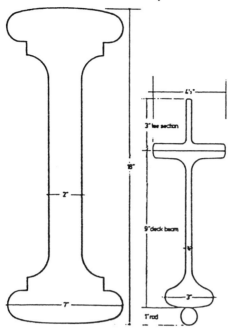

Figure 18. Proposed cast iron rib as per specifications and working drawings (April 1844).
Wrought iron rib as adopted for the Palm House (June 1845).

Fig. 2.

LEGEND TO FIG. 3

1a Arch Rib
1b Arch Rib Tee
1c Wave Moulding Fixing Point
1d Dado Gutter Fixing Strap

2a Glazing Bar
2b Flat Glazing Rail
2c Angle Glazing Rail
2d Tie Rod

3a Glazing Bar
3b Angle Glazing Rail
3c Angle Glazing Rail
3d Tie Rod

4 Dado Gutter

5 Masonry Collar

6 Decorative Scroll

7 Wave Moulding

8a Tubular Purlin
8b Tie Rod
8c Bar Purlin
8d Decorative Rosette

9 Clerestory Tee

10a Cill Beam
10b Cover Plate
10c Gutter/Flashing

11a Pilaster
11b Pilaster Shoe
11c Pilaster Strut

12 Mullion

13 Clerestory Pivotted Window

14 Heating Pipe

15 Window Operating Gear

16a Clerestory Gutter
16b Clerestory Gutter Spigot

17a Glazing Bar
17b Flat Glazing Rail
17c Tie Rod

REDUCED · DO NOT SCALE

Drg NO 3733/ 3072   B

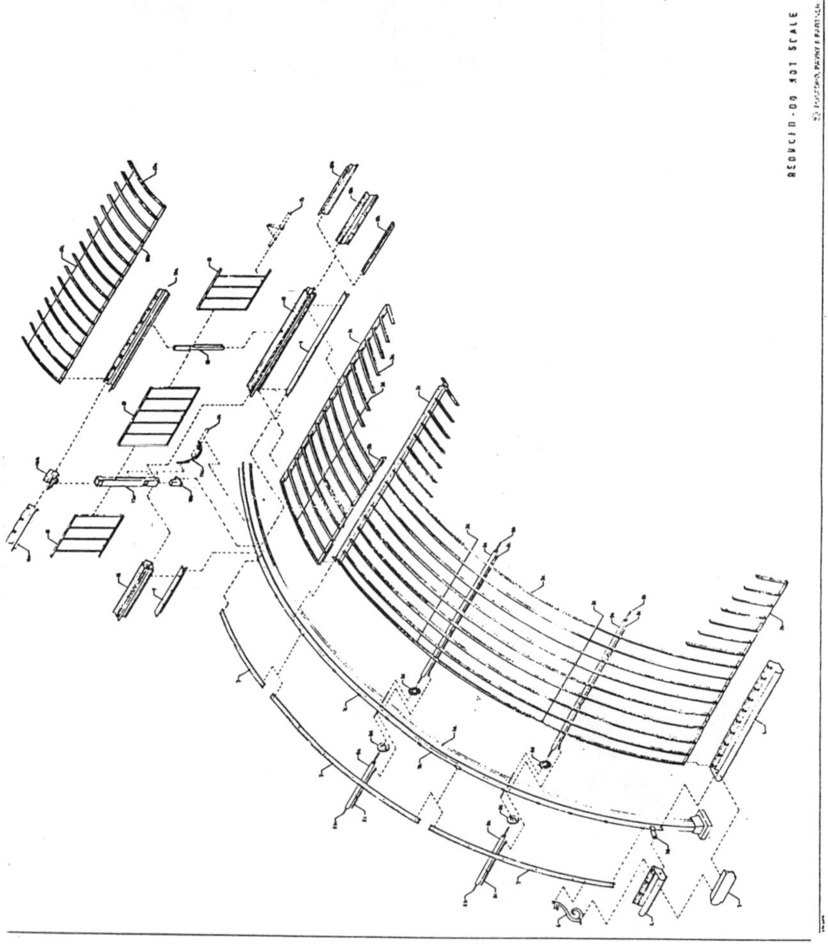

Fig. 3

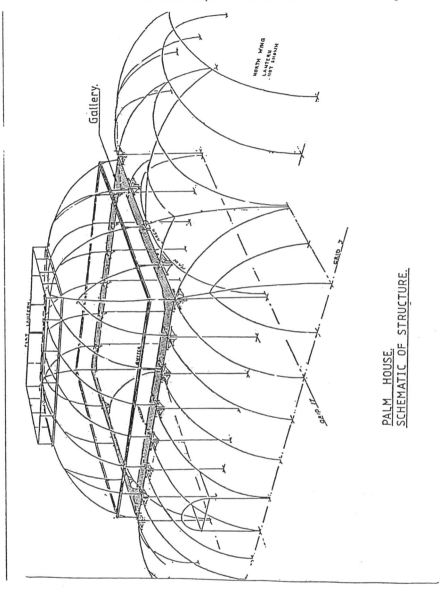

PALM HOUSE.
SCHEMATIC OF STRUCTURE.

Fig. 4.

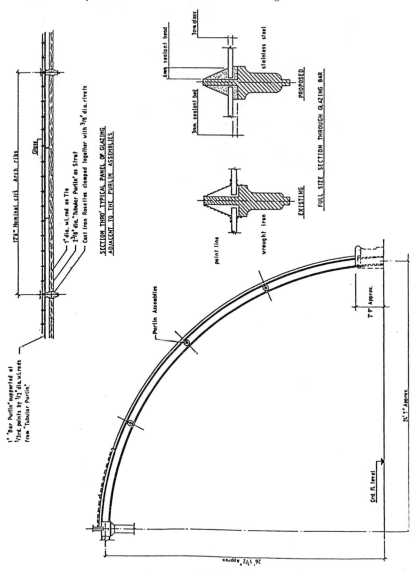

Fig. 5

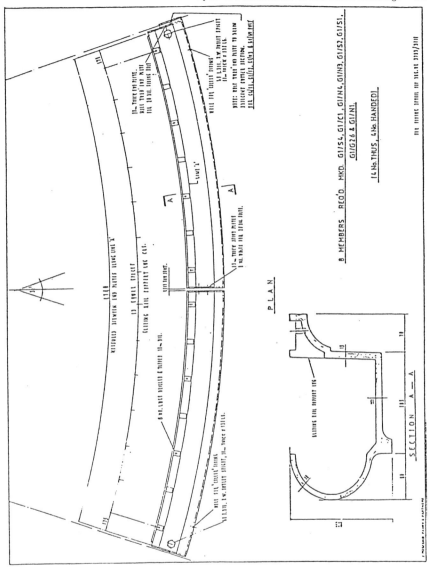

FIG.6

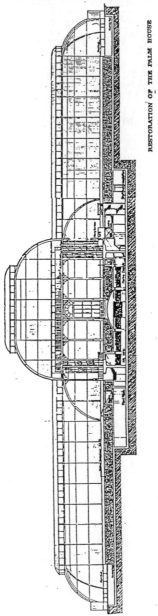

Fig. 7

Case Study: Stanhope Street Convent, Dublin

Ursula Schamberg

Department of Architecture, University College, Dublin 4, Ireland

Introduction

The old Stanhope Street Convent building is a fine 19th century stucture. It has been occupied by the Sisters of Charity up to late 1987.
Since the construction of a new convent the original building is surplus to the needs of the Order. But the building has been well maintained and is in good structural condition. So the Order decided to donate it to a voluntary housing association. It is presently being converted into housing for homeless people in Dublin. It is innovative for a historcal institutional building to be used in this way.

The building has many fine brick and stone features. The interior has fine examples of carved timber doors, wall panelling, window shutters and staircases.

History of Stanhope St Convent

It is difficult to date the building, which is the basis of my report. Although the building is not very old, it was certainly built in the last century. But in those times it was just an addition.
The first house on the site dated back to the 16th century. It was one of the fine manor houses, which were built during the Reformation, when the large estate of Grangegorman was divided up and distributed by Henry VIII to the Protestants (O'Shea Donnelly [1]). In 1814 this manor house was taken over by the Sisters of Charity. Shortly after they moved into the house they built a large extension (Sarah Atkinsen [2]). This structure will now be converted into housing for homeless people. In 1870 a chapel was built by George Coppinger Ashlin. In 1908 he altered the extension which by now was the main building. Since then only small changes have been made (The Irish Builder [3-6]).

The alterations were made by lengthening the front of the building towards Stanhope Street. He designed a symmetrical facade with the main entrance in the centre. George Ashlin composed the elevation very clearly. He was very concerned about the balance in the facade. He designed beautiful features around the windows. He treated the windows of the ground floor, first floor and second floor level all differently (fig.1).

Unfortunately he was not too concerned by the architectual space inside. He did not really try to combine his alterations to the front of the building with the existing older building behind. Of course the decoration and detailing runs through the whole house, but he did not manage to harmonise the two parts of the building. The entrance to the house is very unsatisfactory as you are immediately confronted with a corridor system which gives access to various rooms. These are not nessessarily reception rooms, but are parlours and bedrooms of the nuns. There is no staircase nearby which leads to the upper storeys.

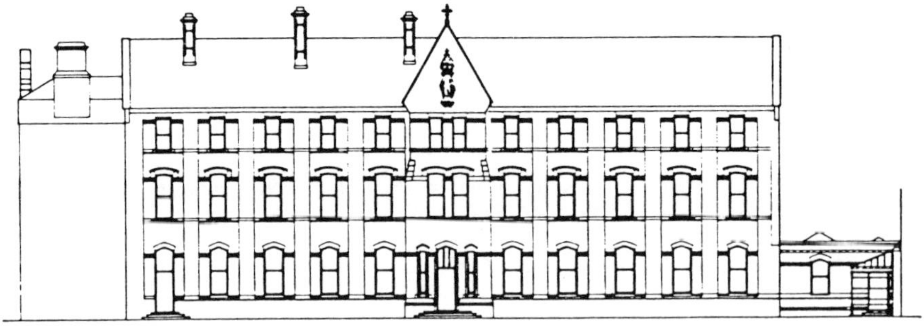

Fig. 1:   South elevation of the old convent

Then about 20 years ago the old convent building became surplus to the needs of the Order, because they no longer took boarders. About that time the Richmond Hospital was looking for rooms. So they rented a number of rooms in the convent. In 1987 when the Richmond Hospital moved to Beaumont they had no longer any use for the rooms in Stanhope Street.

Since then those rooms have been vacant. The nuns, feeling uncomfortable in the big old house, built a smaller house just beside the old one. The architect was Mr. David Crowley. To get space for this new house the nuns made the decision to demolish the old manor house and George Ashlin's chapel (fig.3).

Since that time the nuns have changed their policy. Instead of demolishing the old convent, they decided to donate the building for conversion to residential use for homeless people. An association has been formed to carry out this project. This association will be grant-aided by the Department of the Environment through the administration of Dublin Corporation. The design work is being carried out by Mr. Gerry Cahill.

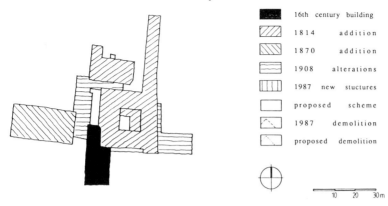

16th century building
1814 addition
1870 addition
1908 alterations
1987 new stuctures
proposed scheme
1987 demolition
proposed demolition

10   20   30 m

Fig. 2: Site plan up to the year 1987

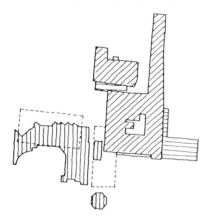

Fig. 3: Site plan in 1987/88

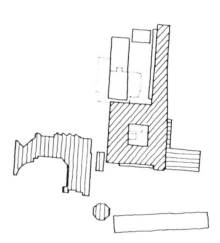

Fig. 4: Proposed site plan

The new design by Mr. Gerry Cahill, architect

Basically Mr. Gerry Cahill will convert the old building into several self contained residential units and communal rooms. The ground floor will contain a caretakers apartment, administration rooms and three residential units, which would be suitable for the disabled.
The centre of the building will be the existing courtyard and it will become a rooflit space, which will contain a restaurant and common room.
The first and second floors will be identical. They will be converted into 25 single and 6 double units on each floor.
In front of the old building a new house will be erected. This new structure will contain 10 2-bedroom houses. They will have their own private gardens.
At the back of the old house the kitchen building will be demolished. In its place another new structure will be built, which will accomodate 8 1-bedroom flats. These flats will look onto a yard to the east and a garden to the west.
The long back wing of the old building, which is at present two storeys high will be raised and another storey will be added.

The issue of conservation and reuse has always been controversial. There is the problem of what to preserve and how to alter a building or structure to adapt it to modern needs. Not everything that is old should be preserved. It is more a question of keeping the character of a place.
The character of Stanhope St Convent is not formed by the architectual space but it is the detailing and decoration of the exterior and interior. So these features should be kept. Where they cannot be preserved they should be replaced by new designs which are based and developed on those old features.

The general idea of housing for homeless people on this site follows on the caring tradition of Stanhope St Convent. The site is suitable, as it is a detached house surrounded by gardens. There is no immediate neighbourhood to be disturbed. The house as it is big was always meant to serve a large number of people and has been divided into a series of small rooms. So there are no major structural changes resulting from the new use.

Today hardly any architectual attractive spaces are left in the building with the exception of a wooden staircase, which once connected the convent with the manor house and the Ashlin chapel, and a front room at second floor level. The staircase is beautiful, because as you ascend it turns around a rectangular centre space which is rooflit. Additional attractive features are wooden steps, carved wooden railings and wall panelling. The front room at second floor level extends over a large space and its attractive feature is the combination of a big room with an arched ceiling. From its windows you have a marvellous view over the area.

The main features of the proposal by Mr. Gerry Cahill will be the rooflit atrium. His design will create an effective entrance and a focal point for the building. The strong centre atrium will help to combine the building and to experience it as one unit. The new design will be a combination of attractive new spaces and beautiful old detailings.

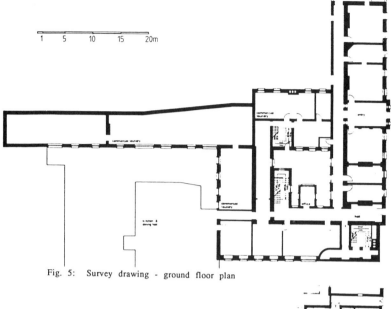

Fig. 5: Survey drawing - ground floor plan

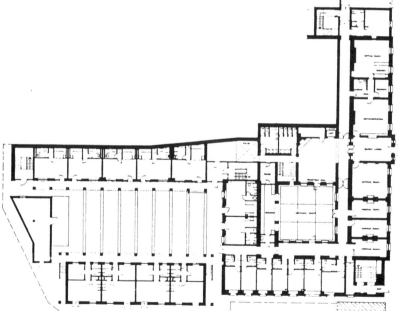

Fig. 6: Proposed design - ground floor plan

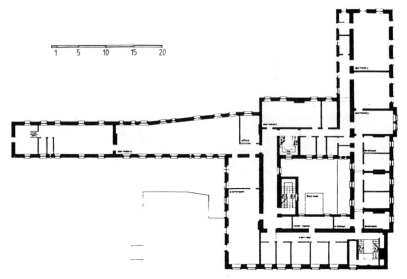

Fig. 7: Survey drawing - first floor plan

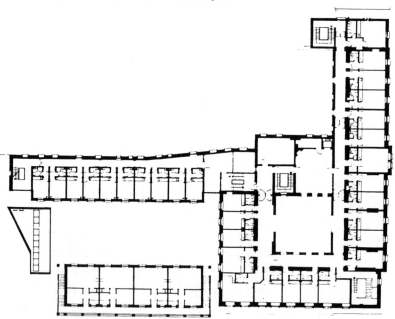

Fig. 8: Proposed design - first floor plan

Structural   and   technical   problems

Together with the architect the structural engineers have spent considerable time opening up the old building. They have analysed the structure, stress graded the timbers and investigated the foundations. The design team has examined the structural potential of the old building for its new uses. Also a detailed examination has been made of the problems associated with adapting the building to comply with modern fire regulations.

Existing roofing timbers and flooring timbers
The report from the structural engineer concerning roofing timbers, flooring timbers and rising damp contains most of the typical problems of a building of this age.
The timber in the front wall and section of the right-hand wall of the quadrangle is attacked by the true dry rot fungus, Serpula (Merulius) lacrymans. The attack affects the first floor and second floor joists of the front corridor, also window and door frames and lintel timbers at ground, first and second floor level. As a result some major structural weakening has taken place.
There is evidence of woodworm attack in the roofing timbers and the ground, first and second floor flooring boards and joists. So far the attacked timber is not structurally weakened.
As well an outbreak of wet rot, Coniophoral. (puteana) cerebella, was noted in a whole range of areas: as in the roof valley rafters over the front entrance projection, roofing timbers over the front left-hand stairwell and embedded bond timbers in the external wall of the stairwell, embedded ends of floor joists at first and second floor levels, window and door frame timbers in the dividing wall between the kitchen and laundry area and dado panelling in general on ground floor level.
In order to get rid of the fungal attack of the timber all structurally weakened timbers are going to be cut out and burned. Timbers which are not structurally weakened will be saved and chemically treated. Replacement timbers will be pre-treated with wood preservative that will resist wood rotting fungi and boring beetles. Where necessary flooring boards will be lifted and joisting and supporting timbers will be chemically treated. All joinery timbers in contact with the damp brickwork will be removed. Bond timbers will be replaced with bricks bedded in mortar.
It has to be mentioned that the installation of the new central heating system-which will be an effective improvement to the existing installation- will not be contemplated before the fungal attacked timber is treated. The introduction of sustained heat will cause the moisture content of damp timber to fall within the limits between which the true dry rot fungus can originate and spread.

Since the sub-floor ventilation is poor additional vents will be fitted in order to provide a "through" circulation of air.

Brickwork
Rainwater penetration has to be stopped. It is caused by the porosity of the exposed brickwork, cracks in renderings, defective window sills and most of all by the poor condition of the rainwater goods.
The roof coverings will be upgraded. Gutters and downpipes will be repaired. Downpipes will be refixed 2" free of wall. The brickwork will be repointed and decaying bricks will be replaced. There is the possibility of using the good bricks of one of the staircases which will be demolished. This staircase was extended into the quadrangle yard some time after 1908. The bricks used here aren't produced anymore.

Foundations and rising damp

While exposing the foundations the ground conditions showed up. Black top soil of about 50mm depth is followed by a clay or rubble fill of about 300 to 900mm depth. Then follows a very moist or wet stoney silty clay.

There is no existance of a damp proof course in this building. This is very common for a structure of that age. But under those conditions it is no surprise that there is considerable evidence of rising damp causing staining of the internal decoration. The moisture meter showed high moisture content in all external and party walls.

Water is the most dangerous chemical to nearly all building materials. Much damage is caused by rising damp. Water is a carrier for water soluble salts and leads to efflorescence, destroys brickwork and joint mortar and may even cause fungus infestation. These salts may be originally present in the brickwork and mortar, or they may be derived from air pollution such as oxides of carbon and sulphur, or they may be carried up from the ground by the water. Rising damp is a result of capillary action, which increases with the decreasing diameter of the capillaries.

The most commonly used method in building repair is chemical protection. Usually good results are achieved by impregnating foundation walls using injection techniques. Of course, the efficiency of chemicals to prevent rising damp depends on the condition of the brickwork and joint mortar as well as on the mechanisms of the chemistry involved. Therefore cracks or gaps, which cause water penetration from the outside, will be sealed with cement grout, mortar or sealants. Crumbling or cracked joints have to be repaired and any other sources of water penetration eliminated.

However the chemicals presently in use to prevent rising damp are either aqueous or solvent systems. Since there are many risks implied using aqueous waterglass products the solvent systems are recommended. In solvent systems film forming low molecular weight organosiloxanes or organosilanes are used, which are highly hydrophobic and show no additional salt formation. These chemicals are assumed to coat the available capillaries and pores due to their high penetration. The resins decrease the surface tension of the coated capillaries pemanently, which reduces the capillary forces (E. Schamberg and H. Fritsch [7]).

Adapting the building to comply with modern fire regulations

Since the statutory controls have not been designed specifically for historic buildings, the application of the regulation depends on the circumstances of the case. Modern fire regulations affect historic buildings in various ways, depending on their use, the way in which these uses change, and the alterations which those buildings undergo.

The old convent building is going to be converted into several self contained units. With this change of use there are various recommendations from the fire department (Alan C. Parnell [8]).

Construction For approval under the Building Regulations, the floors require a more significant fire resistance. Some of the ceilings have plaster cornices and central mouldings. To contribute to the fire resistance the existing ceiling has to be taken down. Decorative features will be carefully cut out. Than two layers of fireline board will be fixed directly to the underside of the timber joists. The fireline board will provide one hour fire resistance. This applies for both existing and new constructions. The fireline board than can either just painted or where existing decorative features will be put up again and adjacent ceilings will be plastered.

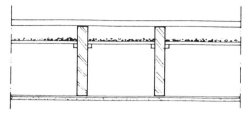

1 "   floorboard

1/2 " boarding on timber beads
          with 1/2" pugging (sand)

          timber joist   300 x 45mm

7/8" lath and plaster ceiling

Fig.9: typical   existing
        floor   construction

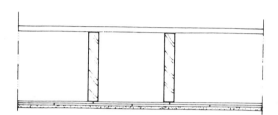

two layers of fireline board

old ceiling

Fig. 10: upgraded   floor
          construction

<u>Wooden doors and dado panelings</u> The old wooden doors have to be upgraded.
The frame, which is 50mm in width, is accepted as fire resistant. But the thin
panels unfortunatelly have to be changed into sheets of insulation board. S o
the doors will be taken out, taken apart. timber will be treated, than they will
be set together and put back again.
Dado paneling will be kept on the public corridores. They will be infilled with
fire resistant material.

<u>New light weight partitons</u> The existing soft board partitons will be taken out
and replaced by light weight metal stud partitons. The system consists o f
tapered edge gypsum plasterboards, which are screw-fixed to the light weight
metal sections. They can provide a high level of fire resistance and sound
insulation.

two layers of 12.5mm
wallboard each side of
48mm metal studs

Fig. 11:   new light weight metal partitions

<u>Means of escape</u> Two of the existing staircases will remain. They will be separated from the building by a lobby. So that from each floor level the enclosed staircase leads directly into open space. Additionally two further staircases will be built. Fortunately they are not external fire escapes, but the old building has enough room to take them.

References

1. M. O'Shea Donnelly "A short history of some Dublin Parishes" Catholic Truth Society Dublin. 1912
2. Sarah Atkinsen "Mary Aikenhead, her life, her work and her friends" Dublin 1906
3. The Irish Builder Dublin 1870 Vol 12 page 205
4. The Irish Builder Dublin May 15 1870 page 114
5. The Irish Builder Dublin Dec 28 1907 no.26-Vol-XLIX and Engineer
6. The Irish Builder Dublin Jan 25 1908 no.2-Vol-L and Engineer
7. E. Schamberg and H. Fritsch "A silicone treatment to prevent rising damp" Goldschmidt *informiert* Th. Goldschmidt AG Dec 1986 no.64 Vol-1/86
8. Alan C. Parnell Historic Buildings The Architectural Press London 1987

SECTION 8 - COMPUTER AIDED SIMULATION

Analytical Model for Masonry using the Finite Element Method

C. Ignatakis, E. Stavrakakis and G. Penelis

Department of Civil Engineering, Aristotle University of Thessaloniki 54 006, Thessaloniki, Greece

ABSTRACT

An analytical model for the behaviour of masonry under in-plane loading is presented. The masonry units and the mortar joints are modelled separately each with its own non-linear material characteristics. The main advantage of the model is the successful consideration of the transverse principal stress which is developed during the in-plane loading of masonry. For this purpose a complete triaxial material model (constitute law and failure criterion) has been developed and is presented briefly. Finally the results from the analysis of masonry models are compared with the experimental findings from the literature and a very good agreement is found.

INTRODUCTION

Masonry is a material which exhibits distinct directional properties because the mortar joints act as planes of weakness. With the advent of computer-based numerical techniques, various attempts have been made to model the in-plane behaviour of masonry (Page-Samarasinghe-Hendry [1]). The main problem encountered by all investigators has been the lack of a representative material model. For convenience, masonry is often modelled as an isotropic, elastic material. Various investigators have used elastic models in conjunction with some allowance for local failure in regions of high tensile stresses. A finite element model capable of predicting joint failure in brick masonry but not a composite failure involving both brick and joint has been developed by Page [2].

The development of the analytical models makes imperative the necessity of reliable experimental data on the behaviour of masonry under in plane loading. Remarkable efforts in this field have been made by Samarasinghe and Hendry [3] and expecially by Page [4] [5]. Page provides failure envelopes of masonry under biaxial stress states for several principal stress ratios and joint orientations and also provides the stress-strain curves for all the specimens tested. Page, Kleeman and Dhanesekar [6] [7], after a numerical investigation of the experimental data mentioned above, have developed an in-plane F.E. model for brick masonry. They make use of a macroscopic continuum model of the stress-strain and failure envelope of masonry which is directly related to the experimental data. Obviously, for a masonry with a different structural layout or for different material properties, there is a need for a new series of both experimental and analytical investigations.

An effort for the development of an analytical model for the in-plane behaviour of masonry until failure, has taken place in the Reinforced Concrete Laboratory of Aristotle University of Thessaloniki Greece. Masonry units and mortar joints have been modelled separately each with its own non linear triaxial constitutive law and failure surface. This model is capable of simulating damages in units, mortar or joints and predicting both joint or composite type failure, due to in-plane stresses in conjunction with the transverse third principal stress which is inevitably developed. This transverse stress (σ_z) proved to be the governing factor of the behaviour of masonry.

PRESENTATION OF THE ANALYTICAL MODEL

At the Reinforced Concrete Lab. of Aristotle Univ. of Thessaloniki a F.E. Program (RECOFIN) has been developed and succesfully used (Penelis et al. [8] [9]) for the analytical representation of the nonlinear behaviour of reinforced concrete for plane stress state, including crack pattern, until failure. The general structure of the RECOFIN program and some of its basic routines are incorporated into the new program for the analysis of masonry (MAFEA: MAsonry Finite Element Analysis).

Geometry of the Model and Loading Pattern
As mentioned above masonry units and mortar joints are modelled separately. Each unit is automatically divided into a certain number of rectangular elements and each one of them is diagonally subdivided into four simple triangular elements. For the sake of limitating the total number of elements the mortar joints are not divided in the sense of their thickness. There are three types of mortar elements (I, II, III, see figure 1) according to their position in a bed or in a header joint or at the intersection of them. The model accepts nodal or self weight loads automatically transformed to nodal forces. The loading is applied incrementally and monotonically.

The Transverse Principal Stress (σ_z)

It is known that the uniaxial compressive strength of masonry is always greater than the corresponding strength of the weaker "associate" (mortar or masonry unit) (Hendry [10]). On the other hand, masonry fails under biaxial compression mainly due to splitting of units (Page [4]). The failure strength of masonry is higher than the corresponding biaxial strength of mortar which, in spite of this, does not fail. At the same time the failure strength of masonry is lower than the corresponding biaxial strength of the masonry units which, in spite of this, fail. These inconsistencies are remedied by the introduction of the transverse stress (σ_z) into the model which proved to be essential for the successful representation of the behaviour of masonry.

Analytical model for the evaluation of transverse stress (σ_z)   Francis

et al. [11] have given a simple model for the evaluation of the transverse stress in uniaxially loaded masonry piers. With a suitable modification of the analytical procedure for in-plane loading, equations for
the transverse stresses of the mortar (σ_{zm}) and of the masonry units
(σ_{zb}) have been derived, in a coordinate system orientated to the directions of the joints (see fig. 1). The equations have the following form:

$$\sigma_{zm} = f(\sigma_{xm}, \sigma_{ym}, \sigma_{xb}, \sigma_{yb}, \nu_m, \nu_b, \lambda_A, \lambda_E) \qquad (1)$$

$$\sigma_{zb} = -(\sigma_{zm} / \lambda_A) \qquad (2)$$

where
$\sigma_{xm}, \sigma_{ym}, \sigma_{xb}, \sigma_{yb}$: The in plane normal stresses of mortar and brick
in contact
ν_m, ν_b : The Poisson's ratios of mortar and brick
λ_A = Ab/Am: The ratio of corresponding surfaces of brick (Ab) and mortar joint (Am) as they are geometrically defined in the figure 1. For a
slender masonry pier this ratio is proved to be the unit/mortar-joint
thickness ratio but for a plane wall it must be defined separately for
each of the three types of mortar elements (I, II, III, see figure 1).
λ_E = Eb/Em: The unit/mortar Modulus of Elasticity ratio.

A parametric investigation proved that the influence of λ_E on the
value of (σ_{zm}) is much greater than the influence of λ_A. On the other
hand, λ_A is a constant geometrical characteristic of masonry, while the
value of λ_E is greatly affected by the stress state of masonry. This
fact is due to the non-linear behaviour of the materials. For a masonry
unit stiffer than the mortar, the value of λ_E approaches very large
values close to failure. For this reason, the equations of (σ_{zm}, σ_{zb})
must be introduced into the analytical model in an incremental form. The
additive process which has been applied for the in plane strains and
stresses must also be applied for the transverse principal stresses (σ_z).
The factor λ_E must now be considered as the unit/mortar ratio of instantaneous values of modulus of Elasticity for the present loading step:
$$\lambda_E^{inst.} = E_b^{inst.} / E_m^{inst.}$$
The transverse stresses (σ_{zm}, σ_{zb}) could be included in the model
only if it has a triaxial failure criterion. On the other hand a reliable
calculation of the transverse stresses depends on a correct value of the
factor $\lambda_E^{inst.}$ for which a triaxial constitutive material model is needed.

Failure Surface for Triaxial Stress State

Due to the lack of experimental data mainly for Bricks and secondly for
Mortars under biaxial and triaxial stress states, it is assumed   that
their behaviour is similar to that of a concrete with equal uniaxial compressive strength. An extensive numerical investigation of the experimental data from the works of Kupter et al. [12], Schickert and Winkler
[13] and Ferrara et al. [14] has been carried out and a continouus failure
surface for triaxial stress state has been composed (see figure 2). The
failure surface is constituted by three families of curves for each one
of the triaxial tension, tension-compression and triaxial compression
region. The surface is closed in the first, instead of being open in
the latest region. The planes defined by couples of equal principal
stresses are planes of symmetry of the failure surface. The figures 2a,

2b and 2c show correspondingly a hydrostatic section, two deviatory sections and a section of the failure surface by the plane ($\sigma_3=\emptyset$). The latest is an analytical representation of the well known biaxial failure envelope of concrete-like materials (Kupfer et al. [11] and it has been used as a guide curve for the formation of the failure surface. In figures 2a, 2c the distinction between the cracking and crushing zone of the failure surface is shown.

Triaxial Constitutive Model
Due to lack of experimental data, the development of a rather simple incremental elastic model has been chosen. The model makes use of the well known equations of linear triaxial elasticity (Hooke's law) in an incremental form. It also requires the uniaxial stress-strain curve (see figure 3) and the failure surface of the material which was presented above. For an element under a given stress state the stress vector $\bar{\sigma}$ (σ_1, σ_2, σ_3) in pricipal streess is known. The corresponding equivalent stress (σ^e) and the equivalent stress-strain curve (see figure 3) are defined as follows:
a.   The ultimate stress vector $\bar{\sigma}_u$ (σ_{1u}, σ_{2u}, σ_{3u}) is defined from the failure surface (see figure 2a).
b.   The safety factor (c) of the element and a multiplier (K), for the uniaxial ultimate strain (ε_{1u}) of the material, defined as follows:

$$c = |\bar{\sigma}_u/\bar{\sigma}| \quad (\text{or } c = f_c/|\bar{\sigma}| \text{ if } f_c > |\bar{\sigma}_u|) \tag{3}$$

$$K = f(\sigma_{1u}, \sigma_{2u}, \sigma_{3u}, f_c) \tag{4}$$

where f_c is the uniaxial cylindrical strength of the material.
c.   Equivalent stress: $\sigma^e = f_c/c$ (5)
d.   Equivalent ultimate strain: $\varepsilon_u^c = K * \varepsilon_{1u}$ (6)

By substituting the ε_{1u} with the ε_u^e in the equation of uniaxial stress-strain curve, the equation of the equivalent stress-strain curve is derived. The slope of the latest curve at the value of the equivalent stress σ^e gives the instantaneous modulus of elasticity ($E^{inst.}$) for the element under consideration at the present loading increment.

Using the data of Kupfer et al. [11] a modification function for the Poisson's ratio is developed (progressive increase from an initial value of about 0.2 to a final value at failure, depending on the stress state).

A very good matching for biaxial stress states and a good one for triaxial stress states has been observed in comparison with experimental data. It has to be mentioned that the experimental data for triaxial stress state shows a considerable scatter.

Failure Criterion for Mortar Joints
A criterion for joint failure is incorporated as a property of mortar elements. Each one of them is checked firstly for its principal stresses using the failure surface for mortar and secondly for the couple of in-plane normal and shear stresses (σ_n, τ) in the direction of joint, using the failure criterion shown in figure 4 (Hamid et al. [15]). The bilinear failure curve needs three parameters to be defined, namely the strength of the joint in direct tension (σ_t), the shear bond strength under zero

normal stress (τ_c) and the coefficient of friction μ (see figure 4).
The joint failure is characterized as unstickingfor $\sigma_n > \emptyset$ or sliding
for $\sigma_n \leq \emptyset$. The post-sliding joint failure criterion is represented
by the dashed line of figure 4.

Types of Damaged Elements

An essential part of the MAFEA program is the subroutine "CHECK" where
all the elements are checked according to the failure criteria presented
above.   The elements library of the model includes seven different types of damaged elements with the following features:

Element α: Intact brick or mortar element.

Element b: Brick or mortar element cracked (smeared model) perpendicular to the direction of the major principal tensile stress in plane. The
cracking stress is distributed to the nodes of the element dropping to
zero from now on. The modulus of elasticity in the direction normal to
the crack and the Shear modulus drop to zero as aggregate interlock assumed to be negligible.

Element c: Mortar element unstuck from the neighboring masonry unit.
The element is treated as a cracked one (type b). In the direction of
the joint.

Element d: Mortar element sliding relative to the masonry unit in contact. The shear stress (τ) drops to the value $\tau_s = \mu * \sigma_n$. The residual shear stress is distributed to the nodes of the element.

Element e: Brick or mortar element cracked in two perpendicular directions. The normal stress· perpendicular to the second crack is treated as
residual stress. The stiffness matrix of the element drops to zero from
now on.

Element f: Brick or mortar element cracked perpendicular to the transverse principle tensile stress (σ_z). The element retains its own stresses with the exception of σ_z, which together with the stiffness matrix
are dropped to zero.

Element g: Brick or mortar element crushed. The element retains its
own stresses but the matrix stiffness is dropped to zero.

Damaging process of the elements. All the physically possible evolutions
of already damaged elements are provided in the checking procedure, and
summarized in the following table.

Table 1. Damaging process of the elements

Type of new damage	Previous state of element						
	a	b	c	d	e	f	g
b	b	e	e	b			
c	c	e	c*	c	Fatal failure		
d	d	b	c*	d	No further checking		
f	f	f	f	f			
g	g	g	g	g			

*No further joint checking

Computational procedure

The well known technique of step by step loading is used. In each step the additional stresses and strains, including the transverse stress (σ_z), of each element are determined by using the resulting stiffness matrices from the stress state of the previous loading step. These stresses and strains are added to those of previous steps and a checking procedure follows. If no changes take place in the state of each element, the next loading step is applied. Otherwise the solution for the present step is repeated after the proper updating of the stiffness matrices of the newly damaged elements and after the addition of the unbalanced forces to the loading vector. Failure is assumed to occur and the computation is terminated when the mathematical procedure becomes unstable.

VERIFICATION OF THE ANALYTICAL MODEL

As mentioned in the introduction, one of the most complete experimental works on the behaviour of brick masonry under biaxial stress state was carried out at the Univ. of Newcastle, Australia (Page et. al. [4], [5], [6]). A total of 180 panels with five different bed joint orientations were tested for a range of principal stresses ratios. Ten of the panels were modelled and analyzed by the MAFEA computer program. The comparison between the experimental findings and the analytical results was very good with regard to the ultimate loads, the damage patterns and the type of failure. The analytical stress-strain curves show a rather constant underestimation of strains at about 25% in all cases, which could be attributed to the lack of information about some of the material properties required by the analytical model. In table 2 these properties are summarised.

Table 2. Material Properties of the Analytical Model

Required Material properties	Brick	Mortar
E_o : Initial modulus of Elasticity (GPa)	12.5	4.5 *
ν : Initial Poisson's ratio	0.15	0.20*
f_c: Uniaxial compressive strength (MPa)	15.0	3.5**
ε_{1u}: Ultimate strain under uniaxial compression	0.0025*	0.0025*
σ_t: Tensile bond strength of mortar joints (MPa)		0.13
τ_c: Shear bond strength (cohesion) of joints (MPa)		0.30
μ : Coefficient of friction of mortar joints		0.75*

 * Based on data from the literature
** Cylindrical strength (at 28 days) calculated from the cube strength (50 MPa) at 7 days.

The experimental failure envelopes in a principal stress system given by Page et al. [6] are shown in figure 5. The analytically determined points of failure of the ten models, analysed with the MAFEA program, are also indicated. The agreement with the experimental results is very good.

In figures 6,7 and 8 the analytical results of three of the models are presented. At the lower part of the figure the panel, the corresponding model with their loadings and the experimental and analytical stress strain curves are presented. At the upper part of the figure the damage patterns at failure and at a previous loading step are drawn following the legend of damaged elements of figure 1.

Figure 6 refers to a model uniaxially loaded perpendicularly to the bed joints ($\Theta=\emptyset^0$). Unsticking of header joints starts at early loading steps ($\sigma_y=3.38$ MPa). Some crushes of previously unstuck mortar elements are observed near failure. Finally, failure occurs at $\sigma_y=8.11$MPa due to crushes of bed joints mortar elements accompanied by vertical cracking of neighboring brick elements.

Figure 7 refers to a biaxially loaded ($\sigma_x/\sigma_y=1.0$) model ($\Theta=\emptyset^0$). The model sustaines the increasing loads without damage. Some crushes of header joint mortar elements are observed near failure ($\sigma_x=\sigma_y=7.89$ MPa). Finally, failure occurs at $\sigma_x=\sigma_y=8.45$ MPa mainly due to splitting and cracking of brick elements accompanied by extensive crushes of mostly bed and secondly header mortar-joint elements.

Figure 8 refers to a biaxially loaded ($\sigma_x/\sigma_y=10.0$) model ($\Theta=\emptyset^0$). Sliding of bed joints starts at early loading steps ($\sigma_x=4.50$ MPa) and is increased from now on. Extensive crushes of header joints observed near failure ($\sigma_x=9.00$ MPa). Finally failure occurs at $\sigma_x=9.60$ MPa due to extensive horizontal cracking and limited splitting of brick elements.

CONCLUSIONS

The analytical model (MAFEA computer program) presented above proved to be capable of predicting the ultimate loads and displacements, the damage pattern and the failure mode of masonry subjected to in plane loading. The main advantage of the model is the succesful consideration of the transverse principal stress. The development of a triaxial constitutive material model and the composition of a failure surface in the space of principal stresses were essential for both the correct calculation and the realistic contribution of the transverse stress (σ_z) to the behaviour of masonry. The model was verified   against experimental data and proved to be a very powerful and reliable analytical tool. The model needs a few and easy to determine material characteristics for bricks, mortar and joints. So the MAFEA program is very suitable for analytical research and it can partially substitute for the expensive experimental paramatric studies of masonry.

REFERENCES

1. Page A.W., Samarasinghe W. and Hendry A.W. The In-Plane Behaviour of Masonry - A Review, Proc. of the British Ceramic Soc., Load-Bearing Brickwork (7), No. 30, pp. 90-100, Sept. 1982.

2. Page A.W. Finite Element Model for Masonry, Structural Div., ASCE, Vol. 104, No. St8, pp. 1267-1285, 1978.

3. Samarasinghe W. and Hendry A.W. The Strength of Brickwork under Biaxial, Tensile and Compressive Stress, Proc. of the British Ceramic Soc., Load-Bearing Brickwork (7), No.30, pp.129-139, Sept. 1982.

4. Page A.W. The Biaxial Compressive Strength of Brick Masonry, Proc. Inst. Civ. Engrs, Part 2, 71, pp.893-906, Sept. 1981.

5. Page A.W. The Strength of Brick Masonry under Biaxial Tension-Compression, Inter. J. Masonry Construction, Vol.3, No.1, pp. 26-31, 1983.

6. Dhanasekar M., Page A.W. and Kleeman P.W. The Failure of Brick Masonry under Biaxial Stresses , Proc. Instn. Civ. Engrs, part 2, 79, pp. 295-313, June 1985.

7. Page A. W., Kleeman P.W. and Dhanasekar M. An In-Plane F.E. Model for Brick Masonry, Proc. of Str. Eng. Cong.,A.S.C.E.,Chicago, Sept. 1985.

8. Penelis G. and Stavrakakis E. Finite Element Analysis of R/C Panels until Failure (in Greek), 2nd Greek Conference on Concrete, Thessaloniki, Greece, May 1975.

9. Ignatakis C.,Stavrakakis E. and Penelis G. Parametric Analysis of R/C Columns under Axial and Shear Loading Using the F.E. Method, A.C.I. Journal, 1988 (accepted for publication).

10. Hendry A.W. Structural Brickwork. The Macmilan Press, 1981.

11. Francis A.J.,Horman C.B. and Jerrems L.E. The Effect of Joint Thickness and other Factors on the Compressive Strength of Brickwork, Proc. of the 2nd Int. Brick Masonry Conf.,Stoke-on-Trent,pp.31-37,Apr.1970.

12. Kupfer H., Hilsdorf H.K. and Rusch H. Behavior of Concrete under Biaxial Stresses, A.C.I. Journal, Vol. 66, No.8, pp. 656-666, Aug. 1969.

13. Schickert G. and Winkler H. Results of Test Concerning Strength and Strain of Concrete Subjected to Multiaxial Compressive Stresses, Deutscher Ausschuss für Stahlbeton, Heft 277, Berlin 1977.

14. Ferrara G., Rossi P., Rossi P.P. and Ruggeri L. Dispositivi di Prova per l' Analisi Sperimentale del Comportamento di Conglomerati Cementizi Sottoposti a Stati Triassiali di Sollecitazione. I.A.B.S.E. Seminar on Concrete Structures Subjected to Triaxial Stresses, I.S.M.E.S. Bergamo, pp. 501-511, May 1974.

15. Hamid A.A. and Drysdale R.C. The Shear Behaviour of Brickwork Bed Joints, Proc. of the British Ceramic Society, Load-Bearing Brickwork (7), No. 30, pp. 101-109, Sept. 1982.

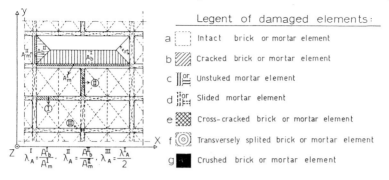

Figure 1.   Finite Element Model of Masonry.

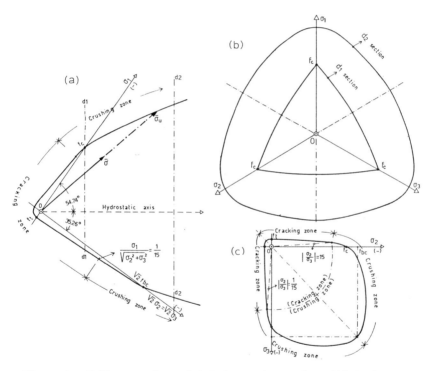

Figure 2.   Failure surface. (a) Hydrostatic section. (b) Deviatory sections. (c) Biaxial section

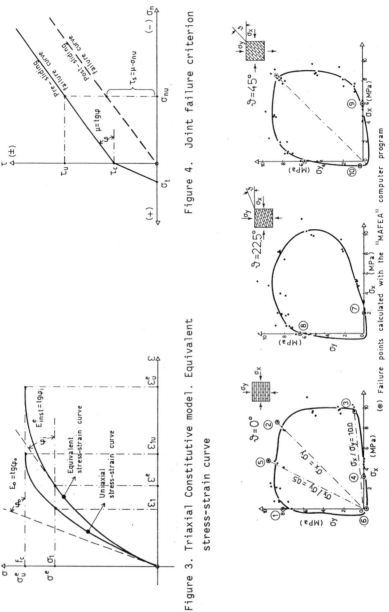

Figure 3.   Triaxial Constitutive model. Equivalent
stress-strain curve

Figure 4.   Joint failure criterion

Figure 5.   Experimental failure envelopes (Page et al. [6]). Analytically determined points of failure

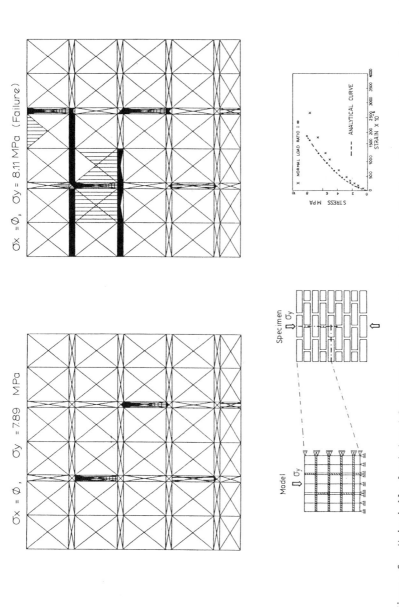

Figure 6. Uniaxially loaded model, perpendicular to the bed joints (θ=∅°): Damage patterns. Experimental and analytical stress-strain curves.

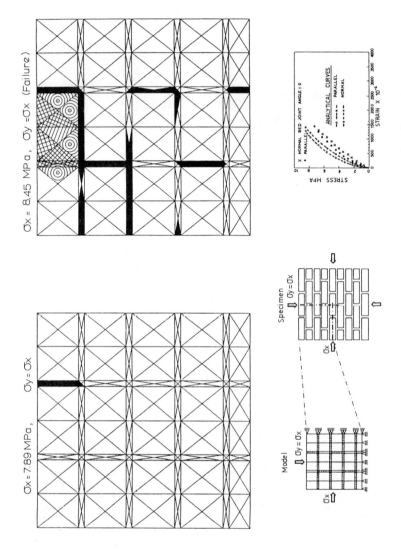

Figure 7. Biaxially loaded model ($\sigma_x/\sigma_y = 1.0$, $\theta = 0°$): Damage patterns. Experimental and analytical stress-strain curves.

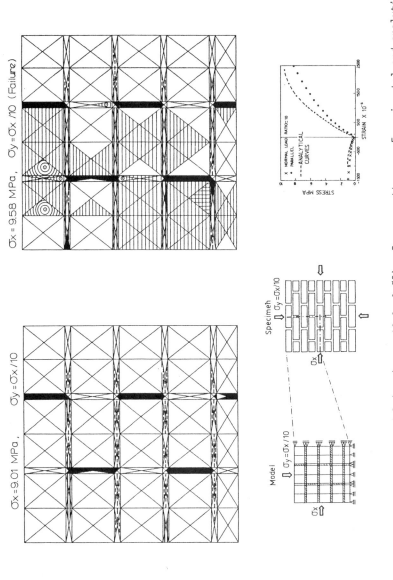

Figure 8.   Biaxially loaded model ($\sigma_x/\sigma_y = 10.0$, $\theta = 0°$):   Damage patterns.   Experimental and analytical stress-strain curves.

Problems Connected with the Arrangement of a Non-Linear Finite Element Method to the Analysis of Masonry Structures

S. Chiostrini, P. Foraboschi and S. Sorace
Department of Civil Engineering, University of Florence, Via di S. Marta, 3, 50139 Florence, Italy

ABSTRACT

A non-linear finite element approach simulating the static behaviour of the masonry structures was developed. The proposed approach is based on a monolateral-friction element coupled with a brick element. After having developed appropriate criteria for proceeding, this method yielded reliable schemes of masonry building structural behaviour. The model permits partializations, monolateral behaviours, shear limited by Coulomb's friction law, fractures, slidings, mechanisms of collapse. The structural behaviour was also analyzed with increasing loads, up to the collapse, obtaining the behaviour at each step and the limit loads with the associated mechanisms of collapse.

The numerical results were compared with theoretical, experimental and photoelasticity results from similar cases, with the purpose of checking the method. The main types of masonry structures were examined in order to improve the reliability of the results. The most appropriate ranges of the involved parameters were produced by carrying out different types of analyses.

INTRODUCTION

A non-linear finite element approach was developed for the analysis of masonry structural behaviour. This approach consists of an appropriate arrangement of a multi-purpose calculation code [1] providing a monolateral-friction element. This element was coupled with a brick element in order to simulate the particular behaviour of the masonry material. This method was developed for the static analyses of the masonry structures. The models obtained by the above described coupling are capable to simultaneously simulate: monolateral behaviours, partializations, fractures, slidings according to Coulomb's law, and mechanisms of collapse.

Initially, the method was checked employing both theoretically and experimentally known results. For that purpose, the known results were compared with the results produced by correspondent cases simulated by this method. The resulting comparison developed, supporting completely the proposed method. The analyses developed in the phase of the comparison regarded: (i) the masonry structures behaviour corresponding to given loads (ii) the collapse load level and the associated mechanisms of a given masonry structure, obtained by increasing the loads in a predetermined pattern.

In order to represent various types of masonry elements, checks also showed that it is impossible to develop an unique arrangement for the model setting. On the other hand, it is clearly demonstrated that elements and restraints positioning and free parameters setting strongly influence the analytical response. So that a second phase was activated.

At the second phase, the main types of structures were analysed in order to obtain criteria for the best simulation of each type of structure and for the appropriate ranges of the parameters used by the method in each situation. These criteria are peculiar to this method, and furthermore some of them are different from those of the "classical" linear finite element approach. The gap setting is the most important aspect which determines the proper functioning of the proposed method. The proper gap setting, nevertheless, strongly depends on the particular situation to be schematized.

THE GAP ELEMENT AND THE BRICK ELEMENT: NUMERICAL MODEL OF MASONRY

Masonry structures were modelled by coupling two different finite elements: the gap element and the brick element. The gap element ("two or three-dimensional interface") consists of two parallel plane surfaces which can mantain ("closed" element) or cut off ("open" element) the physical contact. The element only transmits the compressive stress, in the orthogonal direction to the two surfaces, and, according to Coulomb's law, the shear stress, in the tangential direction. The physical contact is cut off in the gaps in the presence of tensile stress, and fractures occur by separation of the gap's surfaces. In the presence of shear force superior to the Coulomb's friction force, occurs slidings by the shift of the gap's surfaces. Therefore the gap element can be considered a monolateral- friction joint between the brick elements.

In order to generate a gap it is necessary to define:

- two nodes, that may also be coincident;
- an angle, giving the orientation of the two surfaces, and defining therefore the normal direction and the tangential direction;
- the stiffness "k";
- the friction coefficient "f".

The constitutive laws corresponding to these two directions are shown respectively in fig. 1.a and 1.b. The diagram in fig.1.a, corresponding to the normal direction, clearly rapresents the element monolateral behaviour. A residual tensile strenght of 10^{-6} k can be set; this option produces a not perfectly monolateral behaviour, but better numerical behaviour of the method.

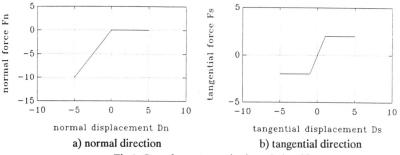

a) normal direction   b) tangential direction
Fig.1: Gap-element constitutive relationships

The constitutive law for the tangential direction presents the same slope as the compressive law. This holds true until the value correspondent to the start of the sliding (this value is: $F_s = f x |F_n|$, according to Coulomb's criterion, where F_n is the compressive force acting on the faces of the element) is reached.

When sliding begins, after having selected the option of tensile strength, the remaining part of the constitutive law is characterized by an elastic stiffness $k' = 10^{-6} k$ (which is only an ideal value); otherwise, this stiffness, as for normal direction, may be put at zero. The introduction of the gap element gives rise to an iterative process to obtain the solution; in fact the method starts from the closed gap situation up to the final close/open gap situation.

The brick element generates the geometry of the structure. It is defined by four nodes, in the bidimensional case, and by eight nodes, in the tridimensional case. The behaviour of the element may be isotropic or anisotropic, linear elastic or non-linear elastic. The results of the presented research support the use of the element in the isotropic and linear elastic version as the appropriate choice for the analyses of masonry structures. In fact, the effects of anisotropy and non-linearity of the masonry are appropriately produced by only the gap elements. The values of the parameters that define the brick element (modulus of elasticity E and modulus of Poisson v) were set following physical considerations, since these parameters have no influence on the numerical process.

One of the main characteristics of the model resulting from the coupling of gap and brick elements consists of concentrating the monolateral-friction behaviour in the gap elements. Only here it is possible to have the separation or the sliding, since it is impossible to have cracks in the brick elements. Therefore this model considers the effect of fractures and slidings on the structural response but the correct representation of the real behaviour is connected with a proper arrangement of the elements. Particular care was employed in the study of the gap disposition and in the parameters setting.

MESH AND PARAMETERS SETTING FOR MONODIMENSIONAL MASONRY ELEMENTS

Mesh generation is the most important problem in the analyses of masonry structures developed by this method. The mesh generation criteria are different from those of linear elastic finite element analyses. The disposition of the gaps is in particular the main problem, and it needs to be studied as first phase. In fact the disposition of the gaps is directly connected to all the non- linearity that the model is capable to perform.

In particular:

- fractures only occur where the gaps are present, and in the normal direction of the gaps contact surfaces;
- the Coulomb's friction and the slidings exist only where gaps are present, and this behaviour only occurs in the tangential direction;
- the mesh exibits monolateral behaviour only in correspondence to the gaps.

Therefore the gap's disposition locates the monolateral behaviour and potentially activates some mechanisms, but inhibits others. These considerations underline the fact that, in order to correctly set the gaps, it is necessary to evaluate the possible mechanisms that the examined structure could be able to perform, the zones with monolateral behaviour and the zones with predominant shear stress. In other words one needs to know a priori roughly how the structure behaves.

Many sensitivities analyses were developed, yielding the result that a good gaps' disposition determines a reliable scheme also employing a few gap elements. Also the parameters setting ned differentiate studies for each type of structure and for each type of analysis.

The most important parameters of the gaps are: stiffness and Coulomb's friction coefficient. The gap stiffness, being not directly related to the physical aspects of the problems but having a great numerical importance that strongly influences the results, needs appropriate evaluations to be properly set. In fact the gaps can link nodes having the same coordinates, or however very close. So that the internal congruence is not substantially altered by the gap's stiffness.

This means that the value of the gap stiffness has to be related only to the numerical analysis to be developed. The first evaluation on this coefficient is that a numerical tensile traction, that is $1/1.10^6$ of the compressive stiffness, needs to be activated to have a quick convergence. In fact that tensile stress produces a stiffness matrix that is numerically easier to manage. This fact implies to not set a high value of k, which can alter the solution, especially the mechanism for that residual tensile strength; on the other hand a too low value of k gives rise to a worse solution. These considerations yield a stiffness range of: 1000-10000 as proper for most cases.

While the gap stiffness derives only from numerical evaluations, the Coulomb's friction coefficient derives from both physical and numerical evaluations, being directly related to both these aspects. In fact this parameter is directly related to the sliding mechanisms, but the applied calculus code allows only to set a unique value in each process. Nevertheless, when the gaps are open, the friction mechanism should have a different coefficient from when they are closed. Therefore the coefficient should be the average of the two situations. It is important to note that one can not predict exactly where gaps will open, so that gaps opening should be roughly guessed. The most appropriate range for the above coefficient is 0.4-0.6 but sometimes it is appropriate to set a value beyond that range.

The setting of the parameters of the elastic linear elements is simpler since they derive only from physical evaluations. The value of the modulus of elasticity, which is the most important parameter, has to be the the same as that of the examined masonry. In fact, when the gaps are closed, only this one produces the strain in the masonry, so that there has to be correspondence between the moduli of elasticity of model and of masonry. Finally it is important to note that it is possible to activate steps of load, which stop at the structural collapse of the structure.

A MASONRY PANEL SHEAR TEST SIMULATION

In order to correctly represent the actual structural behaviour (see Fig. 2) some initial consideration are necessary. To schematize a small masonry element it is possible to introduce in the analytical model all the bricks actually present in the real structure. Moreover, all the actual mortar bed joint planes are represented numerically by an appropriate number of gap elements. Following the above consideration, the problem to correctly simulate the real behaviour is reduced to the evaluation of a correct arrangement for the free-parameters setting [2].

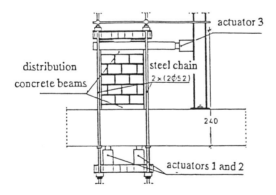

Fig. 2: Actual experimental scheme [3]

Bricks are represented by linear elastic-isotropic four-node elements, which physical constants correspond to those of the real material. The Young modulus E is fixed at the value of 600.000 Pa; the Poisson modulus is 0.13. Gap elements parameter are more difficult to be set directly basing on physical consideration. Free parameters are: (i) k_h horizontal interface gap-element stiffness; (ii) f_h horizontal interface gap-element friction coefficient; (iii) k_v vertical interface gap-element stiffness; (iv) f_v vertical interface gap-elements friction coefficient; (v) N total pre-stress load applied to the panel.

Figg. 3a and 3b show the "microscopic" analytical model behaviour. When C element moves to the right it means that internal friction stresses in the gap-element no 2 exceed the Coulomb limit value. In this conditions, gap no 1 remains in its initial close condition while gaps no 3 and 4 open originating a vertical crack. Gap-element no 2 remain in its close condition also permitting sliding displacements. These simple considerations make it clear that in a correct free-parameter setting procedure, gap physical constants are to be evaluated depending on the gap orientation.

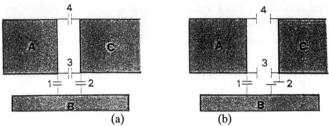

(a)   (b)

Fig. 3: Analytical model microscopic displacements

In the present simulation a value of 0.6 is chosen to represent the friction coefficient for gap elements in both the horizontal and vertical orientations. This value corresponds to the actual mortar-brick contact friction coefficient. The gaps stiffness parameters setting needs some more consideration .

In the real test, pre-stressing vertical load was not directly applied to the panel, due to the presence of the two steel chains (see Fig. 2) which absorbed a part of the vertical load. It is also noted that in the numerical model the vertical load rate relative to the panel directly depends on the relative stiffness between vertical gaps and chain-elements. Assuming steel characteristics for the chains, Fig. 4 shows a diagram which relates gap vertical stiffness with the panel pre-stressing rate. Fig. 4 also shows the variation of the panel compressive stiffness with the kh gap property.

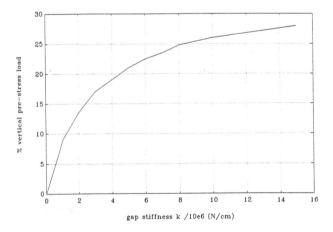

Fig. 4: Gap vertical stiffness - panel pre-stress rate relation

Once fixed the total vertical load rate to be attributed to the panel at the value of 200.000 N, Fig. 5 shows the relation between the gap vertical stiffness and the global pre-stress vertical load.

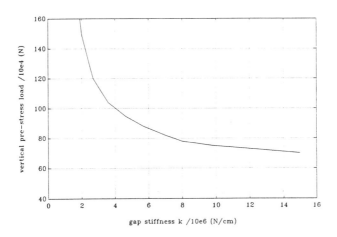

Fig.5: Gap vertical stiffness - global pre-stress vertical load

Once the vertical pre-stress - gap stiffness relation is determined, some analytical tests are performed in order to determine the inflence on the panel's final strength of the vertical pre-stress (see Figs. 6 and 7). Using the preceding relations, the panel pre-stress load rate is at last determined in order to attribute to the panel its actual strength.

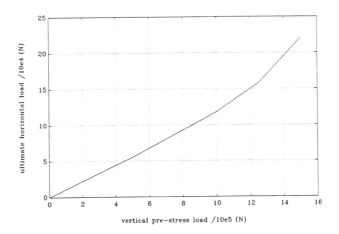

Fig. 6: Panel vertical pre-stress rate - Panel ultimate strenght relation

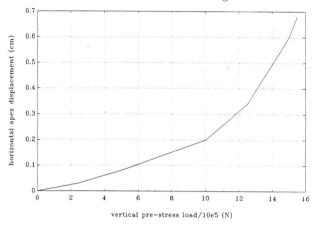

Fig. 7: Panel vertical pre-stress rate - Ultimate apex displacement relation

Since the panel actual vertical strain due to the pre-stress   loading   is about 0.6%, a value of k = 5 10^6 N/cm seems to be the most appropriate to obtain in the numerical model the same pre-stress vertical strain [4].

Once gap stiffness and pre-stress load are determined, some simulations are performed in order to evaluate the friction coefficient influence on the panel global behaviour. Figs. 8 and 9 show both the ultimate collapse load and the panel apex displacements related to the friction coefficient value. It must be noted that the sharp change of the curves at a given value of the friction coefficient is due to the change of the correspondent collapse mechanism, passing from a sliding to a cracking mechanism.

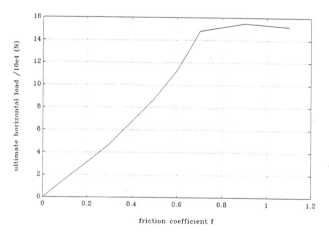

Fig. 8: Friction coefficient - Ultimate collapse loade relation

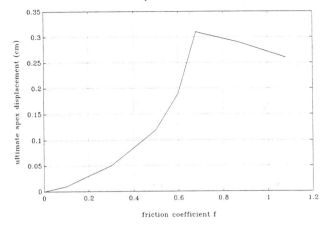

Fig. 9: Friction coefficient - Ultimate apex displacement relation

The choice of m = 0.6 is confirmed as the most opportune in order to represent the actual value of the ultimate apex displacement which is experimentally measured at 0.2 cm.

Once performed the above setting procedure, the analytical model is at last capable to correctly represent the actual panel structural behaviour both at the collapse point and along the load-displacement curve (see Fig. 10). The analytical collapse mechanism also corresponds to the actual fracture situation (see Fig. 11).

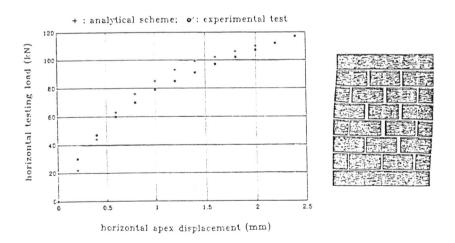

Fig. 10: Load displacement curve   Fig. 11: Collapse mechanism

REFERENCES

[1] AA VV: ANSYS - Engineering Analysis System - User's Manual - Swanson Analysis System Inc. - Houston, Penn., 1986

[2] Gonnelli L. - Modelli numerici per l'interpretazione del comportamento sperimentale di pannelli in muratura - Grad. Thesis - Dept. of Civil Engrg. - Univ. of Florence - Tutors: Chiarugi A. and Vignoli A.

[3] Bernardini A., Modena C. and Vescovi U. - Ricerca sperimentale sui parametri di resistenza e deformabilita' di muarture in laterizio armato ed alveolato - J. "Costruire", no 109, 1978 - no 114, 1979

[4] Chiostrini S. and Vignoli A. - Application of a Numerical Method to Study Masonry Panels with Various Geometry under Seismic Loads - Proc. of STREMA - 5-7th April 1989 Florence

Analytical Model and Numerical Application of the Structural Behaviour of Masonry Walls Under Plane Stress

Rodolfo Antonucci, Massimo Carboni and Giammichele Cocchi
Instituto di Scienza e Tecnica delle Construzioni, University of Ancona, Via delle Brecce Bianche, Italy

ABSTRACT

Based on the F.E. method, the solution of masonry subjected to plane stress is tackled by making use of a macromodel combining the advantages of both micromodelling and macromodelling. The macromodel proposed by the authors has been originated by an assemblage of micromodels of bricks and mortar joints. When the geometry and the elastic characteristics of the bricks and the mortar are known, using the static condensation method it is possible to obtain the masonry response just at prefixed points. Therefore this type of modelling is more accurate than the normal macromodel, but at the same time it has the same flexibility. The model has been implemented in a computer module which allowed the authors to carry out a set of numerical tests on the macroelements, following the progressive behaviour up to failure under several significant load and restrain conditions both in the elastic and non-elastic range. A comparison between the analytical results, the experimental data and the results obtained by other authors show a good agreement of the macroelement analysis with the experimental data and a better representation of the masonry response with respect to the macromodels of other authors.

1. INTRODUCTION

Current numerical application of the structural behaviour of masonry walls under plane stress is examined by making use of MICROMODELLING and MACROMODELLING methods. In the former case, analysis is more detailed using reduced finite elements; whereas in the latter case, the calculation grid is simplified since macroscopic finite elements are used. Both types of modelling have their advantages and disadvantages. On one hand micromodelling provides an accurate response while requiring major input of data; it may use simple constitutive expressions referring to individual material components while it is more difficult to define an adequate standard of material breakage at a microscopic level in view of the complexity of mortar-brick interaction. On the other hand, macromodelling is more simple to apply and requires less

input data, but provides less accurate results; it is however possible
to calculate the breakage criteria of the macromodel easily, while this
is not the case for determining a suitable generalised constitutive
model of the masonry material. The innovation of the proposed modelling consists in its capacity for efficiently combining micromodelling
and macromodelling methods, using the advantages of both.

2. THE FINITE ELEMENT MODEL

The proposed analysis procedure consists, initially, of the analytic
representation of a section of brickwork, called MACROELEMENT; later
the macroelement modelling is simplified using the "static condensation" method [ref. 2] on the external nodes of the internal node
stiffness; the condensed macroelement can, in this way, be used to
describe wider portions of brickwork using the macromodelling method.

Microelement and Macroelement

The brick material was modelled with a three node, triangular finite
plane element (fig. 1). The displacement functions being linear:

$$u(x,y) = \alpha_1 + \alpha_2 x + \alpha_3 y \quad , \tag{1}$$
$$v(x,y) = \alpha_4 + \alpha_5 x + \alpha_6 y \quad , \tag{2}$$

where the constants $\alpha_1, \ldots, \alpha_6$, are calculated by setting the values of
nodal displacement. The field of deformation $(\epsilon_x, \epsilon_y, \gamma_{xy})$ is constant
that is; $\underline{\epsilon}=[B]\underline{s}$ where $\underline{s}$ is the nodal displacement vector and $[B]$ is the
constant matrix which binds the displacement field to the deformations.
Two types of triangular finite elements were adopted which represent a
half-brick; the two deformation-displacements matrixes for the two
elements are respectively:

$$[B_1] = \frac{1}{LD}\begin{bmatrix} 0 & 0 & -D & 0 & D & 0 \\ 0 & L & 0 & -L & 0 & 0 \\ L & 0 & -L & -D & 0 & D \end{bmatrix} \quad ; \tag{3}$$

$$[B_2] = \frac{1}{LD}\begin{bmatrix} -D & 0 & D & 0 & 0 & -L \\ 0 & 0 & 0 & L & 0 & 0 \\ 0 & -D & L & D & -L & 0 \end{bmatrix} \quad . \tag{4}$$

The deformation-stress constitutive   law   for   the   brick   is   of   the following type:

$$[Db] = \frac{Eb}{1-\nu_b} \begin{bmatrix} 1 & \nu_b & 0 \\ \nu_b & 1 & 0 \\ 0 & 0 & (1-\nu_b)/2 \end{bmatrix} . \tag{5}$$

The mortar joint was schematized in diagram form using a four node rectangular plane finite element (fig. 1), suitably simplified; in fact from the original model [ref. 1] the axial component, orthogonal to the joint and the tangential component, parallel to the joint were obtained from the original model.   For the rectangular element we have the displacement functions, which maintain the rectilinear configuration of the edges ($\alpha=x/L$, $\beta=y/d$):

$$u(\alpha,\beta) = c_1\alpha + c_2\alpha\beta + c_3\beta + c_4 \quad , \tag{6}$$
$$v(\alpha,\beta) = c_5\alpha + c_6\alpha\beta + c_7\beta + c_8 \quad , \tag{7}$$

where the constants c_1, .., c_8, are calculated by considering the nodal conditions at the limits. The deformation field (, ϵ) is constant in direction y (β, orthogonal to the joint) and linear in direction x (α, parallel to the joint); the deformation-displacement matrix, is written as follows:

$$[Bm] = \begin{bmatrix} \dfrac{1-\alpha}{d} & 0 & \dfrac{\alpha}{d} & 0 & \dfrac{\alpha-1}{d} & 0 & \dfrac{-\alpha}{d} & 0 \\ 0 & \dfrac{1-\alpha}{d} & 0 & \dfrac{\alpha}{d} & 0 & \dfrac{\alpha-1}{d} & 0 & \dfrac{-\alpha}{d} \end{bmatrix} , \tag{8}$$

obtained by considering "u" and "v" in the deformation expressions (γ, ϵ).
The deformation stress constitutive restraint for mortar is of the following type:

$$[Dm] = \frac{t}{d} \begin{bmatrix} Gm & 0 \\ 0 & Em \end{bmatrix} , \tag{9}$$

The three microelements are combined and constitute the basic module (fig. 1) of the proposed modelling; two basic modules represent a brick with adjacent joint; several modules represent the brickwork macroele-ment (fig. 2). The stiffness matrix of each microelement is obtained by applying the principle or virtual work to the element itself.   By combining the single stiffness matrixes of the microelements, the overall stiffness matrix of the macroelement is obtained; later overall matrix of overall stiffness of the macroelement is simplified using the "static condensation" process of degrees of freedom.

The stiffness matrix obtained with respect to suitable nodes, is that of a finite element which simulates a wider portion of the brickwork. The state of deformation and stress is calculated using the usual methods, on the basis of the nodal displacements.

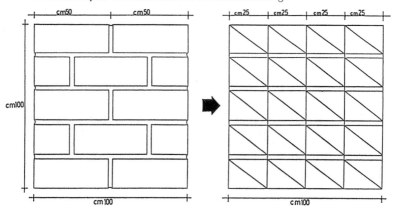

Fig. 2. Macroelement

Material behaviour

For the analytical model of the material the cracking deforming behaviour with integral material (constitutive law), and behaviour during
the post-cracking and breakage stage, are considered.   To achieve the
correspondence between phenomena at a microscopic level and at a
macroscopic level, reference is made to the "macro" in evaluating the
deforming response (response nodes in condensation) and the characteristics of resistance (brickwork material); reference was made to the
"micro" in the evaluation of stress geometry and in assigning constitutive restraints (brick and mortar material).
The constitutive models of materials are introduced using the isotropic
linear and non-linear elastic expression. In the case of the former we
have constitutive matrixes (5) and (9) for the brick and for the mortar
respectively; in the case of the latter the Kupfer expression is
selected [ref. 3].

For the brick, by considering:
K_{sb} = volumetric brick module,
G_{sb} = shear brick module, we have:

$$[Db] = KS \begin{bmatrix} 1 & \dfrac{3K_{sb}-G_{sb}}{2(3K_{sb}+G_{sb})} & 0 \\[2ex] \dfrac{3K_{sb}-G_{sb}}{2(3K_{sb}+G_{sb})} & 1 & 0 \\[2ex] 0 & 0 & \dfrac{3K_{sb}+4G_{sb}}{4(3K_{sb}+G_{sb})} \end{bmatrix} \quad , \qquad (10)$$

where $KS = \dfrac{3K_{sb}+G_{sb}}{3K_{sb}+4K_{sb}}$.

For the mortar by considering:
Ksm = volumetric mortar module,
Gsm = shearing mortar module, we have:

$$[Dm] = \frac{t}{d} \begin{bmatrix} Gsm & 0 \\ 0 & \dfrac{9Ksm}{3Ksm+Gsm} \end{bmatrix} . \tag{11}$$

According to Cedolin's expression [ref. 4] and other authors, Ks and Gs
(secant elastic modules) are functions of the octahedral deformations
(.oct, εoct):

$$Ks = Ko(0,85 \cdot 2,5^{-\mathcal{E}oct/0,0014} + 0,15) \quad , \tag{12}$$
$$Gs = Go(0,81 \cdot 2,0^{-\gamma oct/0,0020} + 0,19) \quad ,$$

where Ko and Go are the initial elastic modules.

As far as the material breakage criteria is concerned, the overall
behaviour of the generic macroelement was considered as being mainly
biaxial and shear. The stresses of each macroelement, are compared with
those for the breakage criteria as follows: mortar is verified at shear
(parallel to the joint), at compression and traction (orthogonal to the
joint); the semi-brick is verified for generic bi-axial stresses
directed according to the orthotropic axes of the macroelement.

The resistance domains for mortar and brick, are experimentally
obtained according to test on real panels of brickwork [ref. 5]. These
domains are indicated in fig. 3, where the values indicated refer to
the overall behaviour of the panel.

In order to verify the joint element of breakage with the parallel
shear stress component to the layers of mortar, a resistance law of the
following type (fig. 3) is adopted:

region I: $fc' \leq \sigma \leq fty$,   (13)
                    $= c - \sigma \cdot tg\phi_1$;

region II: $fcy \leq \sigma \leq fc'$,
                    $= c - fc' \cdot tg\phi_1 + (\sigma - fc')tg\phi_2$;
where
fty = resistance to traction in direction y,
dct = resistance to compression in direction y,
fc' = compression of maximum tangential resistance for the joint,
ϕ_1 = initial angle of friction for mortar
ϕ_2 = final angle of friction for mortar

To verify the brick breakage with the bi-axial stress components according to the orthotropic directions of the macroelement, an experimental
resistance criteria in the stress plane $\sigma_x - \sigma_y$ is adopted, suitable for
verifying the breakage to traction and to compression (monoaxial and
bi-axial).
For a field of stresses such that $1,5 \cdot fc \leq \sigma_x \leq ftx$, the breakage lines
may be expressed as follows (fig. 3) :

```
L1 = fcmy + (-fcmy/ftx)σx ,                                          (14)
L2 = fty ,
L3 = fcmy + σx ,
L4 = 1,35·fc ,
L5 = 2,45·fc - σx ,
L6 = fty + (fty/-fcmx)σx ,
```

```
where:
fc   = medium resistance to compression,
ftx  = resistance to traction in direction x,
fty  = resistance to traction in direction y,
fcmx = resistance to mono-axial compression in direction x,
fcmy = resistance to mono-axial compression in direction y.
```

In order to introduce the anisotropy in the numeric model which occurs in material when cracking and/or local crushing start to occur, the following considerations were made:

1. A diffuse series of cracks is produced in the these areas when one of the main stresses is a traction stress which exceeds the value of resistance to traction ft of the material.
2. Since after the formation of a series of cracks the behaviour of material must express the zero traction stress in the orthogonal direction of the crack, it will be modelled by assuming a value of zero for the stiffness element in the above direction.
3. The material crisis caused by compression occurs when the point representing the state of stress refers to the domain line of resistance in the compression field. This results in the complete disintegration of the element and consequently the cancellation of the stiffness matrix for all other load directions. In addition it is assumed that immediately after compression, the element in question is no longer able to absorb strains and that those previously sustained are released and redistributed to the other resisting elements.
4. The roughness of the surfaces delimiting the generic system of cracks is considered to be such that along the cracks, increases of the tangential efforts are transmitted which are proportional to the corresponding increases in deformation, that is:

$$\frac{1}{Gt}\cdot\frac{\delta}{\delta} = \beta , \quad \text{with } 0 \leq \beta \leq 1 , \qquad (15)$$

since β is a suitable constant to select in the above field, in the case of a single system of cracks or of two systems present at the same time, respectively; Gt being the module of tangential elasticity.

The simulation of post-crack behaviour is produced in three stages:

a) verification of breakage in one or more microelements;
b) reduction of stiffness relative to the type of breakage;
c) redistribution of strains existing in the structure up-dated to the current load conditions.

For the generic joint element, the reduction of stiffness of the material occurs at the following conditions of breakage.

1) Orthogonal traction at the joint: the up-dated constitutive matrix $[Dm_1]$ is zero.
2) Shear (parallel to the joint in traction (orthogonal to the joint): the up-dated constitutive matrix $[Dm_2]$ is again zero.
3) Shear (parallel to the joint) in compression (orthogonal to the joint): the up-dated constitutive matrix $[Dm_3]$ is:

$$[Dm_3] = \begin{vmatrix} \beta m \cdot Kt & 0 \\ 0 & Kc \end{vmatrix} \quad , \qquad (16)$$

where βm is a coefficient less than one, depending on the sliding friction of the joint.

For the generic element of masonry we have the following breakage conditions and relative stiffness reduction.

1) Traction in direction x: the constitutive matrix $[Db_1]$ is:

$$[Db_1] = \begin{vmatrix} 0 & 0 & 0 \\ 0 & E & 0 \\ 0 & 0 & \beta_1 G \end{vmatrix} \quad , \qquad (17)$$

2) Traction in direction y: the constitutive matrix $[Db_2]$ is:

$$[Db_2] = \begin{vmatrix} E & 0 & 0 \\ 0 & 0 & 0 \\ 0 & 0 & \beta_2 G \end{vmatrix} \quad , \qquad (18)$$

3) Traction in direction x and compression in direction y or monoaxial compression in direction y: the constitutive matrix $[Db_3]$ is similar to that at point 1, less coefficient β_1 (now β_3).
4) Traction in direction y and compression in direction x or monoaxial compression in direction x: the constitutive matrix $[Db_4]$ is similar to that at point 2, less coefficient β_2 (now β_4).
5) Biaxial compression according to the two main directions: the constitutive matrix $[Db_5]$ becomes:

$$[Db_5] = \begin{vmatrix} 0 & 0 & 0 \\ 0 & 0 & 0 \\ 0 & 0 & \beta_5 G \end{vmatrix} \quad , \qquad (19)$$

In the previous up-dates the coefficients β_1 , .., β_5, are included between zero and one and vary according to the residual shear resources of the material used.

3. NUMERIC APPLICATION AND COMPARISON

In order to verify the reliability of the model developed, a calculation code called MACMUR was produced which refers to the analysis of the macroelement obtained by combining microelements.

In this analysis MACMUR was applied to the following operations:
1) verification of the breakage point for different combinations of main stresses, slanted with respect to the mortar layers, and applied to the single macroelement;
2) study of the linear elastic behaviour of the macroelement for a history of monotonic load and various restraint conditions;
3) a similar study to the previous, with the introduction of non-linear elastic expression for the behaviour of the material used.

The programme supplies general conditions of the structure to the point of breakage and a series of intermediate data on its behaviour, due to the monotonic increase of loads, (as for example, the convergence of the solution, the methods of a possible breakage and up-dating, the stress and deformation conditions).

The load trials

Coherently with the experimental tests found in literature, a macro-element constituted of 5 rows of bricks and 4 bricks for each row was considered in the numeric analysis. The sizes of the panel were the following: width 100 cm, height 100 cm, thickness 30 cm. as indicated in fig. 2; the "macroelement type" consists of 36 microelements connected to each other by 50 nodes.

Reference is made to the computer numeric tests and the relative obser-vations. In a first series of tests the breakage conditions of the macroelement were verified and compared with the experimental trials. Fig. 4 indicates the trial methods with the main stresses slanted with respect to the mortar layers and the various load courses; the expe-rimental resistance domains were also drawn and the points of breakage obtained by numeric calculation. A second series of tests on the macroelement was carried out to analyse the evolutive behaviour at breakage for significant conditions of load and restraint, with the introduction of both the linear elastic behaviour and the non-linear elastic behaviour. The diagrams obtained were compared with experimental models and those obtained by modelling carried out by other authors. Fig. 5 indicates the graphs of results and test methods.

4. CONCLUSIONS

The following results were obtained from this study:
1) a detailed analytic modelling to finite elements of brickwork portions in plane states of stresses which considers the anisotropy of the material;
2) a calculation algorithm which is closer to the real properties of brickwork so as to simplify input of data.
3) elaboration of modelling to verify the suitability of the model.

Good agreement was found in the results obtained between theoretical and experiment applications. The differences in the results obtained, with respect to those for other modelling studies are due to an improved local representation of the behaviour of materials making up the masonry.

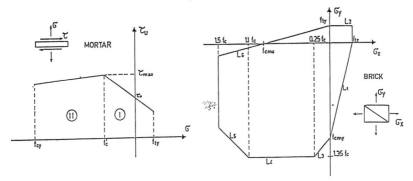

Fig.3 . Adopted failure domains.

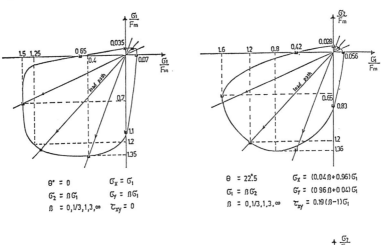

$\theta^{\circ} = 0$ $\sigma_x = \sigma_1$

$\sigma_2 = \beta\sigma_1$ $\sigma_y = \beta\sigma_1$

$\beta = 0, 1/3, 1, 3, \infty$ $\tau_{xy} = 0$

$\theta = 22^{\circ}\!5$ $\sigma_x = (0.04\beta + 0.96)\sigma_1$

$\sigma_1 = \beta\sigma_2$ $\sigma_y = (0.96\beta + 0.04)\sigma_1$

$\beta = 0, 1/3, 1, 3, \infty$ $\tau_{xy} = 0.19(\beta - 1)\sigma_1$

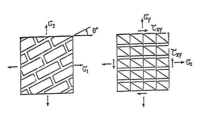

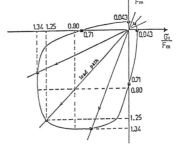

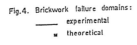

Fig.4. Brickwork failure domains:
——— experimental
▪ theoretical

$\theta^{\circ} = 45^{\circ}$ $\sigma_x = (0.15\beta + 0.85)\sigma_1$

$\sigma_1 = \beta\sigma_2$ $\sigma_x = (0.85\beta + 0.15)\sigma_1$

$\beta = 0, 1/3, 1, 3.$ $\tau_{xy} = 0.35(\beta - 1)\sigma_1$

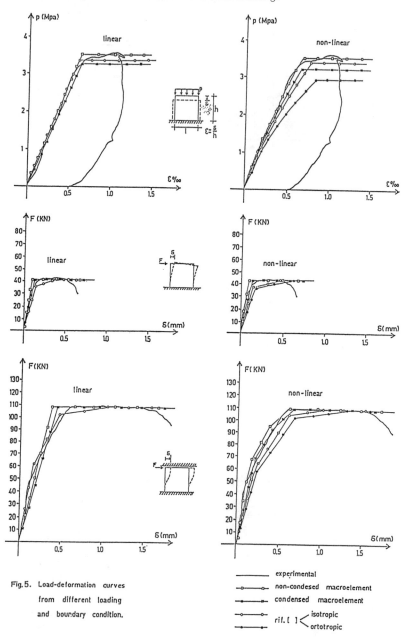

Fig. 5. Load-deformation curves
from different loading
and boundary condition.

experimental
non-condesed macroelement
condensed macroelement
rif. [ ] isotropic
ortotropic

REFERENCES

Book.

1. Przemieniecki J.S., Theory of Matrix Structural Analysis, New York, 1968.

2. Desai S., Abel J.F., Introduction to the Finite Element Method, 1972.

Paper in a journal.

3. Kupfer H.B., Gertle K.H., Behaviour of Concrete Under Biaxial Stresses, Journal of Engineer Mechanics, A.S.C.E., 1973.

4. Cedolin L., Crutzen Y., Dei Poli S., Triaxial Stress-Strain Relationship for Concrete, Journal of Engineer Mechanics Division, A.S.C.E., 1977.

5. Page A.W., The Strength of Brick Masonry Under Biaxial Compression-Tension, International Journal of Masonry Construction, March 1983.

Paper in conference procceding

6. Motta F., Modellazione Numerica del Comportamento Strutturale delle Pareti in Muratura, Atti Seminario C.N.R. su: "Lo Stato dell'Arte in Italia sulla Meccanica delle Murature", Roma, 1985.

7. Motta F., D'Amore E., Analisi Evolutive dei Pannelli Murari in Stati Piani di Tensione, Seminario C.N.R. su: "Lo Stato dell'Arte in Italia sulla Meccanica delle Murature", Roma, 1985.

A Computer Aided Repair (CAR) Case Study: The Hogar Pignatelli Church at Zaragoza.

S. Hernández, J. Mata, A. Solozábal

Department of Mechanical Engineering, University of Zaragoza, Spain.

ABSTRACT

The Church of Hogar Pignatelli was built in the nineteenth century using masonry bricks for its walls and columns, and developed substantial cracks a few years ago. To identify their origin several structural analysis methods were used. F.E. methods were carried out including models of collapsed geometry and soil-structure interaction. From the numerical results obtained, new foundations were designed and restoration work took place to repair the collapsed zones of the transept arches and to construct new foundations.

Description of the Problem

Hogar Pignatelli Church (H.P. Church) in Zaragoza, Spain, was erected in the middle of the nineteenth century (1859-1866). It is shown in Fig. 1, and all of the walls and columns were built using masonry bricks. This Church has only one nave which starts with a vault composed of three stretches of unequal length, next is a transept supporting a drum of octagonal section, and above this is placed a dome. An apse is at the rear where the altar is located.

From the time when the H.P. church was completed until recently, no important fissures had been reported. However, since 1970, (or earlier, because there is no accurate data), a vertical crack has been growing in the keystone of each arch of the transept. The restoration of the church was decided on in 1984: by then the cracks were more than a meter long and a few centimeters wide. The arch next to the apse had three vertical cracks at nearly similar distances, and a horizontal one linking them. Because of this an important part of the masonry of this arch was nearly cut away. The cracks were not only in the arches, they progressed into the lateral chapel, broke the rose window and finally ended at the floor.

The dome, drum, vault and columns are very well preserved and did not have any cracks.

The work, carried out by the authors, has consisted of identifying the origin of the cracks and of deciding on a method for repairing the church.

Fig. 1

Structural Model of the Church of Hogar Pignatelli

The structural model consists of the dome, the drum, the arches, the columns of the transept, and the apse. The complete set weighs up to 1800t. This weight is transmitted to the soil by the columns of the transept and apse. As the dome and the drum (which have eight large windows), are less stiff than the arches of the transept, they have not been included in the model. The vault does not receive loading from the transept but keeps the neighbouring arch from moving in the OX direction. Because of this the stuctural model selected was composed of the arch of the transept, columns and apse and it includes their weight, and the weight of the dome and drum. Wind and snow loading were neglected because their values were insignificant compared with gravity loadings.

The model was discretized using an F.E. mesh containing thin plate, beam and spring elements. Because of symmetry, it was only necessary to discretize half of the model. The meshes are composed of:

Thin plate elements:	68
Beams:	10
Spring elements:	8

All structural analyses were carried out on a VAX/VMS 11/750 computer at the Computer Center of Zaragoza University, using the SAP 4 program [3].

Analysis of the Initial F.E. Mesh

This F.E. mesh is represented in Fig. 2 and Fig. 3, and the problem was studied with infinite stiffness as its boundary condition. The aim of this was to check how the model would work under these conditions, because this must have been the behaviour considered by the designers when the church was built. The mechanical parameters E, v of the brick masonry were calculated as (1)

$$E = 900 f_k; \qquad f_k = 500 \, t/m^2 \qquad \text{hence} \qquad E = 450.000 \, t/m^2$$

$$v = 0.1$$

Several boundary conditions were studied to find out the variations of structural response with each one. The situations included were:

For columns in the X=0 plane

> Translation of nodes in the Y-Y direction allowed.
> Translation of nodes in the Y-Y direction restrained.

For foundation design

> Simply supported columns.

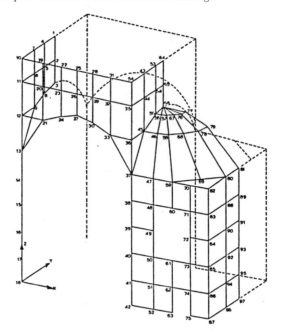

Fig. 2

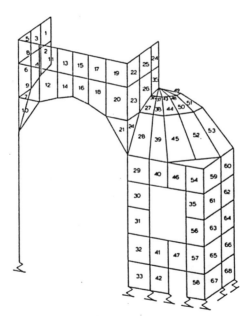

Fig. 3

Built in columns.

The conclusions of this study were that:

- There was little variation on stress material and soil reaction produced by the set of boundary conditions involved.
- Stresses were not high. For instance in the case for which boundary conditions were built-in columns and nodes of columns in the X=0 plane with zero translations in the Y-Y direction the following results were obtained:

Element	σ_{xx} (t/m^2)	σ_{yy} (t/m^2)
27	−16.9	−7.7
28	−56.0	−18.5
36	−0.49	−11.6

- Built-in reactions were very different from each other. As a cross section of a column is about $9m^2$ the resultant stresses were not important for the masonry but too big for the soil foundation.

	Force (t)			Moment (m.t)			
Node	Axial	Shear X-X	Shear Y-Y	Torsion	Bend X-X	Bend Y-Y	σ_z (t/m^2)
18	−670.9	−0.08	0.035	−0.006	0.036	0.25	74.4
42	−476.0	7.0	−0.12	−0.006	−0.12	−31.0	53.0

As allowable stress for this soil is $40t/m^2$, and as the figures obtained were too high, it was necessary to consider the strains in the foundation produced by the loading. To introduce interaction between the soil and structure, a value of ballast module of $13.000t/m^2$ as a string parameter was taken. This value was selected because it was inside the interval proposed by W.E. Schulze [2] for this kind of soil.

Calculating the structure again, we obtained:

Vertical displacement at node 18: -4.2 cm.
42: -1.6 cm.

Stresses at some important elements of the arch and apse were:

Element	σ_{xx} (t/m^2)	σ_{yy} (t/m^2)
27	6.1	44.0
28	−56.0	−61.6
36	26.9	58.9

Results showed that the arch placed in the OXZ plane had rotated in that plane because of differential vertical displacement between nodes 18 and 42. Consequently tension stresses appeared in the arch and apse elements near the keystone. As the material could not undergo this sort of stress this zone of the apse broke away from the adjoining arch, so it could not any longer be included as a part of the structural model. Therefore it was necessary to carry out another F.E. study without this part.

Analysis of the Post-Collapse F.E. Mesh.

A new mesh (shown in Fig. 4) was calculated and the following results were obtained:

Vertical displacement at node 18: -4.2 cm.
42: -1.6 cm.

Element	2	4	14	15	16	17	23	26	28
σ_{xx} (t/m^2)	122.1	121.9	51.4	52.4	6.4	35.8			
σ_{yy} (t/m^2)							37.6	20.1	26.6

When we looked at the results it was found that the central zone of the arches had tension stresses, and that this zone was largest in the arch next to the apse. These results explained the existing cracks and the fact that they were more widely distributed in that arch.

After this analysis the F.E. mesh was refined by creating triangular elements at the keystones of the arches to eliminate collapsed material near the cracks (Fig. 5). When the structure was recalculated the numerical results were quite similar to the former ones and the study ended assuming that convergence had been reached.

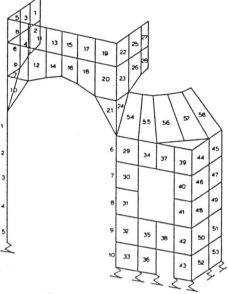

Fig. 4

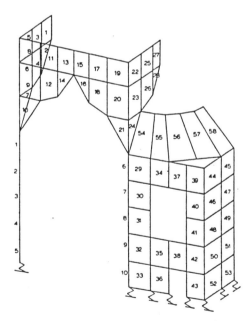

Fig. 5

It is not valid to think that the numerical results obtained for stresses and displacements are exact, because the values of the mechanical parameters of brick masonry and soil are not certain. Nevertheless we think that they are sufficiently accurate to determine the collapse process of the building and to explain the occurrence and layout of the cracks.

A Structural Solution for Restoration

From the results obtained it is possible to point out that the structural collapse of the Hogar Pignatelli Church occurred because:

- Soil stresses were too large.
- This building is symmetric along a longitudinal plane but not along a transverse plane. Because of that there are different soil stresses under nodes 18 and 42; this produces a rotation of the structure in the OXZ plane, a zone of abside is cut away which leads to a weakness of the general structural scheme.

Consequently the desired solution should be to strengthen the structure. This can be done as follows:

- Remove every zone of collapsed masonry and replace it with a material as strong as the brick. It is also necessary to obtain a good link between both materials.

- Improve the current foundation in order to decrease the soil stresses, and ensure that they are quite similar under both node 18 and node 42. In this way future rotations will be avoided.

Design for a New Foundation

Initially, a new formulation was designed by means of four beams of reinforced concrete which would join all the columns of the transept. In this way the foundation area would be larger and therefore soil stresses less than before. The differences between vertical displacements at nodes 18 and 42 would also be reduced, although it was not possible to eliminate them totally. This design for the new foundation ensured that the difference between displacements could be less than a chosen value. Unfortunately this design could not be carried out, because a large well was discovered, as shown in Fig. 6. This well was made before the church was built, and had been used as a water tank until some time ago. When it was discovered it was nearly empty, and it is likely that this well had contributed to the weakening of the soil by leakage.

Another design for the foundation was chosen, avoiding the beam placed between the columns next to the apse. It must be pointed out that these columns do not show different vertical displacements because of the model symmetry. Hence the final design was almost as efficient as the initial one. It is shown in Fig. 7.

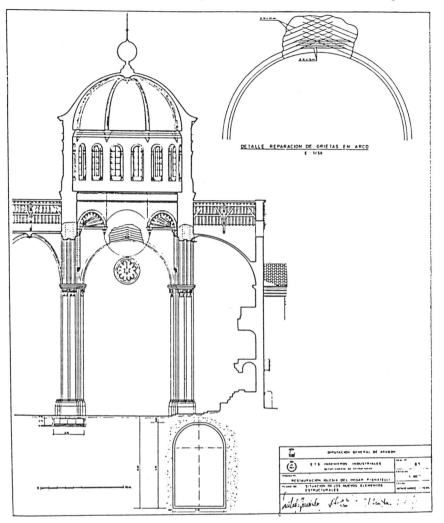

Fig. 6

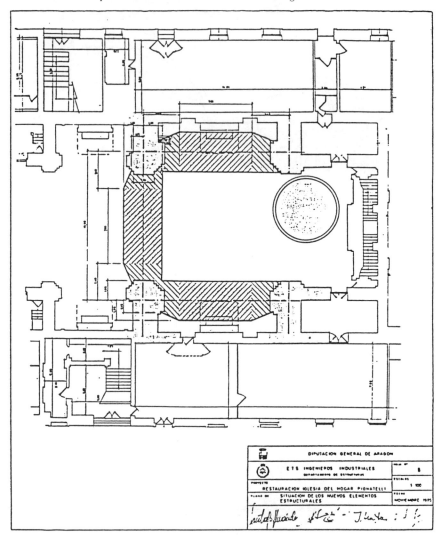

Fig. 7

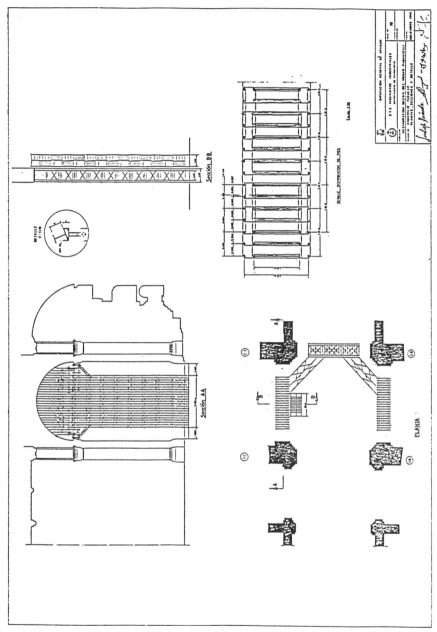

Fig. 8

At this stage another structural analysis of the new foundation, and the initial structural model of the transept and apse were carried out, but avoiding areas of the apse which had collapsed. In those calculations the width of the foundation was fixed and several values for depth were studied. The optimal criterion was to obtain a difference between the vertical displacements of nodes 18 and 42 of less than 1/1000. This criterion was accomplished with a width of 80 cm.

Restoration of the Arches

Before repairing the arches of the transept the zones of masonry brick which were fractured were removed. It did not seem possible to replace the old masonry with similar new material because of the difficulty of achieving a safe bond between them. That is why low density reinforced concrete was chosen. This material had three advantages:

- It is easy to obtain a solid connection with the old masonry brick.
One can introduce steel bars inside the masonry brick, and pour a layer of epoxy resin into the correction.
- It is stronger than the former material.
- It has the same density $(1.6t/m^2)$ as masonry brick.

The scaffold shown in Fig. 8 was erected under each arch for the restoration work. It had to accomplish two objectives:

a) It had to provide a platform for the repair work.
b) It had to support the entire load of an arch. With this facility it was possible to remove the collapsed masonry of the arches safely, and it was also possible to dig foundations under the columns in order to rebuild.

The new foundation served as the foundation for the scaffolding, during the restoration work. After the new material was added to the arches, and the repair work was completed, it started to work as the new foundation for the transept.

The well, which appeared under the arch next to the apse, had to be temporarily filled with sand during the work. After that a provisional foundation was built to support the scaffolding, as we have mentioned. That provisional scaffolding was finally demolished.

References

1. Curtin, W.G.: Structural Masonry Designer's Manual, Granada Publishing Limited, 1982.

2. Schultze, W.E.: Cimentaciones, Ed. Blume, 1970.

3. Bathe, K.J.; Wilson, E.: SAP IV (A Structural Analysis Program for Static and Dynamic Response of Linear Systems), University of California, 1974.

Flexibility Method and its Application to Ancient Structures

W.J. Harvey and F.W. Smith
Department of Civil Engineering, The University, Dundee DD1 4HN, Scotland

SYNOPSIS

Masonry structures built in ancient times and through to the present day depend on gravity for their stability. Most of them are statically indeterminate. The boundary conditions applied are critical to the safety of the structure, but are unknown. An engineer assessing an existing structure must, in the end, use his judgement, there are no "answers" in such analyses.

Jaques Heyman has shown that it is useful, in analysis, to release the structure until it forms a mechanism and analyse the collapse condition. The Flexibility method consists of releasing the structure until it is statically determinate and then studying the **forces** necessary to restore its assumed fixity. The present authors have shown that a statically determinate analysis can be useful in the study of arch bridges. There are two extreme solutions in an arch, one yielding the maximum, and the other the minimum, horizontal thrust. It is possible to explore intermediate possibilities by adopting the flexibility approach and restoring the redundant reactions. An ideal way to pursue this is graphically on a computer screen, when the effect of altering reactions can immediately be observed in changing load paths or lines of thrust.

The application of this approach to arch bridges is demonstrated. The extension to more highly redundant structures is explored in a discussion of multi-span arches, and an approach to more complex structures is suggested.

INTRODUCTION

Thrust lines and elastic analyses

In 1676 Robert Hooke [1] found a solution to the problem of the most important statically indeterminate structure then known. He kept his finding secret for fear of academic rivalry from those whose stature should have precluded such plagiarism. Of course we now know that his solution was of limited value because it provided only understanding, not a scheme of computation. This paper aims to show that understanding can be more useful than essentially meaningless calculated results.

In 1879 Castigliano [2] provided engineers with a computational scheme for indeterminate structures. In various guises his method has held engineers in thrall, and incidentally terrified students, ever since. Many of us recognise that elastic studies may obscure the true behaviour of a structure, but they do allow us to carry out closed form calculations on structures which might otherwise be intractable.

Castigliano's theorems are particularly inappropriate for masonry structures. Masonry is hardly elastic, and arches in particular are very susceptible to small movements of their foundations: movements which must take place.

Load path analysis

For many years, senior engineers have used load path analysis to assist in the conceptual design of complex structures. The approach is one of approximation. The relative stiffness of different paths from point of application to point of support is assessed on the basis of experience. The results are always checked by more "rigorous" methods as the design proceeds.

The zone of thrust

Hooke's line of thrust is of course a load path. The line of thrust ignores material strength, but it can be enhanced to show an area of material which would be required to support the thrust concerned [3].

Graphical indeterminacy

Barlow [4] gave a fine graphical representation of the indeterminacy of arch structures. He demonstrated with a physical model that there are many potential lines of thrust within an arch, any one of which may represent the actual performance of the structure. His lesson has often been lost on more recent investigators who have sought to define the one thrust line. We hope to show that such a constrained view is neither necessary nor desirable.

Indeed, the freedom to investigate all the possible thrust lines in a structure may allow the engineer the flexibility he needs to understand its behaviour. The classical example of an arch will be used to explore this possibility further.

THE INDETERMINATE ARCH

Arches are notionally three times statically indeterminate. In modern structures engineers habitually release these indeterminacies by introducing hinges at the springings and the apex of the arch. Pippard [5] showed that real arches will approach the three hinged condition as they deform after the removal of their centring. Having demonstrated that masonry arches are not elastic rings he proceeded to use Castigliano to produce the MEXE analysis beloved of British bridge engineers. More recently considerable effort has been invested [6-10] in developing complex finite element programs for arch analysis. These still assume that the arch is supported on rigid foundations, which is manifestly untrue.

A force based analytical technique is much more readily adapted to the problem of arches. The Flexibility method consists in releasing indeterminate resultants until the structure becomes statically determinate, then analysing the effect of unit resultants. The much more popular stiffness method which is the root of the FE approach is the converse of this. All "joints" are made rigid in space and the fixity reactions computed. Unit displacements are considered in order to find the "true" deformed shape of the structure. Stress resultants (forces) are computed from the displacements.

A structure which, though notionally statically indeterminate, tends to release its redundant reactions after construction, may be best analysed by the flexibility method. This is especially true if a path can be opened to the exploration of the effect of reactions which cannot sensibly be computed. We will endeavour to demonstrate that such a technique is not just possible but actually easier than some others to implement.

THE RELEASED STRUCTURE

Natural release: the minimum thrust view
We have said that a masonry arch deflects towards a three hinge structure on release of the centring. This must be the case because the arch ring will shorten under stress and the abutments will deflect outwards. The shorter ring will no longer fit perfectly into the springings. As this deformation takes place, the horizontal component of thrust

in the arch will reduce towards a minimum value. The minimum corresponds to the maximum possible rise of the zone of thrust within the arch ring. (Figure 1.) Analysis of the three hinged arch, which is the limit of this process, is very simple. It involves writing and solving two linear simultaneous moment equations. This structure may sensibly be regarded as the released form for the application of redundant actions.

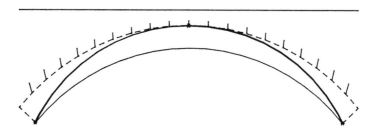

Figure 1.   Arch with minimum thrust

Forced release: the maximum thrust case

It is of course conceivable, and was demonstrated in practice by Chettoe and Henderson [11], that the springings may be forced together by external effects. In the case of arch bridges [11] this is caused by the approach of a heavy vehicle. The limit case of this movement is when the arch begins to lift in a three hinged jacking mechanism. (Figure 3.) The result is still a stable structure which can be analysed as described above. In this case the rise of the zone of thrust is the minimum possible within the arch ring. The horizontal component of thrust in the arch is thus maximised.

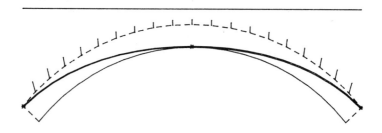

Figure 2.   Arch with maximum thrust

The two cases described are exactly analogous to the limiting active and passive pressures exerted by soil on moving walls.

RESTORING REDUNDANCY

A favoured case: minimum stress

Having produced a released structure, we must now restore its redundant actions and reactions to model the real behaviour. Heyman [12] used the mechanism analysis to compute the line of thrust which had a minimum deviation from the curve of the arch. Both Heyman and the Harvey [3] chose to follow the curve of the intrados of the arch, but the arch centreline might equally well be used. This approach yields a line or zone of thrust which is wholly contained within the arch ring, thus implying the fully redundant structure. (Figure 3.) A gross error is made in assuming that this is the correct solution. Heyman clearly did not fall into this trap. The implication is of minimum value of maximum compressive stress which is not the form a structure naturally seeks.

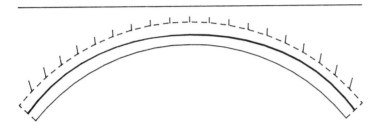

Figure 3.   Arch with minimum stress

The infinity of real solutions

The line of thrust defined by the above method lies at a point between the two extremes already discussed. Barlow [4] showed that these three solutions are only three of the infinite possible set which exist in an arch which is not on the point of failure.

The importance of reactions

The reactions which result at the supports of an arch are important because they control the behaviour of both arch and abutments. In some load cases a larger thrust will be needed, in others the interaction will lead to smaller values. If gross movements are excluded, the arch can deliver whatever reactions are required within the bounds set above. The two limits are reached with a range of abutment movements of less than 0.1% of the arch span [13]

Exploratory analysis

The illustrations presented thus far have all been produced using micro computer software developed at the Wolfson Bridge Research unit in Dundee. We have a program in commercial use based on the minimum stress theme. We have recently developed the maximum and minimum thrust models which were used for the diagrams. The final step has been to allow the user to alter the location, direction and value of the right hand reaction on the arch from the initial calculated value. This encourages the engineer to explore the effect of redundancy by observing the relationship between reactions and the thrustline. Because the only computation involved is vector addition, results are presented as a relatively smooth animation even on an IBM PC AT.

MULTIPLE REDUNDANCY

Most real structures have rather more redundancy than the simple arch described above. It is perfectly practicable to use the exploratory technique on multiple spans and even complex cathedral like structures. The first stages have been made and will be presented below.

Viaducts
A two span arch is the next step in complication. Here there are three reactions and six redundancies. The statically determinate release structure will have both arches descending. (Figure 4.) It will be necessary to

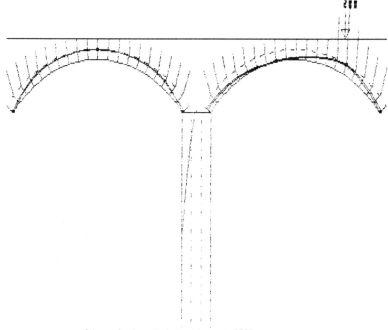

Line of thrust left pier at 7200

Figure 4. Double span – both arches falling

investigate the interaction of two resultants and so they must be changed in turn. Each arch is dealt with separately. Reactions are adjusted to produce an acceptable zone of thrust. The two arches are then combined and the path of the resultant force down the pier is traced. If the two arches are analysed separately, the combined picture can be displayed adequately on a Hercules screen, and very attractively on VGA. Figure 5 is a screen dump of a two span structure on a Hercules screen. It shows the effect of adjusting the reactions in the unloaded arch of Figure 4.

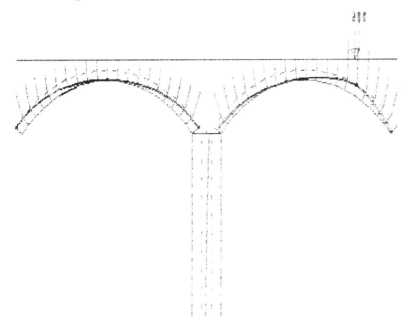

Figure 5. Double span – left arch rising

Extension of the process   The graphical quality available on microcomputers is still somewhat limited. When two spans are being worked on it is usually advantageous to treat them individually before combining the graphics on the screen. A similar approach will, of course, be possible for a viaduct. Each arch can be treated as a separate entity and then the structure combined to show the effect at the piers. As screen resolution improves it will be possible to work on multiple spans on screen.

The mechanistic side of development is also important. It is our aim to use a mouse to adjust the resultants by working with a graphical representation of the vector on screen. This will be particularly appropriate on higher resolution screens working with several redundants.

Cathedrals

The treatment of cathedral type structures is rather more complex. Some of the redundant forces are within the structure and so releases must be made by sectioning.

Decisions on release   The decisions on where to release a complex structure will depend on the graphical representation of that structure. It is clearly possible to treat internal redundants in the same way as reactions, except that the force must be applied to both sides of the release point. This is similar to dealing always with a series of arches before pasting them together to form a viaduct.

Computational considerations   The techniques outlined here are clearly very different from traditional structural engineering computation. The structure must be described geometrically in some detail. That geometric form must allow the division of the structure into sensible segments, and the segmental data must be stored in an effective way. The segmentation must also make sense in terms of the analytical technique. The forces generated in and on each element must add together to produce a sensible continuation of the line of thrust. Where two lines combine this will be particularly complicated, as indicated at the pier heads in illustrations above. A great deal of work remains to be done on data structures and calculation procedures.

THE VALUE OF THE OUTPUT

No doubt many of the readers who have born with us thus far will wish to ask the question "so what?" What does a picture of the polygon of forces offer the engineer. Our view is that it allows him to explore the limits within which his structure is actually working. It will not give an absolute solution to the analytical problem, but the problem is not susceptible to analysis in that way. So many of the parameters concerned can only be defined in terms of limits. It is foolhardy to rely on even a few analytical solutions which don't clearly show what the implications are throughout the structure.

THE NEXT STAGES

A simple extension of the procedure adopted here will be to compute the deformations implied by the thrust lines proposed. Such calculations can be performed many times faster than finite element analysis, so that even complex structures can happily be dealt with on a modern micro computer. This work has already been completed for the simple arch and will be published shortly.

The essential constraint for the time being is graphics resolution. This barrier is being moved every few months and will soon disappear for most real problems. A typical engineering workstation could already handle both computation and graphics for complex structures.

CONCLUSIONS

1   Slender gravity structures are fundamentally different from modern continuous structures and demand unique analytical tools.

2   The line of thrust view has long been popular and load path analysis is its modern descendant.

3   The flexibility method provides a basis for a semi automatic form of load path analysis for masonry structures.

4   The method is capable of considerable development, especially as computers become faster, and as display techniques improve.

REFERENCES

1. Hooke, R, A Description of Helioscopes, and some other Instruments, London, 1676

2. Castigliano, C A P, Theorie de l'Equilibre des Systemes Elastiques et ses Applications, Augustos Frederico Negro, Turin, 1879. Translated by E S Andrews, 'Elastic Stresses in Structures', London, Scott, Greenwood & Son, 1919; also with an introduction by G E A Oravas, The theory of equilibrium of elastic systems and its applications, Dover, New York, 1966

3. Harvey, W J, The application of the Mechanism Analysis to Arch Bridges, J I Struct E, Volume 66, Number 5, March 1988

4. Barlow, W H, On the Existence (Practically) of the line of equal Horizontal Thrust in Arches and Modes of Determining it by Geometric Construction, Min Proc Inst Civ Eng 5, 1846, p162

5. Pippard, A J S, & Chitty, L, A study of the voussoir arch, National Building Studies Research Paper 11, HMSO, London, 1951

6. Chrisfield, M A, A finite element computer program for the analysis of masonry arches, Transport & Road Res Lab, Report LR1115, Crowthorne, Berks, England, 1984

7. Chrisfield, M A, Finite elements and solution procedures
    for structural analysis, Vol 1, Linear analysis,
    Pineridge Press, Swansea, 1986

8. Chrisfield, M A, Plasticity computations using the Mohr-
    Coulomb yield criterion, Engineering Computations, to be
    published

9. Chrisfield, M A, Numerical methods for the nonlinear
    analysis of bridges, Proc 3rd Int Conf on Civil &
    Structural Engineering Computing, Vol 2, Civil-Comp
    Press, Edinburgh, 1987, pp67-74

10.   Chrisfield, M A, Computer methods for the analysis
        of masonry arches, Proc 2nd Int Conf on Civil &
        Structural Engineering Computing, Vol 2, Civil-Comp
        Press, Edinburgh, 1985, pp213-220

11.   Chettoe, C S, & Henderson, W H, Masonry Arch
        Bridges: A Study, Proc Inst Civ Eng, 1957, 8,
        pp723-755

12.   Heyman, J, The estimation of the strength of
        masonry arches, Proc Inst Civ Eng, 1980, 69, Dec,
        pp921-937

13.   Harvey, W J, & Barthel, R, The relationship between
        thrust and springing movement in arches, to be
        published.

The Importance of Phase-by-Phase Limit Analysis of a Monument.
Strengthening of St. Panteleimon Church in Thessaloniki

K. Stylianidis, C. Ignatakis

Department of Civil Engineering, Aristotle University of
Thessaloniki, 540 06 Thessaloniki, Greece

ABSTRACT

If a civil engineer is called upon to contribute to a repair procedure of an old monument which suffers extensive damaging he must not only consider the present structural condition but he must also pay much attention to its historical background. This consideration, accompanied with appropriate analyses, may help him to understand the actual resisting mechanisms of the structure and to interpret the existing damage pattern. The knowledge gained is also valuable for the decicions concerning the repair and strengthening measures. In this paper a phase-by-phase analytical procedure is presented through the case study of St. Panteleimon Church in Thessaloniki, Greece. This procedure follows the historical phases from the structural point of view, i.e. all the basic phases of erection, the partial collapses and the mutilations of the structure during its lifetime. In each phase the "background" stresses and the hinges created during a preceding phase are taken into account. A simultaneous comparison of the results of the analyses and the historical references concerning partial collapses or heavy damaging is performed. This check enables the verification of the analytical models used. In some cases modifications concerning addition of newly activated or subtraction of unactivated or collapsed members are proved to be neccesary. The same concept of modelling and analytical procedure is then used for the analysis of the strengthening measures in their order of application.

ST. PANTELEIMON CHURCH OF THESSALONIKI

Structural form and historical background
The St. Panteleimon Byzantine Church of Thessaloniki was built during the early period of Paleologi (late 13th-early 14th century) (Ioanidou [1]). In its initial form it was a brick and stone masonry crossed compound four-pillar church with a three-aisled perimetric gallery (Fig.1). It had one central dome, one dome on the narthex and two more domes on

the gallery. Wooden tierods resisted the horizontal thrusts developed by the four main arches, the vaults of the narthex and the vaults of the gallery. Wooden beams forming a belting system were found embedded in the surrounding masonry walls and connected with the wooden tierods mentioned above. The walls were resting on deep foundation beams while the pillars were resting on masonry foundation blocks connected with the perimetric foundation beams (Traganou-Deligianni [2]).

The historical documentation of the monument reports successively an early collapse of the western aisle of the gallery, a cutting off of the wooden tierods of the narthex and a collapse of the northern and later of the southern dome of the gallery (Ioanidou [1]). As no attempt has been undertaken to restore the missing architectural and structural elements in the past, all the mutilations and the aging effects are today apparent on the monument (Fig.2,3,4).

Damage pattern

Damages are more extensive in the higher parts of the monument and tend to diminish in the lower parts, including foundations. Taking into account the crack pattern and the structural form of byzantine churches, it is reasonable to conclude that the initial damages were mainly caused by the self -weight thrusts and the accompanying deformations. The damages were later precipitated because of the gradual weakening of the supporting system due to aging and because of earthquakes. Actually, in situ investigations verified that, at the present time, the wooden tierods can not function as they had been designed to, mainly because of sliding of their supports in the masonry.

As a result, the supporting system gives way causing extensive cracking. Some of the cracks can be characterized as hinges since they are very deep and are accompanied by great rotations of the relevant cross-sections. In three main arches, out of the four supporting the central dome, the width and the span have values of the same order of magnitude. These arches, having underneath a front tympanum initially built as an infill, are diagonally cracked, having the typical cracking pattern of a plate supported on three edges and loaded on the free edge. In the so called chapels, which are remainders of the collapsed gallery, great inclinations of the walls supporting the vaults are observed.

Probably the most dangerous cracks are these of the compound pillars where there is a tendency of formation of inclined sliding surfaces due to the combination of normal and shear stresses. These surfaces tend to separate the compound pillars into their components. On the contrary, the cross-sections of the pillars on the foundation appear to be undamaged. In the part of the foundations, where exploratory soil sections were cut, some cracks appeared on the deep beams, but there is no sign of overall instability.

Remedies
Inspite of the structural problems arised during seven centuries of life, it cannot be ignored that the monument is still
standing. Consequently, the remedial measures tend to help
the existing load transferring system, rather than to change
it (Wenzel [3]). As criteria for the proposed interventions,
in addition to the reversibility requirement, the concepts of
modern design codes were used. For the vertical loads and the
design seismic actions, serviceability and strength criteria
were taken into account, which allow for limited cracking but
no formation of hinges. These criteria led to the proposal of
filling the cracks with compatible mortar injections, addition of new metal tierods, lightly prestressed, at the same
level as the existing ones and construction of thin doweled
shotcrete jackets on the outer surface of the arches, given
that the masonry did not have the required strength. Furthermore, the reinforced jackets, combined with the new metal
tierods, can give adequate ductility to the strengthened
structure for the prevention of collapse under severe seismic
actions.

ANALYTICAL PROCEDURE

Analytical possibilities
Although it is beyond the scope of this paper to discuss the
analytical possibilities, it must be mentioned that in such
cases a simple type of static analysis is recommended even
for seismic loads (WG F of UNIDO/UNDP Project RER/79/015
[4]). For the time being, detailed dynamic analyses do not
seem to be feasible mainly because of the difficulties in assessing ground motion characteristics and dynamic properties
of materials and because of their computational cost. The
best that can be expected seems to be a limit-state static
collapse analysis using appropriately simplified models of
the overall structural system (Mainstone [5]). The choice of
a valid model depends on the skill of the analyst. Since it
is often impracticable to analyse a structure as a whole,
more skill is needed to represent boundary conditions.
Foundation soil also calls for a successful model.

Analytical procedure proposed
The analytical procedure performed is a limit-state static
collapse analysis. This procedure has already been successfully used to a limited extent in the past (WG F of UNIDO/
UNDP Project RER/79/015, Case Study [6]).

Model The structure has been divided in four main plane frames. Each frame consisted of arches, vaults, piers, walls,
columns, tierods, struts, foundation beams and soil springs.
Domes were analyzed separately in a previous stage. Elastic
properties of four different materials (masonry, timber, marble and soil) were used to represent the adjacent structural
elements. Regions of practically infinite stiffness were used
to transfer the loads from the arches and vaults on the ec-
centrically loaded piers. Wooden tierods, marble columns and

masonry struts were represented as hinged elements in both
ends. Masonry struts were used to represent infills when it
was assumed that they were activated. Springs with time-
depending stiffness represented the foundation soil. Boundary
conditions were considered to be satisfied when the vertical
displacements of an individual soil spring (belonging in two
perpendicular plane frames) were almost equal.

Loading Dead loads (self-weight and roof load), seismic load
and prestressing loads were considered. It was assumed that
the loading was applied in a monotonically increasing way.

Failure criteria A cross-sectional failure criterion was
adopted concerning combination of normal and shear stresses.
This criterion was derived through Mohr's cycles from the
corresponding Kupfer's criterion for low strength concrete.
The constitutive law of all the materials used was linearly
elastic. A suitable computer program was writen to determine
the safety factor of a polygonal cross-section under biaxial
bending. Deformation failure criteria were not used to inden-
tify local collapses and this is a shortcoming of the analytical methods like the one used (Mainstone [5]). On the other
hand, deformation criteria were used to model the activation
of infills as diagonal struts, when arches or vaults tended
to rest on the infills underneath.

Application of the procedure In each phase the background
stresses and the hinges created in the preceding phase are
taken into account representing the past history effects. A
portion of the loading is applied step-by-step, until a new
hinge forms. The model is then accordingly modified to take
account of the new hinge and another portion of the loading
is then applied. The step-by-step analysis continues until
the total loading is applied. The hinges formed represent
regions of excessive damages during the adjacent phase. A
simultaneous comparison of the analyses results and the historical references concerning excessive damages or collapses
is then performed. An appraisal method, like part of the one
proposed by ICE (Beckmann-Happold [7]) is then applied.

RESULTS

The phases considered and some of the corresponding analytical results are summarised in Table 1. During the phase of
construction, under the total dead loads, hinges were formed
in the foundation and in the arches and vaults, especially at
keystone regions, with the exception that at the gallery
vault, hinges were formed at the origins as well (Fig.5,6).
Under feeble seismic loads, the vault of the western gallery
was proved to be unstable (Fig.6). The collapse of the gallery arch did not affect the remaining structure. The cutting
off of the wooden tierods of the narthex caused many hinges
in the corresponding vault while the rest of the structure
was not affected (Fig.7). Application of seismic loads led to
the formation of many hinges in the arches and vaults which

Table 1.   Analyses results.

PHASES CONSIDERED		FIG.	NEW HINGES	TOTAL HINGES	ANALYS. NEEDED
Phases of construction	Erection of piers	5	1F	1F	3
	Construction of arches and vaults	6	1F/5V	2F/5V	5
Seismic loading : 1.4% Collapse of gallery vault		6	1V	2F/6V	1
Structural modification		7	--	2F/2V	1
Cutting off of the wooden tierods of narthex		7	4V	2F/6V	5
Seismic loading: up to 11.1%		7	2F/5V	4F/11V	9
Seismic loading: increasing		8	MANY	PIERS CHECK	
Phases of intervention	Roof removal	--	--	2F/6V	3
	50% prestressing	--	--	2F/6V	1
	Mortar injections	--	--	2F	-
	50% prestressing	--	--	2F	1
	Roof reconstruction	--	--	2F	1
Seismic loading:up to 18.1%(W-E)		9	6V	2F/6V	9
Seismic loading:up to 17.9%(E-W)		10	6V	2F/6V	7

F: Foundation   V: Vaults

tended to rest on the infills underneath, suffering excessive damaging (Fig.7). Consequently, the ultimate seismic load of the individuale piers can be considered as the upper limit of the ultimate seismic load of the structure (Fig.8).

After the application of the mortar injections, the level of the remedial prestressing forces was calculated using the criterion of no hinges formation under vertical loads. Considerably higher seismic loads were needed to be applied, in relation to the unstrengthened structure, for the formation of the same number of hinges in the masonry arches and vaults. No hinges appeared in concrete jackets under the ultimate seismic loads of the piers mentioned above (Fig.9,10).

From the analytical results presented above it can be concluded that, using the limit-state static collapse analysis, a satisfactory representation of the damage pattern, including partial collapses, can be derived. Consequently, the procedure used is an effective analytical method for the prediction of the future response of the strengthened structure.

REFERENCES

1. Ioanidou, N. Historical Documentation and Intervention Principals of the Conservation Study of the Church of S. Panteleimon at Thessaloniki, pp. 131-145, Proceedings of the Int. Symposium on Restoration of Byzantine and Post-Byzantine Monuments, Thessaloniki, Greece, 1985. 9th Ephorate of Byzantine Antiquities, Thessaloniki, 1986.

2. Traganou-Deligianni, O. Research on Masonry Walls and Foundations during the Conservation Study of the Church of St. Panteleimon at Thessaloniki, pp. 113-130, Proceedings of the Int. Symposium on Restoration of Byzantine and Post-Byzantine Monuments, Thessaloniki, Greece, 1985. 9th Ephorate of Byzantine Antiquities, Thessaloniki, 1986.

3. Wenzel, F. Structural Problems Connected with Restoration and Strengthening, pp. 13-27, Proceedings of the IABSE Symposium on Strengthening of Building Structures-Diagnosis and Therapy, Venezia, Italy, 1983. IABSE, Zurich, Switzerland, 1983.

4. WG F of UNIDO/UNDP Project RER/79/015 Building Construction under Seismic Conditions in the Balkan Region. Vol.6, Repair and Strengthening of Historical Monuments and Buildings in Urban Nuclei. Chapter 4, Methods of Investigation and Analysis, pp. 79-96, UNIDO, Vienna,1984.

5. Mainstone, R.J. Masonry Vaulted and Domed Structures with Special Reference to the Monuments of Thessaloniki, pp. 237 -248, Proceedings of the Int. Symposium on Restoration of Byzantine and Post-Byzantine Monuments, Thessaloniki, Greece, 1985. 9th Ephorate of Byzantine Antiquities, Thessaloniki, 1986.

6. WG F of UNIDO/UNDP Project RER/79/015 Building Construction under Seismic Conditions in the Balkan Region. Vol.6, Repair and Strengthening of Historical Monuments and Buildings in Urban Nuclei. Chapter 9, Case Study:The Church of Hagios Andreas, Peristera, pp.189-195, UNIDO, Vienna,1984.

7. Beckmann, P.-Happold, E. Appraisal-a Cyclical Process of Inspection and Calculation, pp. 31-38, Proceedings of the IABSE Symposium on Strengthening of Building Structures-Diagnosis and Therapy, Venezia, Italy,1983. IABSE, Zurich, Switzerland, 1983.

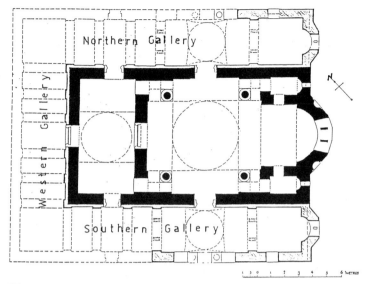

Fig.1 Plan at ground level of St. Panteleimon Church as it was initially built.

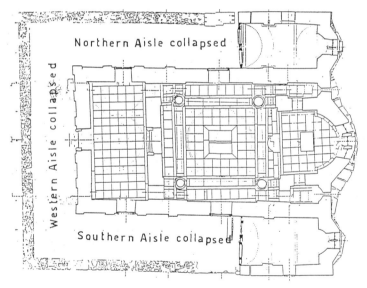

Fig.2 Plan at ground level of St. Panteleimon Church as it is today.

Fig.3   West-East cross section of the Church.

Fig.4   South elevation of the Church.

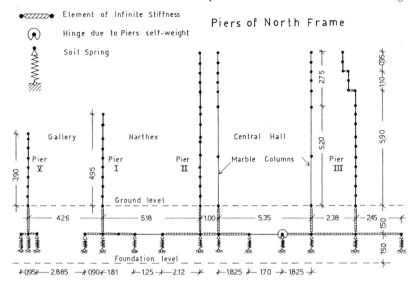

Fig.5 Analytically determined damages during the phase of erection of piers.

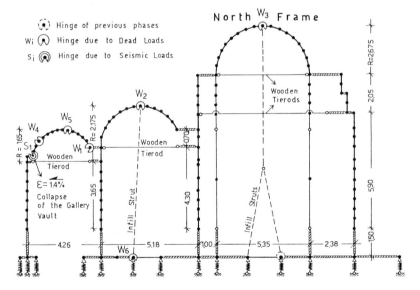

Fig.6 Analytically determined damages during the phase of construction of arches and vaults.

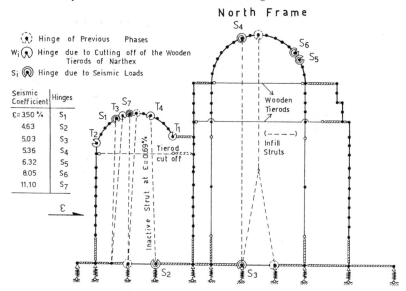

Fig.7   Analytically determined damages of the structure as it is today.

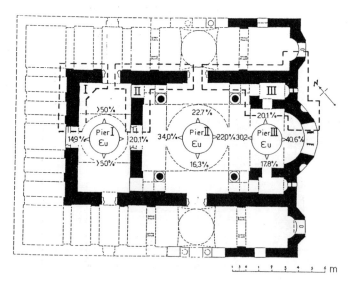

Fig.8   Ultimate seicmic loads of the piers at the present form, after the collapses and mutilations.

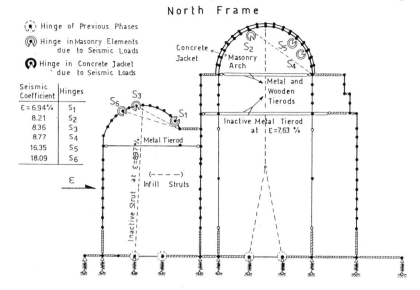

Fig.9   Analytically determined damages of the strengthened structure under West-East seismic loads.

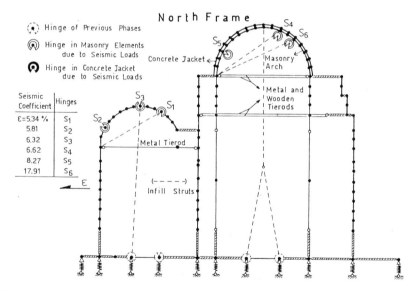

Fig.10   Analytically determined damages of the strengthened structure under East-West seismic loads.

Structural Analysis of the Equestrian Monument to Marcus Aurelius in Rome

G. Accardo, D. Amodio*, P. Cappa*, A. Bennici,
G. Santucci*, M. Torre

Central Institute for the Restoration, Rome, Italy
*Department of Mechanics and Aeronautics, 'La Sapienza' University, Rome, Italy

ABSTRACT

The Marcus Aurelius equestrian monument has been analyzed by the finite element method. The stress and strain fields, relevant to the rider load and thermal effects have been calculated. The finite element model has been used to evaluate the best constraint conditions between the monument and its pedestal and to design an internal stiffening frame. The numerical results have been validated by evaluating experimentally strains and displacements in the horse occuring due to loading by the rider.

INTRODUCTION

Acting on behalf of the'Comune di Roma', the Central Institute for the Restoration of the 'Ministero per i Beni Culturali ed Ambientali' is taking care of the restoration work of the equestrian monument to Marcus Aurelius, the bronze, hand-manufactured in the second century BC placed, during the sixteenth century, on the Capitoline Hill in Rome (Ackerman[1], Gregorovius[2]). The monument, standing on a stone base, is constructed of two different parts: the horse, with a raised front right leg, and the effigy of the emperor, rested on the edge of a large hole localized in the upper part of the animal. The restoration work necessitated the disassembly of the statue into the two constituent pieces, the disconnection of the horse from its ancient pedestal and the transfer of the group to the Physics Laboratory of the Institute. The horse is now resting on a steel frame which has been previously used to protect it during transportation (figure 1).

Before doing any work on the monument, the Central Institute for the Restoration executed a long series of historical and experimental investigations. Among them here we will mention those aiming to obtain a deeper knowledge about the techniques used for casting and assembling the statue (Marabelli[3]); we should also mention the investigations on the chemical composition and

on the chemical-physical and mechanical properties of the alloys
used (Cesareo[4]). Photogrammetry and non destructive (ultrasonic)
techniques have also been used to obtain information on the monument geometry (shape, dimensions and thickness distribution)
(Sena[5], Canella[6]) and on the structural integrity (presence of
holes, inclusions, weldings and cracks) (Micheli[7]). At the same
time the nature and extent of previous restoration work has
been carefully evaluated (Tabak[8]). Finally the temperature field
in the monument has been carefully analyzed throughout the day
and in different seasons (Accardo[9], Caneva[10]).

During such preliminary investigations, the Physics and Environment Control Laboratory of the Central Institute for the Restoration, and the Department of Mechanics and Aeronautics of Rome
University 'La Sapienza' have carried out a study on the structural stability of the monument (Accardo[11], Santucci[12]). The
verification of the stress distribution in the horse, due to the
rider weight, has been the main aim of this study. Then the
thermal stresses due to the non uniform environment temperature
distribution have been evaluated. Looking toward the future,
and the replacing of the monument onto its base, the best restraining conditions have been studied in order to reduce the
stress level in the horse. At the same time investigations have
been carried out on the possibility of creating an internal
stiffening frame to partially release the weight of the rider
on the horse. The study has been carried out using finite element models validated by measuring horse displacements during
loading and unloading.

FINITE ELEMENT MODEL

365 shell elements and 406 nodes have been used to model the
horse body: the tail and the head were not introduced in the
model. The lower part of the three load-bearing legs have been
modelled by beams of circular section. A series of radially
placed high stiffness beams link each lower part of the legs to
the shell elements belonging to the upper part of the legs.
Square section beams have also been used to model the stiffening
cross introduced in previous centuries to consolidate the edges
of the holes on which the rider is resting. The thickness of
each shell element has been obtained by ultrasonic investigations.
The material forming the elements has been assumed to be isotropic and homogeneous. Mechanical tests were carried out on
specimens whose chemical properties were very close to the real
ones. Those tests suggested that one should assume the value of
85 GPa as the Young modulus, 0.3 as Poisson coefficient, 0.000018
$^\circ C^{-1}$ as thermal expansion coefficient and 80 kN/m3 as weight
density.

The restraints linking the monument to its base have been simulated in different ways depending on the aims of the calculation.
As far as the model validation is concerned the leg tips have
been restrained in the same way as they are on the transportation

frame, because the validation measurements have been carried out
in those conditions. In order to evaluate the best way to restrain the legs of the horse when it is standing on its stone
pedestal, a simple supported, a complete restraining or an intermediate solution have been taken into account in the numerical
model. In a further calculation a plate linking the three loaded
leg tips has been introduced in the finite element model. This
plate allows the study of the thermal effect due to different
heating between the bronze monument and the stone base and the
effect due to imposed displacements.

Different loads have been applied to the horse depending on the
aims of the calculations. For the model validation only the rider
weight has been considered. Accurate measurements indicated as
6.2 kN the rider weight. This was subdivided in equal parts and
applied on the 18 nodes placed on the hole edge in the upper part
of the horse. For the constraint optimization also the whole
weight of the monument has to be taken into account; in this
case vertical forces simulated the weight of the missing head and
tail.

RESULTS OF CALCULATION AND EXPERIMENTAL MEASUREMENTS

The calculations have been carried out by the finite element code
SAP. Figure 2 shows the model and its deformed shape, obtained
by loading the structure with the rider weight only and with
simple restraining hypothesis (the displacement scale is 200
times the one used for nodal coordinates). Figure 3 shows a
view of the von Mises equivalent stress level lines on the external surface of the horse. The figure shows that the maximum
stress value is localized on the connection between the front
left leg and the horse body.

The strain and displacement results have been validated by experimental measurements. Displacements have been measured by linear
variable differential transformers on the raised leg; strains
have been measured by using an electrical resistance strain gauge
localized where the calculation results indicated there are maximum values of the three displacement components examined.
Figure 5 shows the experimental and numerical principal strain
localized on the front left leg. The examination of these figures
shows an acceptable agreement between calculated and measured
values so that the finite element model can be considered validated and therefore has been used to perform further investigation.

CHOICE OF BEST CONSTRAINING METHOD

Figure 6 shows the highest equivalent stress values on the external and internal horse surfaces obtained by different constraint
hypotheses. In this figure only the rider weight has been taken
into account while in Figure 7 the whole weight of the monument
has been considered. Among the different constraint solutions
the imposed displacement at the leg tips seems to be the best

of the possibilities. In the finite element model these imposed
displacements have been obtained by a thermal dilatation (positive
or negative) of the base shell element whose stiffness is extremely high. A previous investigation indicated the best imposed
displacement at the leg tips in order to minimize stresses as
shown in Figure 8 for the Rider Weight Load (RWL) and for the
whole Monument Weight Load (MWL). The relative leg tip displacement which gives the minimum stresses is about 0.1% and this value
has been used in Figures 6 and 7 to determine the best constraining solution.

INTERNAL FRAME SUPPORTING THE RIDER

Finally a stainless steel frame structure has been designed to
get the rider supported directly by the horse legs in order to
unload the body of the horse. 22 beams form this frame: their
sections are hollow and circular with 5 mm thickness and 30 mm
diameter. In 1835, G Spagna filled the legs with low casting
temperature alloys so that they are now very rigid and robust
and able to support the rider load with a low stress level.
 Figure 9 shows the frame mounted inside the horse body; the
rider weight is applied on the frame top. A comparison between
the deformed shape of the frame, shown in Figure 9 and in Figure
2, indicates the stiffness increase obtained in the horse; the
stress level reduction is shown in Figure 6. Examination of
Figure 7 indicates that the stainless steel frame weight nearly
eliminates the benefits the frame itself introduces, so that a
lighter weight frame such as an aluminium alloy frame may be
recommended.

CONCLUSIONS

The decision on what type of restoration work to undertake for
the case of composite large dimension monuments such as the
equestrian cast of Marcus Aurelius demands careful analysis of
the mechanical behaviour of the statue structure. The uniqueness
of such a monument and its immense cultural value requires one
to use as little modification as possible. When stiffening
structures are designed it is necessary to analyze their effect
on the monument without actually having to build and mount such
structures. The finite element method provides a valid help to
choose the more effective restoration work on the monument
structure. In this paper one is shown how to use this method
and its integration with experimental techniques. The procedure
adopted in this case can be easily generalised to find a systematic methodology to be followed in the future. To obtain a
reliable finite element model of the monument a deep knowledge
of the geometry, the mechanical properties of the material and
the load nature and intensity are required. Once one has verified, by appropriate experimental techniqeus, that the finite
element model is able to simulate the real behaviour of the
monument it is possible to use this tool in order to undertake
structural restoration.

REFERENCES

1   Ackerman J S, M Aurelius on the Capitoline Hill, Renaissance
    News, Vol 2, PP 69-75, 1957.

2   Gregorovius F, Storia della Citta di Roma nel Medio Evo,
    Einaudi editore, Torino, 1973.

3   Marabelli M, La struttura e le tecniche di fabbricazione,
    Marco Aurelio - Mostra di cantiere (Catalogue), PP 39 - 41,
    ICR, Rome, Italy, 1984.

4   Cesareo R, Ferretti M, Guida G and Marabelli M, Le leghe: il
    metodo e i risultati, Marco Aurelio - Mostra di cantiere
    (Catalogue), PP 42 - 44, ICR, Rome, Italy, 1984.

5   Sena C, Rilievo mediante metodi della 'Fotogrammetria del
    Vicino' della statua equestre di Marco Aurelio in Roma,
    Proceedings of the 1st International Conference on Non-
    destructive Testing in Conservation of Works of Art, Rome,
    Italy, 1983.

6   Canella G, Marabelli M, Marano A and Micheli M, Esame
    ultrasonoro della statua equestre del Marco Aurelio,
    Proceedings of the 1st International Conference on Non-
    destructive Testing in Conservation of Works of Art, Rome,
    Italy, 1983.

7   Micheli M, Indagine radiografica della statua equestre di
    Marco Aurelio, Proceedings of the 1st International
    Conference on Non-destructive Testing in Conservation of
    Works of Art, Rome, Italy, 1983.

8   Tabak G, Nota sul restauro del Marco Aurelio al tempo di
    Gregorio XVI, Rassegna Archivi di Stato, XLII, I, Rome,
    Italy, 1982.

9   Accardo G et al, Il sistema ambiente-monumento, Marco
    Aurelio - Mostra di cantiere (Catalogue), PP 65 - 70, ICR,
    Rome, Italy, 1984.

10 Accardo G, Caneva C and Massa S, Stress monitoring by
    temperature mapping and acoustic emission analysis: a case
    study of Marcus Aurelius, Studies in Conservation, 28,
    PP 67 - 74, 1983.

11 Accardo G, De Santis P, Gori F, Guattari G and Webster J M,
    The use of Speckle Interferometry in the study of large
    works of art, Journal of Photographic Science, Vol 33, No 5,
    PP 174 - 176, 1985.

12   Accardo G, Santucci G, Metodo di calcolo agli elementi finiti
e misure estensimetriche per l'analisi strutturale di
manufatti storico-artistici, 2nd International Conference on
Non-destructive Testing, Microanalytical Methods and Environment Evaluation for Study and Conservation of Works of Art,
Perugia, Italy, 1988.

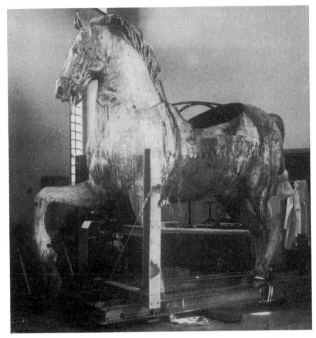

Figure 1. The Horse of Marcus Aurelius

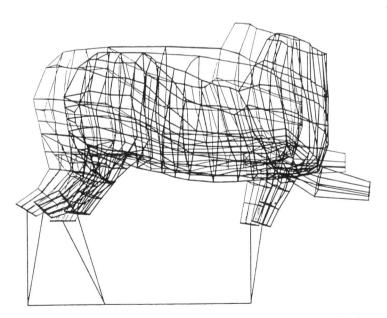

Figure 2. The Finite Element Model and its Deformed Shape

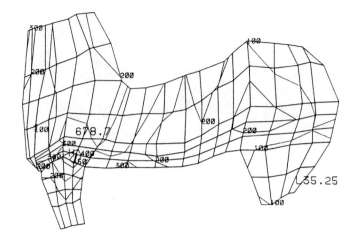

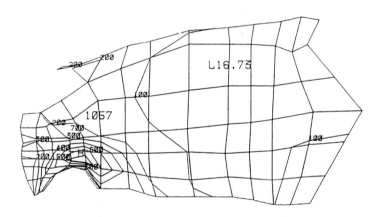

Figure 3. The von Mises equivalent Stress Map
    a) lateral view
    b) upwards from bottom view

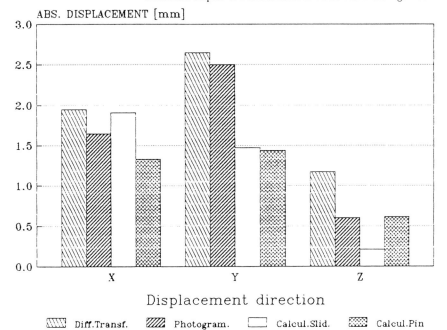

Figure 4. Comparison of displacements

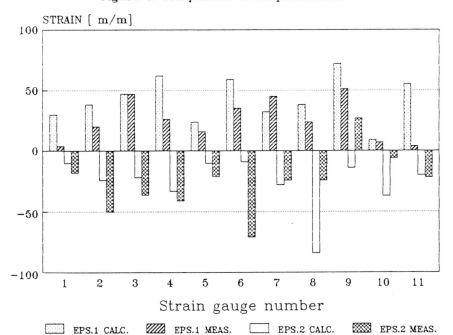

Figure 5.Comparison of principal strains

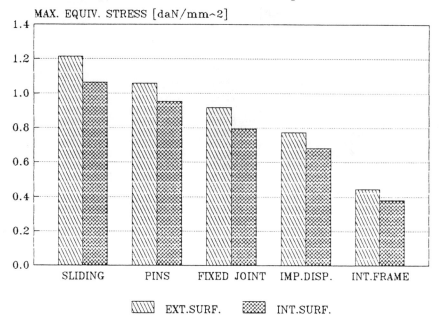

Figure 6. Effect of the constraints
(rider weight RWL)

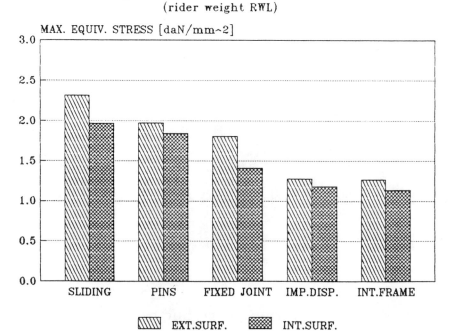

Figure 7. Effect of the constraints
(total weight MWL)

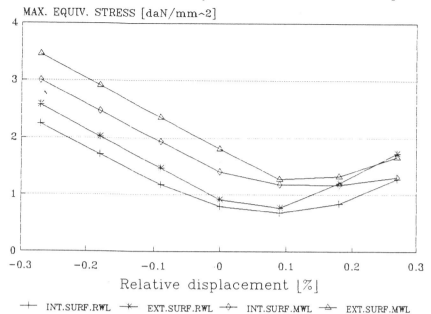

Figure 8. Effect of the imposed
displacement of the constraints

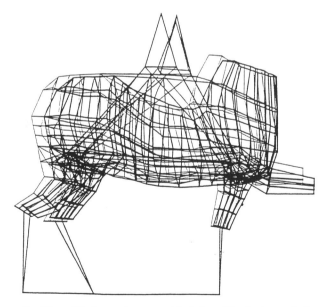

Figure 9. The Finite Element Model with Internal Frame
and its Deformed Shape

The Computational Geometry of the Deterioration of Stone Sculpture

Richard A. Livingston,

Geology Department, University of Maryland, College Park, MD 20742, USA

ABSTRACT

The investigation of the deterioration of sculpted stone on real structures requires a 3-dimensional geometry rather than the simple planar
geometry of test specimens. Computational geometry approximates complex curved surfaces by a set of tangent planes, each defined by a
position vector and local unit normal vector. The tangent planes can be
drawn as a triangular finite element mesh on the surface. The surface
recession produced by erosion is measured as the displacement of the
position vector. The surface recession of a 3-dimensional object
results in both isotropic contraction and distortion of the surface.
A constitutive law, or damage function, can define relating surface
recession to environmental stress. However, the exact form of this law
has not been determined experimentally. Failure to apply the finite
element methodology to actual measurements on stone statues or other
real structures will result in errors in the determination of the
surface recession as a function of position. This will lead in turn to
errors in the inference of the spatial variability of environmental
stresses around real structures.

INTRODUCTION

The concern over the deterioration of stone sculpture due to acid rain
has highlighted the need to treat the process as one occurring in three
dimensions. The conventional one-dimensional approach quantifies the
magnitude of stone deterioration in terms of linear surface recession,
i.e. simple displacement along an axis normal to the plane of the
original surface [1]. This approach effectively depicts the process as
the uniform erosion of a simple planar surface. This is not surprising
since most erosion measurements have been made on simple planar test
specimens. However, this is inadequate to describe erosion on "real
structures", i.e. on 3-dimensional objects. Especially in the context
of the preservation of stone monuments, the erosion of such plane
surfaces is of minor interest. Of greatest concern to the architectural
conservator is the loss of the highly non-planar features such as edges,
corners, sculptural details and inscriptions that are the essence of the
sculpture. A 3-dimensional set of coordinates is required to describe
the geometry of these features.

Moreover, the processes of erosion are not uniform over the surface
of the object. The rate of erosion will vary from point to point because of local differences in exposure to prevailing winds, rainfall,
solar radiation, etc. Even the effect of gravity will vary depending
upon the slope of the surface. Hence, the magnitude of the erosive

forces must also be described as a function of 3-dimensional coordinates in space.

The curves of most sculpted surfaces are too complex to be readily handled analytically. However, the numerical methods of computational geometry and finite element analysis can be utilized. The purpose of this paper is to formulate the problem of the erosion of stone sculpture in a way that permits the application of such numerical approaches.

SURFACE RECESSION IN 3 DIMENSIONS

Erosion is the removal of mass from the stone surface by a combination of mechanical and chemical processes. The loss of mass translates into a loss of the volume of the object, which is observable as a reduction in the linear dimensions, or surface recession. These variables can be measured in several ways, each having a somewhat different physical meaning [2]. Surface recession will be defined as a distance, in this case as the displacement of a given point on the surface relative to its original position. It is a scalar quantity, and in the most general case:

$$w = w(\mathbf{r}, \mathbf{n}, t) \tag{1}$$

where $\mathbf{r}$ is the position vector from the origin to the centroid of the triangular finite element, $\mathbf{n}$ is the unit normal vector for the element, and t is time.

The variation of w with position is a function of the spatial variation in environmental factors. For instance, upper surfaces can be catchments for rainwater, which is a major factor in erosion, while lower surfaces remain dry. The amount of solar radiation received, and hence the thermal expansion and contraction, is also a function of position on the surface. The dependence on the normal, $\mathbf{n}$, is due primarily to gravity, since erosion proceeds faster on an inclined or vertical surface than on a horizontal, upward facing one. This implies that the surface recession is in general anisotropic. Finally, the displacement increases as a function of time.

This problem bears a certain resemblance to plastic deformation analysis. However, it differs in several ways from the usual stress-strain analysis. To begin with, erosion effectively applies no stresses on the object as a whole and thus no strains are imposed. Instead the process consists of the translation and rotation of the surface in space. Consequently, the appropriate measure of deformation is the elongation (or in this case, contraction) which has units of distance, rather than strain, which is dimensionless. This also reflects the fact that the amount of erosion is a function only of surface conditions and is independent of the size of the object. Finally, by the definition of erosion, the mass of the object is not conserved.

APPROACH

The finite element approach consists of approximating the actual curved
surface of the object by a mesh of triangular finite elements, each
representing the local tangent plane. As shown in Fig. 1, the individual tangent plane can be completely specified by two vectors: **r**, the
vector from the origin to the triangle's centroid, P, and **n**, the unit
normal vector to the plane, which gives its orientation. The angle, θ,
between **r** and n is the tilt of the finite element. The nodes of the
finite element are located at the vertices.

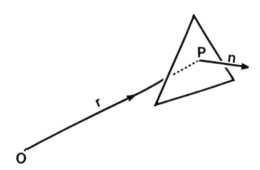

Figure 1: Specification of planar finite element by position
          vector, **r**, and unit normal vector, **n**.

During some time interval, Δt, the finite element is translated and
rotated to a new position, **r'**, as shown in Fig. 2. This displacement is
then given by the vector difference between the initial and final
position vectors, and the surface recession is its magnitude. Hence:

$$w \;=\; |\,r - r'\,| \tag{2}$$

The surface recession can be resolved into two components, one along
the original position vector, **r**, and the other perpendicular to it. The
magnitude of the collinear component, c, can be found from the usual
vector relationships to be :

$$c = w\cos\theta \tag{3}$$

This component describes a reduction in the size of the finite
element, but no lateral change in position or change in shape is
implied. Hence it can be considered an isotropic contraction of the
surface in which the finite element is located.

The other component, d, is given by:

$$d = w\sin\theta \tag{4}$$

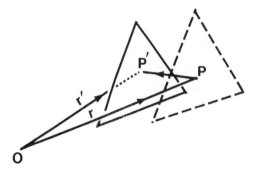

Figure 2:   Displacement of finite element by surface recession.

and represents the rotation of the vector pointing to the centroid of
the triangular finite element. This implies a lateral change in the
position of centroid, which in turn means a change in the shape of the
triangle and a distortion of the shape of the object. Therefore it can
be called the deviatoric contraction.

    It can be seen from equations 3 and 4 that the only case where con-
traction can occur in the absence of distortion of the object is when
$\theta = 0$ everywhere. However, it will be shown below that this condition
holds true only for two unlikely special cases. Thus, for almost all
situations, there will be some distortion, even in the case where w is
constant everywhere on the surface, simply from geometric considerations. Thus distortion is an inevitable consequence of treating
erosion of a surface as a 3-dimensional process rather than a
one-dimensional one.

    The process may be easier to grasp if presented in terms of finite
elements of volume rather than surface. As shown in Figure 3, it is
possible to draw rays from the origin to the vertices of the triangular

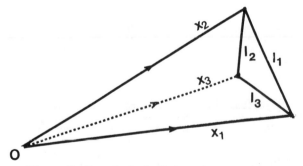

Figure 3: Tetrahedral finite element of volume.

finite element. These rays define a tetrahedral volume within the stone. The apex of the tetrahedron is at the origin, and its base is the surface finite element. The position of the plane is determined by the positions along the three rays, x_i. In general, the base is tilted so that $|x_1| \neq |x_2| \neq |x_3|$. The length of each side of the base triangle is given by the difference between the two adjacent rays. For example:

$$l_1 = x_2 - x_1 \tag{5}$$

It can also be seen that the nodes are located at the intersections of the rays with the tangent plane to the surface.

The centroid is located at the intersection of the three lines connecting the midpoints of the sides of the triangle. The position of the centroid can be specified a vector using the set of six coordinates:

$$r = \{ \; x_1 \quad x_2 \quad x_3 \quad l_1/2 \quad l_2/2 \quad l_3/2 \; \} \tag{6}$$

This is the natural coordinate system defined by Argyris and Doltsinis [3].

After Δt, the base triangle has moved toward the origin to a new position, given by x_i', as shown in Fig. 4. The new position of the centroid is

$$r' = \{ \; a_1 x_1 \quad a_2 x_2 \quad a_3 x_3 \quad b_1 l_1/2 \quad b_2 l_2/2 \quad b_3 l_3/2 \; \} \tag{7}$$

where the coefficients a_i and b_i are all less than one.

Isotropic contraction as described above is simply a translation along r. This is defined as the scalar multiplication of a vector. Therefore, the condition for a simple isotropic contraction without a deviatoric component is:

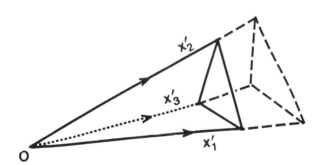

Figure 4:   Effect of surface recession on finite element of volume.

$$r' = ar \qquad (8)$$

By comparison with equation 7, this condition can also be stated as:

$$a_1 = a_2 = a_3 = b_1 = b_2 = b_3 = a \qquad (9)$$

Therefore simple isotropic contraction can occur only if all three sides of the base triangle are reduced by the same proportion, a. This also requires that the distances moved along the rays also be in the same proportion. However, because of the continuity conditions described below, the distances moved along the rays will generally not all be in the same proportion. Therefore, the conditions of equation 9 will not be met, and there will be a deviatoric component, leading to a distortion of the shape.

It can also be seen from Fig. 4 that the volume of stone eroded is the difference in volume between the tetrahedra defined by $Ox_1x_2x_3$ and by $Ox_1'x_2'x_3'$ respectively.

Thus far the discussion has considered only a single isolated finite element. The construction of a mesh requires the specification of continuity conditions among neighboring finite elements. The appropriate condition would be that during the surface recession no gaps or overlaps develop between the finite elements. As shown in Figure 5, this continuity condition means that along a common ray, x_1, between tetrahedral finite elements 1 and 2:

$$_1\Delta x_1 = {}_2\Delta x_2 \qquad (10)$$

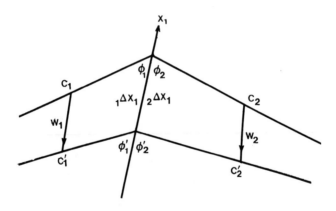

Figure 5: Continuity conditions along common ray between adjacent finite elements

In Fig. 5, the lines representing the surface recession, w_1 and w_2, are shown connecting the centroids before and after displacement, C_i and C_i'. If no rotation occurs around the node, then $\phi_i' = \phi_i$, and the surface element planes before and after erosion are parallel. This is another way of stating the condition of equation 7. Since w_1 is by definition the change in r_1:

$$w_1 = (1-a)r_1 \tag{11}$$

Also, from equation 7:

$$_1\Delta x_1 = (1-a)x_1 \tag{12}$$

Then it follows because of equations 7 and 10:

$$w_2 = (1-a)r_2 \tag{13}$$

In other words, to avoid distortion, the surface recession on both faces must be in the same proportion, $(1-a)$, to the respective position vector. This proportion is the same quantity as strain in the direction of the vector and hence, to avoid distortion, there must be uniform strain on all faces. However, as noted above, strain is not a particularly relevant variable for erosion. The requirement for uniform strain means that, according to equations 11 or 13, the surface recession would have to vary from one finite element to another in constant proportion to the position vector. This implies that the erosion would depend only on the size and shape of the object. However, as discussed above, the erosion is actually a function of environmental factors outside the object. Thus, it is unlikely that this proportionality could be maintained.

The other possible case of isotropic contraction might occur if instead of proportional erosion, uniform erosion were postulated. In this case:

$$w_1 = w_2 \tag{14}$$

Then from equations 11 and 13:

$$r_1 = r_2 \tag{15}$$

but this can only be true for spherical objects.

DISCUSSION

Finite element methods can be applied to this problem for one of two purposes. One is to define a set of reference points on the surface to permit accurate measurement of surface recession. The other is to predict the surface recession given a known distribution of environmental conditions, using an appropriate mathematical model of the deterioration process.

By analogy with elasticity theory, one can propose a relationship between the surface recession and a set of environmental stresses:

$$w(\mathbf{r},\mathbf{n},\Delta t) \quad = D\Delta t\sigma(\mathbf{r}) \tag{16}$$

where $\sigma(\mathbf{r})$ is the environmental stress, a function of such factors as air pollution, wind speed, rainfall intensity , etc. that produce the erosion.   The factor D is a property of the stone and represents its resistance to erosional processes.   This is in effect a constitutive law for stone erosion, or as it is sometimes known, the damage function for stone deterioration.

Unfortunately, the various factors in this relationship are not yet known. Development of $\sigma(\mathbf{r})$ requires a great deal more research into the relationships between the environmental conditions and the resulting stress on the stone.   Similarly, much work remains to be done to determine the variation in D among different types of stone[4]. Thus, for the time being, the computational geometry approach will probably find more use in the measurement process.

In the absence of such a constitutive law, one might attempt to develop an empirical relationship by measuring the spatial variation in surface recession around an object and correlating this with measured values of environmental variables at the same positions. For this approach to be successful, it is necessary to correct for the spatial variation due to geometric considerations. In other words, the true surface recession as defined in equation 2 must be measured, not the isotropic component. In these measurements, therefore, it is necessary to determine the deviatoric component as well. This problem cannot be avoided simply by measuring distance along the local normal, because during the erosion process the direction of the normal will be changing with the distortion of the surface.   Only the use of a finite element mesh in the measurement process can compensate for this distortion.

It should be evident that if surface recession is not correctly, measured, then any inferences about the spatial variability of the environmental stresses derived from this data will be in error. Hence, the results of any investigation of the influence of various environmental factors on erosion that is based on field measurements on "real structures", should be treated with skepticism unless the method for correcting for geometric distortion is stated.

In practice, this measurement process would begin by laying out a triangular mesh on the original surface.   The individual elements would be drawn as close as possible to the local tangent planes.   Therefore, the triangles would vary in shape, size and orientation. This step also defines the initial positions of the centroids and the nodes.   The next step would be to determine the direction cosines from each node to an appropriate origin in a frame of reference, which can be either internal or external.   The spatial position of the centroid would also be recorded. If the object is complex, it may be necessary to subdivide it into several regions, each with its own local origin. After a suitable time period, each node would be relocated by finding the intersection of the new surface with a line to the origin having the original direction cosines.   The finite element mesh would be redrawn from the nodes, and within these the new positions of the centroids would be found.   The true surface recession would then be the difference between the initial position of the centroid and the new one. Although this procedure sounds complicated, in principle it is the same as the pointing frame that has been used by sculptors since antiquity to transfer dimensions from a model to a work in progress.

Finally, surface recession is the correct measure for investigating erosion processes. However, from an esthetics standpoint, its individual components may be more significant than the whole. That is, the distortion of a sculpture may be much more noticeable than a small overall contraction.

CONCLUSIONS

Erosion of stone sculpture is a three-dimensional process that, for almost all cases, results in a distortion of the shape as well as a contraction. This effect can be corrected for through the application of computational geometry and finite element analysis. It is not currently possible to perform computer modelling of the surface recession because the necessary constitutive laws have not yet been developed.

REFERENCES

1. Livingston, R. and Baer, N. Comparative Stone Damage Rates Measured Historic Stone Buildings and Monuments, Paper No. 84-83.2, Proceedings of the 77th Annual Meeting of the Air Pollution Control Association, 1984. Air Pollution Control Association, Pittsburgh, 1984.

2. Livingston, R. and Baer, N. The Accuracy of Stone Weathering Rates Measured on Historic Structures, Wiener Berichte über Naturwissenshaft in der Kunst, Dbl. Vol 2/3, pp. 272-297, 1986.

3. Argyris, J. and Doltsinis, J. On the Large Strain Inelastic Analysis in Natural Formulation, Part I: Quasistatic Problem, Computer Methods in Applied Mechanics and Engineering, Vol. 20, pp. 213-251,1979.

4. Livingston, R. The Application of Petrology to the Prediction of Stone Durability (Ed. Ciabach, J.), pp. 432- 445, Proceedings of the VIth International Congress on the Deterioration and Conservation of Stone, 1988. Nicholas Copernicus University, Torun, Poland, 1988.

Special Finite Element Approaches to the Study of Masonry Domes. Comparative Numerical Analyses and Experimental Researches

C. Blasi and S. Sorace

Department of Civil Engineering, University of Florence, Via di S. Marta n. 3, 50139 Florence, Italy

ABSTRACT

Numerical analyses were conducted on masonry domes,using two different Finite Element procedures.
The first procedure, based on a non-linear calculus program, was able to simulate a monolateral behaviour and the formation of gaps in structures under tensile stress.
A special element was introduced in the numerical model which simulated the masonry structure's non-linearity, non-tensile strength, gaps and slidings.
The second procedure was based on an unconventional application of a numerical program for linear elastic analysis.
The zones under tensile stress were first localized; the physical contact corresponding to these zones was interrupted assuming non-tensile strength for the material.
Results obtained with these two methods were compared with those of in situ experimental tests conducted on the historical dome of the Tempio di Romolo, in Rome.

1. PREMISE

In the last few years the use of numerical models has brought about a fundamental change in working methods in the field of structural calculus.
These models are normally used, with generally good results, for structures built with materials whose behaviour may be described in terms of linear laws, with regard to both small and large displacements.
Until a few years ago attempts were made to find specific systems of calculation for each individual structural typology (calculation of reticular structures, frames, slabs, vaults, etc.).
However, numerical methods have led to unification of the various systems of calculation even in everyday use, and the most recent programmes may be used for an increasingly wide range of problems (although these, natu-rally, include the familiar typologies of "trusses", "beams", "two-dimen-sional elements", etc.).

With regard to those structures built with materials having a decidedly non-linear or anisotropic behaviour, the difficulties of defining "elements" characterized by complex constitutive laws in a way that would provide a reasonably accurate description of the behaviour of these materials, have so far prevented widespread application of similar methods.
This is the case, for example, in the field of masonry structures, where there is much discussion among experts as to the most appropriate system of calculation.

In the present state of research, it is possible to outline three possible approaches to the specific problem of "masonry calculation".

The first system involves the direct study of constitutive laws that describe the mechanical behaviour of masonry with sufficient accuracy and that permit the solution of the problem for sufficiently simple elements. Under this heading, for example, come all those research projects dealing "at continuum" with "materials having non-tensile strength": a vast area of study, now the subject of fierce debate ([1], [2], [3], [7]).

The second method is that of analysing specific structural typologies in masonry, such as panels, architraves, vaults, etc., on the basis of specific hypotheses of behaviour, generally on collapse.
Thus the study of a complex system is approached through the assembly of the individual structural elements listed above, which may constitute it. Examples of these methods of calculation are the one proposed in [4] for the study of panels with openings, the POR method, widely used, and many other with similar characteristics.
These systems of calculation are clearly designed for specific typologies.

Lastly, a third method consists of the application of numerical finite elements methods, with several possible approaches that are distinguished from each other by the varying level of "refinement" in the schematization of structural behaviour.
Any a priori choice of one system in preference to another appears to be unjustified.
One must stress, however, the widely felt need for a close relationship between theoretical procedures and experimental analyses and for constant checking of the one against the other.

The aim of this article is to contribute to the current debate on the subject by presenting a "test" regarding the application of a finite element calculus code (ANSYS, [8]) to a classical structural typology: the hemispherical dome.
The ANSYS program presents, in its vast library, a special element having non-linear behaviour.

This element, the so-called "gap" (or, even, "two" or "three dimensional interface"), because of the characteristics described here, could be used to schematize some fundamental mechanical properties of masonry by concentrating them in the nodes of the structural model.
Among these characteristics, the principle ones are the particular tensile-compressive behaviour and the transmission of shear stress with friction.

A double test was performed.

First, the results obtained from the analyses carried out with the ANSYS code were compared with those obtained by another calculus program, SAP80 ([9]), in widespread use, which adopts a conventional, linear-type analysis.
This program, however, was used in a different way from the usual one.
Once the zones under tensile stresses had been identified, here the physical contact was interrupted by the "manual" introduction of gaps in the structure under study.
In this way it was possible to test, from a purely numerical point of view, the results obtained with the two different codes on a model, in the one example "automatically" and in the other "manually damaged".

Secondly, the results of the two models were compared with the condition of a real building (the dome of the so-called Tempio di Romolo in the Roman Forum), whose cracks and stress state at certain significant points were already known (determined on the basis of a survey carried out by ISMES using the method of flat jacks [5]).

Since the geometrical characteristics of the models are similar to those of the actual dome, the comparison provided an indication of these models' potential for describing the behaviour of real objects.

2. DEFINITION OF THE MODEL

As stated in the first section, the model for comparison was established by using the Tempio di Romolo in Rome as a reference (Fig. 1).
The simplified geometrical model drawn from the building is represented by a hemispherical dome on a cylindrical drum, 90 cm thick, with a radius of 765 cm.
The radius of the circumference of the impost's lantern at the top is equal to 100 cm.
The "equivalent" side of the elements of the mesh is approximately equal to 100 cm.

It should be noted that since the structure had been studied as being subjected only to its own weight, as well as the weight of the lantern, its generally symmetrical condition convinced us that only one quarter of the dome and drum complex needed to be analysed.
Thus the burden of computation was reduced considerably , which is especially important when applying the ANSYS code.

3. "CRACKED LINEAR" MODEL

Fig. 2 reproduces the deformed geometry of the numerical model prepared for the SAP80 code.
The "quad" elements used in defining the model are of the two-dimensional type, bending resistant and having an elastic linear behaviour.

The method adopted here, already partly described in Section 1, is based on the fact that every time a parallel has been subjected to a tensile stress greater than 0.005 N/mm^2, the constraints to the horizontal displacement corresponding to the nodes of extremity of the same parallel have been eliminated.
In this way a repetitive procedure was set up which was concluded when the zones of tensile stress along horizontal "bands" stopped spreading.
The stress state as derived from the computation, is reproduced at its most significant points in Table 1 (the positions of these points are shown in Fig. 1 and 2).

4. NON LINEAR MODEL

Fig. 3 shows the numerical model defined and calculated with the ANSYS code.
The gap elements inserted in the nodes consist of two flat parallel surfaces that can both maintain ("closed" element) and interrupt ("open" element) the physical contact, with the possibility of sliding.

In the actual model, in conformity with the "cracked linear model", the gap elements have been introduced along the meridians, with the surfaces placed horizontally, in such a way as to obtain vertical cracks.
The gap element allows only the transmission of compressive stress, in the normal direction to the two surfaces, and of shear stress, in the tangential one, according to Coulomb's law.
The constitutive laws relating to the two directions are reproduced in Fig. 4.
In this figure Fn, Fs represent, respectively, the normal and shear forces acting on the surfaces of the element; d_n, d_s the correlative displacements between the same faces.
Naturally, the tangential direction law is valid for Fn < 0.
The compressive strength K is also assumed as elastic stiffness in the tangential direction; the value corresponding to the start of sliding, according to Coulomb's law, is: $\mu \cdot |Fn|$, where μ is the coefficient of

friction.

The setting of μ hasn't any numerical implication, being based only on physical evaluations.

For the actual analyses the value : $\mu = 0.5$ has been assumed.

The parameter K has a great influence on the speed of convergence and also on the quality of the numerical solution.

Further information on the characteristics and setting of the parameters relating to the gap elements, are present in [6].

The geometry of the numerical model is generated by the brick elements which are defined by eight modes and have a linear elastic and isotropic behaviour.

One may make the general observation that an element such as the one shown in Fig. 5.a, modelled with the same gap and brick elements described above, subjected to the load represented here, would have a behaviour similar to that shown in Fig. 5.b.

In Fig. 6.a, 6.b are reproduced a general and a detailed view of the deformed geometry of the first and simplest elaborated model, for which the gaps have been placed only on the central meridian.

The "cracks" along this meridian are clearly shown.

The stresses   at the same points set for the analyses with SAP80 are written in Table 1.

5. THE DOME OF THE TEMPIO DI ROMOLO IN ROME

Table 1 also shows the stress state revealed by the ISMES through the use of flat jacks on the Roman monument.

This monument has in fact been subjected to a series of surveys [9] carried out by the Soprintendenza Archeologica of Rome in order to study the static situation, compromised both by a series of vertical cracks on the dome and drum and by rotations and out of plumb of the walls.

6. CONCLUSIONS

The conclusions are summed up in the contents of Table 1, with the most significant numerical results and the corresponding experimental values. The "test" appears on the whole to have been successful as regards both the numerical model (close correspondence, with very slight differences between the two models) and the comparison with the stress and strain state in the actual building.

Although a rough schematic representation has been made of a reality that is complicated by the presence of numerous openings, reconstructions and additions, the fundamental aspects of the actual static state have been collected and described with a fair degree of accuracy from the models, especially from the non linear model.

We thus conclude that the approach to "masonry calculation" by means of finite element numerical methods with non-linear behaviour of the nodes is valid and worth further study.

An effective experimental check is, however, necessary to correctly define the main parameters involved in the numerical analyses.

REFERENCES

Papers in journals

1. Villaggio, P. Stress Diffusion in Masonry Walls, Journal of Structural Mechanics, n. 4, 1981.

Papers in Conference Proceedings

2. Baratta, A. Metodi di calcolo per strutture non reagenti a trazione, Atti VII Congresso Nazionale AIMETA, 1984.

3. Romano, C., and Sacco, E.   Sul calcolo di strutture non reagenti a trazione, Atti VII Congresso Nazionale AIMETA, 1984.

4. Como, M. and Grimaldi A.   Analisi limite di pareti murarie sotto spinta, Atti Convegno Ingegneria Strutturale, C.N.R., Udine, 1983.

5. Blasi, C. and Rossi, P.P. Indagini sulle strutture murarie del Tempio detto di Romolo nel Foro Romano: prove non distruttive con martinetti piatti e analisi numeriche, Atti II Conferenza Internazionale sulle Prove non distruttive per lo studio e la conservazione delle opere d'arte.

6. Chiostrini, S., Foraboschi, P. and Sorace, S. Problems Connected with the Arrangement of a Non-Linear Finite Element Method to the Analysis of Masonry Structures, Proceedings of STREMA 89 - Florence, 1989

Books

7. Di Pasquale, S.   Statica dei solidi murari: teoria ed esperienza, Dipartimento di Costruzioni, Universita' di Firenze, 1984

8. AA.VV.   Ansys - Engineering Analysis   System-User's Manual, Swanson Analysis System Inc. Houston, Pennsylvania, 1986

9. Wilson, E.L.   SAP80 - Finite Element Analysis on Microcomputer, University of California, Berkeley, California, 1980

Point	Stresses	SAP80 Model	ANSYS Model	Experimental Measures
A	fnm	- 0.46	- 0.44	- 0.45
A	fnp	- 0.14	- 0.15	n.m.
B	fnm	- 0.34	- 0.32	- 0.27
B	fnp	- 0.15	- 0.15	n.m.
C	fnm	- 0.27	- 0.26	- 0.33
C	fnp	+ 0.02	+ 0.02	c
D	fnm	+ 0.18	+ 0.19	c
E	fnm	- 0.42	- 0.49	- 0.50
F	fnm	- 0.47	- 0.39	- 0.42
G	fnp	+ 0.78	+ 0.68	n.m.

fnm : Parallel stress (Mpa); (-) compressive stress, (+) tensile stress

fnp : Meridian stress (Mpa); (-) compressive stress, (+) tensile stress

n.m.: Not measured

c   : Crack

Table 1: Comparison between some numerical and experimental results.

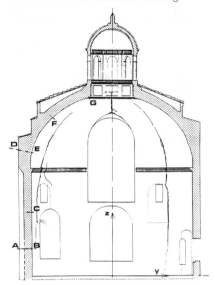

Fig. 1: Vertical section of the Tempio di Romolo in Rome.

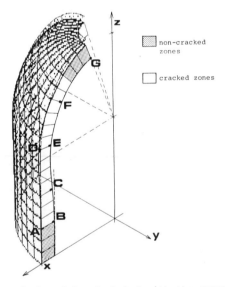

Fig. 2: Numerical model calculated with the SAP80 code:
deformed geometry

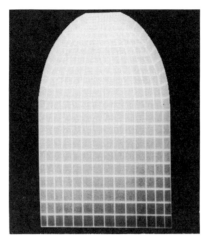

a.

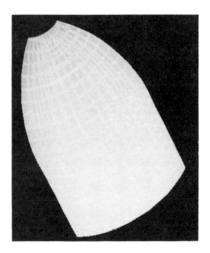

b.

Fig. 3: Numerical model calculated with the ANSYS code:
        undeformed geometry

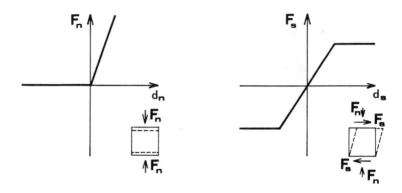

Fig. 4: Constitutive laws of the gap elements.

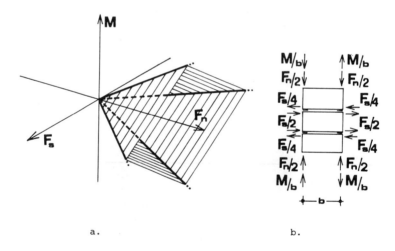

a.   b.

Fig. 5: Limit surfaces for a simple structural   element calculated with
the ANSYS code.

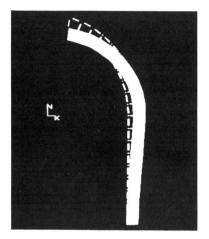

a.

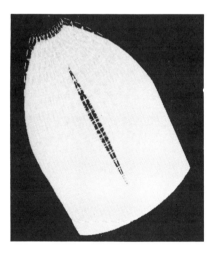

b.

Fig. 6: Numerical model calculated with ANSYS code: deformed geometry
of the simplest elaborated model (gaps placed
only on the central meridian)

Computer Modelling of Moisture Protection Measures in Historic Buildings

H. Garrecht, J. Kropp, H.K. Hilsdorf

Institut für Massivbau und Baustofftechnologie, Universität Karlsruhe, Kaiserstr. 12, 7500 Karlsruhe 1, FRG

ABSTRACT

The effectiveness of moisture protection measures in the restoration of historic buildings and monuments may be substantially improved if these measures are supported by numerical modelling of wetting, moisture movement, and drying in the building materials of a given structural element. For this, in addition to the fundamental laws of moisture movement in porous materials numerous material properties such as sorption isotherms, diffusion coefficients for water vapor as well as capillary flow of water are required, which were determined experimentally for a variety of local sand stones and lime mortars. In these investigations the effect of soluble salts on moisture capacity and moisture movement were taken into consideration. For a given structural element the boundary conditions prevailing on the site determine the moisture as well as the drying conditions. Finite Element Analysis then allows one to perform case studies of possible protection methods, thereby introducing locally modified material properties or partially modified boundary conditions for the element. Different methods then may be compared with regard to cost, effectiveness, and required drying time.

INTRODUCTION.

In historic buildings and monuments the mineral building materials such as natural stones, clay bricks and lime mortars or renderings often suffer serious degradation due to combined physical and chemical action of corrosive agents. Degradation of these materials, however, either requires a high moisture content or is accelerated by excess moisture in the porous materials. Moisture may be taken up by adsorption of the humidity from the atmosphere, however, this mechanism results only in a comparatively low moisture content. In contrast, absorption of driving rain or splash water as well as the capillary rise of water through foundations or sections in contact with earth may lead to a critical moisture load of the materials. Capillary rise of moisture furthermore may introduce dissolved salts into the building materials, hygroscopicity of these salts then drastically increases the equilibrium water content of the materials even through absorption of the ambient air humidity.

In the preservation of historic buildings and monuments effective protection of the materials against excess moisture is required to minimize further decay. This task is related to special problems where older structures are concerned. In most cases these buildings never had any protective measures comparable to modern structures, at the same time their building materials are more vulnerable to decay. Furthermore, the application of modern protection techniques must consider the character of the monument concerned, i.e. necessary alterations of the structure should be minimized, and new materials applied must be compatible with the old materials. In many cases attempts based on trial and error proved to be ineffective, more important, however, accelerated decay and serious damage occured (Fig. 1)[1].

Fig. 1. Rising moisture front after application of a wrong protection method

The selection of protection methods, therefore, should be based on a careful analysis of the structure and its materials, the exposure conditions, and the mechanisms of moisture ingress, moisture movement, and drying of an element. With the help of material parameters the moisture balance of an element then may be modelled numerically for the prevailing boundary conditions. Also different protection techniques can be simulated first by introducing locally modified material properties in a cross section or modified boundary conditions of an element. Based on these case studies effective protection methods can be chosen.

THEORETICAL DESCRIPTION OF MOISTURE BALANCE

In an exterior wall moisture transport may take place through the porous material by diffusion of water vapor or at higher concentrations by capillary flow in the liquid phase. Neglecting the osmotic effects of dissolved salts, the moisture balance of the structural element can be formulated by the expanded Fick's equation for diffusion given by :

$$\frac{\partial c}{\partial t} = \nabla \left(D_V(c, \vartheta) \nabla c + D_L(c, \vartheta) \nabla c + D_T(c, \vartheta) \nabla \vartheta \right) \qquad (1)$$

In this equation the material parameters D_V and D_L characterize the flow of moisture by diffusion and capillarity due to a gradient of the local moisture concentration c. The coefficient D_T describes the moisture flow due to a gradient of temperature ϑ.
All these parameters are functions of the local moisture concentration c and the temperature ϑ and have to be determined experimentally.
The analysis presented in this paper assumes isothermal conditions. Thus eq.(1) is simplified to :

$$\frac{\partial c}{\partial t} = \nabla\left(D_V(c)\nabla c + D_L(c)\nabla c\right) \tag{2}$$

Allthough the concentration gradient is the driving force both for water vapor diffusivity and capillary conductivity, these mechanisms may be effective in different ranges of moisture concentrations. Therefore, they may be superimposed to yield one concentration dependent transport coefficient.
The transient field problem shown in eq.(2) was solved by the Finite Element Method for the two dimensional flow of water. Here, the variational calculation is based on the assumption that the governing differential equation and the given boundary conditions for the structural element are satisfied. Thereby the computational solution is complicated by the strong nonlinearity of the transport coefficients (see fig.4 and fig.5).

MOISTURE PROPERTIES OF THE MATERIALS

Materials
The necessary parameters were determined for different types of sand stones and several types of mortars which were often used in historic buildings in the region of Baden-Württemberg, a state of the FRG.

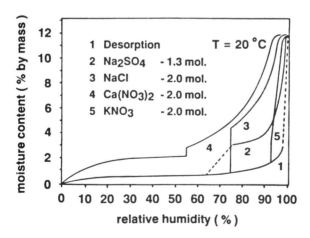

Fig. 2. Effect of salt contamination on sorption isotherms of a yellow sand stone

Sorption Isotherms
Thin discs of these materials were conditioned in 12 different relative humidities at 20°C for several months. The moisture concentration gained through adsorption of the oven

dry material or desorption of initially water saturated material then was determined gravimetrically. Due to the low specific surface area of these materials the hysteresis effect is small.

In order to illustrate the effect of salt contamination of the building materials, samples were also charged with defined concentrations of different salts frequently encountered in historic buildings. Fig. 2 demonstrates the unsteady relation between ambient relative humidity and moisture concentration. For relative humidities higher than a critical value the equilibrium moisture content of the materials rises drastically. This critical relative humidity is governed by the partial vapor pressure of the saturated salt solution. For high salt concentrations and high relative humidities even saturation of the pore system may be obtained [1,2].

Water Vapor Diffusivity
The water vapor diffusivity was determined with the cup method at intervals of approx. 10 % r.h.. Fig. 3 gives some of the results of the tests on some of different types of sandstone. With the help of the sorption isotherms the diffusion coefficients for water vapor then can be calculated as a function of the moisture concentration.

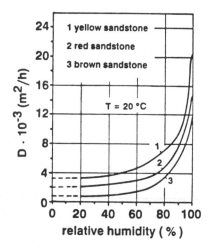

Fig. 3. Water vapor diffusivity of sandstones and mortars.

Capillary Conductivity
At higher moisture concentrations transport of water in the liquid phase occurs as unsaturated or saturated capillary flow in the porous materials [2,3,4,5]. To evaluate the respective transport coefficient we used drilled cores with a diameter of 30mm and a length of 500mm which were sealed along their circumference. One end of the cylinder is exposed to liquid water, and the opposite end is kept at 0% r.h.. For various time steps concentration profiles were taken by splitting the cylinders into small discs with a thickness of approx. 10 mm and subsequent gravimetric determination of the moisture concentration. From these concentration profiles the capillary conductivity was calculated as a function of the moisture concentration [2,5]. As an example, Fig.4 gives the results obtained for the yellow sand stone.

The method described above requires comparatively large specimens, and for each time step several cylinders are needed. Therefore, in future experiments Nuclear

Magnetic Resonance (NMR) will be applied to determine concentration profiles nonde-structively. Kießl and Krus [6] have shown that concentration profiles can be taken with this method with a high accuracy and good reproducibility within a few minutes.

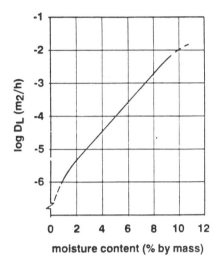

Fig. 4. Capillary conductivity of red sandstone.

RESULTS OF NUMERICAL MODELLING

The system analyzed is given in Fig.5 which shows a cross section of an exterior wall, with a height of 5 m and a thickness of 0.8 m. With the foundation immersed in ground water and the lower portion of the external wall in contact with wet soil, water will be

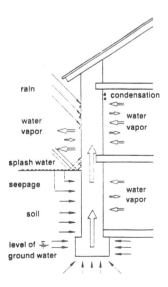

Fig. 5. Analyzed element and boundary conditions.

taken up by capillary activity. In the upper section, the wall surface is exposed to the atmosphere. The relative humidity of the atmosphere and the exposure of the wall to liquid water may vary with time. At the interior surface of the wall evaporation may take place e.g. at 50% rel. humidity in the ground floor and 90% in the basement, respectively. Fig.5 also shows further possible boundary conditions, such as driving rain, splash water, seepage, condensation of water vapor etc..

To simulate the moisture behaviour of real building elements, the cross section of the external wall was divided in up to 7000 elements. This element disposition allows to consider different kinds of building materials used in the structural element. Aside from natural stones, bricks and mortars above and below the ground level, also renderings inside and outside of the external wall as well as coatings may be taken into account. Most important is the possibility to calculate the effectiveness of changes of hygrical behavior of the building materials e.g. due to a chemical injection or other types of moisture protection measures.

Fig.6 shows the moisture distribution within a wall which is exposed to ground water, soil and an atmosphere of a relative humidity of 55, 65 and 85 percent, respectively. These exposure conditions result in a moisture concentration at the bottom of

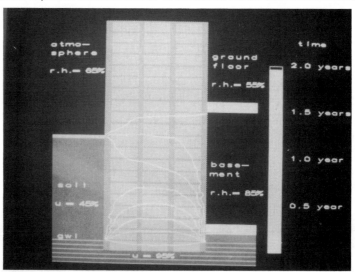

Fig. 6. Equilibrium moisture distribution

the wall of u=95 percent and at the surface of the wall in contact with the soil of u=45 percent. The moisture concentration profiles represent the state of equilibrium starting from saturation, which is a moisture content of 22% by volume for the sand stone and 25% by volume for the mortar. The difference between two adjacent profiles amounts to 10% of the saturation concentration.

Fig.7 shows the effect of driving rain for 1.5 days. This diagram demonstrates how the water front moves into the interior sections of the wall after the exterior surface of the wall has been subjected to driving rain. The ingress of water is much faster in the mortar joints then it is in the sandstone units. The wetting of the sandstone units takes place not only in a horizontal direction but also from the mortar joints.

After approx. 3 days the water front in this wall reaches the interior surface.

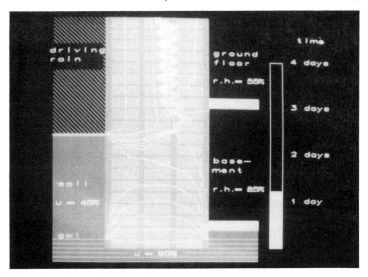

Fig. 7. Effect of 1.5 days of driving rain

Subsequent drying of 5 weeks does not as yet lead to moisture equilibrium as can be seen from Fig. 8. It is well known that drying is much slower then wetting.

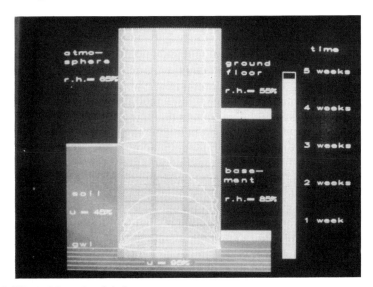

Fig. 8. Effect of 5 weeks of drying

Only in rare cases will a wall be exposed to 3 days continuous driving rain. However, dirty facades of historical buildings may be cleaned by sprinkling water on their surfaces for periods up to 48 hours. This may cause a moisture distribution similar to the one shown in Fig.7.

Fig. 9 shows a structure without basement. Here it was assumed that no moisture transport takes place from the wet soil to the wall. After an equilibrium state is obtained, modified material properties for the socle zone were introduced to simulate the effects of chemical injection or other possible moisture protection measures in this region.

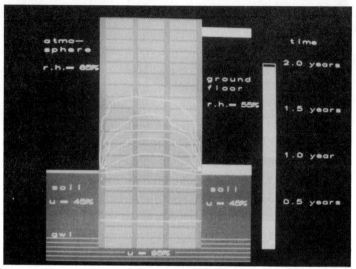

Fig.9. Cross section without basement

In Fig. 10 the effect of a successfully injected socle zone is demonstrated. Again, a redistribution of the moisture profiles after 3 months of drying can be seen.

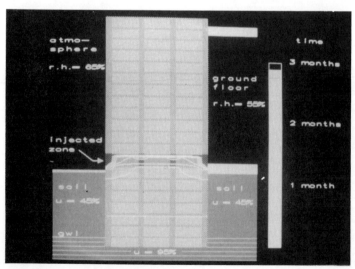

Fig.10. Successful injection measure

In many cases it is difficult to carry out a complete injection, particularly when the moisture content in the pores of the building materials exceeds 50 percent of the saturation moisture content. Fig. 11 shows the moisture distribution 3 months after treatment of the socle zone with an injection which was only 75 percent effective..

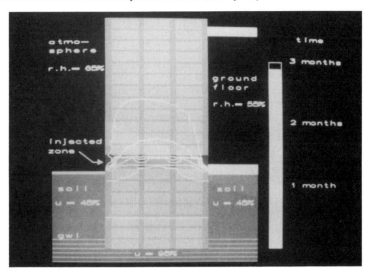

Fig.11. Injection with reduced effectiveness

Especially in historic buildings it often occurs that protection by chemical injection can be done only from the outer side. Then, the entire cross section of the masonry will not be reached. Fig. 12 shows the moisture distribution 3 months after treatment of the socle zone with an injection over only 2/3 of the cross section .

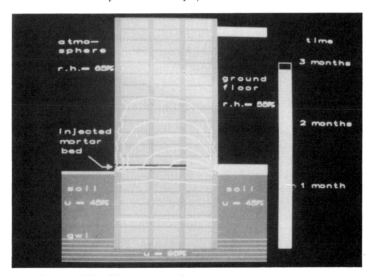

Fig.12. Injection over 2/3 of the cross section

Of course, this method of analysis may also be used to simulate the effectiveness of other protection measures or a combination of several methods.

CONCLUSIONS

The wetting and drying behavior of structural elements in buildings can be simulated by numerical models.These calculations require detailed information on the properties such as sorption isotherms and various transport coefficients for the flow of water. The calculations demonstrated that high moisture concentrations in the building materials can arise due to driving rain or ground water.

Although drying is slower than wetting sections exposed to the free atmosphere will not exhibit sustained high moisture concentrations. Also capillary rise of water can lead to high moisture concentrations. However, the equilibrium condition between capillary rise and evaporation limits the level of the moisture front, and the capillary rise does not always proceed to a considerable height in elements exposed to the atmosphere.

From the sorption isotherms presented in Fig.2 it may be concluded that high moisture concentrations found in elements of historical buildings may also be caused by a contamination of the building materials with hygroscopic salts which will absorb large amounts of water, so that high moisture concentrations are in equilibrium with the air humidity. Although in this case capillary rise is not the immediate cause of a high moisture content dissolved salts are transported into the building materials by this mechanism. Then, protective measures for the foundations or sections in contact with soil will not reduce the high moisture content, however, an impervious moisture barrier applied to the foundation will stop further ingress of salts and a further enrichment of salts in the evaporation zone.

Presently, we attempt to model also such processes by the analytical method described.

REFERENCES

1.   Hilsdorf,H.K; Kropp,J; Garrecht,H; Ursachen und Wege der Feuchtigkeit in Baukonstruktionen; Jahrbuch SFB 315 -Erhalten historisch bedeutsamer Bauwerke, 1986, Verlag Ernst u. Sohn, Berlin, (1987)

2.   Garrecht,H; Kropp,J; Hilsdorf,H.K; Mauerfeuchte als Folge bauschädlicher Salze; Jahrbuch SFB 315 - Erhalten historisch bedeutsamer Bauwerke, 1987, Verlag Ernst u. Sohn, Berlin, (1988)

3.   Krischer,O; Kroll,K; Wissenschaftliche Grundlagen der Trocknungstechnik; Springer Verlag, Berlin (1963)

4.   Kießl,K; Kapillarer und dampfförmiger Feuchtetransport in mehrschichtigen Bauteilen. Rechnerische Erfassung und bauphysikalische Anwendung;Dissertation Universität Essen, (1983)

5.   Sommer,E; Beitrag zur Frage der kapillaren Flüssigkeitsbewegung in porösen Stoffen bei Be- und Entfeuchtungsvorgängen; Dissertation Technische Hochschule Darmstadt,(1971)

6.   Kießl,K; Krus,M; Messung von Wassergehalten und Feuchtetransportvorgängen in Baustoffen mittels kernmagnetischer Resonanz; IBP-Mitteilungen 148,14,(1987), Fraunhofer Institut für Bauphysik, Stuttgart